LIVING LANGUAGE®

JAPANESE
DICTIONARY

JAPANESE–ENGLISH
ENGLISH–JAPANESE

REVISED & UPDATED

THE LIVING LANGUAGE® SERIES

**Living Language Basic Courses,
  Revised & Updated**

Spanish*	Japanese*
French*	Russian
German*	Italian*

Portuguese (Brazilian)
Portuguese (Continental)
Inglés/English for Spanish Speakers

**Living Language Intermediate
  Courses**

Spanish 2	French 2
German 2	Italian 2

**Living Language Advanced Courses,
  Revised & Updated**

Spanish 3	French 3

Living Language Ultimate™
  (formerly All the Way™)

Spanish*	Spanish 2*
French*	French 2*
German*	German 2*
Italian*	Italian 2*
Russian*	Russian 2*
Japanese*	Japanese 2*

Inglés/English for Spanish Speakers*
Inglés/English for Spanish Speakers 2*
Chinese (1999)

**Living Language® Essential Language
  Guides**

Essential Spanish for Healthcare
Essential Spanish for Social Services
Essential Spanish for Law Enforcement
Essential Language Guide for Hotel &
  Restaurant Employees

Living Language Children's Courses

Spanish	French

**Living Language Conversational
  English**

for Chinese Speakers
for Japanese Speakers
for Korean Speakers
for Spanish Speakers
for Russian Speakers

Living Language Fast & Easy™

Spanish	Italian	Portuguese
French	Russian	Czech
German	Polish	Hungarian
Japanese	Korean	Mandarin
Arabic	Hebrew	(Chinese)

Inglés/English for Spanish Speakers

Living Language All Audio™

Spanish	French	Italian	German

**Living Language Speak Up!®
  Accent Elimination Courses**

Spanish   American Regional
Asian, Indian and Middle Eastern

Fodor's Languages for Travelers

Spanish	French	Italian	German

**Living Language® Parent/Child
  Activity Kits**

Learn French in the Kitchen
Learn Italian in the Kitchen
Learn Spanish in the Kitchen
Learn French in the Car
Learn Italian in the Car
Learn Spanish in the Car

*Available on Cassette and Compact Disc

JAPANESE
DICTIONARY

JAPANESE–ENGLISH
ENGLISH–JAPANESE

REVISED & UPDATED

REVISED BY HIROKO STORM, PH.D.

University of Arizona

Assistant Professor of Japanese
Lafayette College

◆

Based on the original

by Ichiro Shirato

LIVING LANGUAGE®
A Random House Company

This work was previously published under the title *Living Language*™ *Common Usage Dictionary—Japanese* by Ichiro Shirato, based on the dictionary developed by Ralph Weiman.

Published by Living Language, A Random House Company, 201 East 50th Street, New York, New York 10022.

Random House, Inc. New York, Toronto, London, Sydney, Auckland

www.livinglanguage.com

LIVING LANGUAGE is a registered trademark of Crown Publishers, Inc.

Printed in the United States of America

Library of Congress Catalog Card Number: 60-15399

ISBN 0-609-80303-4

10 9 8 7 6 5 4 3 2

Contents

Introduction   ix
Explanatory Notes   xi

JAPANESE-ENGLISH   1

ENGLISH-JAPANESE   209

Glossary of Geographical Names   285

INTRODUCTION

The *Living Language® Japanese Dictionary* lists more than 15,000 of the most frequently used Japanese words, gives their most important meanings, and illustrates their uses. This revised edition contains updated phrases and expressions, as well as many new entries related to business, technology, and the media.

1. More than 1,000 of the most essential words are capitalized to make them easy to find.

2. Numerous definitions are illustrated with phrases, sentences, and idiomatic expressions. Where there is no close English equivalent for an Japanese word, or where the English equivalent has several meanings, the context of the illustrative sentences helps to clarify the meanings.

3. Because of these useful phrases, the *Living Language® Japanese Dictionary* also serves as a phrase book and conversation guide. The dictionary is helpful both to beginners who are building their vocabulary and to advanced students who want to perfect their command of colloquial Japanese.

4. The Japanese expressions (particularly the idiomatic and colloquial ones) have been translated to their English equivalents. However, literal translations have been added to help the beginner. For example, under the entry TÉ, hand, you will find: "**té ga aite iru** to be free; to have no work on hand." This dual feature also makes the dictionary useful for translation work.

EXPLANATORY NOTES

NOUNS, VERBS, AND ADJECTIVES. The designation of nouns (*n.*), verbs (*v.*), adjectives (*adj.*), and adverbs (*adv.*) given in this dictionary refers to the word class (part of speech) of the English equivalent and *not* to the Japanese word.

Many nouns in Japanese can be converted into verbs simply by adding *suru*: (e.g., *benkyoo suru* = to study).

A verb which is translated in English in the infinitive form appears in the "plain present affirmative" in Japanese. Beginners are reminded that when such a verb is used as a predicate verb in sentences, it can be changed to the appropriate *-masu* (polite) form: *-masu, -mashita, -masen, -masen deshita, -mashoo*, etc.

Adjectives (*i* = adjectives) are listed in their "plain present affirmative" form. When they are used as predicate adjectives, an appropriate form of *-desu* (*desu, deshita, -ku arimasen, -ku arimasen deshita*, etc.) can be used.

PERSON AND NUMBER. An arbitrary choice has been made for the person (i.e., I, you, he, she, it, we you, they) and number (singular or plural) used in the English translation of a Japanese sentence. Usually a Japanese sentence can be translated in several other ways.

HOMONYM. In Japanese, there are many words which sound and are spelled alike but which have different meanings. In the traditional Japanese writing system, however, such words may be written with different symbols (*kanji*).

COLLOQUIAL AND HONORIFICS. Very colloquial words, phrases, and sentences are marked either *colloq.* or *vulgar*. *Respect* and *humble* designate honorifics. *Respect* is an expression that can be used only in talking about someone else (not about oneself: speaker); and *humble* is used only in talking about oneself (the speaker or the speaker's in-group).

JAPANESE
DICTIONARY

Japanese-English

A

a (*interj.*) O! oh! look! **a to iwaseru** to astonish, surprise. **A taihen.** Oh! heavens! Good Lord!

AA (*interj.*) O! oh! ah! alas! dear me! (*adv.*) in that way; like that; so; **aa suru** to do so (like that); **aa iu** to say so; like that; **aa iu hito** a person like that; **aa iu koto** a thing like that; **aa iu fúu na hito** that sort of person; **aa iu fúu ni** in that way; like that. **Aa kírei da!** Oh, how beautiful! **Aa omoshírokatta.** Oh, it was so interesting! **Aa sóo?** Really? Is it? Did you?

áachi arch.

aa iu = aa yuu that sort of; **aa iu koto** that sort of thing; **aa iu hanashi** that sort of story.

áasu ground wire.

abáku to disclose, to reveal (*a secret*); to expose; to bring to light.

abara ribs; side; **abara bone** rib; side of the chest.

abaráya crumbling house; poor hut.

abare- prefix denoting: rough; rowdy; unruly; **abareuma** runaway horse.

abaremono (*n.*) rowdy; hooligan.

abaredásu to get rowdy, riotous; to break loose; grow restive; to start to behave violently.

abarekómu to force oneself into, burst into, break into; **heyá ni abarekómu** to force an entrance into a room; **ié ni abarekómu** to break into a house.

abaremawáru to rave, to riot.

abareru to act (behave) violent; to rage; to be riotous.

abekobe being topsy-turvy; **abekobe no** opposite; inverse; **abekobe ni** in a contrary manner; upside down.

abiru to pour on oneself; to bathe in; to be under fire; **hitófuro abiru** to have a bath; **chuumoku o abiru** to receive attention.

abisekakéru See abiseru.

abiseru, abisekakéru to pour on; to shower; to lay (something) on; to heap reproaches on.

ábu horsefly; gadfly.

abuku See awa.

abunage na insecure (in appearance).

ABUNAI dangerous, risky, precarious, critical; **abunai mé ni áu** to have a terrible experience. **Abunái!** Look out! Watch out!

abunakkashíi insecure, unsteady; unstable; unreliable; **abunakkashíi tétsuki de** in a clumsy manner.

ABUNAKU nearly; barely; **abunaku náru** to get dangerous. **Abunaku okureru tokoró deshita.** I almost missed the train.

abunasa danger, risk, peril.

abunasoo na dangerous-looking.

ABURA oil; fat; **aburadárake** covered with grease; oil-stained; **abura de ageru** to fry in oil; **abura ga noru** to become interested in; **aburáase** greasy sweat; **aburáase o nagáshite** by the sweat of one's brow; **aburake no áru** oily, fatty, rich (food); **aburake no nái** lean; light; **aburakkói** greasy, fatty, oily (food). **Aburakkói mono ga sukí desu.** I like greasy foods.

aburaáge = age bean curd fried in oil (popular food item).

aburáe oil painting; **aburáe o káku** to paint in oils.

aburagúsuri liniment; ointment.

aburámi fat; fatty part of meat.

aburámushi cockroach.

abúru to place over a fire; to grill; to warm; to dry; **té o abúru** to warm one's hands at a fire.

achikóchi (*adv.*), **achira kóchira** here and there; to and fro.

ACHIRA (*n.*) that direction; other side; over there; yonder; overseas; **achira no shuukan** customs of a foreign country. **Achira e ikimashóo.** Let's go that way.

ACHIRA KÓCHIRA (*n., adv.*) here and there; various places; to and fro; up and down; **achira kóchira kara** from far and near; **achira kóchira o sagasu** to look for (something) here and there; **achira kóchira inaka o ryokoo suru** to travel about the country.

adá enemy; revenge; vengeance; resentment; harm.

adana nickname.

adokenái innocent, artless; naïve (*used when speaking of a child*) **adokenái yoosu** naïve manner; innocent air.

aegi pant; gasp; **aegi aegi** gaspingly; out of breath.

aégu to pant; to gasp.

aen zinc.

aenai untimely; sad; pitiful; **aenái saigo** pitiful end (death); **aenái saigo o togéru** to come to a sad end.

aénaku sadly; unexpectedly; flatly; **aénaku kotowáru** to refuse flatly; **aénaku naru** to die.

áete (*adv.*) boldly; without hesitation; by any means; **áete suru** to dare, venture; **áete iu** I presume; I venture to say.

afuréru to overflow, run over.

agáku to paw; to struggle.

agaméru to revere; to. worship; to respect; to glorify.

aganai atonement; redemption; compensation.

aganáu to buy, purchase.

AGARIGUCHI entranceway in a Japanese-style house.

agaríori (*n.*) ascent and descent; **kaidan no agaríori** going up and down the staircase.

agarisagari rise and fall; fluctuation; **nedan no agarisagari** fluctuation of prices.

AGARU to go up, come up; to rise; to ascend, climb (up); to rise in rank; to improve; to come to an end; to visit (*humble*); to go ashore; to eat, drink (*respect*); to become nervous; **chíi ga agaru** to be promoted. **udé ga agaru** to become more skillful; **áme ga agaru** to stop raining; **riku ni agaru** to go ashore. **Mata agarimashoo.** I will call again. **Okashi o oagari kudasái.** Help yourself to a sweet, please. **Pitchaa ga agaru.** The pitcher (*baseball*) is getting nervous.

age tuck (in Japanese clothes).

ageashi fault-finding; hypercriticism; **ageashi o tóru** to trip (a person) up.

ageku (*adv.*) = **ageku ni; ageku no hate ni** the end; finally, at last; on top of all this; to make matters worse. **Shigoto o nakushita ageku ni byooki ni natta.** He lost his job, and on top of that (to make matters worse), he became ill.

agemono fried food.

agenabe frying pan.

ageoroshi = **agésage** loading and unloading; raising and lowering; **hashi no ageoroshi ni mo kogoto o iu** to find fault with everything [to make comments even on how the chopsticks are handled].

AGERU to raise, elevate, lift (up); to give, present (honorific: used when the speaker gives something to someone else). **Okane o ageta.** I gave her some money.

agésage = **agoroshi** raising and lowering; praise and blame; **háshi no agésage ni mo kogoto o iu** to be (too) particular about trifles.

ageshio flood (rising) tide.

AGÓ jaw; chin.

–agúmu suffix denoting to grow tired of, get (become) weary; **machiagúmu** to grow tired of waiting.

agura o káku to sit cross-legged.

ahen opium.

ahiru duck, drake; **ahiru no ko** duckling.

ahóo fool; idiot; blockhead; **ahóo na** foolish; stupid; **ahorashíi** foolish; silly; ridiculous; **ahóo na koto** foolish affair.

ÁI love; affection; attachment; **ai súru** to love; care for; **fukáku ai suru** to love tenderly (deeply).

ái indigo, blue; **ai-iro no** blue, bluish; **ai nézumi** bluish-gray.

ai- prefix denoting to: mutually; with each other; **ai-mukatte** face to face; **ai-narande tátsu** to stand shoulder to shoulder.

aibiki secret meeting (of lovers); rendezvous.

aiboo partner; accomplice.

aibu caress; fondling; **aibu suru** to caress, fondle, pet.

aichaku deep attachment; passion; **–ni aichaku suru** to love passionately.

AIDA space (between); time (between); distance; interval; **sono aida** in the meanwhile; **nagái aida** for a long time; **hitótsuki no aida ni** in the course of a month; **watakushi ga íkite iru aida wa** as long as I live; **róppun no aida o oite** at intervals of six minutes.

aidagara relationship; terms; **shitashíi aidagara de áru** to be on very friendly terms.

aidoku suru to read for pleasure; **aidókusha** subscriber; reader; reading public; **aidokusho** one's favorite book.

aifuku, aigi lightweight suit.

aijin lover, sweetheart; **aijoo** love, affection; **aijoo no aru hito** affectionate, warmhearted person.

aikagi passkey.

AIKAWARAZU as usual; as always; **aikawarazu isogashíi desu** as busy as ever.

aiko a tie, even game, draw; **aiko ni náru** to end in a tie. **Kore de aiko da.** This makes us even.

aikoku love for one's country, patriotism.

aikótoba password.

aikyóo charm; amiability; **aikyóo no áru hito** charming, amiable person; **aikyóo no nái hito** disagreeable person; **aikyóo o furimáku** to have a smile for everybody.

aima interval; leisure; **aima ni** at intervals; **shigoto no aima ni** in one's spare time.

aimai obscurity; ambiguity; **aimai na** obscure; ambiguous; vague.

AINIKU unluckily; unfortunately; **ainiku na** unfavorable; unfortunate. **Oainiku sama.** I am very sorry (that I do not have it). **Ainkiku áme ga futte kimásiia.** Unfortunately, it started to rain.

ainoko (*n.*) hybrid; Eurasian.

Ainu Ainus (a minority tribe of northern Japan).

airashíi charming; amiable; sweet.

AIRON iron (for pressing); **airon o kakéru** to iron.

áisatsu greeting, salutation; **áisatsu suru** to greet, salute.

aisó sociability, cordiality; **aiso no yói** sociable, cordial; **aiso no nái hito** cold, blunt person; **oaisó o iu** to flatter; **–ni aisó ga tsukíru** to be disgusted with. **Aiso yóku hanashimáshita.** He spoke very pleasantly.

aisuhókkee ice hockey.

aisukuríimu ice cream.

aita empty, vacant; opened; **té ga aita tóki** when he is free.

áitagai ni with each other.

AITÉ companion; partner; adversary; **–o aité ni suru** to challenge; to deal with; **–o aité ni shinai** to pay no attention to; **–no aité ni náru** to keep company with; to become a partner of.

aitsu that fellow; that rascal (derogatory).

áitsuide one after another; successively.

áizu signal; **áizu suru** to signal.

áji horse mackerel, tunny.

AJI taste, flavor; relish; **aji no áru** tasty; **aji no nái** tasteless; **–no aji ga suru** it tastes like; **aji ga kawaru** to become stale, turn sour; **aji o tsukéru** to flavor, season.

ÁJIA Asia; **Ájia no** (_adj._) Asian, Asiatic; **Ajiájin** (_n._) Asian, Asiatic.

ajikenái irksome, wearisome; lonely; **ajikenáku kurasu** to lead a miserable life.

ajina dainty; clever; smart; **ajina kóto o suru** to act cleverly; **ajina kóto o iu** to say something clever.

ajisai hydrangea.

ajitsukénori seasoned seaweed (a popular food item).

ajiwáu to taste; to experience; to enjoy; to appreciate.

ÁKA (_n._) red, crimson, scarlet; communism; communist; **áka no tanin** utter stranger.

aká dirt, filth; **aka dárake** dirty, filthy; **–ni aka ga tsuku** to become dirty; **aká o nagásu** to wash off dirt; to wash (oneself).

AKABOO redcap, porter (for luggage).

AKACHAN = **akago** baby, infant.

akagire chap, crack (in the skin); **akagire ga kiréru** to become chapped.

akágo See **ákachan.**

akahaji disgrace; open shame; **akahaji o kakasaréru** to be put to shame.

AKAI red, ruddy, flushed; **akai kao o suru** to blush.

akaji red figures, deficit; **akaji o dásu** to go into the red; to have a deficit.

akajímita soiled, dirty.

akaku ruddily; redly; **akaku náru** to redden; to flush; to glow.

akanboo baby, infant. (See also **ákachan.**)

akami redness; tinge of red.

akami lean meat.

Akamon Red Gate of Tokyo University; synonym for Tokyo University.

akanuke polish, gloss; refinement; **akanuke no shita hito** polished person; **akanuke no shinai hito** unpolished, uncouth person.

akarámu to turn red; to glow; to ripen (fruit).

akarasama na plain, clear; frank, candid; **akarasama ni** plainly; frankly; without reserve; **akarasama ni iéba** to be frank; to tell the truth in plain terms.

akari light, lamp; **akari o tsukéru** to light a lamp.

AKARUI bright; light; knowing well; versed in; **akaruku náru** to grow light; **akarui heya** well-lighted room; **hooritsu ni akarui** to be familiar with the laws; **akarui uchi ni** while it is light; before it gets dark.

akarumi light place; light; **akarumi e dásu** to bring a thing to light; to expose (something).

akásu to spend the whole night; to sit up all night; to reveal the truth, to confess; to speak one's mind.

akásu to weary, tire; **kane ni akáshite** regardless of the expense; regardless of the cost.

akatsuchi red earth (clay).

akatsuki = **akegata** dawn, daybreak; **akatsuki chikáku** toward daybreak; **–no akatsuki ni wa** when; in the event of; in case of.

akazátoo brown sugar.

akegata See **akatsuki.**

akehanásu to throw open (a window).

akekure morning and evening; day and night; all the time.

AKERU to open; to turn over (pages); to make room (for); to evacuate (a house, premises); to empty (a box); to expire; **ie o akeru** to stay out; **aná o akeru** to make a hole; **mizu o akeru** to pour out water. **Yó ga akeru.** The day is breaking.

AKI room; space; vacancy; **aki o fusagu** to fill a gap.

ÁKI autumn, fall; **akibare** a clear autumn day.

aki- prefix denoting: vacant, unoccupied; spare; **akibin** empty bottle; **akichi** vacant lot; **akidaru** empty barrel; **akima** vacant room.

akimékura illiterate (person).

akínai trade, business; **akínai suru** to do business; **akínai o shite iru** to be in business; to be engaged in a trade; **akínai**

jóozu good at trade; **akinai beta** poor at trade.

akináu to deal in, trade in.

AKÍRAKA NA bright; clear; **akíraka ni suru** to make clear; to account for; **akíraka ni** brightly; clearly; undoubtedly; no doubt. **Akíraka desu.** It is clear.

akirame resignation; relinquishment; **akiraméru** to give up; to resign oneself to; to submit to one's fate; to relinquish.

akireru to be amazed at; to be dumfounded; be disgusted with; **akírete** with astonishment; in amazement; **akírete monó ga ienai** to be dumfounded.

akíru to get tired of, be sick of; to have enough of; **akíru hodo tabéru** to eat one's fill; **–ni akiyasúi** to be soon tired of; **akíru hodo asobu** to play to one's heart's content.

akisu sneakthief.

AKIYA vacant house; unoccupied house; house for rent.

akka suru to go from bad to worse.

akkan rascal, rogue.

akke (*n.*) being dumfounded when an event has happened; **akke nái** too soon; too brief; too sudden; **akke ni toraréru** to be taken aback; to be amazed. **Tsukíhi ga akke náku tátte shimátta.** The days passed all too quickly. **Sore dé wa amari akke nái.** That's too abrupt.

akkoo abuse, insulting remarks; **akkoo suru** to abuse, insult.

akogare longing, yearning; desire.

akogareru to long for, yearn for, yearn after.

áku evil, vice; wrong; wickedness; **áku ni mukuíru ni zén o motte suru** to return good for evil.

AKU to open; to be opened; to become empty, become vacant; **té ga aku** to be free, be disengaged. **Makú ga aku.** The curtain rises.

akubi yawn; **ooákubi** great yawn; **akubi suru** to yawn.

akudói tedious; heavy (color or food); glaring.

akufuu evil practices; evil manners; evil habit.

akuheki bad habit; vice.

akuhitsu illegible handwriting; poor penmanship.

ákui malice, ill will; malicious intent; **ákui de** from malice; purposely; **ákui no áru hito** malicious, evil-minded person.

ákuji evil thing; evil deed; criminal action.

AKUKÁNJOO ill feeling; ill will.

ákumade to the utmost; to the best of one's ability; persistently; **ákumade mo** to the last; stubbornly; to the end; **ákumade**

yaru to do one's utmost.

akunin bad person, villain.

akuratsu na unscrupulous; sharp; crafty; wicked.

akurei bad precedent; bad example; **akurei o tsukúru** to set a bad precedent.

AKURU next, following (time); **akuru asa** the following morning; **akuru toshi** the following year.

ákuseku diligently, industriously; busily; restlessly; **ákuseku suru** to busy oneself; worry about; **–ni ákuseku to suru** to be busy with; **ákuseku to kaségu** to work hard (for a living).

ákusento accent, stress; pitch (of the voice).

ÁKUSHU handshake; **ákushu suru** to shake hands.

akushuu bad habit; evil practices; **akushuu ga tsuku** to develop a bad habit; **akushuu o dassúru** to get rid of a bad habit.

akutóo villain, scoundrel.

akuun ill luck; evil fate.

akuyoo misuse; improper use; abuse; **akuyoo suru** to misuse; abuse.

akuyuu bad friend; bad companion; **akuyuu to maiiwaru** to keep bad company.

áma diving woman (professional pearl-diver).

AMA- prefix denoting: rain; of rain, for rain; **amadare** raindrops; **amádo** rain door; **amagása** umbrella; **amagoi** prayers for rain; **amágu** rain gear; **amagumo** rain cloud; **amámizu** rain water; **amágu o yóoi shite déru** to go out prepared for rain; **amágu no yóoi o suru** to provide oneself with rain gear.

amachua amateur.

amaeru, amattareru to behave like a spoiled child; to coax; to be coquettish; to take advantage of; **amaeru yóo ni** coaxingly. **Okotoba ni amaemashóo.** I'll take advantage of your kind offer.

amaguri roast chestnuts.

AMAI sweet, sugary; not salted enough; indulgent; not strict; **amaku suru** to sweeten; **amai mono** sweets, candy; **amai kotoba** sweet (soft) words; **amaku míru** to have little regard for a person. **Kono sáke wa ama-jio da.** This salmon is not salted enough.

amajio slightly salted.

amakuchi fondness for sweet things; sweet tooth; honeyed words. **Káre wa amakuchi da.** He has a sweet tooth.

amami sweet flavor; sweetness; **amami no áru** sweetish; **amami o tsukéru** to sweeten. **Amami ga tarinai.** It is not sweet enough.

amámori leak in the roof.

amamóyoo signs of rain; **amamóyoo no sóra** a threatening sky. **Amamóyoo desu.** It looks like rain.

AMANÉKU widely, universally; far and wide; **amanéku sékai ni shirarete iru** to be known all over the world; **amanéku zénkoku o jun'yuu suru** to travel all over the country.

AMANJÍRU, amanzúru to be content with, be satisfied with; to put up with; **amánjite** contentedly; willingly; **amánjite seisai o ukéru** to submit willingly to punishment. **Káre wa kore ni amánjite wa inai.** He is not content with this.

Amanógawa Milky Way; Galaxy.

amanzúru See **amanjíru.**

AMARI See **ANMARI**

AMARÍ remainder, rest; surplus, excess; remnants.

AMÁRU to remain, be left over; to be too much; to be in excess; to be beyond one's power; **mini amáru kooei** an undeserved honor; **chikará ni amáru** beyond one's power.

amásu to leave over; to save; **kane o amasázu tsukau** to spend all one's money. **Hitotsu mo amasánakatta.** I didn't leave even one.

ámata (a great) many; many a; a number of; numerous.

amatsusae besides; moreover; what is more; into the bargain; to make matters worse.

amattareru See **amaeru.**

amattarui sweetish; sugary; **amattarui kotoba** honeyed words; **amattarui shibai** sentimental play (drama).

amayádori suru to take shelter from the rain.

amayakasu to pet; to indulge (a child) too much; to spoil.

amayoke shelter from the rain; protection against rain.

amazake sweet drink made from fermented rice.

amazarashi exposure to rain.

ÁME rain; **áme no** rainy; wet; **ame tsúzuki** spell of rainy weather; **áme ni náru** to change to rain; to begin to rain; **áme ni áu** to be caught in the rain. **Áme ga furisóo desu.** It looks like rain.

AME candy; wheat gluten.

AMEFÚRI rain; rainy weather; rainy day; **amefúri ni sóto o arúku** to walk in the rain.

ameiro no light brown.

AMERIKA America; **Amerika no** (*adj.*) American; **AMERIKÁJIN** (*n.*) American; **Amerika Gasshúukoku** United States of America.

ami net; seine; **ami no me** meshes (of a net).

amibári, amíboo knitting needles.

amidana rack (in a train or bus).

amímono (*n.*) knitting; crocheting; **amímono o suru** to knit.

aminome mesh.

ámu to knit; to braid; **kutsúshita o ámu** to knit socks.

án proposal; bill; draft; plan; opinion; idea; **án o dásu** to make a proposal; **án o tatéru** to make a plan; **án o tsukúru** to make a draft; **án ni sooi shite** contrary to expectation; **án no gótoku** as was expected.

án bean paste, bean jam.

ANÁ hole; aperture; den, cave; pit; loss; shortage; fault; **aná o akeru** to make a hole, perforate; **záisan ni aná o akeru** to cut into one's assets; **aná o fusagu** to fill up a hole; stop a gap.

anadori contempt; disdain; **anadóru** to despise; to slight; to make light of; to look down upon; **anadori o ukéru** to be despised; to be scorned; **anadorigatái** formidable. **Shooteki o anadóru na.** Don't despise a weak enemy.

anagachi necessarily, of necessity; always (used with a negative). **Sore wa anagachi múri de wa nai.** It's not altogether unreasonable.

anago sea eel.

an'ánri ni tacitly; by tacit agreement; secretly; **an'ánri ni shoodaku suru** to give tacit consent. **An'ánri ni itchi shita.** It was tacitly agreed.

anaságashi o suru to find fault (with).

ANÁTA you, sweetheart.

ANATAGATA you (*pl.* formal).

ANÁTATACHI you (*pl.*).

anáunsaa announcer.

anbái seasoning; taste; state of health; condition; **anbái suru** to season; to arrange; **yói anbái ni** fortunately.

anbáransu unbalance;
eiyoo no **anbáransu** unbalance of diet.

anchaku safe arrival; **anchaku suru** to arrive safely.

anchoku na cheap, low-priced, inexpensive; **anchoku ni** cheaply, inexpensively.

anchuu mosaku suru to grope in the dark.

ANE older sister.

anemúko husband of an older sister.

ANGAI NA unexpected; unforeseen; surprising; **angai ni** unexpectedly; **angai muzukashii** more difficult than imagined.

ÁNI older brother.

aníyome elder brother's wife.

anji hint; suggestion; **anji suru** to hint; to suggest; **anji o atáeru** to give a hint; **anji ni tónda** suggestive; full of suggestions.

ANJÍRU to be anxious, be concerned; to worry.

ánka cheapness; low price; **ánka na** cheap; inexpensive; **ánka ni** cheaply; at a low price; **ánka na seikatsu** cheap living; **ánka na káiraku** cheap pleasure.

ankéeto questionnaire.

anki suru to learn by heart, memorize.

ANMARI, AMARI too much; excessively; too hard; cruel; unreasonable. **Sore wa anmari desu.** That's too hard. That's too cruel. **Anmari omoshíroku nái.** It's not too interesting.

anma masseur; massage; **anma suru** to massage.

ANMIN quiet sleep; sound sleep; **anmin suru** to sleep well; **anmin o boogai suru** to disturb someone else's sleep.

anmoku tacit consent, tacit understanding. **anmoku no uchi ni** by tacit consent.

ANNA that sort of; like that; such; **anna ni** like that; in that way; **anna utsukushíi musume** such a pretty girl; a girl as pretty as that; **anna hito** a person like that; that sort of person.

ANNÁI guidance; conduct; invitation; **annái suru** to usher, guide; to invite; **annáijoo** letter or card of invitation; **annáiki** guidebook; **annáisha** guide; usher; pilot; **annaisho** guidebook, handbook; **annái náshi ni** unannounced; without knowing; without a guide; **annái o kóu** to ask to see. **Annái náshi ni háitte kita.** She entered the room without knocking.

annei public peace; public welfare.

án ni by hints; tacitly; in secret; implicitly; **án ni shiraseru** to hint; suggest; insinuate.

ANO that; those; **ano yóo na** like that; of that sort; that sort of; **ano kata** he; she; that person. **Ano ne.** You see! I say, Listen!

anoo well; I say; look here.

ano yo other world; next world; **ano yo de in** the world to come.

anpan bean-jam bun; bun.

ÁNPI safety; welfare; health; **ánpi o tazunéru** to inquire after (someone's) health.

anpojóoyaku the (Japan-U.S.) Security Pact.

ÁNRAKU comfort, ease; **ánraku na** comfortable, easy; happy; **anrakú isu** easy chair; **ánraku na seikatsu o suru** to lead a life of ease; **ánraku ni kurasu** to live comfortably.

ANSEI quietness, rest; **ansei ni** quietly; in quiet; **ansei o tamótsu** to keep quiet; to lie quietly.

ANSHIN peace of mind, freedom from anxiety; confidence; **anshin suru** to feel at ease; to feel relieved; **anshin saseru** to set (someone) at ease; **anshin no dekíru hito** reliable person; **anshin no dekinai** unreliable person; **anshin shite** with confidence; with peace of mind.

anshitsu dark room.

anshoo recitation; **anshoo suru** say by rote.

anshutsu invention; contrivance; **anshutsu suru** to think out; to contrive, devise; to invent.

ansoku rest, respose **ansoku suru** to rest; to take a rest.

ansokújitsu Sunday, Sabbath.

anta (colloq.) you.

antei stability; equilibrium; **antei suru** to be stabilized; to be settled; **antei o tamótsu** to keep one's balance; **antei o ushináu** to lose one's balance.

antena antenna.

ANZEN safety, security; **anzen na** safe; secure; **anzen ni** safely; securely; **anzen chitái** safety zone; **anzen kámisori** safety razor.

ANZU apricot.

anzúru to be anxious about, worry about. **Watakushi no kotó o anjínaide kudasái.** Don't worry about me.

ÁO blue; green; **aoáo shita** verdant; freshly green; **áoba** green leaves, foliage.

aodátami new or freshly renovated mat.

aógu to fan; to raise one's eyes; to ask for; to depend upon; **hójo o aógu** to ask for aid. **Sóra o aóida.** He looked up at the sky.

aoj hollyhock.

AÓI blue; green; pale; unripe; inexperienced; **áoku náru** to become blue (pale); **áoku someru** to dye (something) blue. **Aói kao o shite iru.** He looks pale. **Sóra ga áoku hárete iru.** The sky is clear.

aoíki gasp; **aoíki o tsuku** to gasp; to heave a deep sigh; **aoiki tóiki de** gaspingly; with greatest effort. **Aoiki tóiki desu.** I am in great distress.

aojáshin blueprint.

aojírói pale, pallid; sickly.

aomi blueness; blue tint; greenness; **aomi gakátta** bluish; greenish.

aómono vegetables; **aomono íchiba** vegetable market; **aomonoya** greengrocer; vegetable seller.

aomuki ni on one's back. **aomuki ni taoréru** to fall on one's back; **aomúku** to look up, turn one's face up.

aonisai greenhorn; raw youth; stripling.

aónori seaweed processed for food.

aori flapping; bump; **aori o kurau** to feel the influence of; to be hit by; **aóru** to fan; to flap; to stir up, incite; **kaze ni aorárete**

iru to flap in the wind. **Kaze ga kaen o aótta.** The strong wind fanned the flames.

aoténjoo (azure) heaven; vault of heaven; open sky.

aounábara blue expanse of water; ocean.

aozaméru to turn pale. **Aozámeta kao o shite iru.** His face is white as a sheet.

aozóra blue sky.

APÁATO apartment house.

appaku pressure; stress; oppression; **appaku suru** to bear down upon.

ap'páre (n.) being splendid; bravo!; well done! **appáre na** splendid! admirable; **appáre na hataraki** splendid achievement; **appáre na jinbutsu** person of fine (admirable) character.

ára ah! oh! good gracious! oh, my! (used by women).

ará defect, fault, blemish; bony parts (of fish); **ará o sagasu** to look for defects (in others); find fault with others.

ara- prefix denoting: coarse; rough, harsh; **arashígoto** a rough work.

Arabia Arabia; **Arabia no** (adj.) Arabic; Arabian; **Arabiago** Arabic language; **Arabiájin** (n.) Arab; Arabian; **Arabia súuji** Arabic numerals.

aradatéru to excite; to agitate; to exasperate; to inflame; to complicate; **kotó o aradatéru** to complicate matters; to aggravate the matter.

aragyoo asceticism.

ARAI rough; coarse; rude; wild; violent; **arai shimá** a rough pattern; **araku** harshly; roughly. **Úmi ga arai.** The sea is rough.

arai wash; washing; raw fish slices; **araigami** newly washed and untied hair; **araitate** just washed; **araitate no** newly washed; **arai ga kiku** to wash well; to be washable; **arai ga kikanai** not washable.

ARAKAJIME previously; in anticipation; beforehand; **arakajime tsuuchi suru** to inform beforehand; **arakajime yóoi suru** to prepare beforehand.

ARAKATA for the most part; mostly; most of. **Shigoto wa arakata dekiagari máshita.** The work is nearly completed.

arakezuri no roughly planned; rough-hewn.

arakure ótoko (n.) rough; rowdy.

aramashi roughly; nearly, almost; practically; all but; briefly.

aramonóya kitchenware dealer.

aránkagiri as much as possible; **arankágiri ni** every; all; utmost; **arankágiri no chikará o dáshite** with the utmost exertion; **aránkagiri no kóe de** at the top of one's voice; as loudly as possible.

arappói rough; rough-mannered; violent.

arare hail; hailstone; salty rice cracker

(seasoned with soy sauce). **Arare ga fútte iru.** It is hailing.

araryóoji drastic treatment, drastic remedy; drastic measures.

araságashi (n.) fault-finding.

ÁRASHI storm; **árashi no** stormy.

arashígoto rough work; rough labor.

ARASOI quarrel; contention; **arasoi o okósu** to start a dispute; **uchiwa no arasoi** family quarrel; internal troubles.

ARASOU to quarrel; to dispute; to struggle, compete, vie; **saki o arasóu** to scramble for a seat; **arasóu koto no dekínai** indisputable.

ARASU to ruin, to devastate.

arasuji outline, brief summary.

ARATAMÁRU to be changed, be altered; to be improved, be reformed; to take a turn for the worse (in illness); to stand on ceremony. **Soo aratamaránaide kudasái.** Don't stand on ceremony.

arataméru to renew; to renovate, alter, change, revise; to improve; to examine.

aratámete anew; another time; **aratámete tazunéru** to ask again. **Aratámete mairimásu.** I'll come another time. I'll come again.

árata na new, fresh, novel; **árata na súmai** a new house; **árata ni hajimeru** to begin anew.

arate fresh force; new hand.

ARAU to wash; to purify; to cleanse; **ashí o arau** to wash one's hands of a matter; to quit.

araúmi rough sea, stormy sea.

arawaréru to come out; to make an appearance, turn up, show oneself. **Kao ni arawárete iru.** It is written on your face.

ARAWÁSU to show, display; to bring to light, lay bare; to write (a book, novel, etc.); to publish; to make known; **udemáe o arawásu** to show ability; **tookaku o arawásu** to stand head and shoulders above others; **ikarí o kao ni arawásu** to show anger (in one's face); **na o arawásu** to win fame; to distinguish oneself.

ARAYÚRU all; every possible; all sorts of; **arayúru shúrui no hito** all sorts of people; **arayúru shudan o kokoromíru** to try every known method.

ARE that; it; roughness, coarseness; **ARE!** listen! look! see! **are hodo** like that; that (so) much; that degree; **are hodo ittá noni** in spite of all that I have said; **are hodo kane ga átte mo** with all his riches; **are ka kore ka** this or that; **are ya kóre ya** this and that; with one thing or another; **are ya kóre ya de ki o momu** to worry

oneself with one thing or another. **Are!
Nán daroo?** Listen! What can that be?

arebíyori stormy weather.

arechi wasteland; uncultivated land.

arehatéru to be dilapidated; to be utterly
ruined; **areháteta** dilapidated; ruined.

arekkiri since then; any more; all; last.
Arekkiri otosata ga arimasén. I haven't
heard from him since then. **Arekkiri
yoshimáshita.** After that I left off
completely.

aremawáru to rush about furiously.

aremóyoo threatening sky; signs of
approaching storm.

areno wildness; wilds; wild tract of land.

areru to fall into decay; to lie waste; to rush
about furiously; to be rough. **Úmi wa
arete ita.** The sea was rough.

ari ant; **arízuka** an anthill.

ariamáru (*prenoun*) ample; abundant;
ariamáru hodo kane ga áru to have
money to spare.

ariári to vividly; distinctly; plainly.

ariawase potluck; **ariawase no** ready; on
hand; **misé ni ariawase no shinamono**
articles in stock; **ariawase no mono o
tabéru** to take potluck; to eat what is
available.

aribai alibi.

arifureta common; ordinary.

arigáchi frequent occurrence; **arigáchi no**
common; frequent. **Konna kotó wa
arigáchi desu.** Such things are apt to
happen.

arigane cash on hand.

arigatagáru to be thankful, feel grateful;
arigata méiwaku unappreciated favor;
misplaced kindness; **arigata námida** tears
of gratitude. **Anó hito wa watashi no
okurimono o arigatagarimáshita.** She
was thankful for my gift.

ARIGATÁI thankful; **arigatái kotó ni wa**
fortunately; **arigátaku** with thanks.

arigatámi gratefulness, sense of gratitude.

ARIGÁTOO many thanks; I am much
obliged to you. **Arigátoo gozaimasu.**
Thank you.

árika whereabouts; place where a thing is.

arikitari no customary; conventional;
arikitari no hoohoo the customary
method.

ari no mama exact truth; plain fact; **ari no
mamá o iu** to tell the exact truth; **ari no
mamá ni** just as it is; frankly.

arísama circumstances; state; condition. **Soo
iu arísama desu.** That's the situation.

arisóo na seemingly possible; **arisóo mo nái**
unlikely; improbable. **Arisóo na kotó
desu.** It's likely to happen.

aritei as it is; frankly (*colloq.*); **aritei ni iu**
to speak the truth; state frankly.

aritsúku to come by, come upon; to find; to
get, obtain; **shigoto ni aritsúku** to get
work.

arittake all that there is; all that one has;
arittake no chikará o dásu to put forth
all one's efforts.

ariubekarazáru impossible; improbable;
ariubéki possible; probable. **Sore wa
ariubekarazáru kotó desu.** That's
impossible. That could never happen.

ÁRU certain; some; a; an; **áru tokoro de** at a
certain place; **áru hi** one day; once; **áru
hito** a certain person; a person;
somebody; **áru toki** on a certain occasion;
once upon a time.

ÁRU to be at; to exist, live; to be situated; to
lie; to have; to take place; to experience;
to find; to get. **Hón ga tsukue no úe ni
arimásu.** The book is on the desk.
**Oomori wa Tookyoo to Yokohama no
aida ni áru.** Omori lies between Tokyo
and Yokohama. **Tookyoo ni itta kotó ga
arimásu ka?** Have you ever been to
Tokyo? **Kono hón wa dóko ni
arimáshita ka?** Where did you find this
book? **Taihen na kotó ga átta no desu.**
A dreadful thing happened.

ARUBÁITO side job;
ARUBÁITO SURU to do a side job.

ARUBAMU album.

arufabétto alphabet.

ARÚIWA or else; perhaps; probably; maybe.
Arúiwa sóo ka mo shirenai. It may be
so. It is not impossible.

áruji master; host; head of the family.

arukaséru to make walk, let walk (said of a
child, horse, etc.)

arukikáta one's manner of walking.

arukimawáru to walk about; to wander
about; to go around; to gad about.

arukooru alcohol.

ARÚKU to walk, go on foot. **Arúku no wa
karada ni taihen íi desu.** Walking is
very good for your health.

arumájiki improper; unbecoming;
improbable.

arumi, aruminyuumu aluminum.

áruto alto.

ÁSA morning; in the morning; **ása háyaku**
early in the morning; **ása no aida** all
morning; **ása kara ban máde** from
morning till evening; **ásaban** every
morning and evening.

asa hemp; flax; linen; **asaito** hemp yarn;
asanawa hempen cord.

asa- prefix denoting: light; shallow;
asamídori light green.

10

aságao morning glory.

asagi (n.) light blue.

ASAGÓHAN breakfast. Asagóhan wa hachíji desu. Breakfast is at eight.

asagurói dark; dark-skinned; brown.

asáhaka na shallow (of mind); superficial; half-witted.

ásahi morning sun; rising sun.

ASAI shallow; superficial; short, brief; asai kawa shallow river; asai kangáe shallow thought; hi ga asai . . . it is a short time (since).

asakusá nori dried seaweed (food).

asamashíi mean, miserable; wretched; asamashíi yonónaka the wretched world; asamashíi kokoro no otoko a mean-spirited man.

asamídori (n.) light green.

asanagi morning calm.

asáne o suru to lie in bed late; to sleep late; asanéboo late-riser, sleepyhead; asanéboo o suru to oversleep; to get up late.

asáru to fish for; to search for; to hunt for; iró o asáru to philander.

asase shoal; shallows; asase ni noriagéru to run aground.

asatsuyu morning dew.

ASÁTTE day after tomorrow. Asátte ome ni kakarimásu. I will see you the day after tomorrow.

asayake morning glow; sky at dawn.

ÁSE sweat; perspiration; asebámu to become sweaty; to be wet with sweat; asékaki one who perspires profusely; áse ga déru to perspire; áse o káku to perspire; to become sweaty; asemídoro ni nátte in a sweat; soaked with sweat; ásemizu o nagáshite hataraku to sweat with hard work; work by the sweat of one's brow.

asemo prickly heat.

aséru to hurry; to get impatient; to be hasty.

aséru to fade, to discolor. Iró ga áseru. The color has faded.

ASHÍ foot; leg; paw; step; pace; ashi no kóo instep; ashi nó ura sole; ashiáto footprint; ashí ni makásete iku to go without knowing where; ashí ga tsuku to be traced; leave a clue.

áshi reed; rush.

ashiba scaffolding; foothold.

ashibumi step; ashibumi suru to step; stamp one's feet.

ashibyóoshi keeping time with the feet.

ashidamari stand; footing; ashidamari o éru to get a footing.

ashidome confinement; ashidome o suru to keep (someone) indoors.

ashidori gait; manner of walking; tread.

ashikake foothold; pedal. Kite kara

ashikake gonen ni náru. It is five [calendar] years since I came here.

ashikárazu. Please don't take it amiss.

ASHÍKUBI ankle.

ashimóto place where one stands; ashimóto ni at (near) one's feet; ashimóto no akarui uchi ni before it gets dark; before getting caught; ashimóto o míru to take advantage of (someone else's) weakness.

ashinami pace; ashinami o soróete with measured steps; keeping pace with; ashinami o soróete arúku to walk in step.

ashioto footfall, sound of a footstep.

ashirai treatment; reception.

ashiráu to treat, entertain; to receive; to handle; to deal with; to harmonize; to add.

ashi shígeku often, frequently (refers to visits); ashi shígeku kayou to visit frequently.

ASHITA, ASÚ tomorrow. Ashita mata. See you again tomorrow.

ashitemátoi encumbrance, burden, nuisance; ashitemátoi ni náru to become a nuisance; to get in the way.

asobaseru to leave (something) idle; kane o asobasete oku to let money lie idle.

ASOBI play; sport; amusement; pleasure; recreation; sensual pleasure; dissipation; asobi ni iku to go out to play; to seek recreation; asobi gátera for amusement; half in play.

ASOBU to play; to be idle; to go on a spree; to amuse.

ASOKO that place; there; asoko ni over there, yonder.

assaku pressure; compression; assaku suru to press.

ASSÁRI simply; lightly; moderately; briefly; assári shita simple; light; plain; assári katazukéru to make short work of.

assen mediation; assen suru to help, to mediate; arbitrate; asénsha mediator, arbitrator.

ASÚ See ASHITA.

asufáruto asphalt. asufáruto no michi asphalt road.

asupirín aspirin.

ataéru to give; to let have; to present, award; shigoto o ataéru to give work; –ni songal o ataéru to inflict damage on; ataeráreta shigoto work assigned.

átafuta hurriedly; helter-skelter.

atai price; value; atai suru to be worth; to cost; to deserve.

ÁTAKAMO just as if, so to speak. Átakamo Nihonjín no yóoni. Just as if she were Japanese.

ATAMÁ head; top; brains; **atamá o sagéru** to bow respectfully; **atamá ga yói a** clear head; **atamá ga warúi** stupid; **atama gónashi ni** unsparingly; cruelly; **atamá kara ashi no saki máde** from head to foot; **atamákabu** leader; leading member.

atamakázu number of persons.

atamawari equal division; **atamawari ni suru** to divide equally, allot equal shares.

ATARASHÍI new, fresh, novel; recent, latest; **atarashíi sakana** fresh fish; **ataráshiku** newly; anew; afresh; **ataráshiku suru** to renovate; freshen; **ataráshiku hajimeru** to begin anew.

átari neighborhood; vicinity; near; **–no átari ni** in the neighborhood of; near; about; **átari kamáwazu** regardless of the people present.

atari success; hit; **atari doshi** fruitful (successful) year; **atari fuda** price-number ticket; **atari hazure** hit or miss; success or failure; **atari o tóru** to make a hit.

ATARIMAE NO right, proper, reasonable; deserving; natural; usual; **atarimae no kotó** a matter of course. **Okóru no wa atarimae désu.** She has good reason to get angry.

atarisawari consequence; **atarisawari no nái** neutral, noncommittal; **atarisawari no nái kotó o iu** to talk so as not to hurt someone's feelings.

ataru to strike; to come true; to be exposed; to disagree with; to warm oneself; to succeed; to try; **soozoo ga ataru** to guess right; **ataru bekarazáru** irresistible; overwhelming; overpowering. **Keikaku ga atatta.** The plan succeeded. **Tónikaku atatte kudakéro da.** Try anyhow.

ATATAKÁI warm; genial; mild; **atatakái hito** warmhearted, genial person; **atatakai fuyu** warm winter; **atatákaku náru** to become warm; **atatakami** mildness; warmth; geniality; **atatakami no áru** warm, warmhearted.

atatkasóo ni snugly.

atatamáru to get warm; to warm oneself; **Yatto kore de atatamarimáshita.** Now I'm warm.

atataméru to warm up, heat; **kyuukoo o atataméru** to renew an old friendship; **té o atataméru** to warm one's hands (over a brazier).

ate aim, object; **ate ni naránai** unreliable; **ate náshi ni** aimlessly; at random; **atedo náku** aimlessly, without an aim, at random; **ate ni suru** to depend on; **ate ga nái** to find no clue.

–ate addressed to; **watashiate no tegami** letter addressed to me.

ategai appointment; allotment; **ategaibuchi** rations; stipend (*colloq.*).

ategáu to apportion; to allow; to give rations; to supply.

atehamáru to apply to; to hold good for; to conform to; **atehaméru** to apply; to fit; to conform.

atekkosuri, atekosuri sly hint; insinuating remark.

atekomi anticipation; expectation.

atekómu to expect; to hope; **atekónde** in expectation of.

atekosúru to make an insinuating remark; to satirize.

atena address (place); **atena no hito** addressee; **atena o káku** to address a letter.

ateru to hit; to touch; to guess; to expose to; to address to; **múto ni ateru** to hit the mark. **Anó hito ni atete tegami a dishimáshita.** I sent a letter to her attention. **Hí ni atenáide kudasái.** Please do not expose it to the sun. **aterareru** to be hit; to be affected by; to disagree with. **Tábeta sakana ni ateraremáshita.** The fish that I ate didn't agree with me.

atezúiryoo conjecture, random guess; **atezúiryoo o suru** to hazard a guess.

atezuppoo guess; guesswork; **atezuppoo ni** at random; **atezuppoo o iu** to hazard a guess.

ÁTO back, rear; results; **áto ni** behind; **áto de** later; **áto ni nokóru** to stay behind; **áto o ou** to chase after. **Áto ga warúi daroo.** The results won't be good.

atogama successor; **atogama ni suwaru** to succeed (someone).

átokara átokara one after another; in rapid succession.

atokata trace, vestige; proof, evidence; **atokata mo nái** unfounded, groundless.

atokatázuke clearing up; **atokatázuke o suru** to put things in order after a work is completed.

atomáwashi postponement, deferment; **atomáwashi ni suru** to defer, postpone.

atomódori relapse; setback; **atomódori suru** to go back; to degenerate.

atóoshi o suru to push from behind; to back up; to support; to abet.

átosaki fore and aft; first and last; both ends; **átosaki ni náru** to be mixed up; to be in the wrong order; **átosaki no kangáe naku** regardless of the consequences; thoughtlessly.

atoshímatsu settlement (of an affair); **atoshímatsu o suru** to put in order.

atótori inheritor; successor.

atsugami pasteboard, cardboard.

atsugáru to be very sensitive to the heat. **Watashi wa atsugári desu.** I feel the heat.

atsugéshoo heavy makeup; **atsugéshoo shita** thickly made up; heavily powdered.

atsugi many layers of clothing; **atsugi suru** to be warmly dressed.

ATSÚI very warm; hot; **átsuku naru** to become hotter; **átsuku suru** to warm; heat; **onná ni átsuku naru** to run madly after a woman.

ATSUI thick; heavy; **atsui kimono** heavy clothes; **atsui hón** bulky book.

atsukai management; handling; treatment; reception. **Shínsetsu na atsukai o ukemáshita.** I received kind treatment.

atsukamashíí impudent, brazen, shameless; **atsukamáshiku suru** to act shamelessly; **atsukamáshisa** impudence, shamelessness.

atsukau to handle, manage; to transact; **jímu o atsukau** to transact business; **kázoku no shite atsukau** to treat as a member of the family.

atsukurushíí close; sultry; sweltering.

ATSUMARI meeting, assembly; crowd, group.

atsumáru to meet, assemble. **Kúji ni atsumarimashóo.** Let's meet at nine. **Atsumáre!** Line up!

atsuméru to gather, collect; to call together; **hitai o atsuméru** to put two heads together; to talk over something.

atsurae order (purchase); **atsurae no** custom made; **atsuráeru** to order from; to place an order; **atsurae muki no** just the thing; the very thing (person) for . . .

atsureki friction. **Atsureki ga shoojíru.** Friction arises.

atsúryoku pressure; stress; **atsúryoku o kuwaeru** to pressure.

ÁTSUSA heat, warmth; **atsusa átari** heat prostration; sunstroke; **átsusa ni ataru** to suffer from the (summer) heat.

ATSUSA thickness. **Atsusa wa íkura arimásu ka?** How thick is that?

attootéki na overwhelming; **attootéki daitasuu** overwhelming majority.

ÁU to meet; to see; to have an interview with, meet with; **hito ni áu** to meet someone; **hidói me ní áu** to have a terrible time; **áme ni áu** to be caught in the rain.

áu to agree with; to fit in; to be in tune with; **pittári áu** to fit perfectly. **Kono**

tabémono wa watakushi ni wa aimasén. This food doesn't agree with me.

áuto out; out of play (in baseball).

awá bubbles, foam, lather; **awá ga tátsu** to bubble, foam; to ferment; **awá o kúu** to be flustered.

áwa millet.

áwabi abalone.

áware pity; sadness; **áware na** pitiful, poor, sad, miserable; **awaremi** pity, compassion, mercy; **awarému** to pity; **awaremubéki** poor, pitiable, miserable, wretched; **awareppói** pitiful, poor, sad, miserable; **áware ni omoú** to feel pity; **awaremi o kakéru** to treat with tenderness or compassion; **awaremi no fukái hito** person of great compassion.

awase lined lightweight garment.

awaseme joint; seam.

awaséru to put together, unite; **chikará o awaséru** to combine efforts; **hanashi no chooshi o awaséru** to chime in; **tokei o awaséru** to set a watch by; **genbun to awaséru** to compare with the original.

awatadashíí restless; busy; hurried.

awatemono giddy (flighty) person.

AWATERU to be confused; to lose one's head; to hurry.

áwaya exclamation of alarm, agitation, or surprise; **áwaya to míru ma ni** in an instant; in the twinkling of an eye.

awayókuba if things go well.

ayá figure, design; twill; damask; figure of speech.

ayabúmu to fear; to doubt; to hesitate; to have misgivings.

ayadóru to interweave; to embellish; to make designs.

ayamachi fault; mistake; blunder.

ayamári mistake, error.

ayamáru to err. **Sentaku o ayamarimáshita.** He made a mistake in his choice.

ayamáru to apologize.

ayame iris.

AYASHII suspicious; uncertain; **ayashii ningen** suspicious (shady) person; **ayashii eigo** poor English.

ayashimu to suspect; to doubt; to wonder at.

ayásu to amuse; to humor; to caress (an infant).

ayatsuri níngyoo puppet, marionette.

ayatsúru to handle; to control; to pull the wires; **hito o ayatsúru** to play on a person's weakness.

ayaui dangerous; very near; **ayauku** barely; narrowly; on the point of; **ayauku nogaréru** to have a narrow escape; **ayauku suru** to imperil, jeopardize, endanger.

áyu sweetfish (fresh-water game fish).

azá birthmark.

azami thistle.

azamúku to deceive; to cheat; to impose upon; **azamúki yasúi** gullible; **haná o azamúku bijin** a beautiful woman.

azawarai derisive laughter; contempt; ridicule; **azawaráu** to laugh at, ridicule; to sneer at.

azáyaka na clear; splendid; vivid; **azáyaka ni** clearly; splendidly.

azé footpaths between rice fields; low dikes separating rice fields.

azukari taking charge (custody).

azukarimono something left in one's charge.

azukáru to be trusted with; to keep. **Sore o oazukari itashimashóo.** I will keep it for you.

azukáru to participate, to share; **soodan ni azukáru** to be consulted.

azukéru to deposit; to leave in someone's charge; **azukénushi** depositor; **okane o ginkoo ni azukéru** to deposit money in a bank. **Tomodachi ni kodomo o azúkete Nihon e ikimásu.** I'm leaving my child with a friend as I'm going to Japan.

azuki red bean.

azusa catalpa tree.

baabékyuu barbecue.

báagen bargain sale.

BAAI occasion; time; moment; case; circumstances; **–no baai ni wa** when; in case; in the event that; on the occasion of; **baai ni yotté wa** according to circumstances; **hítsuyoo no baai ni wa** in case of need.

BAI double; twice (as large, as many, as much); **bai ni suru** to make twice as large; to double; times; -fold (a counter); **ni bai** twice; two times; **ni bai ni suru** to double.

báibai (*n.*) buying and selling; **báibai suru** to trade in; **baibai kéiyaku** bargain; contract of sale.

baidoku syphilis.

báika selling price.

baikai mediation; matchmatching; **baikai suru** to mediate; to convey; **baikáibutsu** medium; agent; **baikáisha** go-between.

baikin bacillus.

baimei self-advertisement; **baimeika** publicity seeker.

baiorin violin.

baishaku (*n.*) matchmaking; **baishaku suru** to arrange marriages; **baishakunin** go-between; matchmaker.

baishoo compensation, indemnify, reparation; **baishoo suru** to indemnify, make reparation for a loss; **baishookin** money for reparations, damages.

baishuu purchase; bribe; **baishuu suru** to bribe, buy off.

BAITEN stand, stall, booth; store.

baiyaku contract of sale. **Baiyakuzumi!** Sold!

báji toofuu utter indifference; **báji toofuu to kikinagásu** to turn a deaf ear to.

BÁKA fool, blockhead, idiot, folly, nonsense, absurdity; **báka o iu** to talk nonsense; **báka o miru** to be fooled; **báka o suru** to make a fool of oneself; **baka ni suru** to make fun of; make a fool of; **báka na hito** foolish person; **báka ni** awfully. **BAKABAKASHÍI** foolish, silly; **bakabakashíi koto** foolish matter. **Baka yároo** You fool! Idiot! (*vulgar*).

BÁKARI about; some; just; only; almost; on the point of; **–bákari de náku** not only . . . but. **Íma kita bákari desu.** I've just come. **Nakan bákari de átta.** She was ready to cry.

bakashóojiki stubborn honesty; simpleness. **Ano otoko wa bakashóojiki da.** That man is too honest.

bakawárai boisterous laughter; horse laugh.

bakazu experience; **bakazu o fumu** to gain experience; **bakazu o funda** experienced; veteran.

bakemóno ghost, goblin.

baken pool ticket, pari-mutuel ticket; **bakenjoo** grandstand at a racetrack.

bake no kawá dissemblance; disguise; **bake no kawá ga arawaréru** to reveal one's true colors.

BAKETSU bucket.

bakkin fine, penalty; **bakkin o kásu** to levy a fine.

bákku back; background; backer; **bákku suru** to back up (a vehicle); **bakku míraa** rearview mirror (in a car).

bakuchi gambling; **bakuchi o útsu** to gamble; **bakuchíba** gambling place; **bakuchiuchi** gambler.

bakudai na enormous, vast; immense, tremendous.

bakudan bomb; **bakudan tóoka** (*n.*) bombing; **bakuda o tóoka suru** to bomb.

bakuhatsu explosion, detonation; **bakuhatsu suru** to explode, blow up, burst.

bakuon explosive sound; roaring of an engine; buzzing.

bákuro exposure; disclosure; **bákuro suru** to expose; lay bare.

bakushin rush; dash; **bakushin suru** to rush; to dash forward.

bakuzen to shita vague, uncertain; ambiguous, indefinite. **Ími ga bakuzen to shite iru.** The meaning is vague.

BAN evening; night; **ban ni** in the evening; **Nichiyoo no ban ni** on Sunday evening.

bán watch, guard, lookout; number; order; turn; time; round; game; **bán o suru** to keep watch.

BAN– prefix denoting; numerous; innumerable; all; every; **bánji** everything.

BANANA banana.

bánbutsu all things (under the sun); creation; entire universe.

bancha coarse tea; green tea of poor quality; **bancha mo debana** everything in its season.

banchi lot number; address.

bandai all ages; eternity; **bandai ni** through all ages; forever; **bandai fueki no** immutable, eternal.

bando belt; band (music).

bangai (n.) extra; additional turn; **bangai no** (adj.) extra; additional.

bangata evening; nightfall; **bangata ni** in the evening; toward evening.

BANGÓO number; **bangóo o útsu** to number.

BANGUMI program; list.

bánji everything; all things. **Bánji kootsúgoo ni itte iru.** Everything is going well.

bankara Bohemianism; bohemian; **bankara no** unconventional; uncouth; rough and coarse.

banken watchdog.

bankurúwase surprise; expected result; **bankurúwase no** unexpected.

–BANME suffix denoting: ordinal number; **kádo kara sanbanmé no ie** the third house from the corner.

bannen ni in one's old age.

bannín watchman; caretaker.

bánpaa bumper.

banpei sentry, sentinel, guard.

BANSAN supper; dinner; **bansánkai** dinner party.

banshaku evening drink; **banshaku o yaru** to have a drink with supper.

bansoo accompaniment; **bansoo suru** to accompany; **bansóosha** accompanist.

bansookoo adhesive plaster; bandage strip.

bantoo head clerk.

banzái cheers; "long live"; **"banzai"**; "viva"; **banzái o sanshoo suru** to give three cheers.

banzuke list; program, schedule; playbill.

bara rose; rosebush.

barabara (n.) being in pieces, drops; **barabara ni** in bits or pieces; **barabara ni suru** to break up.

barákku barracks; shack.

baramáku to scatter; **kane o baramáku** to spend money recklessly.

baransu balance; **baransu o tóru** to keep in balance.

barásu to break into pieces; to lay bare (a secret); to dispose of; to kill.

báree ballet.

barikan hair clippers.

bariki horsepower; **bariki o kakéru** to get up steam; to make an effort.

básha carriage; coach.

basho space, place; seat; location; situation; room.

bashogara character (of a place); locality; neighborhood.

bassui extract; selection; **bassui suru** to extract; select.

bassúru to punish; to bring to justice.

BÁSU bus; **yuuran básu** sight-seeing bus; **básu de** by bus.

básu bath; basu tsuki no heyá room with a bath.

básu bass (music).

basue outskirts, suburbs.

basuketto bóoru basketball.

BÁTAA butter; **batakusái** exotic, alien (lit: having the smell of butter). **Anó hito wa batakusái.** He acts like a Westerner.

bátabata with a clatter (onomatopoetic); one after another; noisily; **bátabata suru** to flap. **Kaze de to ga bátabata suru.** The wind makes the doors rattle (clatter).

batoo abuse; denunciation; **batoo suru** to abuse; denounce.

bátsu clique, faction; clan.

bátsu punishment, penalty; **bassuru** to punish; **bátsu o ukéru** to be punished.

batsugun no distinguished; conspicuous.

batta grasshopper.

báttaa batter (in baseball); **battaajun** batting order.

BATTARI suddenly; unexpectedly; with a thud. **battári yukíau** to come across, fall in with (a person); **battári butsukaru** to run against, bump into; **battári taoréru** to fall down with a thud; **battári tomaru** to come to an abrupt stop.

batteki selection, promotion; **batteki suru** to select, to promote.

battén demerit; black mark.

bátto bat.

bázaa bazaar.

béddo bed.

Beekoku See **Beigun.**

béeru veil.

beesubóoru baseball.

béi- prefix denoting: of rice, pertaining to rice; **béika** the price of rice.

Bei- prefix denoting: U.S.A. **Beigun** American Army; **Beijin, Beikokújin** (*n.*) American; **béika** American currency; **beikan** American warship; **BEIKOKU =** **Beekoku** America (U.S.A.).

bekkoo tortoise shell; **bekkoo no kushí** tortoise-shell comb; **bekkoo buchi** tortoise-shell rims; **bekkoo buchi no mégane** tortoise-shell glasses; **bekkoo iro** amber color; **bekkoo záiku** tortoise-shell work.

bekkyo separation; **bekkyo suru** to be separated.

bén valve.

bén eloquence; **bén ga tátsu** to speak fluently.

bén feces.

bén convenience; **–no bén o hakátte** for the convenience of. **Básu no bén ga áru.** Buses are available.

bénchi bench.

béngi convenience; facilities; **béngi o atáeru** to provide facilities; to give aid to; **bengijoo** for the sake of convenience.

béngo defense; **béngo suru** to plead; to defend; **bengonin** counsel (for the defense); lawyer; **bengóshi** lawyer; public attorney.

béni rouge; lipstick; **kuchibeni o tsukéru** to put on lipstick.

benímasu red trout.

benjó privy; toilet (*vulgar*); **benjó ni iku** to go to the toilet; to wash one's hands.

benkai explanation; apology; **benkai suru** to explain; to apologize.

benkeijima checks, plaid (pattern).

bénki chamber pot; bedpan.

BENKYOO study; diligence; industry; selling at a small profit; **benkyoo suru** to study; to work hard; **benkyoo suru misé** a shop where prices are cheap; **benkyooka** studious person; hard worker.

benpi constipation.

BÉNRI convenience; facilities; handiness; **bénri na** convenient; handy; useful; **bénri ni** conveniently; **bénri na tokoró ni súnde iru** to live in a convenient location.

bénshi orator, speaker.

benshoo reparation, compensation.

BENTÓO box lunch; **bentóo o tabéru** to eat a box lunch; **bentóobako** lunchbox; **bentóodai** lunch money; cost of lunch.

bentsuu bowel movement.

bénzetsu eloquence; tongue; **bénzetsu sawáyaka na** eloquent; fluent; **bénzetsu**

sawáyaka ni eloquently, fluently. **Bénzetsu ga takumi da.** He speaks fluently.

beppuu separate cover; **beppuu no tegami** a letter under separate cover.

bérabera continually; volubly; **bérabera shabéru** to chatter unceasingly; to talk volubly.

beraboo (slang) blockhead; fool; **beraboo ni** awfully; **beraboo ni samúi** awfully cold. **Beraboo me!** Confound it, you fool you! (*vulgar*).

beranda veranda, porch.

béru bell; doorbell; **béru o narasu** to ring a bell.

béso wry face; **béso o káku** to be ready to cry.

BÉSUTO best; **bésuto o tsukúsu** to do one's best.

bétabeta all over; thickly; sticky (referring to paint or powder); **bétabeta oshiroi o nuru** to powder one's face thickly.

BETSU difference; discrimination; **betsu no** different; another; **betsu no hito** another person; **betsu náku** without discrimination; alike; **dánjo no betsu náku** regardless of sex.

betsu átsurae special order; **betsu átsurae no** made to order; **betsu átsurae no kutsu** custom-made shoes.

BETSUBETSU NO separate; **betsubetsu ni** separately; **betsubetsu ni náru** to become separate; to be separated; **betsubetsu ni suru** to keep separate.

betsudan special; specially; particularly; in particular.

betsujítate specially made or equipped.

bí beauty; prettiness; grace; **bíjin** beautiful woman; beautiful girl; **bidan** beautiful story; fine anecdote.

bideo video.

BIFUTEKI beefsteak.

bigánjutsu facial (beauty treatment); **biganjutsúshi** beautician.

bíiru beer; ale; **nama bíiru** draught beer; **chozoo bíiru** lager beer.

bijinesúman businessman.

bíjutsu fine arts; **bijutsu gákkoo** art school; **bijutsu tenránkai** art exhibition; **bijutsúhin** object (work) of art; **bijutsuka** artist; **bijutsúkan** art museum; **bijutsuteki** artistic; **bijutsuteki ni** artistically.

bíkko lameness; lame person; **bíkko no** lame; crippled; wrongly paired; unsymmetrical; **bíkko o híku** to limp. **Kono tsukue no ashí wa bíkko da.** The legs of this table are uneven.

BIKKÚRI SURU to start (with surprise); to

be surprised; **bikkúri saseru** to startle; **bikkúri gyooten** astonishment, amazement; **bikkúri gyooten suru** to be frightened out of one's wits. **Aa bikkúri shita!** How you startled me!

bikoo incognito; **bikoo suru** to go incognito; to go in disguise.

bíkubiku suru to tremble with fear, be afraid; to feel nervous.

bíku to mo shinai to remain unmoved (calm, composed); to be unflinching; to be unperturbed.

bimyoo na delicate; nice; fine; **hijoo ni bimyoo na ten** a very delicate point.

BÍN opportunity, occasion; message; news; mail; **tsugí no bin de** by the next mail; **kookúu bin de** by airmail.

bín bottle, jar, decanter; **momo no binzume** a jar of peaches.

BÍNBOO NA poor, destitute; **binboonin** poor person; poor (people).

binfíru vinyl.

binkan na susceptible; sensitive.

binkatsu na quick; alert; prompt; **binkatsu na shóchi o tóru** to take prompt measures; **binkatsu ni hataraku** to work rapidly.

BINSEN letter paper; pad of letter paper.

binshoo na quick, sharp, smart, shrewd; **binshoo ni** quickly, etc.; **koodoo ga binshoo da** quick in action.

binsoku na quick, prompt; **binsoku ni** quickly, promptly; **binsoku ni haitatsu suru** to deliver promptly.

binzume no bottled; in a jar; **binzume no sake** bottled sake.

bíri (n.) last; bottom (of the class).

biroodo velvet.

BIRU, BÍRUDINGU building.

biryoku slight ability; humble effort; **biryoku o tsukúsu** to do one's best.

bíshibishi rigorously; severely.

bíshobisho thoroughly drenched, soaked to the skin; drizzling. **Áme ga bíshobisho fúru.** It is drizzling.

bishonure no dripping, drenched; **bishonure ni náru** to get wet through.

bishoo smile; **bishoo suru** to smile; **bishoo shite** with a smile.

bishóonen handsome youth; Adonis.

bisshóri thoroughly; (wet) to the skin; **bisshóri áse o káku** to be soaked with sweat.

BISUKÉTTO cookies; tea biscuits.

bitámin vitamin.

biten, bítoku virtue; good quality.

bíwa loquat (plumlike fruit).

bíwa Japanese musical instrument with four strings; **bíwa o hiku** to play the biwa.

biyoo beauty; **biyóoin** beauty shop.

bóchi graveyard, cemetery.

bodáiju linden tree.

bohyoo gravestone; tomb.

boikótto boycott.

boin vowel (sound).

bokashí gradation; shading, shade (of color); **bokásu** to shade, soften, blend colors.

bóke Japanese quince.

bokéru to be senile; to be in one's dotage; to be weak-minded; to fade; to grow faint. **Kón ga bóketa.** The indigo has faded. **Anó hito wa atamá ga bókete iru.** He is senile.

boki bookkeeping; **bokichoo** account book.

bokkoo sudden rise; **bokkoo suru** to rise suddenly (in power); to spring into existence; **kóogyoo no bokkoo** the growth of industry.

bokkóoshoo (n.) independent; **–tówa bokkóoshoo de aru** to have no relation to; to have no connection (between).

bókkusu box.

bókoku mother country, homeland; **bokokugo** mother tongue.

bókoo alma mater.

BÓKU I (used in men's talk).

bokuchiku stock farming; **bokuchikuka** stock farmer; **bokujoo** stock farm; pasture.

bokumetsu destruction, extermination; **bokumetsu suru** to destroy; stamp out.

bokushi pastor, minister.

bókushingu boxing.

bokutotsu honesty, artlessness, simplicity; **bokutotsu na** artless; simple; plain-spoken.

bon, obon tray.

Bón Feast of Lanterns; Buddhist All Souls' Day in July.

bonchi basin; valley.

bonjín ordinary, mediocre person.

bonnoo passion; lust.

bonsai dwarf tree; miniature garden set in a pot.

bonseki miniature landscape (on a tray).

bon'yári stupid person, blockhead; absentimindedly; vacantly; distractedly; **bon'yári kangaekómu** to be lost in reverie; **bon'yári ichinichí o kurasu** to idle away a whole day; **bon'yarimono** dull-witted, absent-minded person; **bon'yári shita** dull-witted, stupid; absent-minded; vacant; dim. **Imi ga bon'yari shite iru.** The meaning is vague. **Késa wa atamá ga bon'yári shite iru.** My head is not clear this morning.

BOO staff, club, rod, stick; **boo de útsu** to strike with a stick; **shíndai o boo ni furu**

to squander one's fortune; **ichinichí o boo ni furu** to waste a whole day.

bóo- prefix denoting: one; certain (one); **boosho** (a certain) place; **bóoshi** (a certain) person.

boobaku táru vast, boundless, limitless; vague; obscure; **boobaku táru úmi** a vast expanse of sea. **Zénto wa boobaku táru monó da.** The prospects are very dim.

bóobi defense; defensive preparations.

booboo táru extensive; boundless, vast; **bóoboo to** shaggily; thickly; **booboo to hige o nobáshita otoko** a man with a shaggy beard.

boochoo attendance; sitting in conference; **boochóoken** admission ticket (for a visitor to the Diet, a conference, etc.); **boochóoryoo** admission fee.

boodoo disturbance; riot, insurrection.

BOOEKI trade; commerce; **booeki suru** to trade, carry on commerce; **booekifuu** trade wind; **booekíshoo** merchant trader (importer or exporter); **booeki shóokai** trading firm.

booenkyoo telescope.

boofúu storm; stormy weather; typhoon; **boofuu kéihoo** storm warning; **boofúu no** stormy; **boofúu no chuushin** storm center.

boofuzai antiseptic; preservative.

boogai disturbance; obstruction, hindrance, obstacle; **boogai suru** to disturb, etc.

boogen violent language; **boogen a háku** to use violent (abusive) language.

bóogyo defense; **boogyo no** defensive; **bóogyo suru** to defend; **boogyosen** line of defense.

boohatei breakwater.

booka (n.) fireproof; fire prevention; **booka no** (adj.) fireproof; fire-resisting; **booka sétsubi** fire protection; **bookáheki** fireproof walls.

bookán (n.) bully; rough; rowdy.

bookán sha spectator; onlooker; **bookan suru** to remain a spectator.

booken adventure; risk, hazard; **booken suru** to venture, hazard, run a risk; **bookéndan** tale of adventure; adventure; **bookenka** adventurer; **bookenteki** risky, hazardous; adventurous.

bookoo violence, violent conduct; outrage; **bookoo suru** to use violence; **bookoo o kuwaeru** to assault.

bookoo bladder.

bóokun tyrant, despot.

bóokyo violence; violent conduct.

boomei flight; **boomei suru** to flee, take flight, seek refuge; **booméisha** refugee; fugitive; exile.

bóonasu bonus.

boonénkai social gathering at the end of the year.

boorei ghost.

bóori excessive profit; **bóori o musabóru** to profiteer, make excessive profit; **bóori torishimari rei** ordinance to control excessive profits.

booru bowl; ball.

boorubako pasteboard box, carton.

boorugami cardboard, pasteboard.

bóoryoku brute force, violence; **booryokúdan** gang of roughs.

boosatsu sareru to be hard-pressed with business.

booseki spinning; **booseki gáisha** fabric (spinning) company; **booseki kóojoo** fabric mill.

BOOSHI hat, cap; bonnet; **booshi o kabúru** to put on one's hat; **booshi o kabútte míru** to try on a hat; **booshi o núgu** to take off one's hat; **booshíkake** hat rack, hat peg; **booshiya** hatter; milliner; hat store.

booshi prevention.

booshokúzai antiseptic; anti-corrosive.

boosui waterproof; protection against floods; **boosúifu** waterproof cloth.

bóoto mob; insurgents; rioters.

bóoto rowboat; **bóoto o kógu** to row a boat.

bootoo abnormal rise; boom. **Satóo ga bootoo shita.** The price of sugar has gone up enormously.

bóoya (diminutive) my boy; my darling (said of a male infant).

bóozu (derogatory) monk.

bora gray mullet.

bóro rags, tatters; hidden fault; **bóro no** ragged, threadbare; **bóro o kita** in rags; **bóro o dásu** to betray a weakness; show one's true colors; **boroboro no** tattered, ragged; **boroboro ni náru** to crumble, fall to pieces; **borogímono** old (threadbare) clothes; rags.

bóru to charge exorbitant prices; to profiteer.

bosei motherhood, maternity; **boséiai** maternal love.

boseki tombstone.

boshuu levy; recruiting; **boshuu suru** to collect; recruit; raise.

bosshuu confiscation, forfeiture; **bosshuu suru** to confiscate, forfeit, seize.

bossúru to sink; to hide.

bótan tree; peony.

BOTAN button, stud; knob; **botan o kakéru** to button; **botan o hazusu** to unbutton; **botan o osu** to push a button.

bótchan boy (someone else's son); green youth, young master.

botsuraku ruin, downfall, **botsuraku suru** to be ruined.

bottoo suru to be absorbed in; to devote oneself to; to be engrossed with; **shigoto ni bottoo suru** to bury oneself in work.

bóya small fire.

bu rate, percentage; part, portion, section, division; **buai** rate, commission, royalty; **buai o dásu** to give (someone) a percentage. **Ríshi wa sán bu desu.** The interest rate is 3 percent.

bu department; **keiríbu** accountant's department.

–bu copy (a counter for newspapers, pamphlets, etc.).

buáikyoo surliness; curtness; bluntness; **buáikyoo na** surly; blunt; unobliging.

buáisoo inhospitableness; curtness, unsociability; **buáisoo na** unsociable, curt, inhospitable; **buáisoo na henji** a curt reply; **hito ni buáisoo o suru** to be surly.

búbun part, portion, section; **bubunhin** parts (of machines); **bubunteki ni** partially; locally.

búchi spots, specks; patches; **búchi no** spotted, speckled; **buchi neko** tabby cat.

buchoo chief (head) of a department.

budoo grape; grapevine; **budoo no fusa** a bunch of grapes; **budooen** vineyard; **budóoshu** wine; claret; **shiro budóoshu** white wine; **aka budóoshu** red wine.

buénryo rudeness; boldness; **buénryo na** unreserved; rude; bold; **buénryo ni** without reserve, boldly.

buji peace; safety; good health; **buji na** safe, sound; peaceful; **buji ni** safely; peacefully.

bujoku insult, affront; disgrace; **bujoku suru** to insult, disgrace; **bujoku o ukéru** to be insulted.

búka (*n.*) subordinate; under-officer.

bukákkoo clumsiness, awkwardness (in appearance); **bukákkoo na** clumsy, awkward; **bukákkoo ni** clumsily, bunglingly.

búki arms, weapons.

bukíyoo lack of skill, clumsiness; **bukíyoo na** unskillful.

bukka prices; **bukka o toosei suru** to control prices; **bukka chóosetsu** price control. **Bukka ga geraku suru.** Prices are falling. **Bukka ga tooki suru.** Prices are rising.

bukkaku Buddhist temple.

bukkiráboo abruptness; curtness; **bukkiráboo na** curt. **bukkiráboo na kotáe o suru** to make a curt reply; **bukkiráboo ni kotowáru** to refuse curtly.

Búkkyoo Buddhism; **Bukkyóoto** Buddhist.

bukotsu bluntness; roughness; rusticity; **bukotsu na** blunt; rustic; clumsy.

búkubuku bubbling; baggy; bulging; **búkubuku futóru** to become very fat; **búkubuku awadátsu** to bubble up.

bumon class; branch; department; **bumon ni wakéru** to classify.

bún portion, share; social position, lot in life; **bún ni yasunzúru** to be contented with one's lot. **Kore wa watakshi no bún desu.** This is my share.

bún sentence, writing, composition. **Kono bún o yakúshite kudasái.** Please translate this sentence.

bun- prefix denoting: writing, literature; civil life; **bundan** literary circles; **búngaku** literature; **búngaku no** literary; **bungei** literature; **bungo** literary expression; written language; classical Japanese; **bungoo** great writer.

búna beech tree.

bunan na safe, secure; **bunan ni** safely; tolerably well.

bun'an draft, sketch; **bun'an o tsukúru** to make a draft; draw up (a deed, etc.).

bunbóogu stationery; **bunbooguya** stationer, one who sells paper, etc.

bunchoo rice (paddy) bird.

bundori capture, seizure; spoil, plunder; **bundoríhin** trophy, booty, spoils.

bunjoo division; distribution; **bunjoo suru** to divide, distribute; **bunjóochi** land for sale in lots.

búnka culture, civilization; **bunkateki na** cultural.

bunkai analysis; decomposition; **bunkai suru** to analyze; to resolve; to decompose; to break up; to pull to pieces.

bunkan civil official.

bunke branch of a family.

bunken literature; documents, records.

bunko handbox; bookcase; library; collection of works.

bunkóojoo branch factory.

bunmei civilization; **bunmei no** civilized; **bunméikoku** civilized country.

bunpai division, distribution; **bunpai suru** to divide, share; **ríeki no bunpai** a division of profits.

bunpoo grammar. **Bunpoo o machigáeta.** I made a mistake in grammar.

bunpu distribution (geographical).

bunretsu split, rupture; **bunretsu suru** to break up; split.

bunri separation; isolation; **bunri suru** to separate; to isolate.

bunrui classification, assortment.

bunryóo quantity.

bunseki analysis, assay.

búnshi writer.

búnshi numerator, molecule.

búnshoo composition, writing; **bunshooka** good (clear) writer.

bunsúirei watershed.

buntan allotment, share; **buntan suru** to share; **buntánkin** share of expenses.

buntsuu correspondence; **buntsuu suru** to write to.

buppin article; goods, commodities.

búrabura idly, aimlessly; leisurely; **búrabura arúku** to walk leisurely, take a stroll; **búrabura suru** to loaf, be idle; **búrabura shite hi o okuru** to while away one's time.

burakku rísuto black list.

búraku community; village.

búranko swing.

búrashi brush; **búrashi o kakéru** to brush up; to brush.

buratsuku to wander about, walk aimlessly; **machí o buratsuku** to window-shop.

buráusu blouse.

buréeki, buréiki brake. **Buréiki ga kikanai.** The brake does not work.

buréi breach of etiquette; incivility, rudeness; **buréi na** rude, insolent; **buréi na kotó o iu** to speak insultingly; **buréi na kotó o suru** to behave impolitely; to act insultingly.

búri yellowtail, yellowfish.

–buri suffix denoting: way, manner; after (a time); **gonenburi de** after a lapse of five years; **hanashíburi** way of talking.

burikáesu to relapse, have a relapse.

buriki tin plate; **burikíkan** tin can.

buróochi brooch.

–búru suffix denoting: to give oneself airs.

búruburu suru to shiver, shudder.

burui class, order, sort, group; **burui o wakéru** to sort, classify; **burui wake** classification; **burui wake o suru** to catalogue.

burujoa (*n.*) bourgeois.

búryoku military power, armed force.

busahoo mono ill-mannered person, boor.

busata long silence; **gobusata suru** to neglect to write (or visit) for a long time.

búshi warrior, samurai.

búsho appointed post; place of duty.

bushóo laziness, sloth, indolence; **bushóo na** lazy; **bushoo mono** lazy person; lazy-bones.

busoo arms, armaments; **busoo suru** to arm; **busoo káijo** disarmament.

bussan products; produce.

bússhi goods, commodities, raw materials, resources; **bússhi no yútaka na** rich in natural resources.

busshitsu matter, substance; **busshitsuteki** material, physical; worldly; **busshitsuteki ni** materially, physically.

bussóo na unsafe, dangerous; suspicious; **bussóo na yonónaka** restless times (days).

busui na unfashionable; in poor taste; inelegant.

BUTA pig, swine; pork; **buta no abura** lard; **butagoya** pigsty; **BUTANIKU** pork; **tonkatsu** pork cutlet.

bútai stage (theater); footlights; scene; sphere; **butai ni tátsu** to go on the stage; **butáigeki** theatrical drama.

butoo dance; dancing; **bútoo suru** to dance; **butóokai** ball, dance (party).

butsubutsu rash; **kao ni butsubutsu ga dekíru** to get a rash on the face.

bútsubutsu murmuring; grumbling; **bútsubutsu iu** to grumble; to murmur.

butsubutsu kóokan barter.

Butsudan (household) Buddhist altar.

Butsudoo Buddhist teachings.

bútsugi discussion; public censure.

butsukaru to collide with; to clash; to knock (run) against; to fall on; **kónnan ni butsukaru** to encounter difficulties. **Saijitsu ga Nichiyóobi ni butsukaru.** The national holiday falls on Sunday.

butsukeru to throw at; to knock against. **Atamá o hashira ni butsuketa.** I knocked my head against a post.

bútsuri natural laws, physical laws, physics; **butsuriteki** physical.

butsurígaku physics; **butsurigákusha** physicist.

butsuyoku worldly desires.

Butsuzoo Buddhist image.

buttooshi ni throughout; all through; without a break; **tooká kan buttoshi ni** for ten days running.

buttsuke ni directly; personally; outright.

búyo gnat; sandfly.

buyoo ballet; dance; **buyóogeki** dance drama.

buyóojin insecurity. **buyóojin na** insecure, unsafe.

buyúuden heroic story.

búzama na ungainly; uncouth; clumsy.

BYÓO second (of time); **byóo o kizamu** to tick away the time.

byóo tack, rivet; **byóo de tomeru** to tack down.

byóo ancestral shrine, mausoleum.

byoo- prefix denoting: disease, illness; **byoodoku** virus; disease germs; **byoogen** cause of a disease; **byoogénkin** germs; **byóogo** convalescence; **byóogo no hito** a convalescent; **BYOOIN** hospital; **byooin ni háiru** to be hospitalized; **BYOOKI**

illness; **byooki ai kakáru** to fall ill; **byooki no** sick; ill; **atama no byooki** mental illness; **BYOONIN** sick person; **byoosei** condition (of a disease); **byóoshin no** weak, sickly, delicate, in poor health; **byooshitsu** sickroom; ward; **byooshoo** sickbed. **Byoosei ga aratamárimashita.** He took a turn for the worse.

–byoo suffix denoting: disease, illness; **haibyoo** (lung) tuberculosis; **ganbyoo** eye disease.

byoobu folding screen; **byoobu o tateru** to set up a screen.

byoodoo equality; **byoodoo no** equal; **byoodoo ni** equally; without discrimination; **byoodoo ni suru** to make equal; **byoodoo no kenri** an equal right.

byoosha depiction; description, representation; **byoosha suru** to sketch, describe.

CH

CHA, OCHA tea; **ocha o ireru** to prepare tea; **ocha o irekáeru** to make fresh tea; **ocha o dásu** to serve (offer) a cup of tea; **ocha o tsugu** to pour tea; **cha no yu** tea ceremony; art of tea-making; **chabánashi** tea-talk, gossip, chat (over a bowl of tea); **chabashira** tea stalk floating erect in one's cup (foretelling something good, according to superstition); **chadansu** tea cabinet; **chadóogu** tea-things; tea set; **chagara** used tea leaves; **chagáshi** cake, sweets (served with tea); **CHAKA = saka** tea and cake; light refreshment; **chamise** tea stall; refreshment house; **chaseki** place where the tea ceremony is held; **chasen** (bamboo) tea whisk; tea stirrer for tea (used in the tea ceremony); **chashaku** tea ladle; tea scoop, **chataku** tea saucer. **CHAWAN** teacup; rice bowl; **CHAYA** teahouse; roadside snack bar. **Chabashira ga tátte imasu.** A tea stalk is floating erect in his cup.

chabudai low eating-table.

CHAIRO (*n.*) light brown; **chairo no** (*adj.*) light brown; brownish.

chakásshoku light-brown color.

chakásu to laugh, banter; to make fun of.

–chaku suffix denoting: a "counter" for a suit of clothes; **yoofuku itchaku** a suit of Western clothes.

–cháku arrival; **rokúji cháku** arriving at six o'clock.

chakuchaku (*adv.*) steadily; step by step;

chakuchaku shinkoo suru to make steady progress.

chakugánten point aimed at; viewpoint.

chakujitsu sincerity; steadiness and honesty; **chakujitsu ni** honestly; faithfully.

chakuriku (*n.*) landing; **chakuriku suru** to land, alight; **chakurikuba, chakurikujoo** landing field; airstrip.

chakushoku (*n.*) coloring; **chakushoku suru** to color.

chákushu commencement, start; **chakushu suru** to commence, set about, start, begin.

cháme playfulness, sportiness; playful fellow, urchin; **cháme o hakki suru** to be jovial (jolly).

chánpon mixture; **chánpon ni** alternately.

chanoma sitting room; living room; tearoom.

CHAN TO (*adv.*) in good order, neatly; properly; thoroughly; fully, exactly, precisely, correctly; **chan to shita fukusoo** proper dress; **kimono o chan to kiru** to dress properly.

CHASAJI teaspoon.

chazuke rice steeped in hot tea (eaten as a simple meal or after rich food); **chazuke o kakikómu** to eat a hasty meal.

chíkki luggage receipt, baggage check; **chíkki suru** to check one's baggage.

CHI blood; blood relation; **chi ga déru** to bleed; **chi o tomeru** to stop bleeding; **chi no meguri no yói** quick-witted; sensible; **chi no meguri no warúi** dull-witted; not sensible; **chi o wáketa** related by blood; **chibashiru** to become bloodshot; **chibashitta me** bloodshot eyes; **chidarake no** bloody.

chí intellect; **chiteki** intellectual.

chíbi dwarf, pygmy.

chíbusa breast.

CHICHÍ father; **chichikata no** paternal. **Chichikata no shinseki ga áru.** I have relatives on my father's side.

chichí milk.

chichuu ground, earth; **chichuu ni** in the ground; underground.

Chichúukai Mediterranean Sea.

chié wisdom, intelligence; sense; advice, counsel; **chie no áru** wise; **chie no nai** unwise; **chié o kasu** to advise; **chié o shibóru** to rack one's brains; **chié o tsukéru** to suggest.

chífusu typhoid fever, typhus.

chigaeru to change, alter; to make a mistake; to dislocate, put out of joint; **yakusoku o chigaeru** to break a promise.

CHIGAI difference, disparity; distinction; mistake, error; **CHIGAI NAKU** certainly, surely; without doubt; **–ni chigai nái**

there is no mistake about it (that); . . .
undei no chigai ga áru to be as different
as heaven and earth. **Chigai ga áru.**
There is a difference. **Kim wa káre ni
átta ni chigai nái.** You must have seen
him.

CHIGAU to be different, differ (from); to be
unlike; to disagree, not be in accordance
with, to be wrong, be mistaken. **Anó hito
wa chotto hito to chigau.** He is a little
different from other people.

chigiréru to be torn off; to come off. **Sode
ga chigíreta.** A sleeve was torn off.

chigíru to tear off, to pluck, to pick.

chíguhagu no odd, uneven, unequal.

chiheisen horizon; **chiheisen joo ni** above
(on) the horizon.

chihóo locality; country (rural area); **chihóo
no** local; provincial; **chihóoshoku** local
color.

chíi rank, social status, position.

chíiki tract of land; area.

chíimu team.

CHISÁI small, trifling; **chiisáku náru** to
dwindle; to cringe, shrink.

CHÍIZU cheese.

chijimaru = chijimu to shrink. **Keorímono
wa nettoo ni ireréba chijimimásu.**
Woolen fabric shrinks in hot water.

chijimeru to shorten, to reduce, to draw in;
kimono o chijimeru to shorten a dress;

chijimi cotton crepe.

chijimiagáru to tremble with fear, to cringe.

chijimu See chijimaru.

chijin acquaintance; friend.

chijirege frizzled, wavy hair.

chijireru to be wavy; to become curly.

chijoku disgrace, dishonor, shame.

CHIJOO surface of the earth; earth; world;
chijoo no earthly, terrestrial; on the
earth; **chijoo ni** on the ground, on the
earth.

chiká subterranean, underground; **chiká ni**
under the ground; **chiakdoo** underground
passage.

CHIKÁGORO recently, lately; nowadays, in
these days, **chikágoro made** till recent
timès, until lately.

chikai oath, vow; **chikai o tatéru** to make a
vow, swear an oath, give a pledge; **chikai
o mamóru** to keep an oath; **chikai o
yabúru** to break an oath (vow). See also
chikau.

CHIKÁI near; intimate; verging on; akin to;
chikái miyori a near relation; **chikái uchi
ni** before long; one of these days; **kanzen
ni chikái.** It is nearly perfect. It is close
to perfection.

CHIKÁKU nearby place; nearly; in the

neighborhood of; shortly, in a short time;
shóogo chikáku káeru to go home close
to noon. **Súgu kono chikáku ni súnde
imasu.** I live near here.

chikámichi shortcut; **chikámichi o suru** to
take a shortcut.

CHIKARÁ strength, might, power, force;
spirit; vigor; efforts, exertions; ability,
talent; authority; **chikará ga yowái** weak;
chikará ga tsuyoi strong; **chikara no áru**
strong, powerful; **chikara no nái**
powerless, incapable; **chikará ga tsukíru**
to get exhausted; **chikará ni oyobanai** to
be beyond one's power; **chikará o otósu**
to be discouraged; **chikará o tsukéru** to
cheer up, encourage; **chikarazúku** to
recover one's strength or health; to be
cheered up.

chikashíi close, intimate; familiar; **chikashíi
aida de** between friends.

chikáshitsu basement, cellar.

CHIKATETSU subway.

chikatte upon my word, upon my honor.

chikau to swear, vow, pledge one's word.

chikayoru to draw near, approach.

chikazukéru to keep company with; to allow
to come close to; to allow.

chikazuki acquaintance; **chikazuki ni náru**
to get acquainted with.

chikazúku to draw near, approach;
chikazukánai yóoni suru to keep away
from.

chikazukigatái to be inaccessible, be difficult
of access.

chikazukiyasúi to be accessible.

chikei topography; lay of the land.

chikí acquaintance; friend.

chíkkyo confinement in one's house; **chíkkyo
suru** to stay indoors.

chikoku (n.) being late; **chikoku suru** to be
late.

chíkubi teat; nipple.

chikúchiku prickle; tingle; sharp pain.

chikudénchi storage battery.

chikushoo birds and beasts; beast; brute (of a
man); **Chikushoo!** Damn it! Hang it!
(vulgar); **Kon chikushoo me!** You brute!
(vulgar).

CHIKYUU earth; **chikyúugi** globe.

chimayóu to go mad, be crazed.

chímei place name.

chimidoro ni nátte strenuously; desperately.

chín Japanese spaniel.

–chin suffix denoting: charge, price;
densháchin train fare; **yáchin** house rent.

chinámu to be associated with; to call (or
name) after.

chínba lameness; odd pair.

chinbotsu sinking; floundering; shipwreck.

chíngin wages; **chingin seikátsusha** wage-earner.

chinka sinking, submersion; subsidence; **chinka suru** to sink to the bottom; to be put out; to be brought under control; to be extinguished.

chinkyaku rare guest; welcome visitor.

chínmi dainty (thing); delicacy.

chinmoku silence, reticence; **chinmoku suru** to be silent; to hold one's tongue; **chinmoku saseru** to silence.

chinomígo suckling, infant.

chínpu na stale; old-fashioned commonplace; hackneyed.

chinretsu exhibition, display, arrangement; **chinretsu suru** to exhibit, display, show; **chinretsúbako** showcase; **chinretsúkan** museum; gallery; exhibition; **chinretsúmádo** show window; **chinretsúshitsu** showroom. **Sore wa chinretsu shite áru.** It is on view.

chin shígoto piecework; **chin shígoto o suru** to do piecework.

CHÍPPU tip; **chíppu o harau** to tip (a waiter, etc.).

chirabaru to be scattered, be in disorder; **chirakasu** to scatter; to disarrange. **Hón ga chirabatte ita.** Books were scattered about.

chírachira flutteringly; flickeringly; gleamingly. **Yukí ga chírachira fútte ita.** The snowflakes were falling lightly. **Ki no aída kara hikarí ga chírachira shite ita.** The light gleamed through the trees. **Hikarí de mé ga chírachira suru.** The light dazzles my eyes.

chírahora here and there. **Sakura ga chírahora sakidáshita.** The cherry trees have started to bloom here and there.

chirarí to at a glance; by accident; **chirarí to kikikómu** to hear by accident; **chirarí to míru** to catch a glimpse of; glance at (a thing).

chirashi handbill, leaflet.

chirasu to scatter, disperse; **ki o chirasu** to distract (someone's) attention; to divert. (See also **chirabaru**.)

chíri geography; topography.

chirí dust; **chirihárai** duster; **chiritóri** dustpan. **chiri hodo mo nai.** There isn't a bit.

chiribaméru to inlay; to set; **shinju o chiribámeta yubiwa** a ring set with pearls.

CHIRIGAMI toilet paper; facial tissue.

chirijíri ni in all directions; separately; **chirijíri ni náru** to disperse in all directions, scatter; **chirijíri ni nátte iru** to be scattered about, be dispersed.

chirimen crepe; **chirimengami** crepe paper.

chirin chirin tingling; jingle-jangle; **chirín chirin naru** to ring.

CHIRU to fall; to disperse; to be scattered; to be distracted; **ki ga chiru** to be distracted (mentally). **Kúmo ga chitte iru.** The clouds are dispersing.

chiryoo medical treatment; cure; **chiryoo suru** to treat; to cure; **chiryoo o ukéru** to receive treatment.

chisei geographical features; topography.

chishiki knowledge, information, learning; **chishikijín** learned person; intellectual.

chissoku suffocation; **chissoku suru** to suffocate.

chisuji blood; lineage; descent.

chitsújo order; **chitsujo no áru** orderly; **chitsújo no nái** disorderly; **chitsújo ga midárete iru** to be out of order; **chitsújo tadashíi** to be in good order; **chitsujo tadáshiku** in an orderly manner; systematically.

CHITTÓMO (used with a negative) not at all; not a bit. **Góhan ga chittómo oishikunái.** I don't have any appetite at all. **Chittó mo kamawánai.** He doesn't care a bit.

chízu map; topographical chart; atlas.

chochiku savings; **chochiku suru** to save up, store, lay by; **chochiku gínkoo** savings bank; **chochikúshin no áru** thrifty; **chochikúshin no nái** extravagant, prodigal.

chokin savings; **chokin suru** to save money.

chokkaku right angle; **chokkaku ni** at right angles.

chokkei diameter.

chokkoo nonstop trip; direct voyage; **chokkoo suru** to go direct to.

chokkyuu straight ball; line drive.

chóko sake cup.

chókochoko at a trot; with short, mincing steps; **chókochoko komata ni arúku** to walk with short steps; to mince along.

CHOKORÉETO chocolate.

chókuchoku now and then. **Chókuchoku hanáshi ní kúru.** He comes to see us now and then.

chokumen suru to face, confront.

chokuritsu suru to stand up.

chokusen straight line.

chokusetsu directly; **chokusetsu no** direct; immediate; personal; **chokusetsu ni** directly; personally.

chokutsuu direct communication; through traffic; **chokutsuu réssha** through train.

chokuyaku literal translation.

chomei na well-known, famous, noted.

chóo intestines, bowels.

CHOO– prefix denoting: town; street; **chóonai de** in the town.

–choo suffix denoting: government office; **Kikákuchoo** Planning Board.

–choo suffix denoting: chief, director; **shachoo** company president.

chooba counter for Japanese-style establishment (hotel, etc.).

choobatsu discipline; punishment.

choobo account book; register; **choobo o tsukéru** to keep accounts.

choochín paper lantern; **–no choochín o mótsu** to sing someone's praises; boast; **choochín ni tsurigane** an ill-assorted couple (in a marriage); an ill-matched pair.

CHÓOCHOO butterfly; **Chóochoo san** Madame Butterfly.

choodai suru (*humble*) to receive; to drink; to eat. **Koohíi no kawari ni ocha o choodai itashimashóo.** I will take tea instead of coffee.

CHOODO just; right; exactly; **choodo góji ni** exactly at five o'clock; **choodo yói tokí ní** just at the right time; **choodo mannaka ni** right in the middle.

chooetsu superiority, excellence; **chooetsu suru** to surpass; to be superior to.

choogoo (*n.*) compounding, mixing, preparation; **choogoo suru** to mix, concoct, prepare; **choogóozai** compound, mixture.

choohatsu suru to requisiton.

choohónnin ringleader; leader.

choohoogáru to find a thing useful; **chóohoo na** convenient; handy, useful; **chóohoo na hito** handy man. **Kuchi wa chóohoo na monó da.** The mouth is a convenient thing (You can say what you please).

choohóokei rectangle; **choohóokei no** rectangular, oblong.

chooji words of condolence; funeral address, eulogy.

choojin superman; **choojinteki** superhuman.

chójo oldest daughter.

CHOOJÓO top, summit; **choojoo káigi** summit conference.

chooka excess; **chooka suru** to exceed.

chookan morning edition (of a newspaper).

chookeshi cancellation; writing off; **chookeshi ni suru** to square accounts. **Kore de chookeshi da.** Now we're quits.

chookoku engraving; sculpture; **chookokuka** engraver; sculptor.

chookoo sign(s); symptom; **jidai no chookoo** a sign of the times.

chookoo attendance at a lecture; **chookóonyoo** admission fee.

chookyóri long distance; **chookyori dénwa** long-distance telephone; **chookyori hikóo** long-distance flight.

–CHOOME suffix denoting: street (employed when an ordinal number is used to name a thoroughfare or section of town). **Itchoome** First Street; **Nichoome** Second Street.

chóomei long life; longevity; **chóomei no** long-lived.

choomén notebook.

chóomi seasoning, flavor; **choomíryoo** seasoning, condiments, spices.

choomúsubi rosette; bow.

chóonan oldest son.

chóoryoku (power of) hearing.

chooryuu tidal current, tide; tendency, trend.

chóosa examination, investigation, inquiry; **chóosa suru** to investigate, examine.

choosei regulation; adjustment; preparation, drafting, drawing up; **choosei suru** to regulate; to put in order; to prepare, draft, draw up.

choosen challenge; defiance; **choosen suru** to challenge; **choosen ni oozúru** to accept a challenge; **choosenteki** challenging, aggressive; defiant.

CHOOSÉN Korea; **Choosenjín** Korean people; **Choosengo** Korean language. (See also **Kánkoku.**)

choosetsu regulation, control; adjustment; **choosetsu suru** to regulate, control; **bukka o choosetsu suru** to regulate prices.

chooshi tune; pitch; key; rate of stroke; **chooshi ga átte iru** to be in tune; **chooshi ga átte inai** out of tune; **chooshi no yói** harmonious; melodious.

chooshínki stethoscope.

chóosho strong point; one's forte; merit.

chóoshu suru to hear; to listen in.

chooshuu audience; (people in) attendance. **Chooshuu ga óoi.** There is a large audience.

chooshuu collection; levy, assessment; **chooshuu suru** to collect; levy; **zéi o chooshuu suru** to collect taxes.

chootéisha arbitrator, mediator.

chóoten highest point, apex, zenith.

chóoto long distance; long journey. **Chóoto no ryokoo ni tsúita.** He started on a long journey.

chootsúgai hinge.

choowa harmony, accord, agreement; **choowa suru** to harmonize; to agree with; **iro no choowa** harmony of colors.

choozen to aloof; above the world.

choozoo sculpture; statue.

chórochoro trickling (of a brook).

chosaku literary work; **chosakuken**

copyright; **chosákusha, chósha** writer, author.

chósho work (literary); production; publication.

chosúichi reservoir.

CHÓTTO just for a moment; a few minutes; a little; a bit; **chotto no ma ni** in a moment; in no time. **Chótto mátte kudasái.** Just a moment, please. Wait a bit, please. **Chótto dekínai.** It's no easy thing. **Chotto shita kotó de kenka shita.** They quarreled over a trifle. **Chotto shita ié ga aru.** There's a nice-looking house.

chozoomai stored rice.

chuu comment; annotation; footnote.

chúubu central part; center; **Chuubu chíhoo** Central Japan.

chúucho hesitation; indecision; **chúucho suru** to hesitate; waver; **chúucho shite** hesitatingly.

chuudan interruption; break; **chuudan suru** to cut in two, break in the middle.

chúudoku (*n.*) poisoning; ptomaine; **chúudoku suru** to be poisoned; **chuudokusei no** poisonous, toxic.

chuugáeri somersault.

chuugákkoo junior high school.

chuugata medium size; **chuugata no** medium-sized; medium.

chuugen midyear present.

CHÚUGOKU China; **Chuugokújin** Chinese people; **Chuugokugo** Chinese language.

chúui attention, care; warning, caution; advice; hint; **chúui suru** to pay attention to; to attend to; to warn, etc.; **chúui shite** with care; **hito no chúui o hiku** to attract someone's attention; **chúui o ukéru** to be warned; **chúui o unagasu** to call attention to; **chuuibukai** cautious, careful; attentive; **chuui jínbutsu** marked person; suspicious character; **chuuí ryoku** attentiveness; **chúuisubeki** noteworthy, worthy of notice.

chuujitsu faithfulness; honesty; **chuujitsu na** faithful; honest; **chuujitsu ni** faithfully; honestly.

chuujun middle ten days of a month; **Gógatsu no chuujun ni** about (in) the middle of May.

CHÚUKA China; **chuuka ryóori** Chinese food; **Chuuka Mínkoku** Chinese Republic (Nationalist China); **Chúuka Jínmin Kyoowá koku** People's Republic of China (Communist China).

chuukan the middle; midway; **chuukan no** middle, intermediate; **–no chuukan ni** halfway between.

chuuken main body; backbone; center field (in baseball).

chuukoku advice, counsel; warning; **chuukoku suru** to advise; to warn; **chuukoku o ireru** to follow advice; **chuukoku ni somúku** to act against advice.

chuumoku notice, observation; attention; **chuumoku suru** to pay attention to; to watch, keep an eye on.

CHUUMON order; command(s); request; **chuumon suru** to order; **chuumon o tóru** to take an order.

chuumón tori traveling salesman; canvasser.

chuunen middle age; **chuunen no** middle-aged.

chuuníku chuuzei medium build.

chuunyuu injection, pouring into; cramming; **chuunyuu suru** to pour into.

chuuoo center, middle; **chuuoo shíjoo** central market.

chuuritsu neutrality; **chuuritsu chitái** neutral zone.

chuuryuu midstream; middle class; **chuuryuu kaíkyuu** middle class.

chuusai mediation, arbitration; **chuusai nin** mediator, peacemaker; **chuusai suru** to mediate, arbitrate.

chuusan moderate means (wealth); **chuusan káikyuu** middle class.

chuusei neuter gender.

chúusei Middle Ages; **chúusei no** medieval.

chuusen lottery, drawing; **chuusen suru** to draw lots; **chuusen de sadaméru** to decide by lots; **chausénken** lottery ticket.

chuushi suspension, stoppage; steady gaze; close observation; **chuushi suru** to stop, suspend, discontinue; to gaze steadily at; to watch closely; **jígyoo no chushi** work stoppage; **shiai o chuushi suru** to call off a game.

chuushin center, core, heart; balance; **chuushin o tóru** to balance; **machi no chuushin ni** in the center of the city; **chuushin jínbutsu** central figure; leader.

chuushoo defamation, slander.

CHUUTO midway, halfway; in the middle; unfinished; **chuuto de yameru** to stop in the middle of; to drop out of; **chuuto hánpa** (*n.*) halfway; **chuuto hánpa no** (*adj.*) unfinished; **chuuto hánpa ni** (*adv.*) halfway; **chuuto hánpa na kotó o suru** to do things by halves.

chuutóngun army of occupation.

chuutoo medium quality; **chuutoo no** middle grade; medium; **chuutoo no shinamono** goods of medium quality.

chúuya day and night; **chúuya yasumázu hataraku** to work day and night without rest.

chuuyoo moderation; **chuuyoo o mamóru** to

take the middle course; **chuuyoo o éta** moderate; **chuuyoo o énai** immoderate; one-sided.

chuuzai residence; **chuuzai no** (*adj.*) resident; **chuuzai suru** to reside.

chuuzaisho police station.

chuuzetsu interruption; suspension; **chuuzetsu suru** to be interrupted; to be suspended; discontinued. **Shigoto wa chuuzetsu shita.** The work has been held up. **Chuuzetsu shite iru.** It is in abeyance.

D

DA plain present of **desu**, it is. **Kore wa nán da?** What is this? **Fude da.** It is a writing brush. **Are wa dáre da?** Who is he? **Bóku wa yuku nó wa iyá da.** I don't want to go.

DÁASU dozen; **ichi dáasu** one dozen; **dáasu de uru** to sell by the dozen.

dábi cremation.

dabókushoo bruise.

dabora (*colloq.*) big talk; **dabora o fukú** to boast.

dabudabu loose; baggy; **dabudabu no zubón** baggy trousers.

dachin reward; tip; small consideration; **dachin ni** in payment for. **Kore wa otsukai no dachin da.** This is your reward for doing the errand.

dadákko spoiled child; cross, fretful child.

daden (*n.*) telegraphing; **daden suru** to telegraph, to wire.

daeki saliva, spittle.

DAGA but; for all that; all the same; at the same time; on the other hand.

dagashi coarse (cheap) confectionery (candy).

dageki blow; hit; shock; hitting, batting (in baseball); **dageki o kuwaeru** to deal a blow; **dageki o ukéru** to receive a blow.

dáha (*n.*) overthrow; **dáha suru** to break down; to overthrow; to frustrate.

–dai money given in exchange; cost, price; **gasudai** gas bill.

–dai counter for vehicles (machines); **kuruma ichídai** one car.

DÁI time, period, age, generation; reign, dynasty; (one's) lifetime; pedestal, block; stand; rest; table; bench.

DÁI title, heading, theme, subject, topic; question, problem; **dáio o tsukéru** entitle.

dái pedestal, block, stand, rest, table.

dái– prefix which makes an ordinal from a cardinal number; **dáiichi** the first; **dáini** the second.

dái– prefix denoting: big, large, great; grand, high; colossal; **daitókai** a big city; **daibúbun** greater part, for the most part.

DAIBU, DAIBUN greatly, considerably, remarkably, rather, much, many. **Daibu atsúi.** It is pretty hot. **Késa wa daibu yói.** I am much better this morning. **Daibu són o shita.** He suffered a big loss. **Daibu kane ga kakaru.** It takes a lot of money.

dáichi earth; ground.

dáichoo large intestines; colon.

daidai bitter orange.

dáidai successive generations; from generation to generation; **dáidai no** successive; hereditary.

daidaiteki big, grand; splendid; wholesale; **daidaiteki ni** on a large (grand) scale; splendidly; **daidaiteki ni kookoku suru** to advertise extensively.

DAIDOKORO kitchen; **daidokoro dóogu** kitchen utensils.

daidoo énzetsu soap-box oration; street speaker.

daidoo shóoi general similarity; **daidoo shóoi de aru** to be nearly the same. **Yoo súru ni daidoo shóoi de aru.** In short, there is no choice between them.

DAIGAKU university; college; **daigákusei** college student.

daigakúin graduate school.

daigíshi member of the House of Representatives.

daihon text of a play; libretto.

daihyoo representation; type; **daihyoo suru** to represent; **daihyóosha** (*n.*) representative, deputy; delegate; **daihyooteki** (*adj.*) representative, typical.

DÁIICHI NI in the first place, first of all, firstly; **dáiichí no** first, foremost, primary.

DAIJI great enterprise; great thing; serious affair; emergency; **daijí na** important; serious; precious; **daijí na yooji** an important matter; **daijí ni suru** to take care of; **daiji o tóru** to be cautious; **Kimi wa daiji o torisugíru.** You are overcautious. **Odaiji ni.** Take care of yourself.

DAIJÓOBU safe, secure, certain; strong; certainly, undoubtedly, without fail; I am sure; I assure you. **Sono hako wa daijóobu desu ka?** Is that box safe? **Moo daijóobu desu.** I am quite out of danger now. **Daijóobu naorimásu.** You will surely get well.

daika, daikin price, charge; purchase money; **daikin hikikae** cash on delivery; C.O.D.; **daikin hikikae yúubin** C.O.D. **Daika wa íkura desu ka?** What is the price?

daikin See **daika**.

dáikirai hateful, loathsome; abominable, detestable; **dáikirai da** to hate, loathe, have an antipathy to, have a strong aversion to. **Watakushi wa hébi ga dáikirai desu.** I loathe snakes.

daikon white radish; **daikon óroshi** radish grater; grated radish.

dáiku carpenter; carpentry.

daiméishi pronoun.

daimoku title (of a book); heading.

dainamáito dynamite.

dainashi spoiled, ruined; dirty; **dainashi ni suru** to spoil, ruin; to soil; **dainashi ni náru** to become spoiled, ruined. **Kimono ga dainashi ni nátta.** The garment is ruined. **Booshi o dainashi ni shita.** You've ruined your hat.

dairi deputation; agency; **dairi o suru** to act for, take the place of; **dairi no** acting; deputy; **dairinin** proxy; representative, agent; **dairíten** agency.

dairíseki marble.

DAIROKU sixth; **dáirokujúu** sixtieth; **dáirokkan** sixth sense.

DÁISAN third; **DÁISÁNJUU** thirtieth; **DÁISANSHA** third person; bystander; **dáisánsha no tachibá kara kangáeru** to put yourself in a third person's position.

daishárin big wheel, giant swing.

daishi pasteboard, board-mounting; **shashin o daishi ni haru** to mount a photograph.

DÁISHI fourth.

DAISHICHI seventh. **DAISHICHIJÚU** the seventeenth.

daishin doctor's assistant.

daishonin scribe, notary.

daishoo compensation, recompense; **–no daishoo to shite** in compensation for; in recompense for.

daisóreta audacious, bold, insolent; atrocious; **daisóreta mane o suru** to behave atrociously.

dáisuki (*adj.*) favorite, pet; **dáisuki de aru** to have a great liking (for), be extremely fond of; **watakushi no dáisuki na hón** my favorite book.

daisúu, daisuugaku algebra.

DAITAI main points, gist; outline, mainly; on the whole; **daitai ni óite** on the whole, in general; taking all things together; **daitai no mitsumori** rough estimate; **jíken no daitai o hanásu** to give an outline of the case.

daitán bravery; boldness, audacity; **daitán na** brave, fearless; bold, daring; **daitán ni** fearlessly; boldly, audaciously.

daitóoryoo president (of a republic).

daiyamóndo diamond.

daiyaru dial.

daiyoo substitution; **daiyoo suru** to substitute for, use in place of; to serve as, serve the purpose of; **–no daiyoo ni náru** to be used as a substitute; to serve the purpose of; **daiyóobutsu** substitute.

daizai subject matter, theme.

daizáinin great (criminal) offender.

DAIZU soya bean.

dajare poor joke; cheap jest; **dajare o iu** to crack a joke.

DÁKARA accordingly, therefore, so; and so. **Dákara sonna kóto o shité wa ikenai.** That's why you must not do such a thing.

DAKE only; alone; by; as much (many) as; as . . . as; worth; **ni ínchi dake nagái** to be two inches too long; **dekiru dake háyaku** as fast (soon) as one can. **Onegai wa sore dake.** That's all I ask. **Bóku hitori daké de atta.** I was all by myself.

DÁKEDO, DÁKEDOMO, DÁKEREDOMO See **DÁGA.**

dakiagéru to lift up in one's arms.

dakiáu to embrace (each other).

dakikómu to bring over to one's side, win over; to buy off; to entice.

dakishiméru to embrace closely, hug.

dakitoméru to stop by throwing one's arms round another; to hold (a person) back.

dakitsúku to fly into (someone's) arms; to cling to embrace affectionately.

dakiyoséru to draw (someone) close to one's breast.

daku to embrace, to hug; to hatch (eggs).

dákudaku in stream; **dákudaku déru** to gush out, spout forth.

dakuon voiced consonant (such as b, d, g, or z).

dakuryuu, dakusui muddy stream or river; turbid water.

dakyoo compromise; agreement; **dakyoo suru** to compromise; to come to an agreement.

DAMÁRU to be silent. **Damátte kudasái.** Please stop talking.

damásu to deceive, cheat, defraud; to impose upon; to bewitch; to soothe, humor (a crying child).

damátte silently, in silence; without telling; without leave; **damátte kiite iru** to be listening in silence; **damátte hito no monó o tsukau** to use someone else's things without permission.

DAMÉ NA fruitless; hopeless; futile; **damé de aru** to be useless; to be hopeless; to be futile; to be all over (with someone); **damé ni náru** to fail; **damé ni suru** to render useless; spoil.

dámu dam.

dán platform, rostrum, dais; steps, stairs; flight of stairs; grade, class; act; scene; **saídan** altar.

–dan suffix denoting: group, body, party, team; **ryokóodan** account of one's travels; **ichidan o náshite** in a group; **jitsugyóodan** party of businessmen.

dan'an decision; conclusion; **dan'an o kudasu** to make a decision.

dan'atsu suppression; oppression.

danboo heating; **danboo sóochi** heating apparatus.

danchi housing-development apartment.

danchígai de aru to be no match for; to outclass.

danchoo leader of a party.

DANDAN gradually, little by little; by and by. **Dandan kuraku nátte kimáshita.** By and by it became dark.

dandori plan, program, design.

dangai precipice, cliff.

dangan bullet, shot; shell.

dangén assertion; affirmation; **dangén suru** to assert, to declare.

dango dumpling.

dangoo consultation, conference; **dangoo suru** to consult, confer with.

dangoku warm country; warm climate.

DANJITE absolutely; decidedly, on my word; never; by no means. **Danjite ikenai!** Positively no!

dánjo man and woman; both sexes; **dánjo kyoogaku** coeducation.

dankai steps, grade, gradation.

dankoo resolute action; **dankoo suru** to take decisive steps, act resolutely.

dánko taru decisive, resolute, determined, positive; **dánko to shite** decisively, positively.

danmari dumb show; silence; reticence; man of few words.

danna (*colloq.*) master; husband; sir; gentleman; **dannasáma** master (of the house).

dannén suru to abandon (an idea, hope, desire).

dánpan negotiation; parley. **Dánpan ga haretsu suru.** There is a breakdown in the negotiations.

danpatsu bobbed hair.

danpen fragment, piece; odds and ends; **danpenteki** fragmentary.

danran circle; harmony; **danran suru** to sit (around) together.

dánro heating stove; fireplace.

danryoku elasticity; **danryoku áru** elastic, springy.

dánsaa dancer; taxi dancer.

DANSEI male; man; masculinity; **danseiteki** masculine, manly.

dansen disconnection (of a wire). **Dansen suru.** A wire breaks.

DANSHI boy; man; **danshirashíi** manly; **danshiráshikunái** unmanly. **Dánshi.** Men's Room.

dánsu dance, dancing (occidental style).

dantai party, body; group.

dantei decision; conclusion; **dantei suru** to decide; to conclude.

danwa conversation, talk; **danwa suru** to talk, chat; **danwatai** colloquial, conversational style.

danzetsu disconnection, rupture; **danzetsu suru** to be cut off; to become extinct, be disconnected.

danzoku intermission; **danzokuteki no** intermittent; **danzokuteki ni** intermittently, on and off.

dáradara in drops; lazily, sluggishly; leisurely; sloppily; **dáradara suru** to work sloppily; **asé ga dáradara nageréru** to sweat profusely; **daradará zaka** a gentle slope.

–dárake suffix denoting: full of; covered with; **asedárake no** covered with sweat.

darakéru to feel dull, languid.

daraku depravity, corruption.

dararí to loosely; languidly.

darashi nái loose; careless, untidy; **darashi nái fúu o suru** to dress sloppily.

DÁRE who; **dáre no** whose; **dáre de mo** anyone, anybody; whoever; **dáre de mo mina** everyone, everybody; **dáre ka** someone, somebody; anyone, anybody. **Dáre ga shimashíta ka?** Who did it? **Kore wa dáre no desu ka?** Whose is this? **Dáre ni agemashóo ka?** Who should I give it to? **Dáre ka anáta o yonde iru.** Someone is calling you.

daréru to grow listless; to get bored; to relax; to be dull. **Hanashí ga dáreta.** The conversation lagged.

–DARÓO I speculate, I guess. **Ashita áme ga fúrudaroo.** I guess it will rain tomorrow.

DARÚI to be dull; to feel languid; to feel heavy; **Ashi ga darúi desu.** My legs feel heavy.

daruma Dharma; toy image of Dharma.

daryoku See **dasei.**

dasan calculation; **dasan suru** to calculate, count; **dasanteki** calculating, mercenary.

dasei, daryoku inertia; **ima máde no dasei** by force of habit.

dashimóno program; repertoire.

dashin suru to tap, sound.

DASHINUKE suddenness, abruptness; **dashinuke ni** suddenly; abruptly;

unexpectedly; without warning;
dashinuke o kurau to be taken by
surprise.

dashinúku to forestall; to get ahead of.

dashishibúru to begrudge.

dassen derailment, digression; **dassen suru** to
digress; to deviate.

dasshímen absorbent cotton.

dassoo desertion; flight; escape; **dassoo suru**
to desert, run away; **dassóosha** fugitive,
runaway.

dassúru to get out; to escape from; to omit,
leave out; to get rid of; **akushuu o
dassúru** to get rid of a bad habit.

DÁSU to put forth; to take out; to produce;
to turn on; to turn away; to lay bare; to
serve (a meal, tea, etc.); **tegami o dásu**
to mail a letter; **shigoto ni té o dásu** to
throw onself into the job.

datai abortion.

datchoo hernia, rupture.

DÁTTA –ta form (past) of **da**.

dátte (colloq.) but, still; because; for. **Náze
gakkoo e ikanái no desu ka? Dátte
atamá ga itái n desu mono.** Why don't
you go to school? Because I have a
headache.

DE in; at; start; in the matter of; **mikka de in**
three days; **jikan de** by the hour;
Tookyoo dé wa ichiban íi misé desu. In
Tokyo, it's the best store. **Amerika de
kaimáshita.** I bought it in America. **Mizu
de arau.** I wash it in water.

de flow; going out; rise; birth; origin; outset,
start; turnout. **Kyóo wa hito no de ga íi.**
There's a large turnout today.

de áru See **desu**.

dearúku to go out; to gad about.

DEÁU to meet, come across; to happen to
meet.

debaóocho big kitchen knife.

debudebu no fat, plump.

debúshoo one who prefers to stay at home.

dedokoro source; origin.

degarashi tea leaves; coffee grounds.

DÉGUCHI exit.

deiri entrance and exit; **deiri suru** to go in
and out; to frequent, visit regularly;
deiríguchi entrance, doorway.

deisui intoxication; **deisui suru** to be dead
drunk; **deisúisha** drunkard.

DEKAKERU to go out; to start, set out;
degake ni on the point of going, on one's
way; **ryokoo ni dekakeru** to start on a
trip. **Degake ni denwa ga kákátta.** Just
as I was on the point of going out, I
received a phone call.

dekasegi emigration; working in another
country; **dekasegi suru** to work away

from home; **dekaseginin** worker away
from home.

dekáta attitude, move.

deki workmanship; make; tailoring; cut;
result, effect; crop, yield; **deki no yói** of
fine workmanship; **deki no warúi** of poor
workmanship; **deki fúdeki** success and
failure. **Deki fúdeki ga arimásu.** It is not
always successful.

dekiagáru to be finished, be completed, be
ready.

dekiai no ready made.

dekibáe effect, result; manner of execution.
Rippa na dekibáe deshita. It was a fine
performance.

dekigókoro sudden impulse; passing fancy;
dekigókoro de on the spur of the
moment.

dekígoto event, incident; **híbi no dekígoto**
daily occurrence; everyday event; **saikin
no dekígoto** recent event.

dekimóno boil; sore; tumor; ulcer.

DEKÍNAI cannot do; poor. **Nihongo ga
yóku dekínai.** I can't speak Japanese
well.

DEKÍRU can, may; to be able; to be
possible, to be capable of; be done; be
completed; **dekíru kotó nara** if possible
[it is a thing that I can do]. **Shokuji ga
dékita.** Dinner is ready.

DEKIRU DAKE to the best of one's ability;
as . . . as possible; **dekíru dake háyaku**
as soon as possible; as early as possible;
dekiru dake no kotó o suru to do what
one can, to do everything one can.

dekishi drowning; **dekishi suru** to drown;
dekishísha a drowned person.

dekisokonai failure; **dekisokonai no**
defective; bungled; half-baked; clumsy;
deformed.

dekisokonáu to fail; to be a failure; to be
badly done, be botched, be bungled.
Shigoto wa dekisokonátta. The job was
bungled.

dekitate brand-new; just made; fresh.

dékki deck.

dekoboko unevenness; **dekoboko no** uneven,
bumpy; rough; jagged.

demado bay window.

demae catering. **Demae o suru.** They do
catering.

déme protruding eyes; **déme no** goggle-eyed.

demise branch (store); **demise o dásu** to
open a branch.

–DÉMO even, though; even if; as well, also;
but, still. **Watakushi démo dekimásu.**
Even I can do it. **Dónna pén démo íi
desu.** Any pen will do.

demodori divorced woman.

demukae meeting; reception; **demukae o ukéru** to be met (by someone).

DEMUKÁERU to go to meet (on arrival).

denaósu to come again; to go again; to call again.

den'atsu voltage.

denbun telegram, telegraphic message.

dénchi electric cell; battery.

denchuu telegraph or telephone pole; electric-light pole.

dendoo missionary work; **dendóoshi** evangelist, missionary.

den'en country, farms; rural districts; **den'en no** rural, countrified.

denka electrification; **denka suru** to put in electricity; to operate by electricity.

DÉNKI electricity; **dénki no** electric(al); **denkidókei** electric clock; **denkijíkake no** operated by electricity.

DENKYUU electric bulb.

denki biography.

denpoo telegram; cable; **denpoo de** by wire, by cable; **denpoo o útsu** to send a telegram (wire, cable); **denpóoryoo** telegraph fee. (See also **denshin**.)

denryun electric current.

densen infection, contagion; **densen suru** to be infectious; to be infected with; **densenbyoo** infectious, contagious disease; epidemic.

densetsu tradition; legend; **densetsuteki** traditional, legendary.

DENSHA streetcar, train; **densha de iku** to go by streetcar; **densha ni noru** to take a streetcar; **densháchin** streetcar fare; **denshadóori** street with a trolley line.

denshi renji microwave oven.

denshin telegram; **denshin báshira** telegraph pole; **denshínkyoku** telegraph office. (See also **denpoo**.)

denshin gawase wire transfer.

dentoo tradition; convention; **dentooteki** conventional; traditional.

DENTOO electric light; **dentoo o tsukéru** to turn on the lights; **dentoo o kesu** to turn off the lights.

DENWA telephone; **denwa choo** telephone directory; **denwa de** by telephone; **denwá shitsu** telephone booth; **kooshuu dénwa** public telephone; **denwa o kakéru** to call, make a phone call; **denwa o kíru** to hang up; **denwa o hiku** to have a phone installed.

DEPÁATO department store.

DÉRU to come out; to appear; to rise; to be up; to go out; to attend; to flow out; to break out; to issue; **sóto e déru** to go out (outside); **uchi o déru** to leave the house; **shiki ni déru** to attend a ceremony. **Mizu**

ga déru. There is a flood.

desakari height of the season.

desaki place to which someone has gone. **Desakí ga wakaránai.** I don't know where he has gone.

deshabáru to meddle, interfere.

deshí pupil, disciple, apprentice.

–déshita See **desu.**

–deshóo See **desu.**

desoróu to come out fully; to be all out.

–DESU, de aru, da be; it is; equals. **Watakushi wa gakusei desu.** I am a student. **Amerikasei déshita.** It was an American make (product). **Eikokújin deshóo.** Probably he is British.

desuguru to protrude (stick out) too much; to be too far out; to be too strong.

DÉSUKARA, DÁKARA that is why; therefore. **Desukara mínna ni sukarémasu.** That is why she is liked by everyone.

detarame irresponsible remark; nonsense; **detarame o iu** to speak nonsense.

DÉWA then, in that case, if so. **Déwa sayoonára.** Good-bye now. **Déwa mata.** I'll be seeing you. **Déwa soo shite kudasai.** If that is the case, please do so.

DEZÁATO dessert.

dezáin design.

do degree, measure, extent; times; **ichi ni do** once or twice; **do o sugósu** to go to extremes.

DÓA door (Western style).

dobin earthen teapot.

doboku public works; engineering; **doboku gíshi** civil engineer.

dobu ditch.

dobunézumi water rat.

doburoku raw (unrefined) sake.

DÓCHIRA which way; which (of the two); where; what place; **dóchira e?** where? **dóchira démo** whichever; either; both.

dodai foundation, basis.

dógimagi in confusion; **dógimagi suru** to act confused, act flustered.

dohyoo sandbag; Japanese wrestling ring, arena. **dohyoo giwa de** at the last possible moment; at the eleventh hour.

DÓITSU Germany; **Dóitsu no** (*adj.*) German; **Doitsújin** (*n.*) German; **Doitsugo** German language.

dojoo earth, soil.

dókadoka in rapid succession; in crowds; **dókadoka háitte kúru** to come in crowds, to rush in.

dokán to See **dokkári.**

dokata laborer; coolie.

dokeru to remove; to get out of the way.

dóki earthenware.

dóki anger, resentment; **dóki o óbite** in anger.

dókidoki suru to throb violently. **Muné ga dókidoki shimásu.** My heart is beating rapidly.

dokítto suru to be startled, get a shock.

dokkári to = **dokán to** heavily; with a thud.

dókku dock; **dókku ni háiru** to dock (as a ship).

DÓKO where, what place; **dóko e itté mo** wherever you go; **dóko ka** somewhere; **dóko kara** from where; **dóko made** how far; **dóko mo** everywhere.

–dókoro ka far from; to say nothing of; anything but. **Hikooki dókoro ka kuruma mo mótte imásen.** He doesn't even own a car, let alone an airplane.

dokú poison; harm; **doku no áru** poisonous; **dokú ní náru** to be bad for; **doku súru** to harm; to poison. **Oki no doku sama.** I'm sorry for you.

doku to get out of the way; to move aside. **Doite kure.** Clear the way! Get out of my way (rough)!

dokudan arbitrary decision; **dokudanteki** dogmatic, arbitrary.

dokudokushíi malicious, spiteful; poisonous-looking; **dokudokushíi kotó o iu** to say malicious things.

dokuen solo performance, recital.

dokugaku studying by oneself, without a teacher.

dókuja poisonous snake.

dókuji no original; personal; individual; **dokujisei** originality; **dókuji no kangáe** personal opinion.

dokukeshi antidote.

DOKURITSU independence; self-support; **dokuritsu suru** to be independent, stand on one's own feet; **dokuritsu no** independent; **dokurítsu de** independently; **dokurítsukoku** independent state; **dokurítsushin** independent spirit. **Dekuritsu Kinénbi** Independence Day (Fourth of July).

Dokuritsu Kókka Kyoodootai Commonwealth of Independent States.

dokuryoku de on one's own, by oneself, singlehanded; **dokuryoku de yaru** to do something on one's own.

dokusai dictatorship; **dokusai séiji** dictatorship; **dekusáisha** dictator.

dokusatsu suru to poison.

dokusen monopoly; **dokusen jígyoo** monopolistic enterprise, monopoly; **dokusenteki** monopolistic, exclusive.

dókusha reader; subscriber; reading public; **dókusho suru** to read (books); **dokushoka** book-lover; great reader;

dókusho reading.

dokushoo vocal solo.

dokushuu, dokugaku studying without a teacher; **dokushuusho** book for self-teaching; "do-it-yourself" book.

dokusoo originality; **dokusooteki na** original; creative; **dokusoo no sái** creative ability; talent.

dokuyaku poison.

dókyoo spirit; courage; **dókyoo no áru** daring, courageous; **dókyoo no nái** timid, cowardly.

domá earthen floor.

donabe earthen pot.

donáru to shout, thunder at.

DÓNATA who (*respect*), **dónata de mo** anybody. **Dónata desu ka?** Who are you? **Dónata ka ome ni kakarítái soo desu.** Someone wishes to see you.

donburi deep bowl, **donburi meshi** boiled rice served in a deep bowl; **oyako dónburi** chicken, eggs, and rice in a deep bowl.

dóndon rub-a-rub, rat-a-rat; **dóndon susumu** to advance rapidly; **dóndon mookéru** to make money rapidly.

DÓNNA what; what sort of, kind of; **dónna ni** how much; however. **Dónna hón desu ka?** What kind of a book is it?

DÓNO which; what; **dono kurai** to what degree?; how long?; how far?; **dóno hito** which person?

donzoko rock bottom; **donzoko séikatsu** poverty-stricken life.

DÓO how; what; **dóo atte mo** in any case. **Doo itashimáshite.** Don't mention it! Not at all! **Sore wa dóo ni mo narimasen.** It can't be helped.

dóo copper.

dóo torso.

dóo temple, shrine, hall; **dóo ni iru** to attain proficiency, to become an expert.

doo (can also be prefix) the same; the said (aforementioned); corresponding; equal; **doo bánchi** the same street number; **doodan** same, ditto; **dooyoo** the same, ditto; **doo mikka** the third day of the same month.

DOOBUTSU animal; living creature; **doobútsuen** zoo; **doobutsúgaku** zoology.

DOO DE MO in any way; **doo de mo kóo de mo** by any means, at any cost; **doo de mo íi koto** a trivial matter. **Doo de mo ii desu.** It doesn't matter one way or the other.

doodoo suru to go with, accompany.

doofuu enclosure(s); **doofuu no tegami** the enclosed letter.

dóogi morality, morals, principles, ethics.

dóogi motion made during a meeting.

DOOGU tools, implements, utensils; sets; property; household goods; **doogúbako** toolbox; **dooguya** secondhand dealer; curio shop; furniture shop.

doohai equal colleague.

doohan suru to accompany.

dooi consent, approval, agreement; **dooi suru** to consent to, approve.

DOO ITASHIMÁSHITE! Don't mention it. Not at all. The pleasure is mine.

dooitsu equality; **dooitsu no** same; identical, equal.

dooji same time; **dooji no** simultaneous, concurrent; **dooji ni** at the same time; **doojídai** same age; **doojídai no** contemporary; **doojitsu** same (very) day.

dóojoo exercise hall (for Judo, fencing, etc.); arena; Buddhist seminary.

doojoo sympathy, compassion; **doojoo áru** sympathetic, warmhearted; **doojoo no nái** unsympathetic.

DÓOKA, DÓOZO please; somehow or other; **DOOKA KOOKA** somehow or other; some way or other; barely; with difficulty; **dóoka shite** somehow, in one way or another.

dooka assimilation.

dóoka copper coin.

dookaku same rank, status, etc.

dookan same sentiment, same feeling; same opinion; **dookan de áru** to be of the same opinion; to feel the same way.

dooke (*n.*) clowning; **dooke shíbai** farce; **dooke yákusha** clown; **dookéta** comic, foolish; **dookéru** to clown.

dookei aspiration, longing; worship.

dooki motive, incentive.

dooki palpitation; **dooki ga suru** to throb, to palpitate.

dóoki same period; same class; **dóoki no** of the same year; **dookísei, dookyúusei** classmate.

dookokújin fellow countryman.

dookoo pupil of the eye.

dookoo suru to go together; **dookóosha** traveling companion.

doomei alliance; league; **doomei koku** ally.

DÓOMO very; much; rather; quite. **Dóomo arígatoo gozaímasu.** I'm much obliged.

doonen same year; same age; **doonen de aru** to be the same age.

DÓO NI KA somehow or other; **dóo ni ka suru** to manage somehow, try one's best.

DÓORO road.

dooryoku motor power; power.

DOOSE anyway; after all, at best; of course; at all. **Doose yaranákereba naránai desu.** I must do it anyway.

dooséiai homosexuality.

DÓO SHITE why; how; **DÓO SHITE MO** in any case; by any means; whatever may happen. **Dóo shite sore o gozonji desu ka?** How do you know that? **Dóo shite mo ikanákereba narimasen.** Whatever may happen (in any case, no matter what happens) I have to go.

dootoo equality; parity; **dootoo no** equal, equivalent; **dootoo ni** equally; **dootoo ni suru** to make equal, equalize.

DÓOZO please; if you please. **Dóozo moo ichido itte kudasái.** Please say it again.

doozoo bronze statue.

dóra gong.

dórama drama.

dorámu drum (musical); **dorámu kan** drum (for storage).

DÓRE which one? **Dóre ga ichiban íi desu ka?** Which is the best?

doró mud; **doro dárake no** muddy; **dorómizu** muddy water.

doroboo thief.

DÓRU dollar; **doru sóoba** exchange rate of the dollar.

dóryoku effort, exertion; **dóryoku suru** to exert oneself; to endeavor.

dosakusa confusion; tumult; trouble.

dóshidoshi in large numbers; rapidly; in rapid succession.

DOSSÁRI in great quantity or numbers. **Tegami ga dossári kita.** Many letters came.

DOTTO all of a sudden; suddenly; with a rush.

DOYÓOBI Saturday.

dozoo storehouse with earthen walls.

E

E particle denoting: to, toward, in the direction of; **Kyóoto e ikimásu.** I'm going to Kyoto.

e handle, crank, haft, shaft.

É picture, painting; drawing, illustration, sketch; **é o káku** to make (draw, paint) a picture; **é no yoo na** like a picture; picturesque.

ebi lobster; shrimp; prawn.

ebicha maroon; brownish red.

eda branch, bough; twig; **edaburi** spread of branches; **edaha** branches; ramifications; digressions; **hanashí ga edaha ni háiru** to digress; **edaha no gíron** side issue; digression.

ÉE, HAI yes. **Ée, sóo desu.** Yes, that is so. Correct.

eeteru ether.

ee to let me see; well (used when stalling for time). **Ee to, sore wa nán deshita ka?** Let me see, what was it?

égao smiling face; smile; **égao o suru** to smile; **égao de** with a smile.

egatái hard to get; not easily obtainable; **matá to egatái kikái** a rare opportunity.

EHÁGAKI picture postcard.

ehón picture book for children; illustrated book.

Ei– prefix denoting: Anglo-, English, British; **Ei-taishí kan** British Embassy; **Eibúngaku** English Literature.

Éi-Bei England and America; **Éi-Bei no** Anglo-American; **Ei-Béijin** the English and the Americans.

eibin na keen, sharp, smart, clever, quick-witted; **eibin na kansatsu** keen observation; **eibin na mimí** sharp ears.

EIBUN English; English sentence; English composition; English-language text; **Eibun wáyaku** translation from English into Japanese.

eien eternity; permanence; **eien no** eternal; permanent; everlasting; **eien ni** forever, perpetually.

ÉIGA movie; motion pictures; **eigagáisha** film-producing company; **eigákai no meiyuu** movie star; **EIGÁKAN** movie theater.

EIGO English language; English; **Eigo no** (*adj.*) English; written in English; **Eigo ga dekíru, Eigo de hanásu** to speak in English; **Eigo ga wakáru** to understand English.

EIGYOO business, trade; trading; **eigyoo suru** to engage in business; trade in; **eigyóohi** business expenses; **eigyóo jíkan** business (office) hours; **eigyóozei** business tax.

eijuu permanent residence; **eijuu no** settled; resident; **eijuu suru** to reside permanently.

Éika English currency; sterling; British-made goods.

eikan crown of glory; laurels.

éiki high spirits; vigor; energy. **Éiki o sógu.** To dampen one's enthusiasm.

EIKOKU England, Great Britain; **Eikoku no** (*adj.*) English; **Eikokújin** English person (See also **Eigo.**)

EIKYOO influence; effect; **eikyoo suru** to influence; to affect; **eikoo o ukéru** to be influenced, be affected.

eikyuu permanence; eternity; **eikyuuteki** permanent; perpetual, eternal; **eikyuu ni** permanently, forever.

eimin death (human only); **eimin suru** to die.

éiri gain, profit; **eiríteki no** money-making; commercial; **eiri jígyoo** commercial undertaking; **eiri gáisha** commercial concern.

éiri na sharp, keen; sharp-edged.

Eiryoo British dominion.

eisei hygiene, sanitation; health; **eisei ni yói** healthful; wholesome; **eisei ni waruí** bad for the health; **eiseiteki na** hygienic; sanitary.

eisei satellite; **eiséikoku** satellite nation; **jinkoo éisei** man-made satellite; **eisei chúukei** satellite telecast.

eisháki film projector.

eisháshitsu projection room.

eiten transfer on promotion.

EI-WA JÍSHO English-Japanese dictionary.

Eiyaku English translation.

éiyo honor; glory.

eiyoo nutrition; nourishment; **eiyoo áru** nutritious, nourishing; **eiyoo fúryoo** malnutrition; **eiyóobutsu** nutritious food.

eizoku permanence; continuation; **eizokuteki** lasting, permanent; **eizoku suru** to last long, remain permanently.

eizúru to be reflected (as in a mirror in water); to impress.

ÉKI use; good; benefit; advantage, profit; **éki no áru** beneficial, profitable; **éiki no nái** useless; unprofitable; **eki súru** to benefit, do good to.

éki sap, liquid, fluid.

ÉKI = teishajoo railway station; **ekichoo** stationmaster; **ekfin** porter; station employee; **Tokyooeki** Tokyo Station.

ekibyoo epidemic, pestilence, plague.

ékiri dysentery; children's summer diarrhea.

ékisu extract, essence.

ekitai liquid, fluid.

ekkususen X rays.

ekohíiki partiality, favoritism; **ekohíiki no** partial, unfair; **ekohíiki no nái** impartial, fair; **ekohíiki suru** to show partiality to; be partial to.

ekoji na stubborn, perverse, obstinate; **ekoji ni nátte** in spite of; out of spite.

ékubo dimple.

emono game, a catch; trophy; prize, spoils.

ÉN yen (Japanese money); **hyaku en** 100 yen **hyaku én satsu** 100-yen note.

én circle.

én affinity; fate; blood relation, blood connection; **en o musubu** to marry.

én feast, dinner party; **én o haru** to give a dinner party.

enban disk, discus.

enbífuku (male) evening dress.

enboo vista; distant view.

enchaku delayed arrival; **enchaku suru** to arrive late; to be delayed.

enchoo continuation, extension; **enchoo suru** to extend, prolong, lengthen.

endan proposal (of marriage).

endan rostrum, platform.

endoo route; road; **endoo ní** en route; along the road.

en'en in a blaze; **en'en táru** blazing, flaming; **en'en to shite** in (fierce) flames.

enérugii energy.

engan coast; **engan no** on the shore along the coast.

ENGAWA veranda, porch.

engei dramatic performance; entertainment; **engéisha** performer, artist; **engeijoo** variety theater; an entertainment hall; **engéikai** variety show; **engei mókuroku** program; repertoire.

engeki play; theatrical performance.

engi luck; omen; history; legend; **engi no yói** lucky, auspicious; **engi no warúi** unlucky, ominous, ill-omened.

éngi playacting, performance.

éngo support; backing.

engumi marriage; alliance; adoption (of a son); **engumi suru** to marry; to adopt.

énja relative, kinsman.

énjo assistance; help, aid; **énjo suru** to assist, help; to support.

enjuku maturity; mellowness; perfection; **enjuku suru** to grow ripe, mature; to mellow; **enjuku shita** mature; mellow; perfect.

énka exchange rate, value of the yen.

enkai social gathering; feast, banquet; dinner party; **enkai o hiraku** to give a dinner party.

enkai coast, sea (near land); **enkai gyógyoo** inshore fishery.

enkei distant view; perspective; circle; **enkei no** round, circular.

enki postponement; adjournment; **enki suru** to postpone, put off.

enkin distance; far and near; **enkin kara** from far and near.

énko connection; relation; affinity.

enkyóri far distance, great distance; **enkyori de** at a great distance.

enmachoo black list; teacher's record book.

enman perfection; harmony; **enman na** perfect; harmonious; peaceful; **enman ni** harmoniously, smoothly; peacefully; **enman na katei** happy home; **enman ni kotó o osaméru** to settle the matter smoothly.

ennetsu burning (scorching) heat; heat of the sun.

énnichi fete day (of a local deity); fair; festival.

en nó shita ground or space under the veranda or floor in a Japanese house; **en nó shita no chikarámochi o suru** to be engaged in a thankless task; to labor in the background.

enogu paints, oils; colors, pigments; **enogúzara** dish for blending colors.

ENPITSU pencil; **iro-énpitsu** colored pencils; **enpitsu kézuri** a pencil sharpener.

enpoo great distance; distant place.

enrai no kyaku visitor (guest) from a distant place.

énro long way; great distance; long journey. **Énro go-sokúroo o wazurawashimáshite sumimasén.** I thank you for coming all the way.

ENRYO reserve; modesty; respect; **enryo suru** to be reserved; to refrain from; to withhold; **enryo náku** without reserve, freely; **enryo bukái** modest; shy; **–ni enryo shite** out of respect for (someone); **enryo éshaku mo náku** without the least reserve.

ensaki edge of a veranda.

ensei, enséikan pessimism; **enseiteki** pessimistic; **enseika** pessimist.

enshoo inflammation; spread of a fire; **enshoo suru** to each fire.

enshutsu performance (of a play, an opera, a film); **enshutsu suru** to play, perform; to execute.

ensoku excursion (on foot), hike; picnic; **ensoku ni iku** to go on a hike; to take a long walk.

ensoo musical performance; recital; **ensóosha** performer, player; **ensóokai** concert, recital.

entaku round table.

enten blazing (burning) sun; heat of the day.

ENTOTSU chimney; chimney stack; funnel.

en'yoo gyógyoo deep-sea fishing.

en'yoo kóokai ocean voyage.

en'yúukai garden party.

enzetsu speech, address; **enzetsu suru** to make a speech; **enzetsúkai** speech meeting.

enzúku to be married.

episóodo episode.

ERABU to choose, select, elect, single out; to sort; **hón o erábu** to select a book. **Ii no daké o erabimashoo.** Let's choose only a good one.

ERÁI great; extraordinary; worthy; eminent; wonderful; serious; heavy. **Erái kotó ni nátta.** It looks bad.

EREBÉETAA elevator.

ERÍ neck; neckband; collar; **eríkubi** nape of the neck; **erímaki** muffler, scarf; **erí o tadásu** to adjust one's dress; to sit up straight.

éru to gain; to get.

éshaku greeting, salutation; **éshaku suru** to greet; to bow slightly.

esukaréetaa escalator.

etai form, shape; nature; **etai no shirenu** unfamiliar, strange; nondescript; **etai no shirenu hito** a perfect stranger.

eté skill; specialty, one's forte; **eté ni ho o ageru** to sail before the wind; to give scope to one's skill; **–ga eté da** to be a good hand at; **–wa eté de nái** to be a poor hand at.

etoku understanding, comprehension; **etoku suru** to understand, grasp; **etoku shiyói** easy to understand; **etoku shinikúi** difficult to understand.

F

FÁAMASHII pharmacy.

faindaa finder.

fán fan, enthusiast; **eiga fan** movie fan.

fássho fascist.

fáuru foul ball (in baseball).

feruto See **fueruto**.

fíito = fuŝíto feet (a measure).

Fíripin Philippine Islands; **Firipínjin** Filipino.

firumu = fuirumu film.

firutaa filter.

fóoku fork.

–fú suffix denoting: urban prefecture (used only with Kyoto and Osaka); **Kyooto fu** Kyoto prefecture.

fuan insecurity; anxiety; **fuan na** unsafe; insecure; anxious.

fuan ni omóu to feel insecure (uncertain, anxious) about. **Fuan de átta.** I felt uneasy.

fuánnai unfamiliarity; ignorance; **fuánnai na** unfamiliar; ignorant; **fuánnai na tochi** strange place; **tochi ni fuánnai na hito** stranger, person who is not familiar with a place. **Watakushi wa koko wa fuánnai desu.** I am pretty much of a stranger here.

fuántei instability; **fuántei na** unstable; unsteady; insecure.

FÚBEN inconvenience; **fúben na** inconvenient; **fúben o shoozuru** to cause inconvenience; **fúben o shinóbu** to put up with inconvenience; **fúben o kanzuru** to be put to inconvenience.

fúbi deficiency; defect, imperfection; **fúbi no** defective; incomplete; imperfect; **fúbi no ten** defects; imperfections.

fúbin na pitiful; poor; **fúbin ni omóu** to pity, take pity on.

FÚBO parents.

fúbuki snowstorm, blizzard.

fuchakuriku hikóo non-stop flight.

fuchaku suru to stick to; to attach.

fuchí edge, brink, rim; margin, border; **fuchí o tóru** to hem; to fringe; etc.; **fuchí o tsukéru** to frame, border.

fuchi deep pool, deep water; abyss.

fuchin ups and downs; rise and fall; **isshoo no fuchin ni kansuru dáiji** a matter affecting one's whole life.

fuchoo disagreement; rupture; failure; **fuchoo ni owaru** to end in failure.

fuchóowa discord; incongruity; **fuchóowa na** unharmonious, discordant; **fuchóowa de aru** to clash.

FUCHÚUI carelessness; inattention; **fuchúui na** careless; inattentive; **fuchúui ni** carelessly.

fuchúujitsu unfaithfulness, disloyalty; **fuchúujitsu na** unfaithful, disloyal.

FUDA card; label, tag; placard; **fuda o tsukéru** to attach a card (or label); to tag.

FÚDAN usually, ordinarily; habitually; **fúdan no** usual; habitual; common; **fúdan no tóori** as usual.

fundángi everyday clothes.

fude writing brush.

fúdeki failure; poor work; **fudeki na** badly made (done); clumsy. **Kono hako wa fúdeki desu.** This box is badly made. **Íne ga fúdeki desu.** The rice crops is poor.

fudoo difference, diversity, dissimilarity; inequality; **fudoo de aru** to be unequal; to differ; to be irregular.

fudóoi disagreement, difference of opinion.

fudóosan immovable property; real estate.

fudóotoku immorality; **fudóotoku na** immoral, unprincipled.

fue flute, whistle.

fuéisei na unsanitary; unhealthy.

FUÉRU to increase (in number or quantity), multiply. **Mizu ga fúeta kita.** The river is rising. **Okane ga fúeta.** His income has increased.

fueruto = feruto felt.

fúete weak point; unskillfulness; **fúete na** unskillful, inexpert. **Sono hóo wa fúete desu.** I'm a poor hand at it. It's not in my line.

fufuku dissatisfaction, discontent; disapproval; objection; **fufuku ga áru** to be dissatisfied, etc.; **fufuku o iu** to express dissatisfaction.

fugai nái unmanly, effeminate; poor-spirited; cowardly.

fúgi immorality; injustice; adultery; **fúgi no** immoral; improper.

fúgiri ingratitude; dishonesty; **fúgiri no** unjust; dishonest; ungrateful; **fúgiri ga áru** to owe a debt.

fugoo millionaire.

fugoo mark, sign, symbol, cipher.

fugóokaku failure; elimination; rejection; **figóokaku to náru** to fail.

fugóori absurdity; **fugóori na** absurd; irrational, illogical.

fúgu deformity; **fúgu no** deformed, disfigured, crippled; **fúgu ni náru** to become disfigured.

fuguu misfortune, adversity; **fuguu no** unfortunate.

fugyóoseki loose conduct; dissipation.

fuhai decomposition; decay; **fuhai suru** to rot; to be corrupted.

fuhei discontent; dissatisfaction; **fuhei o iu** to grumble, complain; **fuhei de áru** to be discontented; **fuhei o mótte iru** to have a complaint; **fuheika** grumbler, malcontent.

fuhéikin inequality, disproportion; **fuhéikin no** unequal; disproportionate.

fuhen unchangeability; **fuhen no** unchangeable, constant; invariable.

fuhínkoo immoral conduct; dissipation; **fuhínkoo na** loose, immoral.

fuhitsúyoo na needless, unnecessary.

fuhón'i unwillingness, reluctance; **fuhón'i no** unwilling, reluctant; **fuhon'i nágara** against one's will.

fuhoo na unlawful, violent; illegal.

fui unexpectedness; suddenness; **fui no** unexpected; sudden; unlooked for; **fui o útsu** to take by surprise; **fui o kurau** to be taken by surprise.

fuichoo announcement; advertisement; recommendation; **fuichoo suru** to announce; to advertise; to make known.

fuíito See **fíito**.

fuirumu See **fírumu**.

fuiuchi unexpected blow, surprise attack.

fujichaku, fujichakuriku forced landing, emergency landing.

FUJIN woman; lady; **fujinrashíi** womanly; ladylike.

fúji no incurable; fatal.

fujitsu insincerity; faithlessness; lack of feeling; **fujitsu no** faithless; insincere; unfeeling.

fújiyuu inconvenience; want; discomfort; **fújiyuu na** uncomfortable; inconvenient; **fújiyuu o suru** to be short (wanting).

fújo assistance, aid; support; **fújo suru** to assist, aid.

fujóori unreasonableness, irrationality; **fujóori na** unreasonable, irrational.

fujun impurity; **fujun no** impure.

fujun unseasonability, irregularity; **fujun na** unseasonable, irregular.

fujúubun insufficiency; **fujúubun na** insufficient; incomplete.

fuka addition, supplement; **fuka suru** to add, supplement.

fukágen slight illness, indisposition; unsavoriness; **fukágen na** unsavory; indisposed, unwell.

FUKÁI deep, profound; thick, dense; **fukái kangáe** deep thought; **fukái kiri** dense fog; **fukái náka ni náru** to form a close relationship.

fukái unpleasantness. See **fuyúkai**.

fukairi (n.) going too far; addiction; **fukairi suru** to go deeply into; to be taken up too much with.

fukákai mystery; **fukákai na** mysterious; insoluble; **fukákai na kotó** mystery, mysterious affair.

fukakóoryoku act of God; **fukakóoryoku no** unavoidable; inevitable; irresistible.

fukaku negligence, fault; **fukaku o tóru** to be beaten. **Sore wa watakushi no fukaku déshita.** It was my fault.

fukákujitsu uncertainty; unreliability; **fukákujitsu no** uncertain; unreliable.

fukami depth; deep place; **fukami no áru** deep, profound; **fukami ni háiru** to get beyond one's depth.

fukánoo impossibility; **fukánoo na** impossible; impractical. **Hotondo fukánoo de áru.** It is almost impossible.

fukánzen imperfection; incompleteness; **fukánzen na** defective; incomplete.

fukkáppatsu inactivity; stagnation; dullness; **fukáppatsu na** dull; inactive; stagnant.

fukása depth. **Fukása ga go fíito desu.** It is five feet deep.

fukéiki depression; dullness; hard times; **fukéiki na** dull; depressed, gloomy, dismal.

fukéizai na uneconomical; wasteful.

fukénkoo unhealthiness; poor health; **fukénkoo na** unhealthy, unwholesome.

fukénshiki lack of proper judgment; **fukénshiki na** disgraceful, shameful.

fukénzen na morbid, unwholesome.

FUKÉRU to grow old, age; to grow late, advance; **yó ga fukéru made hataraku** to work late into the night. **Yó wa dandan fukéta.** The night wore away. It grew late.

fuketsu dirtiness; **fuketsu na** dirty, filthy; **fuketsúbutsu** dirt, filth.

fukí appendix; **fukí súru** to add.

fukiagéru to blow up; to spout; to throw up.

fukichirásu to scatter about; to blow away.

fukidásu to spout, gush out; to burst out laughing.

fukidemono (body) rash.

fukikakéru to pick (a quarrel); to breathe on. **Kim wa bóku ni kenka o fukikakéru no ka?** Do you want to pick a fight with me?

fukikésu to blow out a light.

fukikómu to blow into (a house, room, etc.); to inspire; to instill in one's mind; to record (make a sound recording); to polish, rub bright.

fukimakúru to blow about; to sweep along.

fukín neighborhood; **fukín ni** in the neighborhood; **fukín no** neighboring, adjacent.

FUKÍN a napkin; dish towel, dishcloth.

fukinshin na indiscreet; immodest.

fukiorósu to blow down.

fukíritsu lack of discipline; irregularity; **fukíritsu na** disorderly; undisciplined; irregular.

fukísoku irregularity; **fukísoku na** unsystematic; irregular.

fukisóoji wiping; cleaning; **fukisóoji o suru** to mop.

fukisusámu to blow furiously.

fukitóru to wipe away; to wipe out.

fukitsu ill omen; ill luck; **fukitsu na** unlucky, ill-omened; ominous.

fukitsukéru to blow against; to beat against. **Ame ga mádo ni fukitsukéru.** The rain beats against the window.

fukiyoséru to drift; to blow together.

fukkatsu revival; **fukkatsu suru** to revive. **Fukkátsusai, Fukkátsusetsu** Easter.

fukkoo revival, renaissance; restoration; **fukkoo suru** to revive, be restored.

fukkyuu restoration; **fukkyuu suru** to restore to the original state; to be restored to normalcy.

fukókoroe indiscretion; misconduct; **fukókoroe na** unwise, indiscreet; **fukókoroe na kotó o suru** to behave badly; to act indiscreetly.

fukoku decree, proclamation; notification; **fukoku suru** to notify; to decree, proclaim.

FUKÓO misery; unhappiness; disaster; mishap; disobedience to parents; **fukóo na** unhappy, unfortunate; miserable; undutiful, unfilial; **fukóo ni mo** unfortunately; **fukóo ni áu** to have a misfortune.

fukóohei unfairness, partiality; **fukóohei na** unfair, partial, unjust; **fukóohei ni** unjustly, unfairly.

FUKU to wipe; to dry; to mop, to rub off;

tenugui de té o fuku to wipe the hands with a towel.

fukú to blow; to breathe; to whistle. **Hídoku fúite iru.** It's blowing hard. **me o fúku** to send out a new shoot; **fue o fukú** to play a flute; **hora o fukú** (colloq.) to boast.

fuku– prefix denoting: assistant, vice-; **fukugíchoo** vice-chairman; **Fukudaitóoryoo** Vice-President (of the U.S.A.).

fuku– sub, double, composite; **fukúri** compound interest.

–fuku suffix denoting: clothes, dress; garment; **yoofuku** European clothes; **fujínfuku** women's clothes.

fukuan plan, idea; scheme. **Watakushi ni fukuan ga arimásu.** I have a good plan.

fukubiki lottery; distribution of prizes.

fukubukushíi happy-looking; radiant.

fukugyoo subsidiary business; side job.

fukúmuu to have (hold) in the mouth; to bear in mind; to include; to imply. **Dóozo kono kóto o ofukumioki kudasái.** Please keep this in mind.

fukurahagi calf (of the leg).

fukuramasu to swell, expand, puff out.

fukurami bulge, swelling.

fukureru to swell, puff out; to be sulky; to become sore.

fukurettsura (colloq.) sulky, sullen look.

FUKURO bag, sack, pouch.

fukurodátaki sound thrashing, drubbing.

fukuryóoji vice-consul.

fukusánbutsu by-product.

fukusáyoo ill effect; secondary reaction; harmful side-effects; **fukusáyoo no nái** harmless.

fukusei reproduction; duplication,

fukusha copying; **fukusha suru** to copy, reproduce; **fukusháki** duplicator.

fukushóchoo vice-president (of a company).

fukushi adverb.

fukúshi welfare.

fukushin devotion; confidence; **fukushin no** devoted; confidential; faithful; **fukushin no tómo** devoted friend.

fukushoku reappointment; **fukushoku suru** to resume office.

fukushuu review; **fukushuu suru** to review, go over.

fukushuu revenge, vengeance; **fukushuu suru** to be revenged.

fukusúu (n.) plural (number); **fukusúu no** (adj.) plural.

fukutsu no inflexible; indomitable.

fukutsuu stomachache; bellyache.

fukuyoo suru to take a dose of medicine.

fukuzatsu na complex, complicated, intricate; **fukuzatsu ni suru** to complicate.

fukuzoo reserve; **fukuzoo náku** without reserve, frankly; **fukuzoo no nái** frank, candid, unreserved; **fukuzoo náku iéba** to be frank with you; **fukuzoo náku íken o nobéru** to express one's views freely, without reserve.

fukyoo business depression, slump, inactivity, slackness, displeasure; ill-humor, disfavor, **fukyoo no** inactive; depressed, weak; in a slump.

fukyuu diffusion, propagation, spread; **fukyuu suru** to diffuse, propagate, spread.

fukyuu immortality, eternity; **fukyuu no** eternal, immortal, undying.

fuman, fumanzoku discontent, dissatisfaction; **fuman na** discontented, dissatisfied; **fuman ni omóu** to be displeased with, dissatisfied with.

fumei obscurity, uncertainty; ignorance; **fumei no** obscure, indistinct, vague; **fuméiryoo** not clear, indistinct. **Yukisaki wa fumei da.** His destination is unknown.

fuméiyo disgrace, dishonor; discredit; **fuméiyo na** disgraceful, dishonorable.

fumetsu immortality; indestructibility.

fumidai step; footstool.

fumidan step; steps, stairs.

fumidásu to step forward.

fumihazusu to miss (lose) one's footing.

fumikataméru to tread; to stamp down.

fumikiri railway crossing; grade crossing.

fumikoéru to step over (a thing).

fumikómi to step into; to make a raid; to rush in; to trespass; to force an entrance.

fumikudáku to trample.

fumímochi dissipation; immoral conduct.

fuminarásu to stamp (one's feet) noisily; to tread; to level by treading.

fumin fukyuu without sleep or rest.

fuminijíru to trample, crush with the feet.

fumínshoo insomnia, sleeplessness.

fumitaósu to kick down; to evade payment; to bargain.

fumitodomáru to stand one's ground, remain.

fumitsukéru to trample; to treat with contempt; **hito o fumitsuke ni shita kotó o iu** to make an insulting remark.

fumoto foot of a hill or mountain.

fumu to step; to tread on; to go through; to value at; **jitchi o fumu** to experience; **tetsúzuki o fumu** to go through the formalities; **shinamono no ne o fumu** to put a price on something.

fúmuki unfit for, unsuitable for.

FÚN, pún minute; **íppun** one minute; **gofún kan** for five minutes.

funaashi speed, draft, headway (of a ship); **funaashi no hayái fúne** fast boat;

funaásobi boat excursion; **funaásobi ni yuku** to go boating.

funáchin passage fare; shipping freight; freightage.

funade ship departure; sailing; **funade suru** to set sail.

funani shóoken bill of lading.

funánori sailor, seaman.

fúnare unfamiliarity; inexperience; **fúnare na** unfamiliar; inexperienced; **roodoo ni fúnare de aru** to be unaccustomed to labor.

funáyoi seasickness.

funbáru to stretch one's legs; to straddle; to make an effort; to persevere; **sáigo made funbáru** to hold fast to the end.

fúnbetsu discretion, good sense; discernment; **fúnbetsu no áru** discreet, prudent; thoughtful; **fúnbetsu no nái** indiscreet etc.; **funbetsu zákari no hito** mature person.

fundan ni in plenty, fully. **Tabemóno ga fundan ni áru.** There is plenty to eat.

FÚNE ship, boat, vessel; **fúne ni noru** to board a ship; to go to sea; **fúne ni yóu** to get seasick.

funésshin indifference; **funésshin na** halfhearted, indifferent, lukewarm.

fungai resentment, indignation; **fungai shite** indignantly; **fungai suru** to be indignant, resent.

funíai unbecoming (to), unsuitable; ill-matched; **funíai no fúufu** ill-matched couple.

fun'íki atmosphere.

funínjoo na unfeeling, coldhearted.

funka eruption, volcanic activity; **funkázan** volcano.

fúnki suru to be stirred up, be inspired by; to rouse oneself to action.

funmatsu powder; **funmatsu ní suru** to pulverize.

funoo impossibility; incompetency; impotency; **funoo no** impossible.

funpatsu exertion, endeavor(s); **funpatsu suru** to exert oneself; to rouse; to make a great effort.

funsai suru to shatter (smash) to pieces.

funshitsu loss; **funshitsu suru** to lose; to miss; to be missing; **funshitú butsu** lost article.

funshutsu spout, gush, jet; **funshutsu suru** to gush out.

funsoo trouble; dispute; difficulties.

funsoo disguise; **funsoo suru = funsúru** to disguise, to impersonate.

funsui fountain; jet.

funsúru See **funsoo suru.**

funtoo hard struggle, desperate fight; **funtoo suru** to struggle, fight desperately.

funzen resolutely; plucking up one's courage; indignantly; in a fit of anger.

fuon unrest; **fuon na** threatening; disquieting; improper; riotous; **fuon na nyúusu** unsettling news. **Keisei ga fuon de áru.** The situation is quite disturbing.

fuóntoo impropriety, inappropriateness; **fuontoo no, fuóntoo na** improper, inappropriate; unjust.

fúrachi outrageousness; insolence; misconduct; **fúrachi na** outrageous, insolent; vicious; **fúrachi na kotó o suru** to misconduct oneself; to act viciously.

fúrafura to dizzy, unsteady; **fúrafura suru** to feel dizzy; to reel, stagger. **Atamá ga fúrafura suru.** My head is swimming.

furai fry; **sakana no furai** fried fish; **furaipan** frying pan.

furanneru flannel.

FURANSU France; **Furansugo** French language; **Furansújin** French person.

furareru to be jilted.

furasshu flashlight.

furekomi announcement, proclamation.

furekómu to announce; to represent oneself as.

furemawásu to broadcast, to spread news.

fureru to touch; to strike against; to refer to; to conflict with; **hooritsu ni fureru** to be contrary to the law; **mondai ni fureru** to refer to the question.

fúri disadvantage, drawback; **fúri na** disadvantageous, unfavorable; unprofitable.

furí appearance; air; pretension; **shiranai furí o suru** to pretend ignorance.

furi– prefix denoting: to shake; to brandish, wave, flourish.

furidashi drawing; start, starting point; issue.

furidásu to begin to fall (as rain or snow). **Áme ga furidáshita.** It began to rain.

furíeki disadvantage; handicap.

furigana Kana (Japanese syllabic sign) attached to *Kanji* to show the pronunciation.

furihanásu to shake free from; to break away.

furiharáu to shake from.

furikae change; transfer.

furikáeru, furimúku to turn around; to look back over one's shoulder.

furikakáru to fall on; to befall, happen.

furikakéru to sprinkle over.

furikazásu to hold aloft; to brandish.

furikíru break away from.

furiko pendulum.

furimawásu to brandish, flourish.

furimúku See **furikáeru.**

furiotósu to shake off.

furishikíru to rain or snow incessantly.

furisutéru to leave, abandon, to shake off.

furitatéru to shake; to toss; to raise one's voice.

furitsuke dance composition; choreography.

furitsuzuku to rain or snow continuously.

FURÓ bath, hot bath; **furó ni háiru** to take a bath; **furoba** bathroom; **furóya** bathhouse.

furoku supplement, appendix.

furoonin wanderer; tramp.

FUROSHIKI wrapping cloth (square piece of cotton or silk used to wrap and carry something); **furoshiki de tsutsúmu** to wrap in a wrapping cloth.

FÚRU to fall, to come down (rain, etc.). **Hídoku áme ga fútte iru.** Rain is falling heavily. **Yukí ga fútta.** There was a snowfall.

furu to shake; to wave, wag; **kubi o táte ni furu** to nod, assent to.

furu– prefix denoting: old; **furuhon** old book; **furuhonya** secondhand book store; **furubíru** to be worn out; to be aged; **furúbita** old, worn-out; **furumono** secondhand goods; **furudóogu** old furniture; **furumono** secondhand household utensils; **furudooguya** secondhand dealer; curio shop; **furugi** old clothes; secondhand clothes; **furugi ya** secondhand-clothes dealer.

furue (n.) shaking, trembling, shivering; **furueagáru** to tremble with fear; **furuegóe** trembling voice; timid voice; **furueru** to shake, shudder, tremble.

furui sieve; **furui ni kakéru** to sift (out) sieve.

furúi old (used when speaking of things); ancient; antique.

furuiokósu to stir up, rouse, awaken; **yúuki o furuiokósu** to summon up courage.

furuitátsu to stir up; to be roused to action.

furukizu old wound; scar; former misdeed.

furukusái stale; old-fashioned; hackneyed.

furumái behavior, conduct, action.

furumáu to behave, act; to treat, behave toward (a person).

furutte energetically; voluntarily; willingly. **Furutte goshusseki kudasái.** Please make every effort to attend.

furúuto flute (Western style).

fúryo no unexpected, accidental; **fúryo no dekígoto** accident; unforeseen event, an emergency.

furyoo no bad; poor; unsatisfactory; deliquent; **furyoo shóonen** bad boy(s); **furyoohin** inferior goods.

furyóoken indiscretion; rash act; **furyooken na** rash; ill-advised.

fusá tassel; tuft; fringe; bunch; cluster.

fusagaru to get blocked; to become choked; to be occupied, engaged; to be filled. **Kono michi wa saki ga fusagatte iru.** This road is blocked. **Sono ié wa fusagatte iru.** That house is occupied. **Kono séki wa fusagatte iru.** This seat is taken. **Íma té ga fusagatte imásu.** I am tied up just now. I am busy now.

fusagikómu to be in low spirits; to mope.

fusagu to close, shut up; to stand in the way; to be dejected, depressed; **basho o fusagu** to take up room; **jikan o fusagu** to fill up the time; **michi o fusagu** to stand in the way.

fusai debt; loan.

fusánsei disapproval; dissent; **fusánsei de aru** to dissent; disapprove; **fusánsei o tonáéru** to raise objections to; to express disapproval. **Kimi wa sansei ka fusánsei ka?** Are you for or against it?

FUSAWASHÍI suitable, becoming.

fuségu to defend, protect, guard against; to prevent; to resist.

fusei dishonesty; injustice; unlawfulness; **fusei na** dishonest; wrong; corrupt; unlawful; **fuseihin** sham (fraudulent article).

fuséijitsu insincerity, dishonesty; **fuséijitsu na** dishonest; false.

fuséikaku uncertainty; inaccuracy.

fuséikoo failure; fiasco; miscarriage; **fuséikoo no** unsuccessful, abortive.

fuséiseki poor (unsatisfactory) result; bad record; poor performance; failure; **fuséiseki de áru** to be unsuccessful, be a failure; **fuséiseki ni owaru** to end in failure.

fusen tag, label; slip.

fuséru to put upside down; to turn over; to be down; to take cover.

fusséssei neglect of health.

fushi joint; knuckle; knot; **fushi ana** knothole.

fushiáwase unhappiness; misfortune, **fushiáwase na** unhappy; unfortunate; unlucky; **fushiáwase ni mo** unfortunately.

fushídara untidiness; looseness, laxity; **fushídara na** untidy; sloppy; irregular; loose; dissipated.

FUSHIGI wonder, miracle; **fushigi na** wonderful; marvelous; mysterious; miraculous; strange; **fushigi ni** wonderfully, miraculously.

fushímatsu mismanagement; carelessness; misconduct; prodigality; **fushímatsu na** lax; wasteful; irregular.

fushin doubt, suspicion; question; **fushin no** doubtful, suspicious, questionable; **fushin ni omóu** to wonder; to think strange.

fushínjin unbelief; impiety; **fushínjin na** unbelieving, irreligious.

fushínjitsu insincerity; faithlessness; **fushínjitsu na** faithless, insincere.

fushínkoo unbelief; **fushínkoo no** unbelieving; freethinking.

fushínsetsu unkindness; **fushínsetsu na** unkind; unobliging.

fushín'yoo distrust, lack of confidence.

fushízen na unnatural, artificial; affected.

fushoo injury, wound; **fushoo suru** to be injured, get hurt; **fushóo sha** injured person.

fushoo báshoo ni reluctantly, unwillingly.

fushóochi dissent; disapproval; **fushóochi o iu** to dissent; to disapprove.

fushóojiki dishonesty; **fushóojiki na** dishonest.

fushóoka indigestion.

fushúbi failure; fiasco; displeasure; **fushúbi ni náru** to fall into disfavor; **fushúbi ni owaru** to end in failure.

fushoku shortage, deficiency; dissatisfaction; **fushoku suru** to want, lack, be short; **fusoku o iu** to grumble, complain; **fusokú gaku** shortage, deficit.

fusóoo na unsuitable, unfitting, unbecoming; undue; **míbun fusóooo na seikatsu o suru** to live above one's means.

FUSUMA sliding screen door covered with paper.

FUTA lid, cover; **futatsuki no** covered; **futa o suru, futa o shiméru** to cover, put on a lid; **futa o tóru** to lift the lid.

futáe double, twofold.

futago twins.

futaoya one's parents.

FUTARI couple, two persons.

futáshika uncertainty; **futáshika na** uncertain; doubtful.

FUTATABI again.

FUTATSU two; **futatsu hénji de** ready enough; most willingly; **futatsu to nái** matchless, unique; **futatsu tomo** both; **futatsú ni wakéru** to divide in two.

futei na uncertain, indefinite; inconstant.

futéisai na unseemly, indecent; unsightly; clumsy.

futeki bold, daring, fearless.

futékinin unfitness, incompetency; **futékinin de aru** to be unfit (for a task), be unsuitable for, be unqualified for; **futekinínsha** a misfit.

futéttei imperfect; inconsistent; unconvincing; not thoroughgoing.

FUTO suddenly; by chance, by accident; **futo omoidásu** to remember in a flash.

futódoki na insolent, rude.

FUTÓI big; thick; deep; sonorous.

futokoro bosom; purse; pocket; **futokoro ga sabishíi** to be short (of money); **futokoro ni suru** to put in one's pocket.

futókusaku poor plan; unwise course; disadvantage; **futókusaku na** unwise, inadvisable, inexpedient.

futomomo thigh.

FUTON mattress; quilt; cushion; bedding, **futon o shiku** to make a bed.

futoo injustice; **futoo na** unjust, unfair; unreasonable; **futoo rítoku** unreasonable profits.

futoppara generosity; broad-mindedness; **futoppara no** generous; broad-minded.

futoraséru to fatten; **FUTÓRU** to grow fat; **shindai ga futóru** to prosper.

futósa thickness; bulk.

FUTÓTTA fat; plump; **futótta hito** fat person.

futsúgoo inconvenience; misconduct; **futsúgoo na** wrong; improper, objectionable; inconvenient; **futsúgoo na kotó o suru** to behave wrongly.

FUTSUKA two days; second day (of the month); **Sángatsu futsuka** March 2.

futsukayoi hangover; **futsukayoi o suru** to have a hangover.

futsúriai incongruity; imbalance, disproportion; **futsúriai no** disproportionate; ill-matched.

FUTSUU usually, normally.

futsuu ni náru to be suspended, cut off, interrupted.

futtei scarcity, shortage; **futei de áru** to be scarce; **futei suru** to run short.

futtémo téttemo rain or shine; no matter what the weather.

futtoo boiling; bubbling; agitation; **futtoo suru** to boil up; to bubble; **futtóo ten** boiling point. **Giron ga futtoo shita.** The discussion became heated.

futtsúri utterly, entirely. **Íto ga futtsúri kireta.** The string snapped.

fúu appearance; customs; manners; way; seal; closing.

fúu seal; **fuu o suru** to seal, to fasten.

fuubun rumor.

fuubutsu scenery; nature; landscape.

fuuchoo trend of the times; fashion, tendency.

FÚUFU husband and wife; married couple; **fúufu ni náru** to marry; **fuufu wákare** divorce; **fuufunáka** married life.

fúuga elegance; refinement; **fúuga na** elegant; refined.

fúugetsu scenery; (beauties of) nature.

fúugi manners; customs; **fúugi no yói** well-mannered; well-bred; **fuugi no warúi** ill-mannered; ill-bred.

fúuha wind and waves; storm; heavy sea; discord; trouble.

fuuhyoo current rumor; report.

FÚUKEI landscape; scenery; **fuukeiga** landscape; seascape (painting); **fuukeigaka** landscape painter.

fuukiri release; **fuukiri suru** to break a seal; to release (a film, etc.).

fúumi flavor; taste; **fúumi no yói** tasty, delicious.

fuurin wind bell (tiny bell that tinkles in the wind).

fúuryuu elegance; taste; **fúuryuu na** elegant.

fuusa blockade.

fuusen balloon.

fuusetsu snowstorm, blizzard.

FUUSHUU manners; custom, usage, practice.

fuusoku wind velocity.

fúutei appearance, looks; dress.

FUUTOO envelope. **Fuutoo ni irete kudasái.** Please put it in an envelope.

fúun misfortune; ill luck; **fúun na** unfortunate, unlucky.

fúuu wind and rain; rainstorm; **fúuu ni sarasareta** weather-beaten; **fúuu ni sarasu** to expose to the weather; **fúuu o okashite iku** go in spite of the storm.

fúuzoku customs; manners; public morals.

fúwa discord; strife; **fúwa de aru** to be on bad terms; **fúwa ni náru** to become estranged.

fúwafuwa light; thin; soft; spongy; lightly; softly.

fuwarí lightly; softly; buoyantly.

fuyakásu to steep, soak.

fuyakéru to swell up; to get soaked; to be saturated.

fuyásu to increase; to add to; to raise.

fuyoo ni náru to be out of use; to fall into disuse.

fuyóoi na unprepared, careless; thoughtless.

fuyóojoo neglect of health; intemperance; **fuyóojoo na** careless of one's health.

FUYÚ winter; **fuyu no** wintry; winter, **fuyufuku, fuyu mo no** winter clothes; **fuyuyásumi** winter vacation.

fuyúkai, fukái unpleasantness; discomfort; **fuyúkai na** unpleasant; uncomfortable; **fuyúkai ni** unpleasantly, uncomfortably.

fuyukitódoki carelessness; neglect; **fuyukitódoki na** careless, negligent.

fuzai absence; **fuzai de áru** to be absent.

fuzoku attached to; belonging to; **fuzoku suru** to be attached to; to belong to; **fuzokúhin** accessories.

G

GA particle marking an emphatic subject; but; and yet; however; although. **Súmisu san ni denwa o kakemáshita ga rúsu deshita.** I phoned Mr. Smith, but he was not in.

ga self, ego; self-will, **selfishness; ga o óru** to give in, to yield; **ga o tóosu** to have one's way; **ga no tsuyói** self-willed, obstinate.

gaarusukáuto girl scout.

gáaze cheesecloth; surgical gauze.

gába to all of a sudden; **gába to okiagáru** to spring out of bed; to spring to one's feet.

gábugabu used only with **nómu** to take long draughts; to swill.

gaburí to used only with **nomu, kuitsuku; gaburí to nómu** to drain at one gulp; to gulp down; **gaburí to kuitsuku** to bite (snap) at.

gáchagacha clattering, rattling; **gáchagacha saseru** to clatter, rattle.

–GÁCHI suffix denoting: apt to, prone to; prevailing; of frequent occurrence; **okotarigáchi** prone to neglect; **byookigachi** prone to illness; ill most of the time; **kumorigachi no** cloudy; gloomy.

gáhaku great painter.

gái injury, harm, damage; **gai súru** to injure, harm, hurt; **gái ni náru** to be injurious to harmful.

gáibu outside, exterior; **gáibu no** external, outer; **gáibu no hito** outsiders.

gaibun reputation; honor.

gaichuu harmful insect; blight; vermin.

GÁIDO tourist guide.

gaihaku suru to stay out, stay away from home (at night).

gaijin foreigner.

gaikai outside world.

gaikan external appearance; outside view; general view; outline.

gaikei external form.

gaiken outward appearance.

GAIKOKU foreign country; **gaikoku no** foreign; exotic; alien; **gaikoku e iku** to go abroad; **gaikoku sei** foreign (product); **gaikoku bóoeki** foreign trade; **gaikoku káwase** foreign exchange (rate); **gaikoku shíjoo** foreign market; **gaikokusen** foreign ships; **GAIKOKUGO** foreign language; **GAIKOKÚJIN** foreigner; **gaikokujín machi** section where many foreigners live.

gaikoo diplomacy; **gáikooka, gaikóokan** diplomat; **gaikooteki** diplomatic;

gaikóodan diplomatic corps.

gaikóoin canvasser

gáikotsu skeleton; bones.

gaimen (*n.*) outside; surface; **gaimen no** exterior, external; outside.

gáimu foreign affairs.

gáinen concept, general idea; conception.

gairai foreign; exotic; imported.

GÁISHITE in general; generally speaking; on the whole.

gaishutsu suru to go out; **gaishutsúgi** street dress.

gaitoo street lamp.

gaitoo street; **gaitoo enzetsu** soapbox oratory; **gaitoo ni tatsu** to go out (in the street).

gaitoo suru to fall under, to correspond to.

gaiyuu suru to travel abroad.

gaka painter; artist.

gake cliff, precipice; **gakekúzure** landslide.

–gake suffix denoting: being on the way to; **toorigake ni** in passing; **negake ni** just before going to bed.

gakka lesson; course of study, subject.

GAKKÁRI SURU to be disappointed; to lose heart; to be tired out, be exhausted. **Kabuki ni ikenákute gakkári shita.** I was disappointed because I could not get to the Kabuki theater.

gakki musical instrument.

gakki school term, semester.

GAKKOO school; college; **gakkoo e yuku** to go to school; **gakkoo tómodachi** schoolmate.

gakkyoku musical piece.

gakkyuu class, grade.

gáku prefix or suffix denoting: learning, studies; science.

gáku amount, sum, denomination.

gaku framed picture; **gaku buchi** picture frame.

gakuha school; academic group.

gákui academic degree.

gakumen face value; par; **gakumen íka ni sagáru** to fall below par.

gakúmon learning; study; **gakúmon suru** to study.

GAKUSEI student; schoolboy (–girl); **gakusei jídai** schooldays.

gakusetsu theory; doctrine.

gakusha learned man; scholar.

gakushiki scholarship; learning.

gakushuu study; **gakushuu suru** to study.

gakutai (musical) band.

gákuto students; scholars.

gakuya dressing room; **gakuyá guchi** stage door.

gakuyuu fellow student; classmate.

gakuzen in amazement; amazed; aghast;

gakuzen to suru to strike with horror; to shock.

GAMAN patience, endurance; pardon; **gaman zuyói** patient; having great endurance; **gáman suru** to bear, endure. **Káre ni wa gáman ga dekínai.** I'm out of patience with him.

gan invocation, prayer.

gán cancer.

gan– prefix denoting: pertaining to the eye; **ganbyoo** eye disease; sore eyes.

ganbáru to persist in; to stand firm, refuse to give in.

gánchuu ni in one's eyes; **gánchuu ni nái** beneath one's notice; **gánchuu ni okanai** to take no notice of; to ignore; to think nothing of.

gángan dingdong; clang; **gángan naru** to clang, ring noisily. **Mimí ga gángan suru.** My ears are ringing. **Atamá ga gángan suru.** My head aches.

GANJITSU New Year's Day.

ganjoo na solid; robust; strongly built.

gánko stubbornness, obstinacy; **gánko na** stubborn, obstinate.

gankyoo stubbornness; persistence; **gankyoo na** obstinate, stubborn; persistent; **gankyoo ni** stubbornly, obstinately.

ganmoo desire, wish.

ganpeki quay, wharf, pier.

gánrai originally; from the first; by nature.

gánseki rock; crag; stones.

ganshiki discernment, insight; critical eye.

gánshó written application.

gánso originator, founder, father of.

GANTAN New Year's Day; morning of New Year's Day.

gan'yaku pill; pellet.

ganze nái innocent, artless; helpless.

ganzoo forgery.

gappei union; combination; amalgamation; **gappei suru** to amalgamate; incorporate.

GARA pattern, design; build; nature (character); **iegara** the family standing.

gáragara clattering; rattling; rattle (toy).

garakuta rubbish; worn-out articles.

garandoo empty, vacant; hollow.

garán to suru to appear empty; to seem deserted.

gararí to completely; with a clatter; suddenly **gararí to kawaru** to change completely.

GARASU (n.) glass; **garasu no** (adj.) glass; glazed; **garasu íta** (glass) pane; plate glass; **garasu kóoba** glass factory.

GARÉEJI garage.

gárigari noisily, with noise; **gárigari kajíru** to munch; **gárigari hikkáku** to scrape; to scratch.

gáron gallon.

–gáru suffix denoting: to wish, want; to be inclined to; **mitagáru** to want to see; **ikitagáru** to want to go; **ureshigáru** to feel glad.

garyoo generosity; tolerance; **garyoo no áru** tolerant; generous; broad-minded; **garyoo no nái** intolerant; ungenerous.

garyuu de in one's own way.

gásagasa suru to rustle; **gasagasa no** rough; loose.

gasatsu na rude, rough, unmannerly; **gasatsu na otokó** unmannerly (rude) man.

gáshi suru to starve to death.

gashitsu studio.

GASORIN gasoline; **gasorin sutándo** gas station.

gassaku collaboration; **gassaku suru** to collaborate, work jointly; **gassákusha** a collaborator.

gasshíri to tightly; closely; **gasshíri shita** massive; well built; sturdy; **gasshíri shite iru** to be massive, etc.

gasshoo chorus; **gasshoo suru** to sing together; **gasshootai** chorus; choir.

Gasshúukoku United States.

gasshuku lodging together; **gasshuku suru** to lodge together; **gasshukusho** training camp.

gassoo playing music together; **nibu gássoo** duet.

gassúru to add (join) together; to unite.

GÁSU gas; **gásu o tsukéru** to light the gas; **gásu o tomeru** to turn off the gas; **gasu sutóobu** gas heater; **gasugáisha** gas company.

gátagata rattling (clattering) sound; **gátagata furueru** to shake, shiver, tremble; **gátagata iu** to rattle, to shake.

–gatái suffix denoting: cannot; hard, difficult; impossible; **egatái** hard to get; unobtainable; **shinjigatái** difficult to believe; incredible.

gátapishi noisily; roughly; with a bang.

gatén comprehension, understanding; consent, agreement; **gatén suru** to understand, grasp the meaning; to be convinced of; to agree, consent; **gatén no ikanai** puzzling; doubtful.

–GATSU counter denoting: month of; **Ichigatsu** January.

gátsugatsu greedily; ravenously; **gátsugatsu tabéru** to eat greedily.

–gawa suffix denoting: side; **soto gawa** outside; **uchi gawa** inside; **minami gawa** south side.

gáyagaya noisily; **gáyagaya sawágu** to make noise, clamor.

gébita vulgar; low; mean.

géemu game; **géemu o yaru** to play a game.

gehin meanness; vulgarity; **gehin na** mean; vulgar; low.

géi arts; accomplishments; feats; tricks; performance; **géi no áru hito** accomplished person.

geijutsu art; fine arts; **geijutsuteki** artistic; **geijutsuka** artist.

geinin professional entertainer.

geisha geisha (girl).

GEJUN latter part of a month; last ten days of a month.

geka surgery; **gekái** surgeon.

gekai this world; earth.

géki play, drama; **gekiteki** dramatic; **gekidan** theatrical world; dramatic company; **gekihyoo** theatrical criticism; **gekihyooka** theater critic; **GEKIJOO** theater, playhouse; **gekisakka** dramatist; playwright. (See also **gikyoku**.)

gékiha suru to defeat, rout.

gekirei encouragement; **gekirei suru** to encourage.

gekiron heated discussion; **gekiron suru** to argue hotly.

gekiryuu rapid stream; swift current.

gekishin severe earthquake. **Sakúban gekishin ga átta.** There was a severe earthquake last night.

gekiyaku powerful medicine; violent poison.

gekizoo sudden increase.

gekkan monthly publication; **gekkan zásshi** monthly magazine.

gekkei menstruation.

gekken fencing (Japanese style).

GEKKOO moonlight; moonbeams.

GEKKYUU monthly salary; **gekkyúu bi** payday; **gekkyuu búkuro** pay envelope; **gekkyúu tori** a salaried man.

gén words; speech; **gén o sáyuu ni takúshite** on one pretext or another.

gen– prefix denoting: original; primary; fundamental; **genbun** original text; **genga** original picture.

génan manservant.

genba the actual place, scene; **genba de on** the spot.

genbaku atomic bomb.

genbatsu severe punishment.

GÉNDAI present time; modern times; **gendaiteki na** modern; **gendaika suru** to modernize.

géngai unexpressed; between the lines; **géngai no ími o toru** to read between the lines.

gengákki stringed instrument.

gengaku reduction, discount; **gengaku suru** to reduce, cut down, curtail.

GÉNGO language, speech; words; **géngo ni**

zessúru to be unspeakable; to be beyond description.

gen'in cause; origin; **–ni gen'in suru** to be due to, attributable to; **gen'in fumei** unaccountable; unknown.

genjitsu reality, actuality; **genjitsu no** real, actual; **genjitsu bákuro** disillusionment; **genjitsu shúgi** realism.

genjoo status quo, existing state of things; **genjoo íji** maintenance of the status quo.

genjuu severity, strictness; **genjuu na** severe, strict; **genjuu ni** severely.

genkai limit, boundary.

genkaku strictness; sternness; **genkaku na** strict; rigorous; stern; **genkaku ni** rigorously.

GÉNKAN, genkanguchi entrance hall.

GÉNKI spirits; courage; vigor; energy; **génki no yói** cheerful; healthy; **génki yóku** in high spirits; cheerfully; **génki no nai** in poor (low) spirits; **génki o dásu** to brace up; **génki o tsukéru** to encourage; to cheer up; **génki na** healthy, spirited.

genkin strict prohibition, ban; **genkin suru** to ban.

GENKIN cash; **genkin de kau** to buy for cash; **genkin bárai** cash payment; **genkin gákari** cashier; **genkin tórihiki** cash transaction.

genko fist; **genko o katameru** to clench a fist.

genkoku plaintiff; accuser.

genkoo words and deeds; **genkóoroku** memoirs; **genkoo itchi suru** to live up to one's words.

genkoo manuscript; draft; **genkoo yóoshi** copy paper; writing pad.

genkoohan flagrant offense. **Genkóohan de káre wa túihosareta.** He was caught red-handed.

génmai unpolished rice, unhulled rice (eaten for high nutritive value).

genmei declaration, statement; announcement; **genmei suru** to make a statement.

genmetsu disillusionment.

genmitsu strictness; precision; **genmitsu na** strict; precise; exact; **genmitsu ni** strictly; closely; **genmitsu ni iéba** strictly speaking.

gén ni actually; before one's eyes. **Watakushi wa gén ni sore o míta no desu.** I saw it with my own eyes.

génpin goods; thing.

génri See **gensoku**.

genryóo raw materials.

gensánchi country of origin; habitat; home.

génshi atom; beginning; origin; **genshi no** atomic; **genshi bákudan** atomic bomb;

genshíro nuclear reactor; **genshíryoko** nuclear energy.

gensho original (work); **Eigo no gensho de yómu** to read in the original English.

genshoo decrease; **genshoo suru** to decrease, diminish.

genshoo phenomenon.

genshoku primary color(s).

génshu strict observance; **génshu suru** to observe strictly; **jikan o génshuu suru** to be punctual.

genshuku gravity, solemnity; **genshuku na** solemn; grave.

genshutsu appearance; disclosure; **genshutsu suru** to appear; to be disclosed.

génso element (chem.).

gensoku, genri principle; fundamental law; **gensoku to shite** as a general rule.

genson no existing, in existence.

gentoo lantern slide.

GÉNZAI (*n.*, *adv.*) present time; at present; actually; at the present moment.

genzei tax reduction.

genzoo (*n.*) developing; **genzoo suru** to develop (photography).

geppoo monthly salary.

geppu monthly installment; **geppu de** by monthly payments.

géragera warau to cackle; to give a horselaugh.

geraku fall; decline; depreciation; **geraku suru** to fall; to decline; depreciate.

geri diarrhea.

gésha suru to dismount.

GESHUKU (*n.*) lodging; boarding; lodging-house; **geshuku suru** to lodge; to board; **geshukunin** lodger; **geshukuya** lodging-house; **geshukúryoo** lodging charge (rate).

geshunin murderer; criminal.

gessha monthly fee; tuition fee.

gesui sewer; drain; sewage.

geta wooden clogs; **geta o haku** to put on clogs; **geta o núgu** to take off clogs; **getaya** clog shop.

getsugaku monthly sum (amount).

getsumatsu end of a month; **getsumatsu kánjoo** end-of-the month payment.

GETSUYÓOBI Monday.

gezai laxative.

gíchoo chairperson.

gidai subject for discussion.

gidayuu ballad drama.

gihitsu forgery (handwriting or picture).

gíin member of assembly or Diet.

gíiji proceedings.

gijoo assembly hall; chamber; conference site.

GÍJUTSU art; useful art; technique; skill;

sentan gíjutsu advanced technology; **gijutsujoo no** technical.

gíkai Diet; assembly.

gíkan chief engineer; technical offical.

gikei older brother-in-law.

giketsu decision, resolution.

gikochinái stiff-mannered; awkward.

gikoo artistic excellence; technical skill.

gikyoku drama; **gikyoku sákusha** dramatist, playwright. (See also **géki**.)

gikyóodai brother-in-law; sister-in-law.

gimei assumed name, false name.

GIMON question; doubt; **gimónfu** question mark.

gímu duty; obligation; **gímu o hatásu** to perform one's duty.

GÍN silver; **gín no** silvered; silver; **gin iro no** silvery; **gíngami** silver paper; tin foil; **gínka** silver coin; **ginkónshiki** silver wedding anniversary; **genmékki no** (*adj.*) silver-plated; **ginpai** silver medal; silver cup.

GINKOO bank; **ginkooka** banker; **ginkoo'in** bank employee; **ginkoo yokin** bank deposit; **ginkoo yokin kooza** bank account; **ginkoo yokin zandaka** bank balance; **ginkoo kawase tegata** bank exchange; **ginkoo kanjoo hookoku sho** bank statement.

ginmí examination, trial.

ginnán fruit of the gingko; gingko nut.

ginoo ability, capacity; skill; **gínoo no áru** able; skillful; talented.

gíragira glittering; dazzling; **giragira suru** to glitter, to dazzle; to glare.

girí obligation; duty; honor; courtesy; **giri no** adoptive; step–; –in-law; **giri no kyóodai** brother-in-law, sister-in-law; **girí o kaku** to fail to do one's duty; **girigatái** having a high sense of duty.

Gírisha Greece; **Girishájin** (*n.*) Greek; **Girishago** Greek language.

gíron argument; discussion; debate; dispute; **gíron suru** to argue, etc.; **gironzúki na** argumentative.

gíryoo ability; talent, skill; **gíryoo no áru** talented.

gisei sacrifice; victim; scapegoat.

gíshi engineer; technical expert; **gishí choo** chief engineer.

gíshiki ceremony, rite; **gíshiki no** (*adj.*) ritual.

gíshu artificial arm.

gisoku artificial leg.

gisshíri closely; compactly; **gisshíri tsumekomu** to pack, jam, cram.

gítaa guitar.

gitei younger brother-in-law.

gizagiza notches.

gizen hypocrisy; **gizénsha** hypocrite; **gizenteki** hypocritical.

gizoo forgery. (See also **gihitsu.**)

go game resembling checkers; **go o útsu** to play "go"; **goban** "go" board; checkerboard; **goban gata no** checkered; **goishi** pieces used in playing "go."

GÓ word, term; language; **Eigo (an)** English word; English language; **gó o tsuyómete iu** to speak emphatically; **góbi** ending (of a word); end (of a sentence); **gobi hénka** inflection.

GÓ five; **DÁIGO** fifth; **GOJÚU** fifty; **CÓJI** five o'clock; **gojuu no tóo** five-story pagoda.

–go suffix denoting: after; **sonogo** after that; since then; **sensoogo** postwar.

gobugari short haircut, crew cut.

gobugobu equally well matched; equal; **gobugobu ni náru** to end in a draw (tie); **gobugobu no tachibá de** on equal terms.

GOBUSATA SURU to neglect to write or call. **Gobusata itashimáshita.** I am sorry I didn't write you. I am sorry I didn't call you earlier.

gochagocha no mixed up, confused; **góchagocha suru** to mix up, jumble; **gochagocha ni náru** to be confused.

GOCHISOO treat; feast. **Kyóo wa watashi ga gochisoo shimashóo.** Let me treat you to dinner today. Be my guest at dinner today. **Gochisoosama.** Thanks for the fine dinner.

gochoo tone of voice; accent.

goei guard; escort; **goei suru** to guard; to escort.

gofuku kimono fabric; **gofukuya** fabric dealer.

gógaku study of languages.

GÓGATSU May.

GÓGO afternoon; **gógo níji** two p.m.

GÓHAN boiled rice; meal; **góhan o tabéru** to eat a meal; **góhan o taku** to cook rice.

gohoo false report.

gójitsu some other day; in the future.

gojuunénsai semi-centennial; jubilee.

gojuúon Japanese syllabary.

gokai misunderstanding; **gokai suru** to misunderstand; to take amiss.

goke widow; widowhood.

góki tone; manner of speaking; **góki surudóku** sharply, in a sharp tone; **góki o tsuyómete hanásu** to speak emphatically.

gókoo halo; glory.

GÓKU very; extremely; **góku mezurashíi** extremely rare; **góku chíisái** very small.

gókui secret; secret principles.

gokuin stamp; hallmark.

gokujoo (n.) first-rate; best quality; **gokujoo no** (adj.) best; first-rate; first-class.

gokuraku paradise; Eden.

goma sesame seed; **goma o súru** to grind sesame seed; to flatter; to fawn upon; **gomaábura** sesame oil.

gomakashi trickery; hocus-pocus; deception; **gomakashi no** fraudulent, sham; **gomakásu** to deceive; to cheat; to cover up; to tamper with.

GOMEN pardon, permission; **GOMEN NASÁI.** Pardon me. Excuse me. **Chótto gomen kudasái.** Excuse me a minute.

GOMÍ rubbish, refuse; dirt; **gomitóri** dustpan; **gomíbako** garbage (rubbish) can.

GÓMU gum; rubber; **gomubándo** rubber band; **gomúhimo** elastic tape; **gomúmari** rubber ball; **gomúnori** mucilage; **gomuwa** rubber tire.

góngo doodan unspeakable; outrageous; absurd.

góo district. **Góo ni itte wa góo ni shitagáeo.** When in Rome, do as the Romans do.

góo fate; **góo no fukai** sinful; **góo o niyasu** to be greatly aggravated.

–góo number; issue; **dái sán goo** issue no. 3; **sono zasshi no Gogátsugoo** the May issue of the magazine.

goodatsu seizure; extortion; plunder; **goodatsu suru** to plunder.

goodoo combination; union; **goodoo suru** to amalgamate; to incorporate; **goodoo no** united; incorporated.

googai "extra"; special issue of a newspaper.

gooi agreement; mutual understanding; **gooi de** by mutual agreement.

goojoo obstinacy, stubbornness; **goojoo na** stubborn, obstinate; **goojoo o haru** to be obstinate.

gookaban deluxe edition.

gookasen luxury liner.

gookaku eligibility; success; **gookaku suru** to be eligible for; to pass; to be successful in.

gookan rape; assault.

GOOKEI sum, total, total amount; **gookei suru** to sum up; **gookei . . . ni náru** to amount to . . . in all; to add up to.

gooketsu hero; great man.

gookin metallic compound; alloy.

gooman haughtiness, arrogance; **gooman na** haughty, arrogant.

goomon torture; **goomon ni kakéru** to torture.

goorei command, order; **goorei suru** to command, order; to rule; **goorei o kakéru** to give a command or order.

gooriki great strength; mountain guide.

góoru goal.

góosha luxury; magnificence; **góosha na** luxurious; magnificent; **góosha o kiwameru** to live in magnificent style.

gootán fearlessness; boldness; **gootán na** fearless; daring; bold.

gootoo burglar, thief.

góou heavy rain.

gooyoku avarice, greed.

gooyuu extravagant pleasures; spree; **gooyuu suru** to go on a spree.

goozen haughtily, arrogantly; proudly.

goraku pleasure; pastime; amusement; recreation; **gorakuyoo no** for amusement; **gorakúshitsu** recreation room.

goran (*n.*) seeing, viewing (used only in reference to the second or third person); **goran ni ireru** to present something for inspection. **Goran kudasái.** Please take a look. **Goran no toori.** As you see. **Chótto kore o goran nasai.** Just look at this. **Máa kangáete goran nasai.** Think it over, anyway.

górira gorilla.

–GÓRO suffix denoting: about (in point of time); around; toward; **nijigóro** about two o'clock; **yoakegóro** toward dawn.

goro sound; **goro ga fí** euphonic.

góro grounder (in baseball).

górogoro rumbling; rolling; gurgling; lying idle; **górogoro korobu** to roll about; **mé ga gorogoro suru** to have a sore (an irritated) eye. **Káre wa máinichi górogoro shite iru.** He idles away his time every day. **Néko ga nódo o górogoro narasu.** The cat purrs.

górufu golf; **górufu o suru** to play golf; **gorufujoo** gold links.

gosai second wife; **gosái o mukaeru** (for a man) to marry again.

gosan miscalculation; **gosan suru** to miscalculate.

goshin suru to diagnose wrongly.

Gósho Imperial Palace.

góshoo daijí ni with the greatest possible care; most carefully; **góshoo daijín ni suru** to take care of; **góshoo daijí ni tsutoméru** to serve most faithfully.

gosoo escort; convoy; **gosoo suru** to escort, to accompany.

gotagota trouble; difficulties; confusion; disorder; **gótagota suru** to be in confusion; to be disordered. **Gotagota ga okorikákete iru.** Trouble is brewing.

gotamaze jumble; muddle.

gotatsuku to quarrel; to be agitated; to be in disorder.

gotcha in confusion.

–GÓTO NI every; every time; at intervals of; **ni mairu góto ni** every two miles; **hi**

goto ni every day; **mikka góto ni** every three days.

gótsugotsu rough; rugged; harsh; stiff; **gótsugotsu iu** to speak harshly; **gótsugotsu shite iru** to be stiff, rough.

gozá mat; matting; **gozá o shiku** to spread a mat (on the floor).

GOZAIMÁSU there is, there are (*humble*).

GÓZEN forenoon; **gózen ni** in the morning.

guai condition; fitness; manner; working order; **guai ga warúi** to feel indisposed, be unwell; to be out of order. **Kono hikidashi wa guai ga warúi.** This drawer does not work smoothly. **Bánji guai yóku itta.** Everything went very well.

guchi idle complaints; **guchi o kobósu** to grumble; complain; **guchippói** grumbling; complaining.

–gumi company, firm; gang; **Fujita gumi** Fujita Company.

gún district; county.

gún crowd; **gún o násu** to crowd; to flock; **gún o nuku** to be far above the crowd (to distinguish oneself); **gunshuu** crowd of people, multitude.

gún (*n.*) military; **gúnbi** arms; **gúnbi shukushoo** disarmament; **gúntai** armed forces.

guntoo archipelago, group of islands.

gúnyagunya flabby; limp.

gúragura suru to be shaky; to totter, waver.

–GÚRAI = **kurai** suffix denoting: about; almost; some; something like; or so. **Anó hito wa sanjuu-gúrai deshoo.** She must be about 30 years old.

gúramu gram.

guratsuku to totter; to be shaky.

guretsu na stupid; ridiculous; absurd; silly.

guron foolish argument; absurd opinion.

gúru conspiracy; collusion; accomplice, conspirator; **gúru ni náru** to conspire with, plot together; **–to gúru ni nátte** in collusion with (someone).

GÚRUGURU round and round; **gúruguru mawaru** to whirl; spin round and round.

gururí circumference; surroundings; **gururí ni** about, around; **gururí to** to round; **ie no gururí ni** around the house.

–gurushíi suffix denoting: to be unpleasant to, repulsive to; **negurushíi** to be sleepless; to sleep badly.

gurúupu group.

guusúu even number; **guusúu no** even-numbered.

gutto considerably; firmly; with great strength; **gutto nómu** to gulp down; **gutto fuéru** to increase markedly.

GUUZEN by chance; accidentally; **guuzen no** accidental; unexpected; casual; **guuzen**

no dekígoto an accident; **guuzen desu to** come across, meet by chance.

guuzoo image, idol, statue.

gúzu imbecile; weak-minded person.

gúzuguzu lazily; idly; tardily; **gúzuguzu suru** to hesitate; to loiter; **gúzuguzu iu** to complain; to murmur.

guzúru to be peevish; to be fretful.

gyakkoo retrogression; **gyakkoo suru** to move back; to run counter to; to retrograde.

gyaku opposite, contrary, reverse, **gyaku ni** contrarily, conversely; **gyaku ni suru** to reverse; to invert; **gyaku ni mawasu** to turn (something) the other way; **gyakumódori** retrogression; reversal; **gyakumódori suru** to go (turn) backward; to have a relapse; to lapse into; **gyakuten** sudden change; reversal; **gyakuten suru** to retrogress.

gyakusatsu slaughter; massacre.

gyakutai ill-treatment; **gyakutai suru** to ill-treat.

gyangu gang.

gyógyoo fishery; fishing industry.

gyokuro sweet green tea (the best and most expensive type).

gyóo line; verse.

gyoogi behavior; manners; **gyoogi no yói** well behaved; well mannered; **gyoogi no warui** poorly behaved; **gyoogi sáhoo** etiquette.

gyóoja devotee; pilgrim; ascetic.

gyóoji observances; functions; proceedings.

gyoojí referee (of Japanese wrestling, sumoo).

gyoojoo behavior, conduct.

gyooketsu coagulation, congealing.

gyóomu business; affairs; duties.

gyooretsu procession, parade; **gyooretsu o náshite** in procession.

gyoosei administration; **gyooséikan** administrator.

gyooshoo peddling; peddler.

gyooten suru to be surprised, amazed, astounded.

gyoozui (n.) taking a shower (Japanese style: pouring water over the body from a small tub); bathing; **gyoozui suru** to take a Japanese-style shower.

gyosen fishing boat.

gyoson fishing village.

gyotto suru to be startled, alarmed.

gyúuba oxen and horses; horses and cattle.

GYUUNIKU beef; **gyuunikuya** butcher shop.

GYUUNYUU cow's milk; **gyuunyuu ya** milkman; **gyuunyúu bin** milk bottle.

gyuutto hard; violently; firmly; **gyuutto osu** to push violently (with force); **gyuutto hiku** to pull with a jerk.

H

HÁ tooth; cog; **há no áru** toothed; cogged; **há no nái** toothless; blunt; **há no tsúita** sharp-edged; **há ga uku** to set the teeth on edge; **há o migaku** to brush the teeth; **há ga itámu** to have a toothache.

ha leaf (of a plant).

háapu harp.

háato heart (in a card game).

HABA width, breadth; **haba ga kiku** to have great influence over; **haba o kikasu** to exert great influence; **haba go ínchi áru** five inches wide.

habakiki influential person.

habátaki suru to flutter, flap wings.

habikóru to spread; to grow thick; to become powerful.

habúku to curtail; to save; to leave out; **jikan o habúku** to save time; **híyoo o habúku** to cut expenses.

HABÚRASHI toothbrush.

haburi influence; power; **haburi ga yói** to be influential.

hábutae glossy silk.

HACHÍ eight; **dái hachí** eighth.

hachi bee; **hachi no su** beehive; **hachimitsu** honey.

HACHÍ bowl, basin; pot.

hachiáwase suru to be brought face to face (bump heads together).

HACHIGATSU August.

HACHIJÚU eighty; **dái hachijuu** eightieth.

hachímaki headband; hand towel tied around the head.

hachiue potted plant.

háda skin; body; disposition; character; **shirói háda** fair skin; **háda ga áu** to get on well (with).

HADAGI underwear.

hadaka nakedness, nudity; **hadaka no** naked, nude, bare; **hadaka ni náru** to strip off one's clothes.

hadashi bare feet; **hadashi de arúku** to walk barefoot; **kuróoto hadashi da** to put even a professional to shame.

hadazáwari touch. **Biroodo wa hadazáwari ga yói.** Velvet feels soft [is agreeable to touch].

HADÉ gaiety; flashiness; display; **hadé na** gay; bright; flashy; **hadé na iro** bright (gay) color; **hade zúki de áru** to be fond of display.

HAE fly.

haegiwa hairline.

haéru to grow; to sprout; to spring up. **Hana no táne ga háeta.** The flower seeds sprouted.

HAGAKI postcard; **hagaki o dásu** to drop (send) a card.

hagami suru to gnash one's teeth.

hagane steel.

hagásu to strip; to tear off.

hagayúi to feel impatient; to feel irritated. **Káre no gúzuguzu shite irú no ga hagayúkatta.** I was irritated by his dawdling.

háge bald spot; bald head; **hageátama** bald head.

hagemásu to encourage; to cheer up; to stimulate.

hagemí stimulation; encouragement; diligence; **hagemí ga tsuku** to be stimulated; to be encouraged; **hagemí o tsukéru** to stimulate; to encourage.

HAGÉMU to endeavor; to exert onself; to be diligent.

hagéru to grow bald; to come off; to fade; **iro no hágeta** discolored; faded.

hageshíi violent, severe, intense; furious; **hageshíku** violently; **hageshíi seishitsu** violent nature (referring to a person); **hageshíi átsusa** intensely hot weather.

hagíshiri suru to grit one's teeth.

hagitóru to strip off; to deprive; to tear off.

hágu to strip; to strip off clothes; **kí no kawá o hágu** to strip the bark off a tree.

háguki gums (of the mouth).

haguréru to stray; to be separated from (one's companions).

hagúruma cog, gear (of a wheel); toothed wheel.

HÁHA, HAHAOYA mother, motherhood; **haha rashíi** motherly; maternal; **Háha no hi** Mother's Day; **hahakata** maternal (side); **hahakata no shinseki** maternal relative.

HÁI yes; yes, sir.

hai lungs; **haibyoo** consumption; **haigan** lung cancer; **haien** pneumonia.

hai ashes; cinder; **hai ni náru** to be reduced to ashes; lungs.

haiagáru to creep (crawl) up; to climb up.

haichi arrangement; **haichi suru** to dispose; to arrange; to station.

haidásu to crawl out, creep out.

haigamai rice with embryo buds.

haigo rear; back (of a person); **–no háigo ni** at the rear of; behind. **Káre no háigo ni shisanka ga hikáete iru.** He has a wealthy supporter behind him.

haigoo harmony; combination; arrangement; **haigoo suru** to harmonize; to combine; to

match. **Iro no haigoo ga warúi.** These colors do not match.

haigyoo suru to close up shop; to give up one's practice; to quit business.

haihíiru high heel.

haiiro ash-gray (color).

haikan discontinuance of publication; **haikan suru** to discontinue publication.

haikara na stylish; foppish; fashionable. **Haikara na yoofuku o kite imashita.** He was wearing a high-styled suit.

haikei background; background scenery.

háikei Dear Sir or Madam (as used in a formal letter).

HAIKEN looking at; inspection (*humble*); **haiken suru** to see; to look at. **Chótto haiken.** Please let me see it. **Haiken shimáshita.** I saw it.

háikingu hiking.

haikómu to crawl (creep) in.

haiku seventeen-syllable poem.

haikyuu distribution; supply; **haikyuu suru** to distribute; supply.

hainichi anti-Japanese.

hairetsu arrangement; distribution; **hairetsu suru** to arrange in order.

hairikómu to get in; to force one's way in.

HÁIRU to enter; to go in; to break into; to join; to hold; to accommodate; **kúrabu ni háiru** to join a club; **oyu ni háiru** to take a bath. **O hairi.** Come in! Walk in! **Hí ga nishi ni háiru.** The sun sets in the west.

haiseki expulsion; exclusion; **haiseki suru** to exclude; to ostracize.

HÁISHA dentist.

haishaku suru to borrow (*humble*). **Haishaku itashimásu.** I'll borrow it.

haishi abolition; **haishi suru** to abolish, discontinue.

haishutsu suru to discharge; to exhaust; **haishutsúguchi** outlet; issue; **haishutsukan** exhaust pipe.

haisui drainage; sewerage; supply of water; **haisui suru** to drain; to pump out.

haitátaki flyswatter.

HAITATSU delivery; distribution; **haitatsu suru** to deliver; to distribute; **haitatsú ryoo** delivery charge; **haitatsunin** distributor; carrier; **haitatsusaki** receiver; destination (of a delivery).

haitoo allotment; dividend; **haitoo suru** to pay a dividend; to allot to; **haitóokin** dividend.

haitori flytrap.

haiyuu actor; actress.

haizara ashtray.

hají shame; disgrace; dishonor; **hají o káku** to be put to shame; **hají o kakaséru** to

put to shame; **haji shírazu** without a
sense of shame; shameless.

hajikéru to split open; to pop.

hajíku to flip; to snap; to repeal; to repel;
yubi o hajíku to snap one's fingers.

HAJIMARU to begin, commence; to be
opened; to originate from.

HAJIME commencement, beginning; outset;
origin; **hajime no** first; original; initial;
hajime kara owari máde from beginning
to end; **hajime wa** at first; **HAJÍMETE**
first; for the first time; for once. **Hajímete
ome ni kakarimásu.** How do you do.
Glad to meet you [I meet you for the first
time]. **Hajímete ikimáshita.** I went there
for the first time.

HAJIMERU to begin; commence; to open;
shóobai o hajimeru to open a business;
benkyoo o hajimeru to begin studying.

hajíru to be ashamed of.

haká grave, tomb; **hakaba** graveyard,
cemetery.

hakadóru to progress rapidly; to make good
progress.

hakai destruction; demolition; **hakai suru** to
destroy, demolish, wreck; **hakáiteki**
destructive; **hakáiryoku** destructive
power.

hakaku no exceptional; unprecedented;
special.

hakamá loose Japanese trousers; pleated
skirt.

hakanái transient, passing; uncertain; vain;
hopeless; **hakanái sáigo o togéru** to meet
with an untimely death; **hakanái nozomi**
vain hope.

hakarai management; arrangement; disposal.

hakaráu to manage; to arrange; to take
measures; **Kono hen wa anáta no
ohakarai ni omakaseshimásu.** I'll leave
the matter to your discretion. **Sore ni
tsúite wa anáta ga yói yóo ni hakarátte
ii desu.** You can do about it as you think
best.

HAKARÁZU MO unexpectedly; by chance.

hakari balance, scales; **hakarí ni kakéru** to
weigh on a scale.

hakarigoto stratagem, ruse; artifice; plan,
scheme; **hakarigoto ni ochíru** to fall for
a trick; **hakarigoto o megurásu** to devise
a stratagem; to form plans.

HAKÁRU to measure; to weigh; to survey;
to sound; to judge (a person's mind);
mekata o hakáru to check a weight;
nágasa o hakáru to measure a length.
**Anó hito no kimochi o hakáru kotó wa
muzukashíí.** It is hard to understand his
mind.

hákase See **hákushi**.

haké drainage; flow; sale; demand; **haké ga
yói** to flow freely; to sell well.

hakéru to drain off; to sell.

haké brush.

haken dispatch; **haken suru** to dispatch,
send; **hakéngun** expeditionary force.

háki breach; annulment; **háki suru** to break
and throw away; to annul.

hakichigaéru to wear someone else's shoes
by mistake; to mistake; to misunderstand.

hakidame rubbish heap.

hakídasu to spit out; to emit; to breathe out.

hakidasu to sweep out.

hakiké nausea; **hakiké o moyoósu** to feel
sick; to be nauseous.

HAKIMONO footgear; clogs.

hakiyoseru to sweep up, gather up with a
broom.

hakka peppermint; mint.

hakka firing; ignition; **hakka suru** to catch
fire, ignite.

hakken discovery; **hakken suru** to discover;
hakkénsha discover.

hakkin platinum.

HAKKÍRI clearly; distinctly; positively;
definitely; exactly; **hakkíri shita** clear,
distinct, positive; **hakkíri shita kóe** clear
voice; **hakkíri shita henji** definite
answer. **Hakkíri zonjimasén.** I don't
know exactly.

hakkoo publication; issue; **hakkoo suru** to
publish; to issue.

hakkoo fermentation; **hakkoo suru** to
ferment.

hakkotsu skeleton; bleached bones.

hakkutsu excavation; **hakkutsu suru** to
excavate.

hakkyuu low (small) salary.

HAKO box; case; chest. **Hako ni irete
kudasái.** Please put it in the box.

hakobi progress; arrangement; **ashi no
hakobi** walking pace.

HAKOBU to carry, convey, transport; to go
on; to progress; **nimotsu o hakobu** to
carry the baggage; **shíbashiba ashí o
hakobu** to make frequent calls. **Súbete
umaku hakobimashíta.** Everything went
all right. Everything turned out all right.

hakozume packed in a box; boxed;
hakozume ni suru to pack in a box.

hakoniwa miniature garden.

HAKU to put on (from waist down; clogs,
sandals, shoes, socks, pants, skirts, etc.);
kutsú o haku to put on shoes.

háku to sweep; **heyá o háku** to sweep the
room.

hakubútsukan museum.

hakuchi idiot; imbecile.

hakuchoo swan.

hakuchuu broad daylight.

hakugai persecution; **hakugai suru** to persecute.

hakugaku erudition, learning; **hakugaku no** erudite; learned.

hakuhatsu white hair; gray hair; **hakuhatsu no roojin** white-haired old person.

hakujaku feebleness, weakness; **hakujaku na** feeble, weak; fragile; **seishin hakujaku jídoo** mentally handicapped child.

hakujin white person; white race (Occidental).

hákujoo confession; **hakujoo suru** to confess, make a clean breast of.

hakujoo coldheartedness; **hakujoo na** unfeeling, heartless. **Anó hito wa hakujoo na hitó desu.** She is a coldhearted woman.

hakúmai hulled (cleaned) rice.

hakumei misfortune; sad fate; **hakumei na** unfortunate; ill-fated.

hakurai imported; **hakuráihin** imported merchandise. **Hakuráihin wa takái kara kaemasen.** I can't buy imported goods because they are expensive.

hakuránkai exposition; fair; **hakurankaijoo** fair grounds.

hákushi, hákase doctor; doctorate degree, Ph.D.; **hakushígoo** doctorate degree; **Yamada Hakushi** Dr. Yamada.

hakushi blank sheet of paper; white paper; clean slate.

hakushiki wide knowledge, erudition.

hákushu applause; **hákushu suru** to clap hands, applaud; to cheer; **hákushu kássai** applause and cheers.

hakyuu propagation, spread; **hakyuu suru** to extend, spread, propagate; to influence; to effect; **zénkoku ni hakyuu suru** to extend over the whole country.

hama seashore, beach; **hama zútai ni** along the beach; **hamabe** seashore; beach.

hamáguri clam.

hamaki cigar.

hamarikómu to fall (sink) into; to become infatuated with; to be addicted to; **onná ni hamarikómu** to be infatuated with a woman.

hamaru to be fixed; to fit; to fall into.

hameru to put in, insert; to fix in; to set; to have (wear) on (one's finger or hand).

hametsu ruin, destruction; **hametsu suru** to be ruined, destroyed.

hamidásu to protrude, stick out.

HAMÍGAKI toothpaste.

hamon suru to excommunicate; to expel.

haamonika harmonica.

hamono edged tool; cutlery.

HÁMU ham; **hamu salada** ham salad.

HÁN stamp; personal seal (used in place of a signature); **hán o osu** to stamp; to seal; **hán de oshita yóo na** stereotyped, cut-and-dried.

hán edition; **hán o kasaneru** to go through many editions; **shohan** first edition.

HAN– prefix denoting: half; **hantoshi** half a year; **hantsuki** half a month.

hán– prefix denoting: opposition; **hankyoo** anti-communism.

HANÁ flower, blossom; essence, spirit; belle; **hana no** floral; **haná o kíru** to cut flowers; **haná o ikéru** to arrange flowers; **hanabásami** flower scissors; pruning shears; **hanaiké** flower vase; **hanatába** bunch of flowers, bouquet; **hanawa** wreath, garland; **hanáya** florist, flower shop; **hanáyaka na** flowery; showy; gay. **Wakái uchi ga haná.** Youth is the springtime of life. **Giron ni haná ga saite kita.** The discussion is becoming heated.

HANA nose, nasal mucus; **hana o susuru** to sniff; **hana o kamu** to blow one's nose; **hana o tarásu** to have a runny nose; **hana ga kiku** to have a good sense of smell; **hana ni kakéru** to be vain; **hana o akasu** to take the conceit out of someone; **hana o tákaku suru** to be proud; **hanasaki ni** under one's very nose; **hanagoe** nasal sound; twang; **hanaiki** (*n.*) breathing through the nose; snoring; **hanaiki ga arai** to be arrogant; **to swagger**; **hito no hanaiki o ukagau** to curry favor with someone; **hanaji** nosebleed; **hanaji o dásu** to have a nosebleed; **hanakaze** head cold. **Hanakaze o hiita.** I have a cold in the head. **hanabáshira, hanappashira, hanasuji** bridge of the nose. **Hanabáshira ga tsuyói desu.** He is haughty.

hanabanashii brilliant; splendid; glorious; **hanabanáshiku** brilliantly; splendidly.

hánabi fireworks display; **hánabi o ageru** to set off fireworks.

hanágata floral pattern; star; **eiga no hanagata yákusha** screen star; **hanagata sénshu** star player.

hanagumori springtime cloudy weather.

hanahadashíi excessive, extreme, exceeding.

hanamí (*n.*) flower-viewing; **hanamí ni iku** to visit places well known for their flower displays (such as cherry blossoms).

hanamúko bridegroom.

hanao clog thong; straps.

hanare detached room; **hanaréya** detached house; **hanarezáshiki** detached guest room.

hanarebánare separation; **hanarebánare ni** separately, apart from each other; **hanarebánare ni náru** to become separated.

HANARÉRU to separate; part from; to come off; **hanáreta** separated, detached, isolated, distant, far off; **hanáreta tokoró kara míru** to watch from a distance; **hanáreta tochi** distant place; **hanárete iru** be distant, live apart from. **Ima shoku o hanárete iru.** He is now out of work.

HANASHÍ talk, conversation, chat; gossip, story; **hanashi jóozu** good speaker; **hanashibeta** poor speaker; **hanashi áite** companion to talk with; **hanashí o suru** to talk, chat; **hanashiburi** way (manner) of speaking; **hanashichuu** busy signal (telephone); **hanashiai** conference, consultation; **hanashiáu** to talk with, consult with; **hanashigóe** voices (in conversation); **hanashí no táne** topic for conversation; **hanashí ga tsuku** to arrive at an understanding; **hanashí o soraseru** to change the subject; **hanashika** professional storyteller; **hanashikómu** to chat for hours; **hanashizúki na** talkative.

HANÁSU to speak, talk, converse; to tell, state. **Eigo de hanáshite kudasái.** Please speak English. **Anáta ni hanashitái koto ga aru.** I have something I'd like to tell you.

hanásu to separate, to part, to set free; **té o hanásu** to loosen one's hold, to let go of someone's hand.

hanauta humming; **hanauta o utau** to hum a song or tune.

hanáyome bride.

hanazákari full bloom.

hanazono flower garden.

hanbai sale; **hanbai suru** to sell, deal in; **hanbainin** dealer, **hanbaigákari** salesman, saleswoman; **hanbáiten** distributor.

HANBÚN half; **hanbún ni suru** to divide into halves.

hándan judgment, interpretation.

handobággu handbag.

handoo reaction; **handoo suru** to react upon; **handooteki** reactionary.

handon half-holiday.

handoru handle; steering wheel.

hane feather; plumage; wing; shuttlecock; **hane búton** feather quilt.

hané (*n.*) splashes of mud, close; **hanné ga agatte iru** to be splashed with mud; **hanekásu** to splash, spatter. **Shibai no hané wa júuji desu.** The theater closes at ten.

hanekáeru to rebound, spring back.

hanemawáru to bounce about, leap about; to romp.

han'enkei semicircle; **han'enkei no** semicircular.

hanéru to leap, spring, bound; to splash, splatter. **Sooba ga hanéta.** Prices jumped. **Abura ga hánete yakedo o shita.** The cooking oil splashed and I got burnt.

hanéru to reject, to throw out, to exclude.

hanetsukéru to refuse; to reject; to repel.

hangaku half (amount); half the sum (price, fare, etc.); half-fare. **Kodomo no joosháchin wa hangaku désu.** Children can travel for half-price. **Kodomo no nyuujóo ryoo wa hangaku désu.** Children are admitted for half-price.

hangen reduction by half; **hangen suru** to reduce by half.

hán'i scope, sphere; limit, bounds.

hanikámu to be shy, bashful.

hánji judge.

HANJÍKAN half an hour.

hánjoo good business; prosperity; **hánjoo suru** to prosper, flourish, do a good business.

hanjuku half-cooked; soft-boiled; half-ripe; **hanjuku no tamágo** soft-boiled egg.

HANKÁCHI handkerchief.

hankan antipathy, ill-feeling; **hankan o idáku** to provoke ill-feeling.

hankéchi See **HANKÁCHI.**

hánkei radius.

hanko seal.

hankoo resistance, opposition; defiance; **hankooteki** defiant, rebellious.

hankyoo echo; response; anti-communism; **hankyoo suru** to echo, resound.

hankyuu half-holiday.

hanmen profile, silhouette; one side; **hanmen no shínri** half truth; **kao no hanmen** one side of the face; **hanménzoo** profile.

hanmoku hostility, antagonism.

hanmon anguish; agony; mortification; **hanmon suru** to be in agony; to feel anguish; to be mortified.

hanne half the price; **hanne de uru** to sell at half the price.

hannichi half a day.

hánnin offender, criminal.

hannoo reaction, response; **hannoo suru** to react, respond; to act upon.

hanpa odds; odds and ends; fragments; **hanpa no odd;** half-done; incomplete; **hanpa mono** a broken set. **Ano hito wa hanpa shigoto shika dekimasen.** He never finishes his tasks.

hanran rebellion, revolt.

hantai opposition; contradiction; **hantai suru**

to oppose; to object to; **hantai no opposite**; opposed; **hantai ni** on the contrary; in the opposite direction; **hantai úndoo** opposition movement, counter movement; **hantáisha** opponent; objector; **hantaitoo** opposition party.

hantei judgment, decision.

hantén spot; speck, dot.

hantoo peninsula.

hantoshi half a year.

hantsuki half a month.

han'yake partly burned; half-roasted, half-baked.

hanzai crime, offense; **hanzai nin** criminal, culprit; **hanzai kóoi** criminal act.

hanzatsu complication; **hanzatsu na** complex, complicated.

hanzen to clearly, distinctly; definitely; **hanzen to shita** clear, distinct; definite. **Sono hanashí o kiite hanzen to simáshita.** Now that I've heard that explanation, the whole story has become clear.

haori Japanese coat.

happóo all directions; all sides; **happóo ni** in all directions; on all sides; all around; **happoo bíjin** everybody's friend.

happun suru to be roused to action.

happyoo announcement; publication; **happyoo suru** to announce; to publish; to make known.

hára field; plain; moor; prairie; wild region.

hará (*colloq.*) belly; bowels; abdomen; stomach; **hará no ookíi** magnanimous; **hará no suwatta** resolute, firm; **hará ga tátsu** to be offended; **hará o kakaete warau** to split with laughter; **harabal ni náru** to lie on one's stomach; **haramaki** belt.

harachígai half brother, half sister.

hárahara suru to feel uneasy; to be in suspense. **Námida o hárahara to nagáshita.** The tears fell in big drops. **Míte ite mo hárahara shita.** I felt nervous just looking at it.

haraí payment; account **haraikomi** payment; installment payment; **haraikómu** to pay in, pay up; **haraimodoshi** repayment; refund; **haraimodósu** to pay back, repay.

haraisage government surplus sale.

harású to clear away; to divert; **uramí o harású** to pay off old scores.

HARÁU to pay (a bill, etc.); to brush off, to clear away; **shakkín o haráu** to pay off a debt. **Námida o harátte shigoto o tsuzuketa.** She brushed away her tears and resumed her task.

harawáta (*colloq.*) intestines; bowels; heart;

character; **harawáta o tátsu** to break (someone's) heart.

hare (*n.*) swelling; **hareru** to swell, **haremono** swelling, boil.

háre fine (fair) weather; **háre no kimono** holiday (Sunday) clothes; **haregi** holiday clothes.

HARÉRU to clear up (weather); to clear away; to be dispelled; **kéngi ga haréru** to be cleared of a charge. **Sora ga haréta.** The sky has cleared.

haretsu explosion; eruption; **haretsu suru** to explode, burst, blow up; to be broken off.

HÁRI needle; pin; hand (of a watch); fish-hook; sting (of a bee); **hári no mé** eye of a needle; **haribako** needlecase; workbox; **harisáshi** pincushion; **harishigoto** needlework; **harishígoto o suru** to sew.

haridásu to post (on a bulletin board); **keiji o haridásu** to post a notice.

harifuda bill; poster; **harifuda o suru** to put up a poster.

harigami label; poster.

harigane wire.

haritsukéru to stick on, paste on; to paste over.

HÁRU spring (season). **Haru ni Amerika e kaerimásu.** I am returning to the United States in the spring.

haru to stick; **kitte o haru** to paste on a stamp.

hasamáru to get in between; to lie between. **Nikú ga há no aida ni hasamarimáshita.** A piece of meat got stuck between his teeth.

HASAMÍ scissors, shears; **niwaki ni hasamí o ireru** to prune bushes.

hasámu to place; to hold between; to pinch; to pick up; **híbashi de monó o hasámu** to pick up something with tongs.

HASHI pair of chopsticks; **háshi o tsukéru** to start eating.

HASHÍ bridge; **hashí o wataru** to cross a bridge.

hashi edge, border; end; **hashi kara hashi máde** from end to end; **dóoro no hashi no hóo o tooru** to keep to the side of the road.

hashigo ladder; flight of stairs; **hashigodan** staircase.

hashika measles.

hashikkói smart, shrewd, sharp.

HASHIRA pillar, post, column; pole; prop; **hashira dókei** wall clock; **daikoku báshira** main pillar; main support (a person).

hashirí (*n.*) running; movement; first (of something); **hashiri mawáru** to run about; **cha no hashirí** the first supply of tea; **hashirigaki suru** to write hurriedly; to scribble; **hashiriyomi o suru** to read hurriedly; to skim; **hashirizúkai** running an errand. **Kono to no hashirí ga yói.** This sliding door moves easily.

HASHÍRU to run; to sail; to move fast. **Káre wa yá no yóo ni hashítte itta.** He was off like a shot.

hashíta fraction; fragment; odds and ends.

hashutsúfu daily houseworker (female).

hashutsusho branch station; police box.

hassha starting (of a train, bus, etc.); **hassha suru** to start; to depart.

hasshin suru to dispatch a message; to send a letter.

hassoo suru to send off; to forward (a letter or package).

hassúru to emit; to radiate; to fire; to discharge (a gun); to issue.

hatá flag, banner, standard; **hatazao** flagstaff.

hata side; neighborhood; **hata de** nearby; beside; **hata no móno** bystanders; outsiders.

HÁTACHI twenty years old (said of a person). **Watakushi wa hátachi desu.** I am twenty years old.

hatairo outlook, circumstances; **hatairo o míru** to see how things go.

hatake field; kitchen garden; farm.

hatakí duster (made of pieces of cloth attached to a stick).

hatáku to dust; to beat; to slap; to empty; to use up; **saifu no soko o hatáku** to spend every penny one has.

hataori weaver, weaving; **hataori kikái** power loom; **hataori kóoba** mill.

HATARAKI action; motion; work, labor; ability; talent; merits; **hataraki no áru hito** an able person; **hataraki mono** a hard worker.

HATARAKU to work, toil, labor; to commit; to do. **Ichinichi juu sóto de hatarakimáshita.** I worked outside all day long.

HATÁSHITE sure enough; just as I expected.

hatásu to accomplish, achieve; to fulfill; **yakusoku o hatásu** to fulfill one's promise; **mokuteki o hatásu** to achieve one's purpose; **gímu o hatásu** to do one's duty.

háta to suddenly; completely.

HATE end, termination; consequence; result; limit; **hate wa** finally; in the end; **hate ga nái** limitless, endless.

haténkoo record-breaking; unprecedented; unheard of.

hateshi end; limits; **hateshi nái** endless,

boundless; **hateshi nái gíron** an endless argument.

háto dove, pigeon.

hatoba wharf, dock, pier.

hatsú first, beginning; **hatsú no** first; initial; new.

hatsuan suggestion, proposal; **hatsuan suru** to suggest, propose.

hatsubai for sale; **hatsubai suru** to offer for sale, put on sale.

hatsubútai debut; first public performance.

hatsubyoo suru to fall ill.

hatsudóoki engine; motor.

hatsufuyu early winter.

hatsugen speech; **hatsugen suru** to open one's mouth; to speak (at a conference); **hatsugénsha** speaker.

hátsugi proposal, motion.

hátsui suggestion; instance; proposal; original idea; **jibun no hátsui de** on one's own initiative.

HATSUKA the twentieth (of the month); (for) twenty days.

hatsukóokai maiden voyage.

hatsumei invention; **hatsuméisha** inventor.

hatsumimi news (to a person). **Kore wa hatsumimi da.** This is news to me.

hatsunetsu suru to have a fever.

HATSUON pronunciation; **hatsuon suru** to pronounce. **Anó hito no Nihongo no hatsuon wa taihen íi desu.** His pronunciation of Japanese words is very good.

hatsuratsu to shita lively; keen; animated.

hattatsu development, progress, growth; **hattatsu suru** to develop, make progress, grow.

hatten development, expansion, growth; **hatten suru** to develop, expand, extend.

háu to crawl, creep.

hayá– prefix denoting: quick; fast; swift; early; **hayáashi** quick steps; trot; **hayagáten** hasty conclusion; **hayagáten suru** to jump to a conclusion; **hayagáwari** quick change (of costume); **hayagáwari suru** to make a quick change.

HAYÁI quick, fast, rapid, swift; early; **háyaku** quickly, promptly, early, etc.; **ki no hayái** excitable (person).

hayaku breach of contract; **hayaku suru** to break a contract.

hayákuchi rapid speech; **hayákuchi de hanásu** to jabber; to speak rapidly; **hayákuchi no** glib-tongued; **hayakuchi kótoba** tongue twister.

hayamáru to be overhasty, be rash; to act hastily; **hayamátta** rash; hasty; **hayamátta kotó o suru** to act rashly.

Sonna ni hayamátte wa ikemasén. Don't be so hasty. Nán to iu hayamátta kotó o shite kureta. What a rash thing you've done!

hayame ni somewhat early, before time; uchi o hayame ni déru to leave home a little early.

hayaméru to quicken, hasten, accelerate; ashí o hayaméru to quicken one's steps.

hayáne o suru to go to bed early; hayáne hayáoki early to bed and early to rise.

hayanómikomi o suru to jump to a conclusion.

hayáoki suru to get up early.

hayari fashion, mode, vogue; hayari no fashionable, popular; hayari no shingata new style.

hayaríuta popular song.

HAYÁRU to be in fashion; to prevail; to rage; to prosper; to be hasty; to be impetuous; hayaránaku náru to go out of fashion; to lose popularity. Ano misé wa yóku hayátte iru. That store is doing a good business.

háyasa quickness, swiftness, rapidity, speed, velocity.

HAYASHI forest, wood, grove.

hayásu to cut into small fragments; to slice up; to hash; to grow; to let grow; hige o hayásu to grow a beard; to grow a mustache.

hayawákari quick understanding; hayawákari no suru to be quick of understanding; to be intelligent; to be easy to understand.

hayawaza clever trick; sleight of hand.

HAZU ought to; is to be; –hazu wa nái cannot be; must not be; there is no reason to believe that . . . Káre wa késa shuppatsu suru hazu déshita. He was to start this morning. Anó hito wa kyoo kúru hazu désu. He is expected here today. Anó hito ga kyóo kuru hazu wa nái. There is no reason to believe that he would come here today.

hazukashigáru to be shy, be bashful.

Hazukashíi to be ashamed; to be shameful; to be dishonorable; to be bashful. Ohazukashíi kotó desu ga . . . To my shame I must confess that . . .

hazukashime shame, disgrace; insult; hito kara hazukashime o ukéru to be humiliated by someone; hazukashiméru to put to shame; to outrage.

hazumi momentum, impetus; hazumi o tsukéru to give impetus to; hazumi ga tsúku to be encouraged; to be stimulated; toki no hazumi de on the spur of the moment.

hazumu to bounce; to rebound; to get lively; to treat oneself to; íki ga hazumu to be out of breath; to pant.

hazure end, edge; outskirts; miss; disappointment; failure (of crops); poor harvest; machi no hazure the end of a street.

hazureru to be disconnected, to be dislocated; to come off; to be out of joint; to fail; to miss; ate ga hazureru to be disappointed in one's expectations.

hazusu to remove; to unfasten; to lose; to avoid; mégane o hazusu to take off one's glasses; kikái o hazusu to lose an opportunity; séki o hazusu to slip out of the room; to leave the table.

hébi snake, serpent.

hedatari distance; difference; gap.

hedatáru to be distant; to become estranged.

hedate distinction; discrimination; reserve; estrangement; barrier; hedate no áru distant; discriminating; hedate no nái candid; openhearted; hedate náku hanásu to speak without reserve.

hedatéru to part from; separate by; to intervene, come between; to alienate; hedátete apart; at a distance; at intervals of; júunen o hedátete after an interval of ten years.

heddofóon headphones.

heddoráito headlight.

hei wall; fence; hei o megurásu to surround with a wall.

heian peace, tranquility; heian ni peacefully, in peace.

heibon commonness; mediocrity; heibon na commonplace, mediocre; tame; uneventful; heibon na tsuki an uneventful month.

heigai evils; evil influence, evil effect.

heihei bonbon commonplace, mediocre.

Héika His (Her) Majesty.

heikai closing, adjournment; heikai suru to adjourn.

heiki coolness, calmness, composure; heiki na cool, calm, composed; indifferent; unconcerned; heiki de calmly; with composure. Heiki na kao o shite imáshita. He looked unconcerned.

heikin average; balance; equilibrium; heikin shite on the average.

heikoo suru to be defeated; to be silenced; to be annoyed; to be embarrassed.

heion tranquility; peace and quiet; heion no, heion na quiet; tranquil; heion ni náru to become quiet.

heisei composure; kokoro no heisei o tamótsu to keep one's presence of mind.

Heisei present era (counted from ascent of

55

present emperor to throne in 1989); **Heisei 4 nen** the year 1992.

heitai soldier.

heiten (*n.*) closing of a shop or business; **heiten suru** to close up shop.

HEIWA peace; **heiwa no, heiwa na** peaceful, peaceable; **heiwa ni** peacefully; **heiwarónsha** pacifist.

heiya plain; moor; prairie.

heizei at ordinary times; usually. **Heizei wa yoru uchi ni imasu.** I am usually at home at night.

heizen to shite calmly, composedly.

hekieki suru to shrink from; to flinch; to be nonplused.

hekomasu to hollow, to depress; to defeat; to silence.

hekomu to become hollow; to become depressed; to be humiliated; to give in, yield.

hekotareru to be discouraged; to be exhausted.

–hen neighborhood; region; side; **kono hen ni** in this neighborhood.

–hén chapter; book, volume.

henden telegram (in reply); **henden suru** to reply by telegram.

hendoo change, alteration; fluctuations; **hendoo suru** to change; to fluctuate.

HENJÍ, bentóo reply, answer; **henjí suru** to reply, answer; **tegami no henjí o dásu** to answer a letter.

henjín eccentric person, odd fish.

hénka change, variation; **hénka suru** to change, alter.

henken prejudice; prejudiced view.

henkin repayment; refund; **henkin suru** to pay back, repay.

henkoo alteration, making changes.

hénkutsu eccentricity; obstinacy; narrow-mindedness; **hénkutsu na** eccentric; narrow-minded; cranky; obstinate. **Anó hito wa hénkutsu na hitó desu.** He is an eccentric person.

henmei alias; assumed name.

HÉN NA odd, strange, queer; **hén na mé ni áu** to have an odd experience; **hén na kokochi ga suru** to have a strange sensation; **hén ni omóu** to think (something) to be strange.

hennyuu admission; assignment.

hénrei return (of a present or call); **–no hénrei ni** in return for.

hensai repayment; **hensai suru** to repay.

hensan compilation; editing.

hensei organization; formation.

hensen change; vicissitudes; **hensen suru** to change, undergo a change.

henshi unnatural death.

henshin change of mind; unfaithfulness; **henshin suru** to change one's mind.

henshoku partiality (weakness) for a particular kind of food.

hensoo disguise.

hentai abnormality.

bentóo See **HENJÍ.**

hentoosen tonsils; **hentoosén en** tonsillitis.

herasu to decrease, lessen, reduce.

herí border, edge, brim, brink; **herí o tóru** to hem, border.

heríkóputaa helicopter.

herikudáru to be modest; to humble oneself; **herikudátte** modestly, humbly.

heríkutsu o iu to quibble; to argue for the sake of arguing.

HERU to decrease, lessen; to be reduced. **Áme de hitode ga hetta.** Because of the rain, the crowds have thinned out.

héru to pass; to elapse; to pass through; to go by way of.

herumétto helmet.

hesokurigane secret savings; pin money.

HETÁ unskillfulness, awkwardness; **hetá na** unskillful, awkward, clumsy. **Watakushi wa Nihongo ga hetá desu.** My Japanese is poor.

heta calyx.

héte after; through; by way of; **ichínen o héte** after a year; **yuujin no té o héte** through a friend; **Róndon o héte** by way of London.

hetoheto ni náru to be reduced to a pulp; to be tired out; to be exhausted.

hetsurai flattery; **hetsurai mono** flatterer; **hetsuráu** to flatter; to fawn on.

hétto beef fat.

HEYÁ room, chamber.

HI sun; day; time; date; **hi no de** sunrise; **hi no iri** sunset; **áru hi** one day; **hiatari** exposure to sun; **hiatari ga yoi** to be sunny, have plenty of sunshine; **hiatari ga warui** to be dark and gloomy; **hi ni yakeru** to be sunburnt; **hi ni sarasu** to expose to the sun; **hi no me o miru** to see the light of day; **hi no me o mínai** to lack sun. **Hi ga nágaku nátte kita.** The days are getting longer. **Hi wa rokúji ni deta.** The sun rose at six.

HÍ fire, flame; spark; light; **hí ga tsúku** to catch fire; **hí ni ataru** to warm oneself by a fire; **hí no ko** flying sparks; **hí no te** flames; blaze; **hí no te ga agaru** to burst into flames; **hí no yoo na** fiery, blazing; **híbana** sparks; **híbana o tobasu** to shoot out sparks. (See also **kasai.**)

hí error, fault; **hí o narasu** to attack, to declaim against; **hi no uchidokoro ga nái** impeccable, unimpeachable.

hi tombstone, monument.

hi– prefix denoting: un–; anti–; non–; **hikínzoku** non-metal.

hiagáru to dry up; to be parched; to starve to death.

hiai sadness; sorrow.

hibachi brazier; charcoal brazier; **hibachi ni ataru** to warm oneself at a brazier.

híban off duty; **híban de aru** to be off duty.

hibí crack; fissure; flaw; **hibí ga iru** to be cracked; to have a flaw; **hibí ga kiréru** to be chapped.

hibikí sound; echo, reverberation; **hibíki watáru** to resound, reverberate.

hibíku to sound; to echo; to affect; to influence; **myóo ni hibíku** to sound strange.

hibon na, hibon no out of the ordinary, extraordinary; uncommon.

hiboshi drying in the sun.

hibúkure blister caused by a burn.

hibúnmei uncivilized; uncultured.

hída fold; tuck; plait; **hída o tóru** to tuck; to fold; crease.

hidachi growth; recovery; convalescence.

HIDARI left; **hidari no** left; left side; **hidari ni** to the left; on the left; **hidarí kiki** left-handedness; left-handed person; winelover, a heavy drinker; **hidarí kiki no** left-handed.

hidarímae adversity; downward course. **Shínshoo ga hidarímae ni náru.** His luck is failing. Luck is deserting him.

hiden secret; trade secret.

hideri drought, dry weather.

HIDÓI severe; excessive; intense; violent; awful; terrible; **hidói mé ni áu** to have a bad time of it.

hídoku severely; intensely; violently; hard.

hidori o kimeru to fix a date, fix on a day; to name a day.

hiéru to grow cold, get chilly.

HÍFU skin.

higaeri return trip made in one day; **higaeri suru, higaeri ni suru** to go and return in one day.

hígai damage, injury; **higáisha** sufferer; victim.

higamí jaundice; warp.

higámu to be jealous; to be prejudiced.

higan other shore (side); goal.

HIGASHI east. **Táiyoo wa higashi kara déru.** The sun rises in the east.

higáshi confectionery.

hige mustache; beard; whiskers; **hige o hayásu** to raise a mustache (or beard); **hige moja no** heavily bearded.

hígeki tragedy, tragic event.

HIGORO always; for a long time; **higoro no** usual; long-cherished. **Káre wa higoro kara kinben da.** He has always been industrious. **Higoro no negái ga kanátta.** My long-cherished dream has been fulfilled.

higoto ni everyday; day by day.

HIGURE twilight; nightfall; **higure ni** toward evening; at dusk.

hihan comment; criticism; **hihan suru** to criticize; to censure.

hihoo sad news.

hihyoo critique; comment; **hihyoo suru** to criticize, comment, review; **hihyooteki** critical; **hihyooka** critic, reviewer.

híiki favor; patronage; partiality; **híiki o suru** to favor, be partial to; **híiki no** favorite; **hiikíkyaku** patron.

HLJÍ elbow; **hijikaké isu** armchair.

hijidéppoo rebuff; cold shoulder; **hijidéppoo o kuwaséru** to give (someone) the cold shoulder.

hijoo extraordinary occasion; emergency; **hijoo na** extraordinary; uncommon; **HIJOO NI** extraordinarily; exceedingly; **hijoo no sái ni wa** in case of emergency; **hijóoguchi** emergency exit; **hijóoji** emergency, crisis; **hijooshúdan** exceptional measures.

hijóoshiki lack of common sense; **hijóoshiki na** eccentric; nonsensical. **Hijóoshiki na hito desu.** He lacks common sense.

hikae note, memorandum; duplicate.

hikaeme moderation; modesty; temperance; **hikaeme ni** moderately; with reserve; **hikaeme ni suru** to be moderate; **bánji hikaeme ni suru** to do all things with moderation.

hikaéru to jot down, note down; to wait; to be moderate, to stop.

hikage shade; shadow; shady spot.

hikaku comparison; **hikaku suru** to compare; **hikakuteki** comparatively.

hikan pessimism; **hikan suru** to be pessimistic; **hikan rónsha** pessimist.

hikarabiru to dry up, shrivel, wither.

hikaraséru to brighten; to polish; to cause to shine; to glimmer.

HIKARÍ light, brightness, brilliancy; glimmer, twinkle, luster, gloss; **hikari tsuushin** fiber-optic communication.

hikáru to shine; to be bright, sparkle; etc.

hikazu number of days; **hikazu ga kakáru** to take many days.

hike weak point; **hike o tóru** to be defeated, be inferior to.

hikeru to be closed; to close; to lose courage; to feel small. **Yakushó ga góji ni hikeru.** The office closes at five. **Watakushi wa sore o kangáeru to ki ga hikeru.** I feel small when I think of it; **hikedoki** closing hour.

hiketsu secret; **seikoo no hiketsu** secret of success.

hikí joy and sorrow; **hikí komógomo** a mixed feeling of joy and sorrow.

hiki (*n.*) pulling; help, backing; influence. **Anó hito wa yói hiki ga áru.** He has good connections.

hiki– prefix denoting: pulling; drawing; **hikishio** to use as an example.

–HIKI counter head denoting (for fish or four-legged animals); **ippikí no ushi** one head of cattle; **níhiki no ushi** two heads of cattle.

hikiage pulling up; evacuation; withdrawal.

hikiagéru to pull up, draw up; to evacuate; to withdraw.

hikiai witness; instance; example; **hikiai ni dásu** to use as an example.

hikiáu to pay (off) well; to make a good return. **Sono shigoto wa hikiawánai.** The work does not pay.

hikiawase introduction; bringing together; comparison; **hikiawaséru** to introduce; to compare with; to check up.

hikicha powdered tea.

hikichigíru to pull off; to tear off.

hikidashi drawer; **hikidashi o akeru** to open a drawer.

hikidásu to draw out; to pull out; **yokin o hikidásu** to draw money from a bank.

hikifune towboat; tugboat.

hikígeki tragicomedy.

hikiharáu to vacate; to remove; **ié o hikiharáu** to move from a house.

hikiiréru to draw into; to pull into; to win over; **mikata ni hikiiréru** to win a person (over) to one's side.

hikiíru to lead; to head; to control; to manage.

hikikae exchange; conversion; **–to hikikae ni** in exchange for.

hikikáeru to exchange; to convert; **sore ni hikikáete** on the contrary; on the other hand.

hikikáesu to come back; to turn back; to return.

hikikomisen railway siding, service wire.

hikikomóru to shut oneself in; to be confined.

hikikómu to retire.

hikimodósu to bring back; to revert to; to restore.

HIKINIKU chopped meat; **hikinikúki** meat grinder.

hikin na familiar; common; popular; **hikin na réi** familiar example.

hikinobású to stretch; to draw out; to enlarge

(a photo); to postpone; to put off. **hikinobashi sháshin** enlarged photograph.

hikiokósu to raise up; to lift up; to cause; to give rise to; to awaken.

hikiorósu to pull down.

hikisagáru to withdraw; to retire.

hikisáku to tear up, tear to pieces.

hikishimáru to tighten; to tie harder; to brace; to be tightened up; to grow tight; to be braced up; **hikishimátta** firm; tight; tense; **fukuro no himo o hikishiméru** to draw the strings of a bag together.

hikitaósu to pull down.

hikitate favor; patronage.

hikitatéru to favor; to patronize; to set off (beauty); to set off to advantage; **ki o hikitatéru** to encourage.

hikitátsu to look well (better); to improve; to become active; **ki ga hikitátsu** to cheer up; to be inspired with hope.

hikite catch; knob.

hikitoméru to detain; to stop.

hikitóru to withdraw; to take back; to take over.

hikitsúgu to succeed in; to take over.

hikitsuke convulsion.

hikitsukéru to draw toward me; to attract.

HIKITSUZÚITE continually; successively; **gonen hikitsuzúite** for five years running.

hikitsuzuki continuation; succession; sequel.

hikitsuzúku to continue; to last.

hikiuke undertaking. **Ano ginkoo wa kono tegate no hikiuke o kobanda.** That bank didn't honor this check.

hikiukéru to undertake; to accept; to take over; to assume; to shoulder the responsibility for.

hikiwake draw, tie; **hikiwake ni náru** to end in a draw.

hikiwakéru to part; to pull apart; to separate.

hikiwatashi delivery; transfer; surrender. **Shoohin no hikiwatashi wa yokka ni súnda.** The delivery of merchandise was completed on the fourth.

hikiwatásu to deliver; to hand over; to surrender.

hikiyoséru to draw near; to bring close; to pull near.

hikízan subtraction.

hikizuru to drag, pull along; **ashí o hikizutte arúku** to drag one's feet; **hikizuridásu** to pull out, drag out; **hikizurikómu** to drag in; to bring in.

hikkabúru to pull (draw) over one's head.

hikkakáru to be caught (on a nail, tree, etc.); to be hooked; to be entangled; to be cheated.

hikkakéru to hook; to hang on; to cheat; to

seduce; to evade payment; **íppai
hikkakéru** to have drink.

hikkáku to scratch; to claw.

hikki transcript; **hikki suru** to write down; to
copy; to take notes; **hikkísha**
stenographer; **hlkkichoo** notebook;
hikkishikén written examination.

hikkoméru to pull (draw) in; to draw back;
to move back.

hikkómu to retire, withdraw; to disappear;
hikkomigachi no, hikkomijían no
retiring (in disposition); **inaka e
hikkómu** to retire to the country. **Ié wa
dóoro kara hikkónde iru.** The house
stands back from the road.

hikkónda secluded; sunken; hollow;
hikkónda basho secluded place.

HIKKÓSU to move (into another house);
hikkoshi no torráku moving van.
Tookyoo e hikkoshimásu. I am going to
move to Tokyo.

hikkurikáeru to tumble down; to be upset; to
tip over; to be overturned.

hikkurikaeshi topsy-turvy; upside down;
wrong side up; inside out. **Uchi no náka
wa hikkurikaeshi ni natte imasu.** The
house is upside down.

hikkurikáesu to overturn; upset; to topple
over; to knock down.

hikkuruméru to bundle (together); to
include.

hikoku defendant; prisoner.

HIKOO flight; aviation; **hikoo suru** to fly;
HIKOOJOO airport; **HIKÓOKI**
airplane; **hikoosen** blimp; dirigible.

hikóoshiki no informal, not official;
hikóoshiki ni unofficially; informally.

HIKU to draw; to attract; to lead; to install;
to quote; to consult; to subtract; **kúji o
hiku** to draw lots; **sode o hiku** to pull
(someone) by the sleeve; **kuruma o hiku**
to draw a cart; **chúui o hiku** to attract
attention; **doojoo o hiku** to win
sympathy; **kaze o hiku** to catch a cold;
denwa o hiku to install a telephone; **jísho
o hiku** to refer to a dictionary; **nedan o
hiku** to cut the price; **chisuji o hiku** to
descend from.

hiku to play (an instrument); **piano a hiku**
to play the piano.

hiku to resign, to retire; recede, ebb. **Hare ga
hikimáshita.** The swelling has gone
down. **Netsú ga hikimáshita.** The fever
has dropped.

HIKÚI low; humble; short; flat; **hikúi hana**
a flat nose; **hikúi kóe** a low voice. **Séi ga
hikúi.** She is short (in stature).

híkutsu meanness; servility; **hikutsu na**
servile; mean.

hikyóo cowardice; **hikyóo na** cowardly;
hikyoo mono coward.

HIMA leisure; (spare) time; dismissal;
leave; interval; recess; **hima de áru** to
be free, be at leisure; **hima ga iru** to
require (more) time; **hima ga nái** to
have no time; **hima o dásu** to dismiss
(a servant); **hima o tóru** to resign; **hi-
madóru** to take (much) time; to delay;
himajín leisured or unemployed person.
Shóobai ga hima de áru. Business is
slack.

himashi ni more and more each day;
himashí ni byooki ga yóku naru to get
better day by day.

himei cry of distress; shriek; **himei o ageru**
to utter a groan.

himitsu secret; secrecy; **himitsu no secret,
confidential, private; **himitsu ni** secretly,
privately; **himitsu o suru** to keep secret;
himitsu o abáku to divulge a secret.

HIMO string, cord; braid; tape; ribbon;
thong; **himo o musubu** to tie a string.
himo de musubu to tie (something) with
string.

himojii to be starved. **Taihen himojíi omoi o
shimashita.** I was very hungry.

himono dried fish.

hín poverty; **hin súru** to be poor.

hin elegance; grace; refinement; **hin ga tsuku**
to be refined; **hin no yói** refined; elegant;
hin no warúi vulgar; uncouth; coarse; **hin
o sagéru** to disgrace oneself.

hinaka broad daylight; daytime.

hínan blame, censure, reproach; **hínan suru**
to blame.

hínan refuge, shelter; **hínan suru** to take
shelter; **hinánsha** refugee; **hinansho**
refugee shelter.

hinata sunny place; sunshine; **hinata ni hósu**
to dry in the sun; **hinata bókko o suru** to
take a sunbath.

hinekuréru to become crooked; **hinekúreta**
distorted, crooked; perverse; **hinekúreta
onna** perverse woman; **hinekúreta
kangáe** distorted view.

hinekúru to twirl; to finger; to toy with.

hinéru to twirl; to turn on (or off); **gásu o
hinéru** to turn on the gas (in a stove).

hiniku sarcasm; caustic remark; **hiniku na**
sarcastic; cynical, ironic; **hiniku o iu** to
speak sarcastically or ironically.

hinin birth control, contraception.

hinjaku meagerness; poverty; **hinjaku na**
meager; shelter.

hinketsu anemia.

hinkoo behavior, conduct; **hinkoo no yói**
well-behaved.

hinmínkutsu slums.

hinobe postponement; extension of time; reprieve; **hinobe suru** to postpone, etc.

hinoki bútai (theater) stage (of cypress); (= first-class stage).

hi no kuruma extreme poverty; **hi no kuruma de áru** to be in great financial difficulty.

hi no maru national flag of Japan; disk of the sun; red circle.

hinpan frequency, **hinpan na** frequent; incessant; **hinpan ni, hinpin to** frequently, incessantly.

hínshi dying; **hínshi no jootai ni áru** to be on the verge of death.

hinshitsu quality.

hínsoo poor appearance; **hínsoo na narí o shite iru** to be poorly dressed.

hippaku pressure (for money); tightness (of money). **Anó hito wa shikín ni hippaku site iru.** She is pressed for funds.

hipparidáko de áru to be sought for eagerly; to be in great demand.

HIPPÁRU to pull, draw, drag, tug; to stretch; to entice; to solicit; **mikata ni hippáru** to win over to our side.

hira– prefix denoting: flat, level; plain, simple; common; **hiraya** one-story house; **hirachi** level land, flat ground.

HIRAGÁNA one of the two sets of Japanese syllabary called **kana.**

hírahira fluttering; flapping. **Kí no ha ga hírahira to chitta.** The leaves fluttered down.

hiráishin lightning rod.

hirakéru to become civilized; to become modernized; to be cultivated; to develop; to grow; **hiráketa** modernized; up-to-date; civilized; **hiráketa hito** person of the world.

hirakí opening; closet; difference; distance; gap.

HIRÁKU to open; to lift (a lid); to unfold; to commence; to set up; to cultivate; to bloom; **tenránkai o hiráku** to open an exhibit. **Haná ga hiráite iru.** The flower is blooming.

hiramekásu to flash; to brandish.

hirameki flash; flashing; gleam.

hiraméku to flash; to gleam; to wave.

híra ni humbly; earnestly; intently. **Híra ni goyóosha o kóu.** I sincerely hope you will pardon me (used in letters).

hirarí to nimbly; lightly.

hiratai, hirrattái flat, level; simple, plain; **hirataku** flatly; evenly; easily; simply, plainly; **hirataku suru** to flatten; **hirataku iéba** to speak plainly.

hirate palm of the hand; open hand; **hirate de útsu** to slap.

hiraya one-story house.

híré fin.

híreniku steak; filet mignon.

hiretsu meanness; baseness.

hírihiri suru to be pungent; to have a burning taste; to smart.

híroba open space; square (of a town).

hirobíro to shita spacious; roomy; open; extensive.

hirogari extension; expansion; spread.

hirogaru to extend; to expand; to spread.

HIROGERU to spread; to extend; to widen; to open; to unfold; to unroll. **Michi o hirogemáshita.** They widened the road. **Mise o hirogeru tsumori désu.** I intend to expand (enlarge) the store.

HIRÓI wide, broad; extensive; roomy; **hirói heya** spacious (big) room.

hiroiagéru to pick up.

hiroiatsuméru to gather, collect; to select.

hiroimono piece of good luck; find; **hiroimono o suru** to find (pick up) (something); to make a rare find.

hiroiyomi o suru to read here and there; to skim; to skip over (details); to pick up the chief points.

híroku widely, extensively; generally; universally; **híroku suru** to widen; to enlarge.

híroma spacious room; hall.

hiromáru to circulate; to be circulated; to be diffused.

hirome announcement; debut.

hiroméru to spread, propagate.

hiroo fatigue; exhaustion; **hiroo suru** to get weary, to be exhausted.

híroo announcement; introduction; **híroo suru** to announce; to introduce.

hírosa width, breadth; area; dimension. **Kono kooen no hírosa wa dore hodo arimásu ka?** How large is this park?

HIROU to pick up; to find; to gather. **Michi de sen én satsu o hirotta.** I found a thousand-yen bill on the road.

HIRU daytime; noon, midday; **hiru hínaka** in broad daylight.

HIRUGÓHAN lunch, midday meal; **hirugohan o tabéru** to have lunch.

hirugáeru to wave; to fly; to float; to flap; **hirugáesu** to wave; to fly; to change.

hiruhan See **hirugóhan.**

HIRUMA daytime; **hirumá ni** in the daytime.

hirumáe forenoon; **hirumáe ni** in the morning.

hirúmu to flinch; to shrink.

hirune midday nap; siesta; **hirune o suru** to take a nap.

hirusúgi shortly after noon.

HIRUYÁSUMI midday recess; lunch hour.

híryoo manure; fertilizer.

hisan misery; distress; **hisan na** tragic; miserable, wretched.

hisashi visor (of a cap); eaves; canopy.

HISASHIBURI DE after a long time; for the first time in many days (weeks, years, etc.); **hisashíburi de áu** to see after a long interval. **Hisashíburi désu née!** It's a long time since I last saw you.

hisashíi long; long continued; of long standing; **hisashíi aida** for a long time.

HISÁSHIKU for a long time. **Káre ni wa hisáshiku awánai.** I haven't seen him for a long time.

hisénron pacifism; **hisenrónsha** pacifist.

hishaku ladle, dipper.

hishíhishi to firmly; tightly; densely; deeply.

hishiméku to clamor, make a noise.

hishóchi summer resort.

hisóhiso in whispers; secretly; **hisohiso bánashi** whispered conversation.

hisoméru to raise or knit (one's brows); **máyu o hisómeta** with a frown.

hisoo na touching, pathetic.

hísshi desperation; **hísshi no** desperate; **hísshi ni** desperately; **hísshi to nátte** in desperation; **hísshi no dóryoku o suru** to make desperate efforts.

hisutérii hysteria, hysterics; **hisutérii o okósu** to go into hysterics.

HITAI forehead; brow.

hitasu to steep; to dip; to soak.

HITO person; people; others; nature; disposition; **hito no yói** good-natured; **hito no warúi** ill-natured; **hito no ooi jíkoku** rush hour.

hitó– prefix denoting: one; **hitóban** one night (evening); all night; whole night; **hitóhako** one box.

HITÓBITO people.

hitochígai mistaken identity.

hitodánomi o suru to depend on someone else.

hitode helping hand; help; **hitode ga tarinai** short of hands; short of help; **hitode o kariru** to ask for help; **hitode ni wataru** to change hands.

hitode, hitogomi crowd; throng. **Taihen na hitode de átta.** There was a large crowd.

hitodenashi inhuman wretch; ungrateful person.

hitodoori pedestrian traffic; **hitodoori no óoi machí** a busy street. **Koko wa hitodoori ga óoi.** It is very crowded here.

hitoemono summer clothes.

hitófude line; stroke; **hitófude de** with one stroke of the brush.

hitogara personal character; personal appearance.

hitogoe voice.

hitogomi (See also **hitode.**) **hitogomi no náka o oshiwákete iku** to push through a crowd of people.

hitogoroshi murder; murderer.

hitogoto other people's affairs. **Hitogoto tó wa omoénai.** I feel as if it were my own concern.

hitóhada núgu to lend a helping hand; to give every assistance possible.

hitóiki breath; **hitóiki tsúite** after a pause; **hitóiki de** in one breath; at a stretch.

hitokata naránu unusual, uncommon; great, immense.

hitokata nárazu not a little; extremely; immensely.

HITÓKIWA especially, particularly; conspicuously; in a high degree; still more.

hitókoto single word; **hitokoto mo iwanai** to be silent; not to say a single word.

hitókuchi mouthful; bite; morsel; **hitókuchi ni tabéru** to eat in one bite.

hitókuse peculiarity; uncommon trait.

hitomae de in public.

hitómaku act; scene; **hitomaku mono** one-act play.

hitomane imitation; mimicry.

hitómatome ni in a lump; in a bunch; **hitómatome ni suru** to put together.

hitómawari turn; round; **hitómawari suru** to go on one's rounds; **kooen o hitómawari sanpo suru** to take a walk through the park.

HITÓMAZU for the present; for the time being; for a while; anyhow.

hitome notice; attention; **hitome o shinóbu** to avoid the public eye; **hitome o shinónde** in secret; secretly; **hitome o hiku** to attract attention.

hitóme look; glance; **hitóme de** at a glance; **hitóme míru** to glance at.

hitomishiri suru to be afraid of strangers; to be bashful.

hitómukashi age; decade.

hitonaka crowd of people; **hitonaka de** in the presence of others.

hitonamí no average; common; ordinary; **hitonami ni** like other people; **hitonami hazureta** uncommon; eccentric.

hitónemuri nap; short sleep.

hitónigiri handful; **hitónigiri no kome** handful of rice.

hitóomoi ni without further hesitation; instantly; at once; without further ado.

HITÓRI (single) person; **hitóri de** alone; unaided; **hitorimono** bachelor. **Hitóri de shimáshita.** I did it myself.

hitori bítori, hitori hitori one by one; one after another (person). **Hitori bítori de kangae ga chigau.** Each person has his or her own opinion.

hitoríde ni spontaneously.

hitorigáten one's own judgment; hasty conclusion.

hitorígo only child.

hitorigoto soliloquy; **hitorigoto o iu** to talk to oneself.

hitorigúrashi living alone; bachelorhood.

hitori hitóri (See **hitori bítori**.) one by one; one at a time. **Hitori hitóri no kangáe o itte kudasái.** Will each of you express your opinion?

hitorimúsuko only son.

hitorimúsume only daughter.

hitori nokórazu everyone.

hitorítabi (*n.*) traveling alone.

hitoriyógari self-satisfaction; self-complacency; **hitoriyógari no** self-satisfied.

hitosárai abduction, kidnapping; kidnapper.

HITOSASHÍYUBI forefinger.

hitosáwagase scare; false alarm.

hitoshii equal to, equivalent to.

hitósoroi set; suit; **hitósoroi no chadoógu** tea set; **fuyugi hitósoroi** winter suit.

hitósuji line; **hitosují michi** straight road; **hitósuji ni** straight, in a straight line; intently.

HITOTONARI personality; character.

hitotoori in a general way; **hitotoori no** general; common; **hitotoori naránu** unusual, uncommon; **hitotoori hanáshite kikaseru** to give a short account.

HITÓTSU one; same; identical; **hitótsu no** one; single; **hitótsu ni suru** to unite, join, combine; **hitotsu bítotsu** one by one; separately; **hitotsu óki ni** alternately.

hitótsukami grain; **hitótsubu no kome** grain of rice.

hitótsukami handful; fistful.

hitóuchi blow; stroke; **hitóuchi ni** at one blow.

hitozuki attractiveness; amiability; **hitozuki no suru** attractive; pleasing; amiable; charming; **hitozuki no shinai** unprepossessing; unattractive.

hitozute hearsay; **hitozute ni** secondhand; by hearsay. **Hitozute ni kiite shitte imásu.** I know it through hearsay. **Sore wa hitozute ni kiitá no desu.** It came to me secondhand.

HITSUYOO necessity; need; **HITSUYOO NA** necessary; requisite, required; **hitsuyoo no sái wa** in case of need. **Ano hón ga zéhi hitsuyoo désu.** I must have that book.

hittakúru to snatch, take by force.

hiwari daily rate; schedule; program; **hiwari de harau** to pay by the day; **hiwari o kimeru** to fix the dates.

hiyaáse o káku to be in a cold sweat.

híyahiya suru to be chilly; to be in great fear.

hiyakashi banter; jeering; ridicule; (mere) inspection.

hiyakásu to make fun of; just to look at. **Chótto hiyakáshi ni íku daké desu.** I'll just go and look at the things. **Anó hito wa anáta o hiyakáshite irú no da.** She is making fun of you.

hiyarí to suru to feel chilled; to be startled, be alarmed at.

hiyásu to cool; to refrigerate; **hiyáshite oku** to keep (something) cool.

hiyáyaka coldness; coldheartedness, **hiyáyaka ni** coldheartedly; coolly; **hiyáyaka na hito** coldhearted person; **hiyáyaka na kaze** chilly wind.

hiyoke screen (against sun); awning; **hiyoke o suru** to screen from the sun.

HÍYOO cost, expense, expenditure; **hiyoo ga kakáru** to be expensive. **Dore hodo híyoo ga kakarimáshita ka?** How much did it cost you?

HIYORI weather; fine weather; condition; state of affairs; **hiryori o míru** to watch which way the wind blows; to sit on the fence. **Hiyori ga kawatta.** The weather has changed.

HIZA knee; lap; **hiza o tsuku** to kneel; **hizagáshira** kneecap; **hizakake** lap robe (rug); **hizamazúku** to kneel; to fall on one's knees.

hízoo treasure, valuable possession; **hizoo no** treasured, valued; dearest; **hizoo suru** to treasure, cherish, keep with great care; **hizóohin** valued possession.

hizuke date; **tegami ni hizuke o suru** to date a letter.

hobáshira mast.

HÓBO almost, nearly; about.

HÓBO kindergarten teacher.

hochoo pace, step; **hochoo o soroéru** to keep pace with.

HODO degree; limit; moderation; some; about; the more . . . the more; as; **hodo yóku** moderately; properly; modestly; **kore hodo** this much; so much; **sore hodo** that much. **Joodán ni mo hodo ga áru.** There is a limit even to a joke. **Háyakereba hayai hodo yói desu.** The sooner the better.

hodoai moderation; golden mean.

hodokoshi alms, charity.

hodokósu to give; to give alms; to practice;

to try; **arayúru shudan o hodokósu** to try every means.

HODÓKU to untie, unfasten; to loosen; to disentangle; **nímotsu o hodóku** to unpack (luggage); **himo o hodóku** to untie a knot.

hodokéru to come loose; to get untied.

HODÓNAKU shortly; before long; by and by.

hodoo footpath; sidewalk; pavement; paved road.

hoéru to bark; to howl; to roar. **Ano inú wa yóku hoéru.** That dog is noisy.

hogáraka melodiousness; cheerfulness; **hogáraka na** sonorous; cheerful, bright; **hogáraka na kóe** in a clear voice; **hogáraka ni** cheerfully.

hógo protection; **hógo suru** to protect; **hogósha** protector, guardian.

hogúsu to unfasten, untie; to disentangle; to unravel.

hógu, hógo wastepaper; **hógu ni suru** to annul, invalidate.

hojíru, hojikúru to pick; to dig; to ferret out.

hójo assistance, aid, subsidy; **hójo no** subsidiary, auxiliary; **hójo suru** to aid, subsidize; **hójo o ukéru** to be subsidized; **hojókin** subsidy, grant-in-aid.

hojuu suru to supplement; to replenish.

HOKA others; rest; besides; another phase; **hoka ni** besides; **hoka no** another; the other; **–no hoka wa** except; **hoka no tokoro** another place; elsewhere; **hoka no hitótachi** other people.

hokan suru to take custody of; to take in charge; **hokannin** custodian.

hoken insurance; **hoken o kakéru** to insure (against accidents); **seimei hóken** life insurance; **kasai hóken** fire insurance.

hoketsu substitute, filling a vacancy; **hoketsu suru** substitute player.

hokki promotion; proposal, suggestion.

hókku hook.

HOKORI dust; **hokori dárake** dusty; **hokori ga tátsu** to be dusty; **hokori o haráu** to dust.

hokori pride. **Kodomo o hokori ni shite imásu.** She takes pride in her children.

hokoróbi rip; run (ravel).

hokorobíru to get ripped; to be torn open; to unravel, run.

hokóru to boast of; to be proud.

hokuro mole (body).

hokyuu supply; replenishment; **hokyuu suru** to supply; to make up the lack.

HOMÉRU to praise, commend; to admire. **Mina anáta o hómete imásu.** Everybody speaks well of you.

HÓN book, volume; **hón'ya** bookstore;

bookdealer; **hónbako** bookcase; **hóndana** bookshelf.

HON– prefix denoting: original; natural; proper; main; head; chief; true; real; regular; genuine; this; present; our; **hónbun** body (of a letter); text; **hóndo** mainland; **honkan** main building; **hónke** head (main) family; originator; original manufacturer; head house.

–hon counter denoting: things which have length, such as pencils, sticks, and poles; **enpitsu níhon** two pencils.

honba home; best place for.

hónbu home office; headquarters.

honburi downpour. **Áme ga iyóiyo honburi ni narimashita.** The rain was coming down in earnest.

honé bone; frame (of a sliding door); spirit; **honé to kawá bakari** to be (only) skin and bones; **honé o óru** to take the trouble to; **honé ga oréru** to be troublesome; to require great effort; **hone no áru otoko** man of courage; **honedárake na** bony; full of bones; **honegumi** build; physique; framework.

honeóri exertion; labor; foil; **honeorizón** (n.) working for nothing. **Honeroizón no kutabire móoke.** It was so much useless labor.

honeóshimi laziness; **honeóshimi suru** to spare oneself.

honki seriousness, earnestness; **honki no** serious, earnest; **honki de** seriously, in earnest. **Anáta wa honki désu ka?** Are you serious?

honkyoku head (main) office.

honmono real thing; genuine article; original article; **honmono no real,** genuine.

hónnin person in question.

HONNO mere; just; little; few; **honno sukóshi** just a little. **Máda honno kodomo desu.** He is a mere child.

honomekásu to allude, hint, suggest.

hónnoo instinct.

hónoo flame.

hónpoo principal salary.

honsai (legal) wife.

hónseki permanent residence.

honshiki regular (orthodox) way; **honshiki no** regular; formal; orthodox.

honshoku one's regular occupation; **honshoku no** professional.

honsoo suru to run about (in pursuit of something); to busy oneself about.

hóntate bookstand; bookrest.

HONTOO truth; reality; fact; **hontoo no** true, real, genuine; regular; **hontoo ni** truly, really; **hontoo ni suru** to accept as fact; to take seriously.

hon'yaku translation; **hon'yaku suru** to translate; **hon'yákusha** translator.

HÓO direction; quarter; side; **migi no hóo ni** on the right side. **Kono hóo ga ii desu.** This is better. **Iku hóo ga ii desu.** It's better to go.

hoo law.

HÓO check; **hoobone** cheekbone; **hoobeni** rouge; **hoohige** whiskers.

hoobáru to stuff one's mouth; to eat in one mouthful.

hoobi prize; reward; **hoobi o morau** to be around.

hóoboo everywhere, in all directions. **Hóoboo anáta o sagashimáshita.** I looked all over for you.

hoochiku dismissal; banishment; **hoochiku suru** to expel, dismiss; to banish; to turn out.

HOOCHOO kitchen knife.

–hóodai suffix denoting: as one pleases; to one's heart's content; **iitaihóodai o iu** to talk as one likes; **shitaihóodai o suru** to act as one pleases.

hoodoo information; report.

hoofu abundance; **hoofu na** rich; abundant.

hóofu ambition, aspiration.

hoofuku zetto suru to be convulsed with laughter, be doubled up with laughter.

hoogai na exorbitant; **hoogai no takáne** exorbitant price.

hoogaku direction; bearing; **hoogaku ga wakaránaku náru** to lose one's bearings; be unable to find one's way.

hoogén dialect; provincialism.

hoohoo no téi de precipitately, hurriedly; sneakingly; **hoohoo no téi de nigedasu** to beat a hasty retreat.

hooka arson.

HÓOKI broom; **hóoki no e** broomstick.

hookoku report; information, direction, course; **hookoku suru** to report; to inform.

hóokoo public duty; service; apprenticeship; **hookoonin** servant; domestic; **hookooguchi** domestic position; **hóokoo suru** to enter (domestic) service.

hookyuu salary; **hookyúubi** payday; **hookyuu seikátsusha** salaried person.

hooman laxity, looseness; **hooman na** lax, loose; reckless; wild.

hoomen release; acquittal; **hoomen suru** to release, liberate, release from custody; to acquit.

hoomén direction; quarter, district; **Shizuoka hóomen** the Shizuoka district.

HOOMON call; visit; **hoomon suru** to call on, visit; **hoomón kyaku** visitor; **hoomon o ukéru** to receive a visit.

hoomotsu treasure; heirloom.

hoomúran home run (in baseball).

hoomushíkku homesick.

hooriagéru to furl up; to throw up.

hooridásu to throw away, cast away, cast out.

hoorikómu to throw in, into.

hooritsukéru to throw at, against.

hooritsu law. **Sore wa hooritsu íhan da.** It's against the law.

hooroku baking pan; earthen pan used for parching tea, etc., at high temperatures.

hooru to throw, fling.

hooshin course, aim; plan; principle; policy; **hooshin o sadaméru** to shape one's course; to decide on a policy.

hóosoo = **shutoo** vaccination.

hoosoo (radio) broadcasting; **hoosóokyoku** broadcasting station.

hóosu hose.

hootai bandage.

hóra boast; brag; tall (big) talk; **hóra o fuku** to blow one's own horn; to boast; **horáfuki** braggart.

horaana cave, cavern; natural cavity.

horebóre suru to be charmed; to be fascinated.

horéru (*colloq.*) to fall in love; to be enamored of.

horidásu to dig out; to unearth, excavate.

horikáesu to dig (turn over the soil).

hóru to dig; to excavate; to burrow; to scoop out; to sink (a well).

HOSHI star. **Sóra ni hoshi ga kagayaite iru.** Stars are glittering in the sky. **Kotoshi wa hoshimáwari ga yói.** I am lucky this year.

hoshigáru to wish for; to long for; to crave; to covet.

HOSHÍI to be desirous of having (something); to want. **Ano hón ga hoshíi.** I want that book.

hoshimóno laundered clothes.

hoshoo guarantee; **hoshóonin** guarantor; certifier.

hosobíki cord, rope.

HOSÓI slender; fine; narrow; thin; **hosome ni** slightly; narrowly; **hosome ni kíru** to cut fine; **hosómichi** narrow path; lane; **hosonagai** long and slender; lanky.

hósu to dry (in the air); to sun; to empty a liquid; to draw off; to pump dry; **sakazuki o hósu** to drink up.

hotéru to feel hot; to burn. **Kao ga hotéru.** My face burns.

HÓTERU hotel.

hotoke Buddha; deceased (person); departed soul.

HOTÓNDO almost, very nearly, all but;

approximately; hardly, scarcely. **Ano bíru wa hotóndo kanseishite iru.** That building is near completion.

hotsuréru to become loose; to be frayed.

hotto suru to sigh with relief; **hotto íki o tsuku** to heave a deep sigh.

hoyoo preservation of health; recreation; relaxation; **hoyoo suru** to take care of oneself; to recuperate; to relax.

HYAKÚ (*n.*) hundred; **hyakú mo shoochishite iru** to know too well; to be well aware of.

hyakushóo peasant, farmer.

hyoo table, chart; **jíkanhyoo** timetable.

hyooban reputation; fame; popularity; report; rumor; **hyooban no** famed; notorious; **hyooban no yói** popular; of good reputation; **hyooban no warúi** unpopular; **hyooban ni náru** to be much talked about.

hyoomén (*n.*) surface; outside; **hyoomén no** (*adj.*) outside, external.

hyoosatsu doorplate; name plate.

HYOOSHI binding; **kami hyóoshi** paper cover, paper binding.

hyooshi time, rhythm; chance; **hyooshi o tóru** to beat time.

hyórohyoro staggeringly; slimly; **hyórohyoro shita** staggering, reeling; slim; lanky.

HYOTTO by chance, by accident; **hyotto shitára** possibly, maybe.

hyúuhyuu whistling; whizzing. **Kaze ga hyúuhyuu fukú.** The wind whistles.

I

I stomach.

iawaséru to happen to be present.

ibáru to be haughty; to brag; to give oneself airs.

ibikí snoring; **ibikí o káku** to snore.

ibúru to smolder, smoke. **Kono sumí wa ibúru.** This charcoal smokes.

ibúsu to smoke; to fumigate.

ICHÍ one; **ICHÍBAN** first; number one; game, round; **ichiban áto de** last of all; at the very end; **ichiban saki no** first, foremost; **ichiban osoi** slowest.

íchi position; situation; location.

ÍCHIBA marketplace, market; **aomono íchiba** vegetable market; **uo íchiba** fish market.

ichíbu part, portion; some part; **ichibu shíjuu** the whole, all the details; from beginning to end.

ichidáiji serious affair.

ICHIDO once, one time.

ICHIDÓO all; all (the persons) present; **kánai ichidóo** all the members of the family.

ICHIGATSU January.

ICHÍICHI in every single case; in detail. **Ichíichi mónku o iwanáide kudasái.** Please don't complain all the time.

ICHÍJI one o'clock; for the present; for a while; **ichijiteki no** temporary.

ICHÍMAI sheet; leaf of a tree.

ICHIMEN entire area, whole surface; one side; other hand; first page (of a newspaper); **ichimenkíji** front-page news; **–no ichimen ní wa . . .** on the other hand . . . **Ichimen ni haná ga saite iru.** Everything is in bloom.

ichimoku glance, look; **ichimoku ryoozen** to be clear at a glance; **ichimókusan ni** at full speed.

ICHÍNEN one year; **ichinen juu** all year round.

ICHINICHI one day; whole day through; all day; **ichinichi óki ni** every other day.

ICHIOO once; for the time being; in the first place; first; in outline. **Ichioo soo shite okimashóo.** We will leave it that way, at least for the time being.

ICHIRYÓOJITSU day or two; **ichiryoojitsu chuu ni** in a day or two.

ichiryuu first class; **ichiryuu no** first rate.

ichiyaku at a single bound.

iden heredity.

ído well (for water); **idobata** side of a well. **idobata káigi** gossiping.

IDOKORO address; residence; whereabouts.

IÉ house; dwelling; cottage; home; family; **ié o tatéru** to build a house; **ié ni káeru** to go home.

iegara birth, lineage.

igai na unexpected; unlooked for; **igai ni** unexpectedly.

igen dignity; prestige; **igen áru fuusai** dignified appearance.

IGIRISU = Eikoku the United Kingdom; **Igirisu no** (*adj.*) British.

igokochi comfortableness; **igokochi ga yói** snug; comfortable; **igokochi ga warúi** uncomfortable.

ihan violation; infringement; **ihan suru** to act against; to infringe upon.

ÍI = yói good; pretty; likable; **íi hito** nice person. **Íi kimi da.** It serves you right.

iiarasóu to dispute, quarrel.

iiatéru to guess correctly.

IIE no. **Iie, moo kékko desu.** No, thank you. (I've had enough.)

iifurásu to spread a story, circulate a tale.

iiháru to insist on; to persist in; to assert positively.

iihiraki vindication.

iikáeru to express in another word; **iikáereba** that is to say.

iikanéru to hesitate to say; to be unable to speak out.

íkata way of speaking; expression.

iikíru to speak positively; to assert.

iimorásu to neglect to tell; to forget to tell.

íin committee; committee member.

íinazuke fiancé; fiancée.

íine de at the price asked.

iinuke excuse; evasive answer.

iisokonai slip of the tongue; misstatement.

iisugi exaggeration.

iisugíru to say too much; to exaggerate.

iitsuke order, command; instruction.

iitsukéru to order, command; to bid.

iitsutae tradition; legend; hearsay.

IIWAKE apology; excuse; pretext; **iiwake o suru** to make an excuse; **iiwake ga tatánai** to be inexcusable.

iiwatásu to tell; to pass judgment; to sentence.

iji temper; disposition; **iji o haru** to be obstinate, be stubborn; **soko iji ga áru** strong-willed.

ijikéru to cower.

ijikitanái greedy.

ijimeru to tease; to treat badly; to torment.

ijippáru to persist in; to be obstinate.

ijirashíi pitiable; pathetic; touching.

ijíru to finger; to play with.

IJIWARU ill-natured person; **ijíwáru** na nasty, mean.

ijiwarúi ill-natured, ill-tempered; **ijiwáruku** spitefully.

ÍJOO more than; above-mentioned; above; upward of, beyond; since, now that; **yottsu íjoo** more than four.

ijoo something unusual; abnormal symptoms; deformity; **ijoo na** unusual, abnormal. **Betsu ni ijoo wa arimasén.** There is nothing unusual.

ijuu suru to move to; to migrate.

ÍKA (*n.*) following; less than, under. **Juunisai íka wa táda desu.** There is no charge for children under twelve. **Sore wa gosen en ika desu.** It costs less than 5000 yen.

IKÁGA how; what (*pol.*). **Kyóo wa okagen wa ikága desu ka?** How do you feel today? **Goíken wa ikága desu ka?** What is your opinion?

ikagawashíi questionable, doubtful.

íkahodo how much; how many.

ikameshíi solemn, grave; stern; authoritative.

IKÁNIMO very; truly; indeed.

ikásu to make good use of; to spare one's life; to keep alive; **kane o ikáshite**

tsukau to make good use of money.

iké pond.

ikedoru to capture.

íken opinon; view; **íken o nobéru** to give an opinion; **íken suru** to admonish; to give advice.

IKENAI be of no use; will not do. **Kore wa ikenai.** This will not do. **Áme ga fúru to ikenái kara.** Lest it rain. **Ikanákereba ikenái.** I must go. [It won't do if I don't go.]

ikéru to arrange flowers.

íki breath; spirit; **íki ga kiréru** to be out of breath; **íki o tsuku** to breathe; to heave a sigh of relief; **íki yoo yóo** to triumphantly.

iki smartness, stylishness; **iki na** smart, stylish, fashionable.

ikidóoru to be angry, be enraged; to be indignant.

ikigomi eagerness; ardor, zeal.

ikigómu to set one's heart on.

ikigurushíi suffocating, stifling, choking.

iki íki shita lively; active; spirited; vivid; fresh; **iki íki shita sakana** fresh-looking fish.

ikímono living thing; creature; animal.

IKINARI suddenly; all at once.

ikinokóru to survive; to outlive.

íkí power, force, energy; **ikíói no nái** spiritless, lifeless; **ikíói no yói** lively; vigorous; **ikíói yoku** vigorously.

IKÍRU to live.

ikiutsushi exact copy; **ikiutsushi no** lifelike, true to life.

íkka whole family.

IKKAI first floor; one floor, one story; **ikkai date no uchi** one-story house. **Kutsú wa ikkai de utte imásu.** Shoes are sold on the first floor.

ikkén affair; matter.

ikkoku moment; second; **ikkoku mo háyaku** as soon as possible.

ikkoo party (of tourists); suite.

ikoo intention; **ikoo o sagúru** to sound; to speak one's mind.

IKU = **yuku** to go; **machí e iku** to go to town. **Háyaku itte kudasai.** Please go quickly.

ÍKU– prefix denoting: now many; **ÍKUDO** how often; how many times; **íkudo to náku** countless times; **íkue** manyfold; **íkue ní mo** many times over; repeatedly; earnestly; on bended knee; **ikunichi** how many days; **íkura** how many; how much; **ikura ka** somewhat; to some extent; **ikura demo** as many (much) as one pleases; any amount; **ÍKUTSU** how many; how old. **Íkura desu ka?** How much? **Kyóo wa ikura ka kíbun ga yói.**

I feel a little better today. **Nihongo ga ikura ka hanasemásu.** I can speak Japanese to some extent. **Íkutsu desu ka?** How old are you? **Íkutsu arimásu ka?** How many are there?

IKUBUN partly; somewhat. **Anáta mo ikubun ka sekinin ga áru.** You, too, are responsible for it.

íku dooon ni unanimously.

íkuji spirit; backbone; **íkuji no nái** spiritless; weak.

ÍMA now; **ima mótte** as yet. **Íma ni kimásu.** She will soon come.

ímada yet (used only with a negative verb). **Imada ni kónai.** It hasn't come yet.

IMADOKI now; nowadays; these days.

IMAGORO about this time. **Imagoro náni o shite irú daroo.** What would she be doing at this time?

imaimashíi provoking; mortifying; disgusting.

ímani very soon; before long; by and by. **Ímani kuru deshoo.** He will probably come very soon.

imasara now; at this time (in a negative sense). **Imasara sonna kotó mo iemasén.** How can you say such a thing now!

imashime instruction; warning, admonition, rebuke, reprimand; **imashiméru** to instruct; to caution, admonish; to warn against; to reprimand, rebuke.

IMÁSU (form of *iru*) there is.

imawashíi offensive; abominable.

ÍMI meaning, sense, significance; **imi aríge na** significant, meaningful; **ími shinchoo** profound meaning. **Sore wa dóo iu ími desu ka?** What do you mean by that?

IMOOTO younger sister.

–in suffix denoting: one who; member of; **jimúin** clerk; **kaisháin** businessman.

inagara without any effort; without stirring.

ÍNAI within; less than; not exceeding. **Gofun ínai ni ome ni kakarimásu.** I will see you within five minutes.

inaka countryside, country; **inaka no** rural, rustic. **Inaka ni súnde imasu.** I live in the country.

inbai prostitution; **imbáifu** prostitute.

ínchi inch.

inchiki na fraudulent; sham; feigned.

Índo India; **Indoyoo** Indian Ocean; **Indójin** Indian; Hindu.

íne rice plant.

inemúri nap; **inemúri suru** to nap; to doze.

infure inflation.

infuruénza influenza.

ínga cause and effect; misfortune; **ínga na** unlucky; **ínga to akiraméru** to resign oneself to fate.

ingin politeness, courtesy; **ingin na** polite, courteous.

ingoo na stubborn; merciless.

inki gloominess; melancholy; **inki na** cheerless, gloomy, dismal.

ÍNKU = INKI ink.

innen affinity; relation; fate; objection.

ÍNOCHI life; **inochi bíroi o suru** to have a narrow esape.

inokóru to remain behind; stay behind.

inóru to pray; **seikoo o inóru** to wish someone every success.

insatsu (*n.*) printing; **insatsúbutsu** printed matter; **insatsujo** printing house; press.

inseki relative by marriage.

inshoo impression; **inshoo o ataéru** to impress; to make an impression.

insotsu suru to lead, conduct, command.

intai retirement; **íntai suru** to retire; to resign.

interi intelligentsia; intellectuals.

INÚ dog; **inugoya** kennel.

in'utsu gloom, gloominess; **in'utsu na** gloomy.

inwai obscenity; indecency; **inwai na** obscene, lewd, indecent.

inzei royalty (on a literary work).

ioo sulphur.

íppa religious sect; school; party; faction.

ÍPPAI cupful, bowlful; full of. **Mizu o íppai kudasái.** May I have a glass of water?

ippaku night's lodging; **ippaku suru** to put up for the night.

IPPAN generality; outline; **ippan no** general; common; **ippan ni** generally.

ippen once.

ippen suru to change completely, to undergo a complete change.

ippon chóoshi monotone; **ippon chóoshi no** monotonous; simpleminded.

ippondachi independence; **ippondachi de** independently.

ippóo one side; one party; **ippóo ni oité wa** on the one hand.

ippuu kawatta curious; funny; queer.

iradátsu to be irritated; to be excited.

irai dependence; reliance; request; **irai suru** to rely on; to request; **irai ni oozúru** to comply with a request.

ÍRAI since; since then.

íra ira suru to be irritated; to be fretful.

IRASSHÁRU to come, go, be at (*respect*). **Yamada-san wa Tookyoo ni irasshaimásu.** Mr. Yamada is in Tokyo. **Tanaka-san wa Kyooto e irasshaimáshita.** Ms. Tanaka went to Kyoto.

ireba artificial tooth.

irechigaéru to misplace, put in the wrong place.

irechigáu to come just as someone else leaves; to leave just as someone else comes in. **Yamada-san wa Tanaka-san to irechigai ni déte itta.** Mr. Yamada had just gone out when Ms. Tanaka came in.

irekáeru to replace; to change; to make (tea, coffee) afresh.

irekawáru to change places; **sekio irekewáru** to change seats with someone else; **irekawari tachíkawari** in rapid succession, one after another.

iremono receptacle; vessel; case.

IRERU to put in; to let in; to hold; to comply with; to listen to; **hito no sétsu o ireru** to take advice; **ocha o ireru** to make tea.

irezumi tattoo.

iri attendance, audience; contents; **ooiri** full house.

iribitáru to be a constant guest; to stay all the time.

irie inlet; creek.

IRIGUCHI entrance; door.

irihi twilight; sunset.

irikómu to enter; to force an entrance.

irikúmu to be complicated.

irimidaréru to be mixed up; to be in confusion.

iritsukéru to parch; to sizzle.

IRÓ color, tint, hue; lover (*colloq.*); **iro age** (*n.*) redying; restoring a color; **iro ótoko** lover; **iro onna** mistress; **iroke** coloring; shade; tone; sexual passion; tender passion; **irozuri** color print; **iroke no áru** seductive; amorous; **iroke no nái** unromantic; innocent; **kaoiro** complexion (facial); **iro age suru** to redye; **iró o nasu** to turn red with anger; **irodóru** to color; to paint.

iróha 47-syllable poem containing all of the 47 syllables in the traditional table of Japanese syllabaries. **Iróha mo shiranai.** He doesn't know even the simplest things (not even the ABC's).

IROIRO NA various; many; diverse; (all) kinds of. **Iroiro shitsumon sareta.** I was asked several questions.

iroméku to be alive; to be stirred; to show signs of uneasiness; to become animated.

irori hearth; fireplace.

irótsuya gloss; luster; complexion; **irótsuya no yói** ruddy; healthy.

irozúku to color; to be tinged; to turn red (as foliage).

IRU to require, want, need. **Watakushi wa kore ga irimásu.** I need this. **Soko e háiru ní wa okane ga irimásu.** You have

to pay [money] to enter. **Sore wa iranai deshóo.** It would not be necessary.

IRU to be at, exist; to be present; to live; to stay. Following a *–te* form verb, it makes a progressive or stative form (describing a state resulting from an action that has taken place). **Sonó hito wa heyá ni imásu.** He is in the room. **Áme ga fútte imásu.** It is raining. **Yamada-san wa kité imásu.** Yamada is here (as a result of having come). **Tookyoo ni imásu.** He is in Tokyo. **Kyóoto ni mikka imáshita.** I was in Kyoto for three days. **Nihongo o benkyoo shite imásu.** I'm studying Japanese. **Tegami ga kité imásu.** There is [has come and is here] a letter for you.

íru to toast; to parch.

írui clothes, garments.

iryoo medical treatment.

iryúuhin lost article; (thing) left behind.

isagiyói clean; pure; upright; brave; manly.

ísai particulars, details.

isakai quarrel.

isamashíi courageous, brave.

isamé admonition; advice, counsel.

isámu to be encouraged; to be in high spirits; to take heart.

isan legacy, inheritance; **isan soozokunin** heir, heiress.

isásaka little; bit; slightly; rather. **Isásaka odorokimáshita.** I was a bit surprised.

iseebi lobster.

isei other (opposite) sex. **Ano hito wa isei no aida ni koosai ga hiroi desu.** He has a large acquaintance among the opposite sex.

isei power, influence.

iséisha statesman.

iseki ruins, remains, relics.

isetsu different view(s); conflicting opinion.

ISHA doctor, physician; M.D. **isha ni kakáru** to go to a doctor; **isha ni míte morau** to consult a doctor. **Isha ni kakáru to nakanaka kane ga irimásu.** Medical expenses are very high.

ísha comfort, consolation; **isháryoo** consolation money.

íshi stone; rock; **ishi dóoroo** stone lantern (in front of a shrine); **ishidan** stone steps; **ishigaki** stone wall; **ishiya** stonecutter.

ishí will, intention; **íshi ga tsuyói** to have a strong will; **íshi ga sotsuu suru** to come to an understanding.

íshiki consciousness; **ishikiteki ni** consciously; **íshiki suru** to be conscious of.

íshin restoration; renovation.

íshin denshin tacit understanding; telepathy.

ishiwata asbestos.

ishizue foundation; basis; groundwork.

isho will, testament.

íshoku food and clothing; means of support; **ishokújuu** food, clothes, and shelter.

ishoku commission; request; charge.

ishoo design; idea.

íshoo clothes, dress, garments.

isobe beach, shore.

isogaséru to hurry up, urge on.

ISOGASHÍI busy, occupied, engaged. **Shikén de taihen isogashíi desu.** I am very busy with my exams.

ISOGI hurry, haste; **isogi no** hasty; urgent, pressing.

ISÓGU to hurry, hasten; to be in a hurry. **Isógu hitsuyoo wa arimasén.** There is no rush.

ísoiso to cheerfully; lightheartedly.

isooróo hanger-on.

íssai all; altogether, every; wholly.

issakúban evening before last.

issakújitsu day before yesterday.

issakunen year before last.

issakúya night before last.

issei ni simultaneously; all at once.

íssha sénri rush; **íssha sénri ni** in a rush; in a hurry; at full speed.

isshiki complete set (of).

isshinfuran whole mind; single heart; **isshinfuran ni** wholeheartedly; intently; with undivided attention.

ISSHO together; at the same time; all at once; **ISSHO NI** together with; simultaneously. **Issho ni ikimashóo.** Let's go together.

isshoo laugh; smile; **isshoo shite** with a laugh; with a smile; **isshoo ni fúsu** to dismiss with a laugh; to laugh one's troubles away.

isshoo lifetime, all through one's life; **isshoo ho nozomi** life-long desire.

ISSHOOKÉNMEI as hard as one can; with all one's might (efforts); with one's whole heart. **Isshookénmei benkyoo shite imásu.** He is studying hard.

ísshu kind, type, variety.

isshuu one round, lap; **isshuu suru** to go round; to make a tour; **sékai isshuu ryókoo** round-the-world trip.

ISSHÚUKAN one week.

isso rather; sooner; preferably.

issoku pair (of shoes or other footgear).

ISSOO much more; all the more.

ISSÚN one *sun* (Japanese unit of length, one tenth of a *shaku*); **issun saki mo miénai** pitch dark.

issúru to miss; to lose; **kóoki o issúru** to miss a good opportunity.

ISU chair; sofa; couch; **isu ni kakéru** to take a seat.

Isuraeru Israel.

isuwáru to remain in the same position (in office); to remain in power.

íta board; plank; plate; sheet; **itábei** wooden wall; board fence.

itabásami fix; predicament; **itabásami ni náru** to be in a fix.

itachi weasel.

ITADAKU to receive; to be presented with; to be given; to accept with gratitude (*humble*). **Juubun itadakimáshita.** I've had enough, thank you.

itade hard blow; severe wound.

itagane sheet metal.

itagárasu plate glass.

ITÁI painful; sore. **Atamá ga itái desu.** I have a headache. **Onaka ga itái desu.** I have a stomachache.

itaitashíi pathetic, sad, pitiful.

itamashíi miserable; touching, sad, pathetic.

itaméru to hurt, injure; to worry; **kokoró o itaméru** to be worried about (something).

itami íru to be greatly obliged; to feel grateful. **Dóomo itamiirimásu.** I'm much obliged to you.

itámu to ache, feel a pain.

ITÁRI = ITARIYA Italy.

itáru to arrive, reach; to result in; to come to; **itáru tokoro** everywhere; throughout; **háru kara áki ni itáru máde** from spring to autumn.

ítasa pain.

itashikata nái it can't be helped; **itashikata náku** necessarily; of necessity.

ITÁSU to do, make (*humble*). **Soo itashimashóo.** Let's do so. **Dóo itashimáshite.** Don't mention it.

itátte exceedingly, extremely, very.

itawáru to pity, sympathize with, console.

itazura mischief; prank; **itazura hánbun** for fun; **itazura na** naughty; mischievous; **itazura ni** needlessly; to no purpose.

itchaku first (in a race); one suit of clothes.

itchi agreement; harmony; **itchi suru** to agree with; harmonize.

itchoo once; one day (*literary usage*); **itchoo isseki ni** in a single day; in a short space of time.

itchókusen straight line; **ítchókusen ni** in a straight line.

iten transfer, removal; **iten suru** to transfer; to move. **Inaka kara machí e iten shimashita.** We moved from the country to the city.

ÍTO thread; yarn; twine; string; **momen íto** cotton thread; **kinu ito** silk thread.

itóguchi clue; beginning; **itóguchi o hiráku** to make a start.

itogúruma spinning wheel.

ITÓKO cousin.

itomá leisure; time to spare; leave of absence; **yasúmu itomá mo nái** to have no time to rest.

itomaki spool, bobbin, reel.

itonámu to carry on; to conduct (business); to run, operate; **seikei o itonámu** to earn a living.

itóosu to shoot through; to pierce.

ÍTSU when; at what time; how soon; **ítsu demo** at any time; at a moment's notice; **ítsu kara** how long; since when; **ítsu made** how long; till when; **ítsu ka** some day; **ítsu mo** always.

ítsu ni solely, entirely.

itsukushimi love; affection; compassion (*literary usage*); **itsukushímu** to love; to treat with tenderness.

ITSÚTSU five.

itsuwa anecdote.

itsuwari lie; **itsuwari no** false, untrue.

itsuwáru to lie, tell a lie.

ittai zentai on earth; in the world. **Ittai zéntai dáre daroo.** I wonder who in the world it can be.

ittán part; outline; one end.

ittan once, if. **Ittan kankyuu áreba . . .** Should an emergency arise . . .

itte hánbai sole agency; monopoly; **itte hanbainin** sole agent; sole distributor.

ittei no fixed, immovable, set; definite; regular.

ittén point; dot; spot.

ittenbari persistency; **ittenbari de** sticking to; solely by.

ITTÓO first class; **ittóo ni noru** to travel first class; **ittoo no kippu** first-class ticket; **nitóo sha** second-class car. **Ittoo fi monó desu.** It is the best.

itsuu one letter.

IU = YUU to say, speak, tell, relate, mention; **ookíku iu** to exaggerate; **iu máde mo náku** of course, naturally. **Iu máde mo nái.** It goes without saying.

iwá rock; **iwa no óoi** rocky.

íwaba in a word; so-to-speak.

iwai celebration; feast; festival.

iwakú reason; **iwakú ga átte** for certain reasons; **iwakú o tsukéru** to find fault with.

iware reason, cause; origin; **iware mo náku** without any cause; **iware no nái** unreasonable; unwarranted.

iwashi sardine.

iwáu to congratulate; to celebrate.

IWAYÚRU so-called; what you call. **Káre wa iwayúru jiyuu shugísha desu.** He is a so-called liberal.

iyá na disagreeable, unpleasant; **iyá na kao o suru** to frown.

iyagáru to dislike, to hate.

iyamí offensiveness, bad taste, sarcasm; **iyami no aru** offensive, disagreeable.

iyashímu to despise, to look down on, to scorn.

ÍYA, IIE no.

iyahóon earphone.

iya iya reluctantly; **iya iya nágara** unwillingly; with reluctance.

íyaku medicine; physic.

iyashíi low; humble; vulgar.

iyáshikumo at all; in the least.

iyóiyo still more; all the more; certainly; positively; no doubt.

íza come now; now then; **íza to náreba** at the last moment; when the time comes; at a pinch. **Íza saraba.** Farewell (*archaic*).

izakaya tavern, saloon, bar.

ízen ago; before; prior to; formerly. **Tooka ízen ni kité kudasái.** Please come before the tenth.

izen as before; as it was.

izon objection; **izon nái** to have no objection; **izon ga áru** to have an objection.

izumi spring; fountain.

IZURE which; someday; sometime; sooner or later; **izure mo** any; all; either; every; both; **izure ni shité mo** in either case; **izure sono uchi ni** one of these days.

J

JA, JÁA well; then; in that case. **Ja, sayonara.** Well, so long.

jaanarísuto journalist.

JAGAIMO potato.

jaguchi faucet, tap; spout.

jáken meanness, unkindness; **jáken na** cruel, unkind.

jáketsu sweater.

jakkan some; little; number of.

–jáku suffix denoting: little less than, little short of. **Yokohama máde wa nijuu máirujaku desu.** It is a little less than twenty miles to Yokohama.

JAMA obstruction, obstacle, hindrance; **jama suru** to obstruct, hinder; **jama ni náru** to stand (be) in the way; **jama o nozoku** to remove an obstacle. **Objama shimáshita.** Excuse me for disturbing you. **Ojama dé wa arimasén ka.** I hope I'm not disturbing you.

jámu jam, jelly.

janen vicious mind; evil thought.

ján jan jingle jingle; dingdong; profusely; a lot (slang).

janken Japanese equivalent of toss-up. **Janken de kimemashóo.** Let's toss for it.

jaratsuku to flirt with.

jaréru to be playful.

jari gravel; pebbles.

jasui distrust; groundless suspicion; **jasui suru** to distrust; suspect without reason. **jasui bukái** suspicious, distrustful.

jázu jazz.

ji piles, hemorrhoids.

JÍ character, letter, ideograph; **jí o káku** to write. **jí o oboéru** to learn how to read and write (characters); **kanji** Chinese characters (used in Japanese writing system).

jí ground, earth, soil; **jimoto** local.

ji– prefix denoting: next; second; vice-; **jikai** next session.

–JI counter denoting: o'clock; hour; time; **ichíji** one o'clock. **Ichíji wa soo omoimashita.** Once I thought that way but now I have a different opinion.

jiban base, foundation.

jibara o kíru to pay out of one's own pocket.

JIBIKÍ dictionary; lexicon; **jibikí o hiku** to look something up in the dictionary; to use a dictionary.

jiboojíki desperation; despair; **jiboojíki ni náru** to become desperate.

JIBUN oneself; **jibun no** my own, your own, mine; personal; **jibun hitóri de** by oneself; **jibun to shite wa** for my part.

jíbyoo chronic disease.

jíchi self-government.

jichoo self-respect; self-love; caution; **jichóoshin** self-respect. **Jichoo shite kudasái.** Take good care of yourself.

jidai time, period, epoch, era; **jidai sákugo** anachronism; **jidaimono** old-fashioned article (furniture, etc.); historical drama; **jidaiókure** one who is old-fashioned; **jidaiókure no** old-fashioned, antiquated.

jídan private settlement; compromise.

jidaraku sloppiness, untidiness; **jidaraku na** sloppy, untidy.

jiden autobiography.

jídoo child; boys and girls; **jídoo no** juvenile.

jidoo automatic action; **jidoo no** automatic; **jidoo hanbáiki** slot machine; **jidoo tóbira** automatic door.

JIDÓOSHA automobile, car; **jidóosha ni noru** to ride in a car.

jiei self-defense.

jifúshin pride; self-confidence.

jigane metal, ore; true character.

jigoku hell.

jígyoo enterprise, undertaking; achievement; dee; work; **jigyóokai** the business (industrial) world.

jihaku confession; **jihaku suru** to confess.

jihatsuteki voluntary; spontaneous; **jihatsuteki ni** voluntarily.

jíhen emergency; disaster; incident.

jihi mercy; benevolence; pity; **jihi bukái** benevolent; charitable.

jihitsu handwriting; autograph.

jihoo time signal; current news.

jíi intention to resign.

jíin Buddhist temple.

jíji current events.

jijíi (collo.) grandfather; old man (derogatory).

jíjitsu fact; truth; **jijitsujóo** practically, virtually; in reality, actually.

jíjitsu time; date.

jijoo circumstances; reasons; state of affairs; **koo iu jijoo dá kara** under these circumstances.

jíka current price.

jikaku self-consciousness; **jikaku suru** to be conscious, aware of; to realize.

JIKAN time; hour; **jikan ni ma ni áu** to be on time; **jikan ni ma ni awánai** to be late. **Máda daibu jikan ga áru.** There is still plenty of time.

jikanhyoo timetable; schedule.

jíkani personally; at firsthand; directly.

jikatsu suru to support oneself.

jíken affair; matter; scandal.

jiketsu self-determination; resignation; suicide.

JÍKI time; period; season.

jiki– prefix denoting: direct; **jikideshi** one's immediate apprentice.

JIKI NI immediately; at once; presently.

jikken experiment; test.

jikkoo practice; action; execution; **jikkoo suru** to carry out; to put into practice; **jikkoo shigatái** impractical; difficult to put into practice.

jiko self; ego; **jiko chúushin no** egocentric.

jíko accident, incident; **kootsuu jiko** traffic accident.

jíkoku time; hour; **jikokuhyoo** transportation schedule.

JIKOO season; weather; current fashion; latest style, vogue; **jíkoo házure no** unseasonable.

jíku phraseology; expressions; wording.

jikú axis; axle; pivot; shaft; stem; stalk.

jíkyoku situation, state of affairs; political situation.

jikyuu self-support; independence.

jiman pride, boast; **jiman suru** to boast; to be conceited.

jíme jime shita damp; wet; moist; humid.

jímen ground; surface of the earth; plot of land; **jímen o kau** to buy a lot of land.

jimí na simple; modest; unpretentious; **jimí na hito** unpretentious person; quiet person.

jímu business; duties; **jimúin** clerk; office worker; **jimúsho** office; **jimúchoo** chief clerk; head official; purser (of a ship).

JIN suffix denoting: people; **Nihonjín** Japanese; **Amerikájin** American.

jínan second son.

jinboo popularity; **jinboo áru hito** idol (of the people).

jínbutsu person; personality; portrait.

jinchóoge sweet-smelling daphne (common garden plant in Japan).

jindai na extraordinary; enormous, huge, great. **Songai wa jindai na monó deshita.** The damage was very great.

jindoo sidewalk, pavement; **jindoo o arúku** to walk on the pavement.

jindoo humanity; morality.

jingúu Shinto shrine (a national monument).

jínja Shinto shrine.

jínji fusei unconsciousness; **jínji fusei ni náru** to faint; **jínji fusei no** unconscious.

jinjoo commonness; **jinjoo no** common, ordinary; **jinjoo ni** commonly.

jinkaku personality; character.

jinken artificial silk; rayon.

jinken juurin infringement of personal rights.

JINKOO population; **jinkoo chuumitsu na** thickly populated.

jinkoo artificiality; **jinkoo no** artificial; **jinkoo kókyuu** artificial respiration.

jinmei the name of a person; **jinmeibo** list of names of persons; directory; **jinmeijísho** biographical dictionary.

jinmín people; public.

jinmon inquiry; examination.

jinrin moral law; human relations.

jínrui human race.

jinryoku human power, human strength; effort, endeavor; help **jinryoku suru** to make an effort; to work on someone's behalf.

jínsei human existence; life.

jinshu (human) race; **jinshuteki henken** racial prejudice.

jinsoku swiftness, rapidity; **jinsoku na** swift, rapid, quick.

jíntai human body.

jinushi landlord.

jinzoo artificial, synthetic; **jinzoo gómu** synthetic rubber.

jínzoo kidney.

jíppa hitókarage ni in a wholesale way; sweepingly.

jippi actual expenses; cost of production; **jippi de** at cost.

jippu one's natural father.

jirásu to provoke, irritate; to tease.

jirei government order; written order; manner of speaking.

jirénma dilemma.

jiréru to be irritated; to fret and fume; to become impatient.

jirettái irritating, provoking; irritated.

JÍRIJIRI slowly; gradually, little by little. **Jirijiri tsume yosemashita.** He edged up to me.

jiriki de by oneself.

jiritsu independence; self-support; **jiritsu suru** to stand on one's own feet.

jíro jiro míru to stare at.

jiron personal opinion; pet theory.

jirorí to with a glance; **jirorí to míru** to glance at.

jiryoku magnetism.

jisan (n.) bringing; carrying; **jisan suru** to bring; to carry along.

jisatsu suicide (the act); **jisatsúsha** suicide (person).

jisei times; mood of the times; **jisei ni okureru** to fall behind the times.

jisei self-control; **jisei suru** to control oneself.

jísetsu season; times; age; **jísetsu házure no** out of season; **jísetsu toorai** the time has come.

jíshaku magnet; compass.

JISHIN earthquake. **Nihón wa jishin ga óoi.** Earthquakes occur frequently in Japan.

jísho land, plot of ground, estate.

JÍSHO dictionary.

jishoku resignation.

jison self-respect; pride; **jisón shin o kizutsukéru** to hurt one's pride.

jishoo self-styled, would-be; **jishoo shíjin.** A would-be poet.

jíssai truth; reality; **jissai wa** in reality; in fact; **jissai no** actual; practical.

jisshi one's natural child.

jisshín hoo decimal system.

jisshitsu substance, essence.

jisúberi landslide.

jisui suru to cook one's meals.

jisúru to decline; to refuse; to resign.

jítai situation; state of affairs.

jitaku house, residence; **jitaku e káeru** to go home.

jiten, jísho dictionary.

JITÉNSHA bicycle; **jiténsha ni noru** to ride a bicycle.

JITSÚ truth; reality; **JITSÚ NI** really; truly;

very, exceedingly; in fact; surely; exceedingly; **jitsú no** true; real; **jitsú wa** in reality; to tell the truth.

jítsubo one's natural mother.

jitsubutsu real thing; actual object; **jitsubutsú dai no** life-size.

jitsugen realization; **jitsugen suru** to realize; to materialize.

jitsugyoo business, industry; **jitsugyoo no** commercial, industrial; **jitsugyóokai** business world.

jitsujoo actual condition; true state of affairs. **Jitsujoo wa kóo desu.** The fact is this.

jitsuyoo utility; practical use; **jitsuyoo ni tekisúru** to be of practical use. **jitsuyoo muki no** serviceable; practical; **jitsuyóohin** necessity; article having practical use.

jitsúzuki adjoining land.

jitto fixedly; firmly; steadily; **jitto mitsuméru** to stare at, look fixedly at; **jitto shite iru** to keep still.

jiyoo nourishment; **jiyó butsu** nourishing food; **jiyoo áru** nourishing, nutritious.

jiyúu liberty, freedom; **jiyuu booeki** free trade; **jiyuu kyóosoo** open (free) competition; **jiyúu na** free; **jiyúu ni suru** to do as one pleases. **Gojiyuu ni.** Help yourself.

jizen philanthropic work; **jizen ka** philanthropist; **jizen jígyoo** philanthropic work.

jobun preface, foreword, introduction.

jochoo promotion; advancement; **jochoo suru** to promote, foster, encourage.

jodóoshi auxiliary verb; inflected particle, i.e., –(r)areru (passive) and –(s)aseru (causative).

jogai exception; **jogai suru** to make an exception of; to exclude; to exempt from.

jogen advice, counsel; suggestion; hint; **jogen suru** to give advice; to suggest.

jóí female doctor.

jójo ni slowly; gradually.

jojóoshi lyrical poem, ballad.

jojutsu description; **jojutsu no** descriptive; **jojutsu suru** to describe; to narrate; **jojutsúbun** description.

jokoo slow pace; **jokoo suru** to go slowly. **Jokoo.** Go slow. Drive slowly.

joo feeling, emotion, sentiment; affection, love; sympathy; **joo ga fukái** affectionate; warmhearted; **joo ga nái** cold, heartless; **joo ni moroi** emotional, sentimental.

joo lock; **joo o kakéru** to lock; **joo o hazasu** to unlock.

–**jóo** article; **Dái Kyúujoo** Article IX.

–**joo** floor mat (Japanese rooms are measured by the number of **joo** mats they contain);

juujoo no ma 10-mat room.

–**joo** suffix denoting: letter; **shookáijoo** letter of introduction; **annáijoo** (letter of) invitation; **shookánjoo** warrant.

jooai affection, love; **jooai no fukái** loving, affectionate.

jooba horseback riding.

jóobu top, upper part, upper surface.

JOOBU good health; soundness of body; **joobu na** durable; robust, strong; **joobu soo na** strong-looking, healthy-looking; **joobu ni náru** to grow strong.

jóocho mood; atmosphere.

joodán joke, prank; fun; **joodán o iu** to joke; **joodán ní suru** to take as a joke.

joodeki good performance; success; good work; **joodeki no** well-done; excellent. **Joodeki!** Well done! Bravo!

jooen suru to put on, perform (a play); to put on the stage.

jóoge top and bottom, upper and lower.

jóogi ruler; square; standard; norm.

jóogo drinker, sake-lover.

jóogo funnel.

joohatsu evaporation; **joohatsu suru** to evaporate.

joohín elegance; refinement; **joohín na** refined; elegant; graceful.

jóoho concession, compromise.

joohoo report; information.

joojiru = **joozuru** to multiply; to take advantage of.

joojitsu personal feelings (considerations).

jóoju accomplishment, achievement; **jóoju suru** to achieve, realize, accomplish.

JOOJUN first ten days of the month; **Ichigatsu joojun** early in January.

jooken condition, term; **jooken zuki** conditional; qualified.

jóoki regular (normal) course; **jóoki o issúru** to deviate, depart from the normal course.

jóoki steam, vapor; **jooki kikán** steam engine.

jookígen good humor; **jookígen de** in a good humor.

jookyaku passenger.

jookyoo state of affairs; conditions.

joomae lock.

joomúin crew.

jóomu torishimari managing director.

joomyaku vein.

joonetsu passion.

jóoo queen.

jooriku suru to disembark, go ashore; **jooriku chitén** point of embarkation.

jóoro watering can.

jooruri Japanese ballad-drama.

jooryokúju evergreen (tree or shrub).

joosei state of affairs; **génka no joosei dé wa** under the present circumstances.

joosha (*n.*) taking a train, bus, etc.; **joosha suru** to take a train; to board a train; **joosháchin** carfare, train fare; **joosháken** ticket (for a train, streetcar, or bus).

jooshiki common sense; **jooshiki o kaku** to lack common sense; **jooshikiteki na** sensible; practical.

jooshúbi success; happy result; **jooshúbi no** successful. **Jooshúbi da.** It's all right.

joosoo upper layer; upper stories (of a building); (top) social class.

jootai condition, state; circumstances; **mókka no jootai dé wa** as matters now stand.

jootatsu suru to improve; advance; progress.

jooténki fine (splendid) weather.

JOOTOO (*n.*) best; first class; **jootóo hin** first-class article; **jootoo no** (*adj.*) best, superior.

jootoogo hackneyed expression, trite saying.

jooyaku treaty, pact, agreement.

jóoyoku lust.

jooyoo kánji ideographic characters included in the Japanese Government's 1945 list of basic symbols for writing.

joozai tablet (medicinal).

JOOZÚ skill, dexterity, proficiency; **JOOZÚ NA** skillful, expert, proficient. **Joozú desu.** He is skillful. **Anó hito wa hanashí ga joozú desu.** She is a good speaker.

joozúru See **joojiru.**

jóryoku aid, assistance; **jóryoku suru** to aid, help.

joryuu sákka female author.

josainái shrewd, clever, smart.

josánpu midwife.

josei womanhood, femininity; **joseiteki** feminine.

josei aid, assistance; **josei suru** to aid, to assist (financially); to subsidize; **joséikin** subsidy.

joshi particle (grammar) e.g., **wa, ga, o,** etc. (used in postposition).

jóshi woman; girl; daughter; female.

JÓYA New Year's Eve.

joyaku assistant official.

joyuu actress.

júgaku = **júkyoo** Confucianism.

JÚGYOO teaching, instruction; **júgyoo o suru** to teach; **júgyoo o ukéru** to take lessons.

jukkoo reflection; careful consideration; **jukkoo suru** to consider carefully; to reflect; to deliberate. **Sono mondai wa jukkoo chuu desu.** That matter is receiving careful consideration.

júkuchi suru to have full knowledge of; to be familiar with. **Watakushi was sono**

kotó o júkuchi shite imásu. I'm fully aware of that.

jukuren skill, dexterity; **jukuren suru** to become skilled; **jukuren o kaku** to lack skill.

jukusui suru to sleep soundly.

juku súru to ripen, mature, become ripe.

júkyoo See **júgaku.**

júmoku trees. **Sono kooen ni wa jumoku ga óoi desu.** There are many trees in that park.

jumyoo life; life span.

jún pureness, purity; **jún na** pure; genuine; innocent; **junkin** pure gold.

jun, junban regular order; turn; **jun ni, junban ni** in regular order; in turn; **jun ni naraberu** to arrange in order. **Junban o mátte kudasai.** Please wait your turn.

júnbi preparation, arrangements; **júnbi suru** to prepare, arrange; to get ready for; **júnbi ga dékite iru** to be prepared.

junchoo favorable, satisfactory condition; **junchoo ni** smoothly; favorably, without a hitch; **junchoo ni iku** to go well; **junchoo ni mukau** to improve.

jun'eki net profit; **jun'eki o éru** to earn a net profit, to clear.

júnjo order, sequence; **júnjo tadáshiku** in good order.

junkan suru to circulate; recur.

junkésshoo semifinals.

junketsu purity; cleanliness; **junketsu na** pure, chaste; clean.

junrei pilgrim; pilgrimage.

júnsa policeman; **junsa hashutsujo** police box; **junsa búchoo** police sergeant. **Keisatsusho de júnsa ni hanashimáshita.** I told it to a policeman at the police station.

junshi inspection tour; **junshi suru** to make the rounds.

junshin pureness; genuineness; **junshin na** pure; unsophisticated.

junsui purity, genuineness. **Kore wa junsui no Nihon no kínu desu.** This is genuine Japanese silk.

juntoo natural; regular; appropriate; normal. **Juntoo ni ikéba tooka ni dekimásu.** If all goes well, it will be done on the tenth.

jushin suru to receive a letter or message.

jutai suru to conceive, become pregnant.

jutsu art; technique; means; way; trick.

JÚU ten, tenth; **júu ga júu made** in every case.

–JUU suffix denoting: all through the course of; during; all over; throughout. **Tookyoojuu** throughout Tokyo. **Uchijuu de dekakemásu.** The entire family goes out together.

juubako pile (nest) of lacquered boxes used as picnic boxes or as containers for foods at festivals.

juban undergarment worn with Japanese clothing.

JUUBÚN plenty; enough; **juubún na** full; sufficient; enough; **juubún ni tabéru** to eat enough.

juubyoo serious illness.

juudai importance; seriousness; **juudai na** important; **juudaishi suru** to take seriously.

JUUGATSU October.

JÚUGO fifteen; **juugoya no tsukí** harvest moon.

JUUHACHÍ eighteen; **juuhachíban** one's forte; hobby; favorite trick.

JUUICHÍ eleven.

JUUICHIGATSU November.

júuji (n.) cross; **júuji ni** crosswise; **júuji no** cross-shaped; **juujígun** crusade.

juujika (See also **júuji.**) **juujiká zoo** crucifix.

júuji suru to engage in, practice, pursue.

juujitsu perfection; enrichment; fullness.

juujun gentleness; obedience; **juujun na** gentle, meek; obedient.

juuketsu congestion (medical). **Mé ga juuketsu shite imásu.** His eyes are bloodshot.

JÚUKU nineteen; **dái juuku** nineteenth.

júukyo dwelling, residence; **juukyonin** resident.

juuman suru to be filled with; to be replete with.

juumin residents, inhabitants.

juumonji cross; **juumonji ni** crosswise. (See also **júuji.**)

júunen decade.

JUUNÍ twelve, dozen; **juunibun ni** more than enough.

JUUNIGATSU December.

júunin ten persons; **juunin nami no** ordinary, average, normal; mediocre.

júurai heretofore; so far; up to now; **júurai no** old, traditional; **júurai no tóori** as in the past.

júurui beast, animals.

juuryóo weight; **juuryoo búsoku** short weight.

juuryoo hunting (with a gun); **juuryooka** sportsman.

JUUSHÍ fourteen.

JUUSHICHÍ seventeen.

juushímatsu lovebird.

juushoku high office; responsible position.

JÚUSHO dwelling, residence; address; **júusho séimei** name and address.

Gojúusho wa dochira desu ka? What's your address?

juushoo serious wound, injury.

juusoo bicarbonate of soda.

JÚUSU juice; **orenji júusu** orange juice.

juutai critical stage; serious condition.

juutaku house, residence; **juutákuchi** residential section.

juuyaku director; board of directors.

juuyoo importance; **juuyoo na** important; **juuyoo de nái** unimportant.

juuzai felony; capital offense.

juuzei heavy taxation; heavy tax.

juwáki telephone receiver.

júyo suru to award (a prize); to confer (a degree).

juyoo demand; **juyoo ga áru** to be in demand; **juyoo o mításu** to meet the demand.

juzu rosary (mainly Buddhist).

K

kabu turnip.

kabu stock, share; **kabúnushi** shareholder.

kabuki classic Japanese play.

kabun superfluous; **kabun no** excessive; undue.

kabureru to be poisoned; to be influenced.

KABÚRU to put on or over one's head; to be covered with; to take upon oneself; **booshi o kabúru** to put on a hat.

kabusáru to get covered; to overlap.

kabuséru to cover with; to put a thing on.

kábuto helmet; **kábuto o núgu** to admit defeat; to throw in the sponge; **kabutó mushi** beetle.

kachí victory, conquest; success.

káchi value, worth, merit; **káchi aru** valuable.

kachiáu to clash with; to knock against; to collide with.

kachikí na unyielding; strong-minded; resolute.

kachiku domestic animals; livestock.

kadai (n.) being too big; **kadai no** too big; exaggerated; too much; too heavy.

kadai subject; theme.

kádan garden; flower bed.

KÁDO corner; turn; angle; edge; **kádo no misé** corner store. **Soo iu to kádo ga tátsu.** That sounds harsh.

kádo excess, immoderateness.

kádo charge; suspicion; grounded; **–no kádo de** on the grounds of, on account of, for the reason that.

kadode departure; **kadode suru** to set out; to leave home.

kadowakásu to kidnap.

kaede maple tree.

kaerigake ni on the way back; upon one's return.

kaerí michi return road; way home.

kaerimíru to look back; to reflect upon; to think of.

KÁERU to return, come back; to go back. **Okaeri nasái.** Welcome back!

káeru to be hatched.

KAERU to change, alter; to exchange; to replace; to convert; **sétsu o kaeru** to change one's opinion; **michi o kaeru** to take another road; **kane o kaeru** to change money.

kaeru frog.

KÁESU to give back, restore, return; to pay back; **okane o káesu** to repay money.

káesu to hatch (eggs).

KÁETTE on the contrary; instead; on the other hand; all the more.

káfuu family customs (tradition).

kafun pollen.

káfusu cuff(s).

kagáisha assailant.

kágaku science; **kágaku no** scientific; **kagákusha** scientist.

kágaku chemistry; **kagákusha** chemist; **kagaku kóogyoo** chemical industry.

kagameru to bend; to bow; **koshi o kagameru** to stoop, bend down.

kagamu to bend, bow; to crouch.

KAGAMÍ mirror; **kagamí o míru** to look in a mirror.

kagaríbi campfire; bonfire.

kagashi scarecrow.

kagayakasu to light up; to make shine; to brighten.

kagayaki luster; brilliance; glitter.

kagayaku to shine, glitter, sparkle, glisten.

káge shadow; silhouette; image; reflection, shade; **káge ni náru** to be shaded; **káge ni** in the shade; **káge ga sásu** to cast a shadow.

kagéguchi malicious gossip; **kagéguchi o iu** to gossip maliciously.

kágehinata two-faced; faithless; **kágehinata no nái** faithful; conscientious.

kúgeki opera; operetta; **kageki dan** opera company; **kagekijoo** opera house.

kageki excessive; extreme; violent; radical; **kagekiha** radicals (political); **kageki shisoo** radical ideas; dangerous thoughts. **Kageki na undoo o shité wa ikemasén.** You must not engage in strenuous physical exercise.

kagemúsha man who pulls strings or exerts influence behind the scenes.

kagen degree, proportion, extent.

kagéroo fly living only one day; **kagéroo no yóo na** short-lived, ephemeral.

kagéru to become shady; to get dark; to darken.

–KÁGETSU counter denoting: (one) month's duration; **ikkágetsu** one month; **nikágetsu** two months; **sankágetsu** three months.

KAGÍ key; **kagi ana** keyhole; **kagí de akeru** to unlock; **kagí o kakéru** to lock.

kagí hook.

kagirí limit, bounds; **kagiri no áru** limited, restricted. **Watakushi no shiru kágiri.** As far as I know.

kagíru to limit, restrict.

kago basket; cage; sedan chair; **kago ni noru** to ride in a sedan chair.

kagoo suru to combine.

KÁGU furniture, furnishings; **kagúya** furniture store.

kagu to smell; to scent; to sniff; **kagitsukéru** to get wind of.

kágura sacred music and dancing in front of a shrine (Shinto).

káhei money; currency.

káhi right or wrong; good or bad; propriety. **Sono káhi wa toohyoo de kimemashóo.** Let's decide the matter by vote.

kahoo ancestral treasure; heirloom.

káhoo luck; good fortune; **káhoo na** lucky.

kai avail, effect, use; **kai ga nai** of no effect; **kai náku** without avail; **kai no nái** useless; fruitless.

kái meeting, assembly; association; society; (society) member; **kai hi** membership fee; subscription; admission fee.

kái time, cycle; **nikái** two times, twice.

kái oar, paddle; **kái de kógu** to row.

kái shellfish.

–kai suffix denoting: stairs; story (of a building); **ikkái** first floor; **nikai-date** two-story house.

–kai suffix denoting: sea, **Nihónkai** Japan Sea.

kaiagéru to purchase, buy; to requisition.

kaibatsu above sea level.

kaiboo autopsy; dissection; analysis.

kaibutsu monster.

kaichiku rebuilding, reconstruction.

kaichuu pocket; **kaichuu mono** purse; **kaichuudókei** pocket watch.

kaidaku willing consent; **kaidaku suru** to give ready consent; to consent readily.

KAIDAN stairway, staircase; flight of steps. **Heyá wa kaidan o agatte hidari no hóo desu.** My room is to the left of the stairway.

kaidashi marketing, shopping; daily needs.

kaidásu to drain off; to ladle; to scoop out.

kaifuku recovery; restoration; re-establishment; **kaifuku suru** to recover; restore.

kaifuu suru to open a letter; break a seal.

káiga pictures; painting(s); **kaiga chinrétsukan** art gallery; **kaiga tenránkai** art exhibition.

káigai (*n.*) abroad; foreign country; **káigai kara** from abroad; **káigai ni iku** to go abroad.

kaigaishíi prompt; brisk; faithful; **kaigáishiku** promptly; briskly; willingly.

kaigan seashore, coast; **kaigansen** coast line.

káigi council; conference; convention.

kaigoo meeting, assembly.

káigun navy; **káigun no** naval.

kaigyoo suru to open a shop; to open a business.

kaihan revised edition.

kaihatsu suru to develop; to exploit; to cultivate; to open up.

kaihen seashore, seaside, beach.

kaihí suru to avoid, shun, evade.

kaihoo liberation, release; **kaihoo suru** to set free.

kaihoo good news.

kaihoo opening; **kaihoo suru** to open to the public.

káihoo suru to nurse (tend) a sick person.

kaihyoo suru to count votes.

kaiín shiki opening ceremony of the Diet (Japanese Parliament).

kaijin ashes; **kaijin ni kisúru** to be reduced to ashes.

káijo cancellation; release, discharge; **káijo suru** to cancel, rescind, etc.

kaijoo sea; **kaijoo no** marine, maritime.

kaijoo circular (letter); **kaijo o mawasu** to send out a circular.

kaijoo ni upstairs; **kaijoo e iku** to go upstairs.

kaikabúru to pay too much; to overestimate; overrate.

kaikaku reformation; reorganization; **kaikaku suru** to reform; reorganize; innovate.

kaikan hall; assembly hall.

kaikata buyer.

kaikatsu cheerfulness; **kaikatsu na** cheerful, gay; jovial.

kaikei accounts; **kaikéibo** account book; **kaikei gákari** accountant; cashier; **kaikei hóokoku** financial report.

kaiken interview, audience; **kaiken o mooshikómu** to ask for an interview; **kaiken suru** to interview.

kaiketsu settlement; solution; **kaiketsu suru** to settle; to solve; to fix up; **kaiketsu ga**

tsuku to come to a settlement; to arrive at a solution.

káiko retrospection; reflection; review; **káiko suru** to look back; to reflect.

káiko discharge; dismissal; **káiko suru** to discharge, dismiss.

káiko silkworm.

kaikómu to hold (carry) under one's arm.

kaikon development; clearing.

kaikoojoo open port.

kaikyoo strait; sound.

kaikyuu class; rank; order; grade.

kaimen surface of the sea.

kaimetsu destruction, ruin.

kaimodósu to buy back, repurchase.

kaimoku entirely, utterly, altogether (used with a negative). **Kaimoku wakarimasen.** I don't understand it at all.

KAIMONO shopping; marketing; purchase; **kaimono o suru** to buy, shop; **kaimono ni iku** to go shopping.

káimu (*n.*) having nothing; having none at all; nil. **Okane wa káimu desu.** I have no money at all.

káin Lower House of the Diet.

kainarásu to tame, domesticate.

káinushi owner of an animal; keeper; master.

kainushi buyer; purchaser. **Watakushi no ie no kainushi ga mitsukarimáshita.** We found a buyer for our house.

káiri nautical mile.

kairiki superhuman strength.

káiro sea route; **káiro o iku** to go by sea.

káiro circuit.

kairoo corridor; passageway; gallery.

kairyoo improvement; reform; **kairyoo suru** to reform; to improve.

kairyuu tide; tidal current; trend.

kaisaku adaptation.

kaisan dispersion; liquidation; breakup; **kaisan suru** to break up; to dissolve; to liquidate.

kaisánbutsu marine products; **kaisángyoo** marine-products industry (processing and selling fish, lobsters, oysters, clams and edible seaweeds).

kaisatsúguchi ticket gate.

kaisei fine weather; clear sky.

kaisetsu explanation; interpretation; **kaisetsu suru** to explain; to interpret; to comment on.

KAISHA company; corporation; firm; **kaisháin** employee of a business firm; businessperson. **Ano kaisha ni tsutómete imásu.** I am working for that firm.

káishaku interpretation; construction; explanation.

kaishiméru to buy up; to corner (the market).

kaishi suru to begin.

kaishoo dissolution; extinction; cancellation.

kaishuu withdrawal; collection; **kaishuu suru** to withdraw; to call in.

kaisoku regulations, rules of an organization.

kaisoo shipping; forwarding; **kaisoo suru** to forward; to transport; **kaisoogyóosha** shipping agency.

kaisoo seaweed.

kaisoo recollection, reminiscence; **kaisoo suru** to recollect, to reminisce.

kaisui seawater; salt water; **kaisuíyókujoo** seaside resort; beach; **kaisúíyoku o suru** to go bathing in the sea.

kaisúu frequency; **kaisúu o kasaneru** to repeat many times.

kaitai dissection; dismemberment.

kaite buyer, purchaser.

kaiten revolution, rotation; **kaiten suru** to revolve, rotate; **kaiténgi** gyroscope.

kaitoo solution; reply; answer; **kaitoo suru** to solve; to reply, answer.

kaitoo president (of an organization).

kaitsumande to make a long story short; in a word. **Kaitsumande ohanashi shimashóo.** I will tell you briefly.

kaiúngyoo marine shipping. (See also **kaisoo.**)

KAIWA conversation.

káiwai neighborhood; **káiwai ni** in the neighborhood.

kaizoku pirate.

KÁJI fire. **Watakushi wa kyónen káji ni aimáshita.** I experienced a fire last year.

kajikamu to be numb with cold; to be numbed.

kajiritsúku to hold on to; to clutch.

kajíru to gnaw; to nibble; to bite; to get a smattering of.

kájitsu fruit; berry; nut.

kajoo article, item; clause; **kajoo o ageru** to itemize.

kajoo excess, surplus.

kajuu overweight.

kakae embrace; employ.

kakaeru to hold under one's arms, to embrace; to employ, to hire.

kakageru to hold up; to raise, hoist.

KAKAKU price; value; **kakaku o tsukéru** to set a price; to fix the value of.

KÁKARI charge(s); duty; **kakaríin** official in charge.

kakariai implication; involvement; **kakariai ni náru** to be involved in.

KAKÁRU to hang; to stand; to rest (against); to set about; to be dependent on; to concern; to catch; to be caught; to begin, start; to take; to need; **byooki ni kakáru** to become ill; **isha ni kakáru** to

consult a doctor. **Soko e ikú no ni ichijíkan kakárimásu.** It takes an hour to get there. **Íkura kakarimásu ka?** How much does it cost?

kakasazu regularly, consistently; without missing; constantly.

KAKATO heel.

KAKAWÁRAZU in spite of, despite; no matter (how, what); regardless of; **áme ni mo kakawárazu** in spite of the rain.

kakawáru to take part, participate in; to concern; to affect; to be at stake.

kaké betting; **kakegoto** gambling; **kaké o suru** to make a bet, wager.

kakeai negotiation; consultation; **kakeai o suru** to negotiate (with).

kakeáu to negotiate; to bargain with.

kakéashi run; double time; gallop; **kakéashi de** on the double; at a run; **kakéashi ni náru** to break into a run; to gallop.

kakebúton quilt; bed-coverlet.

kakedasu to start running; to run out.

kakegae substitute; spare; **kakegae no nái** irreplaceable (most precious) thing.

kakegóe yell, shout; **kakegóe o kakéru** to yell, shout.

kakehi waterpipe, drainpipe.

kakéhiki bargaining; tactics; tact, diplomacy; **kakéhiki o suru** to bargain (with a person).

kakei lineage, genealogy.

kakékin installment; premium; **kakékin o suru** to pay in installments.

kakékko race; **kakékko o suru** to run a race.

kakemochi part-time job; working at two or more jobs at one time.

kakémono hanging picture-scroll.

kakené overcharge; high price; **kakené o iu** to overcharge.

kakeochi elopement.

KAKÉRU to sit, take a seat; to spend; to invest; to gallop; to run; to hang; to suspend; to cover; to spread on; to put on; to pour on; **isu ni kakéru** to sit on a chair; **kane o kakéru** to spend money; **koshi o kakéru** to sit down; **kugi ni kakéru** to hang (something) on a peg; **mégane o kakéru** to wear glasses. **Kono uchi ni wa okane ga kakátte iru.** He spent a great deal of money on this house.

kakéru run, gallop.

–kakéru to begin to; **yomikakéru** to begin to read.

kakeru to be broken; to be cracked; to be short of.

kaketsu approval; adoption; passage; **kaketsu suru** to pass, be approved.

kakézu map, chart.

káki oyster; **kaki fúrai** fried oysters.

kakiarawásu to put in writing.

kakiatsuméru to collect; to rake together; to gather up.

kakiawaséru to adjust, arrange.

kakiire entry; notes; insertion; **kakiireru** to insert; to write in.

kakikae rewriting; transfer; **kakikaeru** to rewrite; to transfer.

kakimawasu to stir (coffee, etc.); to beat; to rummage; to ransack.

kakimidásu to confuse, throw into confusion; to disturb.

kakímono written document; writing.

kakimushíru to tear; to scratch off.

kakíne hedge.

kakinokéru to push aside.

kakinuki extract; abstract.

kakioki will; posthumous letter.

kakiorósu to write down.

kakiotósu to scrape off.

kakisoeru to add a postscript.

kakitatéru to play up; to write up; to make a big story of.

kakitome = kakitome yuubin registered mail. **Kono tegami o kakitome ni shite kudasái.** Please register this letter.

kakitomeru to make notes of; to make a memo.

kakitome yúubin See **kakitome.**

kakitorásu to dictate.

kakitsuke document; bill.

kakiwakéru to push (elbow) aside, to force oneself through.

kákka Your (His) Excellency.

kakké beriberi.

kakki animation; spirit; **kakki no áru** animated; **kakki no nái** lifeless; dull.

kákko parentheses, brackets.

kakkoo shape, form; appearance; style; **kakoo na** suitable; moderate; **kakkoo no yói** well-formed; stylish.

káko (n.) past; bygone days; previous existence; **káko ni oite** in the past.

kakoi enclosure; fence; **kakoi o suru** to enclose; to fence in.

kakomi siege.

kakomu to surround; to enclose; to close in on.

kakotsuke pretense, pretext.

kakotsukeru to make a pretense of; **kakotsukete** under the pretext (pretense) of.

kakou to keep; to store; to preserve.

KÁKU to write; to draw; to paint; **tegami o káku** to write a letter; **é o káku** to draw (paint) a picture.

káku to rake, to scratch; **yukí o káku** to clear away snow.

káku each, every.

káku angle; **chokkaku** right angle.

káku nucleus; **kaku sénsoo** nuclear war.

KAKUBETSU especially, particularly. **kakubetsu no** particular, special.

kakuchoo suru to extend, expand, enlarge.

kakudai suru to magnify; **kakudai kyoo** magnifying glass.

kakugén maxim, saying.

kakugetsu every other month.

kakúgo preparedness; resolution; resignation; **kakúgo suru** to be prepared; to be resolved.

kakuhoo authentic news, definite report.

kákuhoomen in every direction; in all directions.

kakujitsu reliability; authenticity; certainty; **kakujitsu na** reliable; sure; authentic; **kakujitsu ni** certainly.

kakujitsu every other day.

kakumáu to shelter; to protect.

kakumei revolution; **kakumeiteki** revolutionary.

kakunin confirmation; **kakunin suru** to confirm, affirm.

kakunóoko airplane hangar.

kakuran disturbance.

kakuréga hiding place; den.

KAKURERU to hide oneself; to take shelter; to disappear. **Tsukí ga kúmo ni kakúreta.** The moon disappeared in the cloud.

kákuri isolation; **kakuríshitsu** isolation ward.

kakuritsu suru to establish; to fix; to settle.

kakusaku plan, scheme; project; **kakusaku suru** to plan, scheme.

kakusei disillusionment; **kakusei suru** to awake; be awakened; to be disillusioned.

kakuseiki loudspeaker.

kakushidate concealment; **kakushidate o suru** to conceal a fact.

kakushiki social status.

kakushin reform, renovation; **kakushin suru** to believe strongly, to be confident of.

kákusho every place; various places; **kákusho ni** everywhere; in several places.

kakushoo conclusive evidence; proof.

KÁKUSHU every kind; **kákushu no** of every kind.

KAKÚSU to hide, conceal.

kakutei decision; settlement; **kakutei suru** to decide; to settle.

KÁKUTERU cocktail.

kakutoku acquisition; possession; **kakutoku suru** to acquire, obtain, secure.

kakutoo suru to give a definite answer.

kakuu no imaginary; fanciful.

KAKUYASU NA cheap; **kakuyasu ni** cheaply; at a moderate price.

kakuzátoo lump (cube) sugar.

kakuzuke classification, grading; **kakuzuke suru** to classify, grade.

kákyoku melody, tune.

kakyuu no petty; low-grade; low-class; inferior; subordinate.

kakyuu no pressing, urgent; imminent.

kama kettle; iron pot; kiln.

káma scythe.

kamáe structure; appearance.

kamaéru to build, construct; to set up house; to take an attitude.

KAMÁU to care, mind, be concerned about; to trouble oneself about; to give attention to; **kamawázu** regardless of. **Kamawánaidekudasái.** Please don't trouble yourself on my account. Don't bother me.

káme turtle.

kamé jar; jug; vase; urn.

kamei family name; family honor.

kamei alliance, affiliation.

kamen mask; disguise.

KÁMERA camera.

kámi god, deity; **kami dana** family shrine (a shelf in a Japanese house for Shinto tablets).

KAMÍ paper; **kami byóoshi** paper cover; **kami kúzu** wastepaper; scraps of paper; **kamibásami** paper clip; **kamiyásuri** sandpaper.

kamí hair; **kamí o tóku** to comb one's hair.

KAMINÁRI thunder. **Kaminári ga natte imásu.** It is thundering.

KAMISÓRI razor; **kamisóri o ateru** to shave.

kamite upstage (in a theater).

KAMOKU course, subject, lesson.

kamósu to stir up, arouse.

kámotsu freight, cargo; merchandise; **kamotsusen** freighter (ship).

KÁMU = **kami—** to chew; to bite; to gnaw. **Kánde fukuméru yóo ni setsumei shimáshita.** He explained it, taking great pains to make it clear.

kamufuráaju camouflage, disguise.

kán perception; feeling, sentiment, emotion; **kán kiwamáru** to be filled with emotion; to be deeply moved.

kán tin can; **kanzume** canned goods.

kan temper; irritability; **kan o okosu** to become impatient; **kan ga tsuyói** to be hot-tempered; **kan o osáeru** to control one's temper.

–kán counter for volume; reel (motion picture); **dai ikkán** the first volume.

–kan suffix denoting: duration or space between; **isshuukan** one week; **Tookyoo Oosaká kan** between Tokyo and Osaka;

ikkagetsúkan during one month.

kana Japanese syllabary.

kanaboo crowbar; metal rod; horizontal bar.

kanadárai metal basin; washbowl.

kanaéru to grant; to comply with; **negai o kanaéru** to grant one's wishes; to answer one's prayers.

kanagu metal ornaments or fittings.

KÁNAI family; household; wife; **kanaijuu** the whole family.

kanakirigóe shrill, voice; **kanakirigóe o dásu** to scream.

kanamono hardware; ironware; **kanamonoya** hardware store or dealer.

KANARAZU certainly; no doubt, by all means; without fail; invariably. **Kanarazu kité kudasai.** Please be sure to come. Please come without fail.

KÁNARI fairly; pretty; considerably; **kánari no** considerable; **kánari yói** fairly well.

kanariya canary.

KANASHII sad, sorrowful.

kanashími sorrow, grief.

kanashímu to lament; to mourn; to regret.

kanáu to suit; to be suitable; to conform to; to accomplish; to agree with. **Mokuteki ni kanáu.** It answers the purpose.

kanazúchi iron hammer.

kanban signboard, billboard.

kanbashíi sweet; fragrant.

kanbashítta shrill, piercing; sharp.

kanbatsu drought.

kanben na handy; convenient; **kanben ni** simply; easily.

kánben suru to pardon, forgive. **Kánben shite kudasái.** Please excuse me.

kánbi completion; perfection.

kanboo cold; flu.

kanbotsu suru to sink, subside; to cave in.

kánbu staff; management.

kanbutsuya grocery specializing in dried vegetables and fruits.

kánbyoo = **kángo** (*n.*) nursing; **kanbyoonin** nurse.

kanchoo spy.

kánchoo government office.

kandai generosity; leniency; tolerance; **kandai na** generous; lenient; tolerant.

kandánkei thermometer.

kandan nái continual, incessant, endless; **kandan náku** continually.

kandoo emotion; impression; excitement; **kandoo suru** to be moved, be affected; to disown; **kandoo saseru** to move; to impress; to inspire; to appeal to.

kandoo disinheritance; **kandoo suru** to disinherit.

KANE, OKANE money; **kane ga nái** to have no money; **kaneíre** money box;

purse; **kanekáshi** moneylender;
kanemóchi rich person; **kanetsukidoo**
bell tower; **kanezúkai** manner of
spending money; **kane banare no yói**
generous with money; **kane ga kakáru** to
be costly; **kanekáshi suru** to lend money;
ooganémochi very rich man; **kanezúkai
no arai hito** a free spender.

kanegane previously; beforehand.

kánete already; previously; lately; some time
ago.

kangáe thought, idea, opinion.

kangaechígai misunderstanding; mistake;
mistaken ideal; **kangaechígai suru** to
misunderstand.

KANGÁERU to think, consider, deliberate,
believe, be of the opinion; **kangae bukái**
thoughtful; **kangaenaósu** to reconsider.
Sore wa kangáeru no mo iyá desu. I
dislike the very thought of it.

kangei welcome; reception; **kangei suru** to
welcome; **kangei o ukéru** to be received
warmly.

kangeki (*n.*) theatergoing; **kangeki ni
dekakeru** to go to the theater;
kangekíkai theater party.

kangeki emotion; excitement; inspiration.
**Sono hanashi o kiite kangeki
shimáshita.** I was very much moved
when I heard the story.

kángo See **kánbyoo; kangófu** nurse.

kani crab.

kán'i simplicity; **kán'i na** simple; **kán'i ni**
simply.

kan'in adultery.

kanja (*n.*) patient.

kánji manager; staff secretary; executive
committee.

KANJI sense, feeling; **kanji no hayái**
sensitive; **kanji no nibúi** insensitive;
kanjiyasúi sensitive; sentimental.

KANJI Chinese character (ideograph) used
in Japanese writing system.

kanjin na important; essential, vital.

KANJIRU = KANZURU to feel; **átsusa o
kanjiru** to feel the heat; **kónnan o
kanjiru** to find difficulty.

kanjoo feeling, sentiment, passion;
kanjooteki emotional.

KANJÓO calculation, counting; **kanjóo ni
ireru** to take into account; **kanjoogaki**
check, bill. **Háyaku kanjóo shite
kudasái.** Please count it quickly. **Kanjóo
o machigáeta.** I miscalculated.

kanjusei susceptibility; receptivity.

kánka influence.

kankaku space, distance, interval.

kankaku sensation, sense.

kankei relation, connection; concern, interest;

relationship; **–to kankei ga áru** to have a
relation to, be connected with.

KÁNKOKU South Korea.

kankoo sight-seeing; **kankóo kyaku**
sight-seer; **kankoo ni iku** to go
sight-seeing; **kankóodan** tourist party.

kankoo publication; **kankoo suru** to publish;
teiki kankoobutsu periodical.

kankyoo environment, surroundings.

kankyuu emergency.

kankyuu suru to be moved to tears.

kanmei deep impression; **kanmei suru** to
impress deeply; to be deeply impressed;
to be deeply moved.

kanmei terseness; **kanmei na** terse, concise,
simple and brief.

kanmuri crown.

kánnen idea, sense, concept, notion.

kánnin patience; forgiveness.

kannukí bolt, bar (of a gate or door);
kannuki o kakéru to bolt; **kannuki o
hazusu** to unbolt.

kanoo suppuration; infection; **kanoo suru** to
be infected.

kanoo possibility; **kanoo na** possible.

kanpai toast; **kanpai suru** to drink a toast.

kanpan deck; **jookánpan** upper deck;
chuukánpan main deck.

kanraku fall; cave in; **kanraku suru** to fall;
to sink; to collapse; to cave in.

kánri management, administration, control;
kanrísha superintendent; manager.

kanryaku simplicity; brevity; **kanryaku na**
simple; brief; **kanryaku ni** simply;
briefly. **Kanryaku ni shite kudasái.**
Please make it very brief.

kanryoo completion; conclusion.

kansatsu observation.

kansen infection; contagion.

kansen trunk line; main line.

kansetsu indirectness; **kansetsu no**
roundabout, indirect; **kansetsu ni** at
second hand, indirectly.

kansetsu joint; **kansetsu o kujíku** to
dislocate.

kánsha thanks, gratitude. **Kánsha no kotobá
mo arimasén.** I can't thank you enough.

kánsha official residence.

kanshaku passion; temper; impatience;
kanshaku no tsuyói hot-tempered;
irritable; **kanshaku o okósu** to lose one's
temper.

kanshi watch, lookout, vigil; **kanshi suru** to
watch, keep an eye on.

kanshin concern, interest; **kanshin o mótsu**
to be concerned about, be interested in.

kanshin admiration; **kanshin na** admirable,
praiseworthy; **kanshin ni** admirably;
kanshin suru to admire, to be impressed.

kanshoku suru to eat between meals.

kanshoo appreciation; **kanshoo suru** to appreciate; **kanshooteki** appreciative.

kanshoo sentimentality; **kanshoo shúgi** sentimentalism; **kanshooteki** sentimental.

kanshuu spectators.

kansoku observation; survey; **kansokusho** observatory (weather, etc.).

kansoo impression(s); thoughts; **kansoo o nobéru** to give one's impression.

kansoo aridity; **kansoo suru** to dry.

kan súru to be concerned with; to relate to, bear on; to be connected with: **–ni kán shite** in regard to.

kanjoo account.

KANTAN brevity; simplicity; **KANTAN NA** simple, brief; **kantan ni** briefly; in a few words; simply, easily. **Soko e wa kantan ni ikemásu.** You can go there very easily.

kantan suru to admire.

kantei judgment; expert opinion; appraisal.

kantei official residence.

kantoku supervision; control; superintendént; inspector; **kantoku suru** to supervise; control.

kantsuu penetration; **kantsuu suru** to penetrate, pierce.

kan'yoo na important; necessary.

kanyuu entry; joining; admission; **kanyuu suru** to join; to subscribe; to enter; **kanyúusha** member; subscriber.

kanzei customs (duty); **kanzei no kakáru** dutiable; **kanzei no kakaránai** duty free.

KANZEN perfection; completeness; **kanzen na** perfect; complete; integral; **kanzen ni** perfectly.

kanzúku to get wind of; to have an inkling of; to suspect.

KANZURU See **KANJIRU.**

KAO face; looks; complexion; **kao ga urete iru** to be well known.

kaoru to smell; to be fragrant.

kappa old-fashioned raincoat; oilskin.

kapparai shoplifter; pilfering, thieving.

kappatsu activity; briskness; **kappatsu na** active, lively; brisk.

káppu cup (trophy). (See also **koppu.**)

KARÁ (*n.*) being empty; vacant (*adj.*) **kara no** empty; **kará ni suru** to empty. **Kará desu.** It is empty.

kará husks, hulls, shells.

KARA from; out of; since; on; in; and so; because; as; for (following a sentence-ending form of a verb, the copula, or adjective); **kore kara nochi** from now on; **Tookyoo kara Oosaka máde** from Tokyo to Osaka. **Byooki déshita kara ikimasén deshita.** I was sick so I didn't go.

KARADA body; **karada no** physical; bodily; **karada no tamé ni náru** to be good for one's health. **Karada ga warúi.** She is sick. I am sick.

karagéru to tie up, bind; to tuck in.

KARÁI hot; acrid; salty; pungent. **Kono otsúyu wa karái desu.** This soup is too salty.

karaíbari bluff; empty boast.

karakáu to tease; to make fun of; to play a joke on.

karákaze dry wind.

karamáru, karámu to twine around; to coil; to be entangled.

kararí to completely, fully, entirely. **Sóra ga kararí to haremáshita.** The sky has cleared.

kara sáwagi much ado about nothing; **kara sáwagi suru** to make a big fuss about nothing.

karasu to let wither; to dry up. (See also **KARERU.**)

karátto carat.

karazeki dry (hacking) cough.

KARE he; **káre no** his; **kare ni** to him; **káre o mia;** **kárera** they.

kare– prefix denoting: dry; withered; hoarse; **karegóe** hoarse voice.

káree curry; **raisu káree** curried rice; **kareiko** curry powder.

KÁREKORE this and that; one thing and another; some; about; **kárekore ninen bákari** two years or so.

karéndaa calendar.

KARERU to wither, dry up; to die; to get hoarse. **Kóe ga karete kimáshita.** My voice is hoarse. **Ído ga karemáshita.** The well has dried up. **Ki ga karemáshita.** The tree has died. (See also **karasu.**)

kári hunting.

KARI (*n.*) loan; debt; borrowing.

kari no temporary; **kari ni** temporarily; tentatively.

kariru to borrow; **karikata** debtor; **kariukenin** borrower. **Yamada-san ni okane o karimáshita.** I borrowed some money from Mr. Yamada.

kariatsuméru to gather together, muster.

karidásu to hunt out; to round up.

kariiréru to harvest, gather in.

karikomi (*n.*) cutting, pruning.

karikómu to cut, trim, prune.

karikoshi outstanding debt; overdraft.

karinui (*n.*) basting, sewing loosely; **karinui suru** to baste.

KARÓOJITE with much difficulty; barely, hardly.

karu to reap; to cut; to trim; to hunt; to

chase; **kusá o karu** to cut grass; **íne o karu** to harvest rice.

karuhazumi rashness; hastiness; **karuhazumi na** rash; hasty; thoughtless.

KARUI light, not heavy, slight, trifling; not serious; simple; insignificant; **karui shigoto** light work; **karui nímotsu** light baggage; **karuku** lightly; slightly; **karuku suru** to lighten, ease; **karuku útsu** to tap; to pat.

káryoku heating power.

karyuu downstream.

KÁSA umbrella; parasol.

kasa bulk, volume; size; quantity; **kasabátta** bulky.

kasabuta scab.

kasai fire, blaze; **kasai o okósu** to start a fire; **kasai hoochíki** fire alarm; **kasai hóken** fire insurance. (See also **hí.**)

kasamu to swell, increase in volume.

kasanaru to be piled up; to lie one on top of another.

kasaneru to pile up, put one on top of the other; to repeat; **kasanete** in layers; one on the other; repeatedly.

kasanegásane repeatedly, again and again, over and over.

kasei (n.) keeping house; **kaséigaku** home economics.

Kasei Mars.

kasetsu construction; **kasetsu suru** to construct, erect; to lay; **denwa o kasetsu suru** to have a telephone installed; **kasetsuchuu de áru** to be under construction.

kasetsu hypothesis.

kasetsu no temporary, provisional.

kasétto cassette.

kásha freight car.

kashi lending; **kashikata** creditor, **kashikín** loan.

káshi, OKÁSHI cake; confectionery; sweets; candy; **kashíya** confectionery store.

kashigéru to incline; **kubi o kashigéru** to tilt one's head.

Kashi kandánkei Fahrenheit thermometer.

kashikiri charted (bus, etc.).

KASHIKÓI wise, clever, intelligent.

kashikomáru to obey; to assent to; to sit straight. **Kashikomarimáshita.** Yes, sir. I'll follow your instructions.

KASHIMA room to let; apartment; **kashiya** house for rent.

kashimashíi noisy, boisterous.

kashirá (n.) head, chief; ringleader; **kashira dátta** (adj.) chief, leading, principal.

kúshu singer.

kassai ovation.

kásu refuse, dregs, scum; sediment.

KASU to lend; **kane o kasu** to lend money.

KÁSUKA NA faint, dim, vague, indistinct; **kásuka ni** faintly, etc.; **kásuka ni kioku suru** to have a faint recollection.

kasumi haze; mist; **kasumi no kakátta** hazy; misty.

kasumu to grow hazy, grow dim.

kasuréru to get hoarse.

kasuríkizu scratch; bruise.

kasúru to graze, scrape, scratch.

KÁTA shoulder; **katákake** shawl; **káta o mótsu** to take sides. **Káta ga kóru.** I have a stiff neck.

kata form, shape; pattern, model, figure; design, mold.

kata– prefix denoting: single; **katáhoo** one of a pair; **kataashi de tátsu** to stand on one leg.

–kata suffix denoting: person (respect); **kono káta** this person; **ano káta** that person.

KATACHI form, shape; figure; personal appearance; **mime katachi no íi** handsome; shapely. **Sore wa dónna katachi o shite imásu ka?** What kind of shape does it have?

kátachínba odd.

katágata by way of; at the same time; partly; combined with. **Sanpo katagata ikimáshita.** I went there both to take a walk and [at the same time] pay a visit.

katagawa one side; **katagawa tsúuko** one-way street.

katagi no honest; honorable; decent.

KATAI hard; tough; stiff; upright; strong; firm; conscientious; **kataku** strongly; firmly; tightly; strictly; resolutely; stubbornly; **katakurushíi** strict; stiff-mannered; formal; **kataku suru** to harden; stiffen. **Anó hito wa katai hitó desu.** He is a conscientious person. **Kono nikú wa taihen katái desu.** This meat is very tough.

KATAKÁNA one of the two sets of Japanese syllabary called **kana**. **Sore wa katakána de káite kudasái.** Please write it in **katakána.**

katamari lump; clod; mass.

katamaru to coagulate; congeal; to group together.

katameru to harden; to solidify; to stiffen; to consolidate.

katami memento, souvenir; **katami to suru** to keep as a memento.

kátami ga hirói to feel proud.

KATAMICHI one way; one trip; **katamichi joosháken** one-way ticket.

katamukéru to incline, bend, tilt.

katamuki trend; slant; slope; **–no katamuki ga áru** to be apt to, to be inclined to.

katamúku to incline, lean; to decline.

katan íto cotton thread.

kataná sword.

katappáshi (*colloq.*) one by one; one and all; wholesale.

katasa hardness; toughness; solidity.

katasúmi corner; nook; **heya no katasúmi ni** in a corner of the room.

kataware fragment, piece.

katazukéru to put in order; to clear; to put away; to dispose of; to settle.

katazúku to be put in order; to be settled; to come to an end.

KATEI home; family; household; **katei no** domestic; household; house.

katei assumption, supposition; **katei suru** to assume, to suppose.

katoo inferiority; **katoo no** low; coarse; vulgar.

kátsu to conquer, be victorious, win.

katsudoo, katsuyaku activity; **katsudooteki** active; energetic; **katsudooka** active person; **katsudóoryoku** vitality; energy.

katsúgu to shoulder, carry; to carry on the shoulder.

katsuyaku, katsudoo activity; action; boom (rapid, expanding growth); **katsuyaku suru** to be active in; to play an active part.

KATTE one's own way; selfishness; condition; circumstances; **KATTE NA** selfish; willful; **temae kátte ni** selfishly; **katte ni furumáu** to have one's own way; **katte no yói** handy, convenient.

KAU to buy, purchase; to incur; to provoke; **kenka o kau** to pick a quarrel. **Kono hón o hyakuen de kaimáshita.** I bought this book for one hundred yen.

KÁU to keep, raise (an animal or bird). **Watakushi wa inú o kátte imasu.** I have a dog.

KAWÁ skin, hide; leather; bark; peel; etc.; **kawá o hágu** to peel off (skin or bark); **kawazuki no** unpeeled.

KAWÁ river, stream; **kawá o wataru** to cross a river.

KAWAIGARU to love; to pet, fondle, caress. **Káre wa múyami to néko o kawaigátta.** He made a great pet of a cat.

KAWAÍI dear; darling; loving; tiny; **kawaíi akanboo** precious baby; **kawaii kóe** sweet voice; **kawairashíi** sweet; lovely; pretty; charming; amiable; pathetic. **Ano hito ni wa kawaírashii akanboo ga arimasu.** She has a cute baby.

KAWAISÓO NA poor, pitiful, pathetic. **Kawaisóo ha kotó o shita.** That was a pity.

KAWAKÁSU to dry.

KAWÁKU to dry; to get dry; to feel thirsty; **nódo ga kawáku** to be thirsty. **Kuchi ga kawáita.** My mouth felt dry.

KAWAKI thirst.

kawara tile; **kawarabuki no** tile-roofed.

KAWARI substitute, proxy; compensation; **kawari ni** on behalf of; in place of; **kawari o suru** to substitute, take someone's place. **Kawari ga nái.** Nothing is the matter.

kawaru to replace, **kawarugáwaru** in turn, by turns.

kawaru to change; **yoku kawaru** changeable. **Áme ga yuki ni kawarmáshita.** The rain changed into snow.

KAWASE money order; exchange; **kawase sóoba** rate of exchange. **Kawase de gosénen okutta.** I sent a money order for 5,000 yen.

KAYÓOBI Tuesday.

kayou to pass to and fro; to frequent; to go regularly; **gakkoo e kayou** to attend school.

kayowái weak; tender; delicate, fragile.

kayúi itchy.

KAZARU to adorn, decorate, embellish; to display; **kikazáru** dress up.

KAZE wind; breeze; **kásuka na kaze** breath of air; light breeze. **Kaze ga fúite imásu.** The wind is blowing.

KAZE cold; **kaze o hiku** to catch a cold.

kazei taxation; **kazéihin** taxable item; **kazéiritsu** tax rate.

KAZOÉRU to count, calculate; to number; **hi o kazoéru** to count the days.

KÁZOKU family; household.

KÁZU number; **kázu kagiri nái** innumerable, countless; **kázu no óoi** many; numerous.

KE hair ke darake no hairy; **ke no nái** bald, hairless.

–KE suffix denoting: house, family; **Fujiwarake** the Fujiwaras.

–KE suffix denoting: temper, feeling; nature; **hínoke** signs of fire.

kebakebashíi gaudy, showy.

kéchi fault; stinginess; poor quality; **kéchi na** stingy, miserly; **kéchi o tsukéru** to find fault with.

kechirásu to kick about.

kedakái dignified; noble.

kedamono beast.

KEGÁ wound, injury; accident; **KEGÁ O SURU** to get hurt; **kegá o saseru** to injure, hurt; **kega no kóomyoo** lucky mistake; lucky hit.

kegare pollution, contamination; stain.

kegareru to be polluted.

kegasu to stain; to soil; to pollute; to disgrace.

kegírai prejudice; **kegírai suru** to be prejudiced against.

keiba horse race; **keibajoo** racetrack.

keibetsu contempt; slight; insult; **keibetsu suru** to despise; to sneer at.

keiei management, conduct.

keifuku suru to respect; to admire; to look up to.

keiji notice, notification; **keijiban** bulletin board.

keika progress; development; course; **jíken no keika** the course of an event.

keikai watch; guard; **keikai shíngoo** warning signal; **keikai suru** to watch for; guard against.

keikaku plan, project, scheme; **keikaku suru** to plan, etc.

KEIKEN experience; **keiken áru** experienced. **keiken no nái** inexperienced; **keiken suru** to experience; **keikénsha** experienced person.

keiken na pious, devout.

keiki condition, state; times; **kookéiki** business boom. **Keiki ga yói desu.** Trade is brisk.

kéiko exercise, practice, drill; study; **kéiko suru** to practice; to take lessons.

keikoku warning; advice; **keikoku suru** to warn, admonish.

keikoo tendency, inclination; trend.

keimusho prison.

keiniku chicken (as food).

keiran (chicken) egg.

keirei salute, salutation.

keiren convulsions; spasm.

keiryaku stratagem, artifice.

keisan calculation, reckoning; estimation; **keisangákari** accountant; **keisánki** adding machine, calculator.

KEISATSU police station; **keisatsúkan** police officer.

keisha slant, incline, slope.

keishiki forms; formality; **keishikiteki** formal; conventional; **keishikiteki ni** formally.

keiteki foghorn; police whistle; alarm whistle.

keito worsted; woolen yarn.

keitoo system; lineage; **keitoo o tatéru** to systematize; **keitooteki** systematic. **keitoo suru** to exhaust; to concentrate.

keiyaku contract; agreement; promise; **keiyaku suru** to make a contract; **keiyakúsho** written contract.

kéizai economy; finance; **keizaiteki** economical; **keizaijoo** financially.

KEKKA result, outcome, consequence; effect; **sono kekka** consequently.

kekkan blood vessel.

KEKKIN absence (from work); **kekkin suru** to be absent; **kekkínsha** absentee.

kekkon marriage; wedding; **KEKKON SURU** to marry; **kekkónshiki** marriage ceremony.

kékkoo na splendid; fine; good; beautiful; **kékkoo na nikú** delicious meat.

kekkoo suru to take decisive action; to carry out (something) decisively.

KEKKYOKU eventually, finally, ultimately, in the end; **kekkyoku no** final, ultimate.

kemono beast, brute.

kemui smoky.

KEMURI smoke; fumes.

KÉN prefecture; **kénchoo** prefectural office; **kenchíji** prefectural governor; **Chibáken** Chiba prefecture.

kén sword, saber.

–ken house (used as a counter). **Kádo kara sangenme no ié desu.** It is the third house from the corner. (In *sangenme*, "g" takes the place of "k.")

kénage na brave, heroic; manly; **kenage ni** bravely; heroically; nobly.

ken'aku na dangerous; serious; stormy; rough; **ken'aku na sóra** stormy (threatening) sky.

kenasu to abuse, slander.

kenbikyoo microscope.

KENBUTSU sight-seeing; **kenbutsunin** sight-seer; visitor; **kenbutsu suru** to see, look at; to pay a visit to; **kenbutsu ni iku** to go sight-seeing.

kenchiku construction, erection; building; architecture; **kenchiku yóoshiki** architectural style; **kenchiku suru** to build.

ken'etsu censorship.

kengaku observation; inspection; **kengaku suru** to visit (a factory, etc.) for study.

kéngi suspicion; **kéngi o kakéru** to suspect; **kéngi ga kakáru** to be under suspicion.

kéngo na strong; stable; firm, solid; **kéngo ni** firmly; strongly.

kenka quarrel, dispute, brawl; **kenka suru** to quarrel, fight; **kenka o shikakéru** to pick a fight.

KENKOO health; **kenkoo na** healthy.

KENKYUU research, study, investigation; **kénkyuu suru** to study; to do research; **kenkyúukai** learned society; society for scientific research; **kenkyuujo** laboratory; research institute.

kén mo hororo no áisatsu curt, blunt, or brusque reply; rebuff.

kénpoo constitution; constitutional law.

kénpu silk cloth.

kénri right, privilege; **kénri o shuchoo suru** to insist on one's rights.

kénryoku power, authority, influence; **kénryoku no áru** powerful, influential.

kénsa inspection; investigation; **kénsa suru** to inspect, examine.

kensetsu construction; establishment; building; **kensetsu suru** to construct; to found; to establish.

kensoku arrest, restraint; surveillance; **kensoku suru** to restrain, check.

kenson modesty, humility; **kenson na** modest, humble; **kenson suru** to be modest.

kentoo boxing; **kentoo suru** to box; **kentooka** boxer, fighter.

kentóo aim; anticipation; **kentóo o tsukéru** to anticipate; to take aim at; **kentóo ga hazureru** to miss one's aim.

ken'yaku economy; thrift; **ken'yaku suru** to economize; **ken'yaku no** economical, thrifty.

keorímono woolen fabric.

keppaku purity, innocence; **keppaku na** pure, innocent, spotless, clean.

KÉREDOMO but, however, although, yet. **Kyóo wa hídoku atsúi keredomo ikimashóo.** It is hot today, but let's go anyway.

KÉRU to kick.

KÉSA this morning. **Késa wa ikága desu ka?** How are you feeling this morning?

keshikarán outrageous; rude; insulting; insolent.

KÉSHIKI view, sight, scenery, landscape. **Taihen késhika ga yói.** The scenery is very good.

keshitoméru to put out (a fire).

kessaku masterpiece.

kesseki absence (from school or a meeting); **mukésseki** regular attendance.

késshin resolution, determination; **késshin suru** to be resolute, to make up one's mind.

KESSHITE never, by no means; not at all; not in the least. **Kesshite sonna kotó wa itashimasén.** I wouldn't do it for anything. **Kesshite sawatte wa ikemasén.** Don't touch it under any circumstances.

KESU to put out, extinguish; to blow out; to switch off, to erase; to cancel; **súgata o kesu** to vanish, to disappear; **akari o kesu** to switch off the light; to put out the light.

ketatamashíi noisy, loud; piercing; alarming; **ketatamáshiku** frantically; noisily, loudly.

ketsuron conclusion; **ketsuron suru** to conclude; **ketsuron to shite** in conclusion.

kettei determination; decision; conclusion; **ketteiteki** decisive; conclusive; **kettei suru** to decide upon; to be decided.

kettén flaw, defect, blemish; **kettén áru** defective, imperfect; **kettén no nái** flawless; perfect.

kewashíi steep, precipitous.

KEZURU to shave; to sharpen; **enpitsu o kezuru** to sharpen a pencil; **namae o kezuru** to remove a name from a list. **Honemí o kezutte shigoto ni hagénda.** He worked hard without sparing himself.

ki– prefix denoting: air; vapor; atmosphere; **kiatsu** atmospheric pressure; **kion** temperature (of the air).

kibarashi diversion, pastime; **kibarashi o suru** to amuse oneself.

kibaru to exert oneself; to bear down.

kibatsu na original; extraordinary; novel; unusual.

kíbikibi shita vivacious, full of life.

kibin smartness; **kibin na** smart, clever, quick-witted; **kibin ni** cleverly.

kibishíi severe, strict, stern; **kibíshíku** severely, strictly.

kibone care, worry; **kibone no oréru** to be troublesome.

KIBOO wish, desire, hope; **kiboo suru** to hope, wish, desire.

KÍBUN feeling, frame of mind, mood; **kíbun ga yói** to feel better. **Kíbun ga warui desu.** I feel sick.

kichí dangerous situation; **kichí o dassúru** to have a close shave; to have a narrow escape.

kichigái madness, insanity; insane person; **kichigái ni náru** to go mad.

kichín to precisely; neatly; **kichín to shita** orderly, tidy; **kichín to shite iru** to be in good order.

kichoomen na orderly; precise; **kichoomen na hito** one who works in an orderly manner.

kidate disposition, temper; **kidate no yói** good-tempered.

kidoru to assume airs, be conceited; **kidotte** affectedly.

kien tall talk; **kien o ageru** to talk big; to boast.

KIERU to go out; to be put out; to be extinguished; **súgata ga kieru** to disappear. **Hí ga kieta.** The fire has gone out.

kífu contribution, donation; subscription; **kífu suru** to contribute; to subscribe; **kifúsha** contributor; subscriber.

kigae change of clothes.

kigakari anxiety, worry; misgivings.

KIGARU NA cheerful, lighthearted; pleasant, agreeable.

KIGEN state of health; temper; mood; **kigen no yói** good-humored; cheerful; **kigen o sokonáu** to offend.

KÍGEN term, period, time; **kígen ga kúru** to come due; **kígen ga keikasuru** to be overdue.

kigoo sign, symbol, mark, emblem.

kigurai pride; **kigurai no takái** proud.

kihon foundation, basis; standard; **kíhonteki** fundamental, basic.

KIIROI yellow; **kiiroi booshi** yellow cap; **kiiroi kóe** shrill voice.

kíji description; account (in a newspaper or magazine).

kíji grain (of wood), color (of wood).

kíjitsu appointed date; fixed date.

KIKÁI machine; implement; apparatus; machinery; **kikáiteki** mechanical; **kikáigaku** mechanics.

KIKÁI opportunity, chance; **kikái no arishídai** at the first chance; **kikái o toraéru** to seize the opportunity.

kikiawaseru to inquire, make inquiries.

KIKIDÁSU to hear; to find out; to get wind of.

kikiiréru to comply with, assent to, consent to.

kikiíru to listen to.

kikikajiri smattering (of information).

kikikajíru to get a smattering of.

kikikómu to be informed of, get wind of.

kikime effect; efficacy; benefit; **kikime no áru** effective; **kikime no nái** ineffective.

KIKIMORÁSU to fail to hear; not to hear (catch) what is said.

kikín famine.

kikinagásu to pay no heed (to what is said).

kikinaósu to ask someone to repeat (something).

kikinaréru to get used to hearing, be accustomed to hearing.

kikinikúi difficult to hear.

kikioboe recollection (feeling) that one has heard (something) before.

kikisokonai mishearing; misunderstanding.

kikitadásu to ascertain, confirm.

kikitagáru to be inquisitive, be curious.

kikitóru to hear; to get wind of.

kikitsutae hearsay.

kikitsutaéru to hear from others, hear at second hand.

KIKKÁRI punctually; exactly; precisely.

KIKOERU to hear; to be able to hear; to be audible. **Watakushi wa mimí ga yóku kikoemasén.** I'm hard of hearing. **Utá ga kikoemásu.** I hear a song.

KIKOO climate, season; weather; **onwa na**

kikoo mild climate.

KIKU to hear, listen to; to ask; to accept; **kiku tokoró ni yoréba . . .** I hear that. . . . it is said that . . .

kimae generosity; **kimae no yói** generous; openhanded; **kimae yóku kane o tsukau** to be generous with one's money.

kimagure caprice; **kimagure na** capricious, whimsical; **kimagure ni** capriciously.

kimama willfulness; waywardness; selfishness; **kimama na** selfish, etc.

kimari settlement; conclusion; rule; custom; **kimari o tsukéru** to settle, arrange.

kimaru to be settled, to come to an agreement, to be fixed. **Hanashí ga kimaru.** The matter is settled, **kimatta** regular, fixed, routine.

KIMERU to settle, decide; to arrange; to determine; **hi o kimeru** to set the day; **kimeta jikan ni** at the appointed time; **hará o kimeru** to make up one's mind.

kimazui disagreeable, unpleasant.

kimetsukéru to scold, reprimand.

kimi you (used colloq. by men).

kimí egg yolk.

kimijika na short-tempered, touchy.

kimochi feeling, sensation; **kimochi no yói** pleasant; refreshing; **kimochi ga warúi** to feel uncomfortable.

KIMONO Japanese clothing, garment; **kimono o kiru** to get dressed; **kimono o núgu** to get undressed; **kimono o kikáeru** to change one's clothes.

kimuzukashíi hard to please; moody.

KÍN gold; **kin'iro no** golden; **kinpatsu** blond hair.

kinchoku conscientiousness; **kinchoku na** conscientious; scrupulous; discreet; honest.

kinchoo tension, strain; **kinchoo suru** to strain; to become tense.

kíndai modern times; **kíndai shísoo** modern ideas; **kindaika suru** to modernize.

kin'en prohibition against smoking; **kin'énsha** nonsmoker.

kinen commemoration, remembrance; memory; **kinen suru** to commemorate; **kinen no táme ni** in memory of; **kinénhi** monument.

kingan nearsightedness; **kingankyoo** eyeglasses for a nearsighted person. (See also **kinshigan**.)

KÍNJO neighborhood; **kínjo no** neighboring; **kínjo no hitó** neighbor.

kinkán kumquat.

kínko safe; cashbox.

kínniku muscles; **kinniku róodoo** physical labor; **kínniku no** muscular.

kínomi kinomama de in the clothes one is

wearing; without changing clothes;
kínomi kinomama de neru to go to sleep
without changing into pajamas.

KINOO = sakújitsu yesterday; **kinoo no
híru** yesterday at noon. **Kinoo gakkoo o
yasumináshita.** I was absent from school
yesterday.

kinshi prohibition, ban, embargo; **kinshi
suru** to prohibit, forbid; **kinshi o tóku** to
lift an embargo. **Kitsuen kinshi.** No
smoking.

kinshigan = **kingan** near-sightedness;
kinshigan no nearsighted.

kinshu abstinence, teetotalism; **kinshu suru**
to abstain from drinking alcoholic
beverages.

KÍNU silk; **kinu ito** silk thread; **kinu
orímono** silk fabric; **kinu ura** silk lining.

kinuke (n.) being dejected; **kinuke no shita**
dejected, spiritless; absentminded; **kinuke
suru** to be dejected.

KIN'YÓOBI Friday.

kínzoku metal; **kínzoku no** metallic;
kinzoku séihin metal goods; hardware.

kinzúru to forbid, prohibit; to suppress.

kioku memory, recollection; **kioku suru** to
remember, recollect; **kioku subéki**
memorable, noteworthy; **kíoku ga yói** to
have a good memory; **kioku ga warúi** to
have a poor memory.

kippári to explicitly, distinctly; definitely,
decidedly; **kippári to kotowáru** to refuse
flatly.

KIPPU ticket, pass; **kippu o kíru** to punch a
ticket; **kippu úriba** ticket window.

KIRAI dislike, distaste, aversion; **kirai na**
distasteful; abominable. **Kirai désu.** I
dislike it. I don't like it.

kírakira brilliantly; glitteringly; **kírakira
suru** to glitter, to dazzle.

KIRAKU NA easygoing, easy, carefree,
happy-go-lucky; **kiraku na monó**
easygoing person; **kiraku ni kurasu** to
take things easy; to lead a relaxed life.
Dóozo okiraku ni. Make yourself
comfortable!

kiraméku to glitter, sparkle.

kirásu to run out of, be short of; **íki o kirásu**
to be short of breath.

kirau to dislike, to hate, detest.

–kiré counter for: piece, bit, scrap, fragment;
slice. **Pán o hitókire kudasái.** Please give
me a piece of bread.

KÍREI NA beautiful, lovely, pretty;
handsome, good-looking; clean; clear;
kírei na onna no hito a beautiful
(good-looking) woman; **kírei na mízu**
clear water; **kírei ni suru** to clean; to tidy
up; to put in order.

kiremé gap, break; pause, intermission;
kiremé o tsunagu to close a gap.

kiremono cutlery, knives.

kiréru to cut (well), to be sharp; to run out;
to be worn out; to wear out. **Kimono ga
kíréta.** The clothes have worn out. **Náifu
ga yóku kiréru.** The knife cuts well.
Kigen ga kiréta. The term has expired.

kiri fog, mist; **kiri ame** drizzle; **kiribue**
foghorn. **Kíri ga fukái.** It is foggy.

kirí end; limit; **kírí ga nái** unlimited.

–kiri suffix denoting: all (there is); only;
sole; no more. **Korekkiri désu.** This is all
I have.

kiriagéru to stop; to close; to cut short; to
wind up; **hanshí o kiriagéru** to end a
talk; cut a conversation short.

kiridásu to quarry; to cut down (timber) to
break ice; **hanashí o kiridásu** to broach a
subject; to break the ice
(conversationally).

kirihanásu to cut off; to separate.

kiriharáu to cut and clear away; prune.

kirihiráku to cut open; to clear (land).

kirikabu tree stump.

kiríkuchi cut end; opening; slit; section.

kirikuzúsu to cut down; to demolish.

kirimí fish slices, fillets.

kirinukéru to cut one's way through; to find
the way out of (a difficulty); to struggle
through.

kirinuki cutting, clipping, scrap; excerpt.

kirinuku to cut out, clip.

KIRISUTO Christ.

KIRISUTOKYOO Christianity;
Kirisutokyoo Seinénkai Y.M.C.A.,
Kirisuto kyóokai Christian church.

kiritsu order, discipline; rule, regulations;
(n.) standing up; **kiritsu áru** orderly,
disciplined; **kiritsu o mamóru** to obey
the rules; **kiritsu suru** to stand up, get to
one's feet; **kiritsu o yabúru** to break the
rules.

kiritsuméru to shorten, reduce, curtail; **híyoo
o kiritsuméru** to cut down on expenses.

–KÍRO counter denoting: kilometer;
kilogram; kiloliter; kilowatt.

kiroku annals; archives; minutes, record;
kiroku suru to record, write down, keep
records.

KÍRU to cut; to chop; to carve; to break off
(relations); **yubí o kíru** to cut one's
finger; **denwa o kíru** to hang up (the
telephone receiver). **Káre to wa té o
kítta.** I am through with him.

KIRU to wear; to put on; **kimono o kiru** to
put on clothes, dress; **kite iru** to be
dressed in; to have on. **Náni o kite ikóo
ka?** What shall I wear (in going there)?

kiryoku energy, vigor; virility; **kiryoku ga nái** to be languid, lacking in energy; **kiryoku ga otoroéru** to lose one's vigor; to have less energy.

kíryoo personal appearance, looks, features (usually used when speaking of women); **kíryoo no yói** pretty, beautiful, handsome.

KISEN steamship, steamer; **kisen de** by ship; **kisen de iku** to go by ship; **kisen gáisha** steamship company.

kiseru to dress, clothe; to plate, gild, coat; to impute; **tsúmi o híto ni kímeru** to put the blame on someone else.

KISÉTSU season; **kisétsu no** in season, seasonal; **kisetsu házure no** out of season; **kisetsu fuu** monsoon season; **sakura no kisétsu** cherry blossom season.

KISHÁ railroad train; **kishá ni noru** to get on a train; **kishá de iku** to go by train; **kishá o oríru** to get off a train; **kisháchin** train fare; **yógisha** night train.

kishá journalist; **tsuushin kísha** correspondent; **kisháseki** press gallery.

KISHÍ shore, coast; bank; **mukoo gishi** other side of the river.

kishitsu disposition, temperament; **yói kishitsu no hitó** person of good disposition.

kishoku mood, feeling; **kishoku ga yói** to be in a good mood; to feel well; **kishoku ga warúi** to be in a bad mood.

kishoo weather; weather conditions; **kishoodai** weather bureau.

kishú horseman, jockey, rider.

kishuku lodging; room and board; **kishukunin** a boarder; **kishuku suru** to board at; **kishukúsha** dormitory.

KISÓKU rule, regulations; **kisoku tadashíi** regular; systematic; orderly; **kisoku tadáshiku** regularly, systematically; **kisóku o mamóru** to observe the rules.

KISSÁTEN tearoom; coffee shop.

kissúi no pure; genuine.

kisúu odd number.

KITÁ north; **kitá no** northerly; northern.

kitaéru to forge; to drill, train; to discipline; to harden.

kitai expectation, anticipation; **kitai suru** to expect, hope for; to look forward to; to count on; **kitai ni sóu** to meet expectations.

kitaku suru to go home; to come home.

KITANÁI dirty; filthy; nasty; shabby; **kitanáku suru** to soil, make dirty.

kitchíri punctually, sharp; exactly; **kitchíri níji ni** at two o'clock sharp; at two on the dot.

kiteki siren; steam whistle; **kiteki o narasu** to blow a whistle; to sound a siren.

kiten ready wit; tact; **kiten no kiita** tactful; quick-witted; **kiten o kikasu** to be on the alert.

kitoku serious, critical. **Séimei kitoku désu.** She is seriously ill.

kitsuen smoking; **kitsuen suru** to smoke; **kitsuénshitsu** smoking room; **kitsuénsha** smoking car (on a train).

kitsui brave; strong; intense; severe.

KITTE postage stamp; **kitte o haru** to put a stamp on (a letter). **Kono tegami ni wa íkura no kitte o harú n desu ka?** How much is the postage for this letter?

KITTO certainly, without fail; undoubtedly, surely. **Kitto kité kudasai.** Please be sure to come. **Kitto mairimásu.** Certainly I'll come.

kiwadátsu to stand out, be conspicuous; to be in contrast with.

kiwadói critical; dangerous, risky; **kiwadói shóobu** a close game (match); **kiwadói tokoró de** in the nick of time; at the last minute.

kiwaméru to exhaust; to get to the bottom of; to carry to an extreme; **shinsoo o kiwaméru** to get at the truth.

kiwámete extremely, exceedingly; excessively.

kíyoo na clever, skillful; ingenious; **kíyoo na hitó** jack-of-all-trades; handy person.

kiyowai timid, shy.

kíza na offensive; conceited.

kizetsu (n.) fainting; **kizetsu suru** to faint.

KIZU wound, injury, bruise; flaw, defect; **kizuato** scar; **kizugúsuri** ointment for a bruise or wound.

kizutsukéru to hurt, injure, wound.

kizutsuku to be wounded, hurt.

kizúkai fear; anxiety.

kizukare worry; mental fatigue; **kizukare ga suru** to be worried.

kizúku to become aware of.

kizuyoi resolute; brave; **kizuyóku omóu** to be reassured; to be confident.

KO child; infant, baby; cub of an animal.

ko– prefix denoting; little small; **koburi** light rain; light fall of snow; **kozákana** small fish; **kojima** small island.

–ko suffix denoting; lake; **Biwako** Lake Biwa.

kobiritsúku to stick fast, cling.

kobore overflow; droppings; **koborédane** fallen seed.

KOBORÉRU to run over, overflow; to drop; to spill; to be scattered.

kobósu to spill; to drop; to pour out; **námida o kobósu** to shed tears; **mizu o kobósu** to spill water.

kobú bump, swelling, protuberance.

KOCHIRA this place, here; this one;
KOCHIRAGAWA this side. **Dóozo
kochira e.** This way, please. **Tabakoya
wa toorí no kochiragawa désu.** The
cigar store is on this side of the street.

kódachi grove, clump of trees.

KODOMO child; **kodomo rashíi** childish;
kodomoppói childlike; childish.
**Watakushi wa kodomo ga sannin
arimásu.** I have three children.
Kodomoátsukai ni surú na. Don't treat
me like a child.

KÓE voice; **koedaka ni** in a loud voice; **kóe
o kágiri ni** at the top of one's voice;
chiisái kóe de in a low voice; softly;
kogue low voice; whisper; **kogoe de** in a
low voice; in a whisper.

koeda twig, sprig, small branch.

koeru to cross; go across; to pass; to go
beyond; exceed.

kogásu to burn; to scorch, singe.

kogatána small knife; pocketknife.

kogáwase postal money order.

kogechairo dark brown, umber.

kogéru to get scorched, to get burned.

KOGÍTTE (bank) check; **kogítte o kíru** to
issue a check; **kogítte de shiharáu** to pay
by check.

kogoeru to be frozen; to be chilled to the
bone, be numb with cold.

kogoto scolding; blame; **kogoto o iu** to scold;
kogoto o iwareru to be scolded; to be
blamed.

kógu to row; **kogiwatáru** to row across.

kohaku amber.

kói evil intention; evil will; **kói no**
intentional, deliberate; **kói ni** on purpose.
intentionally. **Koi no koto de wa
arimasén.** It isn't anything that was done
intentionally.

KÓI (n.) love; **kói suru** to love; to fall in
love; **koibito** lover; **koishíi** dear; beloved;
koishigáru to yearn for.

kói dark, deep, thick, strong (as tea).

koishi pebble.

koitsu this man (vulgar). **Koitsu!** You rat!

kojíkí beggar.

kójin individual; private citizen; **kojinteki**
personal, private individual; **kojinsei**
individually.

kojínmári to cozily; **kojinmári to shita**
snug, cozy.

kojiréru to go wrong; to get complicated.

kojiakeru to wrench open.

kojitsuke distortion; forced meaning;
kojitsuke no distorted; farfetched.

kojitsukéru to distort, (twist) the meaning.

kokage shade of a tree.

kokiorósu to disparage; to abuse.

kokitsukáu to work like a horse; to drive
(someone) hard.

kókka state, country, nation; **kokka shúgi**
nationalism.

kokkai parliament, national assembly, Diet.

kokkan severe cold; intense cold.

kokkei na comical; **kokkei na hanashí** funny
(comical) story.

kokki national flag.

kokkoo diplomatic relations.

kokkyoo frontier; border; boundaries.

KOKO this place; here; **koko ni** here, in this
place; **koko kara** from here; **koko
shibáraku** for the present; for some time
to come. **Koko da, koko da.** Here we are.
This is the place.

kókoku one's native land.

KOKONOKÁ ninth day of the month.

KOKÓNOTSU nine.

KOKÓRO heart; mind; spirit; **kokoro áru
hito** thoughtful person; **kokoro yukú
made** as one pleases; to one's heart's
content; **kokóro ni kakáru** to be anxious;
kokóro ni ukabu to occur to one; **kokóro
ni tomeru** to bear in mind; **kokóro ga
kawaru** to change one's mind; **kokoro
yásuku náru** to become intimate; **kokóro
no ookíi** broadminded; **kokoro átari** clue;
kokoro átari ga nái to have no idea of;
KOKORO BOSÓI helpless; uneasy;
kokoro bósoku omóu to feel helpless.

kokoroe understanding; knowledge; **kokoroe
chígai** misbehavior, misapprehension.

KOKOROÉRU to know; to think; to
consider.

kokorogákari care; anxiety; concern;
kokorugákari ni náru feel uneasy; to be
anxious.

kokorogake purpose, intention, aim;
attention; **kokorogake no yói** careful;
conscientious.

kokorogakéru to keep in mind; to think
about.

kokorogámae preparedness.

kokorogáwari change of mind; caprice;
kokorogáwari no suru fickle; faithless;
capricious.

kokorogurushíi to be uneasy.

kokoromi trial; experiment; attempt;
kokoromi ni tentatively.

kokoromíru to try, attempt, make an attempt.

kokoromochi feeling, sensation; mood; idea;
shade; **íi kokoromochi ga suru** to feel
comfortable; **kokoromochi yóku**
willingly; **kokoromochi o wáruku suru**
to hurt (someone's) feelings; to displease.

kokoromotonái insecure; apprehensive.

kokoronáki thoughtless; heartless.

kokorone feelings; heart.

kokoroyói pleasant, agreeable, nice; delightful.

kokorozashi will; intention; motive.

kokorozásu to intend; to aim at, aspire to.

kokorozúkai worry, anxiety, concern.

kokorozuke tip, gratuity.

kokorozuyói assuring.

koku– prefix denoting; pertaining to a country, nation, or state; **kokuboo** national defense; **kokufu** national wealth; **kokuhoo** law of the land; **kokúgai** abroad; overseas; outside the country; **kokugo** national language; Japanese language; **KOKUMIN** nation; people; **kokumin kéizai** national economy; **kokumin séikatsu** national life; **kokuseki** nationality, citizenship.

kokuban blackboard; **kokubán fuki** blackboard eraser.

kokubyaku black and white; right and wrong; **kokubyaku o tsukéru** to tell right from wrong; to discriminate between good and bad; **kokubyaku o arasóu** argue the merits (of something).

kokuhatsu prosecution; indictment; accusation.

Kokujin Negro; **Kokujínshu** Negro race.

kokúmotsu cereals, grain, corn; **kokumotsugura** granary.

kokúnai (*n.*) interior; **kokúnai no** domestic; internal; home; **kokunai shoogyoo** domestic commerce.

kokyuu breath; breathing; **kokyuu suru** to breathe.

KOMÁKA NA, KOMAKÁI small, minute; fine, detailed; delicate, thrifty; **komáka na koto** trifling matter; **komakáku chúui suru** to pay close attention.

komaraseru to annoy; to trouble; to muzzle.

KOMÁRU to be distressed; to be embarrassed; to be in trouble; to have a hard time, be hard up.

KOMÉ rice; **komé o tsukúru** to grow (cultivate) rice.

komiáu to be crowded; to be full; to swarm.

KÓMU to be crowded; to be jammed; to be full up. **Kono kishá wa kómu deshoo.** This train will probably be crowded.

kómichi path, lane.

komiíru to be complicated; to get entangled.

komogómo alternately, by turns; reciprocally.

komugi wheat; corn; **komugiko** wheat flour.

kon– prefix denoting: present, current; **KÓNBAN** this evening; tonight; **konchoo** this morning; **KÓNGETSU** this month; **kongetsu tooka** on the tenth of this month; **KÓNNICHI** today; nowadays; the present time; **kónnichi ígo** from now on; from today on. **KONBAN WÁ.** Good

evening. **KONNICHI WÁ!** Good afternoon! Good day!

koná flour; powder; **konagona ni kudáku** to break into pieces; pulverize.

konasu to grind, reduce to powder; to digest; to handle; **joozú ni konasu** to handle with skill.

konboo club, cudgel.

KONDATE menu.

KÓNDO now; this time; next time; new; **kóndo no** this; next; coming; **kóndo iku tóki** the next time I go. **Kóndo no densha de ikimashóo.** Let's take the next train. **Kóndo wa yurúshite agemásu.** I'll forgive you this time.

kongaragáru to get entangled, become involved; to get confused.

kón'i acquaintance; friendship; **kón'i na** intimate, familiar; **kón'i ni shite iru** to be on friendly terms.

konímotsu baggage, luggage.

konki energy; perseverance; patience; **konki no yói** energetic.

konmóri densely; thickly; **konmóri shigétta** densely wooded.

KONNA such; this sort of; **konna fúu ni** in this manner; **konna tóki ni** at a time like this.

kónnan difficulty; difficulties; troubles; **kónnan na** difficult; troublesome; **kónnan suru** to be in difficulty, be in trouble.

KONO this; these; **kono hen ni** in this neighborhood; **kono tsúgi** next time; **kono máe** before this; the last time; **kono saki** hereafter; in the future; **kono yo** this world; this life; **kono yo no** worldly, mundane; **kono yóo na** such; of this sort.

KONOAIDA the other day; recently; not too long ago; **konoaida no ban** the other evening.

KONOGORO these days. **Konogoro wa ikága desu ka?** How have you been lately?

KONOKÁTA since; **júnnen konokáta** these ten years; in the past ten years.

konomí liking, preference, choice.

konómu to like, be fond of; to prefer.

KONPYÚUTAA computer. **dejitaru konpyúutaa** digital computer; **konpyúutaa gengo** computer language; **konpyúutaa puroguramu** computer program; **pasokon** personal computer.

konran commotion, confusion, disorder; **konran suru** to be confused, be in confusion.

KONSHUU this week. **Konshuu no Kin'yóobi ni kité kudasái.** Please come to see me this week on Friday.

konton chaos; **konton táru** chaotic.

kon'yaku (marriage) engagement, betrothal; **kon'yaku suru** to be engaged. **kon'yaku o hákí suru** to break an engagement.

kónzatsu disorder; complication; **kónzatsu suru** to be in disorder, to be confused; to be complicated.

KOO this way. **Koo shite kudasái.** Please do it this way. **Koo nátte wa shikata ga nái.** We can't do much when things go this way.

kooan design, plan; **kooan suru** to design, scheme, plan.

KOOBÁ = **KOOJÓO** factory, mill. **Watakushi wa ano koobá de hataraite imásu.** I am working at that factory.

koobashíi fragrant; savory; favorable.

KOOCHA Western black tea.

koochoo school principal.

koochoo high tide, climax.

koodan platform, pulpit, rostrum.

koodoo lecture hall, auditorium.

koodoo action, movement; conduct, behavior; **koodoo suru** to act, conduct oneself; to move.

kooen support, aid, backing; **kooen suru** to back up, support; **kooénsha** supporter.

KOOEN park, public garden.

KOOEN lecture, address; **kooen suru** to give a lecture; **kooénsha** lecturer.

kóofu workman.

koofuku happiness; well-being; bliss; good fortune; **koofuku na** happy; fortunate; **koofuku ni kurasu** to live a happy life.

koofun stimulation; excitement; **koofun suru** to be stimulated; to be excited.

KÓOGAI suburbs.

KOOGAI public hazard.

koogen plateau.

koogi lecture, discourse.

kóogyoo industry; manufacturing; **koogyóochi** manufacturing district; **koogyooka** manufacturer; **kóogyoo no** industrial.

koohei impartiality; fair play; **koohei na** fair, just, impartial.

KOOHII coffee.

koohyoo favorable criticism; **koohyoo de áru** to be popular, win popularity; to receive favorable criticism.

kóoi kind intentions; kindness.

KOO IU such; this sort of; **koo iu fúu ni** in this way; **koo iu kotó** such a thing as this.

kóoji construction; works; **kooji chuu** under construction.

kóoji alley, lane, narrow street.

koojíru to grow worse, change for the worse.

koojitsu excuse, pretext.

KOOJÓO See **KOOBÁ.**

kóoka effect, result; **kóoka ga nái** not to take effect; to have no result or effect; **kóoka ga áru** to be effective.

kóokai voyage, crossing; **kóokai suru** to sail; navigate.

KOOKAN exchange; **íken kookan** exchange of views; **kookan kákaku** exchange value; **kookándai** telephone switchboard; **kookánshu** telephone operator.

kookan favorable impression, good feeling.

kookei spectacle, sight; scene.

kooken suru to contribute, make a contribution toward; to be conducive to; to go far toward.

kookíshin curiosity; **kookishin no tsuyói** curious.

KOOKOKU advertisement; notice, announcement; **kookoku bíra** poster, placard; **kookoku suru** to advertise; **sangyoo kookoku** classified advertisement.

kóokoo so and so; such and such; **kóokoo iu wáke de** under such (these) circumstances.

kóokoo filial piety, obedience to parents.

kookotsu rapture, ecstasy; **kookotsu to suru** to be in ecstasy; to be enraptured; to be enchanted.

kookuubin airmail.

kookúuki aircraft.

kookyoo (n.) public; society; **kookyoo no** public; common; **kookyóoshin no áru** community-minded.

kookyoo prosperity, business boom.

kookyóogaku symphony; **kookyoogákudan** symphony orchestra.

koonoo effect, efficacy; virtue; **koonoo no nái** ineffective; **koonoo no áru** effective; useful; **koonoo ga áru** to be good for; to be effective, be useful.

KOORI ice; **koori no hatta** frozen, covered with ice; **koorizume no** refrigerated; iced.

kooroo merits, meritorious deed; **kooroo áru** meritorious.

kooron dispute; **kooron suru** to dispute, quarrel.

kooru to freeze.

kóoryoku effect, efficacy; **kóoryoku no áru** valid; effective.

koosa intersection, crossing; **koosa suru** to intersect, cross; **koosáten** intersection, crossroad.

koosai intercourse; association; society; company; fellowship; **koosaika** sociable person; good mixer.

koosan surrender, capitulation; **koosan suru** to surrender, submit; **koosan saseru** to make someone surrender.

koosatsu consideration; contemplation; **koosatsu suru** to consider, weight; to examine; to contemplate.

kooseki distinguished service.

koosen light; beam (ray) of light; **koosen o ireru** to let in the light.

koosetsu public; municipal **koosetsu shíjoo** public market.

kóoshi lecturer.

kóoshi minister (diplomatic service); **kooshíkan** legation; **kooshikán'in attaché**; legation personnel.

kooshiki formula; formality; **kooshiki no** formal; state; official; **kooshiki de arawásu** to formulate.

kooshoo negotation; **kooshoo chuu** under negotiation; **kooshoo suru** to negotiate; **nánra no kooshoo mo nái** to have nothing to do with.

kooshuu (n.) public; **kooshuu bénjo** comfort station, public lavatory; **kooshuu yókujoo** public bath; **kooshuu no** public; common.

koosoku confinement; restraint; detention; **koosoku suru** to confine, detain; **koosoku o úkete inái** to be free from restraint.

koosókudo high speed; rapid transit.

koosui perfume, cologne, scent; **koosui o tsukéru** to use perfume.

kootai relief; substitution; **kootai ni** alternately; in turn; **kootai suru** to relieve; take turns.

Kootáishi Crown Prince.

kootei affirmation; **kootei suru** to affirm; to acknowledge; **kooteiteki** affirmative.

kootei fluctuation, high and low, unevenness, undulations; **kootei áru** fluctuating, undulating.

kootoo oral, verbal; **kootoo de** orally, verbally.

kootoo gákkoo senior high school.

KOOTSUU communication; traffic; **kootsuu kikán** means of communication; **kootsuu o séiri suru** to control traffic; **kootsuu no bén o hakáru** to facilitate communications.

kootsúgoo favorable circumstances; **kootsúgoo no** convenient; **kootsúgoo na** favorable; fortunate; **kootsúgoo ni** conveniently, etc.; **kootsúgoo de áru** to suit one's convenience.

kooun good luck, stroke of luck; **kooun na** lucky, fortunate; **kooun ní mo** fortunately; luckily.

kooza (university) chair, professorship; university course.

kóozan mine; **koozan gíshi** mining engineer; **koozángyoo** mining industry.

koozen openly; in public; **koozen no** open; public; official.

koozoo construction; structure; formation.

kóozui flood, inundation.

KOPPU glass (for drinking). **Koppu o mízu o íppai kudasái.** May I have a glass of water? (See also **káppu.**)

koraéru to bear, endure; to control; to restrain; **itása o koraéru** to endure the pain.

KORE this; these; **kore hodo** this much; so much, so many; **kore kágiri** this is all; once and for all.

korikatamáru to coagulate; to be absorbed in, to be bigoted.

korigori suru, koríru to take warning from; to learn by experience.

koroai suitable; adequate, handy; **koroai o hakátte** just in time.

korobu to fall to the ground.

korogaru to roll; to tumble; to fall; to lie down.

korogasu to roll; to tumble down.

korosu to kill, put to death; **íki o koroshite** with bated breath, breathlessly.

kóru to be absorbed in; to be devoted to; to get stiff; **kenkyuu ni kóru** to be absorbed in one's studies; **tabemóno ni kóru** to be fussy about eating.

kosame light rain, drizzle.

kósei individuality; personality; idiosyncrasy.

KOSHI hip(s); waist; loin; **koshi o suéru** to settle down; **koshikáke** seat, stool, etc.

KOSHIKAKÉRU to sit on a chair.

KOSHIRAERU to make, manufacture; to prepare; to build; to raise; **hako o koshiraeru** to make a box; **kane o koshiraeru** to raise funds; to make a fortune.

koshoo obstacle, hitch; defect; accident; protest, objection; mechanical trouble; **koshoo náku** without a hitch; without any trouble. **Koshoo ga nái.** Nothing is wrong. Nothing is the matter.

KOSHÓO pepper.

kósokoso stealthily, secretly, sneakingly; **kósokoso déte iku** to sneak out.

kosu to go over, go across; to outrun; to move; to pass; **yamá o kosu** to go over the top; to pass the most difficult point.

kosui lake; **kosui no sóba** lakeside.

kosúru to rub; to scrub; to scrape; **mé o kosúru** to rub one's eyes.

kotáe answer, reply, response; solution.

KOTAÉRU to answer, reply, respond; **–ni kotáete** in reply (answer) to; **sóo da to kotaéru** to answer in the affirmative; **shitsumon ni kotaéru** to answer a question.

kotaéru to come home, to strike home, to have an effect on; to be a strain on. **Anó**

hito no kotobá wa mí ni kotaemáshita.
Her words came home to me.

kote iron (for clothes); soldering iron; trowel;
kote o ateru to iron clothes; to solder; to
curl with tongs.

KOTÓ thing; matter, affair; account; event,
occurrence; duty, task; **kotó naku** without
a hitch; uneventfully, peacefully. **Sore wa
nán no kotó desu ka?** What does it
mean? What do you mean? **Sore wa kotó
to baai ni yoru.** That depends on the
circumstances.

kotoyósete on the pretense that; under the
guise of. **Byooki ni kotoyósete jishoku
shimáshita.** He resigned his post on the
pretext of ill health.

KOTOBÁ language; word; term; speech;
expression; **kotobá o kakéru** to speak; to
call to; **kotobá o kawasu** to exchange
words with; **kotobá o nigósu** to give a
vague answer; **kotoba tákumi ni**
persuasively, convincingly. **Kono kotoba
no ími wa nán desu ka?** What is the
meaning of this word?

KOTOGÓTOKU wholly, entirely;
completely; without exception, in every
case. **Koko ni aru hón wa kotogótoku
yomimáshita.** I have read all the books
here.

KÓTO NI especially; above all; moreover.
koto no hoka remarkably, extremely,
unusually.

kotosara ní intentionally, on purpose,
purposely.

KOTOSHI this year; present year. **Kotoshi
no natsú wa taihen atsúi desu.** It is very
hot this summer.

kotowári excuse; denial; refusal; warning;
notice; **kotowári mo náku** without
permission, without one's knowledge.

KOTOWÁRU to make excuses; to refuse,
decline; to ask permission; **téi yoku
kotowáru** to decline politely.

kotowaza saying, maxim, proverb.

kótsukotsu to untiringly; laboriously;
kótsukotsu to arúku to plod; **kótsukotsu
to shigoto o suru** to work untiringly.

kowabáru to stiffen; to get stiff.

kowagáru to fear, be afraid of; to be
frightened; **kowagowa** timidly, fearfully.
Nani mo kowagaru kotó wa nái. You
have nothing to be afraid of.

kowái fearful, frightful, terrible, horrible;
kowái kao angry look; grim face; **kowái
mé ni au** to have a terrible experience.

koware breakage; fragment; **kowaremono**
fragile thing.

KOWARÉRU to break; to be broken; to be
ruined; **Mádo ga kowárete imasu.** The

window is broken. **kowareyasúi** fragile.

KOWASÚ to break down; to destroy,
demolish, smash, wreck; **ié o kowásu** to
pull down a house; **karada o kowásu** to
ruin one's health.

koyá hut, shed, cabin; pen.

koyashí manure; fertilizer.

koyomi calendar; almanac.

KOZÚTSUMI parcel; small package;
kozutsumi yúubin de by parcel post.

KÚ pain; suffering; bitterness; **kú ni náru**
become worried about; bother; to cause
anxiety; **kú ni suru** take seriously; be
concerned about, be worried about. **Áme
wa sukoshi mo kú ni narimasén.** The
rain doesn't bother me at all. **Sonna kotó
o kú ni surú na.** Don't trouble yourself
about such a matter.

KÚ = **KYÚU** nine; **dáiku** ninth.

kubáru to distribute; to deal out; to dispose
(of); **shinbun o kubáru** to deliver a
newspaper.

kúbetsu distinction; classification, division;
kúbetsu suru to distribute; to differentiate
(between good and bad); **kúbetsu o
tsukéru** to make a distinction.

KUBI neck; head; **kubi ni suru** to dismiss;
discharge; **kubi ni náru** to be dismissed;
kubi o nágaku shite mátsu to wait
impatiently; **kubimaki** scarf, muffler;
kubiwa (dog) collar.

kubomi cavity; hollow; dent.

kubomu to become hollow; to be depressed;
to sink.

KUBU DOORI nearly; in all probability; ten
to one. **Kubu doori dekimáshita.** It is
nearly done.

kubun division; **kubun suru** to divide,
partition.

KUCHI mouth; door, aperture; hole; post;
kind; share; **kuchi no tassha na** fluent;
kuchi no karui talkative; **kuchi ga aku**
to open; burst open; **kuchi o kíru** to
break a seal; to open the mouth;
KUCHIBIRU lips; **kuchibue** whistle;
kuchibue o fúku to whistle.

kuchidashi meddling, interference;
kuchidashi suru to meddle; to poke one's
nose in someone else's business.

kuchidome suru to hush up (a matter); to
stop (someone) from speaking.

kuchigótae retort; **kuchigótae suru** to answer
back.

kuchiurusái See **kuchiyakamashíi.**

kuchiyakamashíi = **kuchiurusai** nagging;
critical.

KUDÁMONO fruit; **kudamónoya**
fruit-seller. **Kudámono ga hoshíi desu.**
I want some fruit.

KUDARANAI stupid, foolish; absurd; useless, insignificant; **kudaranai kotó o iu** to talk foolishly.

kudari (*n.*) going down, down; **kudarizaka** downgrade, downhill.

KUDASÁI please give me. **Sore o kudasái.** Please give it to me.

KUDASÁRU to offer; to give (respect). **Kore o watakushi ni kudasáru no desu ka?** Is this for me? **Hitótsu kudasáru wáke ni wa ikimasén ka?** Can't you spare me one of these?

kudói tedious; long-winded.

kudóku to make love to; to attempt to seduce; to entreat; to solicit.

kufuu device; contrivance; plan; scheme; means; expedient; **kufuu suru** to scheme, etc.

KÚGATSU September.

kugi nail; **kugi o útsu** to nail; **kugi o sásu** to remind someone of what he or she must do.

kugirí full stop; pause; period; **kugirí o tsukéru** to settle; to put an end to.

kugúru to pass through; **món o kugúru** to go through a gate.

kui post; stake; pile.

kúiki limit; boundary; **kúiki no** inside the boundary.

kuikomi loss; deficit.

kuikómu to eat into; to encroach upon; to leave a deficit, to go into one's capital. **Séngetsu wa ichi man en kuikomimáshita.** Last month there was a deficit of ten thousand yen.

kuíru to regret; be sorry for.

kuitomeru to check; hold in check; arrest.

kuitsuku to bite; to snap; to take the bait. **Inú ni ashi o kuitsukaremáshita.** I was bitten by a dog.

kuitsuméru to have no means of subsistence.

kujikéru to be disheartened; to lose heart.

kujíku to sprain; wrench; break; crush; discourage; **udé o kujíku** to break an arm; **ashíkubi o kujíku** to sprain an ankle.

KYÚUJUU ninety.

KUKKÍRI clearly; distinctly; plainly; strikingly.

kukyoo adversity; awkward situation; **kukyoo ni ochíru** to be put in an awkward situation.

kumen contrivance; makeshift; **kumen suru** to devise; to contrive; to manage.

KUMÍ class; gang; band; company; team; crew; set, pack; **kumigáshira** head of a group; boss; **kumiawaséru** to combine, join together; to match; **kumiai** association; guild; partnership; **kumiáiin** member (of an association); **kumiai kéisan** joint account.

kumidásu to dip out; to bail out.

kumitate structure, framework; system, organization.

KÚMO cloud(s); **kúmo o tsuku yóo na** lofty; towering; **kúmo o tsukámu yóo na** vague; visionary; **kumogire** break in the clouds; **kumo yuki o míru** to see how the wind blows; to wait for the results.

kumori cloudy, overcast; **kumori náki** clean; clear; cloudless; spotless; **kumoríbi** cloudy day; **kumori gárasu** frosted glass.

KUMÓRU to get cloudy. **Sóra ga kumótte kimashita.** The sky is getting cloudy. **Kará wa kao ga kumorimáshita.** His face became clouded.

kúmu to unite; to associate with; to be in a partnership with; to braid; to fit together; to pair with; **hiza o kúmu** to cross one's legs; **udé o kúmu** to fold one's arms.

–kun suffix denoting: Mr. (same as **san** but usually used for and by men); **Yamada-kun** Mr. Yamada.

KUNI country, land, state, nation; province; territory; **kunimoto** native (home) province; **kuni námari** dialect. **Dóno kuni kara irasshaimáshita ka?** From which country have you come?

kurá warehouse; storehouse; granary; **kurabárai** clearance sale.

KURABERU to compare; to contrast; to match; **ookisa o kuraberu** to compare the size.

kuragari darkness; dark place; **kuragari de** in the dark.

kurai grade, rank; **kurai suru** to stand; to be situated, be located; to lie; **kurai ga tsuku** to gain in dignity.

KURAI dark, dim, gloomy, obscure; **kuraku náru** to become dark. **Totemo kurái desu.** It's very dark.

–kurai See **–GURAI**.

kurashi living, livelihood; **kurashikata** one's manner of living; **kurashi o tatéru** to make one's living; **KURASU** to live; to make a living; **rippa ni kurasu** to live well.

kurayami dark, darkness; **kurayami de** in the dark.

Kuréguremo repeatedly; earnestly.

KURERU to give; to grant. **Anó hito ga watakushi ni sore o kureta.** He gave it to me.

kureru to grow dark. **Hi ga kurete kimáshita.** The day is growing dark.

kuréyon crayon.

kuriagéru to move up; advance; **kíjitsu o kuriagéru** to move up a date.

kuriawase arrangement.

kuriawaséru, kuríawásu to make time; to arrange the time.

kurliréru to transfer; to carry forward.

KURIKÁESU to repeat; reiterate. **Moo ichido kurikáeshite kudasái.** Please repeat it.

kurikómu to carry over; to carry into.

kurikósu to transfer; to carry forward; to bring over.

KURISÚMASU Christmas.

KÚRO black; **kuro nuri no** black-lacquered; painted black; **kuro kumo** dark clouds.

KURÓI black; tanned; dusky; **kurói kamí** black hair. **Anó hito wa iró ga kurói.** He has a dark complexion.

kúroo hardship; suffering; care, concern; **kuróo shoo no** nervous; worrisome; **kúroo suru** to work hard.

kuróoto expert; professional; specialist; connoisseur.

KÚRU to come; to come over; to arrive. **Háru ga kimáshita.** Spring has come. **Otégami ga kimáshita.** Here is a letter for you. **Ashita kúru deshoo.** It will probably come tomorrow.

kuruí disorder, confusion; madness; **kuruí ga kúru** to get out of order.

KURUMA car, vehicle, carriage, cart, wagon; wheel; **kuruma de iku** to go by car.

kurumáru to be wrapped up in; to tuck oneself into or wrap oneself in; **kurúmu** to wrap up; to cover up; to coat, gild.

KURUSHÍI painful; hard; trying; distressing; **kurushíi mé ni áu** to undergo great suffering; **kurushíi tachibá ni iru** to be in an awkward position.

kurushiméru to torment, torture; to persecute; kokoró o kurushiméru to worry; **doobutsu o kurushiméru** to be cruel to (an) animal(s).

kurushimi pain, suffering; hardship; agony; torture.

KURUSHÍMU to feel pain; to suffer from; to be worried; **hín ni kurushímu** to be poverty-stricken. **Náni o sonna ni kurushínde irú no desu ka?** What are you suffering so much from? What makes you suffer so?

kurúu to go mad; to get out of order; to go wrong; to fluctuate. **Kono tokei wa dóko ka kurútte iru.** There is something wrong with this watch.

kusá grass; herb; weed; **kusá o karu** to mow grass; **niwa no kusá o tóru** to weed a garden.

kusái stinking, bad-smelling.

kusamí stink, offensive odor.

kusarásu to corrupt; to cause to decay; to spoil.

kusáru to rot, decay; to turn sour; to corrode; **kusátta** rotten, sour. **ki ga kusáru** to feel low.

kusari chain; tether.

kusé habit, way; characteristic, peculiarity; **kusé ga tsuku** to get into a habit; **kusé o tsukéru** to form a habit; **kusé o naósu** to break a habit.

kushakusha na creased; wrinkled.

kushami sneezing; sneeze; **kushami ga déru** to sneeze.

KUSHÍ comb; **kushí** skewer, spit; **kushí de kamí o tóku** to comb hair.

kushín care; anxiety; struggle; **kushín suru** to take pains; to do one's best.

kushoo bitter smile; forced smile.

kusubúru to smoke, smolder; **uchi ni kusubútte iru** to remain indoors.

KUSURI medicine, drug; remedy; cure; physic; **kusuri o kau** to buy a medicine; **kusuri o nómu** to take a medicine; **kusuriya** pharmacist; druggist; drugstore.

KUTABIRÉRU, TSUKARERU to get tired; to be exhausted; **machikutabiréru** to be tired of waiting.

KUTSU shoes; boots; **kutsu zure ga dekíru** to have one's feet hurt from wearing shoes; **kutsunúgui** doormat; **kutsu himo** shoelace; **kutsúzumi** shoe polish; **KUTSÚYA** shoe store; shoe-repair shop.

kutsurógu to be at ease; to relax; to make oneself comfortable; **kutsuróide hanásu** to have a heart-to-heart talk.

KUTSÚSHITA socks; stockings; **kutsushitadome** garters.

kuttsukéru to join; to attach; to glue; to stick.

KÚUKI air; atmosphere; **shinsen na kúuki** fresh air; **kúuki no ryuutsuu** the ventilation of air.

kuusoo fancy; vision; fantasy; **kuusooka** dreamer; **kuusooteki** visionary; imaginary; **kuusoo o egáku** to build castles in the sky.

kuwadate plan, scheme; attempt, undertaking; **kuwadatéru** to plan, scheme; to devise; to attempt, undertake.

kuwaeru to add (up); to give; to deliver; to offer; **bujoku o kuwaeru** to insult someone. **Ní ni ní o kuwaeru to yón desu.** Two and two are four.

kuwaeru to hold in the mouth; to bite; **yubí o kuwaete** looking wistfully [with finger in the mouth].

KUWASHÍI to be well versed; detailed; minute; particular; familiar with; **kuwáshiku** minutely; to detail; at length;

particularly; **kuwáshiku nobéru** to
explain in detail; to give full particulars.
**Kuwashíí hanashí wa áto de
hanashimashóo.** Later we shall talk about
it in detail. **Anó hito wa rekishi ni
kuwashíí desu.** He is well versed in
history.

KUWAWARU to join; to enter; to
participate, take part in; **ikkno ni
kuwawaru** to join the party; **kyóogi ni
kuwawaru** to take part in the game.

kuyamí condolence; repentance; regret;
kuyamíjoo letter of condolence; **kuyami
o nobéru** to offer one's condolences.

kuyámu to regret; to repent of; to lament.

kuyashíí regrettable; vexing.

kuyáshisa regret.

kúyokuyo suru to worry about; to worry
(oneself); to take to heart; to brood over.

kuuzen no unprecedented; unequaled;
record-breaking. **Sore wa kuuzen no
dekígoto desu.** That is an unprecedented
event.

kúzu waste, refuse, trash; **kuzúkago**
wastepaper basket; **kuzutetsu** scrap iron.

kuzuréru to go to pieces, collapse, give
away; to get out of shape.

KUZÚSU to pull down; to break down; to
destroy; to change. **Kono sen en satsu o
kuzúshite kudasai.** Please break this
one-thousand-yen bill.

KYAKU visitor; guest; customer; patron;
passenger; **kyakusha** passenger train;
kyakusen passenger boat; **okyaku sama**
personal guest; customer (*respect*).

kyakuhon script, scenario; **kyakuhonka**
playwright.

kyakushoku dramatization; adaptation; plot.

kyóhi suru to deny, refuse; to reject.

kyóka permission; leave; admission; license;
kyóka suru to permit, allow; to admit; to
authorize.

kyóku office; department; bureau;
yuubínkyoku post office.

KYOKUTOO Far East.

KYÓNEN = **sakunen** last year; **kyónen no
Ichigatsu** January of last year.

kyoo interest; amusement; **kyoo o samásu**
to spoil the fun; **kyoo o soéru** to add
to the fun; **kyoo ga noru** to become
interested.

KYÓO today. **Kyóo wa nan'yóobi desu ka?**
What day of the week is today?

kyooboo collusion, complicity; **kyooboo suru**
to conspire; plot together; **kyoobóosha**
accomplice.

kyoochoo cooperation; **kyoochoo suru** to
cooperate; to act harmoniously.

KYÓODAI brothers and sisters. **Kyóodai wa**

nánn in arimásu ka? How many brothers
and sisters do you have?

kyoodan teacher's platform; pulpit.

kyoodoo cooperation; collaboration;
partnership; association; union; **kyoodoo
dóosa** united action; **kyoodoo kánri** joint
control; **kyoodoo no** common, joint.

kyoofu fear, fright, dread; **kyoofu o kanjiru**
to fear, etc.

kyoogaku coeducation.

kyóogi game, match; **kyoogijoo** arena;
kyoogíkai tournament, meet; **kyoogísha**
contestant.

kyóogi conference; discussion; **kyóogi suru**
to consult; to confer with.

kyooguu condition; situation; circumstance.

kyoohaku compulsion; threat, menace;
kyoohaku suru to compel; to threaten,
intimidate.

kyoohan complicity; **kyoohánsha**
accomplice.

kyóoi astonishment, wonder; **kyooiteki**
surprising; wonderful.

kyooiku education; training; **kyooiku suru**
to educate; to train; to bring up.

kyooju teaching; instruction; professor;
faculty; **kyoojuhoo** methods of teaching.

kyooin schoolteacher.

kyookai association.

kyookai church; religious association;
kyookaidoo church building; cathedral.

kyookai border, boundary.

kyoomei resonance; sympathy; response;
kyoomei suru to sympathize with; to
echo; respond to.

kyóomi interest, appeal; **kyóomi no áru**
interesting; attractive; **kyóomi no
nái** dull, uninteresting; lacking in
appeal.

kyóoshi teacher, tutor; professor; master.
(See also **KYOOIKU.**)

kyooshitsu schoolroom, classroom.

kyooshuku obligation; humiliation;
kyooshuku suru to be much obliged, be
grateful to, appreciate deeply; to be sorry
for, regret. **Osokunátte kyooshuku désu.**
I am sorry to be late.

kyoosoo competition, rivalry; footrace; sprint;
kyoosoo shikén competitive examination;
kyoosoo suru to compete, contest; to run
a race; **kyoosóosha** rival, competitor.

kyootaku kin securities deposit.

kyootei agreement, pact; **kyootei suru** to
agree; to agree upon; **kyootei nédan**
stipulated price.

kyootsuu no common.

kyootsúuten common feature; thing in
common.

kyooyaku agreement, pact.

kyooyoo extortion; exaction; **kyooyoo suru** to extort.

kyooyoo no for common use; **kyooyoo suru** to use something in common.

kyooyuu co-ownership; **kyooyuu suru** to hold jointly; **kyooyúusha** co-owner, joint owner; **kyooyuuzáisan** common property.

kyoozai teaching materials.

kyóri distance; range; radius; **kyóri ga áru** to be far, distant.

kyozetsu refusal; rejection; **kyozetsu suru** to refuse; reject.

KYÚU = KU, KOKÓNOTSU nine.

kyúu class; grade (in a school); **ikkyuu** first grade; **nikyuu** second grade.

kyuu– prefix denoting: quick, sudden, abrupt; steep; **kyuubyoo** sudden illness; **kyuuhen** sudden change.

KYUU urgency; emergency; **kyuu ni** suddenly; **kyuu ni sonaéru** to provide for an emergency; **kyuu o tsugeru** to be urgent; to become critical; **kyuu o yoosúru** urgent; **kyuuba** critical moment; **kyuuba no shóchi** emergency measure.

kyúuchi difficult situation; fix.

kyuuen rescue; help; **kyuuen suru** to relieve; rescue; to reinforce.

kyuugyoo vacation; suspension of operation; **kyuugyoo suru** to close; to take a holiday; to suspend one's business.

kyúujo relief, help **kyúujo suru** to rescue, save; to help **kyuujoami** safety net; **kyuujosen** lifeboat.

kyuuka holidays, vacation; leave of absence.

kyuukai adjournment; **kyuukai suru** to adjourn.

KYUUKÓO express (train); **kyuukoo suru** to rush; to dash; to go like an express; **kyuukooréssha** express train. **tokubetsu kyuukooréssha** special express train; **kyuukooryóokin** express charges.

M

ma space; room; apartment; time, interval, spare moments; **ma ga áru** to have time; **ma mó naku** before long, in a little while; **magashi suru** to rent out a room; **ma ga wáruku** unfortunately.

ma truth; **ma ni ukéru** to accept as truth, to believe what one hears.

MÁA 1. Indeed! Dear me! (woman-talk) **Máa dóoshita no?** Dear me! What happened? 2. I should say, well. **Máa sóo desu.** Well, it's something like that. 3. Just. **Máa mátte kudasái.** Just wait, please.

maaketingu marketing.

maatarashíi brand-new.

mabara sparcity; **mabara na** sparse, thin, scattered; **mabara ni** sparsely, thinly; here and there.

mabátaki wink, blink; **mabátaki suru** to wink, blink; **mabátaki suru ma ni** in the twinkling of an eye.

mabayúi dazzling, glaring.

mabíku to thin out; to eliminate.

maboroshi phantom; apparition; vision; illusion.

mabúsu to cover with, sprinkle with.

MÁBUTA eyelid. .

MACHÍ town, city; street; **machi házure** outskirts of town; **machí e iku** to go to town.

MACHIÁISHITSU waiting room.

machiawaséru to meet, rendezvous (with); to wait for.

machibooke waiting in vain; **machibooke o kúu** to wait for someone in vain; **machibooke o kuwásu** to keep someone waiting in vain.

machidooshíi to be impatient; to be long in coming.

MACHIGAÉRU = MACHIGÁU to mistake, err, make a mistake, blunder; **hatsuon o machigaéru** to pronounce incorrectly; **michi o machigaéru** to take the wrong road; **machigáete** by mistake, in error. **Futatsu machigaemáshita.** I made two mistakes.

MACHIGÁI mistake, error; fault; accident; **machigái naku** without fail; certainly; **machigái o shoozúru** to cause an accident.

MACHIGÁU, MACHIGAÉRU

machikamaéru to await eagerly; to wait anxiously.

machikanéru to wait impatiently for. **Omachikane no nímotsu ga todokimáshita.** The baggage that you have been waiting for so long has arrived.

machimachi diversity; variety; **machimachi no** diverse, various; divergent, conflicting.

MÁDA as yet; not yet (when used with a negative); still; so far. **Anó ko wa máda honno kodomo désu.** She (he) is still a mere child. **Máda futatsu arimásu.** We still have two.

MÁDE till, until, up to; to; as far as; **Tookyoo máde** as far as Tokyo; **ása kara ban máde** from morning till night.

MÁDO window; **mado gárasu** windowpane; **mádo o akeru** to open a window; **mádo o shiméru** to close a window.

MÁE time before; past; front; since; **máe no** previous, former; **máe ni** formerly, prior;

mae mótte beforehand; **máe kara**
previously; from the front.

máeba front tooth.

maebárai prepayment; **maebárai no** prepaid;
maebárai suru to pay in advance.

maebure announcement; preliminary notice.

maekake apron.

maekóojoo prologue; preamble.

maeoki preliminary statement, introduction.

magari crook, bend, turn.

MAGARU to bend, to yield; to turn; to
wind; **magatta** bent, crooked, etc.;
magarikunétta michi winding (rambling)
road.

MAGERU to bend, curve. **Soko o magete
onegai itashimásu.** Please say yes.
[Please bring yourself to consent (against
your will).]

magirásu to turn away, divert; **ki o
magirásu** to divert (someone's) attention.

magirawashíi confusing; ambiguous;
misleading.

magire confusion; **magire no nái** evident,
unmistakable; **magire mo náku**
undoubtedly.

magirekómu to get mixed with; lost among;
gunshuu ni magirekómu to get lost in
the crowd; to be hidden in the crowd.

magiréru to be mistaken for; to become
confused.

mágiwa verge, brink; **mágiwa ni** on the
verge of; **mágiwa ni nátte** at the last
minute.

MAGÓ grandchild.

magókoro sincerity; devotion; **magókoro no
áru** sincere.

mágomago suru to be at a loss; to be
bewildered.

magureátari lucky hit, lucky shot; fluke.

MAGURO tuna fish.

mahi paralysis; numbness; **mahi suru** to be
paralyzed; **mahi shita** paralyzed.

MAI– prefix denoting: every, each; **maido**
every time, each time; **maigetsu** every
month; **mainen** every year; **máiasa** every
morning; **máiban** every evening.

–MAI counter denoting: sheet; piece; page;
leaf (a counter); **kami sánmai** three
sheets of paper.

majiwari association; relations.

majiwáru to associate with; to mingle with.
**Anó hito wa hito to majiwáru koto o
kiraimásu.** She dislikes mingling with
people.

makaséru to entrust (something to someone);
to leave a person with some matter or
business; **nariyuki ni makaséru** to let the
matter take its course. **Bánji kimi ni
makasemásu.** I leave everything to you.

makasu to beat; to overpower; to beat down
(a price), to bargain; **hyaku yen ni
makasu** to beat down the price to 100
yen. **Káre o iimakásu kotó ga dekínai.** I
can't beat him in an argument.

make defeat, loss; lost game.

makeru to lose, be defeated; to concede,
yield; to be outdone; to reduce (the
price); **makezu otórazu** closely matched.
Makete kuremasen ka? Can't you make
it cheaper?

makijaku tape measure.

makikómu to roll up; to wrap up, enfold in.

makitábako = **shigaretto** cigarette;
makitábako ikko pack of cigarettes;
makitabakóire cigarette case.

MAKKÁ NA crimson, deep red; **makká na
úso** outright lie; **makká ni náru** to turn
red, blush deeply.

makkúra pitch darkness; **makkúra na** pitch
dark.

MAKKÚRO NA deep black, ebony;
makkúro na kami nó ke jet-black hair.

MAKOTO truth; sincerity; honesty;
faithfulness; **makoto no** genuine; real;
sincere; **MAKOTO NI** truthfully;
sincerely; really; greatly, exceedingly.

makú curtain, hanging screen, drapery; act;
shomaku opening act, first act; **makú o
hikishibóru** to pull a curtain aside. **Makú
ga aku.** The curtain rises.

MAKU to wind, roll, coil, reel; **tokei no néji
o maku** to wind up a clock.

MÁKU to scatter, strew, sprinkle; to sow;
shibafu ni mizu o máku to sprinkle the
lawn with water.

MÁKURA pillow, cushion; **mákura o suru**
to rest one's head on a pillow.

makuru to turn (roll, tuck) up; **udé o
makuru** to roll up one's sleeves.

makushitatéru to argue furiously.

MAMA as; as is; as it stands; intact; **sono
mama** just as it is; **sono mama ni shite
oku o leave** (something, or someone)
as is. **Mamá yo.** I don't care. Never
mind.

mamé beans; peas; soybeans; midget; tiny;
mame jidóosha midget car.

mame na healthy, robust; brisk, active;
faithful; **mame ni hataraku** to work
briskly.

mamiréru to be covered, stained with; **doró
ni mamiréru** to be covered with mud.

MAMÓRU to protect, defend, guard; to
obey; **hoo o mamóru** to obey the laws;
yakusoku o mamóru to keep a promise.

MAMÚKOO just opposite; just in front of;
mamúkoo no just opposite; **mamúkoo ni**
right (just) in front of.

MÁN ten thousand; myriad; **mán ni hitótsu** one in ten thousand.

manabu to learn, study.

manben náku without exception; equally; uniformly.

mane imitation, mimicry; **maneru** to imitate; copy, mimic, simulate; **manete in** imitation of.

manekí invitation; beckoning.

MANÉKU to invite; to call in; to bring upon oneself.

maniawase (*n.*) makeshift, expedient; **maniawase no** temporary.

maniawaséru to manage with, make do, serve the purpose.

MÁN'ICHI by any chance; by any possibility; even though; **mán'ichi no baai ní wa** if anything should happen; in case of emergency.

MAN'IN no vacancy; full house; crowded; **man'ín fuda** "sold out" notice; "SRO" notice.

manjoo whole house, hall, assembly; **manjoo ittchi de** unanimously; with one accord.

manki expiration (of a contract); maturity; **manki ni náru** to fall due; to expire; to serve a full term.

manmaru na, manmarui perfectly round.

MANNAKA center, middle; heart; **mannaka ni** in the center; right in the middle.

mannénhitsu fountain pen.

mansei no chronic, confirmed.

manukaréru to escape; to get rid of, be freed from; to be exempt; **ayauku manugaréru** to have a narrow escape.

manuke (*colloq.*) stupid person, ass; half-wit; **manuke na** stupid, foolish.

manzara not wholly; not altogether. **Manzara báka de wa nái.** He is not a complete fool.

manzen at random, aimlessly; vaguely.

MÁNZOKU satisfaction, gratification; **mánzoku na** satisfactory; complete; **mánzoku ni** satisfactorily; **mánzoku shite** contentedly; **mánzoku suru** to be satisfied. **Mánzoku shimáshita.** I am satisfied.

mappádaka nakedness, nudity; **mappádaka no** stark naked.

mappíra not by any means; not for anything. **Sonna kotó wa mappíra desu.** I wouldn't do it for anything.

mapputátsu ni right in two; **mapputátsu ni suru** to cut right in two.

marason marathon (race).

MARE NA rare, unusual, uncommon; **mare ni** rarely, seldom.

marí ball; **marí o tsuku** to play (with a) ball.

maru circle, ring.

MARUI circular, round, spherical. **marui kso (marugao)** round face; **MARUKU** round; in a circle; peacefully; smoothly; **mé o maruku shite** wide-eyed; with the eyes wide open; **maruku osameru** to smooth over (a quarrel); to patch up.

marumeru to make round.

MARUDE quite; thoroughly; almost like. **Marude nátte inai.** It's quite hopeless. **Marude Nihonjín no yóo ni hanashimásu.** He speaks almost like a Japanese.

marukiri = marukkiri completely, entirely.

marumóoke clear profit; cleanup; **marumóoke o suru** make a clear profit.

MÁSAKA by no means, on no account; surely not; you don't say; **másaka no tokí ni** in time of need; in an emergency. **Másaka sonna kotó wa arumái.** It's not at all likely.

mása ni just, exactly. **Mása ni sono tóori desu.** It's exactly true.

masáru to surpass, excel.

masáshiku certainly, no doubt. **Masáshiku anó hito no yatta kotó desu.** There is no question that he has done it.

masatsu rubbing, chafing, friction; **masatsu suru** to rub (against or with), chafe.

máseta precocious; **máseta kodomo** precocious child; **másete iru** to be precocious.

mashi increase; addition; extra; **mashi jikan** overtime; extra time; **ichi warí mashi** a 10 percent increase.

–MÁSHITA verb ending; past of **masu** (*marks ordinary pol. verbs*). **Kinoo gakkoo e ikimáshita.** I went to school yesterday. **Tsukue no ué ni hón ga arimáshita.** There was a book on the table.

mashitáni right under, directly below; **mádo no mashitá ni** right beneath the window.

máshite much more; how much more. **Hawai ní itta kotó mo nái no desu. Máshite Nihón ni wa ichido mo ikimasen.** I haven't been to Hawaii, let alone Japan.

massáichuu in the midst of; at the height of.

massákari height; prime; full bloom; **massákari de áru** to be at the height of; to be in full bloom.

massákasama ni headfirst; headlong; head over heels.

massáki (*n.*) foremost; head; **massaki no** first; foremost; **massaki ni** at the very beginning; first of all.

massáo na deep blue; deadly pale; white as a sheet; **massáo ni náru** to turn as white as a sheet.

masshígura ni impetuously; at full speed; full tilt.

MASSHÍRO NA pure white; snow white; **masshiro na kimono** pure white clothes.

MASSHÓOMEN direct, front; **masshóomen ni** directly in front of; directly opposite; full in the face; **masshóomen no tatémono** the building directly opposite.

MASSÚGU NA straight; direct; upright; **massúgu ni** directly; in a straight line.

MASU to increase; to swell; to raise; to rise. **Jinkoo ga kyónen yóri níwari mashimáshita.** The population increased by 20 percent over last year.

MASUMASU more and more; still more; increasingly. **Masumasu muzukashiku náru deshoo.** It will probably get increasingly difficult.

MATA and; besides; again; too; also; indirect; another; **MATA WA** or else; **mata áru toki wa** on another occasion; **matagiki** indirect information; hearsay; **mata tanomisuru** to ask something (of someone) indirectly (through someone else). **Watakushi mo mata mótte iru.** I have it, too. So have I. **Mata dekakerú n desu ka?** Are you going out again?

matagáru to mount (a horse); to extend over, stretch over, span; **umá ni matagáru** to ride horseback; **sannen ni matagáru** extending over three years.

matágu to step over; to straddle.

matáseru to keep a person waiting.

matatáku to wink, blink.

MÁTCHI match; matches; **matchíbako** matchbox; **mátchi o súru** to light a match; **matchíbako no yóo na ie** tiny house (like a matchbox).

mato target, mark; point; **mato ga hazurete iru** to be wide of the mark; miss the point.

matomari conclusion; settlement; unity; coherence.

matomaru to be settled, decided; to come to a conclusion; to be completed.

matomeru to adjust, settle; to decide; to finish.

matomo ni right in front.

MÁTSU to wait; to await; to watch for, be on the lookout for; to expect; **máte!** wait!; hold on!; **nezu ni mátsu** to sit up and wait for (someone).

mátsu pine (tree); **matsukása** pine cone; **matsubáyashi** pine forest, grove.

matsuri festival; memorial services for one's ancestors.

matsúru to deify; to worship; to enshrine.

MATTAKU completely, entirely, totally;

quite; perfectly; **mattakú no** entire, complete. **Mattaku sóo desu!** You're quite right! **Makkaku fushigi désu!** How strange! **Mattaku wakarimasén.** I don't get it at all.

mattoo suru to accomplish; to fulfill; to complete.

máu to dance.

maue just above, right above; **atama no maué ni** directly overhead. **Anó hito no heya wa kono maué ni arimásu.** His room is right over this room.

MAWARI circumference; surroundings; neighborhood; **mawaridóoi** roundabout; **mawarimichi** detour; roundabout road, roundabout way. **Ie no mawari wa hatake désu.** The farmland surrounds my house. **Mawari wa roku máiru arimásu.** The circumference is six miles.

MAWARU to turn (around); to go round; to come around, revolve, rotate; to spin. **Ichínen ni nido mawatte kimásu.** He comes around twice a year.

maswari awase luck; chance.

MAWASU to turn; to revolve, rotate; to roll; to whirl; to forward; to pass around; **kuruma o mawasu** to turn a wheel; to dispatch a car; **tsugí e mawasu** to pass on to the next.

mayaku drug, narcotic; **mayaku chuudoku** drug addiction.

mayoi delusion; superstition; illusion; infatuation.

mayónaka dead of night.

mayóu to be puzzled; to waver, hesitate; to go astray; to lose one's way.

mayowásu to puzzle, bewilder; to mislead, misguide; to fascinate, captivate; to seduce.

MÁYU eyebrows; **máyu o hisoméru** to frown; **mayúzumi** eyebrow pencil.

mazamáza to clearly, distinctly, vividly.

mazarimono mixture; compound.

mazáru to mingle.

mazéru to mix, adulterate.

mazekáesu to interrupt, butt in; to ridicule, sneer at.

MÁZU first; in the first place; to begin with; about; almost; nearly; anyway; anyhow. **Mázu! Well! Mázu joodeki da.** It is fairly successful.

MAZÚI tasteless, untasty, insipid; plain, homely; poor; awkward, clumsy; **mazusóo na** unappetizing. **Góhan ga mazúi desu.** I don't enjoy eating.

MÉ eye; sight, look, glance; eyesight, vision; notice, observation; point of view; discrimination; insight; bud, sprout, shoot; **mé no todóku kágiri** as far as one can

see; as far as the eye can see; **mé ga
tsubureru** to lose one's sight; to become
blind; **mé ni amáru** to be innumerable; to
be too much for; to be unpardonable; **mé
ni miénai** to be invisible, be unseen; **mé
ni tsuku** to attract (someone's) attention;
to catch the eye; **mé ga warúi** to have
poor eyesight; **mé ga saméru** to wake up;
to be awakened; to have one's eyes
opened; **mé o ageru** to lift one's eyes,
look up; **mé o maruku shite odoróku** to
stare in wonder; **mé o muku** to stare; to
glare at; **mé to mé o miawásu** to
exchange glances; **mé ni háiru** to come
into sight; to come into view; **mé ni tátsu**
to be conspicuous; **mé ga kiku** to
have an eye for; to be a good judge of.
Nagái mé de míte ite kudasái. Time will
tell.

mé bud, sprout, shoot; **mé ga déru** to bud, to
sprout; **mé o tsumu** to nip (something) in
the bud.

–mé suffix denoting; order in which things
are arranged; **sandomé** the third time.

méate aim, object, end; **méate ni suru** to aim
at, aim for.

méboshi objective, aim.

mebúnryoo rough estimation (done by the
eye)

mechamecha ni in disorder, in confusion;
mechamecha ni suru to make a mess of,
upset; to ruin, wreck; **mechamecha ni
náru** to go to pieces; to be spoiled; to get
mixed up.

medátsu to be conspicuous; to stand out;
medátsu iro a loud, gay color; **medátta**
striking, remarkable.

medetái happy; auspicious; successful;
medetái koto happy event; matter for
congratulations; **medétaku** happily,
auspiciously; **medétaku owaru** to end
happily. **Omedetoo!** Congratulations!

meetoru meter (measure); gauge;
meetoruhoo metric system.

MÉGANE eyeglasses; insight; judgment;
meganeya optician. **Mégane náshi de
yomemasén.** I can't read without glasses;
mégane ni kanau to find favorable.

megurásu to enclose with; surround.

meguri circumference, a tour; round;
circulation; flow; **meisho méguri o suru**
to make a tour of famous places.

meguriáu to come across; to happen to meet.

megúru to go around; circulate.

MÉI niece.

meian good idea, good suggestion; bright
(brilliant) plan.

meibo register, roll of names, roster.

méibutsu specialty; noted product; attraction;

feature. **Koko no méibutsu wa nán desu
ka?** What is this place noted for?

meichuu hit; **meichuu suru** to hit the mark;
to tell; **meichuu shinai** to miss, go wide
(of the mark).

méigetsu full moon; **chuushuu no méigetsu**
harvest moon.

MEIGI name; **meigijoo no** nominal, titular;
meigijoo wa nominally; ostensibly.

meihaku na clear, distinct, explicit.

méii famous physician.

meijin expert; master.

meijíru, meizúru to command, to give
orders.

meikaku na clear; definite; distinct; clear-cut;
méiki suru to state clearly; to specify.

meimei christening, naming; **meiméishiki**
christening ceremony; **meimei suru** to
christen, name.

meirei command, order, injunction;
meireiteki na imperative, peremptory;
meirei ni yotte by order of; **meirei suru**
to order, command, decree; to give orders
to.

meisai particulars, details; **meisai na** detailed,
minute; **meisai ni** minutely, in detail;
fully; **meisaigaki** detailed description,
statement, account.

meisaku masterpiece; fine piece of work.

meisan noted product.

meisei fame, reputation; **meisei áru** noted,
renowned.

meishi calling card, visiting card; business
card.

meishin superstition; **meishinteki na**
superstitious.

meisho famous place; famous sight; **meisho o
mawaru** to see the sights.

meishoo place of scenic beauty.

meisoo meditation, contemplation; dream,
illusion; fallacy, erroneous idea; **meisoo
suru** to meditate.

meitei drunkenness; **meitéisha** drunkard;
meitei suru to get drunk.

MÉIWAKU trouble; bother; nuisance;
méiwaku na troublesome, annoying;
méiwaku suru to be troubled; to have
trouble; to get into trouble; **méiwaku o
kakéru** to bother, annoy. **Goméiwaku de
wa arimasén ka?** (Are you sure) I'm not
bothering you?

méiyo honor; glory; fame; **méiyo o hakusúru**
to attain an honor; to attain a reputation;
méiyo o omonzúru to have a sense of
honor; **meiyóshin** ambition; desire for
fame.

meizúru See **meijíru.**

méjiri corner of the eye.

mejírushi mark; landmark; sign; guide.

mekákushi blindfold; screen; blind.

mekásu to primp; deck oneself out; to dress elaborately; to dress up.

MEKATA weight; **mekata de uru** to sell by weight; **mekata o hakáru** to weigh (a thing).

mékimeki more and more; visibly; rapidly. **Nihongo ga mékimeki jootatsu shite imásu.** You are making rapid progress in Japanese.

mekkíri considerably, noticeably.

mekúbase suru to wink meaningfully at.

mekura blindness; blind person; **mekura méppoo ni** recklessly; **mekura ságuri o suru** to fumble; to grope. **Mekura hébi ni ojízu.** Fools rush in where angels fear to tread.

memái dizziness; **memái ga suru** to be dizzy.

memeshíi effeminate, unmanly.

memori graduations (on a thermometer, etc.); gradations; markings.

men face; mask; surface; facet, aspect, phase, side; **men to mukatte** face to face; **men suru** to face, front on; to border on; to look out on. **Heyá wa toorí ni men shimásu.** The room looks out on the street; **menboku (menmoku)** face, countenance; honor; **menboku (menmoku) o isshin suru** to undergo a complete change.

mén cotton (fabric); **ménka** raw cotton; **ménshi** cotton thread.

mendóo trouble, difficulty; troubles; complications; **mendóo na** complicated; troublesome; **mendóo o kakéru** to give trouble; **mendóo o míru** to take the trouble; to look after; **mendookusái** troublesome. **Mattaku mendookusái desu.** It's a great deal of trouble.

men'eki immunity (to disease); **men'eki ni nátte iru** to be immune to; **men'eki chúusha** inoculation.

ménjo exemption; excuse; discharge; **ménjo suru** to exempt (from a tax); to release; to excuse.

menjoo diploma.

menkai interview; **menkai suru** to have an interview; **menkáibi** reception; visitors' day; office day.

menkurau to be confused; to be upset; to be at a loss.

ménkyo = **menkyójoo** license; certificate; **menkyóryoo** license fee; **menkyójoo o mótte iru** to hold a license.

menmitsu na detailed, minute; close; nice; meticulous; **menmitsu ni** minutely, etc.

menshiki acquaintance; **menshiki no áru hito** acquaintance; **ichi ménshiki mo nái**

hito complete stranger.

menshoku discharge, dismissal; **menshoku suru** to dismiss, discharge.

menuki no principal, main; **menuki no basho** busiest section; business center; **menuki no oodóori** main thoroughfare; busy street.

merikómu to cave in; to sink.

mesaki foresight; **mesaki ni** before one's eyes; under one's nose; **mesaki no miénai** stupid; **mesaki no** at hand; immediate.

meshí (*vulgar*) boiled rice; meal; food; **meshí o taku** to cook rice.

MESHIAGARU to eat; to drink (*respect*). **Meshiagatte kudasái.** Please help yourself.

meshita inferior, subordinate.

meshitsúkai servant.

mesu female (animal); **mesu neko** a she-cat.

metsuboo downfall; ruin, destruction.

métsuki expression of the eyes; **kowái métsuki** menacing look.

métta na reckless; inconsiderate; **métta ni** rarely, seldom; recklessly; thoughtlessly.

meue superior, senior; **meue no hitó o uyamáu** to respect one's superiors.

mezamashi dókei alarm clock.

mezamashíi remarkable; brilliant; admirable.

mezáwari eyesore; offense to the eye.

MEZURASHÍI rare, unusual; new; curious; **mezurashíi monó** a novelty, curio.

mi body; person; self; oneself; **mi mo kokoró mo** body and soul; **mi o ayamáru** to lead a dissipated life; **mi no ue** one's station in life; **mi no mawari no mono** personal belongings.

mi fruit, nut, berry.

miageta admirable, praiseworthy; respectable.

miawaséru to exchange glances; to look at each other, to put off, postpone, defer; to abandon.

mibóojin widow.

míbun social position, social standing; identity; **míbun o akásu** to reveal one's identity.

míburi gesture, motion; **míburi o suru** to gesture; make a motion.

mibúrui shivering, trembling; shiver; shudder; **mibúrui suru** to shiver (with cold), to tremble (with fear); to shudder (with horror). **Omótta daké de mo mibúrui ga suru.** The mere thought of it makes me shudder.

MICHI way, road, route, course; highway; **kómichi** path, lane; route; **michi ni mayóu** to lose one's way; **michi o kiku** to ask directions; **michibata** roadside, wayside; **michisuji** route, course.

michibíku to lead, guide.

michigáeru to mistake (by sight) one thing for another; **michigáeru hodo kawaru** to change beyond recognition.

míchi no unknown, strange.

michinori distance, journey; **kishá de ichijíkan hódo no michinori** about an hour's ride by train.

michishírube guidepost; street sign.

michizure fellow traveler, companion on a trip.

mídara na indecent, obscene, lewd.

midare disorder; disturbance; irregularity.

midaréru to be disordered; to go out of order.

midásu to put out of order; to turn upside down; to agitate, disturb; to demoralize.

midashi index; title; headline; heading.

MÍDORI, MIDORIIRO green color; **midorigakátta** greenish; **mídori no** green, verdant.

mié appearance, show, display; **mie no tame ni** for show; **mié ni suru** to do (something) for show or for the sake of appearance; **mié o haru** to show off.

MIÉRU to be visible; to see, catch sight of; to be in sight; to look like; to seem, appear; to be found; **miénaku náru** to disappear, become missing, become invisible. **Toshi no wari ni wákaku miéru.** He looks young for his age. **Mé ga miéru yóo ni nátta.** Now I can see things.

miesuita transparent; obvious, plain.

migaki polish; burnishing; **nihongo ni migaki o kakéru** to brush up one's Japanese.

MIGAKU to polish; to rub; to brush; to improve; to refine; **kutsú o migaku** to polish shoes; **há o migaku** to brush one's teeth; **migakiagéru** to polish (silver, etc.).

migamae attitude (posture) of being ready for action; **migamae o suru** to stand ready; to brace oneself.

migawari substitution; substitute; scapegoat; stand-in; **migawari o tatéru** to put in one's place.

MIGI right, right-hand side; **migi e magaru** to turn to the right; **migi ni déru** to surpass, outdo. **Migigawa kóotsuu.** Keep to the right.

migiwa waterside, water's edge.

MÍGOTO NA beautiful; fine; pretty; brilliant; excellent; superb; **mígoto ni** beautifully, etc. **Mígoto mígoto!** Well done!

migurushíi ugly, unsightly; dishonorable, disgraceful.

mihakarai choice (at one's discretion).

mihakaráu to choose (at one's discretion); to select (something) on one's own. **Sore wa anata no omihakarai ni makasemásu.** I leave the choice to you.

mihárai outstanding (unpaid) account; **mihárai no** outstanding, unpaid, unsettled.

miharashi view, prospect, outlook; **maharashi ga yói** to have a fine view.

mihari watch, vigil, lookout, observation.

miháru to watch, keep watch, stand guard; **mé o miháru** to open one's eyes wide; **mé o mihátte** with wide-open eyes.

mihon sample, swatch, specimen.

MIJIKÁI short, brief; **mijikáku suru** to curtail, shorten, abbreviate.

míjime misery; sadness; **míjime na** sad, miserable, pitiful.

mijin atoms; particles; **mijin ni náru** to be smashed to atoms.

MIJÍTAKU dress; equipment; preparation; **mijítaku o suru** to dress, get dressed; to equip; to prepare oneself.

mijuku immaturity, unripeness; **mijuku na** unripe, green, immature, inexperienced. **Watakushi no Eigo wa mijuku désu.** My English is far from perfect.

mikai no uncivilized, savage.

mikake dáoshi no deceptive. **Sore wa mikake dáoshi desu.** It's not as good as it looks.

mikaku sense of taste; palate; **mikaku o sosoru** to tempt the taste; **mikaku ni áu** to suit one's taste.

MÍKAN tangerine (popular fruit in Japan).

mikan no incomplete, unfinished.

mikáta way of looking at things; point of view, viewpoint; **atarashíi mikáta o suru** to look at something in a new light; to see from a new point of view.

mikawásu to exchange looks.

mikazuki new, crescent moon.

miki trunk, stem.

mikiri abandonment; **mikiri o tsukéru** to wash one's hands of; to have nothing to do with; to give up; to desert.

mikíru to give up, abandon.

MIKKA three days; third day of the month; **mikkákan** three days; **Sángatsu mikka** March 3; **mikka ni agezu** almost every other day.

mikkai secret meeting, rendezvous.

mikkoku suru to inform against, betray; **mikkókusha** informer.

MIKOMI promise, hope, anticipation, prospect; **mikomi no áru** promising; **mikomi ga hazureru** to prove contrary to expectations.

mikónsha unmarried person.

mikósu to anticipate, foresee; to speculate (financially).

mikubíru to make light of; to think meanly of.

mikudasu to look down on; to despise.

mimai sympathy visit; **mimai ni iku** to visit a sick person.

mimáu to visit a sick person.

míman under; below; less than; not more than; **hyakuen míman** less than one hundred yen; **jissai míman** under ten years of age; ten years and under.

mime features; face; looks; **mime yói** good-looking; **mime uruwashíi** beautiful, fair, pretty.

MIMÍ ear; hearing; **mimí ga yói** to have a good ear; **mimí ni ireru** to inform; **mimí ni háiru** to reach one's ears; **mímí o katamukéru** to listen; **mimí o sobatatéru** to strain one's ears; **mimí ni táko ga dekíru** to din into one's ears; **miminari** ringing in the ears; **mimi záwari no** grating, jarring (to the ears). **Miminari ga warúi.** My ears are ringing.

mimochi conduct, behavior; **mimochi ga yói** well-behaved, of good conduct; **mimochi ga warúi** to lead a fast life, be of loose morals.

mimono sight, spectacle; attraction.

mimoto one's birth, parentage; identity; history; career.

mimúki mo sézu without looking around; without a look at; straight ahead.

MINÁ, MINNA all; everyone; everything; **miná de** in all; in a body; all told. **Miná de íkura desu ka?** How much for them all together? How much for the lot?

minage suru to drown oneself.

minagoroshi massacre, extermination, wholesale murder.

minakami source of a river or stream; headwaters.

MINAMI south; **minami no** southerly; southern; **minami ni** to the south; on the south.

minamoto source, fountainhead, origin, root.

minaosu to look at again; to have another look; to take a turn for the better, improve, look up.

minarai apprenticeship; apprentice; **mináru** to receive training, practice as an apprentice; to follow suit, copy; to learn from another.

MÍNARI dress, attire; personal appearance.

minashigo orphan.

minásu to regard as; to consider, think of; to suppose.

minato harbor, port.

mine peak, summit, top; back.

minikúi indistinct, obscure; illegible; difficult to see.

minikúi ugly.

mínji civil affairs; civil case; **minji saibansho** civil court.

minogásu to neglect; to overlook; to forgive.

minoo nonpayment; default in payment; **minoo no** unpaid; in arrears.

minóru to bear fruit; to ripen.

mínu furí o suru to pretend not to see; to wink at; to connive.

min'yoo ballad, folksong, popular song.

MIOBOE recognition; remembrance; **mioboe ga áru** to remember seeing before; to recollect; to recognize.

MIOKÚRU seeing someone off; **hito o miokuri ni iku** to go to see a person off. **Hikoojoo e tomodachi o miokuri ni ikimásu.** I am going to the airport to see a friend off.

miosame last look, farewell look.

miotori unfavorable comparison; **miotori ga suru** to compare unfavorably with; to suffer by comparison; to be eclipsed by.

miotoshi oversight, omission.

MÍRAI (n.) future, time to come; future life; **mírai no** (adj.) future, prospective.

miren cowardice, attachment; regret; **miren ga áru** to be still attached to.

MÍRU to see, look at, glance at, observe; to judge; to read; to look after, etc.; **yóku míru** to have a good look at; **chótto míru to** at first glance; **shinbun o míru** to read (look at) a newspaper. **Íma ni míro!** You'll soon see!

miryoku charm, fascination; (glamour) appeal; **miryoku ga nái** to have no appeal for; to have nothing attractive about.

miryoo suru to fascinate, charm.

misadaméru to make sure of.

misageháteta mean, contemptible.

misaki cape, headland, promontory.

MISÉ store, shop; booth; **misé o hiráku** to open a store, to start a business.

misekake pretense, make-believe; appearance.

misekakéru to pretend, make a show of.

MISÉRU to show, let see, exhibit, display; to make something look like; to give an air of; **isha ni miséru** to consult a doctor, be examined. **Anáta no nóoto o mísete kudasái.** Please let me see your notebook.

miseshime lesson, object lesson, warning, example; **miseshime ni náru** to serve as a warning (lesson) to.

míshimishi iu to creak.

MÍSO soybean paste (food used in daily diet); **míso o tsukéru** to make a mess of; to make a poor showing; **miso shiru**

soybean soup. **Soko ga míso da.** That's the beauty of it.

misoka last day of the month; **oomísoka** New Year's Eve.

misokonai misjudgment, mistaken impression.

misokonáu to misjudge, make a mistake, make a wrong estimation.

missetsu na close, intimate; **missetsu na kankei ga áru** to be closely related to; to be in close connection with.

misshíri, mitchíri severely, seriously; closely, diligently; in earnest.

misuborashíi shabby, ragged, seedy.

misumisu before one's very eyes; in full knowledge of the situation.

mitásu to fill, satisfy, appease, gratify; **kiboo o mitásu** to gratify a desire; **juyoo o mitásu** to meet a demand; to supply a need.

mitate diagnosis (medical); choice; **mitate chigai** wrong diagnosis; mistaken judgment.

mitateru to diagnose; to choose, select.

mitchaku suru to stick, adhere to; to be close together; to be interlocked.

mitchíri See **misshíri**.

mitei no unsettled, undecided.

mitodokeru to verify, make sure of; to satisfy oneself that.

mitomein private seal.

MITOMERU to see, witness; to catch sight of; to observe; to recognize; to admit.

mitooshi perspective, outlook; prospect; unobstructed view.

mitoosu to get an unobstructed view; to see through; to see into.

mitsu honey; **mitsúbachi** honeybee; **mitsúbachi no su** beehive; **mitsuzuki ryókoo** honeymoon.

mitsudan secret conversation, confidential talk; **mitsudan suru** to have a private (confidential) talk.

mitsugi secret; closed conference.

MITSUKERU to find out, discover; to detect; to sight, locate. **Uwagi o mitsukeru kotó ga dekínai.** I can't find my coat.

mitsumeru to stare at, fix one's eyes on.

mitsumori estimate; assessment; evaluation.

mitsumóru to estimate; calculate; evaluate.

mitsurin thick forest, dense woods.

mitsu yúnyuu smuggling; **mitsu yunyúusha** smuggler; **mitsu yúnyuu suru** to smuggle.

mittomonái indecent; disgraceful; unsightly; ugly; plain-looking; **mittomonái otokó** poorly dressed man. **Mittomonái kotó o shité wa ikemasén.** Don't behave so disgracefully.

MITTSU, SAN three. (See also **mikka**.)

miuchi relations; relative; friends; followers.

miwake discrimination; judgment.

miwakeru to discriminate; to discern; to judge.

miwatasu to look over; to gaze out on; **miwatasu kágiri** as far as one can see.

miyage, omiyage souvenir; gift, present; **miyagebánashi** account of interesting or unusual things seen or heard on a trip.

miyako capital; metropolis.

miyasúi evident, easily seen, clear.

mizen ni beforehand; before something happens; **mizen ni fuségu** to prevent (keep from) occurring; to take preventive action prior to something.

mizo ditch, drain, gutter; groove.

mizore sleet. **Mizore ga furimásu.** It's sleeting.

mizou no unheard of; unprecedented.

MIZU water; cold water; **mizu no tooránai** waterproof; watertight; **mizu de yusugu** to rinse with water; **mizu o waru** to dilute; **mizuírazu de kurasu** to live alone (without outsiders in the same house); **mizubúkure** water blister; **MIZUGI** swimsuit; **mizugiwa** water's edge; **mizugiwadátte** splendidly; brilliantly; **mizugiwadátta** splendid; striking; beautiful; wheel; **mizugúsuri** liquid medicine; **mizuhake** drainage; drain; **MIZUKE** dampness; moisture; **mizuke no áru** juicy; watery; **mizuke no nái** dry; parched; **mizukémuri** spray; **mizukoshi** filter; strainer; **mizukasái** watery; **mizasáshi** water pitcher; **mizutame** reservoir; water tank; **mizutori** waterfowl.

mizuhiki colored paper-cord used for tying up formal presents (red and white are chosen for ceremonial occasions).

mizuiro (*n.*) light blue; **muzuiro no** (*adj.*) light blue.

mizukakéron fruitless argument; endless dispute.

mizumizushíi fresh-looking; ruddy.

mizusaki ánnai, mizusaki annainin pilot (of a boat).

mizuúmi lake.

MO particle denoting; as well as; too; also; as many (much) as; no less (fewer) than; neither . . . nor; even; even if; although; in spite of; **dónna ni áme ga hídokute mo** no matter how hard it may rain; **futté no tétte mo** rain or shine. **Watakushi mo ikimásu.** I'll go too. **Hitori mo imasén.** There isn't even one person.

mochi durability; wear; **mochi ga yói** to wear well, be durable.

mochi rice cake.

mochiagaru to be lifted, raised up; to arise; to take place; **MOCHIAGERU** to raise, lift up; to hold up; to praise; to flatter. **Kono hako wa omókute mochiageru kotó ga dekimasén.** This box is too heavy for me to lift up. **Mochiagenáide kudasái.** Please don't lift it up.

mochiáu to balance, keep balanced; to remain steady; to share; to pool (expenses).

mochiawase things on hand, in stock. **Mochiawase ga nái.** There isn't any on hand.

mochiawaséru to have on hand; to have in stock.

mochibá post, station; duty; round, beat, route.

mochidású to take out, bring out; to carry out; to carry away; to remove; to save; to propose; to introduce.

mochiíru to use; to make use of, employ; to adopt; to apply.

mochikáeru to pass from one (hand or person) to another.

mochikakéru to propose; to court.

mochikomi delivery to the door.

mochikomu to carry in, bring in.

mochikotaéru to endure; to hold out; to stand.

mochimóno property, possessions, belongings. **Kono hón wa Tanaka-san no mochimóno desu.** This book is Mr. Tanaka's. This book belongs to Mr. Tanaka.

mochinaósu to improve; to pick up; to recover (usually used when speaking of illness).

mochinige suru to make off with, run away with.

mochínushi owner, proprietor, possessor.

MOCHÍRON, muron of course; naturally; to be sure; certainly; no doubt; needless to say. **Mochíron sukí desu.** Of course I like it! Certainly, I like it.

mochiyóru to contribute one's share; to bring one's quota.

modáeru to be in agony; to be worried; to suffer great agony.

modokashigáru to lose patience.

modokashíi irritating; slow; slow-moving; not quick enough; unsatisfactory.

modori return; temporary recovery.

modóru to return, come back; to go back; to turn back; to recede.

MODOSU to return; to give; to send back; to throw up, vomit.

moeagaru to burst into flames, blaze up; **moegara** embers; cinders.

moekíru to burn out, be burned up.

MOERU to burn, blaze, be in flames; **moetsúku** to catch fire; to ignite; **moesashi** embers; half-burnt stump; **moeyasúi** combustible, inflammable; **moenai** noncombustible; **moeru omói** burning passion. **Ié ga moeru.** The house is on fire. **Hí ga yóku moete imasu.** The fire is burning briskly. (See also **hí.**)

moeru to sprout, to bud.

mofuku mourning clothes.

mogáku to struggle; to writhe; to wriggle.

mógu to break off; to tear off.

moguri diving; diver; unlicensed practitioner.

mogúru to dive (into water); to dip; to creep (into bed); **toko ni mogúru** to get into bed; to crawl into bed.

móji letter, character, ideograph; **moji dóori no** literal; **móji no wakáru** literate, educated; **móji ni akarui** to be learned.

mójimoji suru to hesitate.

mojíru to twist, distort; to parody, mimic.

mokei model, pattern.

MÓKKA now, at present, for the present, currently; **mókka no** present; existing; **mókka no tokoro** for the time being.

mókkyo tacit permission; **mókkyo suru** to give tacit permission.

mokugeki observation; **mokugeki suru** to observe, witness; **mokugékisha** eyewitness.

MOKUHYOO mark, sign; goal, target, objective; **–o mokuhyoo ni suru** to aim at; to have (something) as one's objective.

mokuji table of contents.

mokumoku to silently, in silence.

mokumokutáru silent, dumb; implicit.

mokunin tacit approval; passive consent; **mokunin suru** to tolerate; to give tacit approval; to connive.

mokurei nod; **mokurei suru** to nod; to greet with a nod.

mokuroku table of contents; list; catalogue.

mokuromi plan.

mokusan expectation; calculation; estimate; **mokusan ga hazureru** to be disappointed in one's expectations; to fail to come up to one's estimate.

mokushi revelation.

mokushi suru to overlook; to pass unnoticed.

mokusoku suru to measure with the eye.

mokusoo meditation.

MOKUTEKI aim, purpose, intention; **mokutékichi** destination, end of the journey.

MOKUYÓOBI Thursday.

mokúzai wood, lumber, timber.

mokuzen before one's eyes; immediate; **mokuzen ni** before one's eyes; in the presence of; **mokuzen ni semáru** to be close at hand; to be right in front of one's eyes; to be imminent.

momareru to be tried; to be knocked around, tossed about.

momegoto trouble; dissension.

MOMEN cotton; cotton cloth; **momen íto** cotton thread; **momen mono** cotton goods; cotton clothes.

momeru to get into a dispute; to get into trouble; to have trouble; to feel discord; to be rumpled.

momiáu to shove and push, jostle, to struggle with a person.

momikésu to rub out; to crush out; to smother; to hush up; to stifle.

momiryóoji massage; **momiryóoji suru** to massage.

MOMO peach.

momohiki underwear (shorts), drawers, trunks.

momoiro (*n.*) pink; **momoiro no** (*adj.*) pink, pinkish.

momu to rub, massage; to crumple up, to wrinkle.

MÓN gate; gateway; **mon'ei** gatekeeper.

món crest.

MONDAI question, problem; subject, topic; **mondai ni náru** to give rise to discussion; to be criticized; **mondai ni naránai** to be out of the question, to be insignificant; **roodoo móndai** labor problem.

mondori útsu to turn a somersault.

mongen closing time, lockup time.

monjín pupil, disciple, follower(s).

mónku wording, words, terms, expression, complaint, grievance; objection; excuse; **mónku o iu** to make a complaint; to grumble; **mónku o iwazu ni** without question.

MONÓ thing, object; substance, matter; stuff, article; goods; possession; something; **mono ni suru** to secure; to take possession of; to make something of; **mono ni náru** to come to (anything) good; **mono ni naránai** to come to nothing; to get nowhere; to end in failure.

mono person, somebody.

monohoshiba place for drying clothes.

monohoshízao clothes pole.

monomonoshíi showy, ostentatious; pretentious, pompous.

MONO NO though; although; only; but; about; some; **tó wa iu mono no** for all that; in spite of all that is said; **mono no nífun to tatánu uchi ni** in less than two minutes.

monookí storeroom, storehouse.

monoréeru monorail.

monosáshi ruler; footrule; yardstick.

monoshíri well-informed person; man of great knowledge; scholar.

monosugói dreary, dismal; ghastly, grim, gruesome, terrible; **monosugói arísama** horrible scene; **monosugoi hitode** a terribly large crowd of people.

MÓO already; not any longer; by now; now; soon, before long; presently; **moo sukóshi** a little more, a few more; **moo ichido** once more. **Móo fuyú desu.** It's already winter. **Móo arimasén.** I haven't any more.

moo another. **Mizu o moo íppai kudasái.** May I have another cup of water?

moodéru to visit (a temple): to worship (at a temple or shrine).

móofu blanket.

moojuu wild beast; beast of prey.

móoka raging fire.

mookáru to be profitable; to make a profit; to pay; to be paying.

mooké profit, gains, earnings; **mooké ni naránai** to be unprofitable; **mookéguchi** profitable job, work, undertaking.

mookéru to make, earn profits; to make money; to set up, establish; to frame.

moomoo to dense, thick; dim; **moomoo to shite** thickly, in clouds.

mooretsu violence, fierceness; **mooretsu na** violent, fierce, furious, stormy; strong, intense; **mooretsu ni** violently, strongly, etc.; **mooretsu ni fúru** to rain hard (furiously).

mooshiawase agreement; understanding; appointment.

mooshiawaséru to arrange; to agree upon; **mooshiawásete** by arrangement; **mooshiawáseta jikan ni** at the appointed (agreed-upon) hour.

mooshidéru to make a proposal, make an offer.

mooshikomi offer, proposal; **mooshikomi yóoshi** application form.

mooshikómu to apply for; to propose.

mooshitate statement, declaration; allegation; testimony; plea.

mooshitatéru to state, declare; to testify.

móoshon motion; **móoshon o kakéru** to motion for (a person to do something); to make eyes at; to encourage.

MÓOSU to say, tell (*humble*). **Hái, soo mooshimásu.** Yes, I'll tell him so. **Watakushi wa Yamada to mooshimásu.** My name is Yamada.

MOPPARA chiefly, mostly, principally; solely, exclusively; entirely. **Káre wa**

moppara shigoto ni séidashite imasu.
He devotes himself to his business.

moraigo adopted child.

moraimono present, gift (that is received).

morásu to let leak; to reveal, disclose; to let out, omit, leave out.

MORAU to receive; to get, obtain; to be given; to be presented with; to get a person to do, have a person do (following a –te form). **Kono hón o morau kotó ga dekimasén ka?** Can't I get this book? Couldn't you give me this book? **Tanaka-san ni katte moraimáshita.** I had Mr. Tanaka buy it.

moré leak, leakage, omission; oversight; **moré o fusagu** to stop a leak.

moréru to leak; to escape; to come through; to get out; to get wind of; to be omitted; to be excluded.

mori leak.

móri nursemaid; taking care of a baby.

mori forest; wood.

morikáesu to regain, recover.

MÓSHI MOSHI I say; say; if you please; please. **Móshi moshi.** Hello! Are you there (in a telephone conversation)?

MÓSHI MO in case of; if; provided that; **móshi mo no kotó ga áttara** if anything should happen; in case of emergency.

MÓSHIYA by any chance; by some possibility. **Móshiya to omótte klite mita.** I chanced asking her.

mosu, moyasu to burn.

mosurin muslin.

motaréru to lean on, lean against; to rest against; to recline on; to sit heavily on; to lie heavily on.

motaséru to let (someone) have, let (someone) take; to get (someone) to carry.

moteamasu to be embarrassed at, by; not to know what to do with.

motéru to be welcomed, made much of; to be popular; to receive attention.

MOTO origin, source, cause, root; investment price; cost price; **móto wa** originally, at first; **móto kara** from the beginning; **móto yori** from the first; originally; **motomoto** from the beginning, originally; **motone** original cost; cost price; **motone de uru** to sell at cost.

motó under; **oya no motó de** under parental supervision: **–no shusai no motó de** under the auspices of.

motode capital, funds; stock; **motode o orósu** to invest capital.

MOTOMÉRU to ask for, request, demand; to look for, search for.

MÓTSU to hold; to carry; to have in hand;

to possess, own; **shikkári to mótsu** to grasp firmly; to take firm hold of.

motsure tangle; entanglement; trouble; complications.

motsuréru to get entangled, be in a knot; to become complicated.

mottai artificial importance; **mottai o tsukéru** to exaggerate the importance of.

mottaibúru to put on airs.

mottainái wasteful; extravagant; impious, sacrilegious; gracious; more than one deserves. **Máa, mottainái!** What a waste! **Káre ni wa mottainái hodo no chíi da.** The position is too good for him.

MÓTTE with; by means of; by, through, because, on account of; **tegami de motte toiawaseru** to inquire by letter.

motté kúru to bring; to fetch; to take along.

motte iku to take, carry (away).

motte no hoka out of the question; outrageous; unpardonable.

MÓTTO more; much; still more. **Mótto kudasái.** Give me some more.

MOTTÓMO most, exceedingly, extremely. **Mottómo juuyoo desu.** It is most important.

MÓTTOMO indeed; it is true; but; **móttomo na** reasonable; right; rational; natural.

mottomorashíi plausible.

móya haze, mist.

moyoo pattern; design; appearance, aspect.

moyooshi meeting; gathering.

moyoósu to organize, arrange; to hold (a meeting); to feel; to show signs of; to look like.

MOYORI NO nearest; adjacent, nearby. **Moyori no keisatsusho e shirasete kudasái.** Please notify any police station in your neighborhood.

mozoo imitation; **mozoo suru** to imitate, copy; **mozóohin** imitation, counterfeit.

muboo recklessness; thoughtlessness; **muboo na** reckless, rash; thoughtless, inconsiderate, ill-advised.

múcha nonsense; disorder; **múcha na** disorderly, confused; absurd, unreasonable; thoughtless; **múcha ni** recklessly; excessively, blindly; **muchakucha** unreasonable, absurd; mixed up, jumbled.

múchi ignorance; stupidity; **múchi na** ignorant, illiterate, etc.

muchuu unconsciousness; ecstasy; **muchuu ni náru** to become unconscious; to be carried away; to become ecstatic; **muchuu de** as in a dream; unknowingly; wildly, madly.

muda futility, uselessness; **muda na** fruitless,

futile, no good, of no use; **muda ni náru** to get wasted; to be thrown away; to be in vain; **muda ni suru** to waste, throw away, etc.; **mudaashi** to go for nothing; **mudaashi o suru** to go in vain; to go on a fool's errand.

mudabánashi idle talk, gossip.

mudan without warning; without permission.

muden wireless communication.

múeki no useless, futile.

MÚGI barley, oats, rye, wheat (general term for grain); **mugícha** barley tea; **mugiko** wheat flour; **mugimeshi** rice cooked with barley; **mugiwara bóoshi** straw hat.

mugon silence, muteness; **mugon no** silent, speechless, dumb; **mugon de** silently, in silence.

múhi uniqueness; **múhi no** unequaled, matchless, unique.

muhon rebellion, revolt, insurrection; treason; **muhon suru** to rebel, revolt; **muhonnin** rebel, insurgent; traitor.

muhoo na unlawful, unjust, outrageous.

mushóoshuu without remuneration; **muhóoshuu no** free; **muhóoshuu de** free of charge, without recompense; **muhóoshuu de hataraku** to work without pay.

muígi, muimi senselessness; **muígi na** senseless, absurd, meaningless.

MUIKA sixth day of the month; six days.

muimi See **muígi.**

muíshiki unconsciousness; **muíshiki ni** unconsciously; mechanically, automatically.

mújaki innocence, naïveté; **mújaki na** naive, innocent.

mujin See **mujínzoo.**

múji no plain, unfigured.

mujínzoo, mujin limitlessness.

mujoo heartlessness; **mujoo no** heartless, inhuman; highest; best; supreme.

mujóoken de unconditionally; **mujóoken no** unconditional; absolute.

mujun contradiction; inconsistency; **mujun no** contradictory; conflicting, inconsistent; **mujun suru** to be inconsistent.

mukae meeting (someone).

MUKAERU to meet, go to meet; to greet, welcome, receive; to invite, call for, send for; **Tookyóo eki de hito o mukaeru** to meet a person at the Tokyo station.

mukaiáu to confront someone, to face each other.

mukaikaze head wind, adverse wind.

múkamuka suru to feel sick (nauseous); to feel offended; to get angry.

mukánkaku insensibility; unconsciousness; lack of feeling; **mukánkaku no** insensible; numb; unconscious.

mukánkei no unrelated; unconcerned, disinterested.

mukánshoo non-intervention.

mukashi ancient times, old days, long ago, remote antiquity; **mukashibánashi** an old tale.

MUKAU to face, look out on; to be opposite; to meet, confront; to get toward; to turn toward; **kagamí ni mukau** to look in a mirror; **Beikoku ni mukau** to head for (leave for, go to) America.

mukéiken inexperience; **mukéiken no** green, inexperienced.

mukeru to point at; to turn; to face; **mé o mukeru** to turn one's eyes to.

mukeru to peel, to come off.

muki direction; quarter; situation; aspect; exposure; suitability; **kaze no múki** direction of the wind.

múki without limit in time; **múki no** unlimited, indefinite (service); **múki enki** indefinite postponement.

mukidashi nakedness; **mukidashi no** naked, uncovered, bare; **mukidashi ni** frankly, openly; **mukidashi ni suru** to expose.

mukimi shellfish stripped of their shells; hulled shellfish.

múki ni náru to become spirited.

mukíryoku enervation, lethargy.

múkizu spotlessness; **múkizu no** blameless; flawless; spotless; sound, perfect.

MÚKO son-in-law; bridegroom.

MUKOO yonder; opposite direction; next to come; other party; **mukoo no** opposite, over there; **mukoo ni** on the opposite side, across; **MUKOOGAWA** the opposite side.

mukoo ineffectiveness; **mukoo no** invalid, ineffective, void; **mukoo ni náru** to become void.

mukóomizu recklessness; **mukóomizu no** reckless, foolhardy, rash; **mukóomizu ni** recklessly, head over heels.

muku to face, turn (one's face to); to look, look out on; to point to; to tend toward.

muku to suit, to be fit for.

muku to skin, to peel, to pare, to strip.

múkuchi reticence; **múkuchi no** reticent, closemouthed.

mukui retribution, punishment; reward, compensation.

mukuíru to reward, repay; to revenge; to retaliate.

mukúmu to swell; to become swollen.

mukyóka de without permission.

mukyóoiku illiteracy, lack of education; **mukyóoiku na** uneducated.

mukyuu without salary; without pay; **mukyuu de** gratuitously, freely, without pay, for nothing; **mukyuu no** unpaid, unsalaried.

muménkyo no unlicensed; without a license.

MUNÉ breast, chest; heart; mind; **muné ni ukabu** to occur, come to mind; **muné o uchiakeru** to open one's heart (or mind); to unburden oneself.

mune effect, purport, intention, principle. **Ashita kúru mune shirase ga arimáshita.** There was a report that she intended to arrive tomorrow.

munoo, munóoryoku incompetency, lack of ability; **munoo na** incapable, incompetent; **munoo na hito** a good-for-nothing.

MURÁ village, hamlet, rural community; **muru yákuba** village (municipal) office; **mura házure de** on the outskirts of the village.

mura unevenness, capriciousness; cluster, clump; **mura no áru** uneven, irregular, lacking in uniformity; capricious, fickle.

muragáru to crowd, swarm, flock.

muragi caprice; **muragi na hito** fickle person.

MURÁSAKI (*n.*) purple; **murásaki no** (*adj.*) purple.

murasu to steam; to cook by steam; **gohan o murásu** to steam boiled rice.

muré group; crowd; herd; flock.

murekusái stuffy, musty, moldy.

muréru to be steamed; to be stuffy, to get musty, get moldy; **múreta** moldy, musty; stuffy.

MÚRI compulsion; coercion; unjustness, unreasonableness; **múri na** unreasonable, unjustifiable; unnatural; **múri ni** by force, forcibly; compulsorily; **muri yari ni** by force; **múri no nái** reasonable; natural; **múri na onegai** unreasonable request.

muríkai lack of understanding; **muríkai na** unsympathetic, unfeeling, heartless.

muríshi de without interest, interest-free (money).

muron See **mochiron**.

murui matchlessness; **murui no** matchless, unique; unsurpassable.

múryoku weakness, debility, helplessness; **múryoku na** powerless, helpless, impotent; incompetent.

múryoo without charge; **múryoo no** free of charge, gratis; **muryoo de** free, for nothing, without charge; **muryoo shinryoojo** free clinic or infirmary.

musábetsu making no distinction; indifference; **musábetsu no** indiscriminate; equal; **musábetsu ni** indiscriminately; indifferently; equally.

musabóru to covet, be greedy for; **bóori o musabóru** to profiteer, make an excess profit.

musakurushíi filthy, dirty; shabby.

musan no having no property, unpropertied; **musánsha** a proletarian; person without property; the "have-nots"; **musan káikyuu** proletariat.

musebu to get choked (with tears).

muséifu anarchy; **museifu shúgi** anarchism; **museifu shugísha** anarchist.

muséigen limitlessness; boundlessness; **muséigen no** unlimited, limitless; free, unrestricted; **muséigen ni** freely.

musékinin irresponsibility; **musékinan na** irresponsible.

musendénshin wireless telegraph; radiogram; **musendénshin de** by radiogram; **musendenshínkyoku** wireless telegraph office; wireless station; **musendénwa** radio-telephone.

museru to be choked (with).

muséssoo inconstancy; **muséssoo na** unprincipled; inconstant; unchaste.

mushaburitsúku to seize violently, pounce on; to grapple with.

múshakusha suru to be irritated; to be in an ugly mood; **múshakusha shita** irritated; shaggy, bushy; ragged.

músha musha munching, gobbling; **músha musha tabéru** to munch, to eat greedily.

múshi disregard; **múshi suru** to disregard, ignore, take no account of, close one's eyes to: **-o múshi shite** in defiance of; disregarding.

MUSHI insect, bug; worm; moth, caterpillar; temper; feeling; **mushi no sukánu** disagreeable; **mushi o korosu** to keep one's temper; **mushi no shirase** hunch, premonition; **mushi ni sasaréru** to be bitten by an insect.

mushiatsúi hot and close, sultry.

mushíkaku disqualification; incompetence; **mushíkaku no** disqualified; uncertified; unlicensed.

mushin innocence; request; **mushin no** innocent; involuntary; mechanical; **mushin suru** to make a request; to beg for.

mushínkei apathy; **mushínkei na** dull, apathetic; insensible; **mushínkei de aru** to be insensible to; to be apathetic.

múshiro rather (than); better (than); sooner (than).

mushiru to pull off; to take off; to pluck.

múshoku lack of color; **múshoku no** colorless; transparent.

múshoku no unemployed, out of work.

mushózoku independence; being unattached;

mushózoku no independent; unaffiliated, unattached; neutral.

mushuu no odorless.

musoo dream; dreaming; daydream; **musoo suru** to dream of; to fancy.

músu to steam; to heat with steam; to be sultry.

musubi knot, tie; end, conclusion, close; **musubi no kotoba** closing remarks; **mushubime** knot, tie.

MUSUBU to tie, knot; to close (a bargain); to conclude; to enter into; to join, link; to form; **himo de musubu** to tie with a cord.

MUSUKO son.

MUSUME daughter; young woman; girl.

musúu countless number; **musúu no** numberless, countless, innumerable; **musúu ni** without number; innumerably.

mutéikoo nonresistance.

mutéppoo recklessness; **mutéppoo na** reckless, rash.

mutsumajíi harmonious; intimate, friendly, on good terms; **mutsumájiku** harmoniously; happily.

mutto suru to get offended, take offense; to be stuffy, muggy.

MUTTSÚ, ROKU six.

muttsúri moodiness; moody person; **muttsúri shita** moody; sullen; grim.

muyámi na excessive; indiscreet, thoughtless; rash; unreasonable.

múyoku unselfishness, **múyoku na** unselfish.

muyoo no unnecessary, needless; useless.

múzai innocence (of a crime); **múzai hoomen** acquittal; **múzai no** guiltless, innocent; **múzai ni náru** to be found innocent; to be acquitted.

múzamuza helplessly; recklessly; without much fuss; without regret.

muzei no tax free, duty free, untaxed; **muzéihin** duty-free goods.

muzukáru to fret; to be peevish (said of an infant).

MUZUKASHÍI hard, difficult, troublesome; delicate; doubtful; **muzukashíi mondai** tough (touchy) question; hard problem; **muzukashíi byooki** illness difficult to cure; **muzukashíi tachiba** difficult situation.

múzumuzu suru to be itchy; to be irritated; to be impatient.

MYÓO strangeness; cleverness; **myóo na** strange, queer, curious; miraculous; mysterious; **myóo na hito** strange person; **myóo na kotó o iu** to say strange things; **myóo ni kikoeru** to sound funny.

myóoasa, myoochoo tomorrow morning.

Myóoasa mairimásu. I will come tomorrow morning.

myóoban tomorrow evening, tomorrow night.

MYOOGÓNICHI day after tomorrow.

myóoji surname, family name.

myóonichi tomorrow (See also **ASHITA**)

N

NA, NAMAE name; title; designation; surname; personal name; reputation; fame; pretext, pretense; **na bákari no** nominal, in name only; **na mo nái** nameless, unknown; **na no áru** famous, celebrated; **na ga nái** to be nameless; **na ga shirete iru** to be well known, to be famous; to be popular; **na o kataru** to impersonate; **na o otósu** to lose one's reputation; **na o tsukéru** to name; **nadakái** famous, well known; **nafuda** nameplate; name card.

ná green, leafy vegetables.

NÁBE pot, pan.

nadaméru to soothe, calm.

nudéru to pat; to smooth.

nadetsukéru to comb (hair); **kamí o nadetsukéru** to smooth down one's hair.

–NÁDO and so forth; and the like, etc.; **watakushi nádo** the like of me; a person like myself.

náe seedling, shoot, sapling; **naedoko** seedbed; nursery.

nagabíku to be prolonged; to drag on. **Anó hito no byooki wa nagabíite iru.** Her illness is dragging on.

nagagutsu high boots.

NAGÁI long, lengthy; **nagái aida ní wa** in the long run; **nagái aida** for a long time; **nágaku** for a long time; for many years; **nagáiki** longevity, long life; **nagáiki suru** to live to a great age.

nagamé view, scenery, landscape.

NAGAMÉRU to look at; to watch; **késhiki o nagaméru** to gaze at the landscape; **sóra o nagaméru** to look up at the sky; **hito no kao o nagaméru** to gaze into someone's face.

nagamochí oblong Japanese chest.

nagamóchi endurance, durability; **nagamóchi suru** to last long, endure.

naganága very long; **naganága to kataru** to speak at great length.

NAGANEN many years; **naganen no** long; long standing; **naganen no tomodachi** a friend of long standing.

–NÁGARA suffix denoting: while; as; at the same time that; during. **Asagóhan o tabenágara rájio o kiita.** I listened to the

radio while eating breakfast. **Nenagara
hón o yónde wa ikemasén.** Don't read
books [while] in bed.

NAGÁRAKU for a long time.

nagaré stream, current; lineage.

nagarekómu to flow into.

nagaréru to flow; to run.

nágasa length; measure. **Nágasa wa dono
gurai désu ka?** How long is it? What is
its length?

nagasaréru to drift; to be swept away; **úmi e
nagasaréru** to be washed out to sea.

nagashí kitchen sink.

nagashíme sidelong glance; **nagashíme ni
miru** to look askance at; to look at
(someone) out of the corner of one's
eyes.

NAGÁSU to let flow; to drain; to wash
away; **mizu o nagásu** to pour water; to
drain off; **se o nagásu** to wash one's
back.

nagatarashíi lengthy; tedious.

nagawázurai lingering illness.

nagaya tenement house; block of houses.

nagedásu to throw out, discard; **ashí o
nagedásu** to stretch one's legs.

nagekawashíi sad, lamentable.

nagekí grief, sorrow; **nagekí o kakéru** to be
a source of constant trouble to others.

nagekómu to throw into.

nagéku to weep; to grieve.

NAGÉRU to throw, fling, toss.

nagetsukeru to throw at.

nageyari neglect, negligence; **nageyari ni
suru** to neglect; **shigoto o nageyari ni
suru** to do sloppy work.

nagí lull, calm.

nagori traces, remains; parting; **mukashi no
nagori** remains of the past; **nagori o
oshímu** to grieve at parting.

naguriai fight, scuffle; **naguriai ni náru** to
come to blows; **naguriai o suru** to fight.

naguriáu to fight.

nagúru to strike; to beat.

nagusame comfort, consolation.

nagusaméru to comfort; **mízukara
nagusaméru** to comfort oneself.

nagusami amusement, sport, diversion,
recreation; **nagusami ni** for fun.

NÁI there is not; does not exist; be gone,
missing; not to be found; have not (no);
lack, be devoid of. **Nani mo nái.** There is
nothing. **Okane ga nái.** I've no money.

–NAI suffix denoting; not; negative ending.
Shináide kudasái. Please don't do it.
Kónaide kudasái. Please don't come.

náibu (*n.*) inside, interior.

náichi homeland; mainland; interior.

NÁIFU knife; penknife.

náigai inside and outside; domestic and
foreign; home and abroad.

naijoo internal conditions; real state of
affairs. **Anó hito wa sono kaisha no
naijoo o yóku shitte imásu.** He knows
the internal conditions of that company
very well.

náika internal medicine; **naikái** physician.

náikaku cabinet; ministry; **Náikaku
Sooridáijin** Premier; Prime Minister.

naimen (*n.*) inside, interior.

nainai de secretly; privately; **nainai no
secret**; confidential; **nainai ni suru** to
keep something secret.

náishi from . . . to; between . . . and . . . Sore
wa sen en naishi ni sen en shimásu. It
costs from one to two thousand yen.

naishin inner feelings; **naishin dé wa at
heart**; inwardly. **Naishin wa góku íi hitó
desu.** He is a good man at heart.

naishó secrecy; privacy; secret; **naishó de in
private**; **naishobánashi** confidential talk.

naishoku private occupation; outside work;
sideline.

naishúkketsu hemorrhage.

naitei unofficial decision; **naitei suru** to
decide unofficially; to arrange
tentatively.

naiyoo contents.

najimi familiarity; acquaintance; intimate
friend; **najimi no** familiar; **najimi ni
náru** to make friends with.

najímu to become familiar with; to become
attached to.

najíru to reprove, rebuke.

náka relations; relationship; **náka no íi** to be
on good terms; to be friendly; **náka no
warúi** to be on bad terms; to be
unfriendly; **náka yoku suru** to keep on
good terms with.

NÁKA interior; inside; center; **náka ni**
within; **ie no náka ni** in the house,
indoors; **hako no náka e ireru** to put in a
box.

nakabá half; middle; **natsu no nakabá ni** in
the middle of summer.

nakadachinin broker.

nakágai, nakagáigyoo brokerage;
nakagainin broker; commission merchant;
nakagáiten brokerage house.

nakairi recess, intermission.

nakamá companion; member; (social) set;
circle; **nakamá ni háiru** to take part
(join) in.

nakamaházure ni sareru to be shunned, to
be left out.

nakamí inside, interior; contents.

NAKANAKA very; considerably; rather,
quite; easily; **nakanaka juudai na koto**

(thing) of no small importance;
nakanaka dóoshite on the contrary.

nakanáori reconciliation; **nakanáori o suru**
to become reconciled; to settle
differences; **kenka no nakanáori o
saseru** to patch up a quarrel.

nakaniwa courtyard.

nakaore bóoshi man's felt hat.

nakaseru to move to tears; to make someone
cry.

nakayásumi rest, respite (in the middle of
work); **nakayásumi suru** to take a rest;
to take a coffee break.

nakáyoshi good friend, pal, chum; **nakáyoshi
de áru** to be good friends with.

NAKÁYUBI middle finger.

nakenashi no small amount (of money) one
has. **Nakenashi no kane o yarimáshita.** I
gave her what little money I had.

náki deceased; late (lately deceased); **náki
háha** my late mother; **íma wa náki
Tanaká-shi** the late Mr. Tanaka.

nakigara remains, corpse.

nakigóe cry; scream; **nakigóe de iu** to talk
while sobbing.

nakigoto complaint; whimper; **nakigoto o iu**
to grumble.

nakitsúku to implore, entreat.

nakóodo matchmaker.

NAKU to weep, cry; **nakunaku** tearfully;
naite mé o harásu to cry one's eyes out;
nakitai dake naku to have a good cry.

NAKUNARU to get used up; to run out of.
Moo kane ga nakunarimáshita. I am
short of funds. My money ran out.
**Watakushi no tokei ga
nakunarimáshita.** My watch is missing.

NÁMA NO fresh; raw; unripe; **namazákana**
raw fish.

namanamashíi vivid.

NAMAE, NA name. **Onamae wa?** What is
your name?

namahánka incomplete; superficial;
namahánka no Eigo superficial
knowledge of English.

namahénji vague reply; **namahénji o suru**
to give an evasive reply.

namaiki conceit; **namaiki na** conceited;
affected.

namajii halfheartedly; indifferently; rashly;
namajii na halfhearted.

namajikka ni thoughtlessly; rashly;
halfheartedly; **namajikka na kotó o suru**
to leave something half done.

namakemono lazy person.

NAMAKERU to be lazy. **Kyóo wa ichinichi
namákete shimátta.** I've loafed all day.

namákizu fresh bruise.

namamekashíi charming; coquettish

namanurui lukewarm; **namanurui henji**
halfhearted answer.

namari lead (metal).

namarí dialect, provincial speech.

NAMATÁMAGO raw egg.

namauo raw fish.

NAMÉRAKA smoothness; **naméraka na**
smooth, glassy; **naméraka ni** smoothly.

NAMÉRU to lick; to lap up; to experience;
naméru yoo ni kawaigáru to dote on;
kúroo o naméru to experience a
hardship.

nami average; **nami no** average, common;
namihazurete out of the ordinary,
uncommon.

NAMÍ wave; sea; **nami no oto** roar of the
waves. **Namí ga takái.** The sea is rough.

námida tears; **námida o nagásu** to weep;
námida ni musebu to be choked with
tears; **namidagúmu** to be moved to tears.

namiútsu to undulate, wave.

nán difficulty; trouble; accident, detect; **nán
naku** easily, without difficulty; **nán ni áu**
to have difficulty.

NÁN–, NÁNI prefix denoting: what, which,
how many. **Nánnin imásu ka?** How
many persons are there?

nanáme no diagonal; **nanáme ni** diagonally.

NANÁTSU, SHICHÍ seven.

NÁNBAN what number; what size. **Nánban
desu ka?** What is your (telephone)
number? **Nánban?** Number, please (asked
by a telephone operator).

NÁNBEN how often, how many times;
nánben mo often; many times; over and
over.

nanbutsu tough customer; difficult person.

NÁNDAKA somehow or other; somewhat.
Nandaka tsukáreta. I don't know why,
but I'm somewhat tired.

NÁN DE why; how.

nán de mo any; whatever; anything,
everything, by all means; probably; **náni
ga nán de mo** at any rate; **nán de mo ká
de mo** anything and everything. **Nán de
mo soo iu uwasa désu.** So they say. So I
hear.

NÁNDO how many times.

nándo mo many times, often.

nandoki, ITSU when; **nandoki démo**
whenever.

NÁNGATSU what month.

nangí trouble; hardship; **nangí na** difficult,
troublesome; **nangí suru** to suffer
hardship; **nangí o kakéru** to cause
trouble.

NÁNI what?, why?, which, some, any,
something; what!; well!; **náni wa tomo
are** at all events, in any case; **náni ka ni**

tsukéte in one way or another; **náni yori** more than anything else; **náni yori na** the most desirable; the nicest; **náni ka tabéru mono** something to eat. **Naní kuso.** Damn it! (See also **nán-**.)

nanige náku unintentionally; accidentally; **nanige náku yosoóu** to look innocent; to look unconcerned.

NÁNISHIRO anyhow; at any rate, for. **Nánishiro taihen isogashíi desu.** I am really very busy.

NANIGOTO what; **nanigoto ní mo** in everything; **nanigoto ga aróo to** no matter what happens. **Nanigoto désu ka?** What's the matter? **Nanigoto mo nái** [Nothing has happened.] It's O.K.

nánitozo please (*formal*).

NANJÍ what time. **Nánji desu ka?** What time is it?

nankínmame peanut.

nankuse fault; **nankuse o tsukéru** to find fault with.

nankyoku crisis, difficult situation; **nankyoku ni ataru** to deal with the situation.

Nankyoku South Pole.

Nankyokúkai Antarctic Ocean.

nanmon difficult problem; puzzle; ticklish question.

NÁNNEN what year; how many years. **Nán nen koko ni súnde imásu ka?** How many years have you lived here?

NÁNNICHI what day; how many days. **Kyoo wa nánnichi desu ka?** What date is it?

NAN NO what; what kind; no; not at all; **nan no tamé ni** why; **nán no yooji de** on what business. **Nán no kotó mo nákatta.** Nothing has happened.

nanoka See **nanuka**.

nanpa shipwreck.

nanpasen wrecked ship; **nansen** shipwreck; **nansen suru** to be shipwrecked.

NÁN TO how; what; **nán to itté mo** after all; when all is said and done; **nán to shité mo** at any cost. **Nán to máa!** What! Nihongo de sore o nán to iimásu ka? How do you say it in Japanese?

NANUKA, NANOKA seventh day of the month; seven days.

nanushi village head.

náo more; still; yet; all the more; less; **náo ichido** once again; **náo mata** furthermore; in addition. **Náo machigátte imasu.** It is still wrong.

NAÓRU to be repaired; to be corrected; to recover, get well; **byooki ga naóru** to recover from an illness. **Kono tokei wa súgu naorimásu.** This watch can be

repaired easily.

NAOSARA more; still more; less; still less; **naosara íi** to be so much better.

naoshí correction; mending, repair.

NAÓSU to repair, mend; to correct; to cure. **Kono kutsú o naóshite kudasái.** I want these shoes repaired.

nápukin napkin.

—NÁRA if; in case; provided. **Hitsuyoo nára súgu mairimasu.** I will come if necessary. **Hoshíi nara agemásu.** If you want it. I will give it to you.

NARABERU to arrange, put in order; to line up; to compare with; **káta o naraberu** to be (someone's) equal; **mihon o naraberu** to show samples.

narabi row, line; equal; **narabi náki** unequaled; **narabi ni** together with; besides.

NARABU to be in a row, stand side by side; **itchókusen ni narabu** to stand in a straight line.

naráí custom, habit; **naraí to náru** to form a habit.

narasu to ring; to blow; to sound; to complain; to be famous.

narásu to level; to smooth out; to tame; to domesticate; to train; to get used to; **inú o narásu** to train a dog; **kónnan ni narásu** to inure (someone) to trouble.

NARÁU to learn; to take lessons; to imitate, copy; **ikébana o naráu** to take lessons in flower arrangement. **Anáta wa okáasan ni narátte ryóori ga joozú desu ne.** You are following in your mother's steps as a good cook, aren't you?

narazumono rascal.

NARÉRU to become familiar with; to get used to; to become overly familiar; to become tame; **náreta** domestic; familiar. **Tookyoo no kúuki ni naréru kotó wa muzukashíi.** It is hard for me to adjust myself to the atmosphere of Tokyo.

nari sound; ring; **nari o shizumeru** to be silent, to watch breathlessly.

narí form, shape; size; personal appearance; **narí ga ookíi** to be tall.

naritachi origin; organization.

naritátsu to consist of, be composed of.

nariyuki result, consequence; course (of events); **nariyuki ni makaséru** to let (something) take its own course; **koto no nariyuki** course of events.

NÁRU to become; to make; to get; to grow; to come; to set in; to pass; to attain; to begin to; to come to; to get to; to consist of; to be made of; to turn out; **byooki ga wáruku náru** to take a turn for the worse (in an illness); **byooki ni**

náru to fall ill; **hontoo ni náru** to come true; **sukí ni náru** to begin to like; to develop a fondness for; **toshí ni náru** to come of age. **Sámuku narimáshita.** It is getting cold. **Náru yoo ni shika naránai yo.** Let things go their own way. Take things as they come.

náru to bear fruit, to grow (on a tree). **Ie no ringo ga yóku narimáshita.** My apple tree is laden with apples.

NARU to sound; to ring; to roar; to strike; to resound; to be famous; **mimí ga naru** to have a ringing in one's ears.

NARUBEKU, narutake as . . . as possible; if possible; as . . . as one can; **narubeku háyaku** as quickly as possible; at the first opportunity. **Narubeku kúru yoo ni shimásu.** I'll try my best to come.

NARUHODO really; indeed; I see; certainly. **Naruhodo hontoo desu.** I see it is true. Indeed, you are right.

narutake See **narubeku.**

nasake sympathy; compassion; benevolence; affection; **nasake áru hito** charitable person; **nasaké o kakéru** to show sympathy for; **nasakebukái** compassionate; benevolent; charitable.

NASAKÉNAI unsympathetic; heartless; cruel; miserable; pitiful; shameful; deplorable; **nasakénai arisama** a wretched condition. **Nán to iu nasakénai kotó da!** What a shame!

nasaru to do (*respect*).

násu to do, accomplish; to perform; to achieve; to form; to constitute; to make; to practice; to commit; **áku o násu** to do wrong; **kokorozashi o násu** to accomplish one's purpose; **en o násu** to form a circle. (See also **suru.**)

nasúru to smear; to rub on; to blame.

nata hatchet.

NATSÚ summer; **natsubóoshi** summer hat; **natsukufu, natsumono** summer clothes; **natsuyásumi** summer vacation.

natsukashigáru to long for; to pine for; to languish; **mukashi o natsukashigáru** to think fondly of the past.

natsukashii dear; beloved; longed-for; **natsukáshiku** longingly; fondly; **natsukashíi kókyoo** one's beloved home; one's dear native place; **natsukashíi omoide** fond memories; **natsukashisóoni** longingly; yearningly. **Watakushi wa kókyoo ga natsukashíi.** I long for home. I'm homesick.

natsumíkan Chinese citron; bitter orange (similar to grapefruit).

nawá rope, cord; **nawá ni kakáru** to be arrested; **nawabari** roping off; **nawabari**

o suru to rope off; **nawabari shita zaseki** roped-off seats; **nawabari o arasu** to trespass upon; to encroach upon; **nawatóbi o suru** to jump (skip) rope.

náya outbuildings; shed; barn.

nayamí suffering, pain, anguish, distress, trouble; **nayamí ga áru** to have troubles; **nayamí ga nái** to have no troubles; to be carefree.

nayámu to be worried about; to be troubled with; to suffer from; **nayánde iru** to be in pain, to be in distress.

nazashi designation; calling by name.

nazásu to name; to call by name.

NÁZE why; for what reason; **náze da ka** somehow; without knowing why. **Náze sóo ka?** Why so? **Náze ka shiranai.** I don't know why.

nazo puzzle; riddle; **nazo o kakéru** to drop a hint; **nazo o satóru** to take a hint; **nazo o tóku** to solve a riddle.

nazukéru to tame; to domesticate; to win over.

nazukéru to name; to call.

nazúku to be tamed; to become attached to; to take kindly to.

NÉ root, origin, source, base, foundation, nature; **né mo nai uwasa** a groundless rumor; **né mo ha mo nái koto** a pure fabrication; **né ga tsuku** to take root; **ne ni motsu** to bear a grudge; **né o haru** to spread roots.

NE, NEDAN price, cost; value; **ne ga déru** to increase in price; **ne o kiku** to ask the price; **ne o tsukéru** to set a price on. **Ne ga takái.** The price is high. It is high priced. **Ne ga yasúi.** The price is low. It is moderately priced.

ne sound, tone; **fue no ne** tone of a flute; **kane no ne** sound of a bell.

ne (*n.*) sleep; **ne ga tarinai** to not get enough sleep.

neage price rise; price hike; **neage suru** to raise prices.

nébaneba suru sticky, gluey, gummy, clammy.

nebari stickiness, adhesiveness, perseverance; tenacity; **nebarizuyói** persistent, tenacious; **nebarizúyosa** perseverance, stick-to-itiveness. **Anó hito wa nebari ga nái.** He lacks perseverance. He doesn't stick to it.

nebaru to be sticky, be adhesive; to perservere, to stick to a job.

neboo oversleeping; late-riser, sleepyhead; **neboo suru** to oversleep, to get up late.

nebumi appraisal; estimation; **nebumi suru** to appraise, assess, value.

NEDAN price, cost, terms. **Nedan wa íkura**

desu ka? What is the price? (See also ne.)

nedaru to tease; to coax; to extort; to demand.

nedoko bed; **nedoko ni háiru** to go to bed, to get into bed; **nedoko o koshiraeru** to make a bed.

néesan older sister.

NEGÁI desire, wish; request; **negái ni yori** at one's request; **negái ga kanau** to receive a wish, to have a desire fulfilled.

negaidéru to apply for; to send in (make) a petition.

negaisage withdrawal (of a petition or application); **negaisage ni suru** to withdraw a petition or application.

negau to petition, to beg, to wish; to hope for. **Onegai shitái kotó ga áru.** I have a favor to ask of you. **Sore wa negátte mo nái kotó desu.** Nothing suits (pleases) me more than your proposal.

negawashíí desirable.

négi leek, green onion.

negiru to haggle, beat down the price.

neiro tone; tone quality (of music).

néji screw; **néji de shiméru** to screw down.

nejiáu to contend; to struggle with someone.

nejifuseru to get (someone) down, to overpower (someone).

nejikéru to be crooked, twisted; to become perverse; **neijíketa** perverse, twisted.

nejikíru to twist; to wrench off.

nejikómu to screw in; to stuff into, to demand an apology.

NEJIMÁWASHI screwdriver.

nejíru to twist; to screw; to distort.

nejitóru to wrench off; to twist (someone's) arm (and take something from him).

nekasu, nekaseru to put to sleep; to send to bed; to make (someone) lie down; to lay (something) on the side; to let (something) lie idle; to keep idle; **nekashimono** unsold goods; merchandise that does not sell.

nekkyoo enthusiasm; fanaticism, craze; rage; passion; **nekkyoo shite** frantically, mad with excitement; **nekkyoo saseru** to create excitement, stir up enthusiasm; to thrill; **nekkyoo suru** to go wild over, go crazy over; to grow excited; **nekkyootéki** wild; enthusiastic; mad; hotheaded.

NÉKO cat, kitten; **neko zúki** cat lover; **néko mo shákushi mo** everyone; anybody and everybody.

nekóze hunchback; **nekóze no** stooping, hunchbacked.

NÉKUTAI necktie; **nekutai o shiméru** to tie a necktie; **nekútai o tóku** to untie a necktie.

néma bedroom.

nemaki sleeping apparel, nightgown, pajamas.

NEMUI, nemutai sleepy, drowsy; **nemuku náru** to feel sleepy.

nemuke sleepiness, drowsiness.

nemuri sleep, nap; **fukái nemuri** deep sleep.

NEMURU to sleep; to fall asleep; **yóku nemutte iru** to be fast asleep. (See also neru.)

nemutai, See NEMUI.

nén sense, feeling; idea, notion, thought, desire, wish; concern; **fuan no nén** feeling of uneasiness; **nén o irete** carefully; **nén o osu** to call one's attention to; to remind one of something.

NÉN year; per annum; **nén ni ichido** once a year; **nén ni ichidó no** yearly, annual; **nénjuu** all year round, every day of the year; the whole year, the year through; **nengara nénjuu** all year round; year after year; **néndo** business year, fiscal year; school year; **nenmatsu** at the end of the year; **nenpoo** annual salary.

nendaijun chronological order; **nendaijun no** chronological; **nendaijun ni** chronologically.

nenpyoo chronology, chronological table.

nénga New Year's greetings; **nénga ni iku** to make a New Year's call; **nengájoo** New Year's card.

nen'iri carefulness; **nen'iri ni** carefully, scrupulously, minutely; **nen'iri na** careful, conscientious, attentive.

nenjíru = **nenzúru** to pray.

nenryóo fuel; **ekitai nénryoo** liquid fuel; **nenryoo kiki** energy crisis.

nénshi New Year's Day; **nenshíkyaku** New Year's caller; **nenshi máwari** New Year's calls.

nenzúru See **nenjíru.**

néon neon; **neonsáin** neon sign.

nerai aim, objective; **nerai o sadaméru** to take careful aim. **neraidókoro** one's objective, point aimed.

nerau to aim at; to watch for.

nerí (n.) kneading; **néru** to knead; to soften; to train.

NERU to sleep; to go to sleep; fall asleep; to take a nap; to lie down; **nerarenai** to lie awake, to sleep poorly; **yóku neru** to sleep well. **Neru jikan da.** It's time to go to bed. It's time to go to sleep. (See also NEMURU.)

nesage price reduction.

nesshín zeal, enthusiasm; **nesshín na** enthusiastic; **nesshín ni** eagerly, enthusiastically; earnestly.

nessúru to heat, make hot; to ignite; to get excited.

netámu to be jealous; to be envious of.

netchuu enthusiasm, zeal; **netchuu suru** to be enthusiastic about; **netchuu shite iru** to be devoted to, to be immersed in.

netsú heat; fever, temperature; craze, fad; enthusiasm; **netsú ga déru** to become feverish; **netsú ga áru** to be feverish; to be enthusiastic: **–ni netsú o ageru** to be deeply involved in; **netsuai** passionate love; **netsuai suru** to be madly in love; **netsujoo** fervor, zeal.

nettai tropics; **nettái koku** tropical country; **nettai no** tropical.

nétto (tennis) net.

nettoo boiling water; **nettoo o abiru** to be scalded.

NEUCHI value, worth; price; estimation; **neuchi no áru** valuable; **neuchi no nái** worthless; **neuchi ga agaru** to rise in value; to rise in one's estimation; **neuchi ga ochíru** to fall in value; **neuchi ga áru** to be worthy of; to be worth.

nezumi rat; mouse; **nezumítori** mousetrap.

nezumízan geometrical progression. **Jinkoo ga nezumízan de fuéru.** The population increases by geometrical progression.

NEZUMIIRO (*n.*) gray; **nezumiiro no** (*adj.*) gray.

NI particle denoting: in; at; on; into; for; to; by; and; with; of; **ása ni** in the morning; **gózen sánji ni** at 3:00 A.M.; **hako ni ireru** to put into a box; **hito ni hanashikakéru** to speak to a person; **inú ni kamaréru** to be bitten by a dog; **mádo ni** at the window; in the window: **–ni chiyahoya suru** to make much of; **tana ni noseru** to put on the shelf; **Tookyoo ni iku** to go to Tokyo.

ní load, burden; package; luggage; freight; **ní ni náru** to be a burden to; **ni o tsumu** to load; **ní o orósu** to unload; **ní o koshiraeru** to pack; **ní o tóku** to unpack.

NÍ, FUTATSU two. (See also **FUTSUKA**).

niáu to suit; to become; to match; **niawánai** unsuitable, unbecoming. **Kono kimono wa kimi ni niáu.** This dress (suit) is becoming to you. **Sono tebúkuro wa booshi ni niáu.** Those gloves match the hat.

nibúi dull; dense; slow; thickheaded.

nibúru to become dull, become blunt; to weaken; **késshin ga nibúru** to weaken in one's resolve.

níchanicha suru to be slimy; to be sticky; to be greasy.

nichibotsu sunset; **nichibotsu ni** at sunset;

nichibotsu no nochi after sunset; after dark.

NICHIJOO every day; usually; always; **nichijoo no** daily; usual; ordinary; **nichijoo no koto** everyday occurrence; **nichijoo no shigoto** daily routine; everyday work; **nichijoo go** everyday speech; ordinary language.

NICHIYOO, NICHIYÓOBI Sunday; **Nichiyoo gákkoo** Sunday school.

nichiyóohin everyday necessity; articles used daily.

nidashi broth.

NIDÓ twice, two times; second time; **nidó to shinai** never again; **nidome** second time; **nidome no** second.

nieagáru well done (cooking).

niekiránai vague; undetermined; indecisive; irresolute; **niekiránai henjí** vague answer; noncommittal reply; **niekiránai hito** irresolute (undecided) person.

NIERU to boil; to cook; to be boiled; to be cooked. **Yóku niete imásu ka?** Is it well done? **Kono nikú wa yóku niete inái desu.** This meat is not well done. This meat is half cooked.

nietátsu to boil.

nieyu boiling water; **nieyu o nomaséru** to betray; to deceive; **nieyu o nomasaréru** to be betrayed.

NIGÁI bitter; **nigái keiken** bitter experience; **nigái keiken o shite mé ga saméru** to learn by bitter experience; to have one's eyes opened; **nigái kao o suru** to make a (sour) face; to frown.

nigamí bitterness, bitter taste. **Nigamí ga áru.** It is bitter. It tastes bitter.

niganigashíi bitter; painful; unpleasant; disgusting; shameful. **Niganigashíi kotó da!** What a shame!

nigao portrait; likeness.

nigásu to release, set free; to let escape; to miss; **tomodachi o nigásu** to miss a friend. (See also **nigéru**.)

nigate tough customer; difficult person, weak point.

NIGATSU February.

nigé escape; retreat; **nigé o útsu** to try to escape; to prepare an escape; to excuse oneself from; to shirk, evade; **nigéashi** flight; retreat; **nigéashi ni náru** to be ready to quit; to be inclined to run away. **Anó hito wa ítsumo nigéashi ni nátte iru.** He is always ready to quit. **Nigé o útte mo damé desu.** Such an excuse is no good.

NIGERU to run away, flee; to escape; **mótte nigéru** to make off with something.

nigiru to grasp, take hold of; to grip, seize.

nigiwai prosperity; bustle, activity, stir.

nigiwashíi to be flourishing, prosperous; to be bustling; to be animated.

NIGIWAU to flourish, be prosperous; to be lively, be astir; to be crowded. **Tookyoo no machí wa nigiwátte iru.** The streets of Tokyo are crowded. **Misé wa minna nigiwátte iru.** All the stores are doing good business. All the stores are prospering.

NIGÍYAKA NA prosperous, flourishing, animated, lively; cheerful, gay; **nigíyaka na hito** happy fellow; **nigíyaka na basho** bustling section (place); **nigíyaka ni** gaily; animatedly; **nigíyaka ni asobu** to make merry.

nigori muddiness; impurity; voiced consonant; **nigorí mizu** muddy water.

nigóru to become muddy; to become impure; **nigótta** muddy; cloudy; voiced. **Áme ga futtá no de iké ga nigorimáshita.** The rain has made the pond muddy.

nigósu to make muddy; to answer vaguely, to speak ambiguously; **kotobá o nigósu** to say something ambiguously.

nigúruma cart, wagon.

NIHÓN Japan; **NIHONGO** Japanese (language). (See also **NIPPON**.)

níisan older brother.

nijímu to blot; to run; to spread; to smudge; **inki no nijínde iru** ink-stained. **Arau to iró ga nijímu.** If you wash it, the color will run.

nijínda blurred, smudged, smeared; stained.

NÍJUU twenty. (See also **HATSUKA**.)

nijuu duplication; **nijuu no** double, duplicate; **nijuu no ími** double meaning; **nijuu ni** doubly; twice; **nijuu ni sakusei suru** to make out in duplicate.

NIKAI second floor; twice, two times; **nikai ni** upstairs; **nikai ni agaru** to go upstairs; **nikaidate** two-story house.

NIKKI diary, journal; **nikki ni tsukéru** to record in a diary, make an entry in a diary; **nikki o tsukéru** to keep a diary.

níkkoo sunshine, sunlight.

nikkyuu daily wage; **nikkyuu de hataraku** to work by the day; **nikkyuu de haráu** to pay by the day; to hire someone by the day.

NIKÚ meat; flesh; muscle; **niku no atsui** thick; **niku no usui** thin; **nikú ga tsuku** to get fat; to gain weight; **nikú ga ochíru** to get thin; to lose weight; **nikú o kíru** to carve meat; **nikúya** butcher shop; **nikúrui** meat; **nikushoku** meat-eating; meat diet.

nikúi hateful, detestable; abominable.

nikúmu to hate, abhor, detest; **nikumu béki** hateful, detestable.

–NIKÚI suffix denoting: difficult; troublesome; awkward. **Nihongo dé wa omóu kotó o iiarawashinikúi.** It is difficult to express my thought in Japanese.

NÍMOTSU baggage, luggage; load; belongings, personal effects; **nímotsu no mekata o hakáru** to weigh one's baggage; **nímotsu o azukéru** to check one's baggage.

nín duty; responsibility; task; office; post; **nín ni ataru** to undertake a responsibility; to take on a duty; **nín ni taénai** to be unequal to the task; to be incompetent; **nín ni tsukú** to assume one's post; take up one's duties; **nín o mattoo suru** to fulfill one's duty.

–NIN suffix used as a counter for people; **sanjúunin** thirty people.

NINGEN, HITO human being; **ningen no** human, mortal.

ningyoo doll; puppet; **ningyoo no yóo ni** like a doll (charming, beautiful, handsome); **ningyooshíbai** puppet show; **ningyootsúkai** puppeteer.

NINJIN carrot.

nínjoo humanity; humaneness; kindness; sympathy; **nínjoo no áru hito** humane person, kindhearted person; **nínjoo ga áru** to be humane; to be sympathetic; **nínjoo ga nái** to be inhuman, be heartless.

ninki popular feeling, popular sentiment; popularity; business (conditions); **ninki ni joojíru** to catch the popular fancy; **ninki no áru** popular; **ninki no nái** unpopular; **ninki o tóru** to win popularity; to gain favor. **Ninki ga yói** Business is brisk. **Ninki ga warúi.** Business is slack.

nínpu laborer; **ninpugáshira** foreman.

ninshiki recognition; **ninshiki suru** to recognize; to perceive.

níntai patience; endurance; perseverance; **níntai suru** to be patient; to persevere; **níntai ga dekínai** to have no patience with; to be impatient with; **níntai shite** patiently.

nintei recognition; conclusion; presumption; authorization, sanction; **nintei suru** to admit; to presume; to authorize.

nin'yoo appointment; employment; **nin'yoo suru** to appoint to a post.

nínzuu number of persons; **nínzuu no óoi ié** large family.

NIÓI smell, odor, scent; perfume, fragrance; **íi niói** sweet smell; fragrant odor; **niói ga íi** to be sweet smelling, be fragrant; **warúi niói** bad smell; foul odor; **niói ga warúi** to be foul smelling.

nióu to smell; to be fragrant. **Gásu ga nióu.** I smell gas.

NIPPÓN Japan; **Nippón no** (*adj.*) Japanese; of Japan; **Nippongo** Japanese (language); **Nipponjín** Japanese (person). **Nippongo ga dekimásu ka?** Can you speak Japanese? (See also **NIHÓN**.)

niramí glare; sharp look; influence; authority; **niramí ga kiku** to have authority over; to have influence over; **niramí ga kikanai** to have no authority over; to have no influence over.

nirámu to glare at, scowl; **jitto nirámu** to stare fixedly.

NIRU to boil; to cook. **Watakushi wa nikú wa yóku nita hóo ga íi desu.** I like my meat well done.

niru resemble, be like, be similar to; **totemo yóku nite iru** to be very similar to; to resemble closely; **nite inai** to have no resemblance to; to be dissimilar.

nise (*n.*) imitation, sham; counterfeit, forgery; **nise no** (*adj.*) counterfeit, forged, false; **nisemono** imitation, fake, counterfeit article.

NISHI west; **nishi no** western; **nishi ni** in the west; **nishi gawa ni** on the west (side).

nita like; similar.

–NI TSÚITE of; about; with; on; over; as to; concerning; regarding; on the subject of; in connection with; relating to; in the case of; **kono kotó ni tsúite** about this; with regard to this matter; **kono tén ni tsúite** on this point.

nittei daily routine; day's agenda.

NITTOO daily wages; **nittoo o haráu** to pay daily wages.

NIWA garden; yard; courtyard; **niwáshi** gardener.

níwaka no sudden; abrupt; unexpected; **níwaka ni** suddenly, abruptly; unexpectedly; all at once.

niwakaáme sudden shower, downpour.

NIWATORI chicken, hen; cock.

nizúkuri packing; crating; **nizúkuri suru** to pack; to crate; **nizúkuri ga yóku dékite iru** to be well packed; **nizúkuri ga fukánzen da** to be badly packed; **nizukurinin** packer.

nó field, plain.

NO particle denoting: pertaining to: —'s; of—; —'s own; in; at; on; for; by; **eigo no sensei** teacher of English; English teacher; **Góya no é** a painting by Goya; **ie no iriguchi** entrance to the house; **ishi no hashí** stone bridge; bridge made of stone; **kawa no hashi** bridge over the river; **kyóo no shinbun** today's newspaper; **mondai no hito** man in question; **otooto**

no hón my brother's book; **yuki no hi** snowy day.

nobásu to extend, lengthen, stretch, draw out, prolong; to postpone; to straighten; **issun dake nobásu** to lengthen by one inch; **kanjóo o nobásu** to defer (payment) on a bill.

noberu to express, state; to explain; **íken o nobéru** to express an opinion; **kansoo o nobéru** to give one's impression; **riyuu o nobéru** to state one's reason.

nóbetsu ni ceaselessly, perpetually, continuously.

nobi postponement; spread, growth; **nobí o suru** to stretch oneself.

nobíru to extend, stretch; to be prolonged; to be deferred; to increase, grow, develop. **Watakushi no shuppatsu ga nóbita.** My departure has been delayed.

nobori rise, ascent; uphill road.

nobori streamer, banner.

NOBORU to climb; to go up, rise; to be prompted; **yamá ni noboru** to climb a mountain. **Táiyoo ga noboru.** The sun rises.

nobose dizziness, vertigo.

noboseru to be dizzy; to get excited; to be infatuated with; to be absorbed in; **nobosete iru** in the excitement. **Anó hito wa nobosete iru.** The blood has rushed to his head.

NOCHÍ future time; forthcoming time; **sono nochi** thereafter, since then; **mikka nochi** three days later; **nochi no** subsequent; future; **nochi ni** later on; afterward.

–NÓDE because of. **Kaze o hiitá node atamá ga itái desu.** My headache is due to my cold. [I have a headache because of a cold.]

NÓDO throat voice; **nódo ga yói** to have a sweet voice; **nódo o itaméru** to have a sore throat. **Nódo ga kawakimáshita.** I'm thirsty.

nódoka na quiet, calm; pleasant; **nódoka na ténki** mild weather; **nódoka na kokóro** peace of mind; **nódoka ni** quietly; peacefully.

nogaréru to escape; flee, get away; to avoid, evade; **abunai tokoró o nogaréru** to have a narrow escape; **nogarerarénai** unavoidable, inevitable. **Watakushi wa nogaréru kotó ga deckinai.** I'm in for it; it's inevitable.

nóhara field, plain.

nójuku camping outdoors; **nójuku suru** to camp out.

noki eaves (of a house); **noki o naraberu** to stand side by side; to stand in a row.

nokogíri saw; **nokogíri de hiku** to saw.

nokórazu all, entirely, wholly, without exception; **issen mo nokórazu** to the last cent.

NOKORÍ remainder, rest, balance; **nokori no** remaining; **nokori náku** all, entirely; **nokorimono** remains, leavings, leftovers, remnants, scraps (of food).

NOKÓRU to be left, to remain, to linger. **Okane ga íkura ka nokótte iru.** I have some money left.

NOKÓSU to leave behind; to keep in; to leave over; to save; **kane o nokósu** to save money; **shigoto o nokósu** to leave the work (partly done).

nomaréru to be swallowed up, to be drunk up; to be awed by; to cower.

nomaséru to give a drink, serve a drink; to let (someone) drink, to treat (someone) to a drink; **ippai nomaséru** to entertain with liquor. **Dóozo mizu o íppai nomásete kudasái.** Please give me a drink of water.

nomikomu to swallow; to drink, to gulp; to understand; to take in, to know. **Anáta no iu kotó ga yóku nomikomenai.** I can't grasp your meaning. I don't follow what you say.

nomímizu drinking water.

NOMÍMONO beverage; **tsumetai nomímono** cold beverage.

nominikúi distasteful, disagreeable (to drink), undrinkable.

NÓMU to drink; to take (in); to swallow; to smoke; **ocha o nómu** to drink tea; **tabako o nomu** to smoke.

NONBÍRI easily; **nonbíri to shita** carefree; easy; quiet; **nonbíri to shita seikatsu** carefree life, quiet life; **nonbíri suru** to feel at leisure, to be at ease.

–NÓNI particle denoting: although, though; in spite of, despite. **Wakái noni yóku hatarakimásu.** He works hard despite his young age.

nónki na carefree; easygoing; happy-go-lucky; **nónki ni** leisurely; **nónki ni kurasuto** take life easy.

nóo brain; talent; ability; skill; **nóo o itaméru** to rack one's brains; **noo nashi no** good for nothing.

nóo Noh play (also spelled No).

nooen, noojoo farm; **noonen ni kurasu** to live on a farm.

nooen na charming; engaging; bewitching; voluptuous.

nóofu farmer; farmhand.

nóogu farm equipment.

nóogyoo farming, agriculture; **nóogyoo no** agricultural.

noofkketsu cerebral hemorrhage.

noojoo See **hooen.**

nóoka farmhouse; farmer.

nookoo density, thickness; **nookoo na** thick, dense; heavy; rich; **nookoo ni** thickly, densely; richly; **nookoo na tabémono** rich food.

noómu dense fog.

nooritsu efficiency; capability; **nooritsu no áru** efficient; capable; **nooritsu no agaranai** inefficient; **nooritsu o ageru** to increase efficiency, raise efficiency.

nóoryoku ability; facility; competency; capability; faculty.

noosakúbutsu, noosánbutsu crops, farm produce, agricultural products.

nooson rural area; farm village; agricultural district; **nooson no** rural; agricultural.

nootan shading; tinting; light and shade.

nootén scalp; crown of the head.

noozei tax payment; **noozei suru** to pay taxes; **noozéisha** taxpayer.

nori dried seaweed (a food).

norí paste; glue; starch; **norí de haru** to paste; to glue; **norí o tsukéru** to starch. **Kore ni norí o tsukéte hoshíi.** I'd like this starched.

norikae transfer; change; changing; **norikaéeki** junction, transfer point; **norikaeba** transfer point; **norikaekíppu** transfer ticket.

NORIKÁERU transfer; change (for a train, car, ship. etc.). **Oosaka iki wa koko de norikae désu.** You must transfer here for Osaka. **Shinjuku de básu ni norikáeru hóo ga yói deshóo.** It will be better to transfer to a bus at Shinjuku.

NORIMONO vehicle, conveyance.

noroi (*n.*) curse.

norói slow; lagging; tardy; dull; dense; **norói kishá** slow train; **shigoto ga norói** to be slow at one's work. **Anó hito wa bánji ni norói otokó da.** He is dense about everything.

noróu to curse; to wish (someone) ill.

NORU to ride (in, on); to get (in, on); to go on board; to join; to take part in; to be taken in; to be recorded; **kishá ni notte iku** to go by train; **shinbun ni noru** to appear (be reported) in the newspaper; **soodan ni noru** to take part in a consultation; **umá ni noru** to mount a horse.

noseru to put on top of; to place on, set on; to carry; to load; to take on board; to impose upon; to publish; to record; **jidóosha ni hito o nosete yaru** to give (someone) a lift in a car; **jookyaku o noseru** to take on passengers.

nótto nautical mile, knot.

nottóru to follow; to conform to; to go by; to be in accord with.

NOZOITE except, excepting, with the exception of; but; **hitótsu nozoite minna** all but one; **–o nozoite** with the exception of; excluding; **shoosúu o nozoite** with a few exceptions. **Nichiyóobi o nozoite máinichi benkyoo suru.** I study every day, except Sunday.

nozoku to eliminate, remove, exclude; to abolish; to omit.

nozoku to peep in, to look in.

nozomí wish, desire, hope; expectation, aspiration, ambition; **nozomí o kakéru** to set one's heart on.

nozómu face; to meet; to attend; to be present; **shikí ni nozómu** to attend a ceremony. **Niwa wa yamá ni nozónde iru.** The garden faces the mountains.

nozomu to wish, to desire, to hope for, to aspire to; to expect; to look out on.

nugéru to come off; to slip down.

NÚGU to take off; to pull off; to undress. **Kutsú o núgu no desu ka?** Shall I take off my shoes?

nuíbari needle.

nuká rice bran; **nukamiso** salt and rice bran paste (for pickling).

nukaru to be muddy; to be slushy; to blunder, make a mistake.

nukarumi mud; mud puddle.

nukasu to omit, exclude, leave out; to overlook.

nukedásu to get loose; to sneak out, steal out.

nukigaki selection; excerpt.

nukitóru to pull out, extract; to abstract; to steal.

NUKU to pull out, take out, draw out; to extract (a tooth); to uncork; to unscrew; to select; to leave out, omit.

numá swamp, bog; **numachi** swampy place.

nurasu to wet; to dampen; to soak; to drench. **Ashí o nurasú na.** Don't get your feet wet!

NURERU to become wet, get wet. **Kao ga námida ni nurete iru.** Her face is wet with tears.

nuri coating; varnishing; lacquering; painting; plastering.

NURU to apply; to spread on; to paint; to plaster; to coat; **pán ni bàtaa o nuru** to spread butter on bread.

nurúi lukewarm; dull; sluggish.

nurumáyu lukewarm water.

nusumimíru to steal looks at, look furtively at.

nusúmu to steal; to rob; to snatch a minute's rest; to elude the eyes of others; **hitome o**

nusúnde áu to meet (someone) secretly; **nusubito** thief. **Okan o nusumáreta.** My money has been stolen.

NÚU to sew; **hitogomi o núu** to go through a crowd; **kimono o núu** to sew clothes.

nyóoboo (*colloq.*) wife.

nyuubai beginning of the rainy season.

nyuuden telegram (cable) received; **–no mune nyuuden ga átta.** A telegram has been received to the effect that.

NYUUGAKU (shool) admission, matriculation; **nyuugaku suru** to enter school; to matriculate; **nyuugakushikén** entrance examination.

nyuugoku imprisonment.

nyuuhi cost; expenditure; expenses.

nyuuin suru to enter a hospital; to be hospitalized.

NYUUJOO entrance; admission; **nyuujoo suru** to enter; to be admitted; **nyoojoo múryoo** free admission; **nyuujóoken** admission ticket; **nyuujóoryoo** admission fee.

nyuukai joining (an organization); admission; **nyuukai suru** to become a member (in an organization); **nyuukai o mooshikómu** to apply for membership.

nyuukoo entry (into port); docking; **nyuukoo suru** to enter port; to dock.

nyuumon entering private school; primer; **Nippongo nyúumon** Japanese (language) primer.

nyuusatsu bid; bidding; **nyuusatsu suru** to bid, make a bid.

nyuusen suru to be selected; be accepted.

nyuusha suru to enter a firm.

NYÚUSU news; **kaigai nyúusu** foreign news.

nyuutoo suru to join a political party.

nyuuwa na gentle; tender.

nyuuyoku bath; bathing; **nyuuyoku suru** to bathe.

nyuuyoo need, necessity; requirement; **nyuuyoo na** necessary; required; **nyuuyoo de áru** to be in need of; to want.

ó tail, brush; **ó o furu** to wag the tail; **ó hire o tsukéte hanásu** to exaggerate.

óashisu oasis.

OBA aunt; **obachan** auntie.

OBÁSAN grandmother; old woman.

ÓBI belt, sash; **óbi o shiméru** to do up a sash; **óbi o tóku** to take off an obi; **obiáge** sash-bustle; **obidóme** sashband.

obiéru to become frightened; to have a nightmare.

obikidásu to lure, entice.

obitadashíi immense, vast; **obitadáshiku** abundantly, profusely, in large numbers.

obiyakásu to threaten, intimidate; to scare.

oboé learning; memory; feeling; recollection; expérience; **oboé ga yói** to have a good memory; to be quick to learn.

OBOÉRU to remember; to keep in mind; to memorize; to learn; to recollect; **sámusa o oboéru** to feel chilly. **Yóku oboéte imásu.** I remember it well.

obon See **bon.**

oboreru to drown; to be drowned; to indulge in, to be addicted to.

obotsukanai uncertain, doubtful, almost hopeless; uneasy, weak.

obusáru to ride on someone's shoulders; to ride pickaback; to rely on.

obúu to take (carry) on one's back; **kodomo o obúu** to carry a child on one's back.

OCHA, CHA tea (usually Japanese) (See also **koocha.**)

ochiáu to meet, rendezvous; to come (across) someone.

ochibureru to be ruined, to be reduced to poverty.

óchido fault, error; blame; **óchido ga nái** to be blameless; **hito no óchido ni suru** to lay the blame on someone else.

ochíru to fall; to be reduced. **kiken ni ochíru** to be in danger. **kukyoo ni ochíru** to get into trouble.

ochikomu to fall in, fall into. **Káre wa kawá ni ochikonda.** He fell into the river.

OCHÍRU to fall; to drop; to come down; to collapse; to be left out; to fall short of. **Yáne kara óchite ashí o ótta.** I fell from the roof and broke my leg. **Seiseki ga óchite kimáshita.** My marks are going down.

ochitsuki composure, self-possession. **ochitsuki no áru** calm, self-composed; **ochitsuki no nái** fidgety, restless; **ochitsuki harátte** calmly.

ochitsuku to settle down, become quiet; **ki ga ochitsuku** to feel relieved; to recover one's composure.

odáyaka na quiet, calm, peaceful, gentle; moderate; **odáyaka de nái** alarming, threatening; upsetting, serious. **odáyaka ni náru** to calm down, become calm.

odokashi threat, menace.

odokasu to threaten, menace; to browbeat; to scare.

odori dance; dancing; **odoriagaru** to jump; to dance for joy.

odoróite in astonishment, in amazement.

odorokásu to astonish, surprise, amaze; to startle, frighten.

odoroki amazement, wonder, surprise.

ODORÓKU to be surprised, be amazed, to be frightened. **Káre wa odoróite tobiagátta.** He jumped up in surprise. **Odoróku kotó wa nái.** Nothing is surprising about it. Don't be surprised.

odoru to dance; to step; **bando ni awásete odoru** to dance to a band.

odoshi threat, menace.

odosu to frighten, intimidate; to browbeat.

oeru to end, conclude, finish; **kái o oeru** to bring a meeting to a close; **gyóo o oeru** to finish a course.

ogámu to worship, venerate; to pray for.

ogawa brook, stream.

ogináu to make good, make up for, supplement; **ketsuin o ogináu** to fill a vacancy; **sonshitsu o ogináu** to make up a loss.

ogósoka na grave, solemn, austere; **ogósoka ni** with solemnity.

OHAYOO Good morning! **OHAYOO GOZAIMÁSU.** Good morning. (*vulgar*).

OI nephew.

oi (*colloq.*) hello! hey! look here!

oichirásu to drive out; to scatter.

oidásu to drive out, expel, turn out, evict.

oihagi highway robber.

oiharáu to drive away; to send away.

OIKAKÉRU to chase, run after. **Inú ga néko o oikákete iru.** A dog is chasing a cat.

oikómu to corner; to drive in.

oikósu to outrun; to pass, to outdistance. **Hoka no kuruma o oikoshimáshita.** She passed another car.

oimawásu to run after; to chase around.

oioi gradually, little by little; step by step; eventually.

OISHII delicious, tasty, sweet. **Áa oishii!** It tastes good! **Góhan wa oishíkatta.** The meal was good.

oitatéru to evict; to urge; to drive away.

oitsúku to overtake, catch up with.

oitsuméru to corner, get into a corner.

OJI uncle.

ojigi bow (inclination of the head or body); **ojigi o suru** to bow.

OJÍISAN grandfather; old man.

ojike fear, fright; **ojike ga tsuku** to be seized with fear, be frightened.

OJÓOSAN miss; daughter (*respect*).

OKA hill, mound; land; shore.

OKÁASAN mother, mama (used by children in the family); mother (somebody else's).

OKAGE indebtedness, favor. **Okage sama de.** Thanks to your kindness.

okámi landlady; mistress; hostess (at a restaurant).

OKANE, kane money.

OKÁSHI, káshi cake.

OKASHÍI amusing, laughable, funny; ridiculous; strange. **Nani mo okashíi kotó wa nái.** There is nothing funny. **Okashíi hanashí da.** The story is strange.

okashiya, kashíya cake shop, candy shop.

okasu to commit; to violate; to rape; to infringe on; to desecrate; **kokuhoo o okasu** to break the laws of the land.

okasu to defy; to risk; to damage. **Hidói áme o okashite ikimáshita.** We went despite the heavy rain.

okáwari second helping; another cup; **okáwari suru** to ask for a second helping.

óke tub, tank, pail; **óke íppai no mizu** pailful of water.

oki open sea.

okiagáru to get up; to sit up; **toko no ué ni okiagáru** to sit up in bed.

okidókei table clock.

okikáeru to rearrange; to displace.

okimono small, decorative ornament.

okinaóru to sit up, sit erect.

okinaósu to replace; to rearrange.

–OKI NI at intervals of; **gofun óki ni** at five-minute intervals; **ichinichi óki ni** every other day.

OKÍRU to get up; to rise; to raise oneself; **ása háyaku okíru** to get up early in the morning; **kan ga okíru** to have hysterics.

okite law, regulation, decree.

okizari desertion; **okizari ni suru** to desert; to leave behind.

okkúu na troublesome.

okonai act, deed; conduct; **okonai no yói** well-behaved.

okonáu to act, perform; to carry out; to conduct. **Kekkónshiki wa mikka ni okonaimásu.** We will hold the wedding on the third.

okoraséru to offend; to anger; to irritate (someone).

okorí origin, source, cause, root.

okoríppói touchy, peevish, short-tempered.

OKÓRU to happen, occur, come about; to take place; to arise in; to originate. **Sensoo ga okóru ká mo shirenai.** A war may break out.

okóru to get angry, to lose temper; **okótte iru** to be angry. **Tanaka-san wa sono hanashí o kiite taihen okorimáshita.** Ms. Tanaka got very angry by hearing that story. **Yamada-san ga kónai node okótte imasu.** She is mad because Mr. Yamada hasn't come. **Sonna ni okótte**

wa ikemasén. Don't be angry so much.

OKÓSU to start, begin; to bring about; to establish; to promote; to improve, to awaken; to raise up, lift; to cause; to give rise to; **byooki o okósu** to fall ill; **shíndai o okósu** to make a fortune. **Nánji ni anáta o okoshimashóo ka?** When shall I wake you?

okotari negligence; **okotarigáchi no** negligent, neglectful; **okotari náku** diligently, carefully.

okotáru to neglect; to fail to do.

OKU to put, place, lay, set; to keep; to establish, set up; to open; **fude o oku** to lay down a pen; **otétsudai o hitóri oku** to hire domestic help; **nokóshite oku** to leave; **sono mama ni shite oku** to leave alone. **Kása wa koko ni oite kudasái.** Please leave your umbrella here.

ÓKU back part; inner part; back; inner room; **óku e tóosu** to show a person to the guest room; **yamaóku** the heart of (that part deep inside) a mountain.

ÓKU one hundred million.

okubyóo cowardice, timidity; **okubyoomono** coward.

okufukái deep, profound; of great depth.

okúgai outdoors, in the open air.

okujoo rooftop.

okúnai interior of a house, indoors.

okurasu to delay; to put off.

okure lag; **okure o tóru** to be beaten; to be outstripped; **ki okure ga suru** to feel shy; to lose heart.

OKURERU to be late for; to be behind time; to get (fall) behind; to be left behind; **denshá ni okureru** to miss a train.

okuridásu to send out; to forward; to see (someone) off; to show a person to the door.

okurikómu to see a person home; to escort (someone).

OKURIMONO present, gift; **okurimono o suru** to give (send) a gift.

OKURU to send; to see off; to send off; to escort; to spend, pass (time); **nímotsu o okuru** to send a package; **tanoshíi seikatsu o okuru** to live a happy life. **Éki made ookuri shimashóo.** I will escort you to the station.

OKURU to present. to bestow; **gakúi o okuru** to confer an academic degree. **Kare no sotsugyooiwai ni tokei o okurimashóo.** Let's give him a watch for a graduation gift.

ÓKUSAMA, ÓKUSAN madam, Mrs.

okusoko depth, bottom; **kokoro no okusoko dé wa** in the back of one's mind; in the depths of one's heart.

okusoku guess, supposition; **okusoku suru** to guess, suppose.

okusúru to fear; to shrink; to hesitate; to be shy.

okuyukashíi graceful; refined.

okuyuki depth; length.

okuzáshiki inner room; back parlor.

Omachidóo sama. I'm sorry to have kept you waiting.

omae you (*impolite*).

omedeta happy event.

Omedetoo. Congratulations!

omei slur; bad name; **omei o kiru** to get a bad name; to be dishonored; to have a bad name.

omiyage, miyage souvenir; parting present; gift.

OMÓCHA toy; **omócha ni suru** to trifle with, toy with.

OMOI heavy; wealthy; serious, severe; important; **omoi byooki** serious illness; **ki ga omoi** to have a heavy heart.

OMOÍ thought, idea, mind; sense; heart; feeling; love; care, worry; will, wish; **omoí o kakéru** to take a fancy to; **omoí o kogásu** to burn with love; **omoí o korásu** to tax one's brain.

omoiatáru to occur to; to call to mind.

omoiawaséru to consider (together); put two and two together. **Kárekore omoiawásete yamemáshita.** Taking everything into consideration. I gave up the idea.

omoichigai misunderstanding; **omoichigai o suru** to misunderstand.

OMOIDÁSU to recall, bring to mind, remember. **Dóoshitemo omoidasénai.** Try as I may, I can't recall it.

omoide recollections, memories.

omoigakenái unexpected, unforeseen; least expected; chance, accidental; **omoigakenáku** unexpectedly.

omoikiri resolution.

omoikíru to resign oneself to; to give up; **omoikítte** boldly, resolutely.

omoikítta radical, bold, daring.

omoikómu to be under the impression that, to be possessed with (an idea).

omoinokósu to leave with regret.

omoiómoi each in one's own way; as one pleases.

omoishiraséru to teach someone (make someone learn) a lesson.

omoitsuki plan, suggestion. **Yói omoisuki désu.** That's a great idea.

omoitsuku to recall; to think of, to hit on. **Umái shukoo o omoitsúita.** I got a brilliant idea.

omoitsuméru to brood over; to love passionately.

omoiyari sympathy, consideration; **omoiyari no áru** sympathetic; considerate, kind.

omoiyáru to sympathize with.

omokage features, looks; image, likeness.

omokurushíi heavy, ponderous; clumsy, oppressed.

omomi weight, emphasis, importance.

omomuki effect; taste, elegance, air, appearance; **omomuki no aru** refined. elegant; **omomuki no nái** tasteless, vulgar.

omomúku to go; to proceed to; to grow, to get.

omomuro ni slowly; gently; softly.

ÓMO NA chief, major, leading; **ómo na hitóbito** important persons. **ómo na sangyoo** principal industries.

omoni heavy load.

omonjíru See **omonzúru.**

omonzúru, omonjíru to honor, respect, think much of.

omoomoshíi serious; imposing; dignified; **omoomóshiku** solemnly, seriously.

omori weight, plumb, sinker.

omosa weight, heaviness.

omoshi weight (heavy object used to put pressure on something); **omoshi o oku** to place a weight on.

omoshirogáru to amuse oneself, to be amused; to think (something) funny.

omoshirohánbun half in fun.

OMOSHIRÓI interesting; pleasant, diverting; funny, odd; amusing; **omoshíroku** pleasantly; interestingly, delightfully, etc.; **omoshíroku nái** uninteresting, dull, stupid; unpleasant; unsatisfactory; undesirable.

omoshiromi interest; enjoyment; fun.

omoshirosóo ni with seeming (apparent) interest, enjoyment; like fun. **Kodomótachi wa omoshirosóo ni asonde imasu.** The children are playing, apparently enjoying themselves.

OMOTE face; obverse; right side; exterior; front; first half; **omoté ni** outdoors; **omote no to** front door; **omoté o dáshite** right side up; **Omote Nihón** the Pacific side of Japan.

omotemon front gate.

omotemuki openly, publicly; officially; **omotemuki no** public, open.

omotezáshiki front parlor.

OMÓU to think; to consider; to believe; to wish, desire; to yearn for; to feel; to feel like; to regard (as); to expect; to hope; to imagine; **yóku omóu** to think well of. **Kimi ga koko ni irú to wa omowánakatta.** I had no idea you were

here. **Máa omótte mo minasái.** Just think
of it!

omowaréru to seem, appear; to look; to be
thought of (as). **Áme ga furisóo ni
omowaréru.** It looks like rain.

omowaseburi suggestive manner, coquetry;
omowaseburi na suggestive, coquettish.

omowaséru to make (one) think; to remind
(one) of; to be suggestive of.

omowashíi satisfactory, desirable;
omowáshiku nái unsatisfactory.

omówazu unexpectedly; unconsciously,
unintentionally.

ómoya main house.

ón kindness, goodness; favor; obligation; **ón
ni kanjiru** to feel indebted to; **ón ni kiru**
to be deeply grateful to; **ón o káesu** to
repay a kindness.

on sound; tone; voice.

onaídoshi same age; **onaídoshi de áru** to be
the same age.

ONAJI same, identical; equal, equivalent to,
similar, like; **onaji yóo na** of the same
kind; **onaji yóo ni** alike; **onaji ni** equally,
etc.

ONAKA stomach, belly, abdomen. **Onaka
ga suita.** I'm hungry. **Onaka ga itái.** I
have a stomachache.

ÓNDO temperature.

ongáeshi repayment of a favor; **ongáeshi o
suru** to repay a kindness (or favor).

ÓNGAKU music; **ongakuteki** musical;
óngaku no sensei music teacher; **ongaku
zúki** music lover.

ongi favor, obligation.

oní fiend, devil; ghost; **oni no yóo na**
fiendish, inhuman.

onjín patron, benefactor.

onjoo warm heart, warm feeling; **onjoo áru**
warmhearted.

onjooshúgi paternalism.

onjun na gentle, meek.

onkei favor.

onken moderation; **onken na** moderate,
temperate; sensible; **onken na sétsu** a
sensible opinion.

onkoo na gentle, courteous.

onkyoo sound, noise.

onkyuu pension; **onkyuu o ukéru** to receive
a pension.

ONNA woman, female; female sex; mistress;
onna no woman's; feminine; **onnarashíi**
womanly; ladylike; **ONNÁ NO KO**
young girl; daughter; **onnashújin**
landlady.

óno ax.

onóono each, everyone; all; respectively.

onsen, onsenba hot springs, spa; **onsényado**
hot springs inn.

ónshi (highly respected) teacher (to whom a
special indebtedness is felt).

onshin correspondence; **onshin suru** to
correspond with.

onshírazu ingratitude; **onshírazu na**
ungrateful.

onshitsu hothouse, greenhouse.

ónsu ounce.

ónwa na mild, gentle; genial.

oo oh! how!

ooame heavy rain, downpour.

ooárashi, ooare severe storm.

óobo subscription; application; **óobo suru** to
subscribe to; to apply, make application;
oobósha applicant; subscriber.

ooboo oppression, tyranny; **ooboo na**
arbitrary; tyrannical; **ooboo o kiwaméru**
to tyrannize; to be high-handed.

oobun English or any Occidental written
language or alphabet; **oobundénpoo**
telegram written in the English (or any
Occidental) alphabet.

oobun no appropriate, suitable; reasonable.

ooburi heavy downpour.

oocháku dishonesty; cunning; laziness;
oocháku na dishonest; cunning; selfish;
lazy.

óoda assault and battery; **óoda suru** to
assault.

oodan crossing, intersection; **oodan suru** to
cross, run across.

oodeki triumph, great success.

ooen aid, assistance; **ooen suru** to aid,
support.

OOFUKU going and returning, round-trip;
oofuku ryókoo round trip; **oofuku suru**
to go and return; **oofukuhágaki** return
(post) card; **oofukukíppu** round-trip
ticket.

oogesa exaggeration; **oogesa na** exaggerated;
oogesa na hanashí tall story,
exaggeration; **oogesa na kotó o iu** to
exaggerate.

oogí folding fan; **oogí o tsukau** to fan
oneself.

oogóe loud voice; **oogóe de** in a loud voice,
loudly.

óohei arrogance; **óohei na** arrogant; **óohei ni**
arrogantly.

oohíroma large, grand hall.

ooi cover, covering; shade; screen; **ooi o suru**
to cover, to wrap.

ÓOI lots of, heaps of, plenty, many,
numerous, much. **Nihón ni wa yamá ga
óoi.** There are many mountains in Japan.
**Nihonjín ni wa Eigo o hanásu hitó ga
óoi.** There are lots of Japanese who speak
English. **Anó hito wa kodomo ga óoi.** He
has many children.

óoi yoo hoo!, hello!

ooísogi urgency; **ooísogi de** in great haste, hurriedly; **ooísogi de iku** to hurry to, rush to.

oojíru See **oozúru.**

oojíkake large scale; **oojíkake de** on a large scale.

oojíte in proportion to; according to; in reply to; **hitsuyoo ni oojíte** according to the need; according to the demand.

óojoo death; **óojoo suru** to die; to submit to, give in.

OOKATA probably, perhaps, maybe, almost, in general.

ÓOKEI O.K.

OOKÍI, ÓOKINA big, large, great; heavy; powerful; huge, massive; **hijoo ni ookíi** huge, of great proportions; **óokina kotó o iu** to talk big, brag, **óokiku náru** to grow larger, be enlarged; **óokiku suru** to enlarge, make larger.

óokina See **ookíi.**

ookisa size, dimension, volume, bulk; **ookisa ga onaji** to be the same size; **ookisa ga chigau** to differ in size; **–kurai no ookisa de aru** to be about the size of.

ookoo being rampant; **ookoo suru** to overrun; to be rampant; to swagger; to go sideways.

óoku in many cases, in numerous cases; **óoku wa** mostly; for the most part; largely; **óoku no** a great many; plenty of, lots of; **óoku tomo** at most; generally.

Ookura Dáijin Finance Minister; **Ookuráshoo** Finance Ministry.

ookyuu emergency; first aid; **ookyuu téate** first-aid treatment.

oomata big strides; **oomata ni arúku** to stride; to walk with long steps.

oome overlooking; **oome ni míru** to overlook; to close one's eyes to; to let (something) pass.

oomísoka New Year's Eve.

óomizu heavy flood.

oomúkashi remote antiquity; primitive ages; **oomúkashi kara** from time immemorial.

oonoo anguish, agony; worry; **oonoo suru** to suffer anguish; to be in agony.

oo-oo often, frequently; sometimes.

ooppira ni openly, publicly.

oorai (street) traffic, comings and goings; **oorai suru** to come and go; to rise and fall. **Oorai ga óoi.** Traffic is heavy.

ooryoo usurpation, embezzlement; **ooryoo suru** to appropriate unlawfully; **ooryóosha** embezzler; **ooryóozai** embezzlement.

oosen response; acceptance; **oosen suru** to accept the challenge.

oosetsu reception; **oosetsu suru** to receive visitors; **oosetsuma** reception room, drawing room.

ooshin doctor's visit to a patient; house call.

ooshuu seizure, confiscation; **ooshuu suru** to seize.

ooshuu answer, reply; **ooshuu suru** to answer.

oosóoji general cleaning; **oosóoji o suru** to give a general cleaning.

ootai reception; **ootai suru** to receive, to wait on (a customer).

óoto vomiting; **óoto suru** to vomit.

ootóbai motorcycle.

ootome automation.

ootoo answer, reply.

oóu to reply; to veil; to wrap; to envelop, to hide, conceal; to shelter.

ooúridashi large bargain sale.

ooútsushi close-up (in a movie).

ooyake (*n.*) public; government; **ooyake no** (*adj.*) public, open; official; **ooyake ni suru** to publish; to make known. **ooyake ni náru** to be made known.

ooyasúuri bargain sale.

óoyoo generosity; **óoyoo na** bighearted, generous.

ooyoo practical application; **ooyoo dekíru** applicable; **ooyoo suru** to put into use, to apply; to put to practical use.

oozáppa na rough, loose, **oozáppa na hanashí** roughly outline a story.

OOZÉI crowd, large number of people. **oozéi de** in large numbers; **oozéi no** many, large crowd of; **oozéi no kázoku** large family.

oozóra sky; heavens.

oozúru, oojíru to respond, reply, to comply with; to apply for.

ópera opera.

Oranda Holland; **Orandago** Dutch (language); **Orandájin** Dutch (person).

OREI, REI etiquette, thanks, appreciation; remuneration.

oréru to break, snap, give way, yield; to be folded; **órete déru** to meet halfway. **Tsúe ga óreta** The stick was broken.

orí cage, pen.

orígami paper-folding (popular Japanese pastime).

origamitsuki no certified, guaranteed.

oríibu olive.

orikasanáru to overlap; to lie one on another; **orikasanátte** overlapped; (stacked) in piles.

orímono cloth, textile.

ORÍRU to go down; to come down; to get down, get off; to leave; to get out of; to alight, land; **densha o oríru** to get off a

streetcar; **kaidan o oríru** to descend the
staircase.

óroka not to mention; to say nothing of.

oroshí wholesale business; **oroshí de uru** to
sell wholesale, at wholesale price;
oroshine wholesale price(s).

orósoka careless, negligent; **orósoka ni suru**
to neglect.

ORÓSU to take down; to lower; to bring
down, to drop, let fall; to hand down; to
unload; to let (someone) get off; to sell at
wholesale. **Koko de oróshite kudasai.**
Please let me get off here.

ÓRU to break; to bend, fold; to pick; **haná o
óru** to pick a flower.

óru to weave.

orugan organ.

osaéru to stop; to curb, check, hold down,
suppress.

osamáru to be at peace; to be calmed down,
be pacified. **Kaze ga osamarismáshita.**
The wind has died down.

oséru to govern, rule; **ié o osaméru** to
manage a household.

osanái infant; young; childish; **osanái koro
ni** in childhood.

osen pollution; **kuuki ósen** air pollution.

osháberi chattering; gossip; gossiper;
osháberi na gossipy, talkative; **osháberi
suru** to chatter; to gossip.

oshi deaf and dumb person; deaf-mute.

oshi weight; influence; **oshi no tsuyói**
overbearing, brazen; **oshi ga kiku** to have
influence.

oshiagéru to push; to thrust up.

oshiáu to push, jostle.

oshidashi presence, appearance, look;
oshidashi no yói of fine appearance.

oshidásu to push out; to press forward; to
force out.

oshie teaching, instruction; lesson; **oshiégo**
pupil.

OSHIERU to teach, give lessons; to show; to
tell; **Nihongo o oshieru** to teach
Japanese.

oshihироméru to extend, expand, spread.

OSHÍI regrettable; precious, valuable;
wasteful. **Sore wa oshíi kotó desu.** That's
a pity! **Suterú no wa oshíi desu.** It's too
good to throw away.

OSHIIRE closet.

oshikakéru to force oneself into; to go
uninvited.

oshikoméru, oshikómu to force in; to stuff
into.

oshimázu liberally, freely.

oshíme diaper.

oshímu to value, prize; to spare; to grudge;
to be stingy of; to regret; **kane o oshímu**

to be stingy with money; **wakaré o
oshímu** to be reluctant to leave.

oshinábete generally, in general.

oshinokéru to push away, to push aside.

oshiroi face powder.

oshitaósu to fell; to push down.

oshitatéru to raise, set up, erect.

oshitóosu to push through; to persist to the
end.

oshitsubúsu to crush, smash, squash.

oshitsukéru to press, push against; to
compel.

oshitsumáru to be jammed; to get near the
end of the year. **Kotoshi mo
oshitsumátte mairimáshita.** It's getting
near the end of the year.

oshiuri forcing a sale; **oshiuri suru** to force
a person to buy.

oshiwakéru to push apart; to push through.

oshiyáru to push aside.

oshiyoséru to push to one side; to advance
on.

OSOI late, tardy; behind time; slow; **ashí ga
osoi** to walk slowly; **kaerí ga osoi** to be
late in returning.

OSÓRAKU perhaps, maybe; in all
probability; I'm afraid. **Osóraku móo
Amerika e káetta no deshoo.** I suppose
he has already returned to the United
States.

osoré fear, terror; horror; awe, reverence;
osoré o idáku to be afraid of.

osóreiru to be overwhelmed, be awed.
Osóreirimasu. I'm much obliged to you.
**Osóreirimásu ga, kore o dóko ni
okimashóo ka?** Excuse me—where shall
I put this?

osoreóoi gracious, awe-inspiring; **osoreóoku
mo** graciously.

OSOROSHÍI fearful, awful, terrible;
tremendous; **osoróshiku** terribly, etc;
osoróshiku atsúi terribly hot; **osoróshisa**
fear, terror, horror.

osóu to attack, assault.

osowaru to be taught.

ossháru to say, to speak, to tell, to relay, to
mention (*respect*).

OSU to push, shove; press; to infer, deduce,
guess; to recommend. **Yamada-san o
oshimáshita.** I recommended Mr.
Yamada.

osú (n.) male (animal); **osu no** male (*adj.*);
osu neko tomcat.

osui sewage; filthy water.

otafukúkaze mumps.

otaku your house.

OTEÁRAI See **TEÁRAI.**

oten stain; blot; blemish; **oten o tsukéru** to
stain; to spot; **oten no nái** spotless.

OTÓ sound, noise; roar; tone, note; fame; **otó ni kikoeta** celebrated, noted; **otó o tátete** noisily; **otó o tatéru** to make a sound; to make noise.

OTOKÓ man, male; male adult; manly person; **otokoráshiku** like a man; **otokó ni náru** to come of age; to become a man; **OTOKÓ NO KO** boy; **otokoyáymome** widower.

OTONA adult (male or female).

OTONASHÍI gentle, good, quiet; **otonáshiku suru** to keep quiet.

OTÓOSAN father (used as term of address by the wife as well as chidlren in the family); father (somebody else's).

OTOOTÓ younger brother.

otoróeru to decline; to fall.

otóru to be inferior; to fall behind.

otoshiiréru to trap, capture.

OTÓSU to drop, let fall; to lose; to dump; to remove; to take; to omit; to depreciate; **chikará o otósu** to lose strength, weaken. **Koppu o otóshite watta.** I dropped a cup and broke it.

OTOTOI day before yesterday.

OTÓTOSHI year before last.

otozuréru to call on, visit.

OTSURI = tsurisen small change (money).

otte later on; afterward.

OTTO husband.

OU to drive away, shoo; to pursue, to run after; **hi o otte** day by day; **jun o otte** gradually, in order; **hae o ou** to shoo flies.

óu to bear; to carry on one's back; to owe; to be due. **Watakushi wa anó hito ni óu tokoro ga óoi desu.** I owe him a lot. **Kodomo o senaka ni ótte ikimáshita.** She went there, carrying her child on her back.

OWARI end, termination, conclusion; **owari máde** to the last; **owari ni** in the end; **owari no** final, last; **owari o tsugeru** to come to an end.

OWARU to end, come to an end, finish, complete. **Shigoto ga owatta.** The job is done.

owaseru to make carry; to lay a burden on.

OYÁ parent(s); dealer (of cards); **oyá no** parental; **oyá o uyamáu** to respect one's parents.

ÓYA oh!; oh dear!; my!

óyabun boss; master.

ÓYAJI (*vulgar*) old man; chap, father.

oyakáta boss, chief.

oyako parent and child.

oyáma female impersonator (actor).

oyáshiro Shinto shrine.

OYAYUBI thumb; big toe.

oyayúzuri inheritance; **oyayúzuri no** inherited (from one's parents).

oyobósu to influence, affect; exert; **kooéikyoo o oyobósu** to have a good influence on, to produce a good effect.

oyobu to reach; to amount to; to come up to; to extend; to cover; to match, equal; **oyobanai** to be no match (for); to be inferior (to); **oyobi mo tsukánai** not to begin to compare (to). **Sore ní wa oyobimasén.** Don't bother about that. **Watakushi wa káre ni oyobanai.** I'm no match for him.

oyogí (*n.*) swimming; swim; **oyogí ni iku** to go swimming.

OYÓGU to swim; **yóku oyógu** to swim well. **Hitótsu oyogóo.** Let's go for a swim.

OYOSO about; roughly; as a rule; generally speaking; **oyoso gojúu yen** approximately 50 yen. **Oyoso káre hodo atama no yói monó wa nái.** It's not too much to say that there is no one as sharp as he.

OYU, YU hot water; warm water; bath; **oyu ni háiru** to take a bath.

páatonaa partner.

PÁN bread; **panko** bread crumbs; **pán o éru** to earn one's living (bread); **pán o yaku** to bake bread; **pán'ya** bakery.

panamá boo panama hat.

panku puncture; **panku suru** to puncture.

panorama panorama.

párapara with a clatter; scattering as it falls; pitapat.

pasokon personal computer.

pásu pass, free ticket.

pátapata with a pattering sound; **pátapata suru** to patter; to flutter.

patchi Japanese-style close-fitting trousers (worn by workmen).

pachíri with a click.

pattári suddenly; all of a sudden.

pátto suddenly; **pátto suru** to be gay; to be showy; **pátto moeru** to flare up.

pechánko flattened; crushed; **pechánako ni náru** to be flattened or crushed.

peeji page.

pékopeko cringing; **pékopeko suru** to cringe; to fawn upon.

pekopeko hungry. **Onaka ga pekopeko désu.** I'm awfully hungry.

PÉN fountain pen; pen; **penga** pen-and-ink drawing; **penjiku** penholder; **pensáki** pen point; **pen shuuji** penmanship.

penginchoo penguin.

penki paint; **penki o nuru** to paint; **penkiya** painter.

pérapera fluently, glibly; **pérapera hanásu** to speak fluently; **pérapera shabéru** to chatter, jabber.

perorí to with a quick motion of the tongue; **peroré to naméru** to lick; **shitá o perorí to dásu** to stick out the tongue; **perorí to tabéru** to eat rapidly; to make short work of a meal.

pésuto pest; black plague.

PIANO piano; **piano o hiku** to play the piano.

píipii whistling; piping; **piipii naku** to cheep, chirp (said of birds); **píipii shite iru** to be hard up (for money).

pikáichi number one. (*colloq.*) ace, star.

pikápika glitteringly; **pikápika suru** to glitter, sparkle, flash, twinkle.

PÍN pin; hairpin; **anzénpin** safety pin.

pínpin in a lively manner; **pínpin shite iru** to be full of life, to be in the pink, to be well and sound.

pinsétto tweezers.

pinto focus; **pinto o awaséru** to focus, adjust the focus (of a camera).

pírapira flapping.

píripiri smarting; **píripiri suru** to smart, sting, burn.

pisharí with a bang; **pisharí to to o shiméru** to slam the door shut.

pisutoru pistol, revolver.

pitári, pittári suddenly, closely, flatly; **pittári góji ni** at (five o'clock) sharp; **pittári to áu** to fit to a T; **pitári to tomaru** to come to a dead stop, to stop suddenly.

pítchi pitch (vocal or in a game).

pítchaa pitcher (in a ball game).

pointo point; decimal point; (railroad) switch.

pokán to vacantly; absentmindedly; **pokán to shite iru** to look blank.

pókapoka growing warmer; **pókapoka shite kúru** to grow warmer; **pókapoka suru** to feel warm.

POKÉTTO pocket; **poketto mánee** pocket money.

pónpu pump; **pónpu de mizu o kumiagéru** to pump up water (from a well).

ponchie cartoon; caricature.

póndo pound.

póoru pole.

póroporo in drops, tricklingly.

PÓSUTO postbox, mailbox; **pósuto ni ireru** to mail.

pótapota drop by drop; **pótapota to taréru** to fall in drops; to trickle; to drip.

potchíri just a little, a bit, a drop.

pótsupotsu little by little; in drops; bit by bit. **Pótsupotsu fúru.** It rains in small drops.

pótto in a glow; **pótto kao o akaraméru** to blush.

púnpun piquantly; **púnpun nióu** to smell piquant; to smell fragrant; to stink, reek; **púnpun okóru** to be in a huff; to fume.

puremiamu premium; **puremiamu o tsukéru** to place a premium (on); **puremiamu ga tsúite iru** to be at a premium.

púro pro, professional athlete.

puropagánda propaganda; **puropagánda o suru** to publicize; to spread propaganda.

puropéra propeller.

puroretária proletariat; proletarians.

pyúu to whizzing, whistling; **pyúu to fukú** to whistle; **pyúu to tobu** to whiz through the air.

R

–RA suffix denoting; and others; and the like, etc. **Kimíra ni wa ienái desu.** I can't tell it to you people.

ráchi picket-fence; limit; **ráchi mo nái** foolish, silly; **ráchi ga aku** to reach a settlement; **réhi ga akanaí** to make little headway, remain unsettled; **rachígai ni déru** to go beyond bounds.

rágubii rugby.

–rai suffix denoting; since, the past; **sakunénrai** since last year.

raichoo suru to arrive in Japan.

RÁIGETSU next month; **sarigetsu** month after next.

raiharu = raishun next spring.

raihin guest; **raihínseki** visitor's seats.

raihoo visit, call; **raihoo suru** to visit.

raikai attendance; **raikai suru** to attend a meeting; **raikáisha** audience; attendance.

raikyaku visitor, guest.

raimei thunderclap.

RAINEN next year; **sarainen** year after next.

raion lion.

ráiraku frankness; **ráiraku na** frank; openhearted; broad-minded.

raireki career, history, origin (personal); **raireki o tadásu** to inquire into one's past.

raishun = raiharu next spring.

RAISHUU next week; **saraishuu** week after next.

raisukáree curried rice.

ráiu thunderstorm. **Ráiu ga áru daroo.** There will be a thunderstorm.

raiyuu visit (from abroad); **raiyúusha** visitor; **raiyuu gáijin** foreign visitor.

RÁJIO radio; **rajio hóosoo** radio broadcasting; **rájio o kiku** to listen to the

radio; **rájio o tomeru** to turn off the
radio; **keitai rajío** portable radio.
rakétto racket (tennis, etc.).
rakka falling; **rakka suru** to fall; to drop.
rakkan optimism; **rakkanteki** optimistic;
rakkan suru to be optimistic.
rakkásan parachute.
rakkásei peanut.
RAKÚ comfort, ease; pleasure; **rakú na**
comfortable, easy; **rakú o suru** to take it
easy. **Oraku ni nasátte kudasái.** Make
yourself comfortable.
rakuchaku settlement; **rakuchaku saseru** to
settle, bring to a conclusion; **rakuchaku
suru** to be settled.
rakudai rejection; failure in an exam;
rakudai suru to fail (flunk) an exam; to
be rejected.
rakuen paradise.
rakugaki scribbling.
rakugo comic story.
rakugósha straggler.
rakuséishiki inauguration ceremony;
completion ceremony.
rakusen defeat in an election; failure;
rejection; **rakusénsha** defeated candidate.
rakutan discouragement; despair; **rakutan
saseru** to discourage; **rakutan suru** to be
discouraged; to be disappointed.
rakutenka optimist; **rakutenshúgi** optimism.
ranboo violence, outrage; **ranboo na** violent;
rude; rowdy; disorderly; **ranboo suru** to
behave rudely; **ranboomono** ruffian,
rowdy.
RÁNCHI lunch; **ránchi o tabéru** to have
lunch.
randoku desultory reading.
rankan railing, handrail.
ránpu lamp.
ran'yoo abuse; misuse; **ran'yoo suru** to
abuse.
ranzatsu disorder, confusion; **ranzatsu na**
disorderly, untidy; **ranzatsu ni náru** to
get confused; to be in disorder.
ranzoo overproduction; **ranzoo suru** to
overproduce.
rappa trumpet, cornet, horn; **rappa o fukú** to
blow a horn; **rappa nomi o yaru** to drink
(something) directly from the bottle.
rasen screw; spiral spring; **rasenkei** spiral
form; **rasenkei no** spiral-shaped.
rásha woolen cloth.
–RASHÍI –like; becoming; looking (like);
appear, seem; it seems to me; probably;
kodomorashíi childlike. **Soo rashíi.** I
guess so. **Ame rashíi.** It looks like rain.
Kuru rashíi desu. It seems he is coming.
rashinban compass.
rasshu áwaa rush hour.

réesu lace; race.
RÉI custom, usage, habit, precedent;
instance, case, example; **réi ni yotte** as
usual; **réi no** usual, customary; **réi o
ageru to** for instance; **réi o ageru** to give
an instance; **réi ni náru** to set a
precedent.
RÉI zero.
réi soul, spirit.
réi salutation; **réi o suru** to bow.
REI, OREI thanks, appreciation; **rei o
nobéru** to express thankfulness.
reidai example; exercise.
réido zero; freezing point (Centigrade); **réido
íka** below zero.
reifuku evening dress.
reigai exception; **reigai no** exceptional;
reigai ni suru to except, make an
exception of.
reigí courtesy, etiquette; **reigí tadashíi**
courteous. **Káre wa reigí ga tadashíi.** He
has good manners.
reihai worship; **reihai suru** to worship;
reihaidoo chapel; church.
reijoo letter of thanks; **reijoo o dásu** to send
a letter of thanks.
reikai regular meeting.
reikoku cruelty; **reikoku na** cruel;
coldhearted.
reikoo strict enforcement; **reikoo suru** to
enforce strictly.
reikyaku refrigeration; cooling; **reikyaku
suru** to cool; to refrigerate; **reikyakúhin**
refrigerator, freezer.
reiméiki dawn of a new age.
reinen ordinary year, average year; annually,
every year; **reinen mátsuri** annual
festival; **reinen no tóori** as usual; as
every year.
reiraku ruin, downfall; **reiraku suru** to be
ruined, go to ruin.
reisei coolness, calmness; **reisei na** cool,
calm; **reisei na hitó** coldhearted person;
reisei ni kangáeru to think about
something calmly.
reishoo cold smile, sneer; **reishoo suru** to
sneer at; to mock; to give a mocking
laugh.
reisoo formal wear; ceremonial dress.
reisui cold water; **reisuimásatsu** rubdown
with a cold wet towel; **reisúiyoku** cold
bath; **reisúiyoku suru** to take a cold bath.
reitán indifference, coolness; **reitán na** cool;
cold; indifferent; **seiji ni reitán de áru** to
be indifferent to politics.
reitén zero, zero point; **reitén o tóru** to get a
zero.
reitóoniku frozen meat.
reizen offering to the spirits of the dead.

reizoo cold storage; refrigeration; **reizoo suru** to refrigerate; **reizóoko** refrigerator; **reizóosha** refrigerated freight car.

rekidai successive generations.

reikishi history; **Nippon rékishi** Japanese history; **rekishijoo yuumei na tokoro** place of historical interest; **rekishijoo no jínbutsu** historical personage; **rekishika** historian.

rekizen to clearly, plainly; **rekizen to shite akíraka desu.** It's as plain as day.

rekkoku nations (of the world).

rékkyo enumeration; **rékkyo suru** to enumerate, list.

rekkyoo great (world) powers (countries).

rekóodo record, phonograph record; **rekoodo yáburi no** record-breaking; **rekóodo o tsukúru** to establish a record; to create a new record; **rekoodo o yabúru** to break a record; **rekóodo o kakéru** to play a record (on a phonograph).

renmei joint signature; **renmei suru** to sign jointly.

renpoo federation (of states); union; commonwealth; **renpoo no** united, federated, etc.

REN'AI love; **ren'ai jíken** love affair; **ren'ai kánkei ni náru** to fall in love; to have a love affair.

renchuu party, company.

rénga brick(s).

rengoo combination, union, confederation, amalgamation; alliance, coalition; **rengoo suru** to combine, etc.; **rengoo no** allied, associated, etc.; **rengóokoku** allied countries; **Kokusai Rengoo** United Nations.

renketsu suru to couple, join, connect.

renraku connection; traffic; communication; **renraku suru** to make contact; **renraku o tóru** to get in touch with; **renraku o ushináu** to lose touch, lose contact; **renrakusen** ferryboat (connected with a train).

renshuu practice, training, drill, rehearsal; **renshuu o tsunda** well-trained; **renshuu suru** to practice, etc.

rensoo association (of ideas); **rensoo suru** to be reminded of; to associate (one) with (another).

rentaisékinin joint responsibility.

Rentogen X-ray; **Rentogen ni kakáru** to be X-rayed.

renzoku continuity; succession; **renzoku suru** to continue; to last; **renzoku teki** continuous; consecutive; **renzokuteki ni** continuously.

rénzu lens.

reppuu heavy wind, hurricane. **Reppuu ga**

fúite iru. There's a heavy wind blowing.

resseki attendance; **–ni resseki suru** to attend, be present at.

resseraréru to be ranked with.

réssha railway train.

ressúru to attend, to present; to rank with, take one's place among.

resubian lesbian.

rétsu row, rank, tier, column, line; **rétsu o tsukúru** to form a row, line up.

rettoo archipelago, chain of islands; **Chishima réttoo** the Kuriles.

rettoo inferiority; **rettoo na otoko** man of bad moral character; **rettoo no** inferior, of poor quality; **rettóohin** low-quality goods.

rí advantage; benefit; interest; **rokúbu no ri** 6 percent interest; **rí no áru** advantageous, beneficial; **rí ga áru** to be profitable; **rí o eru** to profit from, gain by.

rí reason, right, truth, principle; **ri no áru** reasonable, justifiable; **rí ni somúku** to be against reason.

ríbon ribbon; **ribon de musubu** to tie with a ribbon.

ríchi intellect; **richiteki na** intellectual.

richigimono upright person.

ríeki benefit, gain, profit; **ríeki no áru** profitable, lucrative; **ríeki o hógo suru** to protect one's interests; **riekíkin** profits, proceeds.

ríen, RIKON divorce; **ríen suru** to divorce.

rifújin unreasonableness; **rifújin na** unreasonable, unjust.

rígai advantages and disadvantages; interests; **rígai ni kankei ga áru** to have an effect on one's interests; to have an interest in.

rigaku hákushi Doctor of Science.

rigákushi Bachelor of Science.

rihatsu haircutting; hairdressing; **RIHATSUTEN** barber shop; **rihatsúshi** barber.

ríido (n.) leading; **ríido suru** to lead.

ríji director; manager; **rijíchoo** chairman of a board of directors; **rijíkai** board of directors.

ríka science.

ríkai understanding, comprehension; **ríkai dekiru** understandable. comprehensible; **ríkai no nái** without understanding; **ríkai no áru hitó** sensible person; **ríkai suru** to understand; to grasp; to appreciate; **rikáiryoku** understanding, comprehension.

rikímu to strain oneself; to brag; to swagger.

rikisaku masterpiece; elaborate work.

rikisetsu suru to emphasize, to lay stress on; to be emphatic.

rikkóoho candidacy (for an election);
rikkóoho suru to run as a candidate;
rikkóoho o happyoo suru to announce
one's candidacy; **rikkoohósha** candidate.

rikoo cleverness, smartness; **rikoo na** clever,
shrewd, bright, intelligent; **rikoo soo na**
bright, intelligent looking.

rikoo suru to carry out, to fulfill.

RIKON, rien divorce; **rikon suru** to
divorce.

rikoshúgi egoism.

rikoteki egoistic, selfish.

riku, rikuchi land; **riku o iku** to go by land;
rikuro land journey, land road (route).
(See also **rikujoo.**)

rikúgun army.

rikujoo land, ground; **rikujoo de** on land.
(See also **riku.**)

rikutsu theory; argument; pretext; reason,
logic; **rikutsu ni áu** to stand to reason;
rikutsu ga tatánai to be unreasonable, be
illogical; **rikutsuppói** argumentative;
rikutsuzeme persuasive reasoning; **nán
toka kán toka rikutsu o tsukéte** on one
pretext or another; **rikutsuzeme ni suru**
to persuade (someone) by reason.

rikuzoku in succession, one after another.

rímen back, reverse, other side; **rímen de**
behind the scenes, in secret; **rímen de
ayatsúru** to pull strings; **rímen o
kansatsu suru** to look at the other side.

rimokon remote control.

RINGO apple; **ringo no kí** apple tree.

ringoku neighboring country.

rinjin neighbor; **rinjin no yóshimi**
neighborliness.

rinjuu one's last (deathbed) moment; **rinjuu
no kotobá** dying words.

rínka neighboring house, house next door.

rinkaku contours, outline; **rinkaku o nobéru**
to give an outline, sketch.

rínri ethics, morality.

rinyuu suru to wean.

RIPPA fineness, richness; **rippa na** fine,
splendid, good, nice, excellent, stately;
rippa ni superbly, admirably, sufficiently;
rippa ni seikatsu suru to make a decent
living. **Rippa désu.** It's splendid.

rippoo legislation; **rippoo no** legislative.

rippuku anger, rage; **rippuku suru** to get
angry; **rippuku saseru** to make angry.

rirei relay race.

rireki personal history, career; **rireki ga yói**
to have a good record of service; **rireki
ga warúi** to have a poor record of
service; **rirékisho** personal history, record
of one's life.

ririku takeoff; **ririku suru** to take off; to get
afloat.

ririshíi imposing; majestic.

riron theory.

ríroseizen logical, valid.

risáichi stricken locality.

risáisha victim, sufferer.

risan dispersion; **risan suru** to be dispersed.

ríshi interest; **yasúi ríshi** low interest; **takái
ríshi** high interest; **ríshi o tóru** to charge
interest; **rishi o shoo zuru** to accrue.

risoo ideal; **takái risoo** high ideal; **risoo
shúgi** idealism; **risooteki** ideal; idealistic.

risookyoo utopia.

risshoo proof; **risshoo suru** to prove,
demonstrate, bear out.

risshun first day of spring.

risurin glycerine.

ritei mileage, distance; **riteihyoo** milestone.

rítsu rate, proportion; **rítsu o ageru** to raise
the rate.

ritsuan plan, device; **ritsuan suru** to plan,
design, devise.

riyoo utilization; **riyoo suru** to use; to make
use of, utilize; to take advantage of; **kikái
o riyoo suru** to take advantage of an
opportunity.

riyuu reason, cause; **riyuu de** for reasons of;
riyuu náku without cause, without
provocation; **riyuu no áru** reasonable;
riyuu no nái groundless; **riyuu o nobéru**
to state one's reason.

rizai finance, economy.

ro hearth, fireplace; **robata** fireside.

ro oar.

roboo roadside, wayside; **roboo no chaya**
wayside teahouse; **roboo no hitó**
passerby; **roboo ni tátsu** to stand by the
roadside.

robotto robot.

rodai balcony (outdoor).

róji alley, lane.

roken discovery, exposure; **roken suru** to be
found out; to be detected.

rokotsu frankness; **rokotsu na** frank, candid;
plain; naked; **rokotsu na atekosuri** broad
hint; **rokotsu ni iéba** frankly speaking.

ROKÚ, MUTTSU six; **dái roku** the sixth;
ROKUJÚU sixty; **rokumai byóobu**
sixfold screen.

rokudenashi (*n.*) good-for-nothing.

ROKUGATSU June.

rokuon recording, transcription; **rokuónki**
recorder (sound recording machine);
rokuon suru to record; to make a
recording.

rón argument; discussion; essay; opinion; **rón
o matánu** to be beyond argument;
ronbun essay, article; thesis; **rongai** out
of the question; irrelevant; **rónri** logic;
ronriteki logical; **ronriteki ni** logically;

rónri ni awánai to be illogical; **ronsetsu** essay; editorial, dissertation; **ronsetsu kisha** editorial writer.

ronjíru, ronzúru to discuss; to argue.

ronkoku prosecution; **ronkoku suru** to prosecute.

ronzúru See **ronjíru.**

róo wax; **róo o hiku** to wax; **roobiki** waxing; **roobiki no** waxed; **róogami** wax paper.

róoa deaf and dumb.

róoba old woman.

róobo aged mother.

roobai confusion, panic; **roobai suru** to be confused; to be in a panic.

rooden short circuit.

roodoku recitation; **roodoku suru** to recite, read aloud.

roodoo manual labor, work; **jikangai róodoo** overtime work; **roodoo jíkan** working hours; **roodoo káikyuu** laboring class; **roodoo kúmiai** labor union; **roodoo kúmiai yakuin** labor leader; **roodoo móndai** labor problem; **roodósha** laborer; **roodoo sóogi** labor dispute; **roodoo úndoo** labor movement; **roodoo suru** to labor, work. (See also **róoryoku.**)

róogo old age.

roohi waste (of time, energy); extravagance; **roohi suru** to waste, squander; **jikan o roohi suru** to waste time.

ROOJIN aged person.

rooka corridor, passageway, hall.

ROOMAJI Roman letters; romanization (anglicization); **roomaji de tsuzuru** to spell in Roman letters.

rómansu romance.

ROOMA SÚUJI Roman numerals.

roonen old age.

roonin unemployed person; **roonin shite iru** to be out of work; to be studying for an entrance examination to a college.

rooren expert; **rooren na** experienced.

róoryoku labor, effort; **rooryoku búsoku** labor shortage. (See also **roodoo.**)

roosóku candle, **roosokútate** candlestick.

róosu sirloin.

rootai old person's body.

Rootarii Kúrabu Rotary Club.

rooyá, keimusho prison, jail.

RÓSHIA. Róshia no (*adj.*) Russian; **Roshiago** Russian language. **Roshiájin** Russian (person).

roten open air; **roten no** outdoor.

rúi kind, sort, variety; description; similar case; parallel. **rúi no nái** unique; unparalleled; **ano rúi no hito** people of that sort.

ruibetsu classification; **ruibetsu suru** to classify.

ruiji resemblance, similarity, likeness; **ruiji no** similar, analogous; **ruijíten** point of resemblance. **–ni ruiji suru** to be like, be similar to.

ruikei total sum. **ruikei suru** to total.

ruirei similar case, analogy; **ruirei no nái** unique; exceptional.

rúnpen tramp, hobo.

RÚSU absence; **rusuchuu ni** during (one's) absence; **rúsu ni suru** to be out (not at home); **rúsu o tsukau** to pretend not to be in. **Sanpo ni itte rúsu desu.** She has gone out for a walk.

rusuban, rusui temporary caretaker (while a person is away from home).

rusui See **rusuban.**

ryáku abbreviation; abridgment; **ryaku sázu ni** in detail (without abbreviating); **ryakú shite** in short; **ryaku súru** to abridge; to abbreviate; **ryakugo** abbreviation; **ryakuji** simplified character; simpler substitute; abbreviation.

ryakudatsu suru to loot; to plunder.

ryakushiki informal way; **ryakushiki no** informal; **ryakushiki de, ryakushiki ni** informally.

ryakuzu rough sketch; **ryakuzu o tóru** to make a rough sketch of.

RYOKAKU traveler; passenger; tourist; **ryokaku annaijo** travelers' aid.

RYOKAN Japanese-style hotel or inn.

ryohi traveling expenses.

ryoken passport; **ryoken o káfu suru** to issue a passport; **ryoken o shinsei suru** to apply for a passport.

RYOKOO travel; trip; tour; **ryokoo suru** to travel; **ryokoo ni dekakeru** to start on a journey; **RYOKOO ÁNNAI** guidebook; **ryokoo annaisho** travel agency.

ryoo- prefix denoting: both, two; **ryooashi** both legs; both feet; **RYOOGAWA** both sides; **RYOOHOO** both; both sides; **ryoogan** both banks of a river; **ryoomen** both sides; **ryoomen o kansatsu suru** to examine both sides; **ryóoshin** both parents; **ryootan** both ends; **ryoote** both hands; **ryoote de mótsu** to hold in both hands. **Ryoohoo tomo shitte iru.** I know both of them.

ryóo hunting; shooting; game; fishing; **ryóo ni iku** to go hunting; to go fishing.

ryóo quantity, volume.

ryóodo territory, possession.

ryoogae money-changing, exchange of money; **Béika o Nihon no okane ni ryoogae suru** to change American money into Japanese money.

ryoohoo remedy; method of treatment.

ryóoji consul; **ryoojíkan** consulate; **soo ryoojíkan** consulate general.

ryooji medical treatment.

ryookai comprehension; **ryookai suru** to comprehend, grasp; to see. **Sore wa watakushi ní wa ryookai dekínai.** It's beyond my comprehension.

ryóoken idea, thought, notion; intention; view; direction; **ryóoken o kiku** to ask (someone) his intention; **ryóoken o suéru** to make up one's mind. **Dóo iu ryóoken de sonna kotó o shitá no desu ka?** What made you do such a thing?

RYÓOKIN charge, fee; fare; **ryóokin o torázu ni** free of charge; **ryóokin o tóru** to charge.

ryookoo na successful; favorable.

RYÓORI cooking, cuisine; dish; food; **ryóori suru** to cook; to prepare food; **Nippon ryóori o tabéru** to have a Japanese meal.

ryooritsu compatibility; coexistence; **ryooritsu suru** to be compatible with; to be consistent with; **ryooritsu shigatái** to be incompatible with, to be inconsistent with.

ryooríya restaurant (Japanese-style).

ryóoshin conscience; **ryooshinteki** conscientious. **Ryóoshin ga togaméru.** My conscience bothers me.

ryooshuushoo receipt.

ryooyoo convalescence; **ryooyoo suru** to convalesce.

ryúuchoo fluency; **ryúuchoo na** fluent; **ryúuchoo ni** fluently, eloquently; **ryúuchoo ni Nihongo o hanásu** to speak Japanese fluently.

ryuudóobutsu liquid diet.

ryuugaku suru to study abroad.

ryuugákusei student studying abroad.

ryuugí style; method.

ryuukan influenza.

RYUUKOO fashion, fad; popularity; **ryuukoo no** fashionable, in fashion; **ryuukoo suru** to be in fashion; to come into fashion; **ryuukoo ni okureru** to be out of fashion, out of style.

ryuumachi rheumatism.

S

–SA suffix added to the stem of an adjective to make a noun (comparable to English -ty, -ness); **bakabakáshisa** stupidity, stupidness; **shitashísa** familiarity.

sa difference; margin. **Sa ga áru.** There is a difference.

SÁA come; now; well; let me see. **Sáa taihen na kotó o shita.** Oh, what have I done! **Sáa ikimashóo.** Let's go now.

sáabisu service (at a restaurant, store, etc.). **Sáabisu ga yói.** The service is good.

saachiráito searchlight.

sáakasu circus.

sabáketa sensible; frank; **sabáketa hito** person of the world.

sabaku desert.

sabáku to judge; to decide; to settle. **Hito o sabáku na.** Don't judge others.

sabáku to sell, to deal with.

sabasába shita refreshing; agreeable.

saaberu Occidental-style sword; saber.

sábetsu distinction; discrimination; differentiation; difference; **sábetsu no áru** discriminating; **sábetsu naku** without discrimination; **sábetsu o tsukéru** to discriminate.

sabí rust; patina; antique look; maturity; **sabí ga tsuku** to become rusty.

sabiréru to cease to flourish.

SABISHÍI lonely, lonesome; deserted, desolate.

sabóru to go slow; to sabotage; to cut classes.

sabotáaju sabotage; going slow.

sadamáru to fix; to become settled; to be determined; to be subjugated; **sadamátta** regular, fixed, definite. **Hi ga sadamarimáshita.** The date is fixed. **Sadmátta jikan ni kimásu.** He comes at a regular time.

sadaméru to establish, to lay down; to decide, to settle; **Shuppatsu no hí o sadamemáshita.** I decided on a date of departure.

sadámeshi surely; doubtlessly; no doubt.

sadámete surely; to be sure.

–SÁE even; only. **Anó hito sae shitte imásu.** Even he knows it. **Okane sáe áreba kaimásu.** I'll buy it if only I have the money for it.

saegíru to cut off; to stop; to interrupt; to hinder, to obstruct, block; **mé o saegíru** to obstruct a view; **hito no hanashí o saegíru** to cut in; to interrupt (someone's) conversation.

saéru to be bright, be clear; to attain a rare skill; **mé ga saéru** to be wakeful. **Tsukí ga saéru.** The moon shines clearly. **Nakanaka sáeta udé desu.** She is quite expert in it.

saezúru to sing, warble (a bird).

safúran saffron.

sagaku balance; difference.

SAGÁRU to hang down; to fall; to go down (in price); to leave; to retire. **Nichiyóohin**

no ne ga sagarimáshita. The prices of ordinary commodities have come down.

sagashidásu to find out, discover.

SAGASU to seek, search for.

SAGÉRU to hang down; to lower, let down; to clear away; to wear (a sword); **akari o sagéru** to lower a lamp; **nedan o sagéru** to lower a price; **ozen o sagéru** to clear a table.

sági fraud; imposture; deceit, cheating; **sági o hataraku** to defraud; **sagíshi** swindler.

saguri probe; **saguri o ireru** to probe.

sagúru to search for; to grope for; to probe; **íken o sagúru** to feel out (someone's) view; **pokétto o sagúru** to fumble in one's pocket.

ságyoo work, operation; **sagyoo chuu** while working; **ságyoo o hajimeru** to begin work; **sagyóoshitsu** workroom.

sáhai agency; management (of housing); **sáhai o suru** to act as an agent; **sahainin** agency.

sáhoo good manners, etiquette; **sáhoo o shiranai** ill-mannered.

sahodo so; so much; much (*often used in the negative sense*); **sahodo ní mo nái** not so much as you think.

SÁI talent; ability; difference; **sái no áru** talented; **gógaku no sái ga áru** to have an aptitude for languages; **sái o tanómu** to put too much confidence in one's own talents.

–sai year (as a counter for age); **sán sai** three years old; **juugó sai** fifteen years old.

saiai no dearest, beloved.

saibai cultivation (of plants); **saibai suru** to cultivate.

SÁIBAN judgment; trial; **saíban suru** to judge; **saibánchoo** chief judge; **saibánkan** judge, bench (legal); **saibansho** court of justice, law court; **Saikoo Saibansho** Supreme Court.

saiboo cell.

sáichi wit and intellect.

saijin sharp-witted person.

SÁICHUU in the midst of; in the course of; at the height of; **shokuji no sáichuu ni** in the middle of the meal. **Íma ga atsúi sáichuu da.** The summer heat is now at its height.

súidaa soda pop, soda water.

saidai greatest; maximum; **saidai no koofuku** to greatest happiness; **saidai sokúryoku** the maximum speed.

saidan altar.

saien talented woman.

SAIFU purse; wallet.

saigai calamity; **saigai o koomúru** to suffer a disaster.

saigen reappearance; **saigen suru** to reappear.

saigén limitation; **saigén ga nái** to be endless.

sáigetsu time; years. **Sáigetsu hito o mátazu.** Time and tide wait for no man.

SÁIGO last; **sáigo no last**, closing; **sáigo ni** lastly; **sáigo no toshí** the last year; **saigo tsúuchoo** an ultimatum.

sáigo one's last moment in life; **hisan na sáigo o togéru** to die a sad death.

saihai (baton of) command; direction, leadership. **saihai o furu** to command.

saihan reprinting, second edition; **saihan suru** to reprint, **saihan ni náru** to run into a second edition.

saihatsu reappearance, **saihatsu suru** to appear again, have a second attack (of a disease).

sáihi adoption or rejection; **sáihi o kimeru** to decide on the adoption or rejection.

saihoo sewing; needlework; **saihoo suru** to sew; **saihóoshi** tailor.

SAIJITSU national holiday.

SAIJOO (*n.*) best, highest; superlative; **saijoo no** (*adj.*) best, highest; **saijóohin** article of the best quality; **saijóokyuu** the superlative degree.

saikai meeting again; **saikai o yakusúru** to promise to meet again.

saikásoo lowest layer.

saiken debenture; **saikénsha** creditor.

saiketsu verdict, decision; **saiketsu suru** to bring in a verdict; to decide.

sáiki pressing creditor.

SAIKIN latest; **saikin no joohoo** latest information.

saikin bacterium.

saikon second marriage; **saikon suru** to marry again.

saikoo maximum, **saikoo no** highest; supreme; **Saikoo Saibansho** Supreme Court.

saikoo revival, restoration; **saikoo suru** to reestablish, to renew.

saikoo reconsideration; **saikoo suru** to reconsider; **saikoo no ué de** on reflection.

saikóoten highest point.

saikóro dice.

saiku workmanship; **saiku o suru** to work; to make; to patch up; to manipulate.

sáikuru cycle.

saikutsu mining; **saikutsu suru** to work a mine.

saimatsu close of the year; **saimatsu no uridashi** year-end bargain.

saimínjutsu hypnotism; **saimínjutsu o kakéru** to hypnotize (someone).

saimitsu smallness; minuteness; **saimitsu na** minute; detailed; **saimitsu ni** in detail.

saimoku details; items; **saimoku ni wataru** to go into detail.

sáimu debt; **sáimu o hatásu** to settle one's debts; **saimúsha** debtor.

sáin signature; **sain suru** to sign.

sainán misfortune, calamity, accident; **sainán ni áu** to meet with an accident (mishap); **sainán o manugaréru** to escape a disaster.

sainin reappointment.

sairai second coming; reincarnation.

sairei festival.

saisai again and again; **saisai no** repeated; frequent.

saisan over and over again.

saisei regeneration; resuscitation; **saisei suru** to come to life again.

saisen offertory; sacred pennies; **saisén bako** offertory box (at a Shinto shrine).

sáishi one's wife and children.

saishiki coloring; painting; **saishiki shita** colored; **saishiki suru** to paint.

saishin rehearing, retrial; **saishin suru** to rehear; to reexamine.

saishin no latest; **saishinshiki** latest model.

saishin no careful, prudent; **saishin no chúui o harátte** most carefully.

SAISHO beginning; **saisho no** first, original; **saisho wa** at first; **saisho ni** at the outset; in the first place; **saisho kara** from the very first.

saishoku living on vegetables only; vegetarian diet; **saishoku suru** to live on vegetables; **saishokushugísha** vegetarian.

saishoo (n.) minimum; smallest; **saishoo no** (adj.) smallest; least.

saishuu (n.) last, final; collection; **saishuu no** (adj.) last, final; **saishuu réssha** last train of a day.

saishuu collection; **saishuu suru** to collect, to gather samples.

sáisoku urging; calling upon; **sáisoku suru** to urge, press; **kane o sáisoku suru** to call upon a person in order to pay off one's debts.

saisoku detailed rules.

saitei no lowest, minimum.

saiten marking, scoring.

saiwai good fortune; happiness; **saiwai na** happy, fortunate; **saiwai ni** happily, fortunately.

saiyoo adoption; appointment; **saiyoo suru** to adopt; to use, employ.

saizen (n.) best; one's best; **saizen no** (adj.) best; utmost; **saizen o tsukúsu** to do one's best.

SAJÍ spoon; **sají de sukuu** to spoon up; **sají o nagéru** to give up.

sajiki stand; gallery; upper boxes (in a theater).

sáka tea and cake; **sáka o dásu** to serve refreshments.

SAKÁ sloping hill; slope; ascent; **saká ni náru** to slope; **saká o noboru** to go up a slope; **saká o kudaru** to go down a slope.

sakadachi o suru to stand on one's head.

sakaéru to prosper, flourish.

sakái boundary, border, frontier.

sakámichi a sloping way (road); sloping grade.

sakan na prosperous; splendid; vigorous; **sakan ni** actively; vigorously; **sakan ni náru** to become active.

SAKANA fish; **sakaná tsuri ni iku** to go fishing; **sakanaya** fishmonger; fish-dealer.

sakanobóru to go up; to go back, retrace.

sakarátte against; in the face of.

sakaráu to oppose, go against.

sakari height, climax; rut, heat; **sakari de áru** to be in full bloom; to be in the prime of.

sakasa, sakasama inversion, inverted order; **sakasa ni** inverted; **sakasa ni** wrong side up; upside down; **sakasa ni náru** to be inverted.

sakasama See **sakasa.**

sakaya sake shop.

sakazúki cup; wine cup; **sakazúki o sásu** to offer a cup (of wine); **sakazúki o hósu** to drink up (a cup of wine or sake); **sakazúki o mawasu** to pass around a cup.

SAKE Japanese liquor, wine.

sáke salmon.

sakebi shout; cry.

sakébu to shout; to cry.

sakei leaning toward the left; **sakei suru** to lean toward the left; to become communistic.

sakeme crack.

sakenómi drinker.

sakéru to split; to be torn. **Kinomo ga sakemáshita.** My dress was torn.

sakéru to avoid, to keep away.

SAKI point; tip; future; destination; front; **saki e itte** later on; **saki no** (adj.) future; coming; former; **saki ni** beyond; previously; **saki ga nagái** to have a long future; **yubi no saki** tip of the finger. **Saki ni itte kudasái.** Please go ahead.

sakidátsu to precede.

sakigake pioneer; **sakigake no** the foremost; **sakigake o suru** to lead.

SAKIHODO, SÁKKI little while ago; **sakihodo kara** for some time.

sakimáwari preoccupation, forestallment; **sakimáwari o suru** to get ahead of.

sakiototoi three days back, three days ago.

sakiotótoshi three years ago.

sakisóhon saxophone.

sakka writer, author; literary person.

sakkaku illusion.

sakki thirst for blood; menace; **sakki dátsu** to look menacing.

SÁKKI See SAKIHODO.

sákku sack; case.

sakkyoku musical composition, musical piece; **sakkyoku suru** to set to music; **sakkyokuka** composer of music.

sáku device; plan; **sáku o megurasu** to devise a scheme; **sáku ga tsukíru** to be at wit's end.

saku to bloom.

SÁKU to rend, split, tear; **náka o sáku** to sever the two.

SAKÚBAN last evening, last night. (See also YUUBE)

sakubun composition.

sakudoo maneuvers; artful management.

sakugen curtailment; retrenchment; **sakugen suru** to cut down.

sakuhin work (literary, musical, etc.).

sákui design; motif.

sakuin index; **sakuin o tsukúru** to provide with an index.

sakújitsu See KINOO.

sákujo omission; **sákujo suru** to strike out; to omit.

SAKUNEN See KYÓNEN.

SAKURA cherry tree.

sakuranbo cherry (fruit).

sakurasoo Japanese primrose.

sakuryaku artifice; device; stratagem; scheme; **sakuryaku ni tómu** to be resourceful in scheming.

sakusei manufacture, production.

sakusen military or naval operation; strategy.

sákusha author; dramatist; poet; composer; maker.

SAKÚYA last night.

sakyuu sandhill, dune.

-SAMA See -SAN.

samásu to wake up, awaken; to make sober; to cool; to bring down. **Kono ocha wa moo sukóshi samáshite kara nomimashóo.** I will drink this tea after it has cooled a bit.

samatage disturbance; hindrance.

samatagéru to obstruct, hinder.

samayóu to wander about; to stray.

samazáma various; **samazáma na hito** all sorts of people; **samazáma ni** in many ways.

SAMÉRU to wake up; to come to oneself; to become sober; **mé ga saméru** to be

awakened; **yoi ga saméru** to become sober.

samezáme to bitterly; without restraint; **samezáme to naku** to weep bitterly.

SÁMO as though, as if; **sámo manzoku soo ni** with evident satisfaction. **Sámo ureshisóo desu.** She looks quite pleased.

samon inquisition, inquiry; **samon suru** to interrogate; **samón kai** court of inquiry.

samugári person who is oversensitive to cold.

samugáru to complain of the cold; to be sensitive to the cold.

SAMÚI cold, chilly.

samuké chill, fit of cold, cold shiver.

samurai knight.

SÁMUSA coldness. **Sámusa ga kibíshiku narimáshita.** The cold has worsened.

SAN, MITTSU three.

-SAN Mr.; Ms. **Yamada-san** Mr. (Mrs., Miss) Yamada.

sanba midwife.

sanbashi landing pier.

sánbi praise; adoration; **sanbi suru** to praise.

sanbika hymn; **sanbika o utau** to sing a hymn.

sanbun prose.

sanbutsu product.

sánchi mountainous region; highlands.

sánchi place of production.

sanchoo summit (peak) of a mountain.

sandán devising ways and means; **sandán suru** to find a means; **kane o sandán suru** to manage to raise money.

sandoítchi sandwiches.

sangaí three stories, third floor.

sangai damage; disaster; **sensoo no sangai** the evils of war.

SÁNGATSU March.

sangyoo (manufacturing) industry; **sangyoo no** industrial.

sangyoo kóokoku classified advertisement.

SÁNJUU thirty.

sanjuu no threefold, triple; **sanjuu no hako** nest (set) of three boxes.

sanjutsu arithmetic; **sanjutsu o suru** to do sums.

sanka participation. **-ni sanka suru** to take part in.

sánkaku triangle; **sánkaku no** triangular.

sankan visit; **sankan suru** to visit and see.

sankei visiting a temple; **sankei suru** to go and worship (at a Buddhist temple or a Shinto shrine); **sankeinin** visitor to a temple, worshiper; pilgrim.

sankoo reference; comparison; **sankoo suru** to refer to; **sankoo ni náru** to serve as a reference; **sankoo no táme ni** for reference; **sankóonin** witness; **sankóosho** book of reference.

sánmai three sheets (of paper, or anything flat and thin); **sakana o sanmai ni orósu** to fillet fish (to make three pieces, i.e., 2 pieces of fish and the bone).

sanmenkíji third-page items of a newspaper; general news.

sanmyaku mountain range.

sanpai worship; **sanpai suru** to visit and worship (at a Shinto shrine).

SANPO a walk; **sanpo suru** to take a walk; **sanpo ni iku** to go for a walk.

sanpu scattering; **sanpu suru** to spread, scatter.

sanpuku side of a mountain.

sanretsu attendance; **sanretsu suru** to attend, be present at.

sanrin forest.

sanrínsha tricycle.

sansei seconding, approval; **–ni sansei suru** to support; to approve of.

sanséiken suffrage; political right.

sanséisha supporter; seconder.

sanshoo comparison; reference; **sanshoo suru** to refer to.

sanshutsu production, output; **sanshutsu suru** to produce.

sánso oxygen.

sanson mountain village.

sansui hills and streams; landscape; landscape painting of mountains and rivers.

santan pitifulness; **santan táru** pitiful; tragic.

santóo third class.

sán'yaku powdered medicine.

sanzai (*n.*) spending (money); squandering; **sanzai suru** to spend money.

sanzai lying scattered; **sanzai suru** to lie scattered.

SANZAN severely; terribly; **sanzan mátsu** to wait a long time; **sanzán na mé ni áu** to have a bitter experience.

saó pole, rod; **saodake** bamboo pole.

SAPPÁRI at all; quite; entirely; **sappári shita** refreshing. **Sappári wakarimasén.** I don't understand at all.

sappúukei tastelessness; **sappúukei na** tasteless; dry.

SARA dish, plate.

sárada salad; **saradáyu** salad oil.

SARAIGETSU month after next.

SARAINEN year after next.

SARAISHUU week after next.

sarakedásu to reveal; to bring shamelessly into view; to lay bare; **múchi o sarake dásu** to expose one's ignorance.

sára ni anew, afresh; once more, again; furthermore.

sárarii salary; **saraíiman** salaried man.

sárasara in the least; smoothly; rustling; murmuring.

sarashi bleaching; refining; exposure; **sarashiko** bleaching powder; **sarashimómen** bleached cotton.

sarasu to bleach.

sarasu to expose; **hají o sarasu** to be put to shame.

sarau dredge; to clean; to sweep away; **ninki o sarau** to win (popularity) by a clean sweep.

sarau to kidnap, to spirit away, to snatch.

sarau (*colloq.*) to review; to repeat; to practice; **piano o sarau** to practice the piano.

sáru to go away, to leave; to take off; to divorce; **gakkoo o sáru** to leave school; **shoku o sáru** to retire from a post.

sáru monkey.

sasaeru to support, maintain; **íkka o sasaeru** to support one's family.

sasageru to offer; to sacrifice; to lift up.

sásai na trifling; small; **sásai na koto** trivial matter.

sasayaki whispering.

sasayaku to whisper.

sasen degradation; **sasen suru** to degrade; demote.

saseru to make; to let; to force; to cause; to get; **kodomo ni benkyoo o saseru** to make a child study.

–(S)ASERU causative ending denoting; cause, to make to, to force to, allow to, let; **ikaseru** to make (someone) go; **tabesaséru** to make eat; to allow to eat; to let eat; to force to eat.

SASHIAGERU to present, offer (*humble*).

sashiatari for the present.

sashidashinin sender (of mail, etc.).

sashidásu to present, offer; to send.

sashidegamashíi impertinent.

sashie illustration; cut.

sashigane instigation; carpenter's square; **–no sashigane de** at the instigation of.

sashihiki deduction; balance; excess; ebb and flow; **sashihiki suru** to balance; to deduct.

sashihiku to subtract, take away.

sashikakáru to come upon; to approach.

sashikómu to insert; to push in; to have a fit of acute pain. **Tsuki no hikarí ga mádo kara sashikomu.** The moonlight floods through the window.

SASHIMI sliced raw fish (popular Japanese food).

sashimukai face to face; facing each other; **sashimukai de** sitting face to face; **sashimukai ni náru** to sit face to face.

sashimukéru to send, dispatch.

sashióku to set aside; to leave; to leave out of consideration.

sashiosae attachment; seizure; **sashiosaéru** to seize; to attach. **Zaisan ga sashiosaerárete iru.** Her property is under attachment.

sashisemátta pressing, urgent; imminent; **sashisemátta yooji ga áru** to have urgent business.

sashitoméru to prohibit, place a ban on.

sashitsukae engagement; hindrance; trouble; inconvenience; objection; **sashitsukae ga nákereba** if you have no objection; **sashitsukae ga nái** to be disengaged.

sashitsukaéru to be hindered.

sashiwatashi diameter.

SÁSHIZU direction; instruction; **sáshizu suru** to direct; to instruct; **sáshizu no motó ni** under (someone's) direction.

sasoi invitation; temptation; **sasoi ni yoru** to call for; **sasoi o kakéru** to sound out (someone) on a subject.

SASOU to invite (someone) to call for; to tempt.

sássato quickly; promptly.

sasshi sympathy; consideration; **sasshi ga tsuku** to make out; to guess; **sasshi no áru** sympathetic.

SASSOKU immediately; directly; **sassoku no henjí** quick answer.

sassúru to perceive; to surmise; to sympathize with.

SÁSU to point at; to pour in; to put in; to hold over one's head; to wear; to measure; to rise; to stream in; to play; to be tinged; to offer a cup (of sake); to stick; to put in; **kitá o sásu** to point to the north; **kabin ni mizu o sásu** to pour water into a vase; **kabin ni haná o sásu** to put flowers in a vase; **higása o sásu** to hold a parasol over one's head; **katuná o sásu** to wear a sword; **sake o sásu** to offer a cup of sake.

sásu to stab, to stitch, to sting. **Hachi ga sashimáshita.** A bee has stung me.

sasuga ni indeed; as one might have expected; true to one's reputation. **Anó hito wa sasuga ni erái desu.** He is indeed a great man.

sasuru to rub; to pat; to strike.

satá notice; news; report; instruction; order; **satá ga áru** to get news from; **satá o suru** to give notice.

sáte well; now; **sáte mata** again; **náni wa sate oki** first of all.

sato village; parent's home (of a married woman); **sato ni káeru** to come back to one's home village; to come back home.

SATÓO sugar (often used with prefix **o-**);

satóo o ireru to sugar; **satóo de katameta** candied. **Osatoo o kudasái.** Please give me some sugar.

satori comprehension; understanding; spiritual awakening (Buddhist term). **satori o hiráku** to be enlightened.

satóru to comprehend; to perceive; **hí o satóru** to be convinced of one's error.

satósu to admonish; to counsel.

satsu, osatsu paper money.

–SATSU (counter for books) volume; copy.

satsubatsu na rough; warlike; violent; bloody.

satsuei taking a photograph; **satsuei suru** to take a photograph of.

sátsui murderous intent; **sátsui o okósu** to seek to kill a person.

satsujin homicide.

SATTO in a quick motion; **satto yuderu** to boil briefly in hot water.

sattoo pouring in; **satto suru** to rush in; **mooshikomi ga sattoo suru** to have a crowd of applicants.

sawagashíi noisy, unquiet; **séken ga sawagashíi** things look dark and ominous.

sawagásu to disturb, agitate.

sáwagi noise; shouts.

SAWÁGU to get noisy; to become agitated; **chiisái kotó ni sawágu** to make a fuss over trifles.

sawari hindrance; impediment; affection; harm.

SAWARU to hinder; to be injurious to; **jikoo ga sawaru** to be affected by the weather; to touch; to feel; **kenkoo ni sawaru** to affect one's health; **hito no ki ni sawaru** to hurt (someone's) feelings.

sawaru to touch.

sawáyaka delightful; refreshing; clear; sweet; fluent, eloquent; **bénzetsu sawáyaka na hito** a fluent speaker; **kíbun ga sawáyaka ni náru** to feel refreshed.

sáyoku left wing.

SAYONÁRA, SAYOONÁRA good-bye.

sáyoo action, process, operation; **–ni sáyoo suru** to act upon.

SAYOONARA See **SAYONÁRA.**

sáyuu (n.) right and left; **sáyuu suru** to influence; **sáyuu ni** from side to side; on the right and left.

SÁZO surely; indeed; how; **sázo otsukare deshóo.** You must be tired.

sazukáru to receive; to be granted; to be taught.

sazukéru to grant; to confer on; **hiden o sazukéru** to teach the secrets.

se back; ridge. **Se ni hará wa kaeraremu.** Needs must when the devil drives. Necessity is a hard master.

sé, séi height (of the body). Sé ga takái
desu. She is tall.

sebaméru to narrow; to reduce; séken o
sebaméru to be humiliated.

sebiro man's suit.

sebíru to importune, to tease into.

sebone backbone, spine.

sechigarái stern; hard; sechigarái yonónaka
hard life.

SÉETAA sweater.

segámu to importune.

segare my son, our son.

sehyoo public opinion, popular judgment;
sehyoo ni noboru to be talked about.

SÉI essence; spirit; vital power; sei ga déru
to work hard; sei o dásu to work hard;
Séi ga tsukíru. His energy is gone.

séi See sé (height).

séi family name, surname.

séi sex, gender.

séi cause, effect; –no séi de owing to,
because of.

séi life, existence; séi o ukéru to be born.

–sei suffix denoting; student; ichinénsei
first-year student; bunkásei student of
literature.

seibo present given at the end of the year (as
a token of thanks for favors).

séibun ingredient; a component.

séibutsu living things.

seichoo growth; growing; seichoo shita
grown-up; seichoo suru to grow up; to be
brought up.

seidai splendor; prosperity; seidai na
prosperous; seidai ni splendidly; on a
grand scale.

séido system; institution; séido no ué no
institutional.

seien encouragement; seien suru to
encourage.

SÉIFU government.

seifuku conquest; seifuku suru to subjugate.

seifuku uniform.

seigaku vocal music.

seigan petition; application.

seigén restriction; limit; seigén suru to
restrict; seigén naku without limitations.

séigi righteousness; justice; séigi no
righteous.

séigo correction of (typographical) errors in
printing.

séigyo control; séigyo suru to control.

seigyoo occupation; livelihood.

seihántai direct opposition; seihántai no
diametrically opposed; seihántai ni in
direct opposition; conversely.

seiheki predisposition; inclination.

seihen political change.

séihi success or failure; result.

seihin manufactured goods; products.

SEIHOKU northwest; seihoku no
northwesterly.

seihon bookbinding; seihon suru to bind a
book.

seihoo method of manufacture.

seihoo west; seihoo no western. (See also
NISHI.)

seihóokei (n.) square; seihóokei no (adj.)
square.

séii sincerity; faith; seii áru sincere; faithful.

seíppai to the best of one's ability; as hard
as possible.

séija right and wrong; good and evil; séija o
wakéru to discriminate between right and
wrong.

SEIJI government; politics; seijígaku
politics; the study of politics; seijika
statesman; politician.

seijin adult; attaining the age of maturity;
séijin shita grown-up; séijin suru to
grow up.

seijin sage, saint; seijin búru to give oneself
a sanctimonious air.

seijitsu sincerity; faithfulness; seijitsu na
sincere, honest; seijitsu ni sincerely.

seijuku ripeness; maturity; seijuku shita ripe;
mature; seijuku suru to ripen.

séika parental home.

seikai political world; seikai ni háiru to
enter upon a political career.

seikaku accuracy; seikaku na correct,
accurate.

seikaku character, personality.

SEIKATSU life; livelihood; seikatsu ga
yútaka de áru to be well off; seikatsu o
tatéru to earn one's living; seikatsu suru
to live; to support oneself.

seiken political power; séiken o nigiru to
take the reins of government.

seiken political view; seiken o happyoo suru
to announce one's political views.

seiketsu cleanliness; purity; seiketsu na
clean; pure; seiketsu ni cleanly; seitketsu
ni suru to clean.

séiki vitality, vigor, life; seiki ga míchite iru
to be full of life.

séiki century.

seikoo success; exquisiteness.

seikoo na fine.

seikoo shita successful; prosperous.

seikoo suru to succeed in.

seikyoo prosperity, boom.

seikyuu claim; demand; seikyuu suru to
claim; to demand.

seimei declaration, statement; seimei suru to
declare.

SÉIMEI life; seimei hóken life insurance;
seimei hóken o kakéru to insure one's

life. **Kono byooki wa séimei ni kakawaru kotó wa arimasén.** This disease will never prove fatal.

seimitsu precision; minuteness; **seimitsu na** minute, detailed; **seimitsu ni** minutely, in detail.

seimon front gate.

séimu government business; administration.

SEINAN southwest; **seinan no** southwestern.

seinen youth, young man; young manhood; **seinen no** young, youthful.

seinen full age; **seinen ni tassúru** to come of age.

seinengáppi date of one's birth.

séirai by birth, by nature; **séirai no** natural, innate.

seirei diligence; **seirei suru** to be diligent.

SEIREKI Christian era; year according to the Christian calendar; A.D. **Kotoshi wa seireki sén kyúuhyaku kyúujuu nínen desu.** This year is 1992.

séiri adjustment; readjustment; putting things into order; **séiri suru** to adjust; to regulate.

seiritsu completion, conclusion; coming into existence; **seiritsu saseru** to bring into existence; **seiritsu suru** to come into being.

seiryaku policy; state policy.

séiryoku energy, vigor; influence, power; **séiryoku no áru** influential, powerful; **séiryoku no nái** uninfluential, powerless; **séiryoku no oosei na** energetic, vigorous; **séiryoku o furuu** to wield power; **séiryoku o ushináu** to lose power; **seiryokuka** energetic person.

seisai restraint; sanctions; **seisai o kuwaeru** to restrain, punish.

seisaku policy; fabrication, manufacture; **seisaku suru** to fabricate, manufacture, produce, make.

seisan feasible plan; **juubún seisan ga áru** to be confident of success.

seisan liquidation; **seisan suru** to liquidate.

seisan production; **seisan suru** to produce; **seisan kájoo** overprodution; **seisán-ryoku** productive power.

seisei dóodoo with dignity and impartiality; fair and square.

seiséi suru to be refreshed; to feel revived.

seiseki results; marks; **seiseki ga yói** to be successful.

séishi life and death; life or death; **séishi fumei no** missing; **séishi no sakái ni áru** to hover between life and death.

seishi rest, repose; stillness; **seishi no** stationary, static, still.

seishi restraint, repression; **seishi suru** to restrain, to check.

seishi paper manufacturer.

seishiki due form; formality; **seishiki no** formal; regular; **seishiki ni** formally; duly.

séishin soul, spirit; mind; will; **séishin shinkei antéizai** tranquilizer; **seishinbyoo** mental disease.

seishin séii with sincerity; with faithfulness.

seishitsu nature, character; property, quality.

seisho fair copy; **seisho suru** to make a fair copy of.

séisho Holy Bible.

seishuku silence, quiet; **seishuku na** silent; **seishuku ni** silently; in an orderly manner.

SEISHUN youth; **seishun jídai** youthful days.

seisoo formal dress; **seisoo suru** to dress up.

seisoo political strife.

seisúru to control; to restrain.

seitai system of administration.

seitei enactment; establishment by law; **seitei suru** to pass a law; to establish.

seiten fine weather; clear sky.

SÉITO student, pupil.

seiton arrangement; regulation; **seiton shitá** orderly; well-organized; **seiton suru** to put in order; arrange; **seiton yóku shite iru** to be in good order.

seitoo justice; **seitoo bóoei** legal defense; reasonable self-defense; **seitoo na** proper; legal; fair and proper; **seitoo ni** legally.

seitoo political party.

seitsuu suru to have a thorough knowledge of.

seiyaku oath; covenant; **seiyaku suru** to swear; **seiyakusho** written oath.

Séiyoo Western (Occidental) countries; **Séiyoo no** Occidental; **Seiyóojin** (n.) Westerner; European; Occidental.

séizei to the best of one's power; at most.

seizen táru orderly; regular; well-organized; **seizen to** in good order.

seizon existence; **seizon suru** to exist.

seizoo manufacture, fabrication; **seizoo suru** to make, manufacture.

seizu drawing; cartography.

seji, oseji compliments; **seji no yói, oseji no yói,** affable.

SÉKAI world, earth; **sekaiteki** being worldwide, international.

sékaseka suru to bustle; to hustle.

séken public; people; world.

sekennami commonness; **sekennami no** common, ordinary; **sekennami ni** according to custom.

SÉKI seat; **séki ni tsuku** to sit down, take a seat.

séki census register, domicile.

séki dam, weir, barrier.

sekí cough; **sekí o suru,** to cough; **sekí ga
déru** to suffer from a cough; **sekibárai**
cough for clearing the throat; **sekibárai o
suru** to clear one's throat.

sekidoo equator; **sekidoo no** equatorial.

sekihi tombstone; stone tablet.

sekihin extreme poverty; **sekihin no** very
poor.

sekiji seating order, seniority; precedence.

sekijitsu former days; old times.

sekikómu to be excited; to be agitated.

sekikónde impatiently; in haste.

sekimen blush (of embarrassment); **sekimen
saseru** to make a person blush; **sekimen
suru** to blush; to be ashamed.

sekinin responsibility; duty; obligation;
sekinin ga áru to be responsible for;
sekinin o hatásu to discharge one's duty;
sekinin o ou to take the responsibility.

sekiryoo lonesomeness; desolation.

sekisetsu accumulated snow.

sekitán coal.

sekitatéru to hurry; to press.

sekitoméru to dam up; to check.

sekiyu petroleum; kerosene.

sekizui spine.

sekkai incision; operation; **sekkai suru** to
incise.

sékkachi impetuosity; impetuousness;
sekkachi na hasty; impetuous.

SEKKAKU with much trouble; with great
pains; especially; kindly. **Sakkaku kitá
noni.** I came in vain.

sekkei plan, design; **sekkei suru** to plan, lay
out; to draw up plans for the construction
of.

SEKKEN soap.

sekkin approach; proximity; **sekkin suru** to
approach.

sekkyóo sermon; preaching; **sekkyóo suru** to
preach; to admonish.

sekkyokuteki positive; **sekkyokuteki ni**
positively.

SEMÁI narrow; limited.

semakurushíi narrow and close.

semáru to press; to urge.

semento cement.

seméru to attack; to torture; to call to
account.

SÉMETE at least; at best. **Sémete moo
ichinichi otomari kudasái.** Please stay at
least one more day.

SÉN line; route; **sén ni nátte** in a line;
Tookaidoosen Tookaidoo Railroad (line);
sén o hiku to draw a line.

SÉN thousand; **sanzén** three thousand.

sén stopper, plug; **sén o suru** to stop with a
cork; **mimí ni sén o suru** to stuff
(something) in one's ears.

sén choice, selection; **sén ni háiru** to be
selected; **sén ni moréru** to be left out.

SENAKA back (of the body).

senbai monopoly (of sales); **senbai suru** to
monopolize (business).

senbatsu selection, choice; **senbatsu suru** to
select; **senbatsu sareta** selected. (See also
sentei.)

senbetsu parting present; farewell gift.

senboo envy; **senboo suru** to feel envy;
senboo no mató to náru to become the
envy of.

sencha green tea.

senchaku first arrival.

senchi-méetoru centimeter.

sénchoo captain; master of a ship.

sendan arbitrary action; **sendan de**
arbitrarily; at one's own discretion.

SENDEN publicity; propaganda;
advertisement; **senden suru** to
propagandize; to publicize.

sendoo guidance, leadership.

SENGETSU last month.

senkyooshi missionary.

SENMENJO washroom.

senmon no special; profession; **-o senmon ni
atsukau** to specialize in.

sénmu torishimari yaku managing director.

senpai (n.) senior; superior.

senpatsu starting out in advance of someone
else; **senpatsu suru** to start in advance;
senpatsutai advance party.

senpoo other person; one's destination.

senpuku concealment; state of being latent;
senpuku suru to lie hidden; to go into
hiding. (See also **senzai.**)

senpukúki period of incubation; latent
period.

senpuu whirlwind; cyclone, tornado.

senpúuki electric fan.

senrei previous instance; precedence; **senrei
no nái** unprecedented.

senrei baptism; christening; **senrei o
hodokósu** to baptize; **senrei o ukéru** to
be baptized.

senren polish; refinement; **senren sareta**
refined; **senren suru** to refine.

senritsu melody; rhythm.

sénro railway line; railroad track.

senryaku strategy; **senryakuka** strategist.

senryoo capture; occupancy; **senryoo suru** to
take a position; to occupy.

senryóo dyestuff, dye.

sensai one's former wife.

sensaku search; investigation; **sensaku suru**
to search into.

sensei oath; **sensei suru** to swear; to take an
oath.

SENSÉI teacher; an instructor; honorific for

professional people (doctors, lawyers, etc.).

SENSÉNGETSU month before last.

sensen kyookyoo with great fear, with fear and trembling; **sensen kyookyoo to shite** living in constant fear.

SENSENSHUU week before last.

senshi death in military action; death on the battlefield.

senshínkoku advanced nation (in technology).

senshítsu cabin.

sénshu champion; (sports) player.

senshutsu election; **senshutsu suru** to elect.

SENSHUU last week.

sensoo war; battle; **sensoo ni iku** to go to the front; **sensoo ni kátsu** to win a battle; **sensoo suru** to make war; to fight.

sensu fan; folding fan.

sensui diving into water; submergence; **sensui suru** to dive; to submerge; **sensúikan** submarine.

SENTAKU wash, washing; laundry; **sentaku suru** to wash; **sentaku ni dásu** to send to be washed; **sentaku ga kiku** to stand and wash; **sentakuya** laundry (shop); laundryman.

sentaku selection, choice; **sentaku ni makaseru** to leave it a matter of choice.

sentan extreme point; extremity.

sente forestalling; the first move (in a game); **sente o útsu** to take the initiative; have the first move.

sentei selection, choice; **sentei suru** to select, choose.

sententeki inherent, congenital.

sentoo head, lead; **sentoo ni tátsu** to head, lead.

sén'ya other night; few nights ago.

sen'yaku previous engagement; **sen'yaku no táme** owing to a previous engagement.

sen'yoo exclusive use, private use; **sen'yoo no** exclusive, private.

sen'yuu exclusive possession; **sen'yuu suru** to enjoy sole possession of.

senzai being latent; **senzai íshiki** subconscious; **senzai no** latent, dormant; **senzai suru** to be latent.

sénzo ancestor, forefather; **sénzo no** ancestral, hereditary.

senzoku specially attached; **–ni senzoku suru** to belong exclusively to.

seóu to carry on one's back; to bear; to shoulder; **omoni o seóu** to be burdened with a grave duty; **sekinin o seóu** to take a responsibility on one's own shoulders.

seppaku pressure; urgency; imminence; **seppaku shita** urgent, imminent; **seppaku suru** to draw near; to be pressed.

seppun kiss; kissing; **seppun o nagéru** to send a kiss; **seppun suru** to kiss, press one's lips upon.

serifu speech, dialogue (in a play).

séro cello, violincello.

sérori celery.

séru light serge.

serufutáimaa self-timer.

sessei temperance, moderation; **sessei suru** to be temperate.

sessen fighting at close quarters; **sessen suru** to fight hand to hand.

SÉSSE TO as much as one can; diligently; **sésse to hataraku** to be busy at work.

sésshi Centigrade thermometer.

sesshoo negotiation; **sesshoo suru** to negotiate with.

SESSHOKU contact, touch; **sesshoku suru** to touch; to come in contact with; **sesshoku o tamótsu** to keep in touch with.

sessúru to touch; to have a contract with.

setchi establishment; **setchi suru** to establish.

setchuu compromise; **setchuu suru** to compromise.

setomono porcelain; chinaware.

sétsu opinion, view; theory, doctrine.

sétsubi equipment, arrangement; **sétsubi o suru** to equip; to provide for.

setsudan cutting off, trimming; **setsudan suru** to cut off; to trim.

SETSUMEI explanation, elucidation; **setsumei suru** to explain; **setsumeisho** instruction booklet.

sétsuna moment, instant; **sétsuna no** momentary; **sono sétsuna** at the very moment.

sétsu ni eagerly, earnestly.

setsuretsu poorness; clumsiness; **setsuretsu na** poor; clumsy; unskillful.

setsuritsu establishment, foundation; **setsuritsu suru** to establish, institute, found.

setsuyaku economy; saving; thrift; **setsuyaku suru** to save; to economize.

setsuyu admonition, reproof; **setsuyu suru** to admonish, warn, reprove.

setsuzoku connection, joining; **setsuzoku suru** to join, connect, link.

séttai reception; entertainment; **séttai suru** to receive; to entertain.

settei establishment, creation; **settei suru** to found, institute (a corporation, etc.).

sétto set.

settoku persuasion; **settoku suru** to persuade, convince.

settoo theft, larceny; **settoo o hataraku** to commit a theft.

SEWÁ help, aid, assistance; good offices;

service; care; trouble; **sewá no yakeru** troublesome; **–no sewá ni náru** to be under the care of; **yokei na sewá o yaku** to poke one's nose where one is not wanted; **sewá suru** to help, aid; to do a kind office; to take care of.

sewashíi busy; busily engaged.

shaba this world.

sháberu shovel.

shabéru to chatter; to prattle.

shabon, SEKKEN soap.

shaburu to suck; to chew.

shachoo president of a company.

shadan interception; isolation; **shadan suru** to cut off from.

shadoo roadway.

shagamu to squat; to crouch.

shagareta hoarse (voice); grating (laugh).

shageki suru to shoot, fire at; **shagekijoo** rifle-range.

shain member of a company.

shajitsuteki realistic, true to life.

shákai society; **sháki no tamé ni** for the good of the public; **shakáigaku** sociology, social science; **shakai-shúgi** socialism; **shakai-shugísha** socialist.

shakkín debt; loan; **shakkín o káesu** to pay a debt; **shakkín o koshiraeru** to fall into debt; **shakkín suru** to borrow money; **shakkíntori** creditor.

shákkuri hiccup, hiccough; **shákkuri suru** to hiccup.

shakoo social life.

shaku Japanese foot; unit of measure corresponding to 3.30 cm. or 1.287 (American) foot.

shakuchi leased land; rented ground.

shákudo measure, gauge, scale.

shákushi wooden spoon.

shakuya rented house; **shakuya suru** to rent a house; **shakuyanin** tenant.

shámen slanting surface; slope.

shanpén champagne.

share play upon words, pun; joke; **share o iu** to crack jokes.

sharei remuneration, reward; thanks; **sharei suru** to reward; to remunerate.

shareru to adorn oneself, to try to look pretty.

shareta stylish, tasteful.

sharin wheel.

sharyoo vehicles, cars.

shasai debentures; bond.

shasei sketching; **shasei suru** to sketch; to make a sketch.

shasetsu editorial, leading article.

sháshi cross-eye.

SHASHIN photograph, **shashin no** photographic; **shashin ni tóru** to take a

photograph of; **shashin o hikinobúsu** to enlarge a photograph; **shashin o tóru** to have a photograph taken; to take a photograph, **shashin o yakitsukéru** to print a photograph; **SHASHÍNKI** camera.

SHASHOO conductor.

shatai body of a car.

SHÁTSU shirt, undershirt.

sháttaa shutter.

shazai apology, **shazai suru** to acknowledge being at fault, apologize.

shazetsu refusal, denial; **shazetsu suru** to refuse, decline.

SHÍ city, municipality; **shí no** city, municipal; **shiyákusho** municipal building; City Hall.

SHÍ four (see also **YÓ, YÓN, YOTTSU**).

–shí Mr., Ms. (*used mostly in writing*).

shí death; **shí ni hínshite iru** to be at the point of death; **shí o osorénai** to face death with calmness.

–SHI particle denoting; in addition to it. **Kane mo áru shi chíi mo áru.** He has wealth and, in addition, high position.

shi poetry, verse.

shiage finish, finishing; **shiage o suru** to give the finishing touches to.

shiagéru to finish, complete.

shiai contest of skill, match; **shiai o suru** to play a match; **shiai o mooshikómu** to challenge to a game; **shiai o shoodaku suru** to accept a challenge (to a game).

shían meditation, consideration; **shían suru** to think; to consider.

SHIASÁTTE two days after tomorrow.

shiawase good fortune, happiness.

shibafu lawn; turf.

shibai play, drama; theater; **shibai ni iku** to go to the theater; **shibai o útsu** to give a performance; to trick someone.

SHIBÁRAKU for a while, for some time; **shibáraku shite** after a while.

shibáru to bind; to tie up; **kizu o shibáru** to bind up a wound; **kisóku de shibáru** to restrict (someone) by a rule.

SHIBASHIBA often, many times, repeatedly.

shibatatáku to blink.

shibire numbness; insensibility.

shibiréru to numb; to be numbed.

shibomu to fade, wither.

SHIBOO death; **shiboo suru** to die.

shiboo wish, desire; **shiboo suru** to wish, to desire.

shiboo fat, grease, suet.

shibóosha applicant, candidate.

shibóru to press out, wring out, squeeze; **chié o shibóru** to rack one's brains; **námida ni sode o shibóru** to weep bitterly; **ushi no chíchi o shibóru** to milk a cow.

shíbu branch; subdivision.

shíbúi astringent; austere; glum; sullen; chaste; simple yet refined (in taste); quiet, sober; **shíbúi kao** glum face; **shibúi konomi** quiet taste.

shibukí spray; **shíbukí o tabasu** to spray, to splash.

shibúru to be reluctant, be unwilling; to become loose with gripping pain (of bowels); not to go smoothly.

shibushibu reluctantly, unwillingly.

shibutói churlish; stubborn.

shichí pawn; **–o shichí ni ireru o** to pawn personal property.

SHICHÍ, NANÁTSU seven.

shichí fatal position; **shichí o dassúru** to have a hairbreadth escape.

SHICHIGATSU July.

SHICHIJÚU seventy.

shichíya pawnbroker, pawnshop.

shichóo city administration building.

shichóo mayor.

shichúu inside a city or town; **shichúu o neriarúku** to walk the streets in a procession.

shichúu stew.

shichúu support.

shída fern.

SHIDAI order; the state of things; as soon as; **shidai ni** gradually; **shidai ni yotté wa** according to circumstances; **tsuki shídai ni** as soon as it comes. **Tenki shídai desu.** It depends upon the state of the weather.

shidoo guidance, leading; **shidoo suru** to guide; to lead.

shidóosha leader, director.

shiei private management; **shiei no** private.

shiei municipal management.

shíeki employment; service; **shíeki suru** to employ.

shifuku private clothes.

shígai outskirts of a city, suburbs.

shígai streets.

shigai dead body, corpse.

shigaisen ultraviolet rays.

shigamitsúku to clasp, cling to.

shígan desire; application; volunteering; **shigánhei** volunteer; enlisted soldier; **shigánsha** applicant; **shígan suru** to apply for.

SHIGATSU April.

shigeki stimulus, stimulation; **shigeki suru** to stimulate.

shigemi thicket, bush.

shigéru to become dense; to grow thick and rank.

shígo after death.

shigoku very, extremely.

shigóku to draw through the hand; to stroke (as a beard).

SHIGOTO work, task; job; **shigoto o suru** to work; **shigoto o tóru** to get a job; **shigotoba** workshop.

shigure wintertime rain; wintry shower.

shigusa manners, behaviors; gesture.

shíhai rule, control, management; **shíhai suru** to govern, rule, manage; **kanjoo ni shíhai sareru;** to be influenced by personal feelings; **shihaikáikyuu** governing class; **shiháinin** manager, director.

SHIHARAI payment; **shiharai suru** to pay; **shiharai o seikyuu suru** to ask for payment; **shiharainin** payer (one who pays); **shiharaisaki** payee.

shiharáu to pay; to discharge; **shiharáu beki** payable.

shíhei paper currency.

shíhen volume of poems; Book of Psalms.

shihóo four sides; **shihóo ni** on all sides; **shihoo háppoo** all directions; **shihoo háppoo e** in all directions.

shihóoken jurisdiction; judicial authority.

shihon capital; fund; **shihon o toozúru** to invest one's capital in; **shihonka** capitalist; **shihónkin** capital; **shihonshúgi** capitalism.

shiin cause of death.

shíin scene.

shiire stocking; laying in, buying up (of goods); **shiire o suru** to stock goods.

shiiréru to stock goods, lay in (goods), to buy up (goods).

shiíru to compel; to force upon.

shiitagéru to oppress, tyrannize.

shíite against one's will, by force.

shíitsu bed sheets, linen.

shíji support, maintenance; **shíji suru** to support; to maintain.

shijin poet, poetess.

shijitsu historical facts.

shijoo market, fair; **shijoo ni déru** to appear in a market; **shijoo ni dásu** to bring to market; **shijoo dookoo** market trends; **shijoo kakatu** market value; **shijoo no jissei** market forces; **shijoo shisuu** market index; **shika** market price.

shijúu forty. (See also **YÓNJUU**)

SHÍJUU whole time, all the time, always.

shiká market price.

–SHÍKA only (used with a negative). **Osakana shíka arimasén.** We have only fish. **Eigo shíka hanasemasén.** I can speak only English.

shikaeshi tit for tat; revenge; **shikaeshi o suru** to take revenge.

shikái municipal assembly; town assembly.

shikai chairmanship.

shikake device, mechanism.

shikakéru to begin; to set to work; to fasten upon; to make advances.

shikaku (sense of) sight, eyesight; shikaku qualification; capacity; shikaku no áru qualified; –no shikaku de in the capacity of; shikaku o ushináu to be disqualified for.

shikaku assassin.

SHIKAKÚ (n.) square; shikakú na (adj.) square; shikakúi hako square box.

shikakubáru to be formal; to stand on ceremony.

shikámo moreover, furthermore.

shikaru to scold; to reprove.

shikáruni however, nevertheless, but, yet (formal); shikáruni mata on the other hand.

SHIKÁSHI however, nevertheless.

SHIKATA method, way, means; shikata ga náku (shikata náshi ni) having no other choice. Shikata ga nái desu. I cannot help it.

shiké stormy weather; scarcity of fish; shiké o kúu to be overtaken by a storm.

shikéi death penalty, capital punishment; shikéi o senkoku suru to pass sentence of death; shikéi o shikkoo suru to execute.

SHIKÉN examination, test; trial; shikén ni tóoru to pass the examination; shikén o okonáu to give an examination; shikén suru to examine, test; shikén o ukéru to take an examination.

shikí command, order; shikí suru to command, give an order; –no shikí no motó ni under the command of.

shikí ceremony; shikí o ageru to celebrate.

shikí four seasons.

–shiki suffix denoting: style; seiyooshiki Western style; Occidental style; suisenshiki flush style (toilet).

shikibetsu discrimination; discernment; shikibetsu suru to discern, distinguish.

shikibúton quiltlike mattress; bedding.

shikichi site, ground.

shikifu bed sheet.

shikii threshold, sill; shikii o matágu to cross the threshold.

shikiishi paving stone; pavement.

shikíkan commander.

shikíkin deposit, key money (for renting a house); shikíkin o ireru to make a deposit on a house; to give key money.

shikimono matting; carpet; shikimono o shiku to lay a carpet.

shikín fund.

shikiri partition; settlement of accounts.

SHIKIRI NI frequently; continually; eagerly.

shikisai color, tint.

shikísha intelligent people; persons of good sense.

shikitsuméru to spread all over.

shikka at one's lap (honorific address to parents, mostly used in letters); –no shikka ni under the care of.

SHIKKÁRI firmly, tightly; strongly; exactly, shikkári shita strong; substantial.

shikkéi disrespect; impoliteness; shikkéi na impolite, rude; shikkéi suru to say good-bye. Shikkéi shimáshita. I beg your pardon (in men's talk).

shikki damp; moisture; shikki no áru wet, damp, moist.

shikki lacquered-ware.

shikkoo execution, enforcement; shikkoo suru to execute, carry out, enforce; shikkoo yúuyo probation; a suspension of execution; shikkoo yúuyo to náru to be released on probation.

shikkoo losing effect; invalidation.

shikkui mortar; plaster; shikkui de nuru to plaster.

shikomi training; teaching.

shikómu to train, to teach.

shikoo enforcement, carrying out; shikoo sareru to take effect; shikoo suru to enforce.

shikoo taste; shikoo ni tekisúru to suit one's taste.

shikóoryoku contemplative faculty, power to think.

shikori stiffness; bump.

shiku to spread, lay; to pave; to issue; to proclaim.

shikujíru to fail; to make a blunder; to be cashiered.

shikyó death.

shikyoku branch office.

shikyoo condition of the market.

shikyoo bishop.

shikyuu urgency; shikyuu no urgent; shikyuu ni at once, promptly.

shikyuu supply, allowance; shikyuu suru to provide; to supply.

SHIMÁ island.

shimá stripes.

SHIMAI end, termination; shimai ni at last; shimai ni náru to come to an end; shimai ni suru to finish.

shímai informal No dance (performed without wearing the formal standard costume).

SHÍMAI sisters.

SHÍMARI tightness; locking, fastening, prudence; shímari no áru firm, locked; prudent; shímari no nái loose, impudent; stupid.

SHIMÁRU to shut, to close; to grow tight; to tighten, to sober down.

shímatsu management; circumstances, result, economy; **shímatsu no oenai** unmanageable; **shímatsu suru** to manage; to put in order.

shimátta compact; firm, well-set.

shimau to close; to finish; to put away.

shimedasu to shut out, exclude.

shimegane buckle; clasp; **shimegane o kakéru** to buckle together.

shímei naming; nomination; **shimei suru** to name; to nominate.

SHÍMEI full name.

shímei mission; errand; **shímei o mattoo suru** to fulfill a duty.

shimekiri close; closed; deadline.

shimekomu to lock in, shut in.

shimekorósu to strangle to death.

shímen space (in a magazine or newspaper).

shimeppói damp; wet; **shimeppói hanashí** tearful story.

shiméru to occupy; **jooseki o shiméru** to occupy the top seat.

SHIMÉRU to tie, to bind; to close, to shut.

shimeru to get damp; to get wet.

shimésu to point out; to show; to indicate.

shimesu to wet, moisten.

shímete altogether; in all.

shimi stain, blot; **shimi no áru** stained; **shimi dárake no** spotty. **Shimi ga demáshita.** There is a stain.

shimijími carefully; fully; heartily; **shimijími kao o míru** to look searchingly into (someone's) face; **shimijími kiku** to listen attentively to.

shímin citizen.

shimínken citizenship.

shimiru to penetrate; to soak into; to smart; to be touched with; **shínsetsu ga mi ni shimiru** to appreciate (someone's) kindness fully. **Kaze ga mi ni shimiru.** The wind is penetrating. **Kono róoshon wa shimiru.** This lotion smarts.

shimizu spring water.

SHIMÓ frost; **shimó de kareru** to be nipped by frost; **shimoyake** frostbite.

shimon trial; inquiry; examination; **shimon suru** to try (hear) a case.

shimon fingerprints; **shimon o tóru** to take (someone's) fingerprints.

shimuke one's behavior toward; one's attitude.

shimukéru to act toward; to treat; to send.

SHÍN heart; mind; core; **shín kara** heartily, sincerely; **shín made** to the core.

shín truth, reality; **shín ni** truly, really, actually; **shín no** true, real; **shín ni semáru** to be true to one's nature.

shína coquetry; **shína o tsukúru** to be coquettish.

shina article; goods, stuff.

shinabiru to wither; to droop.

shinagire out of stock; sold out.

shínai city; inside the city.

shin'ai affection, love; **shin'ai náru** dear, beloved.

shinamono article; goods.

shin'an new idea; new design.

shinario scenario.

shináyaka na pliant, flexible, supple.

shinboku friendship, intimacy; **shinboku o hakáru** to cultivate a friendship.

shínboo patience, endurance, forbearance; **shínboo no nái** impatient; **shínboo no yói** patient; **shínboo suru** to endure; to be patient.

shínboo axle, shaft.

SHINBUN newspaper; journal; **shinbundáne** news matter; **shinbun kisha** journalist.

shinchiku new building; **shinchiku no** newly built; **shinchiku suru** to build, rebuild.

shinchintáisha replacing the old with new; replacement; metabolism; **shinchintáisha suru** to be renewed; to be replaced.

shinchíshiki new knowledge; advanced idea.

shíncho books newly published.

shinchoo care; prudence; **shinchoo na** careful, cautious; **ími shinchoo** having deep meaning; to be of profound significance.

shinchoo height, stature; **shinchoo ga takái** to be tall.

shinchuu brass.

shínchuu true motive; mind; **shínchuu o sassuru** to share (someone's) feelings.

shindai sleeper (on a train).

shíndai fortune, property.

shindan diagnosis; **shindan suru** to diagnose.

shinden sanctuary (in a Shinto shrine).

shindoo tremor, shock, vibration; oscillation; **shindoo suru** to shake, vibrate (from an earthquake or collision); to swing, oscillate, move to and fro.

shingai infringement, encroachment; **shingai suru** to infringe; to make an attack upon.

shingaku theology.

shingari rear; rearguard; **shingari o tsutomeru** to bring up the rear.

shingata new style; new design.

shingénchi seismic center; center of disturbance.

shíngetsu new moon.

shíngi genuineness, authenticity; **shíngi o tashikaméru** to ascertain the truth.

shíngi consideration, discussion,

investigation; **shíngi suru** to consider, to investigate.

shingoo signal; danger signal; **kiken shíngoo** danger signal; **shingoo suru** to signal, give a signal.

shíngu bedding and bedclothes.

shin'i real intentions; true meaning.

shinikakátta dying; at the point of death.

shinime moment of death.

shinimonogúrui death struggle; desperation; **shinimonogúrui de** desperately; **shinimonogúrui no** desperate; **shinimonogúrui ni náru** to make a desperate effort.

shinin dead person.

shinitaéru to die out.

shiniwakaréru to be parted by death.

shínja believer; faithful (person).

shinjín divine worship; devotion; **shinijin bukái** pious, devout; **shinjín suru** to worship; to regard with adoration.

shinjíru See **shinzúru**.

shínjitsu truth; reality; **shínjitsu na** true, real; **shínjitsu ni** truly, really.

shinjitsu sincerity; faithfulness; **shinjitsu na** sincere; faithful.

shinjoo article of faith; creed; (one's) true feelings.

shinju pearl.

shinjuu double suicide; suicide for love.

shínka real value, true worth; **shínka o mitomeru** to appreciate the true value.

shínka evolution; **shínka suru** to evolve.

shinkáichi newly developed district.

shinkan, shinkánsho new publication; new book.

shínkei nerves; **shinkei kábin** nervousness; being overly sensitive; **shínkei no** nervous; **shinkéishitsu** nervous temperament; **shinkéishitsu no** nervous; **shinkei súijaku** nervous breakdown; **shinkeitsuu** neuralgia; **shínkei séishin antéizai** tranquilizer.

shinken na earnest; **shinken ni náru** to be earnest; to become earnest.

shinkíjiku new device; originality; **shinkíjiku o dásu** to introduce a new method.

shinkoku declaration; report (tax return, etc.); **shinkoku suru** to state; to report.

shinkoku na deep, serious.

shinkon new marriage; **shinkon no** newly married; **shinkon ryókoo** honeymoon; **shinkon ryókoo o suru** to go on a honeymoon.

shinkoo faith; belief; **shinkoo no jiyúu** freedom of faith; **shinkoo no nái** unbelieving; **shinkoo suru** to believe in.

shinkoo advance, progress; **shinkoo suru** to advance, to progress.

shinkoo friendship, cordiality.

shínku hardship; tribulation; **shínku suru** to suffer hardship.

shinkuukan vacuum tube.

shinkyuu promotion; **shinkyuu suru** to win a promotion; to be promoted.

shinme sprout, shoot; **shinme o dásu** to bud, sprout.

shínmi blood relation; **shínmi ni nátte sewá o suru** to look after with great kindness.

shinmíri heart-to-heart; earnestly; **shinmíri hanásu** to have a heart-to-heart talk.

shinmitsu intimacy; familiarity; close friendship; **shinmitsu na** intimate, familiar; **shinmitsu na aidagara de áru** to have a strong friendship.

shinmotsu present, gift.

shinmyoo na fair; commendable, conscientious; docile; **shinmyoo ni** commendably; quietly; meekly; fairly.

shínnen new year. **Shínnen omedetoo,** I wish you a Happy New Year.

shínnen faith, belief; deeply rooted conviction.

shinnin confidence, trust; **shinnin suru** to confide in, believe in.

shinnínjoo credentials.

shinnyuu invasion; inroad; trespass; intrusion; **shinnyuu suru** to invade; to intrude into; **shinnyúusha** invader; trespasser.

shinnyúusei new student; freshman.

shinobi stealthy movement; going in disguise.

shinóbu to bear, endure; to conceal; to hide oneself; to steal along one's way; **fujíyuu o shinóbu** to suffer privation; **hitome o shinóbu** to elude observation; **yó o shinóbu** to live in concealment.

shinogiyói genial; nice; mild.

shinógu to endure, bear; to rise above.

shinónde patiently; meekly; secretly.

SHINPAI uneasiness; apprehension; anxiety; worry; care; fear; **shinpai na koto** trouble, difficulty; **shinpai no amari** overcome with anxiety; **shinpai suru** to fear; to be anxious.

shinpan judgment; **shinpan suru** to judge; to umpire; **shinpánsha** umpire; judge.

shinpan new edition, new publication; **shinpan no** newly edited, newly published.

shínpi mystery; **shínpi na** mysterious, mystic.

shínpo progress, advance, improvement. **shínpo suru** to make progress.

shínpu Catholic priest.

shínpu bride.

shinpuku admiration and devotion, honest submission; **shinpuku suru** to acknowledge another's superiority; to obey faithfully.

shinrai trust, reliance; confidence; **shinrai suru** to trust, to place confidence in.

shinratsu severity; poignance; **shinratsu na** severe; poignant.

shinreki new calendar; Gregorian calendar, solar calendar (as distinguished from the lunar calendar used in the past).

shínri examination, trial; **shínri suru** to try, to examine.

shínri truth, truism; **shinri o motoméru** to seek truth.

shínri psychic state; **shinrígaku** psychology.

shinrin forest, wood.

shinroo bridegroom.

SHINRUI relation, relative.

shinryaku aggression; invasion; **shinryaku suru** to invade.

shínryoku fresh green.

shínsa examination, investigation, inspection; **shínsa suru** to examine, inquire into; **shinsáin** jury, committee of inquiry.

shinsai disaster caused by earthquake.

shinsatsu medical examination; **shinsatsu o ukéru** to consult a physician; **shinsatsu suru** to examine a patient.

shinsei sacredness, sanctity; **shinsei na** holy, sacred, hallowed; **shinsei ni suru** to make holy; **shinsei o kegasu** to defile the sacredness.

shinsei application, petition; **shinsei suru** to apply; **shinseinin** applicant, petitioner, claimant.

shinseki relative.

shinsen na fresh, new.

SHÍNSETSU kindness; goodness; friendliness; **shínsetsu na** kind, good, cordial; **shínsetsu o suru** to do a kindness.

shinsetsu new establishment; **shinsetsu no** newly organized, newly formed; **shinsetsu suru** to establish newly.

shínshaku consideration, allowance; **nán no shínshaku mo náku** without any consideration; **shínshaku suru** to take into consideration.

shínshi gentleman; man of position; **shinshi kyóoyaku** gentleman's agreement; **shinshirashíi** gentlemanlike.

shinshiki new style; new system; **shinshiki no** of a new style; modern.

shinshin no rising.

shinshitsu bedchamber, bedroom.

shínshoku food and sleep; **shínshoku o wasurete** forgetful of sleep and other comforts; regardless of oneself.

shinshoku erosion; **shinshoku suru** to erode.

shinshuku expansion and contraction; elasticity; **shinshuku suru** to expand and contract; **shinshuku jízai** elasticity; **shinshuku jízai no** elastic.

shinshutsu marching out; emergence; **shinshutsu suru** to march out; emerge.

shinsoo true state; **shinsoo o akíraka ni suru** to disclose the real state of affairs; **shinsoo o kataru** to lay bare the truth of a matter.

shinsui launching; **shinsui suru** to launch; to be launched; **shinsúishiki** launching (ceremony).

shinsui fascination, infatuation; **shinsui suru** to be fascinated.

shinsui flooding, inundation; **shinsui suru** to be flooded.

shintai image of a god.

shíntai body; person; constitution; **shintai kénsa** physical examination; **shíntai no** bodily, corporal.

shíntai advance and retreat; movement; **shíntai suru** to move, to act.

shintaku trust; **shintaku suru** to entrust with; to leave in trust (property, etc.); **shintaku gaisha** trust company; **shintaku shíkin** trust fund.

shintei presentation; **shintei suru** to present, give.

shinten personal; confidential (written on the envelope of a letter); **shinten no** private, confidential; **shintensho** confidential letter.

shínto believer (religious).

shin to shita silent, still; deserted.

shin to suru prevailing silence.

shintsuu mental suffering; anxiety.

SHINU to die, pass away, expire; **shinu máde** to the end; **shinu kákugo de** at the risk of one's life.

shinwa myth, mythology.

shín'ya dead of night, midnight; **shínya ni** late at night.

Shin'yaku Séisho New Testament.

shin'yoo confidence, trust; credit; **shin'yoo ga áru** to be trusted by; **shin'yoo o éru** to have credit with; **shin'yoo suru** to trust; to credit; **shin'yóojoo** letter of credit; **shin'yoo kúmiai** credit association, credit union.

shin'yuu intimate friend.

shinzen amity, goodwill; **shinzen shísetsu** goodwill mission.

shínzoku relation, relative.

SHINZOO heart; **shinzoobyoo** heart disease; **shinzoomáhi** heart failure.

shinzui essence.

shinzúru, shinjíru to believe in; to accept (something) as true; to trust.

SHIÓ salt (often used with the prefix **o-**); **shiokarái** salty; **shió de aji o tsukéru** to season with salt; **shió ni tsukeru** to salt; to pickle in salt.

shioki punishment; execution; **shioki o suru** to punish; to execute.

shiokuri supply; allowance; **shiokuri o suru** to furnish a person with money (for living expenses, schooling, etc.).

shiorashíi moving, touching; plausible; **shiorashíi kotó o iu** to say pretty things.

shioreru to wither, droop; to be in low spirits.

shippai failure; defeat; **shippai suru** to fail; to be unsuccessful.

shippi useless expenses.

shippitsu writing; **shippitsu suru** to write.

shippó tail; **shippó o dásu** to give (someone) away; to disclose (someone's) identity; **shippó o maku** to acknowledge defeat; **shippó o osaéru** to find fault (with someone).

shippuu violent wind; gale.

shirabakkuréru (*colloq.*) to dissemble; to pretend not to understand.

SHIRABÉRU to investigate; to examine; to prepare a lesson for.

shírafu soberness; sobriety; state of not being drunk.

shirákeru to become chilled; to be spoiled. **Anó hito ga kúru to ítsumo za ga shírakemásu** He is always a wet blanket.

shiranu unknown, unfamiliar; **shiranu kao o suru** to look on with indifference.

shirase information; news; sign; notice.

SHIRASERU to notify; to send a notice; **kekkon o shiraseru** to send a notice of marriage.

shirazu shírazu unawares; unconsciously.

shirei instructions; order, notice.

shíren trial, test; **shíren ni taéru** to stand the test; **shíren o ukéru** to be tried, be tested.

shireru to become known.

shíri private gain; self-interest; **shíri o hakaru** to look to one's own interests.

shirí buttocks; rump; bottom; **shirí ga nagái** to wear out one's welcome; **shirí ga wareru** to be brought to light; to be found out; **shirí o mukeru** to turn one's back upon.

shirikon silicon.

shirime contemptuous glance; **shirime ni kakéru** to look disdainfully at.

shirioshi backing, support; **shirioshi o suru** to back, support.

shíritsu private establishment (school, welfare agency, etc.); **shíritsu no** (*adj.*) private.

shíritsu municipal establishment; **shíritsu no** municipal, city.

shirizokéru to refuse; to reject; to repel, to drive back.

shirizóku to retreat, retire, withdraw; to leave; **íppo shirizóku** to take a step backward.

shiro fortress; castle.

shíro (*n.*) white.

SHIRÓI (*adj.*) white; **shíroku suru** to whiten.

shiróoto amateur.

shirozátoo white sugar, granulated sugar.

SHIRU to learn; to become acquainted with; **shitte iru** to know. **Nihongo mo Chuugokugo mo shitte imásu.** He knows both Japanese and Chinese.

shíru juice, sap; fluid; soup, broth; **shíru no óoi** juicy, succulent.

shirushi sign, mark, symbol, badge; **shirushi o tsukéru** to mark, to tick.

shirusu to write down; to describe.

shíryo consideration; thought; **shíryo no áru** thoughtful; **shíryo no nái** thoughtless.

shíryoku desperate effort; **shíryoku o tsukúshite** with desperate courage.

shíryoku funds, resources, means.

shíryoku eyesight, sight, vision.

shíryoo materials, data.

shiryuu branch stream.

shisai reason; circumstances; details, particulars; **shisai no** minute, detailed; **shisai ni** minutely, in detail.

shisaku speculation; meditation; **shisaku ni fukéru** to be engrossed in thought; **shisaku suru** to think; to speculate.

shisaku trial production; **shisaku suru** to manufacture on a trial (experimental) basis.

shisan property; fortune; assets.

shisatsu inspection; examination; **shisatsu shite arúku** to make a tour of inspection; **shisatsu suru** to visit; to inspect.

shisei carriage, posture, pose; **shisei o tadásu** to hold oneself up.

shisei municipal organization; **shisei chóosa** municipal census.

shiséiji illegitimate child.

shiseki place of historical interest.

shisen line of vision (sight); **shisen o sakéru** to avoid the public gaze.

shisen branch line.

shisetsu institution; institute; **shisetsu suru** to institute; to equip.

shísetsu mission; envoy.

shísha dead person.

shísha branch office.

shisha preview; **shisha o okonáu** to hold a preview.

shishókan post office box.

shíshoo teacher, master (of traditional arts and sports).

shishoo casualties; number of killed and wounded; **shishóosha** dead and injured.

shishúnki adolescence, puberty; **shishúnki no** adolescent.

shishutsu expenditure; payment; **shishutsu suru** to pay; to disburse.

shishuu collection of poems.

shishuu embroidery; **shishuu suru** to embroider.

shisoo thought, idea.

shissaku error, mistake; **shissaku suru** to do (anything) amiss; to make a mistake.

shisseki reproof, reprimand; **shisseki suru** to reprove.

shisshoku unemployment; **shisshoku suru** to become unemployed.

shísso simplicity, plainness, frugality; **shísso na** simple, plain; **shísso ni kurasu** to live a simple life; to live plainly.

shissoo running fast; going at full speed; **shissoo suru** to run away; to run at full speed.

shissoo disappearance (of a person); **shissoo suru** to disappear.

SHITÁ tongue; **shitá o dásu** to put out one's tongue; **shitá o maku** to be astonished.

SHITA foot; bottom; lower place; –**no shitá de** under, below; –**no shitá ni** under, below; **shita e** down, downward; **shita kara** from below, from the bottom; **shita no** lower; downward, subordinate; inferior.

shitabi burning with less intensity; **shitabi ni náru** to reach a low mark, to wane.

shitagáeru to be attended by, to bring under subjection.

shitagaki rough copy, draft; **shitagaki o suru** to draft; to make a rough copy.

SHITAGÁTTE accordingly, consequently; correspondingly.

shitagáu to follow; to accompany; to obey.

shitagéiko preparation; rehearsal; **shitagéiko o suru** to prepare.

SHITAGI underwear, undergarment.

shitagókoro secret desire, intention; **shitagókoro ga áru** to have a secret desire.

shitagóshirae preparation, arrangement.

shitai dead body.

shitaji ground; groundwork, preparation.

shitakénsa previous examination.

SHITAKU preparation; arrangement; **shitaku o suru** to prepare.

shitamachi downtown.

shitami preliminary inspection.

shitamuki downward look, downward tendency; **shitamuki no** downward; prone; **shitamuki ni náru** to look down.

shitanuri undercoating, prime; **shitanuri o**

suru to put on the first coat (of paint).

SHITASHÍI intimate; familiar; **shitashíi aidagara de áru** to be on intimate terms; **shitáshiku** intimately; personally; **shitáshiku suru** to be great friends.

shitashimi friendship, friendly feeling; **shitashimi no áru** familiar, close, affectionate; **shitashimi no nái** unfamiliar; strange; cold.

shitashímu to become friendly with; to become a great friend of.

shitashírabe preliminary inquiry; preparation; doing homework; **shitashírabe o suru** to inquire beforehand.

shitatáru to drip; to drop.

shitate cut; tailoring; getting ready; **shitate no yói** well-tailored; **shitatemono** sewing; tailoring; **shitateya** dressmaker; tailor.

shitate ni déru to treat (someone) with deference; to behave humbly.

shitatéru to make (clothes); to train for a trade.

shitatsúzumi smacking one's lips; **shitatsúzumi o útsu** to smack one's lips; **shitatsúzumi o útte tabéru** to eat with much relish.

shitau to yearn after; to long for.

shitauchi tut.

shitauke subcontract; **shitauke ni dásu** to sublet.

shitayaku subordinate employee.

shitayomi preparation of one's lessons; rehearsal; **shitayomi o suru** to prepare one's lessons.

shitazumi being in the lower layer of something; **shitazumi ni náru** to be in the lower layer; to be placed under something; **shitazumi no seikatsu o suru** to be low in the social scale.

shitchi swampy land; damp ground.

shitei designation; **shitei no** recognized; appointed; **shitei suru** to designate; to name; to appoint.

shitei private mansion.

shiteki pointing out; **shiteki suru** to point out; to show; to indicate.

shiteki poetic.

shiteki private, personal.

shiten branch store.

shitogéru to bring about; to complete.

shitoo na right and proper; fair; reasonable.

shitóshito gently; softly; damp; wet.

shitóyaka na gentle, graceful.

SHITSÚ nature, character; quality.

–**shitsu** suffix denoting: room, chamber; **kyooshitsu** classroom; **shinshitsu** bedroom.

shitsuboku na simpleminded.

shitsuboo disappointment; despair; **shitsuboo**

shite disappointedly; **shitsuboo saseru** to disappoint; **shitsuboo suru** to be disappointed at.

shitsugen slip of the tongue; blunder in speech.

shitsugyoo unemployment; **shitsugyoo suru** to be thrown out of work.

shitsúji steward; manager; butler.

shitsuke discipline; breeding; training; **shitsuke no yói** disciplined, well-bred.

shitsukéru to train, bring up.

shitsukkói, shitsukói obstinate, persistent.

shitsumei loss of eyesight; **shitsumei suru** to lose one's sight.

SHITSUMON question; interrogation; **shitsumon suru** to question.

shitsúmu attending to one's business.

shitsúnai interior of a room; **shitsúnai de in** a room; **shitsunai sóoshoku** interior decoration.

SHITSÚREI breach of etiquette, discourtesy; **shitsúrei na** impolite; **shitsúrei na kotó o iu** to say rude things.

shitsuren broken heart; disappointment in love; **shitsuren suru** to be crossed in love; to become heartbroken.

shittakaburi pretension to knowledge; **shittakaburi o suru** to pretend to know.

SHITTE IRU See **SHIRU**.

shitto jealousy; **shitto suru** to be jealous.

shiwa wrinkles; lines on one's face; creases; rumples; **shiwa ga yoru** to become wrinkled; **shiwa ni náru** to be crumpled; **shiwa o nobásu** to smooth the creases.

shiwaza act, action, deed.

shiyoo use, employ; **shiyoo suru** to use; to make use of; **shiyoohoo** directions for use; **shiyoonin** employee.

shiyoo private business, private use; **shiyoo de** for private use, on private business; **shiyoo suru** to turn to private use.

shízai private fortune, money; **shízai o toojite** out of one's own purse, at one's own expense.

shizen nature; **shizen no** natural, instinctive; **shizen ni** naturally, spontaneously.

SHÍZUKA NA silent, quiet, still, peaceful; **shízuka ni kurasu** to live in peace; **shízuka ni náru** to become still, get calm.

shizukú drop; **shizukú ga taréru** to drip.

shizumaru to become quiet.

shizumeru to quiet, calm, pacify; to quell; to subdue; to sink, send to the bottom.

shizumu to sink; to go to the bottom; to feel depressed.

sho writing; document; calligraphy, penmanship; book.

–sho suffix denoting; public office; **keisatsusho** police station; **Zeimusho** Office of Internal Revenue.

shobatsu punishment; **shobatsu suru** to punish; to impose a punishment.

shóbun disposition; management; punishment; **shóbun suru** to dispose of; to punish.

shóchi management, action; **shóchi suru** to manage; to dispose of; to deal with.

shochuu kyúuka summer vacation.

shoen first public performance of a play.

shóga pictures and writings.

shogen preface, introduction.

shogéru to be dejected, cast down.

shohan first edition of a book.

shóho first step; elements; **shóho no** elementary, rudimentary.

shohoo prescription.

shójo (*n.*) virgin, maiden; **shójo no** (*adj.*) virgin.

shóka early summer.

shokan letter; **shokansen** letter paper.

shokatsu jurisdiction.

shokei punishment.

shóki expectation, anticipation; **shóki no** expected.

shóki heat, hot weather; **shoki ni ataru** to be affected by the heat.

shóki first stage, beginning.

shóki clerk.

shokikán secretary.

shokken authority; official power; **shokken o ran'yoo suru** to abuse one's official authority.

shokki tableware.

shokkoo workman.

shoku office; situation, position; occupation, employment, job; **shoku ni tsukú** to take a post; **shoku o motoméru** to look for employment.

shoku eating; food; appetite; **shoku ga susumu** to have a good appetite.

shokuátari attack of indigestion, food poisoning.

shokuba workshop; place of work.

shokúbutsu plant; **shokubutsúgaku** botany; **shokubutsúen** botanical garden.

shokudai candle-stand.

SHOKUDOO dining room; **shokudóosha** dining car.

SHOKÚEN table salt.

shokugo after a meal.

shokúgyoo occupation, employment.

shokuhi charge for boarding; board.

shukúin staff; personnel.

SHOKUJI meal; diet; **shokuji o suru** to eat; **shokujidóki** mealtime.

shokuji typesetting; typography; composition;

shokuji o suru to compose; shokujikoo typesetter.

shokumin colonization, settlement; colonists; shokumin suru to colonize; to found a colony; shokumínchi colony; shokumínchi no colonial.

shokúmotsu food.

shókumu duties, functions; shókumu o hatásu to discharge a duty; shokumujoo officially, in the line of duty; shokumujoo no official.

shókun Ladies and gentlemen! (used in a speech).

shokunin workman; artisan.

shokupán bread; loaf of bread.

shokuryóohin articles of food, foodstuffs.

shókushi, hitosashíyubi forefinger; index finger; shókushi o ugokásu to be desirous of.

shokutaku person with non-official status; person employed without tenure.

shokutaku dinner table; shokutaku ni tsukú to take one's seat at the table.

shokúyoku appetite; relish; shokúyoku ga nái to have no appetite; shokúyoku o susumaseru to stimulate one's appetite.

shokuyoo no used for food; shokuyoo ni teki súru to be fit for the table.

shomei signature; shomei suru to sign.

shómen document; letter.

shómotsu book.

shonbóri lonely, solitarily.

shonichi first day; opening day.

shóo nature, disposition; character; quality; shóo no yói of good quality; shóo ga áu to be congenial; shóo ga awánai to be incompatible.

shóo chapter, section.

shóo prize, reward; shóo o ataéru to give a prize; shóo o éru to get a prize.

shóo quotient (math).

shóo ministry.

SHÓOBAI trade, business; shóobai ni naránai not to be paying; shóobai o suru to do business; shoobainin merchant.

shóobatsu rewards (honors) and punishment. Gakkoo de shoobatsu o úketa kotó wa arimásen. I have received no honors or punishment in my school days.

shoobén urine; shoobén o suru to urinate.

shóobi admiration; appreciation; shóobi suru to praise; to applaud.

shooboo prevention and extinction of fires; shoobóoshi fireman; shooboosho firehouse; shoobootai fire company. (See also hí.)

shóobu match, contest; game; shóobu o kimeru to fight to a finish; shóobu o suru to have a match (game, sport).

shoobun innate disposition, temperament.

shoochi consent, acceptance; shoochi no ué de by mutual agreement; shoochi suru to consent; to agree to; to understand, to know.

shoochoo symbol; symbolism.

shoodaku consent, acceptance; shoodaku suru to consent to; to comply with.

shoodoku disinfection, sterilization; shoodoku suru to disinfect; shoodokúzai disinfectant; antidote.

shoodoo impulse; impetus.

shoofuda price tag; shoofuda tsuki no marked with a price tag; genuine.

shoogai injury, harm.

SHÓOGAI life; lifetime; all one's days; to the end of one's life; shóogai no lifelong; shóogai o owaru to end one's days.

shoogáibutsu obstacle.

SHOOGÁKKOO grade school, elementary school.

shoogaku small sum.

shoogakukin scholarship.

SHOOGATSU New Year; January.

shoogen testimony, evidence; shoogen suru to testify to.

shoogi game of Japanese chess; shoogi o sásu to play chess.

shoogidáoshi falling in rapid succession one after another; shoogidaoshi ni naru to fall forward, one upon another as when a train makes a sudden stop; to fall like ninepins.

SHÓOGO noon, midday.

shóogyoo commerce, trade; shóogyoo no commercial.

shoohai prize cup; medal.

shoohai victory or defeat; shoohai o arasou to contend for victory.

shoohei engagement (for a position); employment; shoohei suru to engage; to employ.

shoohi consumption; spending; shoohi suru to consume; to spend.

shoohin short piece; sketch.

shóohin goods; commodity; shoohínken gift certificate (issued by retail stores); shoohísha consumer.

shoohyoo trademark.

shooji paper sliding door.

shoojíki honesty, uprightness; shoojíki na honest, upright; shoojíki ni honestly, frankly.

shóojin devotion; aspiration; religious purification; abstinence from animal food; vegetable diet; shóojin suru to devote oneself to.

shoojíru See shoozúru.

shóojo young girl; little girl.

shoojoo certificate of merit; honorary certificate.

shoojóo condition of illness; symptom.

shooka digestion; **shooka fúryoo** indigestion; **shooka suru** to digest; **shookáki** digestive organ.

SHOOKAI introduction; recommendation; **shookai suru** to introduce, recommend; **shookáijoo** a letter of introduction; **shookáisha** introducer.

shookai minute explanation.

shookai company, firm.

shookai inquiry, reference; **shookai suru** to inquire.

shookáki fire extinguisher.

shookaku raising to a higher status; **shookaku suru** to be raised to higher ranks.

shookan summons; call to appear; **shookan suru** to summon, call up; **shookánjoo** summons; a written summons.

shookáryoku digestion.

shookasen fireplug, hydrant.

shooken securities; bond.

shooki soberness; **shooki ni káeru** to come to one's senses; **shooki o ushinau** to lose one's senses; to faint.

shookíbo small scale.

shookin prize (in money); **shookin o kakéru** to offer a cash prize.

shookizúku to come to one's senses.

shooko proof, evidence; **shookóhin** evidence (thing).

shookodatéru to prove; to testify.

shookoo brief tranquility; temporary ease.

shookóogyoo commerce and industry.

Shookoo Kaigisho Chamber of Commerce and Industry.

shookyokuteki negative; passive.

shookyuu promotion; **shookyuu suru** to be promoted.

shookyuu raise in wages.

shoomei proof; certification; **shoomei suru** to prove; to certify; **shoomeisho** certificate; **mimoto shoomeisho** identification card (or other document).

shoomei illumination, lighting.

shoomén front; **shoomén kara míru** to take a front view; **shoomen shóototsu** head-on collision.

shoometsu extinction; disappearance; **shoometsu suru** to disappear; to be extinguished.

shóomi net; **shóomi gókiro áru** to weigh five kilograms net.

shoomon bond; deed; **shoomon o ireru** to give bond; to sign a written agreement.

shoomoo consumption; waste; **shoomoo suru** to consume; to waste; to tire out.

shoonen youth, boy; boyhood.

shóoni infant, baby; **shoonika** pediatrics.

shoonin recognition; acknowledgment; witness; surety; **shoonin suru** to recognize; to admit; **shoonin ni tátsu** to be a witness to.

shóonin merchant, trader; **shóonin ni náru** to become a merchant.

shóorai (n.) future; (adj.) **shóorai no** future; prospective.

shoorei encouragement; promotion; **shoorei suru** to encourage; to promote; to urge.

shóori victory, triumph; **shóori o éru** to win a victory.

shooryaku abbreviation, omission; **shooryaku suru** to eliminate; to omit.

shooryoo small quantity.

shoosai details, particulars; **shoosai ni** in detail; **shoosai no** minute, detailed.

shoosan praise; admiration; **shoosan suru** to praise; to admire.

shoosen merchant vessel.

shoosetsu fiction; romance; novel; **shoosetsuka** novelist, novel writer; **shoosetsuteki** fictitious, romantic.

shooshi death by fire.

shooshin promotion, advancement; **shooshin suru** to rise in rank.

shooshin prudence, caution, timidity; **shooshin na** timid, cautious, prudent.

shoosho bond; document; certificate; diploma.

shooshoku light eating; **shooshokuka** light eater.

shóoshoo little, few; in a small degree.

shooshuu calling out; summons; convocation; draft (into military service); **shooshuu suru** to call out; to summon; to assemble.

shoosoku news; **shoosoku o kiku** to hear from; to have news of (someone); **shoosoku ni tsuujiru** to be well informed; **shoosókutsuu** well-informed person.

shoosoo irritation, fretfulness; impatience; **shoosoo suru** to fret; to fidget, be impatient.

shoosui emaciation, haggardness; **shoosui suru** to become emaciated.

shoosúru to call; to name.

shoosúu decimal, fraction; small number; minority; **shoosúu de aru** to be very few.

shóotai true character; **shóotai náku** out of one's senses; **shóotai o arawásu** to reveal one's true character; **shóotai o tsukámu** to get at the bottom of an affair.

shóotai invitation; **shóotai suru** to invite.

shóoten focus; **shóoten o awaséru** to focus; to bring into focus.

shóoten shop, store.

shootoo putting out lights; **shootoo suru** to put out the light; **shootóorei** curfew.

shoototsu collision, crash; conflict; **íken no shoototsu** conflict of opinions; **shoototsu suru** to run into; to collide.

shóou slight rain, drizzle.

shoouíndoo show window.

shóoyo reward; giving a reward; **shóoyo o ataéru** to give a reward.

shooyoo commerce, business; **shooyoo no** commercial; pertaining to business.

SHOOYU soy sauce.

shoozen sadly, sorrowfully; **shoozen to** with a heavy heart, sadly.

shoozoo portrait; likeness; **shoozoo o kakséru** to have one's portrait painted.

shoozúru to produce; to yield; to grow; to arise; to spring up.

shóri management; transaction; treatment; **shóri suru** to manage; to treat.

shoron preface, introduction.

shorui documents, papers.

shosai study, library.

shóseki, HÓN books.

shosen in the end; after all.

shoshin belief, conviction; **shoshin o hireki suru** to express one's belief.

shoshínsha beginner, novice.

shosúru to conduct oneself; to deal with; to condemn, sentence.

shotái household; **shotaidóogu** household necessities; **shotaijimíru** to be sobered down by household cares; **shotáimochi** family person; **shotáimochi ga íi** to be a good housekeeper; **shotáinushi** head of a household.

shotáimen first interview; **shotáimen no hito** a stranger.

SHÓTCHUU (*colloq.*) always; often; all the time. **Shótchuu kaze o hikimásu.** I catch cold often.

shóten bookshop.

shotoku income; earnings; **shotokúzei** income tax.

shotoo elementary.

shou to carry on the back.

shoyoo no necessary, requisite, needed.

shoyuu possession; **shoyuu suru** to have; to possess; **shoyúuchi** one's land; one's estate; **shoyúuhin** belongings; **shoyúuken** property; proprietorship, ownership; **shoyúusha** proprietor.

shozai whereabouts; site, position; situation. **shozai o hakken suru** to discover (someone's) whereabouts; **shozai o kuramásu** to conceal (one's own) whereabouts.

shozáichi site, locality.

shozaifumei no missing.

shozoku one's post, one's attachment; **shozoku no** attached to, belonging to, **shozoku saseru** to attach; to put under the control of.

shozon opinion; view; intention; **shozon o akásu** to tell one's real intention; **shozon o tazunéru** to ask (someone's) opinion about.

shú lord; chief; principal; master; **shú to shite** mainly, chiefly.

shúbi course of an event; **shúbi yoku** successfully; luckily.

shuchoo assertion; maintenance; opinion, **shuchoo o tóosu** to impose one's opinion on someone else; **shuchoo suru** to assert, to maintain; to advocate; to insist upon.

shudai subject, theme.

SHUDAN means, way; measures, steps. **shudan o miidásu** to find the means to; **shudan o tóru** to take means.

shuei guard; **shuei suru** to keep guard.

shuen feast, banquet; cocktail party; **shuen o moyoósu** to hold a cocktail party.

shuen starring, playing the leading part.

SHÚFU housewife.

shúfu capital, metropolis.

shúgei manual arts; handicraft.

shúgi principle; ism; **shúgi o mamóru** to stick to one's principles.

shúgo protection, guard; **shúgo suru** to protect, watch over.

shuhitsu chief editor.

shúisho prospectus.

SHÚJIN master; employer; one's husband.

shujínkoo hero, heroine (in a novel).

shujín'yaku host, hostess.

shúju no various, several, sundry.

shújutsu surgical operation.

shukan subjectivity; subjective view; **shukanteki** subjective.

shukei paymaster; accountant.

shuken sovereignty; **shukénsha** supreme ruler; chief of state.

shukí memorandum, note; **shukí o káku** to make a memorandum of.

shukka outbreak of fire; **shukka suru** to start a fire.

shukke (Buddhist) priest.

shukketsu bleeding, hemorrhage; **shukketsu suru** to bleed; **shukketsu o tomeru** to stop bleeding.

shukkin attendance (at the office); **shukkin suru** to go to work; **shukkínbo** attendance record, time book; **shukkin jíkan** office-going hour.

shukkoo departure of a ship from a port; **shukkoo suru** to sail.

shukoo plan, idea, contrivance; **shukoo o korásu** to devise a plan.

shukoo handiwork, handicraft, manual work.

shukuboo cherished desire.

shukuboo o tassúru to attain a cherished desire.

shukuchoku night duty; **shukuchoku suru** to keep night watch; to be on night duty; **shukuchokúin** person on night duty.

shukudai homework; **shukadai ni suru** to reserve for future discussion; to keep in abeyance.

shukuden congratulatory telegram.

shukufuku blessing; **shukufuku sareta** blessed, happy; **shukufuku suru** to bless.

shukuhai toast (congratulatory cup); **shukuhai o ageru** to drink a toast.

shukuhaku lodging, accommodation; **shukuhaku suru** to put up for the night; to lodge; **shukuhakunín** lodger; **shukuhakúryoo** room and board; lodging charge; hotel bill.

shukujitsu holiday.

shukumei fate, destiny; predestination; **shukumei no** predestined; **shukuméiron** fatalism; **shukumeirón sha** fatalist.

shukún distinguished service; meritorious deeds.

shukusatsuban pocket-sized edition of a book; monthly bound edition of newspapers.

shukúsha residence; lodging house; billet.

shukusha drawing on a small scale.

shukusho one's address; dwelling place, residence.

shukushoo reduction, curtailment; **shukushoo suru** to reduce; to retrench; to curtail.

shukusúru to congratulate.

shukuten celebration; commemoration; **shukuten o ageru** to celebrate.

shukutoo benediction.

shukuzu reduced drawing; reduced copy.

SHÚMI taste; interest; **shúmi no áru** tasteful; **shúmi no nái** tasteless, dull; **shúmi o mótsu** to have taste for; to like.

shumoku items; article.

shun season; **shun no yasai** vegetables in season.

shunin person in charge; responsible official.

shunkan moment, instant; **shunkan ni** in a moment; **shunkan no** momentary, instantaneous.

shunoo brains; soul; leader. **Tanaka-san wa sono jígyoo no shunoo to nátte iru.** Mr. Tanaka is the driving force of that enterprise.

shunretsu na unrelenting; rigorous; drastic.

shuppan publication; **shuppan suru** to publish, issue; **shuppánsha** publisher.

shuppan sailing; **shuppan suru** to sail, to set sail.

shuppatsu departure; starting; **shuppatsu suru** to depart; to leave; to start; **shuppátsuten** starting point.

shuppei dispatch of troops.

shuren dexterity.

shúrui kind, sort, variety; **arayúru shúrui no** all kinds of; **onaji shúrui no** of the same kind.

shuryoku main force; main body.

shuryoo hunting; shooting; **shuryooka** hunter.

shusai sponsorship; **–no shusai de** under the auspices of.

SHÚU week.

shuukyoku end, conclusion; **shuukyoku no** last, final; **shuukyoku o tsugeru** to come to an end.

shuunyuu income; receipts; revenue; **shuunyuu ga óoi** to enjoy a comfortable income.

shuuréssha last train.

shúuri repair; **shúuri suru** to repair, mend.

shuuryoo completion; **shuuryoo suru** to complete the course of.

shuusai genius; talented person.

shuusaku study.

shuusan gathering and dispersion.

shuusánchi distributing center.

shuusei amendment; revision; modification; **shuusei suru** to amend; to revise; to modify; **shuuséian** amendment (to a bill).

shuusen recommendation; mediation; **shuusen suru** to recommend; to mediate.

shuusen end of war; **shuusen ni náru** to come to the end of a war.

shuuséngyoo brokerage; commission agency; **shuusénryoo** commission; brokerage; **shuusenya** broker, commission agent; real estate agency; employment agency.

shuusennin go-between; middleman.

shuushi religion; sect, denomination.

shúushi income and expenditure. **Shúushi ga tsugunawanai.** We cannot make ends meet.

shúushi from beginning to end.

shúushin morality, ethics.

shuushin lifetime; all one's life; **shuushin chóoeki** penal servitude for life; **shuushin káiin** life member.

shuushoku securing employment; **shuushoku suru** to secure a position in an office; to enter into service.

shuushuku contraction, shrinking; **shuushuku suru** to contract; to shrink.

shuushuu collection; **shuushuu suru** to collect; to gather.

shuutai unseemly sight; shameful conduct; scandalous condition; **shuutai o enzúru** to behave disgracefully.

shuuten terminal point.

SHUUTO father-in-law; **SHUUTOME** mother-in-law.

shuutoo na cautious; scrupulous, thorough; **shuutoo na chúui** scrupulous (meticulous) care.

shúuu shower; **shúuu ni áu** to be caught in a shower.

shuuwai acceptance of a bribe; graft; **shuuwai suru** to take a bribe.

shúuya all night; whole night through; **shuuya únten** all-night service (for trolley cars, buses).

shuuyoo culture; cultivation; **shuuyoo o tsumu** to make a constant effort to improve oneself; **shuuyoo suru** to cultivate.

shuuyoo accommodation, reception; **shuuyoo suru** to take in; to quarter.

shuuyóoryoku capacity.

shuuzei collection of taxes; **shuuzei suru** to collect taxes; **shuuzéiri** tax collector.

shuuzen repair; mending; **shuuzen suru** to repair; to mend.

shuwan ability, skill, talent; **shuwan no áru** able, capable, talented.

shuyoo na chief; important; essential.

shúzoku race; family; class.

shuzooka sake-brewer.

soaku na crude, coarse; inferior.

SÓBA buckwheat; dark buckwheat noodles; **kake soba** buckwheat noodles served in soup; **mori soba** buckwheat noodles served with soup but in a separate container.

SÓBA side; neighborhood, proximity; **sóba ni, sóba de** at hand, beside; **sóba no** neighboring.

sobadatéru to prick up one's ears; **mimí o sobadátete kiku** to strain one's ears to listen.

sobiéru to rise; to tower; to soar. **Yamá ga tákaku sobiéru.** The mountain towers.

SÓBO grandmother.

soboku simplicity, artlessness; **soboku na** simple, artless.

sóburi behavior; bearing; manner; **sóburi o suru** to behave oneself; to assume the air of.

sobyoo rough sketch.

sóchi management; disposal; dealing.

SOCHIRA, SOTCHI there; that way.

sodachi breeding, bringing up; **sodachi no warúi** ill-bred; of slow growth; **sodachi no yói** well-bred; of good social background.

SODATÉRU to bring up, raise; to train; **haná o sodatéru** to grow flowers; **kodomo o sodatéru** to bring up a child.

SODÁTSU to grow; to be brought up.

SODE sleeve; **sode ni sugáru** to hang on a person's sleeve; to beg for mercy; **sode o hiku** to pull (someone) by the sleeve.

soen long negligence; **soen ni náru** to neglect to visit.

soéru to add; to affix, attach; **chikará o soéru** to give a person assistance; **kyoo o soéru** to liven up the entertainment.

SÓFU grandfather; **SOFÚBO** grandparents.

sogai check; obstruction, impediment; **sogai suru** to check; to obstruct, impede.

sogeki sniping; **sogeki suru** to aim and shoot; to fire at; to snipe.

sógo discrepancy; disappointment, failure; **sógo suru** to go wrong; to be in disagreement.

sógu to chip; to cut aslant; to diminish, reduce; **kyóomi o sógu** to spoil the pleasure.

sokkenái cold; blunt; dry; curt; **sokkenái áisatsu** curt salutation.

sokki shorthand, stenography; **sokkíroku** shorthand records; stenographic transcript; **sokkísha** stenographer.

sokkin spot cash; **sokkin de haráu** to pay cash.

sokkoojo meteorological station, weather bureau.

SOKKÚRI whole; just as it is; altogether; **jitsubutsu sokkúri** to be true to life.

sokkyóokyoku improvisation (in music).

SOKO that place, there; **soko e** there, to that place; **soko kara** from there; **soko ni, soko de** there, in that place.

soko bottom, depth; sole (shoe); **sokoshirenu** bottomless, unpredictable; **kokoro no soko kara** from the bottom of one's heart.

sokode now; then; thereupon; accordingly.

sokói underlying motive; true intention.

sokoiji spite, malice; **sokoiji no warúi** malicious, spiteful.

sokojíkara latent (potential) energy; reserve of force; **sokojíkara no áru** strong; energetic **sokojíkara no áru kóe** deep (tone of) voice.

sókoku one's native land; **sokokúai** love of the native land.

sokonáu to harm, hurt, injure, damage, spoil, ruin.

sokonuke sáwagi boisterous merrymaking.

sokoo conduct, behavior; **sokoo ga osamaránai** to conduct oneself improperly.

SOKÓRA, SOKORA ÁTARI thereabouts; about there.

soko soko ní hastily, hurriedly.

sokotsu carelessness, heedlessness; **sokotsu na** careless, heedless.

–SOKU counter denoting: pair (for shoes, socks, and stockings); **kutsu issoku** one pair of shoes.

sokubai suru to sell on the spot.

sokubaku restriction, restraint; **sokubaku sareru** to be restricted; **sokubaku suru** to restrict.

sókudo speed, velocity.

sókui accession to the throne.

sókuji at once, immediately.

sokujitsu same day; on the very same day.

sokumen side, flank; **sokumen no** lateral, flanking.

sokúryoku speed, velocity; **sokúryoku o choosetsu suru** to regulate the speed.

sokuryoo land survey; **sokuryoo suru** to measure; to survey; **sokuryóoshi** surveyor.

sokusei rapid completion; quick mastery; **sokusei kóoza** intensive course.

sokuseki footprint.

sokushi instantaneous death; **sokushi suru** to die instantly.

sokushin promotion; acceleration, hastening; **sokushin suru** to promote; to further; **shokúyoku o sokushin suru** to stimulate the appetite.

sokutatsu, sokutatsu yúubin special delivery; **sokutatsu de** by special delivery; **sokutatsu de dásu** to send by special delivery.

sokutei measurement; **sokutei suru** to measure.

sokutoo prompt answer, ready reply; **sokutoo suru** to reply at once.

SÓKUZA NI at once, immediately, instantly.

somaru to be dyed, be colored; to be infected with.

SÓMATSU crudeness, coarseness; **sómatsu na** crude; coarse; poor; **sómatsu ni suru** to treat lightly; to handle roughly.

some dye, dyeing; **some ga yói** to be well dyed, **someko** dyestuff, dye.

someru to dye; to stain.

sometsuke dyeing; printing; blue-and-white porcelain.

SÓMOSOMO in the first place.

somukéru to turn away, avert; **kao o somukéru** to turn one's face away.

SOMÚKU to revolt against; to rise against; to act contrary to; to disobey; to violate; **ryóoshin ni somúku** to go against one's principles.

són loss, damage; disadvantage; **són na** disadvantageous; **són ni náru** to be disadvantageous to; **són o suru** to suffer a loss.

sonaeru to prepare; to provide for; **igen o sonaéru** to possess great dignity;

man'ichi ni sonaéru to prepare for the worst.

sonaéru to offer (to the altar).

sonaetsukéru to provide with; to equip with.

sonawáru to be furnished with, be supplied with.

sonboo existence; life or death fate; **sonboo ni kansúru mondai** a question of life or death; **sonboo ni kansúru** to decide the fate.

sonchoo esteem, respect; appreciation; **sonchoo suru** to esteem, respect.

sónchoo village headman; mayor.

sondai haughtiness, arrogance; **sondai na** arrogant, haughty; **sondai ni kamaéru** to have a haughty bearing.

son'eki profit and loss; loss and gain; **son'eki o keisan suru** to calculate profit and loss.

sonemí jealousy, envy.

sonému to be jealous of; to envy.

songai damage, injury; loss; **songai báishoo** compensation for damages; **songai báishoo o yookyuu suru** to sue for damages; **songai o atáeru** to do damage; **songai o koomúru** to suffer a loss.

sonjíru See **sonzúru**.

sonkai village assembly.

SONKEI respect; high regard; honor; **sonkei suru** to respect, esteem, honor; **sonkei sareru** to be respected.

sonmin villagers.

SONNA that sort of, such; of the kind, of the sort; **sonna hito** such a person; a person like that; **sonna ni** so; in that way; so much; **particularly**.

SONO that, those; **sono ba** that place; **sono ba de** then and there; on the spot; **sono go** after that, afterward; from that time on; **sono go no** later; **sono hen** about, thereabouts; **sonó hoka** besides, beyond, moreover; **sonó hoka no** other, another; **sonó hoka wa** the rest, the others; **sono kóro** around that time; in those days; **sono kóro no** of that time; **sono kuse** and yet, notwithstanding; **sono mama** as it is, in that condition; **sono mama ni shite oku** to leave as it is; **sonó ta** besides, moreover; beyond; **sono te** that trick [that hand]; that device; **sono tóori** just so; exactly in that way; **sono uchi** by and by; by all means; in the meantime; **SONO UE** in addition; moreover. **Sono té wa kuwánu.** None of your games! I'm not so easily cheated. **Sono ue no kotó wa yakusoku dekimasén.** I can't promise any more than that.

sonryoo hire, rent (tools, articles); **sonryóo de kariru** to hire; **sonryóo de kasu** to hire out; to rent out.

sonshitsu loss, damage; disadvantage.

sonshoo injury, damage, casualty; **sonshoo o koomúru** to be damaged; **sonshoo suru** to injure, damage.

sonsúru to exist; to remain.

sóntoku loss and gain, profit and loss; **sóntoku no mondai de wa nái** not to be a question of money.

sonzai existence; **sonzai suru** to exist; to remain.

sonzoku continuance; **sonzoku suru** to continue; to last.

sonzúru to be worn out, be damaged.

SÓO that way; so; idea; **soo iu** that sort of; **soo iu wáke de** for that reason. **Sóo desu.** That is so. **Soo shite kudasái.** Please do so.

sóo thought, conception; **sóo o néru** to meditate, to work on a plan.

sóo bronze; priest, monk.

sóo layer, stratum, seam.

sooan draft; rough cast.

sooba current price; quotation; speculation; **sooba ni té o dásu** to engage in speculation; **soobáshi** speculator.

sooban sooner or later; by and by.

soobétsukai farewell meeting; farewell dinner.

sóochi arrangement, equipment; **sóochi suru** to equip with; to arrange.

sóochoo university president.

soochoo early morning; **soochoo ni** early in the morning.

soochoo na solemn; sublime.

sóoda soda; bicarbonate of soda.

soodai representative; deputy; **soodai ni náru** to represent.

soodan consultation, conference; **soodan no ue** after consultation; **soodan suru** to consult, confer; **soodan ni noru** to take part in a consultation.

soodásui soda water.

sóodoo confusion, disorder; disturbance; **sóodoo o okósu** to raise a disturbance.

soodóoin general mobilization.

soofu sending; **soofu suru** to send; to forward.

soogákari de full force; with a united force; everybody participating.

soogaku musical performance; music.

soogaku total amount. sum total.

soogankyoo binoculars.

soogawa whole leather.

soogei sending off and welcoming (people).

soogi funeral service; **soogi o okonáu** to hold a funeral service; **soogísha, soogiya** undertaker.

sóogi dispute; quarrel; conflict; (labor) strike; **soogidan** strikers.

sóogo reciprocity; **sóogo no** mutual, reciprocal.

soogon grandeur; solemnity; **soogon na** magnificent; grand; solemn.

soogoo looks, features; **soogoo o kuzúshite warau** to smile gleefully; to be radiant with joy.

soogoo synthesis; putting together; **soogoo suru** to put together.

soogoo dáigaku university.

soogyoo start of an enterprise.

soohaku paleness; **soohaku na** deadly pale.

sóohoo both parties; both sides; each side; **sóohoo no** either; both; mutual.

sooi difference, disparity; **–ni sooi nái** must be, it is certain that; **sooi náku** certainly; without fail; **–to sooi suru** to differ; to disagree; to be contrary to.

sóoi new device; novel idea; originality.

SOOJI cleaning; sweeping; **sooji o suru** to clean; to sweep.

soojíshoku general resignation; **soojíshoku o suru** to resign in a body.

sóojite generally; in general; for the most part.

soojuku premature growth, precocity; **soojuku no** precocious.

soojuu management; control; manipulation; **soojuu suru** to manage; to handle; to control; **kikái o soojuu suru** to operate a machine; **otto o soojuu suru** to manage one's husband; **soojúushi** pilot; manipulator.

sookai freshness; exhilaration; **sookai na** refreshing, enlivening; **sookai ni suru** to refresh; to exhilarate, enliven; **sookai ni náru** to be refreshed.

sookai general meeting; general assembly.

sookan first publication (of a new magazine, paper, etc.); **sookángoo** initial number (issue) of a magazine.

sookan deportation; **sookan suru** to send back; to deport.

sookan grand sight.

sookatsu summary; **sookatsu suru** to sum up; to summarize.

SOOKEI total; sum total; **sookei de** in all, as a total; **sookei suru** to sum up; to total.

sooken healthiness; **sooken na** healthy, sound, stout.

sookin remittance; **sookin suru** to remit money; to send money.

sóoko warehouse; **sóoko ni azukéru** to store in a warehouse; **sóoko ni hokan suru** to store.

sookon early marriage.

sookoo manuscript; copy; **sookoo o tsukúru** to draft; to make a draft.

SÓO KOO SURU UCHI NI in the meantime; meanwhile.

sookutsu den, lair; nest; **doroboo no sookútsu** den of thieves.

sookúzure collapse, complete rout. **sookúzure ni náru** to be routed.

sóokyo daring enterprise.

soomei wisdom, sagacity; **soomei na** wise, clearheaded.

sóomen Japanese noodle (popular in summer).

soomoku plants and trees.

soomókuroku general table of contents.

sóomu general affairs; director; manager.

soonan meeting with an accident; mishap. **soonan suru** to meet with an accident; **soonánsha** victim of an accident; **soonan shíngoo** signal of distress.

soonen prime of life.

soonyuu insertion; **sooyuu suru** to insert, put in.

sooon noise, hubbub.

soooo fitness, suitability; **soooo na** appropriate, adequate; **soooo suru** to be suitable, to be fitting.

sooran superintendence, control; **sooran suru** to superintend, manage.

soorei splendor, magnificence; **soorei na** magnificent, splendid.

sooretsu funeral procession.

sooretsu na heroic, tragic; **sooretsu na sáigo o togéru** to die a heroic death.

sooritsu establishment, foundation; institution; organization; **sooritsu suru** to establish, institute, found; **soorítsusha a** founder.

sooron introduction; general remarks; quarrel, dispute; **sooron suru** to quarrel; to argue.

sóoryo priest, monk, bonze.

sooryóoji consul-general; **sooryoojíkan** consulate-general.

sóosa search, investigation; **soosa suru** to search, look for, hunt for.

sóosa process, operation, management.

soosai general manager; president; governor.

soosaku creation; original work; **soosaku suru** to create; to originate; to write an original work; **soosakuka** person of originality; fiction writer; **soosakuteki** creative, original.

soosaku search. investigation; **soosaku suru** to search, to look for, to hunt for; **soosakutai** search party.

soosénkyo general election.

sooshiháinin general manager.

sooshiki funeral; funeral services.

sooshin transmission of a message; telegraphic service.

sooshíngu personal ornaments, furnishings.

SOOSHITE, SOSHITE and then; and in addition.

sooshitsu loss; forfeiture; **sooshitsu suru** to lose; to be lost.

soosho series (of books); collected works.

sooshoku ornamentation, decoration, adornment; **sooshoku no nái** plain, unadorned; **sooshoku suru** to ornament, adorn, decorate.

sooshúunyuu total income.

soosoo early; as soon as possible; without delay.

sóosu Worcestershire sauce.

soosúu total number.

sootaiteki relative; correlative.

sootatsu conveyance; delivery; **sootatsu suru** to send; to forward; to convey.

sootei binding; design; **sootei suru** to bind; to design.

sóoto daring enterprise.

sootoku governor-general; viceroy.

SOOTOO fitness, suitability; **sootoo na, sootoo no** suitable; respectable; reasonable; moderate; considerable; **sootoo ni kurashite iru** to be comfortably off; **sootoo suru** to be fit for.

sootoo sweeping away; **sootoo suru** to sweep away.

soowa episode.

soozái daily dishes.

soozen noisily; uproariously; **soozen to in** a noisy manner.

soozoku succession; inheritance; **soozoku suru** to inherit; to succeed; **záisan o soozoku suru** to inherit an estate.

soozokunin heir, heiress.

soozoo creation; **soozoo suru** to create.

soozoo imagination; fancy; **soozoo ni tómu** imaginative; **soozoo suru** to imagine, fancy; **soozóoryoku** power of imagination.

soozooshíi noisy, full of noise.

sopurano soprano.

SÓRA! there! **Sóra míro!** There! You see! I told you so (*colloq.*)!

SÓRA sky; air; heavens; **sóra de** by heart, by memory; **sóra tákaku** high up in the sky; **sóra de oboéru** to learn by heart; **sóra de yómu** to recite from memory.

soradánomi hoping against hope; vain hope.

sorairo sky-blue, azure.

soramóyoo look of the sky; weather; situation.

sorásu to evade, elude, dodge; to turn aside; to draw off; **hanashí o wakí ni sorásu** to turn the talk away; **mé o sorásu** to look away; to avert one's eyes from; **shitsumon o sorásu** to parry a question.

sorásu to bend, to curve; to turn backward.

sorazorashíi feigned; false; hypocritical;
sorazoráshiku in obvious dissimulation,
hypocritically.

SORE it, that; sore dá kara therefore,
accordingly; sore dake that much, so
much; sore ná noni yet, in spite of that;
sore démo still, yet; sore hodo so
much, so; sore kara and then, after that;
sore máde till that time; sore nára then,
if so; sore ni besides that; sore tómo or
else.

soréru to stray; to glance off.

sorí warp; curve; bend; sorí ga áu to get
along (with each other) very well; sorí ga
awánai not to be on good terms (with
someone).

sorimi straightening oneself up; holding one's
head high; sorimí ni náru to throw back
one's head.

soroban abacus; finance; soroban ga toréru
to pay; to be profitable; soroban o hajíku
to move counters of an abacus; to
calculate. Soroban ga awánai. The
accounts do not square.

soroéru to put in order, arrange in order.

soroi set; suit; sorói mo sorótte without
exception; sorói no of the same pattern,
uniform.

SÓROSORO slowly, gradually; gently.

soróu to become complete; to be arranged in
order; to gather, assemble; to agree, be in
accord.

sóru to bend; to warp; to bend backward. Hi
ni atatte íta ga sorimáshita. The sun has
warped the board.

sóru to shave; kao o sóru to shave oneself.

soryaku roughness; soryaku no rough,
cursory; soryaku ni roughly.

sosei resuscitation; reanimation; revival; sosei
suru to revive, come to life again; sosei
no omoí o suru to feel revived, to feel a
great relief.

soséihin article of inferior quality.

sósen ancestor.

soshaku chewing, mastication; soshaku suru
to chew, masticate.

soshakúchi leased ground.

soshakúken lease.

sóshi obstruction; check, prevention; sóshi
suru to check; to hold in check; to
hinder, impede.

soshiki system; organization; formation;
composition; soshiki suru to form; to
organize; to constitute; soshikiteki
systematic; methodical; soshikiteki ni
suru to systematize.

soshíru to slander; to blame, speak ill of.

SOSHITE See SOOSHITE.

soshitsu predisposition; nature; makings. Anó

hito ni wa shijin no soshitsu ga áru.
He is very poetic. (He has the poet in
him.)

soshoku plain diet; soshoku suru to eat
poorly (live on poor fare).

soshoo lawsuit; action; case; soshoo o okósu
to sue; soshoo suru to sue; to start a
lawsuit; to go to law; soshoonin plaintiff.

sosogu to pour into; to pour on; to water; to
pour (itself) into.

sosokkashíi hasty; careless; heedless;
sosokkashíi kotó o suru to act carelessly;
to make a stupid mistake.

sosonokásu to tempt, entice; to stir up.

sosoru to incite, stir up, to excite.

sossen suru to take the lead; to take the
initiative.

sosui drainage.

SOTCHI, SOCHIRA there; that way.

sotchinoke laying aside; neglecting;
sotchinoke ni suru to neglect; to leave
out in the cold.

sotchoku plainness, frankness, candidness;
sotchoku na simple and honest; sotchoku
ni hanásu to speak frankly.

SÓTO out-of-doors, outside; sóto e iku go
outside.

sotobori outer moat (around Japanese
castles).

sotogawa outer side; outside.

sotoúmi open sea.

sotsu waste; bungling; fault; sotsu ga nái to
be faultless.

sotsugyoo graduation; completion of a course
of study; sotsugyoo suru to complete a
course; to graduate from; sotsugyóosei
graduate, alumnus; sotsugyóo shiki
graduation ceremony; commencement;
sotsugyoo shóosho certificate; diploma.

sotsuu understanding; sotsuu suru to
understand (each other); íshi ga sotsuu
suru to come to a good mutual
understanding.

SOTTO quietly; softly; gently; secretly; sotto
shite oku to leave it as it is.

sottoo fainting; sottoo suru to faint.

sówasowa nervously; restlessly; sowasowa
suru to be restless; to be nervous.

soyógu to rustle; to wave.

soyoo grounding; elementary knowledge;
culture; soyoo ga áru to be well grounded
in.

sóyosoyo to softly, gently (said only of the
blowing of the wind); sóyosoyo fúku
kaze gentle breeze.

sozei taxes; taxation.

sú sandbank; shallow; sú ni noriagéru to run
aground.

sú vinegar.

su nest; den; **su ni tsúku** to brood, incubate; **su o tsukúru** to build a nest.

suashi barefoot; **suashi de** barefoot(ed).

subarashíí splendid, magnificent.

subashikkói, subayái nimble; active, smart; quick-witted.

subayái See subashikkói.

subekkói smooth; slippery; velvety.

suberikómu to slide into; to slip into.

subéru to slide; to slip; to glide.

súbesube shita smooth; velvety.

SÚBETE whole, all; altogether, **súbete no** all; whole; every.

sudare bamboo blind; **sudare o kakéru** to hang a bamboo blind; **sudare o maku** to roll up a bamboo blind.

sude empty hand; **sude de** unarmed, empty-handed.

SÚDENI already.

sudoori passing by without calling. **sudoori suru** to pass by without calling (at someone's house).

SUE end; future; **sue ní wa** in the long run, **sue no** last; final; youngest, **sue no áru wakamono** a promising youth.

suekko youngest son, youngest daughter.

suéru to set, place, lay.

suetsuke fitting up; installation, **suetsuke no** fixed, stationary.

suetsukéru to fit up; to set, place in position.

súgao unpainted face.

sugáru to cling to; to lean on.

súgata form, figure, shape; **súgata o kaeru** to disguise oneself; **súgata o kakúsu** to disappear.

sugenái cold; rough; flat; **sugenáku** coldly, roughly; flatly; **sugenáku kotowáru** to refuse flatly.

sugi cryptomeria; Japanese cedar.

sugíru to pass by; to go too far.

–SUGÍRU suffix denoting: be excessively, do (something) excessively; **omosugiru** to be too heavy; **tabesugíru** to eat excessively.

SUGÓI uncanny, weird; ghastly, lurid; **sugói hikarí** lurid light.

sugósu to pass, spend (time); to take too much.

súgosugo dejectedly; disconsolately; with a heavy heart.

SÚGU soon; immediately; close by; near; **súgu hana no saki ni** just under one's nose; **súgu ni** immediately, instantly.

suguréru to surpass, excel; to be excellent; to be strong.

sugúrete eminently; conspicuously; by far.

súhada bare skin; **súhada ni náru** to bare oneself; **súhada ni kiru** to wear next to the skin.

suhádaka nudity; state of being stark naked; **suhádaka de** stark naked.

súi essence; pith; elegance; fashion; **súi na** fashionable; refined, tasteful; **súi o kikasu** to pardon (someone else's) folly.

súi sour, acid; **súi mo amai mo shirinúita híto** person who has tasted the bitter and the sweet of life.

suiagéru to suck up.

suichoku no perpendicular, vertical.

suichuu (n.) being in the water; **suichuu no** (adj.) underwater; **suichuu ni** (adv.) underwater.

suidásu to suck out.

suiden paddy field, rice field.

SUIDOO water service; waterworks; city water; channel; **suidoo o hiku** to have water pipes laid; to have water supplied; **suidookan** water pipe.

suiei swimming; **suiéigi** bathing suit; **suieijoo** swimming place.

súifu sailor, seaman; **súifu ni náru** to become a sailor.

suigai damage by flood; flood-disaster; **suigáichi** flooded district.

suigen, suigénchi source of a river; fountainhead.

suihei water level; horizon; **suihei no** level, horizontal; **suihei ní** horizontally.

súihei sailor (in the navy); **suihéifuku** seaman's uniform.

suiheisen horizon; sealine; horizontal line.

suihen waterside.

suijaku emaciation, debility; **suijaku suru** to be weakened; to grow weak.

suiji cooking, cookery; **suiji gákari** person in charge of cooking; cook; **suiji suru** to cook; **suijiba** kitchen.

suijóoki vapor, steam.

suijun water level.

suika watermelon.

suikan drunken fellow.

suiki moisture, humidity; dropsy; **suiki no áru** moist, humid; **suiki ga dekíru** to become dropsical.

suikómu to inhale; to draw in; to absorb; to suck in.

suikoo execution; **suikoo suru** to execute, carry out.

suikuchi mouthpiece; cigar holder.

súikyo recommendation; **súikyo ni yotte** through (someone's) recommendation. **súikyo suru** to recommend.

súikyoo drunken frenzy; whim, vagary; **súikyoo de** out of mere pique; just for kicks; **súikyoo na** frenzied with drink.

suimen water surface; **suimen kara ichi méetoru ue** one meter above the water; **suimen ni ukabu** to rise to the surface.

SUIMIN sleep; **suiminbúsoku** want of sleep.
suimon floodgate.
SUIMÓNO soup (Japanese-style); **suimonó wan** soup bowl. (See also **súupu.**)
suinan calamity by water; casualty at sea.
súiri reasoning; induction; **súiri suru** to reason; to induce.
súiro waterway; watercourse.
suiron reasoning; **suiron suru** to reason; to deduce.
suiryoku hydraulic power; **suiryoku dénki** hydroelectricity.
suiryoo guess, conjecture; **suiryoo suru** to guess; to presume; to consider.
suiryoo quantity of water. volume of water.
suiryuu stream; water current.
suisaiga watercolor painting; **suisaigáka** watercolor painter.
suisánbutsu marine products: fish, crabs, lobsters, clams, oysters, seaweeds.
suisángyoo fishery; marine-products industry. (See also **suisánbutsu.**)
suisatsu guess, conjecture; sympathy; **suisatsu suru** to conjecture, to guess, to infer from.
suisenbénjo flush toilet.
suisen recommendation; **suisen suru** to recommend; **suisénjoo** letter of recommendation.
suisen daffodil.
súisha water mill, water wheel.
suishin depth of water.
suishínki propeller; screw.
suishoo recommendation; approval; praise; **suishoo suru** to recommend; to praise.
súishoo crystal; **súishoo no yóo na** crystalline, crystal-like.
suisoku conjecture, supposition; inference; **suisoku suru** to conjecture; to suppose.
suisoo water tank, cistern.
Súisu Switzerland; **Súisu no** (*adj.*) Swiss; **Súisujin** Swiss (person).
suitai decline; decay; **suitai suru** to decline; to decay; to fall.
suítchi switch.
suitei presumption; conclusion; **suitei suru** to presume; to conclude.
suitoo canteen.
suitoo gákari cashier, teller.
suitorígami blotting paper, blotter.
suitóru to suck up; to absorb.
sultsúku to stick fast to, adhere.
suiun transportation by water; **suiun no bén** facilities for transportation by water. **Oosaka wa suiun no bén ga íi desu.** Osaka City has very good facilities for marine transportation.
súiyaku liquid medicine.
suiyoku cold-water bath.

SUIYÓOBI Wednesday.
suizókukan aquarium.
SÚJI line; strips; muscle; sinew, tendon; fiber; plot; source, quarter.
sujigaki plot of a play.
sujimúkai no See **sujimúkoo no.**
sujimúkoo no diagonally opposite; **sujimúkoo no ié** a house diagonally across the street.
sujoo past career; one's past; birth; blood; origin; **sujoo no iyashíi** of low birth; **sujoo no shirenai** of unknown character; **sujoo no yói** of good family; of good birth.
sukáafu scarf.
sukáato skirt.
sukashi watermark; transparency; openwork; **sukashi no** watermarked.
sukasu to look through; to hold to the light; to thin out; to leave an opening.
SUKÉETO skating; pair of skates; **sukéeto o suru** to skate.
sukétchi sketch, sketching; **sukétchi ni iku** to go sketching; **sukétchi suru** to make a sketch.
SUKÍ fondness; love; fancy; taste; **sukí na** (*adj.*) favorite, pet; **sukí ni** as one pleases; at one's pleasure; **sukí ni náru** to become fond of; **sukí ni saseru** to let (someone) do as he or she pleases. **Sukí desu.** I like it.
suki opening; crack; chance, opportunity; leisure; unguarded point; **suki ga nái** to find no chance; **suki o nerau** to watch for a chance.
suki spade, plow.
sukihara empty stomach.
sukíi ski.
sukíkirai likes and dislikes; **sukíkirai no óoi** squeamish; finical, finicky, too particular.
sukima space; crevice; intermission; **sukima náku** leaving no space; compactly.
sukitóoru to be transparent, be clear; **sukitóotta** clear, transparent.
SUKIYAKI Japanese dish of meat and vegetables usually cooked on the table.
sukízuki taste, liking, fondness; matter of taste; **sukízuki ga áru** each to one's own taste. **Sore wa sukízuki desu.** It is a matter of taste.
SUKKÁRI completely, entirely.
sukobúru very, highly, extremely, awfully.
SUKÓSHI little, few, bit; **sukóshi demo** any, even a little; **sukóshi no** a little, a few, slight; **sukóshi mo** not in the least (*used with a negative verb*); **sukoshi zútsu** little by little.
Sukottorándo Scotland; **Sukottorando no**

(*adj.*) Scots; of Scotland;
Sukottorandójin Scot (person).

SUKU become empty; become sparse; aida
ga suku to become separated; té ga suku
to be disengaged. Onaka ga sukimáshita.
I'm hungry. Kono densha wa suite
imásu. This streetcar isn't crowded.

sukui help, rescue, relief, salvation; sukui o
motoméru to ask for help, call for help;
to seek salvation; sukuínushi savior,
deliverer.

sukuidásu to help (someone) out of; to
rescue.

sukumu to be cramped; to be paralyzed with
fear.

SUKUNÁI to be few, little, scanty, scarce.
Shuunyuu ga sukunái desu. Her income
is small.

sukunakaránu not a little; not small;
considerable; much; sukunakaránu
méiwaku considerable inconvenience;
much trouble.

SUKUNAKUTOMO at least, to say the
least.

sukúramu scrimmage; sukúramu o kúmu to
line up for a scrimmage.

sukurfin movie screen.

SUKUU to help, save, rescue; to relieve;
sukuu kotó no dekínai hopeless.

sukuu to scoop, to ladle; to trip up.

súmai dwelling, residence, abode.

sumánai to be sorry for; to have no excuse
for.

sumaséru to bring to an end.

sumáshita affected, stuck-up; indifferent.

SUMÁSU to finish, conclude, get through.
Góhan wa sumashimáshita. We have
finished our meal.

sumásu to clear, to clarify; to look demure,
to be affected.

sumáu to live, dwell.

SUMÍ India ink; ink-stick (cake of ink used
to prepare ink for brush writing); sumí o
súru to rub an ink-stick; sumí o tsukéru
to dip in ink; to smear with ink.

súmi corner, nook; súmi kara súmi made
every nook and corner; súmi ni oku to
put in the corner.

SUMÍ charcoal; sumíya charcoal dealer.

sumika dwelling, residence.

sumikómu to live in an employer's house.

SUMIMASÉN pardon me; I'm sorry.
Sumimasén ga enpitsu o kashite
kudasái. Pardon me—may I borrow your
pencil?

sumíyaka na quick, rapid, swift, speedy,
prompt.

sumízumi all the corners; every nook and
corner. Kono hen wa sumízumi made

shitte imásu. I know every nook and
corner of this neighborhood.

sumoo Japanese wrestling; sumoo o tóru to
wrestle.

SÚMU to reside, live. Kono machi ní súnde
imasu. I live in this town. Dóko ni súnde
imásu ka? Where do you live?

súmu to end; to come to an end.

súmu to become clear (liquid).

sun Japanese inch (corresponds to 1.193
American inches).

SUNA sand; suna de migaku to polish with
sand; suna o máku to scatter sand.

súnao meekness, gentleness; súnao ni
obediently, meekly; súnao na meek,
gentle; súnao ni suru to obey; to be
obedient.

SUNÁWACHI namely, that is to say;
nothing but; neither more nor less;
thereupon.

suné leg; shin; suné ni kizu mótsu mi
someone having a guilty conscience; oya
no suné o kajíru to sponge off one's
parents.

sunéru to be peevish; to sulk; to be in a pet.

súnka moment's leisure; little time to spare;
súnka mo nái to have no time to spare.

su nó mono vinegary dish; vegetables
seasoned with vinegar.

sunpoo measure, dimensions; sunpoo o tóru
to take measurements (for a new suit);
sunpoo no tóori ni according to the
measurements; sunpoogaki measurement,
specification.

Supéin Spain; Supeingo Spanish (language);
Supeinjín Spaniard.

supóotsu sports; supootsubángumi sports
program.

suppádaka nudity, nakedness.

SUPPÁI sour, acid, tart. Kono míruku wa
suppáku nátte imasu. This milk has
turned sour.

suppanúku to expose; to disclose.

suppokásu to leave undone; to neglect.

suppon snapping turtle.

SUPÚUN spoon.

–súra particle denoting: even, so much as.
Kodomo súra shitte imásu. Even a child
knows it.

surarí to shita slender, graceful.

súrasura smoothly; without a hitch.

surechigau to pass by each other.

surekkarashi pert person.

suréru to rub; to graze; to be worn out.

súri pickpocket, cutpurse.

suriherásu to wear down; to wear away.

surikiréru to get worn out; to become
threadbare.

surikómu to rub in.

surímono printed matter; **surímono ni suru** to print.

surimúku to rub off; to chafe.

suríppu slip (woman's undergarment).

súriru thrill.

suritsubúsu to grind down; to rub out of shape; to dissipate one's fortune.

SURU to do; to play; to practice; to make; to change one thing into another; to act as, officiate as. **Suru kotó ga nái desu.** I have nothing to do. **Nihongo no benkyoo o shimáshita.** I have studied Japanese. **Kyóoto e iku kotó ni shimáshita.** I have decided to go to Kyoto. **Anó hito wa kyóoshi o shite imásu.** He is a teacher. **Sore wa sen en shimásu.** It costs one thousand yen.

súru to print; to duplicate. **Meishi o sútte moratái desu.** I would like to have visiting cards printed.

súru to pick (someone's) pocket.

súru to grind, to bray.

súru to rub, to file.

súru to lose one's fortune. **Kabu de okame o surimáshita.** She lost her fortune on the stock market.

surudói sharp, acute, keen, cutting.

SURUTO whereupon, just then; then, well. **Suruto minna de goman en désu ne?** Then the total will be fifty thousand yen, won't it?

susamajíi alarming, dreadful, fearful, terrible.

susamu to grow in intensity or violence; to go to ruin; to grow wild; to be addicted to.

susanda ruined, desolate, dreary. **Susanda seikatsu o shite imásu.** He is living a wild life.

suso skirt (of a dress); bottom (of a mountain); **zubon no suso** trouser cuff.

súsu soot; **susu dárake no** sooty.

susukeru to be stained with soot; **susubóketa, susúketa** smutty.

susugu to rinse; to wash.

susumeru to promote; to advance, put forward; to put on (a watch); **kooshoo o susumeru** to proceed with the negotiations.

susumeru to recommend; to advise, to counsel; to encourage, to present, to offer.

susumu to progress, advance, go forward.

susunde of one's own accord; willingly.

susurináku to sob; to whimper.

susurinaki sobbing; **susurinaki o suru** to sob.

sutáa star (of movies or stage).

sutáato (n.) start (in a sport); **sutáato o kíru** to start.

sutajio studio (for movies, broadcasting).

sutánpu stamp: datemark.

sutareru to fall into disuse; to go out of use or fashion.

sutásuta to quickly, hurriedly.

sutebachi despair; self-abandonment; **sutebachi ni náru** to abandon oneself to despair.

sutebasho dumping ground.

sutéeshon railway station.

sutego deserted child; foundling.

SUTEKI NA splendid, brilliant, fine, remarkable, superb; **SUTEKI NI** exceedingly, remarkably; **suteki na gochisoo** a fine dinner.

sutékki walking stick, cane.

sutemi disregard of one's life; desperation; **sutemi ni náru** to abandon oneself to despair.

sutene bargain price; **sutene no** ridiculously cheap; **sutene de uru** to sell at a sacrifice; to sell dirt cheap.

SUTERU to throw away, abandon; to give up.

suteuri sacrifice sale; a less-than-cost bargain; **suteuri ni suru** to sell at a sacrifice.

sutezérifu menace; parting shot; **sutezérifu o nokósu** to leave with a parting remark.

suto See **sutoráiki.**

sutóobu stove.

sutoráiki, suto strike (walkout of labor).

sutoraiku strike (baseball).

sutóroo (beverage) straw.

SUU to breathe; to inhale; to sip; to absorb; to smoke; **iki o súu** to breathe the air; **tabako o súu** to smoke a cigarette.

súu number, figure; **daitasúu** majority.

SÚU– prefix denoting: several; **suujitsu** several days; **suunin** several persons.

suugaku mathematics; **suugaku no** mathematical; **suugákusha** mathematician.

suuhai worship; adoration; **suuhai suru** to worship, venerate.

SUUJI figure, numeral; **suuji no** numerical; **suujijoo** numerically.

suukoo loftiness, sublimity; **suukoo na** lofty, sublime.

SÚUPU soup (Occidental style); **suupu zara** soup plate. (See also **shíru** and **tsúyu.**)

suusei trend; drift; tendency; tide, current; **yó no suusei ni tomonátte** with the trend of the times.

suwari stability; **suwari ga yói** to sit well; to be stable.

SUWARU to sit; to squat; to be set; **chan to suwaru** to sit straight; **rakú ni suwaru** to sit comfortably.

suyaki unglazed pottery; **suyaki no** unglazed.

súyasuya to quietly, gently, peacefully; **súyasuya to nemuru** to sleep quietly.

súzu tin.

suzu bell, handbell; **suzu no otó** tinkle of a bell; **suzo o narasu** to ring a bell.

suzume sparrow.

suzumí enjoying the cool air; **suzumí ni iku** to go out to cool off.

suzúmu to cool oneself; to enjoy the cool breeze.

suzunari cluster (of fruit); **suzunari ni nátte iru** to hang in clusters.

suzuri ink stone (used in preparing ink for brush-writing) (see also **sumí**); **suzuríbako** ink-stone case.

SUZUSHÍI cool, refreshing; **suzushíi kao o suru** to assume a nonchalant air; to appear calm and unconcerned.

T

tá rice field, paddy field; **tá o tagayásu** to till a rice field; **tá ni mizu o hiku** to irrigate a rice field.

tá others, rest; **tá no** other, another.

tá– prefix denoting: many, much; **tagaku no okane** large amount of money.

TABAKO cigarette; **tabakó ire** cigarette case; **tabako o súu** to smoke a cigarette; **tabakoya** cigar store (stand).

tabanéru to bundle; to tie up in a bundle.

tabeakíru to become tired of (a food).

tabehajiméru to begin to eat.

tabekáta how to eat. **Nihonshoku no tabekáta o setsumei shite kudasái.** Please explain how to eat Japanese food.

TABEMÓNO food; provisions; edibles. **Nani ka tabermóno wa arimásu ka?** Can we get something to eat? **Nihón de wa ómo na tabemóno wa okome désu.** In Japan, rice is the staple food.

TABÉRU to eat; to take; to live on; **gekkyuu de tabéru** to live on the salary; **hitókuchi tabéru** to have a mouthful (of food). **Yooshoku bakari tábete imasu.** I am eating only foreign (Occidental) food.

tabesugí overeating, surfeit.

tabesugíru to overeat.

tabetsukéru to be accustomed to eat. **Chuuka ryóori wa tabetsukéte imasén.** I am not accustomed to Chinese food.

tabezu gírai disliking (a food) without tasting; food prejudice.

tábi (Japanese) socks; **tábi issoku** pair of tabi; **tábi o haku** to put on socks; **tabihádashi** wearing socks but no shoes; **tabihádashi de** in one's socks.

tabí journey; **tabí o suru** to travel; **jínsei no tabí** life's journey.

–tabi times, occasion; **–tabi góto ni** whenever, every time when.

tabikóogyoo local performances (of a theatrical company); road performances.

tabisaki while on journey. **Sono tegami wa tabisaki de uketorimáshita.** I received that letter while I was on a trip.

TABITABI often, many times, repeatedly. **Sono kotó wa tabitabi hanashí ni demáshita.** That subject came up often in our conversation.

taboo being fully occupied with; being busy; **taboo na** busy; **taboo ni torimagíre** on account of the pressure of business; **taboo de áru** to be busy.

TÁBUN perhaps, probably. **Kón'ya tábun kúru deshoo.** He will probably come tonight.

tabun reaching (others') ears; **tabun o habakáru** to be afraid of publicity.

tabyoo being sickly; being weak and feeble.

TÁCHI nature, character, quality, disposition. **táchi no yói** of good quality; **táchi no warúi** of bad quality.

tachiagáru to stand up, rise to one's feet.

tachiai presence, attendance; **–ni tachiai o motoméru** to request (someone's) presence as a witness.

tachiáu to stand by; to fight with; **–ni tachiáu** to attend; **–to tachiáu** to fight with.

tachíban standing on sentry duty; **tachíban o suru** to stand watch; **tachíban o oku** to place a guard.

tachibánashi o suru to talk standing; to stand chattering together.

tachidokoro ni on the spot, instantly. **Tachidokoro ni késshin shimáshita.** He made up his mind in an instant.

tachidomáru to stop short, to halt, stand still; **kyuu ni tachidomáru** to come to a sudden halt.

tachidooshi (n.) standing the whole way. **Ueno máde tachidooshi déshita.** We had to stand the whole way to Ueno.

tachifusagáru to block (someone's) passage.

tachige going (said of a charcoal fire, etc.); being dropped (said of matters); half-burned. **Sono keikaku wa tachige ni narimáshita.** The plan has fallen through.

tachigiki eavesdropping, overhearing; **tachigiki o suru** to eavesdrop.

tachigui eating while standing; **tachigui o suru** to eat standing.

tachigusare dilapidation (of a building); **tachigusare ni náru** to fall into ruin.

tachiíru to enter; to penetrate; to interfere. **Shibafu ni tachiránai de kudasái.** Keep off the grass. **Tachiítta kotó o otazune shimású ga . . .** It might be too personal, but may I ask . . .

tachikí standing tree.

tachikoméru to screen, envelop. **Kasumi ga tachikoméru.** The mist envelops all things.

tachimachi at once; in an instant. **Nihon ni kúru to tachimachi yuumei ni narimáshita.** As soon as he came to Japan, he became prominent.

tachimawáru to go round; to play one's part; to maneuver; **joozú ni tachimawáru** to play one's part well; **zúruku tachimawáru** to act in a cunning way.

tachimí seeing a play from the gallery (from standing room).

tachimukáu to fight against.

tachinaóru to regain one's footing; to recover.

tachinoki removal; vacation; evacuation; **–ni tachinoki o meizúru** to order to vacate; **tachinoki méirei** order for removal; deportation order; an eviction order; **tachinokisaki** refuge.

tachinóku to quit; to leave; to vacate.

tachiokure being late in getting started.

tachiokuréru to be tardy, be behind time.

tachióojoo standstill, deadlock, being kept standing; **tachióojoo o suru** to come to a standstill; to be in a dilemma.

tachisukúmu to stand petrified with fear.

tachiyóru to call at; **–no uchí ni tachiyóru** to drop in.

tachizume being kept standing.

táda merely, only, simply; free of charge.

tadachi ni at once, immediately, directly; without any delay. **Tádachi ni kité kudasái.** Please come immediately.

tadagoto trivial matter; commonplace (thing). **Tadagoto de nái.** It is no trivial matter.

TADÁIMA now, just now; I'm home (greeting); **tadáima no tokoro** for the present; **tadáima de wa** now, nowadays.

tadai no heavy, great; serious; **tadai no songai** heavy loss; **tadai no eikyoo o koomúru** to be seriously affected.

tadanori free ride; stealing a ride.

tadare sore; inflammation; **tadaruer** to break out in sores; to be inflamed.

TÁDASHI however; provided that. **Tádashi kodomo wa hangaku désu.** (But) children are (charged) half-price.

TADASHÍI right, proper.

tadásu to examine, investigate; to inquire into; to question.

todayóu to drift about; to wander; **kao ni ureí o tadayowásete** with a worried look; **namí ni tadayóu fúne** a boat drifting at the mercy of the waves.

tadóoshi transitive verb (one which can take the particle **o**).

tadóru to go on wearily.

taedáe brokenly; feebly, faintly.

taegatái intolerable, unbearable.

taemá break; gap; pause.

taéru to bear; to bear up; **kónku ni taéru** to bear up under privation; **nín ni taéru** to be equal to one's duty; **juunen no shiyoo ni taéru** to be good for ten years.

taéru to become extinct; **onshin ga taéru** to hear nothing from (someone). **Kyookyuu ga táeru.** The supply is cut off.

táezu constantly; **táezu dóryoku suru** to make a constant effort.

tagá hoop; **tagá o hazushite sawaide iru** to go on a spree.

tagaéru to break; to violate; **yakusoku o tagaéru** to break a promise.

tagai ni with one another; with each other; mutually.

tagaku large sum.

tagayásu to till, plow, cultivate; **hatake o tagayásu** to farm; to work on a farm.

tagei varied accomplishments; **tagei na** highly accomplished; **tagei na hito** person of many talents; **tagei no** many-sided.

tagon telling others; **tagon suru** to tell others.

tagui kind, class, sort; **tagui náki** matchless, unique.

tagúru to haul in (hand over hand); to follow up; to trace to its source.

táhata farm; field; cultivated land.

tahóo another side; other side; **tahóo de wa** on the other side; **tahóomen** many directions; many sides; different subjects.

tái opposite; even, equal; versus, against; **ni tai súru** versus, against, toward, to; **sán tai gó no seiseki** a score of 3 to 5; **tai Bei bóoeki** trade with the U.S.A.

tái body, form; **tái o kawasu** to dodge; **tái o nasánai** to be in bad form.

tái party, corps, band; **tái o kúmu** to form in a line, to form a party; **tái o tóku** to disband.

tai– prefix denoting: great, large, grand; general, main, principal; serious; **taínin** important mission; **taiyaku** important task.

–tái suffix denoting: be desirous of, want to do (something). **Tabetái desu.** I want to eat. **Mitái desu.** I want to see it.

taibetsu general classification; **taibetsu suru** to classify roughly.

táibu bulkiness; greater part; **táibu no** voluminous.

táibyoo serious illness.

táida idleness, laziness; **táida na** idle, lazy.

táido attitude; **táido o ippen suru** to change one's attitude completely.

taifúu gale, typhoon.

TAIGAI generally; almost; probably.
Doyóobi wa taigai uchi ni imásu. I am usually at home on Saturdays.

taigaku, taikoo leaving school.

taigan opposite force, great army.

taigen, taigen sóogo bragging, boasting; **taigen sóogo o suru** to boast.

táigi toil, exertion, labor; **taigi sóoni** languidly; **táigi desu** to feel tired.

táigo ranks; **táigo o midáshite** in confusion.

táigotettei spiritual awakening.

taigun large crowd (herd, flock, school, etc.); **kujira no taigun** large school of whales.

taigun large force, great army.

taiguu treatment; service; rating; **taiguu ga warúi** to treat coldly; to be paid poorly; **taiguu ga yói** to treat well, be hospitable, pay well.

taigyoo slow-down strike.

taihai crushing defeat; **taihai suru** to meet with a crushing defeat.

taihai decay, corruption; **taihai suru** to be ruined.

taihan great part.

taihei peace, tranquility.

TAIHÉIYOO Pacific Ocean.

TAIHEN very, extremely, remarkably; **taihen na** serious, dreadful; innumerable; **taihen ni** very. **Taihen omoshirói desu.** It is very interesting.

táiho arrest; apprehension; **taihójoo** warrant of arrest.

táiho deterioration; retrogression, going backward.

taihoo gun; cannon; **taihoo o útsu** to fire a gun.

táii general idea; résumé; outline.

táii abdication.

táiiku physical education.

taiin suru to be released from (leave) a hospital.

taiji subjugation; wiping out; control.

taijoo leaving, exit; **–ni taijoo o meizúru** to order (a person) out of the room; **taijoo suru** to leave.

taijuu weight (of the body); **taijuu ga masu** to gain weight.

táika authority, distinguished person (in any circle; i.e., master painter, great musician, eminent scholar, etc.).

táika great fire.

taika degeneration.

taika fireproof; **taika kénchiku** fireproof building.

taikai withdrawal of membership (from an association or society).

taikaku, taiku physique; **taikaku kénsa** physical examination.

taikan high official.

taikánshiki coronation.

taika rénga firebrick.

taikei system; **taikei o tatéru** to systematize.

taiken personal experience; **taiken suru** to experience.

taiketsu conformation; **–to … to a taiketsu saseru** to confront (someone) with (another).

táiki standing by; being ready; **táiki no shisei** in a position of readiness.

táiki atmosphere.

taikin large sum of money.

taiko drum.

taikobara potbelly, paunch, bay window.

taikoo opposition; rivalry, confrontation; **taikoo úndoo** a countermovement; **taikoo suru** to oppose; to face; to counteract; **taikóosaku** counterplan, countermeasures; **taikóosha** rival, antagonist.

taikoo fundamental principle, code.

taikoo See **taigaku.**

táiku See **taikaku.**

taikutsu ennui; dullness; **–ni taikutsu suru** to be bored; to become weary of; **taikutsu saseru** to bore.

taikyaku retreat; **taikyaku suru** to retreat.

táikyo, taishutsu leaving, quitting; **táikyo suru** to leave, quit; **taikyo méirei o dásu** to issue an order for departure.

taikyoku general state; general situation; **taikyoku ni mé o tsukéru** to take a large view of things.

taikyoo leaving the capital.

taikyúuryoku durability; endurance.

taiman negligence.

taimen dignity, honor, reputation; **–no taimen o sonjíru** to bring disgrace on; **taimen o omonzúru** to have a sense of honor; to make much of one's dignity; **taimen o tamótsu** to keep one's reputation.

taimen interview, meeting; **taimen suru** to interview, to meet.

taimoo great ambition; **taimoo o idáku** to harbor an ambition.

tainin important mission; **tainin o hatásu** to carry out an important mission.

tainoo nonpayment; **tainoo suru** to be delinquent in payment; **tainookin** arrears; **tainóosha** delinquent payer.

taion body temperature; **taion o hakáru** to

take the (body) temperature; **taiónki** clinical thermometer.

taipísuto typist.

taipuráitaa typewriter.

taira evenness; level; flatness; **taira na** flat; **taira ni suru** to level, flatten.

tairagéru to subdue; to subjugate.

tairiku continent; **tairiku no** continental.

tairitsu opposition; rivalry.

tairyaku outline; summary; **tairyaku o nobéru** to give an outline.

tairyoo large quantity; **tairyoo séisan** mass production.

tairyoo big catch (of fish).

tálsa great difference; **táisa o shoojíru** to make a great difference; **táisa ga áru** there is a great difference.

taisai grand festival; great fete.

taisan dispersion; **taisan saseru** to break up; **taisan suru** to take flight; to be dispersed.

taisei structure; system; organization; trend of affairs; general situation; **sékai no taisei** international situation; **taisei ni tsuujíru** to be conversant with the trend.

taisei completion, accomplishment; **taisei suru** to complete.

TAISÉIYOO Atlantic Ocean.

taiseki accumulation; heap; **taiseki suru** to accumulate.

taisen great war; **Dái niji sekai táisen** World War II.

TAISETSU NA important, precious. **Hakkíri káku kotó ga taisetsu désu.** It is important to write clearly. **Taisetsu ni shite kudasái.** Please take good care of it.

taishaku loan; **taishakuhyoo** balance sheet.

taishíkan embassy; **taishikán'in** embassy attaché.

taishin kénchiku earthquake-proof building.

táishita great; important; remarkable.

táishite very, greatly; importantly; remarkably (used with negative expressions).

taishitsu physical constitution.

taishoku gluttony; **taishoku no** gluttonous, greedy; **taishoku suru** to eat (too) much.

taishoku resignation; **taishoku téate** retirement allowance; **-o taishoku suru** to resign from an office; to retire from service.

taishoo object.

táishoo title of the highest officers of the army and navy; general; admiral; leader; head.

taishuka heavy drinker.

taishutsu leaving; **taishutsu suru** to leave, retire from. (See also **táikyo.**)

TÁISOO very; exceedingly; many; much. **Taisoo omosirói shibai desu.** It is an exceedingly enjoyable play.

TAISOO physical exercise, gymnastics; **taisoo o suru** to exercise.

taisúru to front; to oppose; to be opposite to; to correspond to.

TAITEI generally; usually; mostly; **taitei no hitó** most people. **Taitei wa arukimásu.** Usually I walk. **Nichiyóobi wa taitei uchi ni imásu.** Generally I stay at home on Sundays.

taiteki powerful enemy. **Yudan taiteki.** False security is a great foe.

taitoku suru to master; to comprehend.

taitoo equality, equal footing; **taitoo ni** on equal terms; **taitoo no** equal.

táitoru title.

táiu heavy rain, downpour.

taiwa dialogue; conversation; **to taiwa suru** talk with.

TAIWAN Formosa; **Taiwán no** Formosan.

taiya tire.

taiyaku important task; heavy role.

taiyoo summary; general principle; résumé.

taiyoo ocean; **taiyoo no** oceanic.

TAIYOO sun; **taiyóoreki** the solar calendar; Gregorian calendar.

taizai stay; **taizai suru** to stay.

taizen calmness, composure; **taizen to shite** calmly, composedly.

tájitsu one day in the future; some day.

tajoo na amorous; wanton; of loose morals.

takabúru to be proud; to be haughty; to hold up one's head.

takadai height; upland.

takadáka at the height; **takadáka to** aloft, proudly.

takai another world; **takai suru** to die.

TAKÁI high, tall; **takái tatémono** tall building; **takái yamá** tall mountain. **Nedan ga takái.** The price is high.

takafbiki loud snore.

takamáru to rise; to swell; to be raised.

takara treasure.

takaru to swarm; to gather, assemble; to crowd.

tákasa height.

takatobi high jump; running away; **takatobi suru** to run away (to avoid).

takawárai loud laugh; ringing laughter.

take bamboo.

také length; measure; height; **také ga takái** to be tall.

takenawa being at its height, being in full swing.

taki waterfall.

takibi bonfire; wood fire; **takibi o suru** to make a fire.

takidashi boiling rice for sufferers in an emergency.

takimono fuel; firewood.

takitsuke kindling wood; **takitsukéru** to light, kindle; **kenka o takitsukéru** to fan a quarrel; to incite; **sutóobu ni hí o takitsukéru** to make a fire in the stove.

tákkuru tackle; **tákkuru suru** to tackle.

táko kite; **táko o ageru** to fly a kite.

takokujín foreigner.

TAKU to boil rice.

takuchi house lot; residential land.

takuetsu excellence; superiority; **takuetsu suru** to be distinguished, exceed in.

takuhatsu religious begging.

takujisho day nursery.

takujoo denwa desk telephone.

takumashii robust, strong

takumi skill, adroitness, cleverness; **takumi na** skillful, dexterous.

takurámu to scheme, plan; to play a trick; to design, devise; to invent; **muhon o takurámu** to conspire.

TAKUSAN much, many, a lot; **takusán no** numerous. **Moo takusán desu.** No, thank you (I've had enough). **Takusan tabemáshita.** I ate a lot.

takusetsu excellent opinion; enlightened views.

TÁKUSHII taxicab.

takusúru to trust; to entrust.

takuwae store, reserve, savings; **issen no takuwae mo nái** to have not a penny saved.

takuwaéru to save, amass, lay by, hoard; **hige o takuwaéru** to wear a mustache; **kane o takuwaéru** to save money.

tamá ball; globe; bead; jewel; **tamá no áse** beads of perspiration; **mé no tamá** eyeball; **teppoo no tamá** bullets; **tamá o nagéru** to throw a ball.

TAMA rare; seldom, not often; **tama ni** rarely, once in a while.

TAMÁGO egg; **tamágo no kimi** yolk of an egg; **tamágo no shiromi** white of an egg; **tamágo o káesu** to hatch an egg.

TAMANEGI onion.

tamaranai to be unbearable; cannot help; be dying for.

tamari pool; waiting room.

tamarimizu stagnant water.

tamaru to collect, accumulate, gather; **haraí ga tamaru** to be in arrears; **shakkín ga tamaru** to run up debts.

támashii soul; spirit; **támashii o ubáu** to enchant.

tamatama by chance. **Tamatama káre wa byooki déshita.** It so happened that he was ill.

tamátsuki billiards.

tamázan calculation on the **soroban** (an abacus).

TAMÉ benefit; consequence; aim; reason; for the purpose of; for the sake of; because of; **hoomon shita táme ni** as a result of his visit; **tamé ni naránai** to be of no good; **tamé ni náru** to do good.

tameíke irrigation pond; reservoir.

tameíki sigh; **tameíki o tsúku** to heave a sigh.

tameráu to hesitate, waver.

tameru to save, put by, store; to accumulate, collect.

tameshi experiment; attempt; **tameshí ni** by way of experiment.

tameshí example, precedent. **Sonna tameshí wa nai.** There is no precedent for this.

TAMÉSU to try, attempt; to make a trial of; to put to the test; **yúuki o tamésu** to put one's courage to test.

tamoto sleeve of Japanese dress; foot; **hashi no tamoto** foot of a bridge.

tan phlegm; **tan of háku** to expectorate; to spit out.

–tan measure of land (about .245 acres); roll of cloth (about 12 yards).

TANA shelf, rack; **jibun no kotó wa tana ni ageru** to criticize others without recognizing one's own defects; **tana ni ageru** to put up on a shelf.

tanagókoro palm of the hand.

tanako tenant.

tanaoroshi inventory; stock-taking; fault-finding; **tanaoroshi suru** to take stock; to pick holes in (someone else's) character.

tanazarashi shopworn merchandise; secondhand merchandise; **tanazarashi ni náru** to be shopworn.

tanbo field, rice field.

tanchoo monotony, lack of variety; **tanchoo na** monotonous, dull.

tandoku being by oneself; **tandoku hikóo** solo flight.

táne seed; stone or pit of a fruit; breed; child; cause, sources; secret of a trick; **táne o máku, tanémaki o suru** to sow (seeds); **námida no táne** source of grief.

taneábura seed oil, rape-oil (used in cooking).

tanegire being incapable of supplying something, being exhausted; **tanegire ni náru** to run short of (something).

tanen many years.

tangan entreaty, supplication, petition; **tangan suru** to entreat, supplicate, petition; appeal.

tán'i unit.

tani, tanima valley.

tanigawa stream running through a valley.

tanin stranger; (other) person.

tanin gyóogi standing on ceremony. **Tanin gyóogi ni naránaide kudasái.** Please don't stand on ceremony.

tanisoko bottom of a valley.

tan'itsu singleness; **tan'itsu no** single, sole, simple.

tan'itsuka unification.

TANJÓO birth; **tanjóo o iwáu** to celebrate a birth; **tanjóo suru** to be born; **TANJÓOBI** birthday.

tanjun simplicity, plainness; **tanjun na** simple, naïve, unsophisticated.

tanjuu pistol; revolver.

tánka, wáka Japanese verse of 31 syllables.

tanken exploration; expedition; **tanken suru** to explore; **tankenryokoo** an expedition.

tánki quick temper; **tánki na** irritable, quick-tempered; **tánki ni okósu** to become impatient.

tankoo coal mine; **tankóofu** coal miner.

tankoobon separate volume; **tankoobon to shite shuppan suru** to publish in book form.

tánmei short life, early death.

tanmono cloth, piece goods, drapery.

tannin charge, duty; **tannin suru** to take charge of.

tanomí request; solicitation; reliance; **-o hito no tanomí de suru** to do something at the request of (someone else); **tánomi ni naránai** to be unreliable.

tanomoshíi reliable, trusty; **sue tanomoshíi wakamono** a promising youngster.

TANÓMU to ask; to beg, to desire; to trust to; to rely on (someone to do something); **isha o tanómu** to call a doctor; **kodomo o tanómu** to entrust someone with the care of a child. **Yamada-san ni tanónde kudasái.** Please ask Mr. Yamada to do it.

TANOSHÍI to be pleasaant, delightful, enjoyable.

tanoshími pleasure, enjoyment, amusement.

tanoshímu to take pleasure in; to enjoy oneself; to amuse oneself with; **jínsei o tanoshímu** to enjoy life.

tánpaku quality of being simple; frankness; **tánpaku na** simple, unaffected, plain (as a diet).

tanpen short piece; **tanpen shóosetsu** short story.

tanrei na graceful.

tánren temper; forge; training; **seinen no íshi o tánren suru** to train the mind of a young person; **tetsu o tánren suru** to temper metal; **tánren suru** to temper; to forge; to train.

tansei sigh; groan; lamentation; **tansei o morásu** to lament; to sigh deeply.

TANSHIN alone.

tánsho weak point or defect (in personality); **tánsho o ogináu** to remedy a defect; **-ga tánsho de áru** –is one's weak point.

tanshootoo searchlight.

tanshuku shortening, curtailment; **tanshuku suru** to shorten, cut off.

TANSU Japanese-style chest of drawers.

tantei detective, undercover person; **himitsu tántei** private detective; **tantei shóosetsu** detective story.

tantóo dagger.

tantoo suru to take charge of.

tanzúru to lament, deplore; to regret.

taoréru to fall; to fall down, tumble down; **taóreta ié** tumble-down house; **taorekakátta ginkoo** insecure financial institution.

TÁORU towel.

taósu to throw down; to bring down; to beat; **kí o kiritaósu** to fell a tree; **shakkín o taósu** to fail to pay a debt.

tappitsu elegant penmanship.

TAPPÚRI much, great deal, plentifully, full. **Go fiito tappúri aru.** It is a good five feet.

–tara suffix denoting; if, when, in case; **áme ga futtára** if (in case) it rains; **Yamada-san ga kitára** if Mr. Yamada should come.

tarásu to drop; to let drop; to dribble; to let fall; to hang down; to suspend; **makú o tarásu** to hang a curtain; **yodare o tarásu** to drool; **yuka e mizu o tarásu** to spill water on the floor.

tarazu not enough, insufficient, short of; **ni man en tárazu de** for less than 20,000 yen.

taréru to drip, trickle down, fall in drops. **Amadare ga nokí kara taréru.** The rain drops from the eaves. **Kí no eda ga hikúku tárete iru.** The branches of the tree are drooping low.

tariru, taru to be enough, be sufficient; **shinrai surú ni tariru** to be worthy; to be trusted.

taru barrel, cask.

tarumu to become slack, loose, lax. **Nawá ga tarunde imásu.** The rope is slackening.

tasatsu murder.

TÁSHIKA if I remember right; **táshika na** certain, sure. **Táshika desu.** It is certain. **Táshika soo iimáshita.** I think (I'm pretty sure) he said so.

tashikaméru to make certain, authenticate, verify.

tashimae supply, complement, supplement.

tashinami circumspection; self-control; accomplishments secretly enjoyed; **tashinami ga nái** lack of self-control. **Anó hito wa é no tashinami ga áru.** She can paint.

TASHOO more or less; in some measure, a little; somewhat. **Tashoo no chigai wa áru deshoo.** There will be some difference, but not much.

tasogare evening, twilight.

TASSHA healthiness; **tassha na** healthy, strong; **tassha ni kurasu** to enjoy vigorous health; **tassha ni náru** to get well. **Otassha désu ka?** Are you well?

tassúru to reach, arrive at, get to, attain; **mokutékichi ni tassúru** to arrive at a destination; **sen en ni tassúru** to run into 1000 yen.

TASU to add; **ní ni san o tasu** two plus three; **moo sukóshi mizu o tasu** to add a little more water.

tasukáru to be saved, be rescued; to be of help; **fushigi ni tasukáru** to have a miraculous escape; **taihen tasukáru** to be greatly relieved.

tasuke salvation; preservation; deliverance; succor, help, aid, assistance; **kámi no tasuke** help from God; **tasukébune** lifeboat.

TASUKÉRU to help, aid, assist; to reinforce; **komátte iru hitó o tasukéru** to help a person in need.

tasúu large number, majority; **tasúu no** many; **tasúu o shiméru** to command a majority; **tasúuketsu** decision by the majority.

tataeru to fill up to the brim; to be brimful; **mizu o óke ni tataeru** to fill the tub with water.

tatakau to fight with; to fight against; to fight a battle; **yuuwaku to tatakau** to struggle with temptation.

tataki striking, beating, pounding, chopping fine; concrete; **tataki no iké** concrete-lined pool.

tatakiáu to scuffle.

tatakifuséru to knock down.

tatakikómu to strike into; to train hard.

tatakikowásu to knock to pieces.

tatakinomésu to knock down.

tatakiotósu to strike (fruit) from a tree; to attack (someone) so violently that s(he) is obliged to resign her/his post.

tatakitsukéru to throw a thing against something; to throw to.

TATÁKU to strike, beat, hit; to knock; **taiko o tatáku** to beat a drum; **to o tatáku** to tap at the door.

TATAMI floor mat made of rice straw tightly bound together and covered on the upper surface with matting; **tatami o shiku** to lay down a **tatami.**

TATAMU to fold; to shut up; to wind up; to do away with; **ié o tatamu** to shut up one's house; **kamí o yottsú ni tatamu** to fold a paper into four.

tatari evil consequence.

tataru to bring evil upon, to cast an evil spell on; to inflict a calamity on.

táte shield; **–ni táte o tsuku** to set oneself against, oppose, defy (someone).

TÁTE length; height; **táte no** lengthwise.

–tate suffix denoting: just; fresh from; **takitate** just boiled; **kitate** just arrived; **dekitate** just completed.

tatéfuda sign, signboard.

tatégu furnishings (of a house); fixture. **tatégu o ireru** to furnish a house.

tateguya shop where house furnishings are made and sold.

tatekae defraying the expense for another person; **tatekaékin** the sum defrayed temporarily for another person; advance (payment).

tatekakeru to rest, stand, lean, set, place something against.

tatekomoru to shut oneself up, confine oneself, remain in seclusion.

tatekómu to be crowded (with people); to be pressed with business; to be crowded with buildings; **shigoto ga tatekónde iru** to be pressed (with business.)

tatemae ceremony of putting the framework (in a Japanese house or other building).

tatemáe principle; policy; rule; **–o tatemáe to suru** to make a point of.

tatemashi extension of a building.

TATÉMONO building, house. **Nihonshiki no tatemono ni súnde imásu.** I live in a Japanese-style house.

tatenaosu to build again; to reconstruct.

TATÉRU to build, construct, erect, set up; to shut, close; **hatá o tatéru** to hoist a flag; **ié o tatéru** to build a house; **kinénhi o tatéru** to erect a monument; **to o tatéru** to shut the door.

tatétsubo floor space of a building. **Kono uchí wa tatétsubo ga hyakú tsubo áru.** The floor space of this house is 100 **tsubo** (**tsubo**: about 6 feet by 6 feet).

tatetsuke opening and shutting of doors and windows. **Kono uchí wa tatetsuke ga yói.** The doors and windows of this house open and shut smoothly.

táteyoko length and breadth; lengthwise and crosswise.

TATOE even if, even though; **tatoe dónna**

kotó ga átte mo whatever may happen; tatoe joodan ni mo sévo even in jest.

tatoé simile, metaphor, example; tatoé ni iu yóoni as the saying goes.

TATÓEBA for instance, for example.

tatoéru to compare; to give an example.

tatoogami folding paper-case; portfolio; tissue handkerchief.

TÁTSU to sever, cut off; to chop off; to break; futatsú ni tátsu to cut in two; sake o tátsu to abstain from sake.

TÁTSU to stand up, to rise, to get on one's feet; to leave; asu Tookyoo o tátsu to leave Tokyo tomorrow; séki o tatsu to leave the seat. Kemuri ga tátsu. The smoke rises.

tatsujin master; expert; one who is adept; yumi no tatsujin archery expert.

tatsumaki waterspout, sand pillar.

TATTA only, merely; tatta íma just now, a moment ago.

tatte earnestly; tatte no negái earnest request.

tattóbu to value; to set a value on.

tattói noble, august, high (in rank); valuable.

taue rice transplantation; taue doki the rice-planting season; taué uta the rice-planting song; taue o suru to transplant rice.

tawagoto silly talk, nonsense.

tawainái easy; innocent; droll.

tawamuréru to play; to frolic; to jest; to dally; onná ni tawamuréru to flirt with a woman.

tawara straw bag for rice; bale.

tawashi scrubbing brush.

tayásu to exterminate; to eradicate; to put an end to.

TAYASÚI easy, simple. Tayasúi goyóo desu. It's an easy thing. I'll be glad to do it for you.

tayoo pressure of business; many things to do.

táyori intelligence, news, tidings; letter; táyori ga nái to hear nothing from; táyori o suru to write a letter.

táyori reliance, dependence; táyori to náru hitó one's second self, a reliable person.

tayóru to rely on, depend on.

tayúmu to flag, slacken one's efforts, relax one's attention.

tazei great number.

tazuna rein, bridle; tazuna o shiméru to tighten the reins; tazuna o yuruméru to slacken the reins.

TAZUNERU to look for, search for, hunt for; ask; ánpi o tazunéru to inquire after a person; michi o tazunéru to ask the way to.

TÉ hand; arm; paw; helping hand, possession; handwriting; means, way, trick; hand (in card-playing); té ga aite iru to be free; to have no work on hand; té ga tarinai to be shorthanded.

–te suffix denoting; one who performs; direction; kamite upper part; shimote lower part; yarite clever fellow, cunning fellow; yomite one who reads.

teaká dirt from the hands; teaká ga tsukú to become soiled from handling.

tearai rough, violent; tearai kotó o suru to act violently.

TEÁRAI, OTEÁRAI toilet, bathroom.

téashi hand and foot. Watakushi no téashi to nátte hataraite kuremáshita. He was my right-hand man.

teatari shídai ni at random.

téate recompense; allowance; medical care; rinji téate temporary allowance; kizu no téate o suru to dress a wound; téate o dásu to give an allowance.

teatsui hospitable; courteous.

tebánashi de with the hands free; openly; broadly; kodomo o tebánshi de asobaseru to leave children by themselves; tebánashi de jiténsha ni noru to ride a bicycle without using the handlebars.

tebanásu to let go of, release.

tebáyaku quickly, rapidly.

tebikáe note, memo.

tebikaéru to withhold from, hold off (buying goods, etc.).

tébiki leading another by the hand to show the way; guidance; guidebook; Yamada-san no tébiki de through Mr. Yamada's good offices.

tebiroi wide, roomy; on a large scale; tebiróku shóobai o suru to carry on a large trade, do a big business.

tebúkuro gloves; tebúkuro o hameru to put on gloves.

tebura empty hands; naked fist; tubura de hoomon suru to call on (someone) without bringing a present.

téburi gesture; customs.

tebúsoku too short of helping hands.

techígai something amiss, something wrong; techígai ni náru to go wrong.

techoo notebook, memorandum book.

tédashi meddling; interference; tédashi o suru to poke one's nose into.

tedásuke aid, assistance; tedásuke ni náru to be of help to.

tédate means, measures, steps; method.

tedori net receipts; tedori juuman en to receive 100,000 yen net.

TEEBURU table (Occidental).

téepu tape; **téepu rekóodaa** tape recorder.

tefuki hand towel.

tegai no self-sustained, self-fed; **tegai no inú ni té o kamaréru** to be bitten by a pet dog; to be betrayed by a favorite person.

tegákari hold; clue, trace; **tegákari o éru** to find a clue to.

tegakéru to engage in; to have experience in; to bring up.

TEGAMI letter, note, correspondence; **tegami o dásu** to send a letter, write to; **tegami o morau** to receive a letter.

tegará merit; achievement, distinguished service.

tegaru na easy (not difficult) to do; **tegaru na shokuji** light meal; **tegaru ni hoomon suru** to make an informal call.

tegata draft, bill, note; sign; **hyakuman en no tegata** draft for one million yen; **yakusoku tégata** promissory note.

tegatái safe; steady and honest; reliable; prudent; of good reputation (said of a shop).

tegáwari substitute. **Watakushi wa tegáwari o sagashite imásu.** I am looking for someone to relieve me. I am looking for someone to take my place.

tegiwa workmanship, skill (in doing or making); **tegiwa yóku** cleverly, skillfully; **tegiwa ga waríi** unskillful.

tegókoro discretion, consideration; **tegókoro o kuwaeru** to use one's discretion.

tegore handy; convenient; moderate (in price or size); just right. **Tegoro na uchí ga mitsukarimáshita.** We've found a house just right for us.

tegótae reaction, response; resistance; **tegótae ga áru** to be responsive; to be effective.

tegowái strong; handy.

tehái arrangement.

tehájime beginning; **tehájime ni** first, to begin with; **tehájime no** opening, first.

téhazu order, arrangement, plan; **téhazu o suru** to make arrangements.

tehódoki rudimentary lesson.

tehón model, pattern.

téi appearance, style; **téi yoku kotowáru** to decline politely.

teiboo dike; bank, embankment.

teichi lowland, low ground.

teiden power failure.

téido degree, standard, measure, extent; **téido no takái** of high standard; **téido móndai** a question of degree.

TEIEN formal garden.

teigi definition.

téigi proposal; **téigi suru** to propose.

teihaku anchorage, mooring; **teihaku chuu**

no fúne vessels in the harbor; **teihaku suru** to be at anchor.

teihyoo settled opinion; reputation; **–tó no teihyoo ga áru** to have the reputation of.

teiin regular staff; capacity (of a car); quorum.

teijuu suru to live (at a permanent address).

teika fixed price, list price; **teikahyoo** price list.

teika suru to grow worse, deteriorate.

teikei cooperation; **teikei suru** to join hands with; to act in concert with.

teiken definite view, fixed opinion.

teiketsu conclusion, contract; **shakkan o teiketsu suru** to arrange a loan.

téiki fixed (regular) time, definite period, time; **teiki joosháken** season ticket; commutation ticket; **teiki kankóobutsu** periodical; **téiki ni** periodically.

teikíatsu low atmospheric pressure.

teikoku fixed time, appointed time.

téikoku empire; **téikoku no** imperial.

teikoo resistance, opposition; **–ni teikoo suru** to resist, oppose, fight.

teikyoo offer; **teikyoo suru** to offer; to put at (someone's) disposal.

teikyuu, ténisu tennis; **teikyuu o suru** to play tennis.

teikyuu na low; cheap; vulgar.

teikyúubi periodic holiday observed by stores.

TÉINEI NA polite, courteous; careful, scrupulous. **Téinei na táido de hanashimáshita.** He spoke very courteously. **Teinei na shigoto o shimáshita.** He did a very careful job.

teinen retirement age.

teinoo feeblemindedness, imbecility; **teinóoji** imbecile child, idiot.

teíppai one's utmost.

teiraku fall; depression; **teiraku suru** to fall, go down.

teiré care; keeping; repairing; trimming (a garden); **teire no ikitodóita uchi** carefully kept house; **tieré o suru** to repair, to renovate.

téiri low rate of interest.

teiryoo fixed quantity.

TEIRYUUJOO bus stop, streetcar stop.

teisai appearance, show; style; **teisai o tsukúru** to keep up appearances; **teisai ga yói** pleasing in appearance.

teisatsu reconnaissance.

teisei correction; revision; **teisei suru** to correct, revise.

teisetsu faithfulness, constancy, devotion.

teisha stopping a vehicle (car, train, etc.); **hijoo teisha** emergency stop; **teisha suru** to stop at; **teisha o meizuru** to order a vehicle to stop.

teishaba, teishajoo, ÉKI railway station.

teishi stop, stoppage, suspension; **shiharai o teishi suru** to suspend payment; to stop payment.

teishoku regular occupation.

teishoo discourse; lecture.

téishu head of a family; husband; innkeeper.

teishuku virtue; **teishuku na** virtuous and refined (woman).

teishutsu presentation (in the formal, official sense); **teishutsúsha** introducer, presenter.

teishuu regular income; **teishuu ga nái** to have no regular income.

teisoo chastity, faithfulness.

teisúru to present, offer; to pass; **ikan o teisúru** to be a grand sight.

teitai accumulation, piling up; indigestion; **teitai suru** to accumulate, pile up.

teitaku mansion.

téito metropolis; imperial capital.

teiton standstill; stagnation; **teiton suru** to come to a standstill.

teitoo mortgage, security; **teitoo ni tóru** to hold (something) as security.

TEIJIKA NA nearby; **teijika na tokoro** place nearby.

téjina parlor tricks, conjuring tricks; **tejinashi** juggler.

tejoo handcuff.

tejun order; systematic plan; **tejun ga kurúu** to go out of order; **tejun o sadaméru** to arrange for.

tekágen discretion, consideration; **tekágen ga wakaránai** to be little used to; **tekágen o suru** to use one's discretion; to make allowances for.

tékazu trouble; **tékazu o kakéru** to give trouble.

teki enemy, opponent, antagonist; **teki mikata** friend and foe; **tekichi** enemy's land.

tekibishíi severe, strict, stern, rigorous, intense.

tekichuu hit, hitting the mark.

tekigáishin hostile feeling.

tékigi suitability for an occasion; **tékigi na** suitable; **tékigi ni** suitably; **tékigi no shóchi o suru** to act as one thinks fit.

tekigoo conformity, agreement; **tekigoo suru** to conform to.

tekihatsu disclosure, exposure; **tekihatsu suru** to disclose, expose; **fusei jíken o tekihatsu suru** expose.

tékihi fitness, suitability. **Tékihi wa wakarimasén.** I cannot tell whether it is suitable or not.

tekihoo proper method; legality.

tekihyoo apt remark; **tekihyoo o kudasu** to make a pertinent comment.

tekikaku, tekkaku exactness; acuteness; **tekikaku na** exact, acute.

TEKIMEN NI immediately.

tekin security (money), deposit; **tekin o útsu** to give a deposit.

tekinin competence, fitness.

tekioo fitness; adaptability.

tékipaki actively; briskly; promptly.

tekirei good example.

tekiryoo proper quantity.

tekisei kénsa test for quality; aptitude test.

tekisetsu fitness, appropriateness; **tekisetsu na** appropriate.

tekishi, tekitai hostility, animosity.

tekishutsu extraction; quotation; **tekishutsu suru** to extract.

tekisúru to fit, suit, agree; **kenkoo ni tekisúru** to be good for one's health; **shokuyoo ni tekisúru** to be fit to eat.

tékisuto text, textbook.

tekitai (see **tekishi**) –ni **tekitai suru** to stand against.

TEKITOO NA appropriate, suitable; **tekitoo ni** in an appropriate fashion. (See also **tekisetsu**.)

tekiyoo summary, résumé; application; **tekiyoo suru** to apply.

tekizai tékisho right person in the right place. **Kare wa tekizai tékisho desu.** He is the right man for that place.

tékizu wound; **tékizu o ou** to be wounded (in a fight).

tekkai withdrawal; **takkai suru** to withdraw.

tekkaku See **tekíkaku.**

tekkan iron pipe.

tekken clenched fist.

tekkin konkuríito concrete reinforced with steel.

tekkíri surely, without doubt.

tekkoojo iron foundry, ironworks.

tekkotsu iron frame, steel skeleton.

tekkyoo iron bridge.

tekozúru to be at one's wit's end; to have much trouble with. **Anó hito ni wa zúibun tekozurimáshita.** He was an awkward customer to deal with.

tekúbari preparation.

TÉKUBI wrist.

tékuchi way, means.

tekúru to go on foot.

tekuse no warúi light-fingered, thievish.

TEMÁ time; wages; **temáchin** wages, service charge. **Kono shigoto wa temá ga kakáru.** This job takes a lot of time. **Temá wa íkura desu ka?** How much do I owe you (for your services)?

temae this side.

temaegátte willfulness, selfishness; **temaegátte na yátsu** selfish fellow.

témane gesture; **témane o suru** to gesticulate.

temáneki beckoning.

temáwari one's personal effects.

temáwashi preparation, arrangement; **temáwashi ga yói** to be fully prepared in advance; **temáwashi suru** to get ready.

TEMIJIKA NI in short; **temijika ni iéba** to describe briefly.

temochibúsata feeling awkward, or ill at ease.

temotó money on hand; **temotó ga kurushíi** to be short of cash.

TEMPURA See **TENPURA.**

temúkai resistance.

ten dot; mark; point; **ten no uchidokoro no nai** faultless; **ookisa no ten de** in point of size.

tén heaven, sky.

tenami skill; **tenami o miséru** to show one's skill.

tenboo view, observation; **tenboo suru** to view, look upon; **tenbookyoo** periscope; telescope; **tenbóosha** observation car; parlor car.

ténbun natural endowment; **ténbun no yútaka na** highly gifted.

tenchi change of air; **tenchi suru** to go (to another place) for a change of air.

ténchi heaven and earth; universe; sphere.

TENDE (always used with a negative) at all; altogether; **tende hanashí ni naránai** to leave no room for negotiation. **Tende yóku nái.** It is no good at all.

téngoku heaven, paradise.

tenímotsu luggage, hand baggage; **tenímotsu toriatsukaijo** baggage room.

ten'in store clerk.

tenioha grammatical particles such as **wa, ga, o, ni,** etc.

tenisu See **teikyuu.**

tenji braille (dots).

tenjoo ceiling.

ténka entire country.

tenkai development, expansion; **tenkai suru** to develop, expand.

tenkan conversion; **tenkan suru** to convert, divert, turn.

tenkei model, specimen; **tenkeiteki Amerikájin** typical American.

tenken inspection; **tenken suru** to inspect.

TÉNKI, tenkoo weather; humor; **TÉNKI YÓHOO** weather forecast. **Kyóo wa ténki ga warúi.** The weather is bad today. He is ill-tempered today.

tenki turning point.

tenkin change of office; **–ni tenkin ni náru** to be transferred to.

ténko roll call.

tenkoo weather (see also **ténki**); **tenkoo fujun** unseasonable weather.

tenkoo turn, shift; **tenkoo suru** to turn.

tenkyo change of residence; **–ni tenkyo suru** to move to.

ténmatsu details (of an event).

ténmei providence, fate; **ténmei o shiru** to resign oneself to fate.

tenmon astronomy; **tenmóndai** astronomical observatory; **tenmongákusha** astronomer.

tennen nature; **tennen no bi** natural beauty; **tennen gásu** natural gas.

tennentoo smallpox.

tennin transfer; change of post.

tennóo emperor; **Tennoo Héika** His Majesty the Emperor.

ténnyo heavenly maiden.

TENÓHIRA palm of the hand.

tenpen chíi natural disaster (earthquake, flood, typhoon, etc.).

tenpin gift of heaven; innate nature; **tenpin o hakki suru** to bring all one's talents into play.

tenpuku downfall; **tenpuku suru** to turn over, capsize.

TENPURA, TEMPURA deep-fried fish, shrimps, and vegetables.

tenránkai exhibition.

tensai genius; natural gift. **Tensái hada no hitó desu.** He is something of a genius.

tensai calamity.

tensai reproduction of something which was once published.

tensaku correction (of a composition, poem, etc.).

ténsei nature; by nature. **Tensei shoojiki desu.** He is honest by nature.

tenseki suru to transfer one's legal domicile. (See also **tentaku.**)

tensen dotted line.

tensha transcription; **tensha suru** to copy, transcribe.

ténshi angel.

tenshin ranman naïvete; artlessness, innocence.

tensho letter of introduction.

ténshu shopkeeper, storekeeper.

tenshúkaku castle tower.

tensoo transmission; forwarding; **yuubínbutsu o Kyóoto ni tensoo suru** to forward mail to Kyoto.

tensui óke rainwater tank.

tentai heavenly bodies.

tentaku, tenseki change of residence.

tentan unselfishness.

tentekómai o suru to be in a business boom.

tentoo shop; overturning; fall; **ki ga tentoo suru** to lose one's presence of mind; **tentoo suru** to fall; to overturn.

tentoo shop; **tentoo ni dásu** to put something on sale.

tenguí Japanese towel; **tenguí kake** towel rack.

tenúkari fault; oversight.

tenurúi slow, dilatory.

tenzai suru to be dotted with.

teochí fault; slip; omission.

teoke wooden pail.

teókure ni náru to be too late.

teppén top, summit; **atama no teppén** crown (of the head).

teppítsu stylus (for handwritten mimeograph work).

tera Buddhist temple.

terasu to shine on, shed light on; to refer to; **jíjitsu ni terashite** in the light of the facts.

TÉREBI television.

terekkusu telex.

terikaesu to reflect.

terikómu to shine into.

teritsukéru to shine down upon.

téro terrorism.

TÉRU to shine; to be fine; **tétte mo futté mo** rain or shine. (See also **terasu**.)

teryóori homemade dish.

tesage handbag.

teságuri groping; **teságuri de iku** to grope (in the dark).

TESAKI hand; finger; agent; follower; tool; **tesaki no kíyoo na** dexterous.

tesei handmade; homemade.

teshita follower; agent, vassal. (See also **tesaki**.)

tesóo line in the palm; **tesóo o míru** to read a palm.

tessaku iron railing.

tessúru to pierce, penetrate.

tesuri handrail.

tesúu trouble, care; **tesúu ga kakáru** to require care, be troublesome.

tesúuryoo fee, commission.

tetsu iron; **tetsubin** iron kettle.

TETSUDÁI help, assistance; assistant, helper.

TETSUDÁU to help, assist, lend a hand; **shigoto o tetsudáu** to help (someone) with work.

TETSUDOO railway, railroad.

tetsugaku philosophy; **tetsugaku joo** philosophically.

tetsujóomoo wire entanglements; barbed-wire entanglements.

tetsuke(kín) advance (money), deposit; **tetsukékin o útsu** to pay a deposit.

tetsuya all night through; **tetsuya suru** to be up all night.

tetsúzuki process, formalities, proceedings;

tetsúzuki o suru to take steps.

tettei suru to get to the bottom; to be thorough.

tetteiteki na thoroughgoing.

tettoo tétsubi thoroughly (from beginning to end).

tettoribayái quick; rough and ready.

tewaké o suru to divide work.

tewátashi handing over personally.

tezáiku handiwork.

tezema narrowness; smallness. **Koko wa tezema de komárimasu.** We are cramped for space here.

tezúkami ni suru to take with the fingers.

tézuru connection; **tézuru o motoméru** to hunt up a connection.

tezuyói firm, resolute.

TO particle denoting: and; with; along with; if, when; as soon as. **Asoko wa háru ni náru to komimásu.** That place gets very crowded in spring. **Kyóoto e Yamada-san to ikimáshita.** I went to Kyoto with Mr. Yamada. **Tookyoo to Kyóoto e ikimáshita.** I went to Tokyo and Kyoto.

TO door.

tobaku gambling.

tobasu to let fly; to omit; to hurry; **kaze ni booshi o tobasu** to have one's hat blown off by the wind.

tobiagáru to fly up; to take wing, take flight; to jump to one's feet.

tobiarúku to run about.

tobidásu to fly out; to take wing; to run out.

tobidóogu firearm.

tobihi flying sparks; leap of flames; chicken pox.

tobiiri open contest.

tobikakáru to spring (leap, jump) upon.

tobikiri extra fine; best, choicest; **tobikiri jooto no shina** top-grade article.

tobikómu to jump (spring) into; to rush; **heyá ni tobikómu** to burst into the room; **mizu ni tokibómu** to dive into water.

tobikósu to jump over, leap over.

tobimawáru to fly about; to jump about.

tobinóku to jump back; to spring aside.

tobiokíru to jump out of bed; to start up; to jump for.

tobioríru to jump down, leap down.

tobira leaf of a gate (or door); title page of a book.

tobisáru to fly away.

TOBI TOBI NI here and there; at intervals; at random, without order; **tobi tobi no** sporadic.

tobitsúku to fly at, spring at, leap at.

tobokéru to pretend ignorance.

toboshíi to be scarce; to be short.

TOBU to fly; to jump, leap, bound.

tochi ground, land; **tochi no mono** a native, a villager.

TOCHUU on the way; halfway; **tochuu de yameru** to give up halfway; **tochuu gésha suru** to stop over (on a train trip).

todáeru to cease, stop, end; to drop.

TODANA cupboard, closet.

TODOKÉRU to report; to send. **Okome o todókete kudasái.** Please send me the rice.

todokoori hitch, hindrance; being in arrears; **todokoori náku** duly, regularly; smoothly.

todokóoru to be in arrears; to be left undone; to be stagnant. **Shigoto ga takusan todokóotte imasu.** There is a good deal of work left undone.

todóku to reach, get to; to attain; **mé no todóku kágiri** so far as (anyone) can see; **omói ga todóku** to realize one's objective.

todomáru to stop, halt, stand still.

todome finishing stroke, *coup de gráce.*

todoméru to stop, cease, put an end to.

togaméru to censure, to rebuke; to disapprove; **kí ga togaméru** to feel uneasy.

togarásu to sharpen; to point; to pout; **enpitsu o togarásu** to sharpen a pencil.

togáru to be pointed, come to a point; **togátta hana** hawk nose.

togé splinter; thorn; **togé ga áru kotoba** stinging words; **yubí ni togé ga sasaru** to get a splinter in one's finger.

togéru to accomplish, achieve; to attain, gain, realize; to commit; **yakusoku o togéru** to fulfill one's promise.

togiréru to break; to pause; to be interrupted.

tógu to whet, grind, sharpen; **naifu o tógu** to sharpen a knife.

toguchi doorway.

tóho going on foot.

tohoo ni kureru to be bewildered.

toiawaséru to inquire, to refer. **Taishíkan de toiawásete kudasái.** Please inquire at the Embassy.

toitsuméru to press for an answer.

tojikoméru to confine, shut in; **áme ni tojikomeraréru** to be house-bound by rain.

tojikomóru to confine oneself to; to shut oneself up.

tojimari o suru to lock a door.

TOJÍRU to bind; to file; to sew up.

TOJÍRU to shut, close.

tokai city, town; **tokaijín** city people, townsfolk.

tokaku (to be) apt to; in one way or other;

tokaku suru uchi ni in the meantime. **Wakái mono wa tokaku keisotsu de áru.** Young people are apt to act hastily.

tokásu to melt, liquefy; to fuse; **koori o takásu** to melt ice; **satóo o mizu ni tokásu** to dissolve sugar in water.

tokeáu to be melted together; to come to a mutual understanding.

TOKEI clock, watch; **oki dókei** clock; **ude dókei** wristwatch; **tokeiya** a watchmaker.

tokéru to melt; dissolve; **mizu ni tokéru** to be soluble in water; **netsú de tokéru** to melt by heat.

tokéru to get loose, come untied. **Musubime ga tóketa.** The knot has come untied.

TOKI time; hour; moment; time when; **toki házure** no out of season; **tokí o éta** seasonable, timely. **Kyooto e itta tóki kaimáshita.** I bought it when I went to Kyoto.

TOKIDOKI now and then; occasionally. **Tokidoki aimáshita.** I met him occasionally.

tokifuseru to persuade; to convince; to argue down; to prevail upon.

tokitsukéru to persuade, prevail upon.

tokka special prices; **tokka hánbai** sale at reduced prices.

tokken exclusive right or privilege.

tokki projection; **tokki suru** to project.

tokkoo special virtue, efficacy.

tukkumiáu to grapple with each other.

tokku ni (*adv.*) long time ago.

tokku no (*adj.*) long time ago; **tokku no mukashi** long ago, ages ago.

tokkuri sake bottle.

tokkyuu special express (train).

TOKO alcove; floor; bed; bedding; **toko no ma** guest-room alcove in a Japanese house where hanging scrolls, flower arrangements, etc., are displayed; **toko o shiku** to spread out bedding, make a bed; **toko ni tsúite iru** to be in bed; **tokokázari** alcove ornament.

tokoage to leave a sickbed.

tokoo voyage, passage; **–e tokoo suru** to make a voyage to; **tokóosha** passenger, emigrant.

TOKORO address, place; **tokoro o éru** to find a right place.

tokoróde then, well, now.

TOKORGA but, however, on the contrary.

tokoya barbershop, barber.

toku profit, gain; **toku na** profitable, advantageous; **toku o suru** to gain, profit, benefit.

toku virtue, morality.

tóku to untie, undo, unbind; to melt; to fuse; to smelt.

TOKUBETSU NO special, particular, exceptional; **TOKUBETSU NI** specially.

tokuchoo characteristic.

tokudane exclusive news, scoop (newspaper).

tokuden special telegram.

tókugi morality; **tokugijoo** morally; from the moral point of view.

tokuháin special representative, special correspondent (of a newspaper).

tokui pride, self-complacency; one's forte; customer, patron.

tokumei anonymity; **tokumei de** anonymously.

TÓKU NI especially. **Ashita wa tóku ni háyaku kité kudasái.** Please come especially early tomorrow.

tokusaku better way, wiser way.

tokusan speciality of a locality.

tokusei special make; deluxe.

tokusetsu specially set up, specially organized.

tokushi benevolence, charity; **tokushika** charitable or self-sacrificing person.

tokushi special envoy.

tokushoku special feature, speciality.

tokushu na special.

tokuten score (sports).

tókuto carefully, attentively.

tokutokuto proudly; with a triumphant air.

tokutóoseki special seat.

tokuyaku special contract.

tokuyuu no peculiar; characteristic.

tomádoi suru to be bewildered.

TOMARU to stop (at or in). **Itamí wa tomarimáshita.** The pain is gone. **Kono densha wa shinagawa de tomarimásu ka?** Does this train stop at Shinagawa Station?

tomaru to lodge; **hitóban tomaru** to stay overnight.

tomásu to enrich, make wealthy.

TÓMATO tomato.

tomeru to stop, bring to stop; **gásu o tomeru** to turn off the gas; **kuruma o tomeru** to stop a car.

tomeru to give lodging (to a person), give shelter.

–TOMO of course; even though; **dónna kotó ga okóru tomo** whatever may happen. **Ikimásu tomo.** Of course I will go.

tómo attendant; suite; **tómo ni** together with; including; **tómo o suru** to follow (someone). **Daika sóoryoo tomo ni sen en désu.** The price is 1000 yen, including postage.

TOMODACHI friend. **Tomodachi ni ái ni ikimásu.** I am going to see a friend.

tomodaore common ruin.

tómokaku at all events, at any rate.

tomokasegi suru to work (both husband and wife) for a living.

tomonáu to accompany, go with; **heigai ga tomonáu** to be attended with evil.

tomosu to burn, light, turn on (a lamp).

tómu to grow rich. **Anó hito wa keiken ni tónde imasu.** He has great experience.

tomurai funeral, burial.

tomuráu to mourn for the dead.

tón ton, tonnage.

tonaéru to recite; to repeat; to chant.

TONARI neighboring house; next-door neighbor; **tonari no** adjoining; next; **tonari átte iru** to be next door to each other.

tonbo dragonfly.

tonda surprising; extraordinary; shocking, terrible; unexpected; **tonda mé ni áu** to meet with a misfortune.

tondemonái surprising; extraordinary; unexpected; awful; abused; **tondemonái kotó ni náru** to become serious; to take an unexpected turn.

TÓNIKAKU in any case.

tónjaku care, heed, regard; **jikan ni tónjaku náku** regardless of time.

tónkyaku ludicrousness; wild screech or act (to scare or make others laugh); **tónkyoo na** freakish.

tonneru tunnel.

tonogata men, gentlemen; **tonogata no** men's, gentlemen's.

tonshi sudden death.

tonto not at all, not in the least; entirely. **Anó hito wa tón to kónai.** She does not come at all.

tonton byóoshi without a hitch. **Kotó ga tonton byóoshi ni hakonde imásu.** Things are going along swimmingly.

ton'ya wholesale shop, wholesale dealer.

tóo political party; **Shakaitoo** Socialist Party.

TÓO ten, ten years old.

tóo counter for cattle (denoting: head); **ushi háttoo** eight cows.

tóo rightness, propriety, justness; **tóo no hónnin** person in question; **tóogetsu** this month.

–tóo tower, pagoda.

–too suffix denoting: grade, class; **ittóo** first class.

tooa East Asia.

tooben answer; explanation; defense.

tooboe (*n.*) howling; **inu no tooboe** the howling of dogs; **tooboe suru** to howl.

tooboo flight, desertion; **tooboo suru** to run away; **toobóosha** a fugitive.

TOOBUN for the time being. **Toobun áme**

wa furánai deshoo. It won't rain for a while.

tóobun sugar content, **tóobun o fukúnda** sugary.

toochaku arrival; **toochaku jun ni** in order of arrival; **toochaku shídai** immediately on arrival; **toochaku suru** to arrive.

tóochi this place, here.

toochoku being on duty; on watch.

toodai lighthouse.

toodori president, director.

tooen a distant (blood) relation.

toogé mountain pass, defile; crisis; **Hakone no toogé** Hakone Pass; **toogé o kosu** to pass the critical stage.

tóogi debate, discussion; **tóogi suru** to discuss, debate.

toogoku imprisonment.

Toogíu Crown Prince.

tóogyo rule, management.

tóoha party, faction; school; clique. **tóoha suru** to traverse; to travel on foot; to tramp.

tooheki thievishness; kleptomania.

toohi escape, flight; **toohi suru** to escape, fly.

toohyoo voting; poll; **–ni toohyoo suru** to vote for; **toohyoo de kimeru** to decide by vote; **toohyoo ni iku** to go to the polls.

TOOI far; far away. **Tanaka-san no uchí wa koko kara tóoi desu.** Mr. Tanaka's house is far from here.

tooin party member.

tooitsu unification, uniformity; **tooitsuteki** unifying.

tóoji at that time; at this time.

toojíru See **toozúru.**

toojísha person concerned; **toojísha ni kakeáu** to negotiate with the persons concerned.

tóojitsu day in question; appointed day; day of issue (for a ticket, etc.).

toojoo suru to get on board a ship or plane.

toojoo stage entrance; **toojoo suru** to go on the stage.

TOOKA ten days; tenth day of the month.

tookan mailing, posting; **tegami o tookan suru** to mail a letter.

tookárazu before long, in the near future.

tookei statistics; **tookei o tóru** to make a survey.

tóoki registration; **tooki suru** to register.

tóoki earthenware.

tookoo suru to contribute to a periodical.

tookoo suru to go to school.

tookoo suru to surrender.

tooku a distant place; **ki ga tooku náru** to faint, swoon.

tookyókusha authorities concerned.

tookyóri equal distance.

tookyuu class, grade; **tookyuu o tsukéru** to grade.

toomáwari detour; roundabout way; **toomáwari o suru** to detour.

toomáwashi na roundabout, indirect; **toomáwashi ni** indirectly; in a roundabout way.

toome distant view; **toome ga kiku** to be able to see a long way off.

toomei na transparent.

toomen no present; urgent; immediate; **toomen no mondai** matter in hand.

toomichi long way, great distance.

toonan robbery, burglary.

tooni long ago; already.

tóonin person in question.

toonóku to recede; to get away. **Ashí ga toonóku.** Her visits are becoming rarer.

toonori long ride, long drive; **toonori o suru** to take a long drive; **jiténsha no toonori o suru** to go on a long cycling excursion.

toorai suru to come, arrive; to occur; to come to hand. **Kikái ga toorai shita.** An opportunity presented itself.

toorei returning a salute; returning a call.

TOORÍ road, street; traffic; **toorí o yoku suru** to clear a passage; **toori ippén no** casual; indifferent.

–toori kinds. **Iku toori mo áru.** There are many kinds.

–TÓORI like, as; **watakushi no iu tóori** as I say.

toorigakari passing, chance; **toorigakari no hito** passersby.

toorikakáru to happen to pass (come by).

toorikósu to go beyond; to walk past; to pass.

toorinuke passing through.

tooroku registration; **tooroku suru** to register.

tóoron debate, discussion; **tóoron suru** to debate; **toorónkai** forum.

tooroo fixed stone lantern, dedicatory lantern.

TÓORU to go along; to pass; to go by the name of; to be admissible; to get through; **shikén ni tóoru** to pass an examination; **sujimichi ga tóotte iru** to be consistent; to be logical. **Kono básu wa Ginza o toorimásu.** This bus goes through Ginza.

tooryuu suru to stay at.

tóosa exploration; survey.

toosei management, control; regulation; **toosei suru** to bring under government control; to regulate, govern.

toosen winning a prize; success in a lottery; **toosen bángoo** winning numbers; **toosénsha** successful candidate.

tooshaban mimeograph, duplicator.

tooshi investment; **–ni tooshi suru** to invest in; **tooshisha** investor.

toosho contribution; **tooshóran** letters-to-the-editor column.

tóoshu present master; head of a family.

toosoo escape.

TÓOSU to let (someone) pass through; to admit; to carry; to realize; to make; to usher in; **mé o tóosu** to run over, glance over; **món o tóosu** to admit a person within the gates.

tóosutaa toaster.

tóosuto toast (bread).

TOOTEI by no means (used with a negative); after all. **Sonna kotó wa tootei dekimasén.** I can't possibly do such a thing.

tootói precious, valuable; high; noble; sacred, holy. **Tootói ojikan o sáite kudasaimáshite arígatoo gozaimáshita.** Thank you for spending your precious time on me.

TÓOTOO finally. **Tóotoo sono shigoto o shite shimaimáshita.** I've finally finished that work.

tootoo to flowing in torrents; eloquently; **tootoo to nagaréru** to flow majestically (as a river); **tootoo to nobéru** to speak fluently.

toowaku suru to be perplexed, be puzzled; to be embarrassed; to be at a loss.

tooyoo appointment, promotion; **tooyoo suru** to appoint, promote.

TÓOYOO Orient; **Tóoyoo no** (*adj.*) Oriental; **Tooyóojin** (*n.*) Oriental.

tooyoo kánji (ideographic) characters included in the official list of 1850 (**Tooyoo Kanji Hyoo**) designated by the Japanese Government as the basic symbols in writing (replaced by **jooyoo kánji** in 1981).

tooza present time; current deposit; **tooza no kózukai** pocket money adequate for the present.

toozakáru to become more distant; to go away; **akuyuu kara toozakáru** to keep away from bad companions.

toozakéru to keep clear of, away from; to keep at a distance.

toozen matter of course; naturally.

toozoku thief, robber, burglar.

toozúru to throw; to throw away, throw off; to abandon; **íppyoo o toozúru** to cast a vote.

toppatsu outbreak; **toppatsuteki** unexpected, sudden.

toppi na extravagant, fantastic, venturesome.

toppuu gust of wind.

tora tiger.

toraéru to catch, seize, take hold of; **eríkubi o toraéru** to seize (someone) by the neck.

torahóomu trachoma.

toraí suru to come over the sea; to visit (a country).

TORÁKKU truck; track field.

toránpu playing cards; **toranpu o suru** to play cards.

TORI bird, fowl; **TORINIKU** chicken meat, poultry.

toriáezu in haste; for the time being.

toriageru to take up, take in one's hand; **fuhei o toriageru** to listen to a complaint.

toriatsukai handling (of a thing); arrangement (of a business); treatment (of a guest). **Toriatsukai chúui.** Handle with care.

toriáu to hold each other; to struggle for; to take notice of.

toriawase assortment; combination.

torichigaeru to mistake; to misunderstand; to misapprehend.

torichirasu to scatter about, put in disorder. **Heyá ga torichiráshite áru.** The room is untidy.

torié worth, merit, useful (strong) point; **torié no áru** useful, valuable, worthy; **torié no nái** worthless, good for nothing.

torihakaráu to manage; to arrange; to dispose of; to settle; to deal with.

toriharau to remove, take away, clear away; to clear by taking (things) away.

torihazusu to remove; to take to pieces.

toríhiki transaction, dealing; **toríhiki o suru** to do business with; **torihiki o hajimeru** to open an account with; **torihikisaki** customer; business connection.

torii open front gate of a shrine, often painted red.

toriire harvest, crop; **toriire dóki** harvesttime.

toriíreru to take in; to harvest, gather in; to accept; to adopt.

toriisógi in a hurry; with dispatch.

torikaeru to change, exchange; to renew.

torikaeshi recovery, retrieval; **torikaeshi ga tsukánai** irrevocable.

torikáesu to get back; to regain, recover; to recall.

torikakaru to begin, commence; to set about.

torikawasu to exchange.

torikesu to cancel, revoke; **chuumon o torikesu** to cancel an order; **zenhánketsu o torikesu** to revoke a former decision.

torikimeru to arrange; to agree upon, settle, decide upon.

toriko captive, prisoner of war.

torikomu to take in; to bring over; to be in

confusion; to get in favor with; **sentakumono o torikomu** to take in washing. **Kyóo wa sukóshi torikonde imásu.** This place is upset today.

torikoshigúroo unnecessary worry; **torikoshigúroo o suru** to run to meet trouble; to be overanxious.

torikowásu to pull down; to take down; to break down; to break up.

torikúmu to wrestle with; to grapple with; to be matched against.

torimagiréru to be in confusion; **zátsumu ni torimagiréru** to be under the pressure of routine business.

torimáku to surround, hem in, encircle, enclose; to fawn upon.

torimatomeru to gather all together; to collect; to pack; **kazai dóogu o torimatomeru** to collect one's household goods.

torimidásu to disturb; to lose one's composure. **Heyá wa torimidáshite atta.** The room was in disorder.

torimodósu to take back; to regain, recover; to resume.

torimótsu to treat; to receive; to entertain.

torinaósu to recover; to mend; to alter.

torinashi mediation, intercession; **torinásu** to plead for; to mediate; to recommend.

torinigású to fail to catch; **kikái o torinigású** to miss an opportunity.

torinokeru to remove, take away; to clear away, get rid of.

toriotósu to let fall, slip, drop; to miss one's hold.

torishimari management, supervision, control; **torishimaríyaku** manager, director.

torishimáru to manage, control, superintend, oversee.

torisoroéru to put together; to gather; to assort.

toritate no fresh (from); **toritate no momo** fresh peaches; **toritate no sakana** fish fresh from the sea.

toritateru to collect; to promote; to patronize; **kashikín o toritateru** to collect loans; **yakunin ni toritateru** to appoint (someone) to a post.

toritomeru to ascertain, make sure; to make definite; **ínochi o toritomeru** to have a narrow escape.

toritsugi intermediation; receiving a thing and handing it to another; agency; agent; answering a knock (or bell); usher; **toritsugi o suru** to act as an agent, to transmit; to convey.

toritsuke run on a bank.

toritsukeru to fit; to furnish; to install; to draw out (of the bank); **kikái o toritsukeru** to set up an apparatus.

toritsuku to hold fast to, cling to; to catch hold of; **toritsuku shima mo nái** to be left helpless.

toritsukuróu to mend, repair, patch; **teisai o toritsukuróu** to keep up appearances.

toriya bird-fancier; poultry dealer.

toriyóseru to get, obtain, procure.

tororo grated yam.

tórotoro suru to doze; to take a nap.

TÓRU to take; to take in one's hand, take hold of; to get; to fetch; to hand; to pass; to receive; to gain; to accept; to adopt; to choose; to buy; to gather; to pick; to eat; to charge; to manage; to interpret; to take away; to catch; to deprive a person of; to possess; to take possession of; to need, require; to preserve; to engage; to subscribe to; to insist; **eiyóobutsu o tóru** to take nourishing food; **fude o tóru** to take a pen in hand; to write; **jikan o tóru** to take time; **jímu o tóru** to do business; **ichiban chiisái no o tóru** to pick the smallest one; **kane o toraréru** to have one's money stolen; **kí no mi o tóru** to pick fruit from trees; **kusá o tóru** to weed; **hyaku man en no gekkyuu o tóru** to receive a salary of one million yen; **ríshi o tóru** to charge interest; **sakana o tóru** to catch fish; **shashin o tóru** to have a picture taken; **shibai no séki o tótte oku** to reserve a seat at a theater; **shinbun o tóru** to subscribe to a newspaper; **tsuyói taido o tóru** to assume a fair attitude toward; **wairo o tóru** to accept a bribe; **wáruku tóru** to take amiss. **Heyá o tótte okimáshita.** I have engaged a room for you. **Káre wa kataku tótte ugokánai.** He tries to carry his point and won't yield. **Shió o tótte kudasái.** Will you pass me the salt? **Yasai wa ano misé kara torimásu.** We buy vegetables from that store.

Tóruko Turkey; **Torukogo** Turkish (language); **Torukójin** Turk.

tóryoo paints.

tóshi towns and cities; **toshi kéikaku** city planning.

TOSHÍ year; age; **toshi to tómo ni** with age; **toshí o mukaeru** to welcome the New Year; **toshí o okuru** to pass the years; **toshí o tóru** to grow old; **toshigoro** marriageable age; **onaji toshigoro no** of about the same age; **toshigoro no musume** daughter of marriageable age; **toshishita** younger; junior; **toshíue** senior; older; **TOSHIYÓRI** old person. **Tanaka-san yóri mittsu toshishita désu.**

He is three years younger than Mr. Tanaka. **Yamada-san yóri mittsu toshiue désu.** He is three years older than Mr. Yamada.

–to shite as; for; in the capacity of; **orei to shite** as a token of thanks; **soodai to shite shusseki suru** to attend as a representative.

tósho books; **tosho gákari** librarian; **toshókan** library; **tósho etsuránshitsu** reading room.

toshikoshi New Year's Eve.

toshimawari luck attending one's age. **Kotoshi wa toshimawari ga warúi.** This year is an unlucky one for me.

TOSSA NO AIDA NI in a moment; quick as thought; on the spur of the moment.

tosshin suru to rush; to dash; to charge.

totan zinc.

totan'ita galvanized iron sheets.

–totan ni just as; in the act of. **Watakushi ga háiru totan ni káre wa déte itta.** He went out just as I entered.

TOTEMO very, awfully; extraordinarily.

TÓOTOO at last, finally, at length.

totonoéru to prepare, get ready; to arrange.

totonóu to be prepared; to be arranged; to be in good order; to be ready, be settled.

TOTSUZEN suddenly, abruptly; all of a sudden; **totsuzen no** sudden, abrupt. **Totsuzen jishoku shimáshita.** She resigned without giving notice.

totté handle; knob; **totté o tsukéru** to fix a handle.

tottei jetty, breakwater.

TÓU to ask, question.

tózan mountain climbing.

tozetsu stoppage, cessation; interruption; **tozetsu suru** to be stopped; to be interrupted.

tsúba saliva; **tsúba o kakéru** to spit at.

tsubasa wings.

tsubo land measure of six **shaku** (Japanese feet) square. **Kono niwa wa sanbyaku tsubo arimásu.** This garden has an area of three hundred tsubo.

tsubo jar; **tsubo ni ireru** to pot (plant).

tsubomeru to make narrow; to pucker up; **kása o tsubomeru** to shut an umbrella; **kuchi o tsubomeru** to pucker up the lips.

tsubomi flower bud.

tsúbu grain; drop (of liquid).

tsubureru to be crushed; to be smashed, be broken; to break; **menboku ga tsubureru** to be put out of countenance. **Ginkoo ga tsubureta.** The bank failed.

tsubusu to crush; to smash, break; **shíndai o tsubusu** to dissipate one's fortune; **jikan o tsubusu** to kill time.

tsubuyáku to mutter, grumble; to murmur.

TSUCHÍ ground, earth; mud; clay.

tsuchikusái rustic; boorish.

tsúe cane, walking stick; **tsúe o tomeru** to make a stopover; **tsúe o tsukú** to walk with a walking stick.

tsugeguchi talebearing; **tsugeguchi suru** to carry tales.

tsugeru to tell; to inform; to bid; **itomá o tsugeru** to bid farewell.

TSUGÍ next, succeeding, adjacent; **tsugí no ma** next room. **Kono tsugí wa dáre desu ka?** Who comes next to her?

tsugi patch; **tsugi o ateru** to patch.

tsugime joint; seam; **tsugime náshi no** seamless.

TSUGOO circumstances; **tsugoo ni yori** for certain reasons; **tsugoo yóku** fortunately; **tsugoo ga yói** to be convenient; **tsugoo suru** to arrange; to manage.

tsúgoo in all; together.

tsugu to pour out; to fill; **ocha o íppai tsugu** to pour a cup of tea.

tsugu to join, to piece together; **ki ni take o tsugu** to graft bamboo onto a tree; to be incongruous.

tsugu to rank next to, to be next to, to rank second to.

tsugu to succeed, to accede; to inherit.

TSÚI unintentionally; by mistake.

tsui pair, couple.

tsuide order, sequence; **tsuide ni** by way of, incidentally, when, as; **tsuide no sétsu at** your convenience.

tsuihoo banishment, exile.

tsuika supplement, appendix; **tsuika suru** to add, supplement.

tsuikyuu investigation; **tsuikyuu suru** to inquire closely into (a matter).

TSÚINI at last, finally; at length.

tsuiraku crash; fall; **tsuiraku suru** to fall; to crash.

tsuiseki pursuit, chase; **tsuiseki suru** to pursue.

TSUITACHÍ first day of the month.

tsuitate screen.

TSÚITE (always used following **ni**) of, about, concerning; **kono ten ni tsúite on** this point. **Kono mondai ni tsúite dóo omoimásu ka?** What do you think about this?

tsuitoo mourning; **tsuitoo suru** to mourn (a death); **tsuitoo no kotobá** memorial address; eulogy.

tsuitotsu bumping into the rear; **tsuitotsu suru** to collide (from behind).

tsuiyásu to spend, expend, lay out; **monó o mueki ni tsuiyásu** to be wasteful.

tsujitsuma consistency; **tsujitsuma no awánu** inconsistent.

tsukaéru to be clogged, be obstructed, be blocked; to be barred; **kotobá ga tsukaéru** to stammer, to stick in one's throat; **muné ga tsukaéru** to feel heavy in the stomach. **Kúda ga tsukáete iru.** The pipe is choked.

tsukai message; errand; messenger.

tsukaihatásu to squander, spend all (one's money).

tsukaikata usage, application. **Kono kikái no tsukaikata ga wakarimasén.** I don't know how to use this machine.

tsukaikómu to embezzle.

tsukaimichi employment, use.

tsukaimono present, gift; **tsukaimono o suru** to give a present; to send a gift.

tsukainaréru to be accustomed to using.

tsukaisugíru to use excessively; to spend too much.

tsukamaeru to catch; to seize; to take hold of.

tsukamaru to be caught, be taken; to be arrested.

tsukamaséru to let (someone) grasp; to bribe.

tsukamiai grappling, fighting (without a weapon).

tsukámu to seize, catch, grasp, hold.

tsukaré weariness, fatigue.

TSUKARÉRU to get tired, grow weary, become fatigued.

tsukaru to soak in; to be soaked in, be steeped in; **kaisui ni tsukaru** to take a dip (in the sea).

tsukasadóru to rule, govern, administer; to take charge of.

TSUKAU to use, put to use, employ; to take; to spend; **atamá o tsukau** to use one's brain; **yú o tsukau** to take a hot bath. **Anó hito wa rippa na Nihongo o tsukaimásu.** He speaks good Japanese.

tsukeiru to take advantage of (someone); to presume on (someone's) good nature; to impose on (someone's) kindness.

tsukekomu to enter; to take advantage of another's weakness.

tsukemono pickles; pickled vegetables.

tsukenerau to prowl, to dog, shadow; to hang about.

tsukeru to soak in, steep in.

TSUKÉRU to attach one thing to another, to set one thing on another, to stick on, to sew on; to wear, to make an entry (in a book); **katá o tsukéru** to make an end (of something); **ki o tsukéru** to take care; **mikomi o tsukéru** to form a judgment; **kusuri o tsukéru** to apply a medicine; **na**

o tsukéru to name; **pán ni bátaa o tsukéru** to spread butter on bread; **té o tsukéru** to put one's hand to a task; to eat.

tsuketodoke fee, payment of money, bribe; occasional presents.

TSUKÍ moon; month; **mikazuki** crescent; **tsukí ni nikai** twice a month; **tsuki no de** rising of the moon.

–tsuki suffix denoting: assigned to; attached to; per. **Hitóri ni tsuki gosen en désu.** The charge is 5000 yen per person.

tsukiagéru to thrust up; to push up; to toss.

tsukiai keeping company; association; intercourse; **tsukiai no tamé ni** for the sake of friendship; **tsukiai nikúi** to be difficult to get along with; **tsukiai o suru** to keep company with.

tsukiáu to keep company with, associate with.

tsukiatari dead end (street); collision, crash.

tsukidásu to thrust out, stick out, push out, stretch out.

tsukihájime beginning of a month.

tsukihi days and months; time; years; date.

tsukikáesu to thrust back.

tsukimatóu to follow, shadow (someone); to hang on; to pursue.

tsukímono accessory, adjunct, appendage; part; anything which is attached to or is an indispensable part of something.

tsukinami na commonplace; conventional.

tsukinúku to thrust through, pierce, penetrate.

tsukiókure no of the previous month; **tsukiókure no zasshi** back numbers of a magazine.

tsukiotósu to throw or push (someone) down or off.

tsukíru to become exhausted; to be used up, be consumed. **Okane ga tsukimáshita.** I ran out of money.

tsukisoi attendant; nurse; chaperon.

tsukisóu to attend (someone); to accompany.

tsukitaósu to knock down.

tsukitoméru to ascertain, make sure of; to assure, convince, satisfy oneself of.

tsukitóosu to thrust, pierce.

tsukitsukéru to thrust before; to put (place) under (someone's) nose; to point at.

tsukíyo moonlit night.

tsukizúe end of a month.

tsukízuki no monthly; **tsukízuki no téate** monthly allowance.

tsukkakáru to fall on, pick a quarrel with (someone).

tsukkakéru to slip on.

tsukkíru to cross; to go (run) across; to go through.

tsukkómu to thrust in; to plunge in; to poke into.

TSÚKU to arrive at. **Fúne wa íma tsukimáshita.** The ship has just arrived. **Kóobe ni tsukimáshita.** He arrived at Kobe.

tsúku to adhere to, to stick to. **Té ni penki ga tsúite iru.** There is paint on her hand.

tsuku to pierce, to thrust, to stab; **tantoo de tsuku** to stab (someone) with a dagger.

TSUKUE table, desk.

TSUKÚRU to make, manufacture; to prepare, produce; to turn out; to frame; to build, erect; to form; to raise; to cultivate; to constitute; **ié o tsukúru** to build a house; **kane o tsukúru** to make a fortune; **rájio o tsukúru** to make a radio; **rétsu o tsukúru** to form in line.

tsukúsu to exhaust; to come to the end of; to serve (someone); to make efforts.

tsukuzúku thoroughly, utterly, quite; **tsukuzúku iyá ni náru** to become utterly disgusted; **tsukuzúku kangáeru** to reflect carefully.

TSÚMA wife.

tsumadátsu to stand on tiptoe.

tsumahájiki suru to flick; to disdain; to shun; to scorn.

tsumamidásu to pick out, drag out, turn out.

tsumamu to pick, pinch, take a pinch of.

TSUMARÁNAI trifling, worthless, commonplace; **tsumaránai kotó** matter of no importance; **tsumaránai mono** trifling thing.

TSÚMARI in the end; in the long run; finally; in a word.

tsumáru to be blocked up; to be full, be packed; to be shortened; **hentóo ni tsumáru** to be at a loss for a reply; **kane ni tsumáru** to be pressed for money; **ki ga tsumáru** to be oppressive.

tsumashíi frugal, thrifty, economical.

tsumazúku to take a false step; to lose one's footing, stumble, fall.

TSUME nail; claw; hoof; hook; **tsume o kíru** to cut one's nails.

tsumekakéru to crowd (a house); to throng to (the door).

tsumekiri constant attendance; staying at one's post without a break.

tsumekómu to cram; to stuff; to jam; to pack; **heyá ni hito o tsumekómu** to crowd people into a room.

tsumémono o suru to stuff, pack.

tsuméru to cram; to stuff; to fill; to pack; to charge; **kaban ni tsuméru** to pack a suitcase.

TSUMETAI cold (to the touch), chilly; icy; **tsumetai kokóro** cold heart; **tsumetai mízu** cold water.

tsúmi crime, offense; sin; fault; **tsúmi na** sinful, cruel, inhuman.

tsumiagéru to heap up, make a pile; to accumulate.

tsumidásu to send off, ship off.

tsumihóroboshi atonement of sins, expiation.

tsumikaéru to reship.

tsumikómu to load; to put on board; to take in.

tsumini cargo, freight.

tsumitatéru to save up (money); to lay by; to reserve, amass, accumulate.

TSUMORI intention; motive, expectation; understanding. **Harátta tsumori désu.** I believe I've paid for it. **Iku tsumori désu.** I intend to go.

tsumorigaki written estimate; written measurement.

tsumóru to accumulate; to be piled up; to amount to. **Tsumóru hanashí ni yó o fukáshita.** We had much to talk about and sat up far into the night. **Yukí ga tsumóru.** Snow is piled up on the ground.

tsumu to pile up, heap up; to load; to accumulate; to take on board; to pick; to pluck; to pull out.

tsumujíkaze whirlwind, tornado.

tsuná cord, rope, line. **Tanomi no tsuná mo kíreta.** The last ray of hope is gone.

tsunagi connection, link.

tsunagu to tie, fasten, chain, connect, join.

tsunami tidal waves.

tsúne usual state; **tsúne no** usual, ordinary, common; **tsúne ni** always.

tsunéru to pinch.

tsunó horn; **tsunó o hayásu** to become jealous.

tsunóru to solicit (a subscription); to collect; to grow violent, severe, intense, fierce; to become worse.

tsunzáku to rend, break; to pierce; to split.

tsuppáru to stretch (an arm or leg against something); to plant one's feet on the ground.

TSURAI hard; painful; bitter; **tsuraku** bitterly, harshly.

tsuranáru to range; to lie in a row; to be present at. **Matsuda-san no kekkónshiki ni tsuranátta.** I attended Mr. Matsuda's wedding.

tsuranúku to pierce; to pass through.

tsurara icicle.

tsurasa pain, painfulness.

tsure companion.

tsuréai (*colloq.*) spouse, husband, wife.

tsuredátsu to go along with.

TSURERU to take (with). **Tomodachi o tsurete ikimáshita.** I took a friend of mine with me.

tsuresóu to be married, be man and wife.

tsuri change. **Gohyakú en no tsuri o moraimáshita.** I received change of 500 yen.

tsuri fishing (with a hook and line). **Tsuri o shi ni ikimáshita.** I went fishing.

tsuriai balance, equilibrium; harmony; **tsuriai o tóru** to balance oneself.

tsurusu to hang, suspend; to swing.

tsutaeru to convey; to report; to deliver; to communicate.

tsutawaru to be handed down; to be transmitted.

tsuté intermediary; good offices; **tsuté o motoméru** to hunt up connections.

tsutomáru to be fit for; to be equal to (a position).

TSUTOME duty; service; **tsutomé o hatásu** to discharge one's duties; **tsutoméguchi** place of employment; **tsutomenin** salaried person.

TSUTOMÉRU to serve, to hold (fill) a post; to exert oneself; to make an effort; to endeavor; to labor, work; **tsutomesaki** one's place of employment. **Takagi-san wa ginkoo ni tsutómete imásu.** Takagi works for a bank.

tsutsu pipe, tube; gun barrel; gun.

tsutsúku to poke at; to pick at, to peck.

tsutsumashíi modest, reserved.

TSUTSUMÍ package, parcel; **tsutsumígami** wrapping paper, a packing sheet.

tsutsuní dike, embankment.

TSUTSÚMU to wrap, to do up, to pack.

tsutsushimi prudence, discretion, caution; **tsutsushimi no nái** immodest, indiscreet; **tsutsushimi o wasureru** to lose one's self-control.

tsutsushimu to be discreet; to be careful, be prudent; to restrain oneself.

tsuttátsu to stand; to stand up straight.

tsúu connoisseur, authority, expert judge.

–tsuu counter for letters, telegrams; **tegami o ittsuu dásu** to send a letter.

tsuuchi information; **tsucchi suru** to inform.

tsuuchoo official communication, notification.

tsuufuu ventilation.

tsuugaku suru to go to school.

tsuuji bowel movement; **tsuuji ga tomaru** to become constipated; **tsuuji o tsukéru** to loosen the bowels.

tsuujiru to pass; to run; to be opened (to traffic); to be understood.

tsuujoo usually; ordinarily; as a rule.

tsuukai na extremely delightful; pleasant; **tsuukai na otokó** a man of spirit. **Sore wa tsuukai de átta.** It was a delightful sensation.

tsuukan passing through customs.

tsuukan suru to feel keenly, feel acutely.

tsuukin suru to go to the office.

tsuukoku announcement, notice, information; **tsuukoku suru** to notify.

tsuukoo passing; transit; **tsuukoodome no** thoroughfare; **tsuukoodome ni suru** to close a road; to stop traffic.

TSUUREI as a rule; commonly.

tsuusan sum total.

tsuusetsu na keen, acute.

tsuushin correspondence, communication; **tsuushínsha** news agency.

tsuushoo common name.

tsuutatsu notification; **tsuutatsu suru** to notify.

tsuuun transportation, moving van; **tsuuun gáisha** a mover.

–TSUUWA counter denoting: phone-call unit. **Ittsúuwa wa sánpun desu.** One telephone call unit is based on three minutes' conversation.

tsuuwáryoo charge for a telephone call.

tsúuyaku interpretation, interpreter; **tsúuyaku suru** to interpret.

tsuuyóomon public gate; side gate.

tsuuyoo suru to pass for; to circulate; to be current; to hold good.

tsuya gloss, luster.

TSUYÓI strong, powerful, robust, healthy.

tsuyoki firmness; **tsuyoki o shimésu** to show firmness.

tsuyoméru to strengthen; to invigorate; to intensify; **ími o tsuyoméru** to emphasize.

tsuyomí strength, power; strong point.

tsúyosa strength, power.

tsuyu rainy season (June–July); **tsuyu no iri** start of the rainy season; **tsuyu no ake** end of the rainy season.

tsúyu, otsúyu soup, broth; gravy (Japanese style).

tsúyu dew, dewdrop. **Tsúyu ga oríru.** The dew falls.

TSUZUKERU to continue; to keep on.

tsuzuki continuation; connection; succession.

TSUZUKU to go on; to follow, go in succession; to last. **Á me wa mikka tsuzukimáshita.** The rain continued to fall for three days.

tsuzumeru to contract; to condense; to reduce, shorten, cut short.

tsuzuri spelling.

tsuzuru to spell words; to compose (a tune); **bún o tsuzuru** to write.

U

úba wet nurse.

ubagúruma baby carriage.

ubáu to take by force, snatch; to rob (someone of something).

úbu naïveté; greenness.

UCHI house; home; inside, interior; **sono hí no uchi ni** in the course of that day; **uchi no kotó** household matters; **uchi de asobu** to play indoors.

uchiageru to shoot up; to send up; to set off.

uchiakeru to disclose, reveal; to confide (a secret); **himitsu o uchiakeru** to give secret information; to disclose secrets.

uchiáu to exchange blows.

uchiawase previous arrangement; consultation; **uchiawase o suru** to make arrangements for.

uchiawaséru to strike (one thing against another); to make arrangements for something.

uchidashi close; closing time (of a theater). **Uchidashi wa góji deshita.** They closed at five o'clock.

uchidásu to begin to beat; to strike out; to close.

uchideshi apprentice; private pupil.

uchigawa inside.

uchikáesu to strike, beat, hit back, return a blow.

uchikesu to deny; to negate; to contradict.

uchiki retiring disposition; shyness.

uchikiru to close; to discontinue; **kooshoo o uchikiru** to drop negotiations.

uchikomu to drive in; to strike into; to shoot into; to fall deeply in love with; to be absorbed in; **kugi o uchikomu** to drive a nail into; **tamá o uchikomu** to send bullets into.

uchimaku real state of things; inside facts; **uchimaku o abáku** to see behind the scenes.

uchiotósu to strike down, knock down, floor; to shoot down.

uchitaósu to knock down, strike down, overthrow.

uchitokeru to open one's heart; to be frank, to be candid.

uchitomeru, uchitóru to kill, slay, shoot dead.

uchiúmi inland sea.

uchiwa family circle; private circle (of friends); **uchiwa dóoshi** those who are of the same party (or family, etc.); member of the inner circle.

uchiwake item breakdown (of an account); details.

uchooten ni náru to be in ecstasy.

úchuu universe, cosmos; **uchuu hikóoshi** astronaut; **uchuu káihatsu** space development; **uchuusen** spacecraft.

UDÉ arm; ability; **udé o furuu** to exercise a talent; **udé o kasu** to lend a helping hand; **udé o tamésu** to test one's ability; **udekiki** able man; man of ability.

udon noodle; **udonko** wheat flour; **udonya** restaurant where Japanese noodles are the specialty.

UE upper part, surface, topside; top, summit, head; after, on, upon; **ichiban ue no** uppermost; **shikén no ué de** on examination; **ue ni tátsu hitó** one who stands in authority over others; **ue no** higher; upper; superior.

ué hunger; starvation; **uejini** death by starvation.

uekáeru to transplant, replant; **hoka no hachí ni uekáeru** to transplant into another pot.

ueki plant; potted plant; **uekiya** gardener.

uekomi thicket, shrubbery.

ueru to plant.

uéru to become hungry; to starve; to be famished; to hunger for.

uéshita up and down; shirts and trousers; **uéshita ni náru** to be upside down; **uéshita ni suru** to turn upside down.

uetsuke planting; transplanting.

ugai gargling, rinsing the mouth; **ugai suru** to gargle; **ugaigúsuri** a gargle.

ugátsu to dig; to cut through; to pierce; **ugátta kotó o iu** to make a pointed remark.

UGOKÁSU to move; to shift; to remove, to set in motion; **chooshuu o ugokásu** to move an audience; **hito no kokóro o ugokásu** to touch the heart.

ugokí movement, motion.

UGÓKU to move; to shift; to sway; to work; to be transferred to another position. **Ugóite wa ikemásen.** Don't move.

ugoméku to wriggle, squirm.

uisukii whiskey.

ukaberu to float, keep afloat.

ukabu to float; to come to the surface, appear. **Ií kangáe ga ukanda.** I hit upon a good idea.

UKAGAU to pay a visit; to inquire (*humble*). **Sono kotó wa Yamada-san ni ukagaimáshita.** I asked Mr. Yamada about it. **Yamada-san no otaku ni ukagaimáshita.** I visited Yamada's house.

ukagau to watch for, to look for, to be on the lookout for; **hito no kaoiro o ukagau** to study a person's face; **kikái o ukagau** to look for a chance.

ukareru to make merry; to be gay.

ukasareru to be carried away, be captivated; **netsú ni ukasareru** to be delirious with fever.

ukatsu carelessness, thoughtlessness; stupidity.

uke reputation, popularity; acceptance, assent, consent. **Anó hito wa uke ga íi.** She has a good reputation.

ukedásu, ukemodósu to redeem, take (something) out of pawn.

ukekotae reply, answer; **ukekotae o suru** to reply, answer.

ukemi acting on the defensive; passive (in grammar).

ukemochi charge.

ukemodósu See **ukedásu.**

ukenagasu to ward off, turn aside; **shitsumon o takumi ni ukenagasu** to ignore a question diplomatically.

ukeoi contract for work.

ukeóu to undertake; to take upon oneself; to assume.

UKÉRU to receive; to accept; to have, to obtain; to take; **hoomon o ukéru** to receive a visit; **shújutsu o ukéru** to have an operation (surgical). (See also **uketoru.**)

uketomeru to stop; to catch; to ward off. **tamá o uketomeru** to catch a ball.

UKETORI receipt; acceptance; **uketorinin** receiver, recipient.

UKETORU, UKÉRU to receive; to accept. **Tegami o uketorimáshita.** I received a letter.

uketsugi succession; inheritance.

UKETSUKE receiving; accepting; reception desk; **uketsuke gakari** receptionist.

ukewatashi delivery, transfer; **ukewatashi o suru** to deliver, transfer.

uki float, buoy.

ukiagáru to rise to the surface; to float.

ukiashi unsteadiness; wavering, faltering; **ukiashi ni náru** to waver, become unsteady.

ukibúkuro air bladder (of a fish), life buoy, life belt.

uku to float; to come to the surface; to be left over; to be saved; **ki ga uku** to be gay, to be exhilarated.

UKKÁRI vacantly; carelessly; without attention.

UMÁ horse, mount; **umakata** driver of a pack horse; **umaya** stable.

UMÁI good; nice; tasty; skillful; successful; profitable; **umái mono** delicious, dainty food.

umami deliciousness, flavor; **umami no áru hanashí** a nice speech.

umare birth, lineage; **umare no vói** to be

well-born, be high-born.

UMARERU to be born; **hínka ni umareru** to come from a poor family; **umareru to súgu** at birth.

umaretsuki by nature; by temperament.

umaru to be filled up; to be hurried.

umeawase amends, compensation; **sonshitsu no umeawase o suru** to make up for a loss.

umekí moan, groan.

uméku to groan, moan.

umeru to bury; to reclaim; to fill up.

umetate reclamation; filling up; **umetatéchi** reclaimed land; **umetate kóoji** reclamation work.

ÚMI sea; ocean; **hí no umi** vast sheet of fire; sea of fire; **úmi de oyógu** to swim in the ocean; **umibe** beach, seashore.

umí pus; **umí o mótsu** to form pus.

umu to form pus, fester.

umi no háha one's natural mother.

umitate fresh (said of an egg).

únmei destiny, fate, fortune; doom; **únmei no chóoji** fortune's favorite.

unpan transportation; **unpan suru** to transport.

UMU to bear, give birth to, be delivered of. **Anzúru yori umu ga yasúi.** Fear often exaggerates danger.

úmu existence, presence; yes or no; **úmu o iwasezu** forcibly; whether one will or not. **Ayamari no úmu o shirasete kudasái.** Let me know whether there is any mistake.

ún fortune, lot, destiny, fate; **ún no warúi** unlucky; **ún no yói** lucky.

ún (*colloq.*) yes; h'm; well; groan.

unadareru to hang one's head.

unagásu to urge, press, demand, to call upon; to stimulate.

unarí groan; roar; humming.

unaru to groan; to roar; to howl, to hum.

unasaréru to have a nightmare, have bad dreams.

unazúku to nod, bow one's head in assent.

únchin freight; portage; shipping expenses.

undei no sá all the difference in the world.

UNDOO movement, motion; physical exercise; **undoo suru** to move; to exercise; to walk; to campaign; **undooka** athlete.

uné furrow.

unéru to wind; to undulate; **nami ga unéru** to swell.

únga canal; **ungachitái** canal zone.

unomi ni suru to gulp down.

unsoo carrying, transport; **unsoo suru** to carry, transport; **unsooya** mover, forwarding agent.

UNTEN operation; driving; working; **unten suru** to drive, operate, work; **unténshu** engineer (operator of an engine); chauffeur; motorman; **unten menkyo** driver's license.

únto (*colloq.*) with great force; with all one's might; soundly; liberally; **kane ga únto áru** to have lots of money; **únto osu** to push with all one's might.

unubore self-conceit; **unubore ga tsuyyói** to be full of conceit.

unuboreru to be vain: to be conceited, to think highly of oneself.

ún'yu traffic; transport.

unzan operation, ...lculation; **unzan suru** to calculate.

unzári suru to be disgusted with.

UO fish; **uogashi** fish market.

uppun resentment, grudge, enmity.

URÁ reverse side; back, sole of the foot; lining of clothes; hidden meaning of an expression; second half of baseball inning.

uradana house in an alley.

uradóori back street.

uragaki endorsement; **uragaki suru** to endorse.

uragiri treachery, perfidy.

uragíru to betray, turn traitor, go over to the enemy.

uraguchi back entrance.

uraji lining; cloth for lining.

urameshíi reproachful; resentful; hateful.

urami resentment; grudge; hatred; malice; **urami o idáku** to bear a grudge.

urámu to bear a grudge; to feel bitter against; to think ill of.

urámichi byway; back road.

uramon back gate.

uranái fortune-telling; fortune-teller.

uranáu to divine, forecast; **minoue o uranáu** to tell (someone's) fortune.

uraniwa backyard; rear garden.

urate rear of a building.

URAYAMASHÍI enviable. **Anáta ga urayamashíi desu.** I envy you.

urayámu to envy, be envious of, be jealous of; **hito no koofuku o urayámu** to envy a person his good luck.

urekko popular person; lion; **bundan no urekko** popular writer.

urekuchi market.

ureshigáru to be glad; to take delight in; to feel happy.

URESHII glad, joyous, delighted, happy. **Ome ni kakárete ureshíi desu.** I'm glad to be able to see you.

uríage proceeds (returns) of a sale.

URIBA sales counter.

uribagákari sales clerk.

uridame proceeds, cash in a money box.

uridashi bargain sale; opening sale.

uridásu to offer for sale, place on the market, put on sale.

urikire sold out.

uriko salespeople.

urimono for sale; **urimono ni dásu** to put up for sale.

URINE sale price.

urioshimi holding (hoarding) goods for future sale; **urioshimi o suru** to hoard goods for future sale.

urotáeru to be confused, be thrown into confusion; to be upset.

urotsuku to loiter, hang about; to wander about.

URU to sell; to deal in; to offer for sale. **Sore wa dóko de utte imásu ka?** Where is it sold?

úru to gain; to get.

urúmu to be wet; to be moist; to be blurred; to be dimmed.

uruoi moisture, damp; enrichment; grace, charm; **uruoi no áru** moist; profitable; tasteful.

uruósu to wet, moisten; to dip; to be moistened, be wet; to benefit (someone).

URUSÁI annoying, tiresome, harassing, irksome.

urúudoshi leap year.

uruwashíi beautiful, pretty; fine; **gokigen uruwáshiku** in good humor; in excellent health.

úryoo rainfall; **uryookei** rain gauge.

usankusái suspicious-looking; uncanny.

USHI cattle; cow; bull; ox.

USHINÁU to lose; to miss; to part with; to be deprived of.

USHIRO (*n.*) back, rear; (*adj.*) **ushiro no** back, hind, rear; **ushiroashi** hind legs; **ushiro ni** behind; **ushiro e mawaru** to get behind.

ushirogurái shady; not aboveboard; **ushirogurái kotó** underhanded, shady transaction.

ushiromuki standing with the back toward another.

ushiroyubi o sásu to point a finger of scorn at; **ushiroyubi o sasaréru** to be talked about as an object of scorn.

úso lie, falsehood; **makká na úso** a pack of lies; **úso no** false; **úso o tsukú** to lie; **úso happyaku o naraberu** to tell all sorts of lies.

usugurai gloomy, dim, dusky, dark.

USUI thin; light; weak; **nínjoo no usui hito** coldhearted person.

usukimi warúi dismal; weird, eerie.

usuppera na thin; flimsy; superficial.

usurágu to thin; to fade, grow pale; to be toned down; to become dim.

usurasamúi chilly; rather cold.

UTÁ ode, poem; song; **utá o utau** to sing a song; **utá o yómu** to compose a poem.

utagai doubt; **utagai náku** beyond doubt; **utagai o harásu** to clear away suspicion; **utagai o idáku** to harbor suspicion; **utagai o tóku** to clear up all doubts.

utagáu to doubt; to be doubtful of. **Utagáu yóchi ga nái.** There is no room for doubt.

UTAU to sing, chant, carol; to recite; **hanauta o utau** to hum a song.

úten rainy weather; rainy day.

útouto suru to doze off, to slumber.

ÚTSU to strike, hit, beat; to fire, shoot; to drive in; to give a performance; to attack, assault; to send a telegram; **denpoo o útsu** to send a telegram; **fui o útsu** to make a sudden attack; **kugi o útsu** to drive in a nail; **pisutoru de útsu** to shoot with a revolver; **shibai o útsu** to give a play; to play a trick. **Tokei ga nji o útta.** The clock struck two.

utsubuse ni on one's face.

UTSUKUSHÍI beautiful, fair; **utsukushíi hanashí** a beautiful story; **utsukushíi késhiki** beautiful scenery.

utsumúku to look down; to stoop; **utsumúite arúku** to walk with one's head bent.

utsurígi caprice, whim; **utsurígi no** capricious, changeable.

utsúru to be reflected; to fall upon; to be becoming; to be taken; **kagamí ni utsúru** to be reflected in a mirror; **shashin ni utsúru** to be photographed. **Ano káta ni wa ano kimono ga yóku utsúru.** That dress is very becoming to her.

utsúru to remove; to change, shift; to be infectious.

utsushi copy.

UTSÚSU to remove; to transfer; to pour; to carry; to turn; to direct; **jimúsho o utsúsu** to move the office; **miruku o hoka no bín ni utsúsu** to pour milk from one bottle into another.

utsúsu to copy, to transcribe; to describe, to picture.

utsuwa vessel; caliber; **sono utsuwa de nái** to be by no means qualified.

uttae accusation, charge; lawsuit; complaint; petition; **uttae o kiku** to hear a case.

uttaéru to sue; to complain to; **hootei ni uttaéru** to take legal proceedings against someone; **rísei ni uttaéru** to appeal to reason; **yóron ni uttaéru** to appeal to public opinion.

uttooshíi depressing, oppressive, gloomy.

uwabe surface, exterior.

UWAGI upper or outer garment; coat; jacket.

uwagoto o iu to be delirious.

uwaki fickleness, inconstancy; flirtation; **uwaki na** fickle, flirtatious; **uwakimono** licentious man, wanton woman.

uwame upward glance.

uwamuki upward trend. **Sooba ga uwamuki de áru.** Prices show an upward trend.

uwamúku to look up, to turn one's face upward.

uwanosóra absentmindedness; **uwanosóra de kiku** to listen absently.

uwanuri final coating (of plaster or paint); **són no uwanuri o suru** to add to one's loss; to suffer loss upon loss.

uwasa rumor, report, talk; **uwasa o suru** to spread a rumor.

uwate better hand; **uwate ni déru** to get the upper hand.

uwayaku superior official.

uyamáu to respect; to honor.

uyamuya ambiguity; vagueness; **uyamuya ni suru** to obscure an issue; **uyamuya ni hoomúru** to suppress a matter.

uyauyáshiku respectfully.

úyoku right wing; right field (in baseball).

úyo kyokusetsu much meandering; **úyo kyokusetsu o héte** after aimless wandering.

uzoo múzoo rabble; all sorts and conditions of men.

uzukumáru to crouch, squat down.

uzúmaki eddy, whirlpool.

uzumáku to whirl, swirl; to flow in whirls; to curl.

uzumaru to be filled up; to be buried.

uzumeru to bury.

uzumoreru to be covered with; to live in obscurity.

V

vaiorin violin.

véeru veil.

viníiru plastic, vinyl.

W

WA particle denoting: sentence topic: = as for. **Doitsugo wa benkyoo shimáshita.** [As far as German is concerned] I studied German (but not French). **Kinóo wa ikimáshita.** I went yesterday (but not today). **Watakushi wa ikimasén.** As for me, I'm not going.

wá circle; ring; wheel; **wá ni wá o kakéru** to exaggerate.

waapuro word processor.

wabiru to apologize for; to make an excuse; to beg pardon.

wabishíi miserable, poor, wretched; **wabishíi kurashi o suru** to lead a lonely life.

wabun text in Japanese; **wabun éiyaku** translating into English from Japanese; **wabun dénpoo** telegram in Japanese.

wadachi rut, wheel track.

wadai topic, subject; **wadai ni noboru** to be talked about.

wadakamari ill feeling; reserve; **wadakamari ga áru** to be vexed at something.

wadakamáru to be coiled up (as a snake); to be rooted; to be harbored.

Wa-Ei jísho, Wa-Ei jiten Japanese-English dictionary.

wafuku Japanese clothes; kimono.

wagamáma willfulness; waywardness; **wagamáma na** willful, wayward; **wagamáma o suru** to have one's own way; **wagamamamono** wayward person.

wagoo suru to harmonize with; to agree with each other.

wáiro bribery, bribe; **wáiro o tsukau** to bribe, corrupt; **wáiro o tóru** to be bribed; to take a bribe.

waishatsu man's dress shirt.

wáiwai noisily, clamorously.

wáka, tánka Japanese verse of 31 syllables; Japanese verse.

wakagaeri rejuvenation.

wakage youthful spirit.

WAKÁI young, youthful; **wakái hito** young person; **wákakatta toki** when she was young; **wakamono** young man.

wakai suru to make up, settle amicably; to accommodate with.

wakarazuya blockhead; incorrigible person.

WAKARE farewell, parting; division; branch; **wakaré no sakazúki** a parting cup; **wakaré o oshímu** to be reluctant to part; **wakaré o tsugeru** to say good-bye.

WAKARÉRU to branch off, split, part; to break up, be divided; to get separated; **eikyuu ni wakaréru** to part forever.

wakari understanding; **wakari no yói** intelligent, sensible; **wakari no warúi** slow to understand.

wakarikítta well-known; obvious.

WAKÁRU to understand, realize, comprehend; **wakarí nikui** hard to understand.

wakasu to boil; to heat; **cha o wakasu** to make tea; **yú o wakasu** to boil water.

WÁKE reason; ground; meaning; circumstance; **wáke no wakaránai hanashí** a strange story; senseless talk;
wáke no wakátta hitó a person amenable to reason; **wáke o tazunéru** to ask the reason. **Sore wa doo iu wáke desu ka.** What do you mean by that?

wakehedate partiality, favoritism; **wakehedate no nái** impartial, fair; **wakehedate o suru** to be partial, to discriminate.

wakemáe share, portion.

wakemé dividing line, decisive event.

WAKÉRU to divide, separate; to distribute; to distinguish; **itsútsu ni wakéru** to divide into five parts. **Tochi o kodomo ni wakemáshita.** He divided his estate among his children.

wakí side; other way; supporting role; **waki no** other, another; side, lateral; **wakí ni yoru** to step aside; **wakí e oku** to lay aside; **wakí o tsutoméru** to support the leading actor (in a No play).

wakimáe discernment, discrimination; judgment; understanding; **wakimáe no nái** thoughtless, indiscreet.

wakimé sidelong glance; **wakimé mo furazu** without looking aside, devoting oneself entirely to.

wakimi o suru to look aside; to look off.

WAKU to boil. **Furó ga wakimáshita.** The bath is ready. **Yú ga waite imásu.** The water is boiling.

waku to gush out; to spring; to grow.

wakú frame, tambour.

waméku to cry; to scream, yell, shriek.

wán bay; inlet; gulf.

wanpaku kozóo spoiled child; naughty boy.

wánpaku na willful; naughty.

wánryoku physical strength.

warai laughter; smile; ridicule; **waraigao** smiling face; smile; **waraigusa** laughingstock, butt of ridicule; **warai jóogo** ticklish person.

WARAU to laugh; to smile; to chuckle; to deride, jeer.

waraji straw sandals; **waraji o haku** to put on straw sandals; to fly from (official) pursuit; **waraji o núgu** to take off straw sandals; to settle down.

wareme crack, crevice, fissure.

wari rate, proportion, percentage; allotment; **wari no yói** profitable; **wari ni** comparatively; **nén ichíwari no risoku** interest of 10 percent annually.

wariai rate, proportion; **wariai ni** comparatively.

waribiki discount, price reduction; **waribiki suru** to allow a discount.

waridásu to calculate, compute; to deduce from, conclude from.

warikiréru to be divisible. **Sánjuukú wa**

júsan de warikiréru. Thirty-nine can be divided by 13.

WARU to split; to crush; to divide; to get lower than; to dilute; to open one's heart; to cut; to halve; to cleave; to rend; **juuní o rokú de waru** to divide 12 by 6; **maki o waru** to split wood for fuel. **Kono sake wa mizu o watte áru.** This sake is mixed with water.

warubíreru to act timidly; to fear; **warubírezu** with good grace; without fear.

warudákumi evil design, machination; **warudákumi o suru** to conspire.

warugashikói cunning, artful.

warugi ill will; **warugi no nái** without malice; **warugi no nái hito** good-natured person. **Watashi wa warugi de shitá no de wa arimasén.** I meant no offense at all.

WARÚI bad, ill, evil; unlucky; wormy; rotten; wrong; defective; detrimental; slanderous; **wáruku nátta tabemóno** spoiled food; **warúi kotó o suru** to do wrong; to commit a sin, commit a crime; **karada ni warúi** to be injurious to the health; **wáruku suru** to make a thing worse; **wáruku suru to** if things go wrong; **wáruku tóru** to take amiss. **Anó hito wa mé ga warúi.** He has poor eyesight.

warujie (*n.*) craftiness, cunning; **warujie no áru** (*adj.*) cunning; **hito ni warujie o tsukéru** to put a person up to mischief.

warúkuchi abuse, abusive language; **káge de warúkuchi o iu** to backbite; **warúkuchi o iu** to speak ill of.

warumono bad fellow; rogue.

wárusa mischief; trick.

wasei of Japanese make.

wasen Japanese rowboat.

washizúkami grasping, clutching; **washizúkami ni suru** to grasp, clutch.

wasuregachi na forgetful.

wasuremono thing left behind; **wasuremono o suru** to leave (something) behind.

wasureppói to have a poor memory.

WASURERU to forget; to lose sight of; to leave behind; **shinshoku o wasureru** to forget sleep and food, be devoted to.

WATÁ cotton; cotton wool; **wata íre** padded clothes; **wata no ki** a cotton plant; **wata no yóo ni tsukaréru** to get dog-tired.

WATAKUSHI I; secrecy; privacy; **watakushi no** my; private; personal; **watakushi no nái** disinterested, unselfish; **watakushítachi** we.

watari passing; crossing; **watari ni fúne** opportune rescue; **watari o tsukéru** to pave the way; to establish some connection.

watariáu to cross swords with; to quarrel with.

wataru to go over; to go; **Chúugoku kara Nippón ni wataru** to come from China to Japan; **hashí o wataru** to cross a bridge; **úmi o wataru** to sail across the sea.

watashi ferry; place where passengers take a ferryboat; **watashibúne** ferryboat.

WATASHI (*more informal than* **WATAKUSHI**).

WATASU to pass (a person) over; to carry across; to take over; to ferry over; to hand deliver; to transfer; to make over; to pay; **kyúuryoo o watasu** to pay wages; **mukoogawa ni watasu** to take over to the other side (of the river).

wátto with a sudden outcry; **wátto nakidásu** to burst into tears.

wayaku suru to translate into Japanese.

wáza to purposely, on purpose; **wazatorashíi** artificial, unnatural; studied; **wazatoráshiku** artificially.

wazawai misfortune, adversity, calamity.

WÁZAWAZA intentionally, on purpose; **wázawaza iku** to take the trouble to go.

WÁZUKA NA small (quantity); few (in number); slight.

wazurawashíi vexatious, troublesome, wearisome; **yonónaka ga wazurawashíi** to be weary of life.

wazurawasu to trouble; to keep a person busy; to exercise; to cause inconvenience.

–YA particle denoting: and (used when a list is incomplete); or; as soon as; **are ya kóre ya de** with one thing or another; **tori ya kemono** birds and beasts; **Tookyoo ni tsukú ya** as soon as I got to Tokyo.

–ya suffix denoting: store; **sakanaya** fish market; fishmonger.

yáa oh; hallo.

yáado yard.

yábo boorishness; want of taste; **yábo na** uncouth, vulgar, unrefined; senseless; rusty; **yábo na otoko** boor, silly fellow.

yabuisha quack doctor.

yábun evening, nighttime. **Yábun ni demáshite osóreirimasu.** I must apologize for calling on you so late at night.

yabunirami squint; cross-eye; **yabunirami no** cross-eyed.

yabure rupture, breach; rent, tear; **kimono no yabure** rent in a garment; **yabure kábure** desperation, self-abandonment.

yaburéru to be torn, be rent; to be broken; to be beaten; to fail in one's design.

YABÚRU to tear, rend; to break, destroy, crush; **heiwa o yabúru** to disturb the peace; **kamí o yabúru** to tear a sheet of paper. **Káre no keíkaku wa yabúreta.** His attempt had failed. **Kimono ga yabúrete iru.** The clothes are torn.

yáchin house rent; **yáchin no todokoori** rent arrears. **Yáchin ga agarimáshita.** The rent has been raised.

yádo, yadoya hotel, inn, lodging; **ichíya no yádo o kasu** to give a night's lodging; **yádo o kóu** to ask for lodging; **yádo o tóru** to stay at an inn for the night.

yadonashi homelessness; homeless person, vagrant.

yadoya, yádo inn, hotel; **yadoya ni tomaru** to stay at an inn; **yadoya no híyoo** hotel expenses.

yagai field; **yagai úndoo** outdoor exercise; **yagai no** open air, outdoors.

yagaku night study; evening school, **yagákkoo** night school.

yagate presently, soon; before long.

yágoo shop name; firm name.

yágu bedclothes, bedding.

yagura tower, turret; **hinomiyágura** fire tower.

yagyoo night work; **yagyoo téate** overtime (for night work); **yagyoo o suru** to work at night.

YAHÁRI too, also; as well; still; all the same. **Démo yahári yamemashóo.** I won't do it, notwithstanding your persuasion. **Yahári damé desu.** That won't do, either.

yáiyai hey!; hard; pressingly; **yáiyai itte sáisoku suru** to press (someone) for.

yáji heckling; cheering; rooting.

yajíru to cheer; to support; to disturb; to heckle; to interrupt; to obstruct. **Bénshi o yajiritaóshita.** The speaker was hissed down.

yajiuma mob, busybodies, bystander.

yakai evening party; ball; **yakai o moyoósu** to give a party.

YAKAMASHÍI noisy, uproarious; rigorous, strict. **Ano heyá wa taihen yakamashíi desu.** That room is very noisy.

yákan night, nighttime.

yakan kettle.

yáke despair, desperation.

yakeato ruins left after a fire.

yakedo scald, burn.

yakei night view; **Kóobe no yakei** the view by night of Kobe.

yakei night watch.

YAKERU to burn; to be burned; to be destroyed; to be roasted; to be broiled; to be scorched; **hi ni yaketa kao** sunburned face; **yakeru yóo na átsusa** burning heat of day; **muné ga yakeru** to have heartburn.

yakeshínu to perish by fire.

yaketsúku to scorch, burn; **yaketsúku yoo na táiyoo** burning sun.

yaki baking, roasting; firing of porcelain; tempering of a sword. **Kono tóoki wa yaki ga íi desu.** This porcelain is well fired.

yakimashi further copies (prints) of a photograph.

yakimóchi toasted *mochi* (rice cake); jealousy; **yakimochi yáki** jealous person; **yakimóchi o yaku** to be jealous.

yákimoki suru to be impatient; to be nervous.

yakimono ceramic-ware, pottery; broiled, baked, or roasted dish.

yakin night duty, night work; **yakin o suru** to be on night duty.

yakinaoshi warming (of cooked food); literary rehash, adaptation; **yakinaoshi suru** to adapt from, to rehash. **Kore wa furui Nihon no shoosetsu no yakinaoshi desu.** This is an adaptation from an old Japanese story.

yakinaósu to bake for the second time; to roast again; to imitate.

yakiniku roast meat.

yakitori roast fowl.

yakizákana broiled fish.

yákkai trouble; support; dependence; **yákkai o kakéru** to give trouble; to be under the care of; to be welcomed by; **yákkai na** troublesome, difficult, annoying; **yakkaimono** person, thing; nuisance. **Yakkaibárai.** Good riddance to bad rubbish.

yakki ni náru to get warm; to become excited.

YAKKYOKU pharmacy; dispensary.

yakoo réssha night train.

YAKU to burn; to set something on fire; to broil; to roast; **imó o yaku** to bake potatoes; **nikú o yaku** to roast meat; **sakana o yaku** to broil fish; **sumí o yaku** to make charcoal; **té o yaku** to burn one's fingers or hand; to be at a loss.

YÁKU translation, version; **yákusha** translator; **yákusu, yaku súru** to translate.

YÁKU about, approximately.

yakú office; duty; part in a drama; **yakuba** public office; **yakumé** duty; business;

mission; **yakumé o hatásu** to discharge one's duties; **yakunin** government official; **yakusha** actor, actress; **yakusho** public office; **yakú ni tátsu** to be of use; **yakú o tsutoméru** to play the part of.

yakuhin drugs, chemicals.

yakusoku promise; engagement; appointment; **yakusoku suru** to promise.

yakyuu baseball; **yakyuu o suru** to play baseball.

YAMÁ mountain; hill; mine; crown (of a hat); pile; speculation; climax (of a drama); **yama no yóo na** mountainous; **yamakúzure** landslide; **yamámichi** mountain road; **yamanóbori** mountain climbing; **yamabíraki** the opening of a mountain to pilgrims or climbers for the year; **yamadera** temple in the mountains; **yamaguni** mountainous country. **Koko ga kono shoosetsu no yamá desu.** Here is the climax of this novel. **Yamá ga atatta.** The speculation has turned out well.

yamadashi bumpkin, rustic.

yámai illness; **yámai ni kakáru** to become ill.

yamakaji forest fire.

yamamori heap; heaping up anything in measuring; heaping full; **yamamori ni suru** to heap up; to fill to overflowing.

yamashíi to feel ashamed; to have qualms of conscience.

yamawake ni suru to divide equally into two parts.

yame end, conclusion, finish; abolition, stop, discontinuance; **yame ni suru** to be discontinued.

YAMERU to stop; to break; to give up, abandon; to resign; to discontinue; **gakkoo o yameru** to leave school; **hanashi o yameru** to cease talking; **shoku o yameru** to retire from office; **toríhiki o yameru** to close an account.

yamiagari convalescence; **yamiagari no** convalescent.

yamitsuki infatuation; feeling ill; **yamitsuki ni náru** (*colloq.*) to develop into a passion; to be wholly given up to.

yamitsúku (*colloq.*) to be taken ill; to be wholly given up to; to run madly after.

yamíyo dark night.

yamome widow.

YAMU to stop, cease, abate; to clamp down; to drop down; **yamu o énai** unavoidable; necessary; **yamu o ézu** unavoidably. **Áme ga yamimáshita.** The rain has stopped.

yanami row of houses.

yáne roof; **yaneura** attic.

yánushi owner of a house; landlord.

yanwári softly; gently.

YAOYA fruit and vegetable market; greengrocer.

–YARA and so on; and the like; **náni yara ká yara de** with one thing or other.

yariba disposal place; **yariba ga nái** to be at a loss as to where to put (something); **yariba ni komáru** to be at a loss as to what to do with (something).

yaridásu to begin to do.

yarikake half-done, half-finished.

yarikakéru to begin; to set about; to proceed to make.

yarikanéru to hesitate to do. **Ano hito wa dónna kotó demo yarikanénai otokó da.** He is up to all sorts of things. He will go to any extreme.

yarikata manner of doing; **yarikata ga íi** to go about one's task in the right way. **Sore wa yarikata shídai desu.** It depends on how you do it.

yarikoméru to silence; to snub; to put down; to argue down.

yarikuchi manner of acting; policy. **Yarikuchi ga shaku da.** I am displeased with his way of doing things.

yarikuri to make shift; **yarikuri o suru** to live by one's wits.

yarinaósu to do over again; to try again; to start over again; to resume.

yarippanashi ni suru to neglect; to leave in disorder.

yarisokonai failure.

yarisugíru to overdo; to go too far; to do too much.

yarisugósu to go past.

yaritogéru to accomplish, perform, achieve; to finish.

yarítori exchange; **yarítori suru** to exchange.

YARU to give, present (something to someone). **Inú ni mizu o yatta.** I gave water to the dog.

yaru to do, to undertake.

YASAI vegetables.

YASASHII gentle, tender; easy, simple; **yasashii mondai** easy question; **yasashii kotobá o kakéru** to speak kindly (words) to (someone).

yasegáman suru to endure (anything) because of pride.

yasei wildness; **yasei suru** to grow wild (without being cultivated).

YASERU to become lean (thin); to lose freshness.

yashiki mansion; premises; grounds; home site.

yashin ambition, aspiration; schemes; **yashin manman** highly ambitious; **yashin o**

idáku to be ambitious; **yashinka** ambitious person.

yashinai nutrition; bringing up; **karada no yashinai ni náru** to be nutritious.

yashináu to bring up; to support; to subsist; to maintain; to feed.

yashinaioya foster father; foster mother.

yáshiro, oyáshiro Shinto shrine.

yasuágari (*n.*) being inexpensive, being cheap, being economic.

yasubúshin flimsily constructed building.

YASÚI cheap, inexpensive; **yasúi hon** cheap book; **yasumono** low priced (cheaply made) article. **Bukka ga yásuku nárimashita.** Prices have come down. **Yasumonókai no zeni úshinai.** Penny-wise and pound-foolish.

–YASÚI suffix denoting: easy to, simple to; **kowareyasúi** to be easy to break; **yomiyasúi** to be easy to read.

yasumáru to be rested; to feel at rest; **karada no yasumáru tokí ga nái** to be too busy to relax for a moment.

yasuméru to rest (oneself); to give rest; to ease; **kadara o yasuméru** to rest from work; **ki o yasuméru** to set (one's mind) at ease.

YASUMI rest; recess; holiday; vacation: **natsuyásumi** summer vacation.

YASÚMU to rest; to go to bed; to take a vacation; **gakkoo o yasúmu** to be absent from school; **yóru háyaku yasúmu** to go to bed early in the evening.

yasunzúru to be content (with); to rest satisfied; to be at ease; **í o yasunzúru** to set (someone's) mind at ease.

yasuppói cheap, flashy; mean; **yasuppóku miéru** to look cheap.

yasúraka na peaceful, calm; **yasúraka ni** peacefully, at rest.

yasuri file, rasp; **yasuri o kakéru** to file.

yasuúkeai ready promise; irresponsible promise; **yasuúkeai o suru** to promise readily; to promise without due consideration.

yasuuri bargain sale; **yasuuri o suru** to sell at a bargain price.

yasuyado lodging house; cheap inn.

yasuyásu easily, with ease.

yátai float (in a festival); one's fortune; **yátái mise** open-air stall (or booth).

yatara na careless; indiscriminate.

YATOI employment; employee; **yatoi gaikokújin** foreign employees; **yatoiire** employment, hire; **yatoinin** employee; servant; **yatoínushi** employer.

yatóu to engage, employ, hire.

yatsuátari ni indiscriminately, recklessly.

yatsugibaya ni in rapid succession.

yatsuréru to get thin; to be worn out, to waste away; **míru kage mo náku yatsúrete iru** to be a mere shadow of one's former self.

yatte míru to try, attempt.

YATTO at last; with difficulty; **yatto kurashite iku** to have great difficulty making both ends meet; **Yatto kippu ga kaeta.** I could buy a ticket only with difficulty.

yattoko pincers, nippers; wrench.

YATTSU, HACH eight. (See also **yooka, hachigatsu.**)

yattsukeru to attack.

yawarageru to soften, lessen, lighten; to moderate; to relax; **kóe o yawarageru** to speak softly; **kotobá o yawarageru** to speak gently (with soft words).

yawaragu to soften; to be softened; to become mild, become moderate. **Árashi ga yawaragimáshita.** The storm has abated.

YAWARAKÁI soft, gentle, tender, mild; **yawarakái nikú** tender meat.

yáya to some degree, somewhat. **Yáya shina ga ochíru.** It is somewhat inferior in quality.

YAYAKOSHÍI difficult, complicated, intricate. **Yayakoshíi hanashí desu.** It is a complicated story.

yayamo suréba to be apt to, be liable to.

–yo above, over; more; **san mairu yo** over three miles; three miles plus.

YÓ night; **yó o akasu** to pass a night without sleep. **Yó ga akeru.** The day is breaking.

YÓ world, age, times; **yó ni déru** to see the light, to rise in the world; **yó o itou** to be weary of life; **yó o sáru** to depart this life, to die.

yoakashi sitting up all night.

YOAKE dawn, daybreak; **yoake ni** at dawn, at daybreak.

yobawari calling (someone) by name; **doroboo yóbawari suru** to brand as a thief.

yóbi reserve; preparation; **yóbi no** reserve, spare; **yobíhin** spare store, reserve supply; **yobíkin** reserve fund, emergency fund.

yobiageru to call out, call up; **namae o yobiageru** to call out (someone's) name.

yobiatsuméru to call together, assemble, summon.

yobidashi subpoena; calling out; summoning.

yobidásu to call out; to call up.

yobigoe cry; cry of street hucksters.

yobiiréru to call (someone) in; to hale (someone) into.

yobikakéru to call (out) to; to speak to, address.

yobiko whistle; birdcall; **yobikóbue** (police) whistle.

yobikomu to call a person in.

yobiokosu to wake, rouse; to call; **kioku o yobiokosu** to call to mind.

yobimono chief attraction; feature attraction; **kyoogi chuu no yobimono** feature attraction of the tournament.

yobirin (call) bell; buzzer.

yobitateru to call out; to call to; to ask to come.

yobitomeru to call and stop; to call to (someone) to stop; to call (someone) back.

yobiuri hawking.

yobiyoseru to call, summon, send for; to call together, assemble.

yoboo prevention, precaution; **yoboo chúusha** preventive injection, inoculation; **yoboo suru** to prevent; to keep as a precaution against.

yoboyobo tottering.

YOBU to call; to call out to; to call after; to send for; to invite; **isha o yobu** to send for a doctor.

yobun (n.) surplus, extra; **yobun no** (adj.) surplus, extra, remaining.

yobyoo complication.

yóchi foresight; **yóchi suru** to know beforehand.

yochi room, space.

yodan digression; **yodan ni wataru** to digress; **yodan wa shibáraku oki** to return to the main subject.

yodare saliva; **yodare o tarasu** to slobber.

yodooshi all night, all night through.

yofukáshi o suru to keep late hours; to sit up late at night.

yofuke late hours; **yofuke ni** late at night.

yogen prediction, prophecy; **yogen suru** to foretell, predict.

yógi bedcover.

yogi nái unavoidable.

yógisha night train.

yogore dirt, filth, soil; **yogoreme** visible stain.

yogoreru to become dirty, become filthy; to be stained; **yogoreppói** easily soiled; liable to be soiled.

YOGOSU to make unclean; to stain; to soil, foul.

yóha aftermath; tail end; **taifuu no yóha** the end of a typhoon.

yohaku space; margin.

YOHODO to a great degree; very greatly; for a good while; **yohodo máe** quite a while ago; **yohodo no** large number of, great deal of.

yohoo forecast, prediction; **tenki yohoo** weather forecast; **yohoo suru** to forecast, predict.

yoi evening; **yoi no kuchi ni** in the early evening; **yoi no myoojoo** evening star; Venus.

YÓI, ÍI good, right, fine; **yói kangae** a good idea. **Sore de yói.** That will do. **Itte yói.** You may go.

yoí intoxication; **yoí ga deru** to become intoxicated; **yoí ga mawaru** to get tipsy; **yoí ga saméru** to sober up; **yoidore** drunkard; **yoidore ni náru** to be drunk.

yoigoshi overnight.

yoin trailing note, reverberation; agreeable aftertaste, suggestion; **yoin no áru** trailing; suggestive; pregnant.

yoippari sitting (staying) up very late; **yoippari no asanéboo** late to bed and late to rise.

yoizame sobering up.

yojiréru to be twisted, be contorted.

yojiru to twist.

yóka spare time; **yóka ni** in spare time; **yóka ga áru** to have leisure; **yóka o riyoo suru** to take advantage of spare time.

yokan presentiment, premonition; **yokan ga suru** to have a premonition.

yokan chill in the air (early spring).

yokare ashikare right or wrong; rightly or wrongly.

yókaze night wind.

–yoke suffix denoting: shelter, screen; **hiyoke** sunshade.

YOKEI NA extra; unnecessary; enough and to spare; superfluous; **yokei na mono** unnecessary (thing); **yokei na híyoo** extra expenses. **Yokei na oséwa desu.** Mind your own business.

yokéru to avoid, shun; to keep off from; to keep aloof.

yóki expectation, anticipation; **yoki ni hanshite** contrary to expectation; **yóki shinai** unexpected; unlooked for; **yóki suru** to expect, anticipate.

yokin money deposited; **yokin suru** to deposit money in the bank.

YOKKA four days, fourth day of the month.

yokkaku bathers; visitors at a spa (or hot spring).

yokkyuu craving, desire.

YOKO width; side; flank; **yoko no** sidelong; horizontal; **yoko ni** across, crossways; **yoko kara kuchi o dásu** to cut in; to put in a word; **yoko ni náru** to be down; **yokobai ni náru** to lie on one's side.

yokochoo lane; side street.

yokodori suru to snatch.

yokogíru to cross, traverse; to sail across;

toorí o mukoo e yokogíru to go across
the street.

yokoku notice, announcement; yokoku náshi
ni without warning; yokoku no tóori as
previously announced; yokoku suru to
give notice in advance.

yokome sidelong glance; yokome de míru to
look askance at; yokome o tsukau to cast
a sidelong glance.

yokomichi byroad; wrong direction;
digression; yokomichi ni háiru to deviate
from.

yokomoji Occidental script or letters.

yokoo rehearsal; preliminary exercise.

yokoppara side (of the body).

yokoshima wickedness; yokoshima na
wicked.

YOKOSU to send; to forward; to hand over,
give over, deliver.

yokotaéru to lay down (something); mi o
byooshoo ni yokotaéru to become ill; to
lie down in a sickbed.

yokotaoshi ni náru to fall sideways.

yokotawáru to lie down; to lie across;
nagaisu ni yokotawáru to lie on a sofa.

yokoyari interruption (of conversation); –ni
yokoyari o ireru to break in; to cut in.

yokozuke ni suru to bring alongside (a pier,
etc.).

YÓKU well; finely; often; thoroughly. Kono
hón wa yóku kákete iru. This book is
written well.

yokú greed, desire; yoku no fukái avaricious,
greedy; yokú o hanárete without ulterior
motive; yoku toku zuku de for gain; for
self-interest; yokúbari greedy person.

yokubáru to be avaricious, be greedy.

YOKUASA following (next) morning.

YOKUBAN following (next) evening.

yokuboo desire, ambition.

YOKUCHOO next morning.

YOKUGETSU next month.

YOKUJITSU next day.

yokujoo public bath.

yokumé partiality, prejudice; yokumé de
míru to show prejudice. Ikura yokumé
de míte mo. Even if I give it the benefit
of the doubt.

YOKUNEN next year.

yokusei control, suppression; yokusei
dekínai uncontrollable; yokusei suru to
control; to suppress.

YOKUSHITSU bathroom.

YOKUSOO bathtub.

yokusúru to bathe; to take a bath; onkei ni
yokusúru to be favored with; onten ni
yokusúru to receive a special favor.

yokuyoku very, extremely; carefully;
yokuyoku iyá ni nátta being quite sick

of; yokuyoku no kotó de nákereba
unless driven to extremes; yokuyoku no
riyuu a very strong reason.

yokuyokujitsu next day but one; two days
later.

yokuyokunen next year but one; two years
later.

yokuyoo intonation, modulation; yokuyoo no
áru modulated; yokuyoo no nái
monotonous; yokuyoo o tsukéru to
modulate.

yokyoo entertainment; extra show, side show.

yomáwari night watch; night watchmen.

yómei remainder of one's life; yómei
ikubaku mo nái to have only a few years
left (to live).

yoméru to be able to read; to read well; to
see; to understand; to see through. Kono
shoosetsu wa chótto yoméru. This novel
is rather interesting (reading).

yomí reading, Japanese reading of a Chinese
character (kun reading).

yomiagéru to read out, read aloud; to finish
reading, read through; hón o yomiagéru
to read through a book.

yomiayamari misreading; mispronunciation.

yomiayamáru to misread; to mispronounce.

yómikaki reading and writing; yómikaki ga
dekíru to be able to read and write.

yomikáta reading, pronunciation; reading
lesson.

yomikikaséru to read (a book) to
(someone).

yomikonásu to digest what one reads.

yomímono reading, reading matter; kodomo
no yomímono children's books; juvenile
literature.

yominaósu to reread.

yominikúi illegible; difficult to read;
yominikúi jí illegible handwriting.

yomiótōsu to overlook (miss) in reading; to
skip (over).

yomiowaru to read through; to finish reading.

yomité poet; reader.

yomiyói easy to read; legible; yomiyói jí
legible handwriting.

YÓMU to read; to recite; to understand; to
see; hito no kaoiro o yómu to read
(someone's) face; hito no shínchuu o
yómu to guess what a person means;
musabori yómu to devour (a book); utá
o yómu to recite a poem; to compose a
poem; zatto yómu to run one's eyes over;
to scan.

yómichi night journey; yómichi o iku to go
by night.

yomigáeru to come to one's senses; to be
freshened; to be brought to life; to rise
from the dead. Yomigáetta yóo na

kokochi ga suru. I feel myself again (a new man).

YÓN, YOTTSÚ, SHÍ four; juuyón fourteen; yónjuu forty.

yonabe night work; yonabe o suru to do night work.

YONAKÁ midnight; yonaká ni in the dead of night; in the middle of the night.

yonaréru to get used to the world; to grow accustomed to the ways of the world; to grow worldly; yonarénu inexperienced; green; yonáreta hito man (woman) of the world. Káre wa máda yonarénai. He has seen little of life.

yondokoronái unavoidable; urgent, pressing; necessary; yondokoronáku unavoidably; out of necessity; unwillingly.

yonen nái wholly engrossed; earnest; eager; kenkyuu ni yonen nái to be absorbed in study.

yonónaka world; public; times; yonónaka e déru to start life; yonónaka ga iyá ni náru to be sick of the world.

–YÓO manner, style, way, appearance; –no yóo na of the manner of, like; –no yóo ni in the manner of; –no yóo desu it's like. Kúru yoo desu. It appears that he is coming.

yóo main point; essence; yóo wa in brief.

yóo business; task; use; service; yóo ga áru to have business on hand; yóo o tasu to go to the bathroom.

yóobo foster mother.

yooboo expectation; urgent request; yooboo suru to demand.

YOOCHÍEN kindergarten.

yoodan business talk.

yoodatéru to lend, advance (money); to accommodate.

yóodo iodine.

yoofúbo foster parents.

YOOFUKU Occidental clothes.

yoogísha suspect, suspected person.

yóogo protection, safeguard; yóogo suru to protect, defend.

yoogo wording; terms.

yóogu tools, implements.

yoogúruto yogurt.

yoohínten Occidental goods shop.

yoohoo directions for use; uses.

yóoi preparation, provision; prudence; mán'ichi no yóoi o suru to prepare for an emergency; yóoi suru to get ready.

YOOI easiness, simplicity; yooi de nái difficult; yooi na easy, simple.

yooiku suru to bring up; to rear.

YOOJI, YÓO business. (See also yookén.)

yóoji infant, baby.

yóoka adoptive family.

yóojin care, prudence; yoojin bukái careful; yóojin no tamé as a precaution; yóojin suru to be careful; yoojínboo bodyguard.

yoojin high official.

yóojo adopted daughter.

yoojóo suru to take care of one's health.

YOOKA eight days; eighth day of the month.

yookai dissolution; melting, smelting, fusion; yookai suru to dissolve; melt; to smelt; to fuse.

yookan Occidental-style building.

yóokan bittersweet jelly of beans (popular snack or dessert item).

yookén, YOOJI business; matter of business. Náni ka goyooken ga arimásu ka? Do you have any business to transact?

yooki weather; gaiety; yooki na bright; cheerful (of disposition); yooki ni atarareru to be affected by the weather; yooki ni náru to be merry, become lively.

yooki receptacle; vessel.

yookoo traveling abroad; yookoo suru to go abroad.

yookyuu claim; demand; request; yookyuu suru to claim; to demand; yookyúusha claimant.

yóomu important mission.

yoomuki business; mission; errand; yoomuki o tazunéru to inquire into (someone's) business; to ask (someone) his or her business.

yoorei example.

yóoro important position; high office; yóoro ni tátsu to occupy an important position.

yooróoin old-age home, nursing home.

yooróokin old-age pension.

YOORÓPPA Europe; Yooroppajín European.

yoosen letter paper.

yoosha náku without ceremony; mercilessly.

yóoshi point, gist; essential (important) points; summary; blank printed forms; denpoo yóoshi telegraph form.

yooshi adopted son; yooshi ni suru to adopt a child.

yooshiki mode; form; style.

yoosho Occidental books.

yooshoku Occidental food; yooshokuya restaurant serving Occidental food.

yooshoku shínju cultured pearl.

yooshu (Occidental) wine.

yóoso essential element; important factor.

yoosoo Occidental-style books, clothes, dress; yoosoo suru to be dressed in European style.

YOOSU condition; circumstances; appearance; –no yoosu o suru to show

signs of; **yoosu o ukagau** to observe; to
see how things stand.

yoosúru require; need.

yootáshi transacting business; **yootáshi ni
iku** to go out on an errand.

yootén gist; main point.

yóoto use; **yóoto ga hirói** to have various
(many) uses.

YOOYAKU at last; at length; gradually;
narrowly; **yooyaku ma ni áu** to be barely
on time. **Yooyaku áme ga yanda.** At last
the rain stopped.

yopparai drunkard, drunk.

yoréru to be twisted, get twisted.

yoreyore no worn out; seedy; threadbare.

–YORI from; out of; at; in; since; than;
before; **úmi no kánata yori** from beyond
the sea. **A wa B yori sé ga takái.** A is
taller than B. **Kái wa gógo yóji yori
hajimaru.** The party is to begin at four in
the afternoon.

yorí twist, ply; **yori ito** twisted thread; **yorí o
kakéru** to give a twist.

yoriai meeting; gathering.

yoridásu to pick out, single out; to sort out.

yoridokoro ground; source; authority;
reliance; **yoridokoro no áru** sure,
reliable, authentic; **yoridokoro no nái**
groundless, unfounded, unreliable.

yorikakáru to lean (stand) against.

yorimichi stop (on the way); **yorimichi o
suru** to visit on the way; to break a
journey.

yorinuki no (*adj.*) choice, select.

yorinúku to choose, select, pick out; **tasúu
no uchi kara yorinúku** to pick (a few)
out of a large number.

yorisóu to draw close, draw near; to nestle.

yoritóru to choose.

yoriwakéru to sort out, assort, classify; to
pick out; to separate.

yorokeru to totter; to stagger.

yorokobashíi glad, joyous, delighted. **Konna
yorokobashíi kotó wa arimasén.** Nothing
gives me as much pleasure.

yorokobásu to delight, rejoice; to bring joy,
gladden.

YOROKÓBI joy, delight; congratulations;
yorokóbi o nobéru to congratulate.

YOROKOBU to be glad; to rejoice; to be
delighted (at). **Yorokónde.** Gladly. With
pleasure.

yóron public opinion.

YOROSHÍI to be good; to be permissible; to
be acceptable.

YOROSHIKU well; properly; in an
appropriate way; best regards. **Aoki-san
ni yoroshiku.** Please remember me to
Aoki.

yóroyoro unsteadily; **yóroyoro to arúku** to
walk unsteadily (feebly or drunkenly).

yorozuya general store.

YÓRU night.

yoru to depend on; to hang on; to be based
upon, be founded on; **goirai ni yori** at
your request; **saikin no chóosa ni yoréba**
according to the latest information.

yoseru to let approach, let come near; to
bring near; to draw near; to add; **isu o
yoseru** to draw up one's chair; **–ni mi o
yoseru** to become dependent on.

yóshi all right; well; good; now; even if,
though; **yóshi nanigoto ga okoróo tomo**
whatever may happen. **Yóshi bóku ga
yatte miyóo.** Now I'll try.

–no yóshi I hear . . .

yoshin preliminary tremors.

yoshin preliminary examination.

yoshuu preparation; rehearsal; **yoshuu suru**
to prepare lessons; to rehearse.

YOSÓ somewhere else; another place; **yosó
de** elsewhere, somewhere else; **yoso goto**
another's affair; **yosó mi** looking off,
aside, away.

yosoku estimation, estimate; forecast; **yosoku
suru** to estimate, to forecast, predict.

yosoo anticipation, expectation; **yosoo suru**
to expect, anticipate; **yosóogai ni**
unexpectedly; **yosóogai no** unexpected.

yosoóu to dress (attire, equip) oneself in.

YÓSU to stop, to drop; to leave off; to give
up; to cut off; **tabako o yósu** to stop
smoking. **Joodán wa yóse.** None of your
jokes.

yosutébito hermit; monk.

yótayota unsteadily.

yotei plan; schedule; **yotei no tóori** as
prearranged.

yótsugi heir; heiress.

yotsukado crossroads; corner of the street.

YOTTE and so, consequently, therefore.

yótto yacht.

YOTTSU, YÓN, SHÍ four. **Yottsu
kaimáshita.** I bought four of them.

yóu to get drunk; to feel sick (from motion);
fúne ni yóu to get seasick; **hikooki ni
yóu** to get airsick; **sake ni yóu** to get
drunk.

YOWÁI weak; feeble (in body);
poor-spirited; delicate (things); mild,
gentle; **ki no yowái** fainthearted;
softhearted, limited; **karada ga yowái** to
have a weak constitution; to be in poor
health.

yowamí weakness, feebleness; **yowami ni
tsukekómu** to take advantage of
(someone's) weak point; **yowami o
miséru** to display cowardice.

yowámushi weak person; crybaby.

yowané weakness; confession of weakness; **yowané o háku** to betray weakness; to complain.

yowakí (stock-market term) bears; shorts; selling spirit.

yowátari going through the world; living; **yowátari no hetá na** dull-witted, shiftless; **yowátari no joozú na** shrewd, hardheaded.

yoyaku reservation; advance booking; **yoyaku suru** to book in advance; to subscribe to; **yoyaku mooshikomíkin** subscription (money); initial installment; **yoyákusha** subscriber.

yoyuu spare, reserve (money, time, etc.); **yoyuu shakushaku** to have a good deal in reserve.

YÚ, OYU hot water; **yú ni háiru** to take a bath; **yú o tsukawaseru** to bathe (a child or invalid); **yú o sásu** to pour hot water; **yú o wakasu** to boil water.

YUBÍ finger, toe; **yubí o kuwaeru** to look with envy; **yubíwa o yubí ni hameru** to put a ring on a finger.

YÚBUNE bathtub.

yudan negligence; inattention; carelessness; imprudence; unguarded moment; **sukoshi mo yudan ga nái** to be always on one's guard; **yudan suru** to be negligent. **Yudan taiteki.** Danger comes soonest when it is despised.

YUDAYÁJIN Jew, Jewish.

yudéru to boil; to seethe.

yudono bathroom (for bathing only).

yuen lampsoot, lampblack; **yuen ga tátsu** to smoke.

yugaméru to distort; to contort; to crook, bend; to curve; to warp; **kao o yugaméru** to make a wry face.

yugámu to warp; to swerve, deflect; to be crooked, be distorted.

yúge jet of stream, vapor; **yúge o tátete okóru** to fume (with anger).

yuigon testament, will; one's dying wish; **yuigon o káku** to make a will; **yuigon o sézu ni shinu** to die intestate; **yuigon suru** to leave a will.

yúiitsu only, sole; unique.

yuisho lineage, blood; history.

YUKA floor; **yuka o háku** to sweep the floor, **yukaita** floorboard.

yúkai pleasure; happiness; merriment; **yúkai na** pleasant, happy, merry, joyful.

yukashíi attractive; amiable; winning, engaging.

yukata light, unlined cotton garment worn in summer.

yuketsu blood transfusion.

YUKI, IKI going; bound for; **Oosaka yuki no densha** the Osaka train.

YUKÍ snow; **yukí o itadaku** snowcapped; **yukí o káku** to shovel away the snow; **yukidoke** thawing (of ice and snow); **yukidoke suru** to thaw; **yukí ga fúru** to snow. **Yuki ga tsumóru.** The snow covers the ground.

yukiatari báttari rashly; impetuously; on the spur of the moment; **yukiatari báttari ni yaru** to take chances, to act impetuously.

yukichigai crossing. **Kimi no tegami wa bóku no to yukichigai ni nátta.** Your letter crossed mine.

yukidomari blind alley; dead end (of a street); impasse.

yukigakari circumstances; convention.

yukigake ni on one's way to.

yukiki going and coming; traffic; **yukiki no hito** passersby; acquaintances; **yukiki suru** to come and go; to associate.

yukisaki one's destination.

yukitodóku to be scrupulous; to be prudent; be careful; to be attentive.

yukitsuke no favorite; regular; **yukitsuke no mise** one's favorite shop.

yukiwatáru to extend; to prevail; to spread; to penetrate; to pervade.

yukizumáru to stand still; to arrive at a deadlock; **kotobá ga yukizumáru** to be at a loss for words.

YUKKÚRI slowly, at leisure, leisurely; **yukkúri suru** to enjoy one's free time. **Yukkúri nasái.** Stay as long as you can.

YUKU, IKU to go, proceed; to travel; **kishá de yuku** to go by train; **úmaku yuku** to go well; to be successful.

yukue whereabouts; **yukue fúmei** missing; **yukue o kuramasu** to conceal oneself; **yukue o sagasu** to trace (someone).

yukusaki destination; future.

yukusue future.

yukute way; path; **yukute o saegíru** to stand in the way; **yukute o terasu** to light the way.

yukuyuku on the way; **yukuyuku wa in the end, in the course of time.

yumé dream; **yume no yó** dream world; **–o yumé ni míru** to see in a dream; **yumé kara saméru** to wake from a dream; to be disillusioned; **yumé o míru** to dream.

YUNOMI mug, cup.

YUNYUUHIN imports, imported goods.

yurai origin; history; **yurai suru** to originate.

yure shake, sway, rock, jolt, roll, pitch.

yureru to shake, rock, pitch; to tremble.

yuriokósu to shake up; to wake up by shaking.

yuru to shake; to swing; to joggle.

yurúi relaxed, loosening, slack.

yuruméru to loosen, unloose; to unbend, relax; **té o yuruméru** to loosen one's hold of.

yurúmu to loosen, become (get) loose; to abate. **Ki ga yurunde iru.** His attention is wandering.

yurushí permission, leave; license; initiation; pardon, forgiveness; **yurushí o éte** with permission; **yurushí o kóu** to ask permission.

YURÚSU to permit, allow; to approve; **jikan no yurúsu kágiri** so far as time permits.

yurúyaka na lenient; mild; **yurúyaka na saká** a gentle slope.

yúruyuru slowly, leisurely.

YUSHUTSU export, exportation; **yushutsu suru** to export; **yushutsúhin** exports.

yusoo transportation, conveyance; **yusoo suru** to convey, transport.

yusuburu to shake; to swing.

YUSUGU to wash out; to rinse.

yusuri extortion, blackmail; blackmailer; **yusuru** to extort (money), blackmail; to squeeze.

yútaka na abundant, plentiful, copious; **yútaka na seikatsu** rich living.

yutánpo hot-water bottle. **Yutánpo o irete oyasuminasái.** Get into bed with a hot-water bottle.

yutori room, margin; elbow room; spare (money, time); **yutori o tóru** to leave some room for.

yuttári shita easy; composed; **yuttári shita kimochi ni náru** to feel easy; to feel at home.

YUU, IU to speak, talk; to mention.

yuu to tie; to dress; to arrange; **kamí o yuu** to dress one's hair.

YUUBE last night; yesterday evening. (See also **sakúban**.)

yuuben eloquence; **yuuben na** eloquent, fluent; **yuuben o furuu** to speak eloquently; **yuubenka** eloquent speaker.

yúubi grace, elegance; refinement; **yúubi na** graceful, elegant.

YUUBIN mail, post; **gaikoku yúubin** foreign mail; **yuubin chókin** postal savings; **yuubin haitatsunin** letter carrier; **yuubin káwase** money order; **YUUBIN KÍTTE** postage stamp; **sokutatsu yúubin** special delivery; **yuubin o dásu** to send a letter by mail; **YUUBÍNBAKO** mailbox, letter box; **yuubínbutsu** mail, postal matter; **dái ísshu yubbínbutsu** first-class mail; **dái níshu yuubínbutsu** second-class mail; **YUUBÍNKYOKU** post office. (See also **yuusoóryoo**.)

yuuboo hopefulness; **yuuboo na** hopeful, promising; **zénto yuuboo na seinen** a promising youth.

yúuchoo na sedate, calm, composed; tedious, wearisome, slow.

YUUDACHI shower; **yuudachi ga kúru** to have a shower; **yuudachi ni áu** to be caught in a shower.

yuudai na magnificent, imposing.

yuudoku na poisonous, venomous.

yuudoo inducement; **yuudoo suru** to draw, lure, lead.

yuueki usefulness; benefit, advantage, instructiveness; **yuueki na** useful, advantageous; **yuueki désu** to be useful; to be beneficial; **yuueki ni tsukau** to make the best use of.

yuuénchi recreation ground, public playground.

yuuetsu superiority, supremacy; **yuuetsu suru** to be superior to, to surpass; **yuuétsukan** sense of superiority.

yuugai na bad, harmful, injurious; **kenkoo ni yuugai de áru** to be bad for the health.

YUUGATA evening.

yúugi play, game, amusement; **yúugi o suru** to play a game.

yuugoo melting, fusion, union, harmony; **yuugoo suru** to melt down, to harmonize; to fuse, unite.

yuuguu warm treatment; **–ni yuuguu sareru** to be received cordially by; **–o yuuguu suru** to give a warm reception to.

YUUHAN supper, evening meal.

yuuhi setting sun.

yúui na capable, able, efficient; **shóorai yúui na** promising.

YUUJIN friend, companion.

yuujoo friendliness; friendly feelings.

yuujuufudan irresolution, indecision; **yuujuufudan na** irresolute.

yuukai abduction, kidnapping; **yuukai suru** to kidnap; **yuukáisha** kidnapper.

yuukan evening issue, evening paper.

yuukan na brave, courageous, daring; **yuukan ni** courageously.

yuukénsha elector, voter.

yúuki courage, valor; **yúuki rinrin** spiritedly, bravely; **yúuki o dásu** to gather one's courage; **yúuki o ushinau** to lose courage.

yuukoo na efficient; meritorious, **yuukoo de áru** to be effective, to hold good; **yuukoo ni tsukau** to make good use of.

yuukyuu no salaried.

yuumei na famous, noted, celebrated; **yúumei ni náru** to become famous.

yúumoa humor; **yúumoa ni tomu** to have a sense of humor.

YUURANBÁSU sight-seeing bus.

yúuretsu superiority; inferiority; merits; difference; **yúuretsu ga nái** to be equal; **yúuretsu o arasóu** to strive for superiority.

yúuri being profitable.

yúuryo anxiety, concern; **yúuryo subéki** serious, grave; **yúuryo suru** to become anxious about, become troubled.

yuuryoku na powerful, influential; controlling; **yuuryókusha** influential person.

yuuryoo na superior, excellent, choice; **yuuryoo na seiseki** excellent result.

yuusénken priority, first claim.

yúushi volunteer; supporter; interested person.

yuushoo victory; superiority.

yuushuu superiority; sublimity, excellence; **yuushuu na** superior, best, excellent.

yuusóoryoo postage. (See also **yuubin, yuuzei.**)

yuutai generous treatment; hospitality, welcome; **yuutai o ukéru** to be welcomed at.

yuutai voluntary resignation, voluntary retirement; **-o yuutai suru** to resign or retire voluntarily from . . .

yuutoo superiority; excellency; top grade; **yuutoo no** high-grade, superior, excellent, first-rate; **yuutoo de sotsugyoo suru** to graduate with honors.

yuuutsu na melancholy, cheerless, gloomy.

yuuwa suru to melt; to soften; to soothe; to conciliate, placate, propitiate; to be reconciled with.

yuuwaku temptation, enticement; **yuuwaku suru** to tempt, entice; **yuuwaku to tatakau** to resist temptation.

yuuyake evening glow; afterglow.

yuuyami twilight, dusk; **yuuyami semáru kóro** in the gathering dusk.

yúuyo delay; hesitation; extension of time, grace, reprieve; **yúuyo náku** without delay; without allowing an extension; **yúuyo o atáeru** to give an extension; **yúuyo suru** to hesitate, give time.

yuuyoo usefulness; **yuuyoo na** useful, serviceable; **yuuyoo ni** usefully, effectively.

yuuyúu leisurely; deliberately; serenely, placidly, calmly.

yuuzai guiltiness; conviction; culpability; **yuuzai no** guilty.

yuuzei postage. (See also **yuubin, yuusóoryoo.**)

yuuzuu circulation (of a bill or note); accommodation; versatility; adaptability; **yuuzuu o kikasu** to adapt oneself; **yuuzuu suru** to advance money.

yuzuriáu to compromise, concede mutually, meet halfway.

yuzuriukéru to obtain by transfer; to take over; to inherit.

yuzuriwatashi alienation; conveyance; transfer.

yuzuru to make over; to hand over; to transfer; to part with; **hito ni séki o yuzuru** to make room for; **ippo mo yuzuranai** not to yield a step.

Z

záazaa plenty, freely, profusely (said of rain or water); **záazaa mizu o nagásu** to let water run freely. **Áme ga záazaa fútte iru.** It is pouring.

ZABÚTON cushion to sit on; **zabúton o shiku** to seat oneself on a cushion.

zadan familiar conversation, table talk; **zadánkai** (discussion) meeting.

záiaku sin, transgression, offense, crime; **záiaku o okasu** to commit a sin; to commit a crime.

zaibatsu powerful financial group.

zaichuu containing. "**Insatsúbutsu zaichuu.**" "Printed matter only."

zaidan foundation; financial group.

zaigai abroad, overseas; **zaigai nipponjín** Japanese residents abroad.

zaigaku in school; **zaigaku chuu** while in school; **zaigaku suru** to be in school, at school.

zaigen source of revenue; resources; **zaigen ni toboshíi** to lack financial resources.

zaigoo sins, sinful acts; **zaigoo no fukái** sinful.

ZAIJUU residence; **Nyuuyóoku zaijuu no Nipponjín** Japanese residents in New York.

zaikyoo being in the capital; staying in Tokyo; **zaikyoo no yuujin** a friend in the capital (in Tokyo).

zaimoku wood, timber, lumber.

zaínin criminal, offender, malefactor.

záirai existing hitherto; **záirai no** usual, ordinary, conventional.

záiryoku financial status.

zairyóo raw material; data.

zairyuu residing, dwelling; **-ni zairyuu suru** to reside in.

zaisan property; fortune; **zaisan o tsukúru** to make a fortune; **zaisanka** wealthy person.

zaisei finance; financial affairs; **zaisei joo** financially, from a financial point of view; **zaisei joo no** fiscal.

zaishoku service; tenure (of office);

zaishoku chuu during one's term of office.

ZAITAKU being at home. **Myóonichi wa gozaitaku deshóo ka?** Will you be at home tomorrow?

zakka miscellaneous goods; **zakkashoo** grocer; general dealer.

zákkubaran na frank, plain, outspoken; **zákkubaran ni** frankly, plainly; **zákkubaran ni hanásu** to speak plainly.

zánbu remainder, rest, balance.

zanbú to with a great splash.

zangé repentence; penitence; confession of sins; **zangé suru** to repent, be penitent.

zangén slander; false charge.

zankoku cruelty, brutality; harshness, coldheartedness; inhumanity; **zankoku na** cruel, brutal, merciless, harsh; **zankoku ni atsukau** to treat cruelly.

zánmu remaining business; **zánmu o séiri suru** to wind up affairs.

zannén regret, chagrin; mortification; **zannén na** regrettable; mortifying; **zannén ni omóu** to regret; to be sorry for.

zannin brutality, cruelty; coldheartedness; **zannin na** brutal, cruel; **zannin ní mo** brutally, cruelly; **zanninsei** cruel nature.

zanpai rout, crushing defeat; **zanpai suru** to be routed, be beaten to the ground.

zanshi suru to be killed in an accident.

zánsho heat of late summer, lingering summer, Indian summer.

zansónsha survivor.

zanson suru to survive; to subsist; to remain, be left.

zappaku na loose; unsystematic, incoherent; crude; **zappaku na gíron** poor argument.

zappi miscellaneous expense; incidental expense.

zappoo general news; **zappóoran** news columns.

ZARA NI in plenty; plentifully; everywhere; **zara ni áru** to be very common; to be found everywhere.

zárazara rough feeling; **zárazara suru** to feel rough.

ZASEKI seat; room.

zasetsu breakdown; setback; collapse; discouragement; **zasetsu suru** to break down, receive a setback; to become discouraged; to collapse. **Keikaku wa chuuto de zasetsu shita.** The plan collapsed before it was completed.

ZASHIKÍ room; living room in a Japanese house; **kyaku o zashikí e tóosu** to show a visitor into the living room.

zashoo suru to run ashore, run aground; to be stranded.

ZASSHI magazine, periodical, journal; **zasshi o tóru** to subscribe to a magazine.

zasshu crossbreed, hybrid; variety; various kinds; **zasshu no** mixed, crossbred, hybrid; **zasshu o tsukúru** to cross, interbreed.

zatsudan chatting, gossiping; **zatsudan suru** to gossip, chat.

zatsuji miscellaneous affairs.

zátsumu routine work; miscellaneous business; **zátsumu ni owareru** to be kept busy with miscellaneous business.

zatsu na rough, coarse; miscellaneous; **zatsu ni káku** to write carelessly, scribble; to draw roughly; **zatsu na kotobá o tsukau** to speak roughly; **zatsu na tatekáta** crude (flimsy) construction.

zatsuon hubbub; murmur; static (on the radio).

zatsuyoo miscellaneous business.

zatsuzen disorder, confusion; indiscriminately; desultorily; **zatsuzen to shita** disorderly; desultory; indiscriminate. **Zatsuzen to tsumikasánete áru.** They are heaped in disorderly fashion.

zatta no sundry, miscellaneous, various, diverse; all sorts of; **zatta no mono** all sorts of things.

ZATTO roughly; hastily; briefly; approximately; **zatto shita** rough, cursory, coarse; **zatto shita mitsumori** rough estimate; **zatto mé o tóosu** to glance cursorily through (a book); **zatto setsumei suru** to explain briefly.

zattoo bustle; congestion; confusion; **zattoo shita machi** busy street; **zattoo suru** to bustle; to be crowded (with).

zawameki to be noisy; to rustle.

zawatsuku to be noisy; to rustle; to murmur, to be agitated.

záwazawa murmuringly, rustlingly; noisily; **záwazawa suru** to be noisy; to be agitated.

zé ga hi demo whether right or wrong; by hook or by crook; by all means. **Zé ga hi demo sore o té ni irenákereba naránai.** By hook or by crook, I must get it.

ZÉHI by all means; under any circumstance.

ZÉI tax, duty; rate; **zéi o chooshuu suru** to collect taxes; **zéi o kasúru** to impose a tax (on); to levy a tax; **zéi o osaméru** to pay taxes; **zeikan** customs, customhouse.

zeitáku, zeitakúhin luxury; extravagance; **zeitáku na** luxuriant, extravagant; **zeitáku ni** luxuriantly, extravagantly; **zeitáku ni kurasu** to live in luxury; **zeitáku o iu** to ask too much; **zeitáku o suru** to indulge in luxury.

zekkoo severance of a friendship or acquaintanceship.

zekkoo no finest, best; capital, splendid; **zekkoo no kikái** splendid opportunity, golden opportunity.

zekkyoo exclamation, ejaculation; **zekkyoo suru** to exclaim; to shout, yell.

zen Buddhist sect emphasizing religious meditation.

zén'aku good and bad; right and wrong.

zenbu first part; front; forepart.

ZÉNBU all parts, whole, entire lot; **zénbu de** altogether; in all.

zenbun complete sentence; full text.

zénchi complete recovery; perfect cure; **zénchi suru** to be completely cured or recovered.

zenchoo presage, omen; sign, symptom.

zéndai mimon no unprecedented, unheard-of, record-breaking.

ZENGAKU total amount, sum total.

ZÉNGO before and after; order; thereabouts, somewhere about; **zéngo no kankei** context (of a sentence); **zéngo o tsúujite** from the first to the last.

zéngo fukaku being unconscious; **zéngo fukaku ni** quite unconsciously.

zengósaku remedial measures; **zengósaku o koozúru** to consider the remedies.

zén'i good intention; good faith; **zén'i no** well-meant, well-intentioned, in good faith.

zenin approval; **zenin suru** to approve.

zen'in everybody present; all members.

ZENJITSU previous day, day before.

zenjutsu no previously mentioned, above-mentioned.

zénka previous criminal record; **zenkamono** ex-convict.

zenkai complete recovery of health.

zénkai last occasion; previous installment; **zénkai ni** last time, previously; **zénkai no** last, previous.

zénkan whole volume, entire book.

zenkei whole view; panoramic view; bird's-eye view.

zenken full power; full authority; **zenken o inin suru** to entrust a person with full power (or authority).

zénki previous period; first term; first half of the year.

zénki no aforementioned, above-mentioned; **zénki no tóori** as mentioned above.

zénkoku whole country, whole land; **zénkoku ni** throughout the country; **zenkokuteki ni** national, country-wide.

zenkoo good conduct, good deed.

zénkoo whole school; **zenkoo seito** the whole student body.

zenmai spring (of clocks, etc.).

zenmai flowering fern.

zenmetsu annihilation, extermination; **–o zenmetsu saseru** to annihilate.

zennan zénnyo pious men and women, pious people.

zennín virtuous person.

zennoo advance payment; **zennoo suru** to pay in advance.

zenpai complete defeat, crushing defeat; **zenpai suru** to suffer a crushing defeat.

zenpai total abolition; **zenpai suru** to abolish, to make a clean sweep of.

zenpan first half.

ZENPOO front; **zenpoo ni** ahead, in front; **zenpoo no** front, forward.

zenpuku no utmost, greatest; wholehearted; **zenpuku no dóryoku o suru** to exert oneself to the utmost.

zenrei precedent; previous example; **zenrei no nái** unprecedented.

zénretsu front rank.

zénryoku all one's energy (strength, power); **zénryoku o tsukúsu** to do one's best.

zenryoo goodness, integrity; **zenryoo na** good, virtuous, honest.

zensei height of prosperity; zenith of power; **zensei jídai** golden age; age of prosperity; **zensei o kiwaméru** to be at the height of prosperity.

zensékai whole world; world at large; **zensékai ni** all over the world.

zénsha no former, prior.

zénshi whole city; all over the city; **zénshi itáru tokoró ni** everywhere in the city; **zenshímin** all the citizens; all the residents of the city.

zenshin whole body; full-length photo (of the body); all over the body; **zenshin fuzui** total paralysis; **zenshin fuzui ni náru** to become paralyzed.

zenshin advance, progress; **zenshin suru** to advance.

zenshin gradual (slow but steady) advance; **zenshin suru** to move step by step.

zenshin antecedents; (one's) past.

zenshin one's whole heart; **zenshin o kómete** with all of one's heart.

zénsho taking proper measures; **zénsho suru** to manage tactfully.

zenshoo complete destruction by fire; **zenshoo suru** to be entirely destroyed by fire.

zenshoo complete victory, unbroken series of victories; **zenshoo suru** to win a complete victory.

zenshóogai one's whole life; **zenshóogai o tsuujite** throughout one's life.

zensokúryoku full speed, top speed; **zensokúryoku o dásu** to go at full speed.

ZENTAI whole body; entirety; naturally; as a

matter of course; on earth; **zentai de in all**, altogether; **zentai to shite** in general; **zentai ni** wholly, entirely, generally; **zentai no** whole, entire, complete.

zénto future; prospect; future career; **zénto ni nozomi o kakéru** to pin one's hopes on one's future; **zénto ryooen** the goal which is a long way off.

ZÉN'YA previous night; **sono zén'ya** night before.

zen'yaku complete translation.

ZENZEN entirely, completely, wholly; thoroughly; exactly; at all. **Zenzen shiranai.** I don't know at all.

zeppan out of print.

zeppeki precipice, cliff.

zéro zero, nought, nothing.

zessei matchless, peerless.

zesshoku fasting, abstention from food; **zesshoku suru** to go without food.

zessoku cessation of breathing; expiration; **zessoku suru** to die, expire.

zessúru to go out of existence, become extinct; to exceed, be beyond (something).

zetchoo highest point, summit, zenith; **zetchoo ni tassúru** to reach the summit.

zetsuboo despair, hopelessness; **zetsubooteki no** hopeless, desperate; **mattaku zetsuboo de áru** to be utterly hopeless; **zetsuboo suru** to despair, give up hope.

zetsudai no gigantic, colossal, enormous; **zetsudai no dóryoku o suru** to make a supreme effort.

zetsuen isolation; insulation; **zetsuen suru** to sever connections with; to insulate; **zetsuen'sen** insulated wire.

zetsumei death; **zetsumei suru** to die, expire.

zetsumetsu extermination; extinction; **zetsumetsu suru** to exterminate, stamp out; to die out.

zétsumu nil, nought, nothing; **–wa zétsumu de áru** there can be no such.

ZETTAI absoluteness, positiveness; **zettai ni** decidedly, absolutely; **zettai no** absolute, positive; **zettai zetsumei** desperation, last extremity.

zokkai world; life; laity; **zokkai no** worldly, mundane.

zokkoo continuation; **zokko suru** to continue, proceed with.

zokkoku dependency; subject state; tributary.

zokuaku na being coarse, vulgar, gross, unrefined.

zokuhatsu, zokushutsu successive occurrence; **zokuhatsu suru** to occur in succession.

zokuhen sequel.

zoku na worldly; popular; common; vulgar; **zoku ni** commonly, popularly.

zokusetsu common saying; popular view; tradition.

zokushoo popular designation; popular name.

zoku súru to belong to; to pertain to; to come under. **Beikoku ni zoku súru.** It belongs to the United States.

zókuzoku successively, in rapid succession.

zókuzoku suru to feel chilly; to shiver; to thrill.

zonbun to the full; to one's heart's content; **omóu zonbun naku** to cry to one's heart's content.

zonjiru See **zonzúru**.

zonmei living, being alive; existence; **zonmei chuu ni** during one's lifetime; **zonméisha** survivor.

zonzái na careless, inattentive; rough; rude; **zonzái ni** roughly, crudely, carelessly; **zonzái na mono no iikata o suru** to be rough spoken; **zonzái ni káku** to write carelessly.

zonzúru to know; to be aware of, be conscious of; to think; to be acquainted with. **Kono fukín wa yóku zonjíte imásu.** I know this neighborhood well. **Sonó hito o go-zónji desu ká?** Are you acquainted with him?

zóo image, statue, statuette; figure.

zóo elephant.

zoochiku extension; addition; **zoochiku suru** to enlarge; to build an extension.

zoochoo presumption; **zoochoo suru** to become arrogant.

zooen reinforcements; **zooen suru** to reinforce.

zoofuku ki amplifier.

zoogaku increase, augmentation; **zoogaku o suru** to increase, raise (money, salary, etc.).

zoogen increase and/or decrease.

zóoho supplement, enlargement; **–o zóoho suru** to enlarge, supplement.

zooin increase in personnel; increased staff.

zooka increase, augmentation; **zooka suru** to increase, augment; **zookáritsu** the rate of increase.

zoohéikyoku mint (for money).

ZOOKIN cleaning rag; mop.

zookyuu wage increase, pay increase; **zookyuu suru** to increase wages.

zóoo hatred, spite, antipathy.

ZOORI sandals; **zoori o haku** to wear sandals.

zoosaku fittings; furniture; alterations; features; **zoosaku no sorótta kao** regular features, comely face; **zoosaku o suru** to make alterations in a house. **Zoosakuzuki kashiya.** Furnished house to let.

ZOOSA NÁI not difficult, easy, simple; **zoosa náku** easily, without difficulty.

zoosen shipbuilding; **zoosenjo** shipyard, dockyard.

zooshi increase in capital; **zooshi suru** to increase the capital.

zooshin promotion; betterment, increase; **zooshin suru** to promote; to increase; to be conducive to; **nooritsu o zooshin suru** to increase efficiency.

zoosho collection of books.

zooshuu additional income, increase of receipts.

zoosui rise (swelling) of a river;

zootei presentation, offer; **zootei suru** to present; to give a present; **zootéihin** gift, present; **zootéisha** giver.

zootoo exchange of presents; **zootoo suru** to exchange presents; **zootóohin** presents, gifts.

zoowai bribery, corruption; **zoowai suru** to bribe; to offer a bribe; **zoowai jíken** bribery case; **zoowáisha** briber.

zóoyo presentation; donation, present, **zóoyo suru** to present; to donate; **zooyósha** donor.

zoozei increase in taxation, tax increase; **zoozéi an** bill for an increase in taxation; **ichíwari no zoozei** a 10 percent increase in taxation; **zoozei suru** to increase taxes.

zórozoro dragging along, trailing along, going with many followers. **Minná ga zórozoro tsúite arúku.** They follow at her heels.

zotto suru to shudder, shiver, to feel shocked; **hito o zotto saseru** to make (someone) shudder; **kangáete mo zotto suru** to shudder at the thought of.

zu drawing, picture; diagram; map; **zu de setsumei suru** to illustrate by a diagram; **zu ni noru** to be puffed up; **zu o hiku** to draw a diagram.

–zu a negative-ending denoting: not, without. **Góhan o tabézu ni ikimáshita.** She went there without eating.

zuan plan, design; sketch; **zuan o tsukúru** to prepare a design; **zuanka** designer, draftsperson.

zúbazuba (*colloq.*) frankly, candidly; **zúbazuba itte shimau** to speak frankly.

ZUBÓN trousers, pants.

zubora negligence; nonchalance; slovenliness; **zubora na** negligent, slovenly; **zubora ní** negligently; with nonchalance; **zubora ní náru** to become negligent.

zuboshi bull's-eye, mark; **zuboshi o sásu** to hit the mark.

zubunure ni náru to become soaked (drenched) to the skin.

zubutói bold, daring, audacious; impudent; **zubutói hito** bold fellow; **zubutói kotó o suru** to do a bold thing.

zudón to with a bang, with a thud. **Zudón to teppoo no otó ga shita.** Bang! went the gun.

zugayóoshi drawing paper.

ZÚIBUN fairly, pretty, tolerably; extremely; **zúibun na** very disagreeable; **zúibun samúi** very cold.

zuihitsu stray notes; essay; jottings; miscellaneous writings.

ZUII liberty, freedom; absence of restraint; **zuii ni** freely, voluntarily; **zuii no** free, voluntary, optional. **Gozuii ní meshiagatte kudasái.** Please help yourself.

zúiichi (*n.*) best; foremost; **Nippon zúiichi no sakura no meisho** the most famous place for cherry blossoms in Japan. **Sékai zúiichi desu.** It is the largest in the world.

zuiji at any time; as occasion demands.

zuikoo accompanying; attendance on a journey; **zuikoo suru** to accompany (someone) **zuikóoin** staff (personnel), attendants.

zujoo overhead; over one's head; **zujoo ni óchite kuru** to fall on one's head; **zujoo o tobu** to fly overhead.

zukai illustration, graphic representation; **zukai suru** to illustrate; **zukai shite setsumei suru** to illustrate with a diagram.

zúkazuka straightly, directly.

zúkizuki itámu, zúkizuki suru to throb with pain.

zumen drawing, plan, map.

–zumi suffix denoting; maximum weight capacity of; shipment by; **kisenzumi** shipment by freight; **kyuutonzumi kásha** nine-ton freight car.

zungúri shita dumpy, stocky.

ZÚNOO head, brains; **zúnoo meiseki no** clearheaded; **zúnoo o yoosúru shigoto** brain work.

zunúkete exceptionally, extraordinarily; far above the average; **zunúkete sé no takái kodomo** an exceptionally tall child.

zúnzun rapidly; apace; in leaps and bounds; **zúnzun saki e iku** to go ahead at a rapid pace; **zúnzun susumu** to proceed rapidly.

zurarí to all in a row; in a long row; **zurarí to narabu** to stand in a long row; to sit in a long row.

zuréru to slip down; to slip off.

zúru to slip down. **Zubón ga zúru.** His trousers are slipping.

zúru cheating.

zurúi sly, crafty; unfair; **zurúi otokó** foxy fellow; **zurúi kotó o suru** to do a tricky thing.

zurukéru to shirk (neglect) one's duty; to be tardy; to be idle; **gakkoo o zurukéru** to play truant from school.

zushín to with a thud; with a heavy sound.

zutazuta pieces; **zutazuta ni** in pieces, stripes; **zutazuta ni hikisáku** to tear to shreds; **zutazuta ni kíru** to cut to pieces.

–ZÚTSU each, apiece; **hí ni sankai zútsu** three times a day; **hitóri ni mittsu zútsu** three pieces to each person; **ni sannin zútsu** by twos and threes; **sukoshi zútsu** little by little, bit by bit.

ZUTSUU headache; **wareru yóo na zutsuu** a splitting headache; **zutsuu no táne** a cause of worry; **zutsuu ga suru** to have a headache.

ZUTTO directly to the point; straight to the spot; very much; by far; all the time; **zutto íi** very much better; **zutto ízen** long time ago; **zutto tsuzuite** all the time. **Zutto massúgu ni itte kudasái.** Keep straight on.

zúutai body, frame, physique.

zuuzuuben dialect spoken in the northeastern part of Japan.

zuuzuushíi impudent, audacious; shameless; **zuuzúushiku** impudently, audaciously, shamelessly; **zuuzúushiku náru** to become impudent; **zuuzuushísa** impudence, audacity, effrontery; shamelessness. **Zuuzuushíi otokó da.** He is impudent.

English-Japanese

A

a (an) hitótsu, ichí (*but no word is usually used for this*).
  There is a man. Otoko no hitó ga imásu.
  He is a policeman. Júnsa desu.
abandon (to) suteru (*give up*); misuteru (*forsake, desert*); yameru (*relinquish*).
abbreviate (to) ryaku suru (*simplify*); shooryaku suru (*omit, cut out*).
abbreviation ryáku, ryakugoo.
ability shúwan (*capacity*); gíryoo (*skill*); nóoryoku, sainoo (*talent*).
able dekíru; binwan na, yuunoo na.
able (to be) dekíru.
abortion datai.
abolish (to) haishi suru.
about góro (*point in time*); kúrai, gúrai, hodo, bákari (*quantity*); mawari (*nearness of a place*); –ni tsuite (*concerning*).
above –no ué (*higher than, over*); –fjoo (*more than*).
abroad káigai ni (*overseas*).
absence rúsu (*from home, from the office*); kesseki (*from school, from a meeting*).
absent (to be) rúsu no, kesseki no.
absolute zettaiteki.
absorb (to) suiagéru (*suck up*); suitóru (*take in*).
abstain (to) kiken suru (*from voting*).
abstract chuushooteki.
absurd okashii, báka na.
abundant takusán no.
abuse akuyoo.
abuse (to) akuyoo suru.
academy akádemii, gakkai.
accent ákusento.
accent (to) kyoochoo suru (*emphasize*).
accept (to) ukéru, osaméru (*take in*); shoodaku suru (*agree to*).
acceptance shoodaku.
accident jíko.
  by accident guuzen ni.
accidental guuzen no.
accidentally guuzen ni; omoi gake náku (*unexpectedly*).
accommodate (to) tekioo saseru (*adapt, adjust*); shuuyoo suru (*take in*).
accommodation tekioo (*adaptation*); shisetsu (*facilities*).
accompany (to) isshoni tsuite iku.
accomplish (to) shitogéru, kansei suru.
accord itchi, choowa (*harmony*); íshi (*choice, will*).
according to –ni yoréba; –ni yotte (*depending on*).
account kanjoo (*statement of money*); hanashí (*narration*).

accountant kaikei gákari.
accrue (to) rishi o schoozuru.
accuracy seikaku sa.
accurate seikaku na.
accuse (to) hínan suru.
accustom (to) narásu; shuukan o tsukéru (*habituate*).
ache itami
ache (to) itámu
achieve (to) shitogéru (*accomplish*).
achievement kooseki.
acid *adj.* suppái. –*n.* sán.
acknowledge (to) mitoméru.
acknowledgment uketori (*receipt*).
acquaintance shirai.
acquire (to) éru (*gain*); té ni ireru (*acquire property or rights*).
across mukoogawa (*across the street*).
  go across yokogíru.
  come across mitsukéru (*happen to find*).
act makú (*of a play*); okonai (*deed*).
act (to) suru (*do*); furumau (*behave*).
active katsudooteki, sakan na.
activity katsudoo.
actor yakushá; eiga háiyuu (*movie actor*).
actress joyuu.
actual hontoo no.
actually hontoo ni.
acute surudoi (*sharp*); kyuusei no (*opp. of chronic*).
adapt (to) tekigoo saseru (*make fit*).
add (to) kuwaéru.
addition tashizan (*math.*); kuwáeta mono (*thing added*).
address júusho (*of a place*); hanashí (*speech*).
address (to) hanashikakéru (*speak to*).
  to address a letter tegami ni atena o káku.
adequate tekitoo na.
adjective keiyóoshi.
adjoining tonari no.
administer (to) kánri suru.
admiral kaigun táishoo.
admiration kanpuku, kanshin.
admire (to) kanshin suru, uyamáu.
admission nyuujóoryoo (*charge*).
admit (to) mitoméru (*recognize*); ireru (*let in*).
admittance nyuujoo (*entrance*).
  No admittance. Tachiiri kinshi.
adopt (to) toriiréru.
adult otona.
advance (to) susumeru.
advanced technology sentan gijutsu.
advantage ríeki (*benefit*).
adventure booken.
adverb fukushi.
advertise (to) kookoku suru.

advertisement kookoku.
    classified ad sangyoo kookoku.
advertising kookoku.
    agency kookoku dairi ten.
    campaign kookoku sen.
    research kookoku choosa.
advice chuukoku.
advise (to) chuukoku suru.
affair koto, kotogara.
affect (to) eikyoo suru (*influence*).
affected kidotta (*in manner*).
affection aijoo.
affectionate aijoo no áru.
affirm (to) dangen suru (*state as a fact*).
affirmation dangen.
afloat ukabiagáru.
afraid kowái.
after áto de (*later*); áto (*next to*); sorekara
    (*and then*).
afternoon gógo.
afterward sono go.
again mata, moo ichido.
against –ni táishite.
age (to) toshí o tóru (*said of a person*);
    furuku náru (*said of a thing*).
agency dairíten (*office of an agent*).
agent dairínin (*person*).
aggravate (to) motto wáruku suru (*make
    worse*).
ago máe.
agree (to) sansei suru.
agreeable kokoroyói (*pleasing*).
agreement keiyaku, kyootei, dooi.
agricultural nóogyoo no.
agriculture nóogyoo.
ahead máe mi (*in front of*); saki ni (*of time
    or place*).
aid énjo.
    first aid ookyuu téate.
    first-aid station ookyuu teatesho.
aid (to) énjo suru.
aim mokuteki (*purpose*).
aim at (to) neráu.
air kúuki.
airfield hikoojoo.
air force kuugun.
airmail kookuubin.
airplane kikóoki.
airport kuukoo.
aisle toorímichi.
alarm odoroki (*sudden fear*); keihoo
    (*warning*).
    alarm clock mezamashi-dókei.
alcohol aurkooru.
alike onaji yóo ni (*in a similar way*).
all minná, súbete, zénbu.
alliance doomei.
allow (to) yurúsu (*permit*); ataeru (*give*).
ally mikata.

almost taitei, hotóndo.
alone hitóri de; tandoku de.
along –ni sotte (*parallel to*); issho ni
    (*together with*).
already súde ni, móo.
also yahári, matá, –mo.
altar saidan.
alter (to) kaeru.
alternate *adj.* hitotsu oki no. –*n.* kawari no
    hito (*person*); kawari no mono (*thing*).
alternate (to) hitotsu oki ni suru; kóogo ni
    suru.
although kéredomo.
altitude tákasa.
altogether miná de (*in all*), mattaku
    (*completely*).
    It's five hundred yen altogether. Miná
    de gohyaku en désu.
always itsu mo (*at all times*); ítsu demo (*at
    any time*).
amaze (to) odorokaséru.
amazement odoroki.
ambassador táishi.
ambitious haki no aru, yashin no aru.
amend (to) teisei suru.
America Beikoku, Amerika.
    American Beikokújin, Amerikájin
    (*person*); Amerika no (*pertaining to the
    U.S.A.*).
among –no náka no, –no naka ni, –no naka
    de.
amount gáku; soogaku (*total*).
ample juubún na.
amplifier zoofuku ki; anpu.
amuse (to) tanoshimaséru, omoshirogaraséru.
amusement goraku.
amusing omoshirói.
analyze (to) bunseki suru, kentoo suru.
ancestor sósen.
anchor ikari.
ancient furúi, mukashi no.
and to, ya, shoshite.
anecdote itsuwa.
angel ténshi.
anger ikari.
anger (to) okóru.
angry (to be) okótte iru.
    to get angry okóru.
animal doobutsu.
animate (to) kappatsu ni suru.
annex bekkan (*building*).
annihilate (to) zenmetsu saseru.
anniversary kinénbi.
announce (to) koohyoo suru (*publish*);
    seimei suru (*declare*).
annoy (to) komaraséru.
annual maitoshi no.
annul (to) torikesu.
anonymous tokumei no.

another hoka no.

answer henjí, kotáe.

answer (to) kotáeru, henjí o suru.

antenna antena.

anticipate (to) yosoo suru.

antique kottoohin.

anxiety shinpai.

anxious (to get) shinpai suru.

any náni ka, dáre ka; sukóshi mo (*not even a little*).

anybody dáre ka, dáre demo.

anyhow tómokaku.

anything náni ka, nán demo.

anywhere dóko demo.

apart betsu betsu ni.

apartment apáato.

apiece –zutsu.

apologize (to) ayamáru.

apparent akíraka na (*obvious*).

appeal (to) uttaéru.

appear (to) arawaréru (*make an appearance*).

appearance mikake (*mien*).

appease (to) nadameru.

appendix furoku (*of a book*); móochoo (*of the body*).

appetite shokuyoku.

applaud (to) hákushu kassai suru.

applause kássai.

apple ringo.

application mooshikomi (*request*).

apply (to) mooshikómu.

appoint (to) ninmei suru.

appointment ninmei (*assignment to office*); yakusoku (*engagement*).

appreciate (to) kánsha suru (*thank*); arigátaku omóu (*feel gratified*).

appreciation kánsha.

appropriate tekitoo na.

approve (to) sansei suru (*agree*); yói to omóu (*think well of*).

April Shigatsu.

apron épuron, maekake.

arbitrary dokudanteki na.

arcade aakéedo.

architect kenchikuka.

architecture kenchiku.

ardent nésshin na.

area akichí (*open space*); chíiki (*region*).

argue (to) iiarasóu; gíron suru.

argument iiarasói, ronsoo.

argue (to) okóru (*start, originate*).

arithmetic sanjutsu.

arm udé (*of the body*); búki (*weapon*).

    armaments buki.

    arms reduction gunshuku.

arm (to) *v.t.* busoo saseru; *v.i.* busoo suru.

army rikúgun.

around –no mawari ni.

arouse (to) me o samaséru (*awaken*); sawagaseru (*stir up*).

arrange (to) seiton suru (*set in order*); uchiawáseru (*make an arrangement*).

arrangement uchiawase (*plan*).

arrest táiho.

arrest (to) táiho suru, tsukamaéru.

arrival toochaku.

arrive (to) toochaku suru, tsúku.

art geijutsu (*art in general*); bíjutsu (*fine arts*).

article shinamono (*commodity*); kíji (*writing*).

artificial jinzoo no (*not natural*).

artist geijutsuka, geinóojin (*performing artist*); bijutsuka (*person skilled in one of the fine arts*).

artistic geijutsuteki.

as –to shite (*in the capacity of*); –no yoo ni (*in such a manner*); –hodo (*as . . . as*).

ascertain (to) tashikaméru, kakutéi suru (*determine*).

ash hai.

ashamed (to feel) hazukáshiku omóu.

aside sóba ni; wakí e (*nearby*).

ask (to) kiku, tazuneru.

asleep (to be) nemutte iru.

aspire (to) netsuboo suru.

aspirin asupírin.

assault shuugeki, bookoo.

assemble (to) atsuméru (*bring together*); atsumáru (*come together*).

assembly shuukai, kumitate; **assembly line** nagare sagyoo retsu.

asset shisan.

assign (to) ategáru (*allot*); shitei suru (*designate*).

assist (to) tetsudáu, tasukéru.

assistant tetsudái, joshu.

associate (to) koosai suru (*mingle with*); rensoo suru (*relate in thinking*).

assume (to) hikiukeru (*undertake*); katei suru (*suppose*).

assurance hoshoo, ukeai.

assure (to) hoshoo suru.

astonish (to) odorokásu, bikkúri saseru.

astound (to) bikkúri gyooten saseru.

astronaut uchuu hikóoshi.

asylum seishin byóoin.

at ni, de.

athlete undooka.

athletics undoo.

atmosphere fun'íki.

attach (to) tsukéru.

attack (to) koogeki suru, seméru, osou.

attain (to) tassúru (*gain*); toochaku suru (*reach*).

attempt (to) kokoromíru.

attend (to)–ni shusseki suru (*be present at*).

attention chúui.

attic yane ura.

attitude táido.

attorney bengóshi (*lawyer*).
   power of attorney ininken, dairinin.

attract (to) chuui o hiku (*draw attention*); miwaku suru (*entice*).

attraction miwaku.

attractive miryokuteki, aikyoo ga aru.

audience choshuu.

audit kaikei kansa suru.

August Hachigatsu.

aunt oba, obasan.

author chósha (*writer of a book*).

authority táika (*great expert*); tookyokúsha (*government*).

authorize (to) kengén o ataeru.

automatic jidóoteki.

automobile jidóosha.

autumn áki.

average heikin.

avoid (to) sakéru.

awake (to be) me ga sámete iru.

awaken (to) okósu (*arouse*).

award shoohin, shóoyo.

award (to) shóoyo a dásu.

aware (to be) shoochi shite iru.

away achira ni, atchi ni.
   Go away. Atchi e itte.

awful osoroshíi, taihen na.

awkward fúben na, bukíyoo na.

B

baby akanboo.

back senaka (*of the body*); urá (*of a house, etc.*).

background haikei.

backward ushiro ni (*toward the back*); gyaku ni (*in a reverse direction*).

bacon béekon.

bad warúi.

badge kishoo.

bag fukuro.

baggage nímotsu (*heavy, such as trunks*); tenímotsu (*hand luggage*).

bake (to) yaku.

baker pán'ya.

bakery pán'ya.

balance tsuriai; nokorí (*remainder*).

balcony barukónii, rodai.

ball tama (*sphere*); marí, booru (*for a game*).

balloon keikikyuu (*lighter-than-air-craft*); fuusen (*toy*).

banana bánana.

band bando, gakudan.

bandage hootai.

banister tesuri.

bank ginkoo (*financial institution*); dote (*of a river*).
   bank account ginkoo yokin kooza.
   bank balance ginkoo yokin zandaka.
   bank charge ginkoo tesuu ryoo.
   bank check ginkoo kogitte.
   bank letter-of-credit ginkoo shin-yoo joo.
   bank loan ginkoo kashitsuke.
   bank note satsu.
   bank statement ginkoo kanjoo hookoku sho.

banker ginkooka.

bankruptcy hasan.

banquet enkai.

bar baa (*for drinks*); kanaboo (*rod*).

barber rihátsushi, tokoya.

barbershop rihatsúten.

bare hadaka no.

barefoot suashi no.

barge tenmasen.

barn ushigoya.

barrel taru.

barren ko o umanai (*sterile*); fumoo no (*land*).

basin tarai.

basis kiso, kónkyo.

basket kago.
   wastepaper basket kuzu-kago.

bath o-fúro (*hot*); mizu-buro (*cold*).
   to take a bath furó ni háiru.

bathe (to) kaisúiyoku o suru (*in the sea*); mizu o abiru (*in running water*).

bathroom furoba, yudono (*bath*); tearai (*toilet*).

battle ikusa, sensoo.

bay wan.

be (to) iru, óru (*there is: animate*); áru (*there is: inanimate*); da (*it is—*).

beach umibe, kaigan.

bean mamé.

bear kumá.

bear (to) gáman suru (*endure*); úmu (*give birth to*).

beard hige.

beat (to) útsu.

beautiful utsukushíi, kírei na.

beauty utsukúshisa; bijin (*beautiful woman*).

beauty parlor biyóoin.

because kara, node (*used after a sentence or clause*).

become (to) –ni náru.

becoming (be) niáu (*befitting*).

bed nedoko, beddo; shindai (*berth*).

beef gyuuniku.

beer bíiru.

beet bíitsu, kabu.
before máe, máe ni.
beg (to) tanómu.
beggar kojikí.
begin (to) *v.t.* hajimeru; *v.i.* hajimaru.
beginning hajime.
behave (to) furumau.
behavior furumai.
behind ushiro ni, áto ni.
belief kakushin (*conviction*); shinkoo (*faith*); íken (*opinion*).
believe (to) shinjíru.
bell kane, béru.
belong (to) –ni zokusuru.
below shita ni.
belt beruto; óbi (*sash*); kawa-óbi (*leather*).
bench bénchi.
bend (to) *v.t.* mageru; *v.i.* magaru.
beneath shita ni.
benefit ríeki (*good advantage*); onkei (*favor*).
bequest izoo.
beside –no sóba ni, –no sóba de.
besides –no hoka ni, sono ue (*moreover*).
best ichiban íi.
bet kaké.
bet (to) kakéru.
betray (to) uragíru (*act treacherously*); azamuku (*deceive*).
better motto íi.
between –no aida ni.
beware (to) yóojin suru.
beyond –no mukoo ni.
bicycle jiténsha.
bid (to) ne o tsurkéru (*offer a price*); nyuusatsu suru (*make a bid*).
big ookíi, óoki na.
bill denpyoo (*grocer's bill, restaurant bill of fare*).
billion júu-oku.
bind (to) yuwaéru, shibáru (*tie*).
bird tori.
birth tanjoo.
　　to give birth umu.
birthday tanjóobi.
biscuit bisuketto (*tea biscuit, cookie*).
bishop kantoku (*Protestant*); shikyóo (*Catholic*).
bit sukóshi.
bite kamikizu (*dog bite*); sashikizu (*mosquito bite*).
bite (to) kámu (*chew*); sásu (*said of insects*).
bitter nigái.
bitterness nigami.
black kurói.
blade ha.
blame semé (*censure*); tsúmi (*crime, sin*).
blame (to) seméru; hihan suru (*criticize*).

blank hakushi (*blank sheet of paper*).
　　fill in a blank form yooshi.
blanket móofu.
bleed (to) shukketsu suru.
bless (to) kiyoméru (*consecrate*); agameru (*praise, glorify*).
blessing shukufuku (*benediction*); kami no megumi (*God's blessing*).
blind *adj.* moomoku no.
blindness moomoku.
block katamari (*bulky piece*); kukaku (*row of houses*).
block (to) fusagu, samatagéru.
blood chi.
bloom (to) haná ga saku (*flowers*).
blossom haná.
blotter suitórigami.
blouse buráusu.
blow (to) fúku (*wind*).
blue aói.
blush (to) sekimen suru, akaku náru.
board ita (*plank*); makanai (*food*).
boardinghouse geshukuya.
boarding pass toojóoken.
boast (to) jiman suru.
boat bóoto (*rowboat*); fúne (*powered by motor*).
body karada (*living or dead person*); shigai (*corpse*).
boil (to) wakasu (*water*); yudéru (*cook in water*).
boiler bóiraa.
bold daitan na.
bomb bakudan.
bomb (to) bakugeki suru.
bond shooken (*document*).
bone honé.
book hón.
　　textbook kyookásho.
bookseller hón'ya.
bookstore hón'ya.
border kokkyoo (*frontier of a country*); kyookai (*boundary, limit*).
boring omoshíroku nái (*uninteresting*).
born (to be) umareru.
borrow (to) kariru.
boss awayaku.
both futari tomo (*people*); ryoohoo (*things*).
bother (to) nayamásu (*annoy*); jama suru (*trouble*).
bottle bín.
bottom soko.
bounce (to) hanekáeru.
bowl donburi, bóoru.
box hako.
boy shoonen, otokó no ko.
bracelet udewa.
braid uchihimo, amigami.
brain atama (*intellectual ability*).

brake buréeki.
branch eda (*of tree*); shiten (*office, etc.*).
brave yuukan na.
brassière burájaa.
bread pán.
break (to) kowásu (*destroy*); yabúru (*tear, rip*).
breakfast asagohan.
breast mune (*human*).
breath íki.
breathe (to) íki o suru.
breeze soyókaze.
bribe wáiro.
     to take a bribe wáiro o tóru.
brick rénga.
bride hanáyome.
bridegroom hanamúko.
bridge hashí.
brief mijikái (*short*).
bright akarui (*with light*); hade na (*of color*).
brighten (to) akaruku suru (*with light*).
brilliant mígoto na.
bring (to) motté kuru.
     to bring up sodatéru (*a child*); mochidasu (*for discussion*).
Britain Eikoku, Igirisu. See also **English.**
     British Eikoku no. Igirisu no.
broad hirói.
broadcast hoosoo.
broadcast (to) hoosoo suru.
broil (to) yaku.
broken kowáreta.
brook ogawa.
broom hooki.
brother níisan, oníisan, ani (*older*); otootó (*younger*).
brother-in-law gi-kei, giri no áni (*older*); gitei, giri no otootó (*younger*).
brown chairo.
bruise uchikizu.
bruise (to) *v.t.* uchikizu o ukéru.
brush fude (*for writing*); haké, burashi (*for sweeping*).
bubble awá.
buckle bakkuru, bijoo.
bud tsubomi.
Buddha Hotoke.
     a statue of Buddha Butsuzoo.
     Buddhism Búkkyoo.
budget yosan.
build (to) tatéru.
building tatémono.
bulletin keiji (*pinned on a board*); kaihoo (*publication*).
     bulletin board keijiban.
bundle tsutsumí.
burn (to) yaku; moyasu (*throw into a fire*).
burst (to) sakéru (*pipes, etc.*).
bus básu.

bush shigemi.
business yooji (*errand*); shigoto (*work*); shóobai (*profession*).
businessperson kaisháin.
busy isogashíi.
but ga, shikáshi, kéredomo (*however*).
butcher nikúya.
     butcher shop nikúya.
butter bátaa.
button bótan.
buy (to) kau.
buyer kaite, baíyaa.
by sóba ni (*nearby*); de (*by means of*).

C

cab tákushii (*taxi*).
cabbage kyábetsu.
cable kéeburu (*rope, wire*); kaigai dénshin (*cablegram*).
cage tori kago (*for birds*); orí (*for animals*).
cake kéeki.
calculator keisanki.
calendar karéndaa, koyomi.
calf koushi.
call (to) hoomon suru (*to make a call, visit*).
call (to) yobu.
calm shízuka na, odáyaka na.
calm (to) shízuka ni suru.
camera kámera, shashínki.
camp kyánpu.
camp (to) kyánpu suru.
can kán.
can (be able) dekíru (*can do*); –kotó ga dekíru (*can—*).
can opener kan-kíri.
cancel (to) torikesu (*revoke*); sákujo suru (*delete*).
candidate koohósha.
candle roosoku.
candy kyándii, ame.
cap booshi (*hat*); futa (*lid*).
capital shúto (*city*); shihon (*money*).
     capital punishment shikéi.
capricious kimagure na.
captain rikugun táii (*army*); sénchoo (*merchant ship*); kaigun táisa (*navy*).
captive toriko.
capture (to) toriko ni suru, tsukamaeru.
car kuruma (*vehicle*); jidóosha (*automobile*).
carbon paper kaabon péepaa.
card hagaki (*postcard*); e-hágaki (*illustrated postcard*); toránpu (*playing card*).
care (to) kamáu (*be concerned*); sewá o suru (*care for a child*).
     to take care daijí ni suru.
careful chuuibukái.

careless fuchúui na.
caress aibu; hooyoo.
carpenter dáiku.
carpet júutan.
carry (to) mótte iku (*take to*); hakobu (*transport*).
carve (to) kíru (*meat*); chookoku suru (*sculpture*).
case hako (*box*); jíken (*matter*).
cash genkín.
    to cash a check kogítte o genkín ni kaeru.
cashier genkin gákari, genkin suitoo gákari.
cassette kasétto.
castle shiro.
cat néko.
catch (to) toraeru.
    I have caught a cold. Kaze o hikimáshita.
    I could not catch the train. Densha ni ma ni aimasén deshita.
category shúrui (*kind*); búrui (*class*).
cathedral jfin.
Catholic Kyúukyoo, Katorfkku.
cattle ushi (*cow*); kachiku (*livestock*).
cause gen'in.
    without cause gen'in náshi ni.
cause (to) gen'in to náru (*bring about*); –sa seru (*cause a person to do...*).
cease (to) yamu, owaru (*come to an end*).
ceiling tenjóo.
celebrate (to) iwáu.
cellar chikáshitsu.
cement semento.
cemetery bóchi, hakaba.
censorship ken'etsu.
center chuushin (*of a circle*).
central chuushin no, chuuoo no.
    central heating danboo-sóochi (*heating system*).
century séiki.
ceremony shikí.
certain táshika na (*without doubt*); áru (*a certain*).
certainty táshika na kotó.
certificate shoomeisho.
chain kusari.
chari isu, koshikaké.
chairperson gíchoo.
chalk hakuboku, chóoku.
challenge choosen.
challenge (to) choosen suru.
champion chánpion, sénshu (*athletic*); tóoshi (*fighter*); yoogosha (*defender*).
chance chánsu (*opportunity*); guuzen (*coincidence*); únmei (*luck, fortune*).
    to take a chance chansu o tóru.
change hénka, kawari (*alteration*); komakái

okane (*small change*); otsuri (*money returned as change*).
change (to) kaeru (*make different*); kawaru (*become different*).
chapel reihaidoo (*place of worship*).
chapter shóo.
character tokuchoo (*unique feature, distinctive mark*); seishitsu (*disposition*).
characteristic *adj.* dokutoku no.
charge (to) tsuké ni suru (*accuse*); tsuké ni suru (*charge to an account*).
charitable omoiyari no áru (*sympathetic*).
charity jizen.
charming miwakuteki na (*fascinating*); taihen utsukushíi (*very attractive*); aikyoo no áru (*engaging*).
chase (to) oikakéru.
chat (to) shabéru, uchikutsuroide hanásu.
cheap yasúi.
cheat (to) damásu.
check kogítte (*bank check*).
check (to) kuitoméru (*hold back, hamper*).
check chíkki (*claim check*).
cheer (to) nagusaméru (*comfort*); genkizukéru (*enliven*).
cheerful akarui (*disposition*); génki na (*lively*).
cheese chíizu.
chemical *n.* kagaku séihin. *–adj.* kágaku no.
chemistry kágaku.
cherish (to) daijí ni suru.
cherry sakura no haná (*blossom*); sakura no kí (*tree*); sakuranbo (*fruit*).
chest muné (*of the body*); hako (*box*).
chestnut kúri.
chew (to) kámu.
chicken niwatori, chíkin.
chief *n.* shunin (*head person*). *–adj.* ómo na.
chimney entotsu.
chin agó.
China Chúugoku.
    Communist China Chuukyoo.
    Chinese Chuugokújin (*person*); Chúugoku no (*pertaining to the country*).
chip kirehashi, kakera.
chocolate chokoréeto.
choice sentaku (*selection*); yorigonomi (*preference*).
choke (to) *v.t.* chissoku saseru (*suffocate*); *v.i.* chissoku suru.
choose (to) erábu (*make a choice of*); yóru (*pick out*).
chop (to) kizamu (*mince*).
chopsticks háshi.
Christian Kirisutokyoo-shínja (*person*).
    Christianity Kirisutokyoo.
Christmas Kurisúmasu.
church kyookai.

cigar hamaki, shígaa.
   cigar store tabakoya.
cigarette makitábako, shigarétto.
circle maru; enshuu (*circumference*).
circular *adj.* marui. *–n.* kaijoo.
circulate (to) kubáru (*distribute*).
circumstances jijoo (*conditions*); baai
   (*case*).
citizen shímin.
city shí.
city hall kookaidoo.
civilization bunmei.
civilize (to) buméika suru.
claim seikyuu (*demand*); yookyuu (*request*);
   shuchoo (*insistence*).
claim (to) seikyuu suru (*demand*); shuchoo
   suru (*insist*).
clamor sáwagi (*loud noise*).
clap (to) hákushu suru (*applaud*).
class shúrui (*kind*); kaikyuu (*social status*);
   kúrasu (*school*).
   first class ittoo (*in plane, etc.*).
classic koten.
classify (to) bunrui suru.
   classified ad sangyo kóokoku.
clause jookoo, sétsu (*grammar*).
clean kírei na.
clean (to) sooji suru (*rooms, etc.*).
   to make clean kírei ni suru.
cleaner kuriíninguya (*laundry*).
cleanliness seiketsu sa.
clear kírei na.
   The sky is clear today. Kyoo wa sóra ga
   hárete imásu.
   This is clear. Kore wa kírei desu.
   clear soup osúmashi.
clerk jimúin (*office*); ginkóoin (*bank*).
clever rikoo na (*intelligent*); joozú na
   (*dexterous*); kayoo na (*skillful*).
climate kikoo.
climb (to) noboru.
clip kuríppu.
clip (to) karu.
clock tokei.
   alarm clock mezamashi dókei.
close *–no soba ni* (*nearby*); no chikáku ni
   (*close to*); kínjo ni (*in the neighborhood*).
close (to) *v.t.* shiméru; *v.i.* shimáru.
closed kyuugyoo (*business*); heiten (*store*).
closet todana (*cupboard*); oshiire (*for
   storage*).
cloth kiré, nuno (*general term*).
   cotton cloth momen mono.
   silk cloth kinú mono.
clothes kimono (*Japanese*); yoofuku
   (*Occidental*).
cloud kúmo.
cloudy kumótte iru.
clover kuróobaa.

club boo (*heavy stick*); kúrabu (*association*).
coal sekitán.
coarse arai, sómatsu na (*roughly made*);
   katoo na (*rude*).
coast kaigan (*beach*); engan (*shore*).
coat kóoto (*Japanese*); uwagi
   (*Occidental-style jacket*).
cocktail kákuteru.
code kisóku (*set of rules*).
coffee koohíi.
coffin hitsugi, kan'oke.
coin káhei.
cold samúi (*weather*); tsumetai (*to the
   touch*).
   to catch a cold kaze o hiku.
   It is cold. Samúi desu.
   I am cold. Watashi wa samúi desu.
coldness sámusa, tsumetasa.
collaborate (to) kyoodoo de hataraku (*work
   together*).
collar káraa (*for men*); kubiwa (*for animals*),
   erí.
collect (to) *v.t.* atsuméru (*gather, get
   together*); *v.i.* atsumáru (*come together*).
collection shuushuu (*of stamps, etc.*);
   kashikin chóoshuu (*of debts*).
college daigaku (*university*).
colonial shokumínchi no.
colony shokumínchi.
color iró.
color (to) iró o tsukéru (*add color*).
column enchuu (*pillar*); rán (*newspaper*).
comb kushí.
comb (to) kushí de tóku, kushí o kakéru
   (*one's hair*).
combination kumiawase.
combine (to) kumiawaséru (*join together*).
come (to) kúru.
   to come around yatte kúru.
   to come back káette kuru.
   to come in háiru.
comedy kígeki.
comet suisei.
comfort nagusame (*consolation*).
comfort (to) nagusameru (*console*).
comfortable kokochi yói, rakú na.
comma kónma, kuten.
command shikí (*military direction*); meirei
   (*order*).
command (to) meizúru (*direct*); shíhai suru
   (*control*); meirei suru (*give orders*).
commander shikísha.
commercial *adj.* shóobai no, shóogyoo no; *n.*
   komáasharu (*advertisement*).
commission nínmu (*charge, duty*); toritsugi
   (*agency*); tesúuryoo (*for service*).
commit (to) okasu (*a crime*).
common futsuu no (*ordinary*); atarimae no
   (*usual*).

common sense jooshiki.
Commonwealth of Independent States Dokuritsa Kokka Kyoodootai.
communicate (to) renraku suru (*contact*); tsuushin suru (*correspond with*).
communication renraku, tsuushin; shomen (*written message*).
   mass communication masukomi.
community shákai (*society*).
compact disk konpakuto dísaku.
companion nakama (*comrade*); aite (*partner*); tsure (*traveling*).
company kyaku (*social*); kaisha (*firm*).
compare (to) hikaku suru, kuraberu.
comparison hikaku.
compete (to) kyoosoo suru, kisóu.
competition kyoosoo (*rivalry*); shiai (*contest*).
complain (to) fuhei o iu (*make a complaint*).
complaint fuhei, kujoo.
complete zénbu no (*entire*); kanzen na (*perfect*).
complex fukuzatsu na (*complicated*).
complexion kaoiro.
complicate (to) fukuzatsu ni suru.
   to get complicated fukuzatsu ni náru.
compliment sánji (*praise*); oseji (*flattering speech*).
compose (to) sakkyoku suru (*music*); shi o tsukúru (*poetry*).
composer sakkyokuka (*of music*).
composition sakubun (*as a school subject*); sakuhin (*prose or poetry*); sakkyoku (*music*); haigoo (*arrangement*).
comprise naritátsu, fukúmu.
compromise jóoho (*concession*); dakyoo (*agreement*).
compromise (to) dakyoo suru.
computer konpyúutaa.
   computer language konpyúutaa gengo.
   computer program konpyúutaa purogúramu.
   digital computer dejitaru konpyúutaa.
   personal computer pasokon.
conceit unubore (*overweening, excessive self-importance*).
conceited unuboreta.
conceive (to) jutai suru (*become pregnant*); kokóro ni idáku (*form a conception of, imagine*).
concentrate (to) shuuchuu suru.
concern jígyoo (*enterprise*); shinpai (*anxiety*).
   a matter of great concern juudai na mondai.
   to be concerned shinpai suru.
concerning –ni tsúite.
concert ongákkai.
concrete konkuríito (*for building*).

condemn (to) hínan suru (*censure*); senkoku suru (*sentence*).
condense (to) asshuku suru (*compress*); mijikáku suru (*shorten*).
condition jootai (*aspect*); jooken (*terms*).
   critical condition kiken jóotai.
   on condition that –no jooken de.
conduct furumai (*behavior*); okonai (*deed*).
   bad conduct waruí okonai.
   good conduct yói okonai.
conduct (to) okonáu (*perform*).
   to conduct a business shóobai o keiei suru.
   to conduct an orchestra ookésutora o shikí suru.
conductor shashoo (*of trains, etc.*); shikísha (*of an orchestra*).
confess (to) jinin suru (*acknowledge*); mitomeru (*admit*); hákujoo suru (*make a confession*).
confession kokuhaku, hákujoo.
confidence shin'yoo, shinrai (*trust*); jishin (*self-confidence*).
confident jishin no áru.
confidential himitsu no.
confirm (to) tashikaméru (*establish firmly*); kakushoo suru (*verify*).
confirmation kakunin (*corroboration*); kakushoo (*proof*).
congratulate (to) iwáu, shukúsu.
congratulations omedetoo gozaimásu.
connect (to) tsunagu (*join*).
connection kankei (*relation*); tsunagari (*link*).
conquer (to) seifuku suru.
conquest seifuku.
conscience ryóoshin.
conscientious ryooshinteki na.
conscious kizuite iru (*aware*).
consent dooi (*assent*); itchí (*unanimity*).
conservative hoshuteki na.
consider (to) yóku kangáete míru (*contemplate*); kóoryo ni ireru (*to take into account*); kangáeru (*think*).
considerable kánari no (*much*).
consideration kóoryo (*careful thought*); omoiyari (*thoughtful regard*).
consist of (to) –kara náru (*be composed of*).
consistent shubi ikkan shita.
constant kawaranai (*unchanging*); chuujitsu na (*faithful*).
constitution kénpoo (*of a state*); taikaku (*of the body*).
constitutional kenpoojoo no.
consul ryóoji.
consulate ryoojíkan.
contagious densensei no.
   a contagious disease densenbyoo.
contain (to) ireru (*include*); háitte iru (*have within*).
container iremono.

contemporary géndai no (*of the day*); doojídai no (*existing at the same time*).
contented manzoku shita.
contentment manzoku (*satisfaction*).
contents naiyoo.
continent *n.* táiriku.
continual taema no nái (*unceasing*).
continue (to) *v.t.* tsuzukeru; *v.i.* tsuzuku.
contraception hinin (*birth control*).
contract keiyaku (*agreement*); keiyakusho (*written document of an agreement*).
contractor keiyakunin, ukeoinin.
contradict (to) hanbaku suru (*rebut*); mujun suru (*conflict with*).
contradiction hanbaku (*rebuttal*); mujun (*inconsistency*).
contradictory mujun shite iru.
contrary hantai no.
  on the contrary hantai ni, káette.
contrast taishoo.
contrast (to) taishoo suru.
contribute (to) kífu suru (*money, etc.*); kikoo suru (*to a publication*).
contribution kífu (*donation*); kikoo (*something written for a publication*).
control toosei (*government*); yokusei (*restraint*).
  birth control sánji seigen.
control (to) tóogyo suru (*govern*); toosei suru (*regulate*).
controversy ronsoo, gíron (*dispute*).
convenience bénri, tsugoo.
convenient tsugoo no yói, bénri na.
convent shuudóoin.
convention kyoogíkai, káigi, shuukai.
conversation kaiwa (*dialogue*); hanashí (*talk*).
converse (to) hanásu.
convert (to) kaeru (*change into*); kaishuu saseru (*to a religion*).
convict (to) yuuzai to senkoku suru (*declare guilty*).
conviction kakushin (*firm belief*); yuuzai hánketsu (*verdict of guilty*).
cook ryoorínin (*of Japanese or any other kind of food*); kókku (*for other than Japanese food*).
cook (to) ryóori suru, ryóori o tsukúru.
cool suzushíi (*temperature*); tsumetai (*to the touch*); reisei na (*unexcited*); reitán na (*lacking in zeal*).
cool (to) tsumetaku suru.
copy utsushi, kópii (*of a letter, etc.*); mosha (*of a picture*).
corporation kaisha (*firm*); shadan-hóojin (*corporate body*).
correct tadashíi (*right*); táshika na (*sure*); seikaku na (*accurate*); machigai no nái (*without error*).

correct (to) naósu; koosei suru (*proofread*), tensaku suru (*school papers*).
correction teisei (*of an error*); koosei (*in proofreading*); tensaku (*of a school composition*).
correspond (to) buntsuu suru, tsuushin suru (*exchange letters*); itchi suru (*agree*).
correspondence tsuushin; buntsuu.
correspondent tsuushin'in (*of a periodical*); tokuháin (*mass media*).
corrupt (to) fuhai suru (*rot*); daraku suru (*morally*).
corruption daraku (*moral deterioration*).
cost nedan (*price*); híyoo (*expense*).
costume fukusoo, kimono; yoofuku (*Occidental*); íshoo (*fancy dress*).
cotton watá (*raw*); momen (*woven*).
cough sekí.
count keisan (*reckoning*).
count (to) kazóeru.
counter kauntaa (*restaurant, etc.*); chooba (*in Japanese-style hotel*).
countless kazoekirénai.
country inaka (*rural region*); kuni (*nation*).
countryman inaka mono (*a rustic*); dookokújin (*compatriot*).
couple futatsú (*of things*); futarí (*of people*); futsuka (*of days*); fúufu (*husband and wife*).
courage yúuki.
  to have courage yúuki ga áru.
course kamoku, katéi (*of study*); kóosu, michi (*road followed*); yarikatá (*line of conduct or action*).
court saibanshó (*tribunal*).
  law court hootei.
courteous téinei na; teichoo na (*polite*).
courtesy téinei (*politeness*); kóoi (*favor*); reigi (*civility*).
courtyard nakaniwa.
cousin itóko.
  second cousin mata ítoko.
cover futa, kábaa.
cow meushi.
crack wareme (*split*); sukimá (*chink*); hibí (*flaw*).
crack (to) *v.t.* waru; *v.i.* wareru; hibí ga háiru (*break without separating*).
  to crack a nut kurumí o waru.
  to crack a joke joodán o tobasu.
  a hard nut to crack nan móndai.
cradle yurikago.
crash shoototsu (*collision*).
crash (to) shoototsu suru.
crazy kichigai jímita (*half-crazed*).
  crazy about muchuu ni nátta.
cream kurfimu.
create (to) tsukúru (*bring into being*); soosaku suru (*produce*).

creature ikímono (*living thing*).
credit kuréjitto, shin'yoo (*trust*).
creditor kashi nushi, saikénsha.
crime tsúmi.
    to commit a crime hanzai o okasu.
crisis kikí (*crucial time*); tooge (*of a sickness, etc.*).
    political crisis seiji no kikí.
    financial crisis kéizai no kikí.
critic hihyooka (*reviewer*).
critical hihyooteki (*inclined to criticize*); kikí no (*serious*).
criticism hihyoo, hihan.
criticize (to) hihyoo suru (*discuss critically*); hinan suru (*find fault with*).
crooked magatte iru (*bent*); nejíreta (*twisted*); fushóojiki na (*dishonest*).
crop shuukaku (*yield*); toriire (*harvest*).
cross juuji (*lines that intersect*); juujika (*religious symbol*).
crossing tokoo (*ocean*); koosáten (*intersection*).
crossraods koosáten; yotsukado.
crouch (to) kagamu.
crow kárasu.
crowd hito gomi.
    to be crowded kónde iru.
crown kanmurí.
crown (to) eikan o sazukéru (*reward or honor*).
cruel zankoku na.
cruelty zangyaku.
crumb pan kúzu.
crumble (to) kuzuréru (*collapse*); mú ni kisúru (*come to nothing*); koná ni suru (*break into crumbs*).
crust pán no kawá.
crutch matsubazúe.
cry sakebi góe (*shout*); naki góe (*crying*).
cry (to) sakébu (*shout*); naku (*weep*).
cunning warugashikói (*sly*); zurúi (*crafty*).
cup yunomi (*teacup*); koppu (*glass*); káppu (*trophy*).
    a cup of coffee koohíi íppai.
    a cup of tea o-cha íppai.
cure (to) naósu.
    to be cured of naóru.
curiosity kookíshin.
curious kookíshin ga tsuyói (*inquisitive*); kímyoo na (*strange*).
curl káaru (*of hair*).
current *adj.* génzai no (*present*); ryuutsuu shite iru (*in general circulation*). –*n.* nagaré (*stream*).
curtain madó kake, káaten (*for a window*); makú (*theater*).
curve yumi nari (*arched shape*); kyokusen (*curved line*).
curve (to) *v.t.* mageru; *v.i.* magaru.

cushion kússhon; zabúton (*for sitting*).
custom shuukan (*habit*); fúuzoku (*convention*).
customhouse zeikan.
customs official zeikánri.
customary futsuu no (*ordinary*).
customer kyaku.
cut kiríkizu (*wound*); kirehashi (*a piece of something*).
cut (to) *v.t.* kíru; *v.i.* kiréru.

dagger tantóo.
daily máinichi no.
    daily newspaper nikkán shínbun.
dainty kyasha na.
dam dámu, séki.
damage songai (*loss*); hígai (*injury, harm*).
damage (to) damé ni suru.
damp shimeppói (*of things*); shikki no óoi (*of atmosphere*).
dance dánsu (*foreign*); odori (*Japanese*).
dance (to) odoru.
danger kiken.
dangerous abunái.
dark kurai (*little light*); kói (*color*); kurói (*person*).
dash (to) tosshin suru (*rush*).
data déeta.
    data processor joohooshori kikái.
date yakusoku (*appointment*); hizuke (*on a letter*).
daughter musumé (*plain form*), ojóosan (*respect form*).
dawn yoake.
day hi, hirú (*daytime*).
    day after tomorrow asátte.
    day before yesterday ototoi.
    yesterday kinóo.
    today kyóo.
dazzle (to) mé o kuramasu.
dead shinda (*lacking life*).
    dead leaves kareha.
deaf mimi no kikoenai.
deal toríhiki (*business*).
    a great deal hijoo ni takusán.
deal (to) toríhiki suru (*trade*); tsukiáu (*associate with*).
dealer shóonin.
dear takái (*price*); kawaíi (*beloved*).
death shí (*loss of life*); shiboo (*act or fact of dying*).
debate ronsoo.
debit ka rigata.
debt shakkín (*sum due*); sáimu (*liability*).
debtor karínushi.
decanter tokkuri.
decay fuhai (*rot*).

decay (to) kusáru (rot); otoroéru (decline); táika suru (deteriorate).

deceased shiboo.

deceit azamuki.

deceive (to) damásu (cheat); azamúku (delude).

December Juunigatsu.

decent óntoo na (proper); joohín na (modest); kánari rippa na (respectable).

decide (to) kimeru.

decision kettei.

decisive ketteiteki.

deck kanpan, dékki (of a ship); hito kumi (of playing cards).

declare (to) shinkoku suru (report); mooshitatéru (state).

decline jítai (refuse).

decline (to) jítai suru.

decrease genshoo.

decrease (to) v.t. herasu, sukunáku suru; v.i. heru.

decree hanketsu (judicial decision); hoorei (ordinance).

dedicate (to) sasageru (consecrate); yudanéru (give oneself to one's work).

deed kóoi (action); jikkoo (performance); okonai (act); shoosho (document).

deep fukái (opp. of shallow); kói (color).

deer shiká.

defeat haisen (military); shippai (failure).

defeat (to) v.t. makasu; to be defeated v.i. makeru.

defect kettén.

defend (to) mamóru.

defense booei.

defiance choosen (challenge); múshi (setting at naught).

define (to) téigi suru.

definite hakkíri shita.

defy (to) choosen suru (challenge); múshi suru (set at naught).

degree do (on a thermometer, etc.); gákui (diploma); by degrees dandan.

delay chien.

delay (to) v.i. okureru.

delegate daihyoo (representative).

delegate (to) haken suru (depute); inin suru (entrust); daihyoo suru (represent).

deliberate (to) shían suru (consider); shíngi suru (discuss).

deliberately shinchoo ni, yuuyuu to.

delicacy bimyoosa (of coloring, etc.).

delicate yowái (in health); kowareyasúi (fragile); a delicate situation muzukashíi tachiba.

delicious oishii.

delight uréshisa.

deliver (to) todokéru (goods); watasu (hand over).

deliverance kyuushutsu (from bondage, etc.) sukui dásu kotó.

delivery haitatsu (forwarding).

demand yookyuu, motomé (request); juyoo (for goods).

to be in demand juyoo ga áru.

democracy minshushúgi, demokuráshii.

demonstrate (to) jitsuen suru.

demonstration jitsuen (exhibition); jíí úndoo, démo (mass meeting, protest parade).

denial hitei (negation); hinín (disavowal); kyóhi (refusal).

denounce (to) kokuhatsu suru (inform against); háki suru (repudiate).

dense fukái (as fog); oishigétta (as forest); kónda (crowded).

density mítsudo.

dentist háisha.

deny (to) uchikesu.

depart (to) déru.

department bumon (section); depáato (department store).

departure shuppatsu.

depend (to) tayóru (for support); tánomi ni suru (rely on).

dependent tayótte iru (on one's parents, etc.).

deplore (to) nagéku (lament).

deposit tetsukekin (as a binder); yokin (in a bank).

depreciation genka shóokyaku.

depress (to) kíochi suru.

depression fukéiki (in business); yuuutsu (of mind).

deprive (to) ubaitóru.

depth fukása.

deride (to) azakéru.

descend (to) kudaru (go down); oríru (alight from); kudari ni náru (slope down).

descendant shíson.

describe (to) setsumei suru, nobéru (give an account of).

description setsumei, jojutsu (of a person).

desert sabaku.

desert (to) suteru (one's family or friend); dassoo suru (from the army or prison).

deserve (to) shikaku ga áru (be entitled to); káchi ga áru (be worthy of).

design zuan (sketch); kooan (idea, scheme); dezáin (dress, etc.).

designer zuanka (of patterns); kooánsha (of ideas); dezáinaa (of dresses).

desirable nozomashíi.

desire yokuboo (craving); nozomi (wish, hope).

desire (to) nozómu (long for); kiboo suru (wish).

desk tsukue, désuku.

desolate wabishíi, sabishíi.

despair zetsuboo, rakutan (*despondency*).

despair (to) zetsuboo suru (*lose hope*); rakutan suru (*be disappointed*).

desperate zetsuboo teki na (*beyond hope*); kiken na (*dangerous*); hisshi no (*frantic*); mukóomizu no (*reckless*).

despise (to) misageru.

despite ákui (*malice*); bujoku (*insult*); keibetsu (*scorn*).

despite –ni mo kakawárazu.

dessert dezáato.

destiny únmei.

destroy (to) kowásu; hakai suru (*demolish*); dainashi ni suru (*ruin*); zenmetsu saseru (*annihilate*).

destruction hakai.

detach (to) hikihanásu (*unfasten, separate*).

detail saimoku (*item*); kuwashíi kóto, shoosai (*particulars*).

in detail kuwáshiku.

detain (to) hikitoméru.

detect (to) tantei suru.

detective tantei.

detective story tantei shóosetsu.

determination saiketsu (*decision*); késshin (*resolution*); ketsudán ryoku (*firmness of purpose*).

determine (to) kakutei suru (*ascertain*); kimeru (*decide*).

detest (to) kirau.

detour mawari michi.

deterimental furíeki na, yóku nái.

develop (to) hatten saseru (*cause to grow*); keihatsu suru (*unfold*); genzoo suru (*photo negatives*).

development seichoo (*growth*); hatten (*gradual progress*); kakuchoo (*expansion*).

device kufuu.

devil oní, ákuma.

devise (to) kufuu suru.

devoid kakete iru (*lacking in*).

devote (to) sasageru (*give up, direct*).

devour gátsugatsu tabéru (*eat hungrily and greedily*); horobósu (*destroy*).

devour a book musabori yómu.

dew tsúyu.

dial daiyaru, mojiban.

telephone dial daiyaru.

dial (to) diayaru o mawasu.

dialect hoogen.

dialogue kaiwa, taiwa.

diameter chokkei.

diamond daiyamóndo, kongóosekí.

diary nikki.

to keep a diary nikkí o tsukéru.

dictate (to) kakitoraséru (*a letter*).

dictation kakitori (*practice in spelling*); koojutsu (*business*).

dictionary jísho, jíten, jibiki (*lexicon*).

English-Japanese dictionary Ei-Wa jíten.

Japanese-English dictionary Wa-Ei jíten.

die (to) shinu.

diesel diizeru.

diet shokuji ryóohoo (*prescribed allowance of food*); dáietto (*to lose weight*).

Diet gíkai (*Japanese Parliament*).

differ from (to) chigau.

difference chigai (*dissimilarity*); sábetsu (*distinction*); íken no sooi (*disagreement*).

different (be) chigau.

difficult muzukashíi.

difficulty kónnan, mendoo.

dig (to) hóru.

digest (to) shooka suru (*food*); kanryaku ni suru (*abbreviate*).

dignity igen (*of bearing*).

dim usugurai.

dimension ménseki (*area*); ookisa (*size*).

diminish (to) v.i. chiisáku náru (*in size*); sukunáku náru (*in number*).

dine (to) shokuji o suru.

dining room shokudoo.

dinner hirú no shokuji, hirugohan (*noon meal*); ban no shokuji, yuuhan (*evening meal*).

dip (to) tsukeru, hitasu.

diplomacy gaikoo (*between nations*); kakehiki (*tactful dealing*).

diplomat gaikóokan.

direct massúgu na (*straight*); jíka no (*direct rays, etc.*).

direct (to) shíji suru (*point the way*); sáshizu suru (*order*).

direction hoogaku (*way*); shidoo (*guidance*); kánri (*control*); sáshizu (*instruction*).

director shiháinin (*manager*); juuyaku (*of a company*); shunin (*chief*).

directory juushóroku.

telephone directory denwachoo.

dirt óbutsu (*filth*); doró (*mud*); hokori (*dust*).

dirty kitanái.

disability múryoku.

disabled múryoku ni nátta.

disadvantage fúri.

disagree (to) itchi shinai.

disagreeable fuyúkai na.

disagreement fuítchi (*discord*); fuchóowa (*disharmony*); íken no sooi (*dissent*); fúwa (*quarrel*).

disappear (to) miénaku náru.

disappearance miénaku náru kotó, shooshitsu.

disappoint (to) shitsuboo saseru.

disapprove (to) sansei shinai.

disaster tensai (*calamity*).

disastrous hisan na, saigai no ookíi (*flood, etc.*).

discharge káiko (*release from duty*); jotai (*army*).

discharge (to) funaóroshi o suru (*cargo*); hassha suru (*a gun*); hima o dásu (*dismiss*).

discipline kúnren (*drill*); kiritsu (*order*).

disclaim (to) hóoki suru.

disclose (to) arawásu (*expose*); abáku (*reveal*); happyoo suru (*make known*).

disclosure bákuro.

discomfort fukái.

disconnect (to) kíru (*sever a connection*).

discontent fumánzoku na.

discontinue (to) chuushi suru.

discord fúwa.

discoteque dísuko.

discount waribiki.

discount (to) waribiki suru.

discourage (to) rakutan saseru
to be discouraged gakkári suru.

discouragement rakutan.

discover (to) mitsukeru (*find small things*); hakken suru (*find more important things*).

discovery hakken.

discreet shíryo no áru (*judicious*); shinchoo na (*prudent*); yoojinbukái (*wary*).

discretion shíryo (*prudence*).

discuss (to) tóogi suru (*talk over*); tóoron suru (*argue*).

discussion tóogi (*debate*); tóoron (*argument*).

disdain keibetsu.

disdain (to) keibetsu suru.

disease byooki.

disgrace fuméiyo (*dishonor*); hají (*shame*).

disguise hensoo.
in disguise hensoo shite.

disguise (to) hensoo suru.

disgust iyake.

disgust (to) muné o wáruku suru (*nauseate*); kimochi wáruku saseru (*create an aversion*).
be disgusted unzári suru.

dish sara.

dishonest fushóojiki na.

disk enban.

dislike kirai.

dislike (to) kirau.

dismiss (to) ikaseru (*allow to go*); menshoku suru (*expel*); hima o dásu (*discharge*).

dismissal hima.

disobey (to) somúku.

disorder ranzatsu (*lack of order*); kónzatsu (*confusion*).

dispense with (to) shóbun suru (*dispose of*).

display chinretsu (*show*); hyoogen (*manifestation*); misebirakashi (*ostentation*).

displease (to) ki ni sawaraseru (*offend*).

displeasure fuman (*dissatisfaction*).

disposal shóbun.

dispose (to) naraberu (*arrange*); –ki ni náru (*be inclined to*).
to dispose of shóbun suru.

dispute kóoron (*debate*); sóogi (*controversy*); kenka (*altercation*).

dispute (to) tóogi suru (*argue about*); hanbaku suru (*contest*); teikoo suru (*oppose*).

dissolve (to) tokásu (*melt*); torikesu (*annul*).

distance kyóri.

distant tooi (*far off*).

distinct hakkíri shita (*clear*); tokushu na (*different*).

distinction tokuchoo (*individuality*).

distinguish (to) miwakéru (*through sight*); kikiwakéru (*through sound*).

distort (to) yugaméru (*twist*); kojitsukéru (*pervert*).

distract (to) ki o toraréru.

distress nayami (*worry*); nageki (*grief*); kutsuu (*pain*).

distribute (to) wariatéru (*allot*); makichirásu (*spread out*); bunpai suru (*apportion*); kubáru (*deal out*).

district chihóo (*region*); kú (*city ward*).

distrust fushín'yoo.

distrust (to) shinjínai.

disturb (to) jama suru.

disturbance jama.

ditch mizo, horiwari (*trench*).

dive (to) tobikómu.

divide (to) wakéru (*separate, part*); waru (*by cutting*); shikíru (*by partition*).

divine shinsei na.
divine being kámi.
divine service reiháishiki.

division warízan (*math.*); bunkatsu (*separation*).

divorce (to) rikon suru.
divorced rikon shita hito.

dizziness memái.

dizzy memái ga suru.

do (to) suru (*act*); tsukúru (*make*).

dock hatoba, dókku.

doctor isha (*medical*); hákase (*academic*).

doctrine shúgi.

document shórui (*papers*); shoosho (*deed*); búnsho (*official letter*).

dog inú.

doll ningyoo.

dome maru ténjoo.

domestic katei no (*household*); kainarasareta (*domesticated, tame*); kokúnai no (*native, pertaining to one's country*).
  domestic affairs káji (*of a household*).
  domestic animal kachiku.

dominate (to) shihai suru (*govern*).

door to, dóa (*Occidental-style*).
  Japanese sliding door shooji.
  entrance door génkan no to.
  back door uraguchi no to.

dose fukuyooryoo (*medicine*).

dot ten.

double nibai.

double (to) nibai ni suru.

doubt utagai (*lack of certainty*); fushin (*misgiving*).

doubt (to) utagáu (*disbelieve*); fushin ni omóu (*question*).

doubtful táshika de nái (*uncertain*); hakkíri shinai (*ambiguous*); utagawashíi (*questionable*).

doubtless utagai nái.

down shita.

dozen dáassu.

draft kawase tégata (*bank order*); shitae (*sketch*); shitagaki (*of a plan*).
  draft (draught) of wind sukimá kaze.

drag (to) hiku (*draw forcibly*); hikizuru (*pull*).

drain (to) haisui suru (*carry away water*); nomihosu (*drink up*).

drama engeki, dórama (*a play*); gekiteki jíken (*event*).

draw (to) káku (*pictures*); hikitsukéru (*attention*).
  to draw back shírizóku.

drawer hikidashi (*of a table, etc.*).

drawing room zashiki.

dread osore.

dread (to) osoréru.

dreadful osoroshíi.

dream yumé.

dream (to) yumé o míru.

dreamer kuusooka, musooka.

dress kimono (*Japanese*); dóresu, yoofuku (*Occidental*).

dress (to) *v.t.* kimono o kiseru; *v.i.* kimono o kiru.

dressmaker yoofukuya, yoosáishi (*of Occidental clothes*); shitateya.

drink nomímono.
  drinking water nomímizu.

drink (to) nómu.

drip (to) shitatáru.

drive (to) unten suru.

driver unténshu.

drop itteki (*of liquid*).

drop (to) *v.t.* otósu (*let fall*); *v.i.* ochíru (*from a height*).

drown (to) oboreru.

drug kusuri (*medicine*); mayaku (*narcotics*).

drugstore kusuriya.

drum taiko; dorámu (*Occidental-style*).

drunk yótte iru.
  a drunken person yopparai.

dry kawáita (*of things*); kansoo shita (*of climate*).

dry (to) kawakásu (*make dry*); nugúu (*wipe one's eyes, etc.*); kawáku (*become dry*).

dryness kawakí (*thirst*).

duck ahiru (*domestic*); kámo (*wild*).

due manki (*payable*); toozen no (*fit, proper*).
  due to –no tamé ni.

dull nibúi (*blunt*); bonyári shita (*stupid*); omoshiróku nái (*uninteresting*).

dumb oshi.

during –no aida, –kan, –chuu (juu).
  during ten years juunen kan.
  during one's absence rúsu no aida, rusu chuu.

dust chiri; hokori (*a finer dust than* chiri).

dust (to) sooji suru, hokori o haráu.

dusty hokori no óoi.

Dutch Oranda no.

duty tsutomé (*work to be done*); gímu (*moral or legal obligation*); kanzei (*on imported goods*).

duty free muzei no.

dwarf kobito (*person*); kogata no (*undersized*).
  dwarf trees bonsai no kí.

dwell (to) súmu.

dye senryóo.

dye (to) someru.

E

each káku (*prefix*) –zútsu.
  each person méi mei.
  each person or thing sorézore (*of several*).
  each other otagai ni.
  each time –tabí ni.

eager nésshin na (*ardent*).

eagle washi.

ear mimí.

early *adj.* hayái. –*adv.* háyaku.

earn (to) kaségu (*by labor*).

earnest majime na (*serious*); nésshin na (*intense*).

earth tsuchí (*soil*); chikyuu (*world*).

ease rakú, kiraku.

ease (to) rakú ni suru.

easily yasashíku; tegaru ni (*readily*); súrasura to (*smoothly*).

east higashi.
  the East Tóoyoo.
  East Asia Higashi Ájia.
Easter fukkátsusai, íisutaa.
eastern higashi no.
easy yasashii.
eat (to) tabéru; meshiagaru (*honorific; respect*).
echo yamabiko (*a phenomenon of nature*); hankyoo (*in other cases*).
echo (to) hankyoo suru.
economical keizaijoo no, keizaiteki na.
economize (to) setsuyaku suru (*use eeonomically*).
economy class ekónomii kurasu.
edge há (*of blade*); hashi (*of cloth*); kishí (*of cliff, etc.*).
edition hán.
  first edition shohan.
  new edition shinpan.
  revised edition kaiteiban.
editor henshúusha (*of books or magazines*); shuhitsu (*of newspaper*).
editorial shasetsu.
education kyooiku.
  to receive an education kyooiku o ukéru.
effect kekka (*consequence*).
effective yuukoo na (*operative*); yuunoo na (*efficient*).
efficiency nooritsu.
effort dóryoku (*strenuous attempt*); honeori (*exertion*); róoku (*strain*).
  with an effort hone ótte.
  without any effort dóryoku sézu ni.
egg tamágo.
egoism jiko chuushin shúgi.
eight yattsú, hachí.
eighteen juuhachí.
eighteenth juuhachí ban.
eighth dái hachí.
eightieth hachijúu ban.
eighty hachijúu.
either dóchiraka no (*one of the two*); dóchira mo (*each of two*).
  either ... or –ka ... ka, –ka arúiwa ... ka
elastic shinshukusei no áru, shináyaka na (*flexible*).
elbow hijí.
elder toshiue no.
elderly nenpai no.
eldest ichiban toshi ue no.
elect (to) erábu (*choose*); sénkyo suru (*by vote*).
election sénkyo.
electric dénki no.
electrical dénki no.
electricity dénki.

elegant yúuga na (*graceful*); joohín na (*tasteful*).
element yóoso (*component part*).
elementary shóho no.
elephant zóo.
elevator erebéetaa.
eleven juuichí.
eleventh dái juiichí.
eliminate (to) nozoku (*exclude*); sákujo suru (*get rid of*); habúku (*omit*).
eloquence yuuben.
eloquent yuuben na.
else hoka ni.
  something else hoka ni náni ka.
  anyone else hoka ni dáre ka.
elsewhere hoka ni dóko ka.
elude (to) nogaréru (*evade*); sakéru (*escape adroitly from*).
embark (to) joosen suru (*board a ship*); shuppan suru (*depart*).
embarrass (to) komaraséru.
  I was embarrassed. Komarimáshita.
embarrassing toowaku saseru.
embarrassment toowaku (*perplexity*).
embassy taishíkan.
embody gutaika suru (*make concrete*).
embrace (to) daku (*a person*); torimáku (*encircle*); hoogan suru (*contain*).
embroidery nuitori, shisuu.
emerge (to) arawaréru (*come out into view*).
emergency hijóoji.
eminent kéncho na (*distinguished*).
emotion kanjoo (*feeling*).
  with emotion kandoo shite.
  appeal to the emotions kanjoo ni uttaéru.
emperor tennóo.
emphasis kyoochoo.
emphasize (to) kyoochoo suru.
emphatic tsuyói.
empire téikoku.
employee yatoinin, shiyoonin, juugyóo in.
employer yatóinushi.
employment shokúgyoo (*occupation*); shigoto (*work*); koyoo.
empty kara no.
enable (to) –ga dekíru.
enamel enameru.
enclose (to) kakomu (*surround*); kakou (*shut in*), doofuu suru (*in a letter*).
enclosure kakoi (*fence*); doofúubutsu (*enclosed materials*).
encourage (to) genki zukéru (*hearten*); yuuki zukéru (*put courage into*).
encouragement hagemashi.
end sue (*latter part*); owari (*the close*); ketsumatsu (*conclusion*); shimai (*finish*).
end (to) owaru, shimau.
endeavor jinryoku, dóryoku.

endeavor (to) dóryoku suru (*try hard*); kokoromíru (*attempt*).

endorse (to) uragaki suru.

endure (to) gáman surú (*bear bravely*); mochikotaéru (*hold out*).

enemy teki.

energy chikará (*power*); génki (*vigor*).
    atomic energy genshíryoku.
    energy crisis nenryoo kíki
    mental energy seishin nóoryoku.
    solar energy taiyoo enérugii.

enforce (to) shiiru (*press*).

engage (to) yatóu (*hire*).

engaged isogashíi (*busy*); kon'yaku shite iru (*betrothed*).

engagement yakusoku (*formal promise*); kon'yaku (*betrothal*); yooji (*business*).

engine kikái (*machine*); kikán (*boiler*), énjin (*of car, etc.*).

engineer gíshi (*of factory*).

English eigo (*pertaining to the language*); Igirisu (Eikoku) no (*pertaining to the country*); Igirisújin (Eikokújin) (*pertaining to the people*).

engrave (to) hóru; insatsu suru (*print*).

enjoy (to) tanoshímu.

enjoyment tanoshimi.

enlarge (to) ookíku suru (*make bigger*); hikinobásu (*a photograph, etc.*).

enlist (to) gúntai ni háiru (*in the army*); hito no shíji o éru (*secure one's support*).

enormous kyodai na.

enough juubún.

enter (to) háiru.

entertain (to) tanoshimaséru (*amuse*); motenasu (*guests*).

entertainment goraku (*amusement*); yokyoo (*public show*).

enthusiasm nésshin.

enthusiastic nésshin na.

entire kanzen na (*complete*); zentai no (*whole*).

entitle (to) na o tsukéru.

entrance iriguchi.

entrust (to) makaséru (*a duty, etc.*); azukéru (*a thing to another person*).

enumerate (to) kazoéru (*count*).

envelope fuutoo (*for letters*).

envious urayamashíi.

envy urayami, shítto (*jealousy*).

envy (to) urayámu (*feel envy of*); shítto suru (*begrudge*).

episode soowa, episóodo.

equal onaji (*the same*); byoodoo no (*equitable*).

equal (to) –ni hitoshíi.
    A equals B. A wa B desu.

equality byoodoo.

equator sekidoo.

equilibrium tsuriai.

equip (to) yóoi suru (*supply*); sóobi suru (*fit*); mijítaku suru (*array*).

equipment shitaku, júnbi, sóochi.

era jidai.

erase (to) kesu nuguikésu (*wipe out*).

eraser keshi gomu.

erect (to) tatéru (*set up*).

err (to) machigáeru.

errand tsukai.

error machigái.

escalator esukaréetaa.

escape toosoo (*running away*); datsugoku (*from prison*).

escape (to) nigéru (*get free*); nogaréru (*get off safely*).

escort (to) goei suru (*with military*); tsukisóu (*accompany*).

especially tókuni.

essay ronbun, zuihitsu.

essence yootén (*main points*); hóntai (*a thing in itself*); yóoso (*element*).

essential kanarazu iru, nákute wa naránai (*necessary*); honshitsuteki no (*of essential character*).

establish tatéru, setsuritsu suru (*found*); kakutei suru (*ascertain*); seitei suru (*prove*).

establishment setsuritsu (*business firm*).

estate shoyúuchi (*property*); jísho (*ground*).

esteem sonkei (*respect form*).

esteem (to) sonkei suru.

esthetic fúuryuu na, biteki na.

estimate mitsumori (*of the cost*); hyóoka (*of the value*).

estimate (to) hyóoka suru (*appraise*); mitsumóru (*compute*); hándan suru (*judge*).

estimation mitsumori, hyóoka.

eternal eikyuu no (*everlasting*); huhen no (*immutable*).

eternity eikyuu, eien (*infinite time*); fumetsu (*immortality*).

ether eeteru.

European Yoorappájin (*people*); Yooróppa no (*pertaining to Europe*).

evade sakéru.

evasion káihi.

eve yuugata (*evening*); zénya (*the evening or day before a festival*).

even mo, démo (*also*); taira na (*level*); choodo (*just*).

evening ban, yóru, yuugata.
    Good evening! Konban wá.
    yesterday evening sakúban, yuube.
    tomorrow evening myóoban, ashita no ban.

event dekígoto, jíken.

ever ítsu demo (*always*); táezu (*incessantly*);

ima máde ni (*up to now*); ítsu ka (*on any occasion*).

every mai–, dónna –démo; zénbu (*all*).
everyday máinichi.
every year maitoshi.

everybody dáre mo (*referring to members of a group*); dáre demo (*no matter who*); minna (*all*).

everything nán demo (*no matter what*); zénbu, minna (*all things*).

everywhere dóko de mo (*no matter where*); hóoboo (*all over*).

evidence shooko (*proof*).
evident akíraka na (*obvious*).

evil *adj.* warúi, akushitsu na (*wicked*); fukitsu na (*unlucky*). –*n.* áku (*vice*); jáaku (*wickedness*); warúi kotó (*bad thing*).

evoke (to) hikiokósu (*draw forth*).
evolve (to) tenkai suru (*unfold, unroll*); hatten suru (*develop*).

exact seikaku na (*accurate*); genmitsu na (*precise*); genkaku na (*rigorous*).

exaggerate (to) kochoo suru, oogesa ni iu.
exaggeration kochoo, oogesa.

exalt (to) takaméru (*raise high*); homesoyásu (*extol*).

exaltation takaméru kotó.

examination kénsa (*inspection*); chóosa (*investigation*); koosatsu (*consideration*); shikén (*test*).

examine (to) shirabéru (*inspect*); shikén suru (*give a test*).

example réi (*illustration*); tehón (*model, pattern*).

exceed sugíru, kosu (*go over*).

excel (to) sugúréru.
   She excels in English. Eigo ni sugúrete iru.

excellence subaráshisa, kesshutsu (*superiority*); chóosho (*great merit*).

excellent sugúreta.

except –no hoka wa.
except (to) nozoku (*omit*).
exception reigai.
exceptional reigaiteki na.
exceptionally reigaiteki ni (*unusually*); hijoo ni (*very*).

excess yobun.

excessive yobun no (*surplus*); hoogai na (*exorbitant*).

exchange kookan (*of things in general*); ryoogae (*of coins*).

exchange (to) torikaeru, kookan suru (*barter*).
   exchange rate kawase réeto.

excite (to) *v.i.* sawágu (*a body of people*); *v.t.* ugokásu (*arouse a feeling*).
   to get excited koofun suru.

excitement koofun.

exclaim sakebu (*cry out*); zekkyoo suru (*speak vehemently*).

exclamation zekkyoo (*outcry*); kantánshi (*an interjection*).
   exclamation mark kantánfu.

exclude (to) nozoku.

exclusive dokusenteki (*monopolistic*); –o nozoite (*not including*).

excursion ensoku (*picnic*); yuuran ryókoo (*pleasure tour*).

excuse koojitsu (*bad*); iiwake (*apology*).

excuse (to) yurúsu (*forgive*); benkai suru (*vindicate*).
   Excuse me. Gomen nasái.

execute (to) jikkoo suru (*carry out*); suikoo suru (*perform*).

execution shikkoo, suikoo.

exempt (to) menzúru (*free*).

exercise undoo (*of the body*); renshuu (*lesson*).

exercise (to) undoo suru (*engage in athletics*); renshuu suru (*practice*).

exert (to) tsukúsu (*put forth*); mochiíru (*use*).

exertion dóryoku, jínryoku (*vigorous effort*).

exhaust (to) kará ni suru (*empty*); tsukai tsukúsu (*use up*); tsukarehatesaséru (*tire out*).

exhaustion hiroo (*extreme fatigue*).

exhibit (to) tenji suru (*show publicly*).

exhibition hakuránkai (*exposition*); tenjíkai (*show*).

exile tsuihoo (*banishment*); tsuihoonin (*person in exile*).

exile (to) tsuihoo suru.

exist sonzai suru, áru (*be*).

existence sonzai (*being*); seizon (*life*).

exit déguchi.

expand hirogeru (*spread out*); kakuchoo suru (*extend*); kakudai saseru (*amplify*).

expansion kakuchoo (*dilation*); hirogari (*expanse*).

expansive koodai na (*extensive*); kokoro no hirói (*comprehensive*).

expect (to) kitai suru (*look forward to*); –to omóu (*suppose*).

expectation kitai (*anticipation*); yosoo (*probability*).

expedition tanken (*for exploration*).

expel (to) oiharáu (*drive out*); menshoku suru (*dismiss*).

expense híyoo.

expensive takái, kóoka na (*costly*).

experience keiken (*personal observation*).

experience (to) keiken suru (*undergo*).

experiment (to) shikén suru (*test*), tamésu (*try out*).

expert *adj.* kuróoto (*in doing something*). –*n.* senmonka (*specialist*).

expire (to) kikan ga kireru (*come to an end*), íki o hikitóru (*breathe one's last*); kieru (*die out*); shoometsu suru (*become extinct*).

explain (to) setsumei suru (*give an explanation*); káishaku suru (*interpret*); benmei suru (*justify by an explanation*).

explanation setsumei.

explanatory setsumeiteki, setsumei no.

explode (to) bakuhatsu suru.

exploit tegara (*brilliant achievement*).

exploit (to) kuimono ni suru (*take advantage of for one's own ends*).

explore (to) tanken suru (*search through*); chóosa suru (*inquire into*).

explosion bakuhatsu.

export yushutsu.

export (to) yushutsu suru.

expose (to) sarasu (*leave unprotected*); chinretsu suru (*exhibit*); roshutsu suru (*in photography*); abáku (*disclose, reveal*).

express sokutatsu (*special delivery*); kyuukoo (*train*).

express (to) iiarawásu (*state*).

expression hyoojoo (*facial*); hyoogen (*verbal*).

expressive hyoojoo ni tómu.

expulsion hoochiku.

exquisite sensai na (*delicate*).

extend (to) nobásu (*in length or term*); hirogeru (*in breadth*); okuru (*an invitation, greetings*).

extensive koodai na (*far-reaching*).

extent han'i (*space, scope, degree*).

    to some extent áru téido.

exterior sóto, hyoomen (*surface*).

exterminate (to) tayásu.

external gáibu no (*outside*).

extinct horóbite shimatta.

extinction shoometsu.

extinguish kesu (*put out*); tayásu (*put an end to*).

extra betsu no.

    an extra googai (*edition of a newspaper*).

extract bassui (*excerpt*).

extract (to) nuku (*pull out*); nuki-tóru (*pull out with difficulty*); tekishutsu suru (*draw forth*).

extraordinary futsuu de nái (*exceptional*); hibon na (*uncommon*); ichijirushíi (*remarkable*).

extravagance zeitakú (*lavish wastefulness*); hoojuu (*unrestrained excess*).

extravagant zeitakú na (*profuse, wasteful*); múcha na (*unreasonable*); hóogai na (*exorbitant, excessive*).

extreme kyokután na (*utmost*); ichiban tooi (*outermost*).

extremely taihen, hijoo ni.

extremity hashi (*extreme point*).

eye mé.

eyebrow máyuge.

eyeglasses. mégane.

eyelid mábuta.

F

fable otogibánashi, guuwa.

face kao.

face (to) mukau.

facilitate rakú ni suru.

facility yooi (*ease*); béngi (*convenience*).

fact kotó; shidái (*of an occurrence*); jikoo (*particulars*).

    in fact jitsú wa.

factory kooba, koojoo.

faculty shuwan (*aptitude*); gakubu (*of a university*).

fade iró ga saméru.

fail (to) shippai suru (*be unsuccessful*); hasan suru (*become bankrupt*).

    without fail machigái náku, kitto, zéhi.

faint usui (*of color*); yowái (*wanting in courage*); kásuka na (*of sound, etc.*).

faint (to) kizetsu suru.

fair *adj.* kírei na (*pretty*); iro no shirói (*of complexion*); koohei na (*impartial*). *—n.* ichi (*market*); jizen íchi (*bazaar*).

faith shinkoo (*belief*); shinjoo (*creed*); kyóogi (*religious doctrine*); shinrai (*trust*).

faithful chuujitsu na.

fall tsuiraku (*drop*); taki (*cascade*); áki (*autumn*); kanraku (*surrender*); gakai (*of a government*).

fall (to) ochíru (*drop*); fúru (*rain, snow*); sagáru (*prices*).

    fall down korobu.

false úso no, hontoo de nái (*not true*); fujitsu na (*not faithful*); sorazorashíi (*feigned*); nise (*counterfeit*).

fame meisei.

familiar yóku shirarete iru (*well known*); kikináreta (*to the ear*); mináreta (*to the eye*); arifureta (*common*); shitashíi (*intimate*).

family kázoku.

    family name myóoji.

famine bússhi no ketsuboo (*scarcity of food*); kikín (*failure of crops*); kíga (*starvation*).

famous yuumei na.

fan sensu (*folding*); uchíwa (*nonfolding*).

    electric fan senpúuki.

fancy soozóoryoku (*imagination*); kangáe (*idea*).

fantastic kuusooteki na (*extravagant*); iyoo

na (*grotesque*); soozoojoo no
(*imaginary*), subarashíi (*wonderful*).
far tooi.
  as far as máde.
  so far ima máde (*up to now*).
fare ryóokin (*cost of transportation*).
  one-way fare katamichi ryóokin.
farm hatake (*field*); noojoo (*ranch*).
farmer nóofu, hyakushoo.
farming nóogyoo (*agriculture*).
farther mótto tooi.
farthest ichiban tooi.
fashion tsukuri káta (*shape*); ryuukoo,
  fásshon (*style*).
fashionable (to become) ryuukoo suru.
fast hayái.
fasten (to) shikkári tomeru (*make fast*);
  kukuri tsukéru (*attach securely*).
fat adj. futótta. –n. abura.
fatal ínochi ni kakawáru.
  fatal wound chiméishoo.
  fatal accident chimeiteki jíko.
  fatal disease fúji no yámai.
fate únmei (*destiny*); ún (*appointed lot*).
father otóosan (*respect*); chichi (*plain*).
faucet jáguchi.
fault kettén (*defect*); tánsho (*weak point*);
  machigái (*mistake*).
favor onegai (*request*).
  Could (will) you do me a favor? Onegai
  dekimásu ka?
favor (to) ekohíiki o suru (*be partial to*);
  shíji suru (*support*).
favorable kooi áru (*well disposed*); shoodaku
  no (*consenting*).
favorite adj. ki ni iri no (*preferred*); dáisuki
  na (*liked greatly*). –n. ninkimono
  (*person*).
fax fákkusu.
fear osore (*dread*); shinpai (*anxiety*).
fear (to) osoréru.
fearless daitán na.
feather hane.
feature tokuchoo (*characteristic*); yootén
  (*striking point*); kaodachi (*appearance*).
February Nigatsu.
federal chuuoo séifu no (*pertaining to the
  central government*).
fee gessha (*monthly*); shinsatsúryoo
  (*doctor's*).
feeble yowái (*weak*); bonyári shita
  (*indistinct*).
feed (to) tabesaséru.
feel (to) sawaru (*touch*); kanjiru (*perceive a
  sensation*).
feeling kankaku (*sense*); kimochi (*sensation*);
  kanjoo (*emotion*).
fellow adj. nakama no. –n. nakama
  (*associate*).

fellowship shoogákukin (*grant*); shinboku
  (*friendliness*).
fellow worker shigoto nákama.
female onna (*woman*).
  female sex josei.
feminine onna no.
fence kakíne (*enclosure for garden*); kakoi
  (*for other purposes*), hei.
fencing kéndoo (*Japanese-style*); fénshingu
  (*foreign*).
ferocious kyooboo na (*fierce*); yaban na
  (*savage*).
ferry watashibúne (*ferryboat*); renrakusen
  (*connected wtih trains*).
fertile kóeta (*productive*).
fertilize (to) híryoo o hodokósu.
fertilizer híryoo (*manure*); kagaku híryoo
  - (*chemical*).
fervent netsuretsu na (*ardent*).
fervor netsu joo (*ardor*).
festival saijitsu (*feast day*); omatsuri, matsuri
  (*of shrine or temple*).
fetch moté kuru.
fever netsú.
few ní san (*two or three*); sukóshi (*not
  many*).
fiber sén'i.
fiber optic communication hikari tsuushin.
fiction shoosetsu, fíkushon.
field nóhara (*open country*); bokusóochi
  (*meadow*).
  rice field tá.
fierce araarashíi (*ferocious*); mooretsu na
  (*violent*); hageshíi (*furious*).
fiery hí no yoo na (*glowing*).
fifteen júugo.
fifteenth dái júugo; júugo nichi (*of the
  month*); júugo ban.
fifth dái go.
fiftieth dai gojúu.
fifty gojúu.
fig ichíjiku.
fight kenka (*brawl*); sensoo (*battle*).
fight (to) sensoo suru (*wage war*); dóryoku
  suru (*struggle for*); kenka suru (*quarrel*).
figure suuji (*number*); katachí (*form*); súgata
  (*body*); moyoo (*design, pattern*).
file yasuri (*tool*); rétsu (*row*); fáiru (*official
  file*); tojikomi (*for letters*).
fill (to) v.t. ippai ni suru; v.i. ippai ni náru
  (*become full*).
film fuirumu (*for camera*); éiga (*motion
  picture*).
filthy kitanái (*unclean*); gehín na (*obscene*).
final sáigo no (*last*); shuukyoku no
  (*conclusive*).
  finally tóotoo.
finance zaisei.
finance (to) kane o dásu.

financial zaiseijoo no.

find (to) mitsukeru.

fine *adj.* komakái (*small*); hosói (*slender*); usui (*thin*); utsukushíi (*beautiful*); ii (*good*); génki na (*healthy*).

fine *n.* bakkin (*penalty*).

finger yubí.

finish (to) shimau, oeru; dekiagaru (*complete a piece of work*); shiagéru (*get a thing done*).

fire hí; káji (*conflagration*).

fireworks hánabi.

firm *adj.* katai (*compact*); shikkári shita (*rigid*).

firm shóokai, kaisha (*commercial*).

first *adj.* dái ichí no, ichí ban no (*ordinal number*). –*adv.* hajime.
    at first hajime wa.
    for the first time hajímete.

fish sakana, uo; sashimi (*slices of raw fish*).
    raw fish namazákana.

fish (to) tsuri o suru.
    go out fishing tsuri ni iku.

fisherman ryóoshi.

fist nigiri kóbushi.

fit *adj.* tekitoo na (*appropriate*); datoo na (*proper, right*). –*n.* hossa (*convulsion*).

fit (to) tekigoo suru (*be fit for*); awaséru (*make to suit*); júnbi suru (*qualify*); áu (*be adjusted to fit*).

fitness tekitoo.

five itsútsu, gó.

fix (to) kimeru (*determine*); toritsukéru (*arrange*); naósu (*mend*).

flag hatá.

flame honoo.

flank sokumen (*side*).

flank (to) sokumen o mamóru.

flash hirameki (*lightning*).

flat hiratai (*level*); kin'itsu no (*unvarying*); ki no nuketa (*stale*).

flatter oseji o iu.

flattery oseji (*insincere compliment*).

flavor aji (*taste*); kaori (*smell*).

fleet kantai (*navy*).

flesh nikú (*meat for eating*); nikutai (*of the human body*).

flexibility shinayákasa.

flexible shináyaka na (*pliable*).

flight hikoo (*trip by air*); tooboo (*a fleeing*); kaidan (*of stairs*).

fling (to) tosshin suru (*dash, rush*); nagetsukéru (*hurl, toss*).

flint hiuchí ishi.

float (to) uku (*on water*); ukabu (*on water or in air*).

flood oomizu, koozui.

flood (to) shinsui saseru (*inundate*); shinsui suru (*be inundated*); hanran suru (*overflow*).

floor yuka (*of a room*).

floppy disk furoppii dísuku.

flourish (to) sakaeru (*thrive*).

flow nagaréru.

flower haná.
    flower arrangement ikébana, kádoo.

fluid ekitai.

fly hai.

fly (to) tobu.

foam awá.

foam (to) awá ga tátsu.

fog kiri (*mist*); móya (*haze*).
    thick fog nóomu.

fold hída (*in a garment*).

fold (to) tatamu, óru.

foliage ha.

follow (to) –ni shitagáu (*go or come after*); –ni tsúite kúru (*come traveling with someone*); –ni tsúite iku (*go accompanying someone*); issho ni iku (*accompany*).

following sono tsugí no (*next*).
    the following day akuru hi.

fond (be) konómu.

fondness sukí.

food tabémono.

fool báka.

foolish báka na (*silly*); bakarashíi (*nonsensical*); bakágeta (*ridiculous*).

foot ashí (*of the body*); ffito (*measure*).

football futtobóoru, shuukyuu.

footstep ashidori (*tread*); ashiáto (*footprint*).

for –no kawari ni (*in place of*); –o daihyoo shite (*representing*); –ni táishite (*in return for, in contrast with*); –no tsugunai ni (*in compensation for*); –no tamé ni (*on behalf of, in support of, for the purpose of, because of*); –ni mukatte (*in the direction of*); –no wari ní wa (*in respect of*).
    for example tatóeba.
    for the first time hajímete.
    for the most part daibúbun.
    for the present ima no tokoro.

forbid kinjíru.

force chikará (*strength*); gúntai (*troops*).
    by force múri ni.

force (to) bookoo suru (*use force upon*); kojiakéru (*break open*); oshiyáru (*impel*); múri ni, shíite (*when followed by a causative verb*).
    I forced her to go. Múri ni ikaseta.

ford (to) asase o wataru (*wade across*).

foreground zenkei.

forehead hitai.

foreign gaikoku no (*pertaining to foreign countries in general*); séiyoo no (*of the Occident*).

foreigner gaikokújin, gaijin (*foreigners in general*); oobéijian (*Occidental*).

forest hayashi, mori (*grove*); shinrin (*dense growth*).

forget (to) wasureru.

forgetfulness wasureppói kotó.

forgive yurúsu.

forgiveness yurushi.

fork fooku (*for eating*); wakarémichi (*parting of the ways*); shiryuu (*of a river*); matá (*of a tree*).

form katachi (*shape*); keishiki (*formality*); yóoshi (*blank*).

form (to) katachizukúru (*shape*); tsukúru (*organize*); –ni náru (*constitute*); tsukuriagéru (*build up*).

formal seishiki no.

formation sóshiki.

former máe no, saki no (*previous*).

formerly máe ni (*previously*); móto (*originally*).

formula hooshiki, yarikata (*method*).

forsake (to) misuteru (*abandon*).

fort yoosai.

fortieth yonjuu ban mé no; dái yónjuu.

fortunate ún ga íi.

fortunately ún yoku, shiawase ní mo (*luckily*).

fortune shiawase (*good luck*); zaisan (*wealth*); únsei (*fate*).

forty shijúu, yónjuu.

forward zenpoo e (*onward*).
    move forward zenshin suru.

forward (to) okuru (*goods*); kaisoo suru, tensoo suru (*letters*).

foster yoo—.
    foster daughter yóojo.
    foster mother yóobo.
    foster father yóofu.
    foster son yooshi.

found (to) setsuritsu suru (*establish, start*); kisó o okú (*lay the base of*).

foundation dodai (*groundwork*); kónkyo (*basis*); shuppátsuten (*beginning*); zaidan (*endowed institution*).

founder soorítsusha (*one who establishes or lays a foundation*).

fountain funsui.

four yottsú, shí, yón.

fourteen juushí, juuyón.

fourteenth juuyon ban mé no (*place*); júuyokká (*of the month*).

fourth yottsu mé, dái shí, dái yón; yokka (*of the month*).

fowl torí (*bird*).

fox kitsuné.

fragment kakera, kirehashi.

fragrance yói niói.

fragrant nioi no íi.

frail yowayowashíi.

frame gakubuchi.

frame (to) é o gaku ni ireru (*a picture*).

frank sotchoku na (*openhearted*); koozen no, akarasama na (*without guile*).

frankness sotchoku.

free táda (*gratis*); jiyúu na (*liberated*); múzei (*without tax*).

free (to) *v.t.* hanásu (*let go free*); *v.i.* jiyúu ni náru (*be set free*).

freedom jiyúu (*liberty*); dokuritsu (*independence*).

freeze (to) *v.t.* kooraseru; *v.i.* kooru.

freight kámotsu (*goods*).

French furansu no (*pertaining to France*); furansugo (*language*); furansújin (*people*).

frequent tabitabi no (*recurring often*).

frequent (to) yóku iku (*visit often*).

frequently tabitabi (*often*); yóku (*at short intervals*).

fresh mizumizushíi (*newly grown*); dekitate no (*just made*); shinsen na, atarashíi (*said of foods*).

friction masatsu, atsureki.

Friday Kin'yóobi.

friend tomodachi; yuujin.

friendly aiso no íi.

friendship yuujoo (*friendly attachment*); yúugi (*intimacy*).

frighten (to) odorokásu;
    be frightened bikkúri suru, odoróku.

frightening kowái.

fringe fusá (*tuft*); herí (*border*).

frivolity fumájime.

frivolous fumájime na.

frog kaeru.

from –kara.
    from now on íma kara.

front máe, zenmén (*forward part*); zenpoo (*forward place*); shoomen (*of a building*); sensen (*line of battle*).

frost shimó.

fruit kudámono.

fry (to) furai suru, ageru.

frying pan furái pan, age nábe.

fuel nenryóo.

fugitive *n.* toosóosha (*runaway*); booméisha (*political refugee*).

fulfill (to) hatásu (*perform*); jikkoo suru (*execute*).

full ippai no (*filled to capacity*).

fully mattaku.

fun tanoshimi (*amusement*).

function hataraki.

function (to) hataraku.

fund kikín.

fundamental kisoteki na.

funds shikín (*sum of money*).

funny kokkei na.

fur kegawa.

furious okótte iru (*angry*).

furnace ro.

furnish (to) kyookyuu suru (*provide*); sonaéru (*equip*).

furniture kágu.

furrow áto (*track*); wadachi (*rut*); fukái shiwá (*deep wrinkle*).

furrow (to) kao o shikameru (*make a wrinkle in the face*).

further sonó ue (*besides*).
    further away mótto saki.
    further on mótto saki e.

fury gékido (*wild anger*); kyooboo (*violence*).

future *adj.* mírai no. *–n.* mírai (*time to come*); shóorai (*prospect*).
    in the future mírai ni, shoorai.

G

gaiety nigiyákasa (*mirth*).

gain ríeki (*opposite of loss*); mooke (*earnings*); zooka (*increase*).

gain (to) té ni ireru, éru (*obtain*); masu (*increase*).

gallant isamashíi.

gallery gyáraii (*of fine arts*); tachimí-seki (*standing room in a theater*).

gamble (to) kakegoto o suru, kakéru.

game yúugi (*amusement*); kyóogi (*sporting contest*); shoobugoto (*of chance*).

garage garéeji.

garden niwa.
    public garden kooen.

gardener uekiya, niwáshi.

garlic ninniku.

gas gásu.

gasoline gasorin.

gate món.

gather *v.t.* yoseatsuméru (*bring together*); atsuméru (*collect*); saishuu suru (*pick up*); tsumu (*as flowers*); *v.i.* atsumáru (*assemble*).

gay yooki na (*said of people*); hade na (*said of colors*).

gem hooseki (*jewel*).

gender séi.

general *adj.* ippan no, ippanteki no (*belonging to the whole*); taitei no (*common to many*).
    in general, generally ippan ni.

general táishoo (*military*).

generalize (to) ippanka shite kangáeru.

generation sédai (*used when referring to people, as in "young generation"*); jidai (*period of time*).

generosity kandaisa, kimae no yósa.

generous ki no ookíi, kandai na.

genius tensai.

gentle otonashíi (*said of people*); yasashíi (*said of manners*); odáyaka na (*quiet*).

gentleman shínshi.

genuine honmono no (*authentic*); senjitsu na (*sincere*).

geographical chiriteki no.

geography chíri.

germ baikin.

German dóitsu no (*pertaining to Germany*); doitsugo (*language*); doitsújin (*people*).

gesture míburi.

get (to) náru (*become, turn*); té ni ireru (*get hold of*).

ghastly zotto suru.

giant *adj.* óoki na, ookíi. *–n.* oоótoko (*big man*).

gift miyage (*souvenir*); okurimono, purézento (*present*); sainoo (*talent*).

gifted sainoo no áru (*talented*).

girl onná no ko.

give (to) sashiageru (*to others: humble*); ageru (*to others*); yaru (*to others: fam.*); watasu (*hand over*); kudasáru (*from others: respect*); kureru (*from others: fam.*).
    give back káesu.

glad ureshíi (*delighted, happy*).
    be glad yorokóbu.

gladly yorokónde.

glance hitóme.
    at a glance hitóme de.

glance (to) chirátto míru (*look rapidly*); zatto mé o tóosu (*read rapidly*).

glass garasu (*material*).
    looking glass kagamí.
    drinking glass koppu.

gleam kagayaki (*shine*); hirameki (*of intelligence*).

gleam (to) kagayáku.

glitter kagayaki.

glitter (to) pikápika hikaru.

globe tamá (*round object*); chikyuu (*the earth*).

gloomy kurai (*dark*); usugurai (*somber*); inki na (*depressed*).

glorious kooei áru (*illustrious*); soogon na (*majestic*); subarashíi (*delightful*).

glory kooei (*honor*); sookan (*splendor*).

glove tebúkuro.
    a pair of gloves tebúkuro hitókumi.

go (to) yuku, iku; máiru (*honorific: humble*); irassháru (*honorific: respect*).
    to go away itte shimau.
    to go back káeru.
    to go down oríru (*stairs, etc.*).
    to go down kudaru (*mountains, etc.*).

to go into háiru.
to go out déru.
to go up noboru, agaru.
god kámi (*deity*); guuzoo (*idol*).
gold kín.
golden kin'iro no.
good íi, yói.
  Good afternoon! Konnichi wá.
  Good evening! Konban wá.
  Good morning! Ohayoo gozaimásu.
  Good night! Oyasumi nasái (*said when going to bed*).
good-bye sayonara.
goods shinamono.
goodwill kóoi.
goose gachoo.
gossip goshíppu, uwasabánashi.
gossip (to) uwasabánashi o suru, hito no uwasa o suru.
govern (to) osaméru (*rule*); kánri suru (*control*).
government seiji (*politics*); seitai (*form of government*); kánri (*management*); toochi kikán (*governing body*).
grace shitoyákasa.
graceful shitóyaka na.
grain kokúmotsu.
grammar bunpoo.
grand subarashíi (*magnificent*); rippa na (*splendid*).
  Grand! mígoto desu.
grandchild magó.
granddaughter mago músume.
grandfather ojíisan, sófu.
grandmother obáasan, sóbo.
grandson mago músuko.
grant kyóka (*permission*); joseikin (*funds*).
grant (to) kikitodokéru (*consent to*); ataeru (*give*); júyo suru (*bestow*); yurúsu (*allow, permit*).
grape budoo.
grapefruit gureepu furúutsu.
grasp (to) nigiru (*in the hand*); tsukámu (*with the hand or mind*).
grass kusá.
grasshopper inago.
grateful arigatái.
gratitude kánsha.
grave *adj.* juudai na (*serious*).
grave haká (*place of burial*).
gravel jari.
gray nezumi iro, hai iro.
grease abura.
great ookíi (*large*); idai na (*much above the average*).
greatness idaisa.
greedy kuishínboo na (*for food*); yokufukái (*for gain*).
green mídori.

greet (to) áisatsu suru.
greeting áisatsu.
grief fukái kanashimi (*deep sorrow*); shintsuu (*distress*).
grieve (to) *v.t.* fukáku kanashimaséru (*cause grief to*); kurushimaséru (*distress*); *v.i.* fukáku kanashímu (*feel grief*); nagéku (*lament*).
grin (to) niyátto warau.
grind surikudáku.
groan unari góe.
groan (to) unáru, uméku.
grocer shokuryoohin'ya.
grocery store shokuryoohin'ya.
grope teságuri suru.
gross juuni dáasu (*12 doz.*).
ground jímen (*surface of earth*); dodai (*foundation*).
group gurúupu; shuudan (*assemblage*).
group (to) matomeru.
grow (to) hattatsu suru (*develop*); seichoo suru (*said of animate things*); haéru (*flourish in earth*).
growth seichoo.
grudge urami.
  hold a grudge against uramu.
gruff bukkiráboo na.
guard hoshoo (*sentry*); shashoo (*of a train*); bannín (*watchman*).
guard (to) mamóru.
guardian kookennin (*legal*); hogósha (*keeper*).
guess suiryoo, ate zuiryoo.
guess (to) soozoo suru.
  guess right iiatéru.
guide annáisha (*tourist*); michi annaisha (*one who shows the way*); shidóosha (*leader*).
guide (to) annái suru (*lead the way*).
guilt tsúmi.
gum norí, gómu.
  chewing gum chuuíngamu.
gun júu (*firearm*); teppoo (*rifle, shotgun*); kenjuu (*revolver*).
gush (to) fukidéru.

H

habit shuukan.
habitual shuukanteki na (*customary*); jooshuuteki (*regular*).
hail arare (*small hailstone*); hyóo (*large hailstone*).
hail (to) arare ga fúru.
hair ke (*in general*); kamí (*of the head*).
hairdo heya sutáiru.
hairdresser biyóoshi.
half hanbún.
  half-hour hanjíkan, sanjippun.

hall hiroma, hóoru.

ham hámu.

hammer kanazúchi.

hand té.

hand (to) watasu (*hand over*).

handbag handobaggu, tesage.

handful té ippái.

handkerchief hankachi.

handle té, hikite (*of a door*); e, té (*of a tool*).

handle (to) atsukau.

handsome tanrei na (*good-looking*); yooboo no utsukushíi (*beautiful*).

handy kíyoo na (*said of persons*); chóohoo na, bénri na (*said of things*).

hang *v.t.* kakéru (*something*); kubi o kukuru (*a person*); *v.i.* sagáru (*hang down*).

happen (to) furikakáru (*befall*); okóru (*occur*).

happening dekígoto (*event*); jíken (*incident*).

happiness koofuku (*well-being*); shiawase (*fortune, luck*).

happy ureshíi, koofuku na (*felicitous, joyous*); shiawase na (*favored by luck*).

harbor minato.

hard katai (*solid, as opposed to soft*); muzukashíi (*difficult*).

harden (to) *v.t.* katameru, kataku suru (*solidify*); katamaru (*become solid*).

hardly hotóndo (*used with a negative expression*).

hardness kenroo.

hardship kónnan.

hardware kanamono.

    hardware store kanamonoya.

hardy joobu na.

hare no-úsagi.

harm gái (*damage*); songai (*loss*); sonshoo (*injury*).

harm (to) gaisúru.

harmful warúi.

harmless gái no nái.

harmonious tsuriai no tóreta (*balanced*).

harmony wáon (*musical*); haigoo (*of colors*); enman, choowa (*between persons*).

harsh soaku na (*coarse*); fuchóowa na (*discordant*); kibishíi (*stern*).

harvest shuukaku.

haste isogi.

hasten (to) isógu (*hurry*); isogaséru (*hurry a person*); hayaméru (*a result*); isóide suru (*hurry to*).

hat booshi.

hate nikumi.

hate (to) nikúmu, kirau.

hateful nikurashíi.

hatred nikushimi.

haughty gooman na.

have (to) mótsu (*possess, hold*); nómu (*drink*); tabéru (*eat*); uketoru (*receive*).

haven minato, hinansho.

hay karekusa.

he káre, anó hito.

head atamá (*of the body*); kashiró (*leader*), shunin (*chief*).

headache zutsuu.

head up tsumu.

heal *v.t.* naósu (*mend*); *v.i.* naóru (*be mended*).

health kenkoo.

healthy kenkoo na, joobu na.

heap yamá.

hear (to) kiku.

hearing kiku chikara, chooryoku.

    hard of hearing mimí ga tooi.

heart shinzoo (*organ of the body*); kokóro (*as seat of the emotions*).

heat (to) atataméru, átsuku suru.

heaven téngoku (*Christian*); gokuraku (*Buddhist*).

    Heavens! óya máa!

heavy omoi.

hedge iké gaki.

heed (to) shitagáu.

heel kakato.

height tákasa.

heir soozokunin.

heiress soozokunin.

helm káji.

help tetsudái.

help (to) tetsudáu (*give a helping hand*); sewá o suru (*take care of*); tasukéru (*rescue*).

helper tetsudái.

helpful yakú ni tátsu.

hem fuchí (*margin*); heri (*edge*); sakái (*border*).

hen mendori.

henceforth kore kara.

her, hers kánojo no. See also *him*.

herb yakusoo (*medical*).

herd muré.

here kokó (*this place*); kotchi, kochira (*this side*).

herewith koko ni.

hero eiyuu (*of a battle*); shujínkoo (*of a novel*).

heroic eiyuuteki.

heroine jojóofu (*person of great deeds*); onna shujínkoo (*of a novel*).

herring níshin.

herself jibun (*self, same word is used for both male and female*).

    by herself hitóri de, jibun de.

hesitate (to) tameráu, chúucho suru.

hide (to) kakúsu (*conceal*); himitsu ni suru (*keep secret*); kakuréru (*conceal oneself*).

hideous zotto suru yóo na.
high takái.
higher –yóri mo takái.
hill oka (*small mountain*); saká (*on a road*).
him ano káta ni, anó hito ni (*to him*); ano
    káta o, anó hito o (*as object of
    sentence*).
himself jibun (*same word used also for
    "herself"*).
    by himself jibun de.
hind ushiro no.
hinder (to) jama suru, samatagéru.
hinge chootsúgai.
hint hinto, honomekashi (*allusion*); atekosuri
    (*insinuation*).
hint (to) honomekásu (*allude to*); atekosúru
    (*insinuate*).
hip oshiri, koshi.
hire (to) yatóu (*servants, etc.*); kariru (*cars*).
his anó hito no, káre no.
historian rekishika.
historic rekishijoo no, rekishiteki no.
history rekishi.
hit (to) útsu, tatáku, nagúru.
    to hit against butsukeru.
hoarse shagare góe no.
hoe kuwa.
hold (to) mótsu (*have*); okonáu (*a
    ceremony*); kaisai suru (*an exhibition or
    conference*); tamótsu (*maintain*).
hole aná.
holiday yasumí (*period of recreation or
    rest*); matsuri (*festival*); saijitsu (*national
    holiday*).
hollow *adj.* kara no (*empty*). –*n.* kubomi
    (*cavity*).
holy shinsei na (*sacred*); koogooshíi (*divine*);
    shinkóoshin no fukái (*deeply pious*).
homage kéi (*respect*).
home uchi, katei (*family*).
    hometown kókyoo, kuni.
honest shoojíki na (*truthful*); seijitsu na
    (*sincere*); sotchoku na (*frank*).
honesty seijitsu.
honey hachi mitsu.
honor méiyo (*fame*); shin'yoo (*credit*);
    sonkei (*esteem*).
honor (to) meiyo o ataeru (*exalt*); hijoo ni
    sonkei suru (*venerate*).
honorable tootói, sonkei subéki.
hood zukín (*garment*).
hoof hízume.
hook kugi (*to hang things on*).
hope kiboo (*opp. of despair*); kitai (*confident
    anticipation*); mikomi (*probability*).
hope (to) nozomi o kakéru (*count on*);
    nozomu (*desire*).
hopeful kiboo ni míchite iru, ate ni shite iru.
hopeless nozomi no nái.

horizon chiheisen (*of land*); suiheisen (*of
    sea*).
horizontal yoko no.
horn tsunó (*of animals*); tsuno bue (*wind
    instrument*), horun (*English horn*).
horrible osoroshíi (*terrible*); monosugói
    (*ghastly*).
horror kyoofu.
horse umá.
horseback (on) umá ni notte iru.
hosiery kutsúshita.
hospitable motenashi no yói.
hospital byooin.
host shújin (*one who entertains another,
    hotel-keeper*).
hostess hósutesu, onna shújin (*in a hotel or
    restaurant*); okámi (*in an inn*); shújin (*at
    home*).
hostile tékii no áru.
hot atsúi.
hotel hóteru (*Occidental-style*); yadoya,
    ryokan (*Japanese-style*).
hot spring onsen.
hour jikan.
    two hours ni jíkan.
house ié (*the structure*); uchi (*home, one's
    abode*).
household shotái, katei (*home*).
housekeeper kaséifu.
how dóo, dónna ni.
    how much íkura.
    how many dono kurai, íkutsu.
    how long dono kurai nágaku.
    how often nando kúrai.
    How beautiful! Máa kírei desu ne.
    How are you? Ogénki desu ka?
however ga, keredomo; dónna ni –mo, íkura
    –mo (*in whatever way, to whatever
    degree*).
howl (to) hoéru (*said of animals*); unáru
    (*said of the wind*).
human *adj.* ningen no (*characteristic of
    people*). –*n.* ningen, hito.
    human being ningen.
    human race jínrui.
    human nature ningensei.
humane nínjoo no áru (*compassionate*);
    jihibukái (*merciful*).
humanity jíndoo.
humble kenson na (*modest*); hikaeme na (*not
    pretentious*).
humid shimeppói (*damp*); shikki no takái (*of
    high humidity*).
humiliate jisónshin o kizutsukéru, hají o
    kakaséru (*mortify*).
humility kenson (*humbleness*).
humor kishitsu (*disposition*); kíbun (*mood*);
    kimagure (*caprice*); kokkei, yúumoa
    (*jocularity*).

in good humor jookígen.
hundred hyakú.
hundredth hyakubanme no.
hunger ue (*famine*); kuufuku (*craving for food*).
hungry (be) onaka ga suita.
hunt kári ryóo (*hunting*).
hunt (to) kári o suru (*shoot animals*); sagasu (*look for*).
hunter ryóoshi.
hurry n. isógu kotó, isogí.
be in a hurry isóide iru.
hurry (to) isógu.
hurt n. v.i. itámu; v.t. itaméru.
husband otto.
hush (to) shízuka ni saseru (*quiet*); damaraséru (*silence*); osaéru (*restrain*).
hyphen háifun.
hypocrisy gizen.
hypocrite gizénsha.
hypothesis kasetsu.

I

I watakushi, watashi, bóku (*used by men among friends*).
icy koori.
icy koori de tsúrutsuru shita.
idea kangáe (*thought*); chíshiki (*knowledge*); inshoo (*impression*); shínnen (*belief*); omoitsuki (*intention*).
ideal n. risoo. –adj. risooteki na.
idealism kannénron.
idealist risooka.
identical dooitsu no.
idiot hakuchi.
idle shigoto no nái (*unemployed*); hima de áru (*not active*); namáketa (*lazy*).
idleness namakéru kotó.
if móshi.
ignoble iyashíi, gehín na.
ignorance múgaku (*lack of education*); múchi (*lack of knowledge*).
ignorant múgaku na (*without education*); múchi na (*unthinking, uninformed*); fuánnai no (*unaware*).
ignore (to) múshi suru.
ill kagen ga warúi, byooki no (*sick, unwell*); warúi (*bad, evil*).
illness byooki.
illusion sakkaku (*optical*); moosoo (*delusion*).
illustrate (to) sashie o ireru (*pictures and diagrams*); réi o shimesu (*give examples*).
illustration sashie (*picture*); réi, tatoe (*example*).
image súgata (*form*); chookokúzoo (*carved statue*); guuzoo (*idol*).

imaginary soozoo no.
imagination soozoo.
imagine (to) soozoo suru (*form a mental picture*); omóu (*think*); kangáeru (*suppose*).
imitate (to) maneru, mane o suru.
imitation mane (*copy*); magaimono, nisemono (*fake*).
immediate súgu no, chokusetsu no.
immediately súgu ni.
imminent sashisemátta (*impending*).
immobility fudoosei.
immoral fudóotoku na.
immorality fudóotoku.
immortal fújimi no, shinu koto no nái.
immortality fúshi, fukutsusei.
impartial koohei na.
impatience tánki.
impatient (be) ki ga hayái (*of character*); tánki na (*quick tempered*).
imperfect fukánzen na (*incomplete*); kekkán no áru (*faulty*).
impertinence shitsúrei.
impertinent shitsúrei na (*rude*); namaiki na (*insolent*).
impetuosity sékkachi.
impetuous gekiretsu na, nesshín na.
impious fushínjin na.
import yunyuuhin (*goods*).
import (to) yunyuu suru.
importance juuyoosei.
important daiji na (*of consequence*); kan'yoo na (*essential*); chomei na (*eminent*).
impossible fukánoo na.
impress (to) osu (*imprint*); inshoo zukéru (*produce a vivid impression*); kandoo saseru (*move deeply*).
impression inshoo
be under the impression that –to omótte iru, ki ga suru.
imprison (to) keimusho ni ireru.
improve (to) v.t. jootatsu saseru (*ameliorate*); yóku suru (*better*); kairyoo suru (*reform*); v.i. jootatsu suru (*become better*).
improvement kairyoo (*reform*).
improvise (to) sokkyoo de suru.
imprudence fukínshin.
imprudent fukínshin na.
impulse shoodoo (*propulsion*); shigeki (*impetus*).
impure fujun na (*adulterated*).
in ni, de; tame ni (*in order to*); –no nakani (*inside*); –no uchi ni (*within*).
inadequate fujúubun na, futékitoo na.
inaugurate v.t. hajimeru (*begin*); v.i. hajimaru (*be inaugurated*).
incapable –ga dekínai, múryoku na.
incapacity munoo, futékitoo.

inch ínchi (*American measure*).
incident dekígoto (*occurrence*).
include fukúmu, fukuméru
  to be included háitte iru.
income shuunyuu (*earnings*).
incomparable hikaku no dekínai.
incompatible ki no awánai (*inharmonious*);
  itchi shinai (*inconsistent*); ryooritsu shinai
  (*not able to coexist*).
incompetent chikara no nái, munoo na.
incomplete fukánzen na.
incomprehensible ryookai dekínai.
inconvenience fúben.
inconvenient fúben na (*not suitable*); tsugoo
  ga warúi (*troublesome*).
incorrect machigátte iru (*inaccurate*); datoo
  de nái (*improper*).
increase zooka.
increase (to) v.t. fuyásu (*quantity*); ookíku
  suru (*size*); ageru (*price*); v.i. fuéru (*in
  quantity*); ookíku náru (*in size*); tákaku
  náru (*in price*).
incredible shinjirarénai.
incur ukéru (*meet with*); áu (*run into*).
indebted kari no áru (*owing money*); sewá ni
  nátte iru (*obliged*).
indecision fukétsudan.
indecisive niekiránai.
indeed hontoo ni (*in fact*).
independence dokuritsu (*self-government*).
independent dokuritsu no.
index sakuin (*of books*).
index finger hitosashí yubi.
indicate (to) shimésu.
indicative –o shimésu (*giving an indication
  of*); –o honomekásu (*giving a hint*).
indifference mukánshin.
indifferent reitán na (*pertaining to feelings*);
  mutónjaku na (*pertaining to appearance*).
indignant fungai shita (*angered*).
indignation fungai.
indirect toomáwashi no (*devious*); kansetsu
  no (*not straightforward*).
  indirect answer kansetsu no henji.
indirectly kansetsu ni.
indiscretion shiryo no nái kotó
  (*imprudence*).
indispensable zettai hitsuyoo na (*absolutely
  necessary*); sakerarénai (*unavoidable*).
individual adj. kóko no (*separate*); dokutoku
  no (*peculiar*). –n. kójin.
indivisible wakéru koto no dekínai (*entity*).
indolence bushóo (*sloth, idleness*).
indolent bushóo na (*idle, lazy, slothful*);
  mukátsudoo no (*inactive*).
indoors okúnai.
  to go indoors náka e háiru.
induce (to) sasoikomu (*attract*).
induct (to) hikiiréru (*introduce into a place*).

indulge (in) –ni fukéru.
indulgence kimama, wagamáma.
indulgent tenurui (*not severe*).
  indulgent parent yasashii.
industrial sangyoo no.
industrious kinben na (*hardworking*).
industry sangyoo.
inexhaustible tsukínai (*limitless*); taénai
  (*unfailing*); tsukarénai (*unwearied*).
inexplicable fukákai na (*incomprehensible*).
inexpressible iiarawasénai (*indescribable*).
infallible zenzen ayamari no nái (*free from
  error*); kesshite machigawánai (*never
  mistaken*).
infamous hyooban no warúi (*notorious*);
  fuménboku na (*shameful*).
infancy akanboo no tokí (*babyhood*); shóki
  (*beginning of existence*).
infant n. akanboo, chiisái kodomo (*very
  young baby*). –adj. akanboo no
  (*pertaining to a baby*).
infantry hohei.
infection kansen (*contagion*).
infer (to) súiri suru (*conclude by
  reasoning*); ketsuron o hikidásu (*draw
  conclusions*).
inference ketsuron (*conclusion*); suiron
  (*deduction*).
inferior adj. shita no (*less important*);
  sómatsu na (*poor quality*). –n. shita no
  kaikyuu (*lower in rank*).
infernal meido no, jigoku no (*hellish*); hidoo
  no (*inhuman, devilish*).
infinite kagiri no nái (*endless*); hijoo na
  (*very great*).
infinity mugen (*boundlessness*).
inflation infure.
inflict (to) ataeru (*impose*).
influence eikyoo (*effect*); séiryoku
  (*personal*).
influence (to) eikyoo suru.
inform (to) shiraseru.
information shirase (*news*); hoochi (*report*);
  chíshiki, joohoo (*knowledge*).
ingenious rikoo na (*clever*); kíyoo na
  (*skillful*); koomyoo na (*cleverly
  contrived*).
ingenuity rikoosa (*cleverness*).
ingratitude onshírazu.
inhabit kyojuu suru (*reside*); súmu, yadóru
  (*live in*).
inhabitant kyojúusha.
inherit (to) soozoku suru.
inheritance isan (*thing inherited*); soozoku
  (*an inheriting*).
inhuman zannin na.
initial adj. hajime no (*beginning*). –n. kashira
  ji (*letter*).
  initial stage shóki.

initiate (to) hajimeru (*begin*); seishiki ni kanyuu saseru (*admit*).

initiative dokusóoryoku (*originality*).

injurious yuugai na (*harmful, hurtful*).

injury kegá (*wound*); songai (*damage*).

injustice fuhoo, fusei (*iniquity*), fukóohei (*unjust act*).

ink sumí (*Japanese only*); ínki, ínku (*other*).

inkwell inkítsubo.

inland kokúnai no (*domestic*).

inn yadoya, ryokan.

innate umaretsuki no (*inborn*).

innkeeper ryokan no shújin, yadoya no shújin.

innocence mújaki (*freedom from wrong*).

innocent múzai no (*not guilty*); mújaki na (*guileless*).

inquire tazunéru.

inquiry toiawase.

inscription káite aru kotó.

insect mushi.

insensible mukánkaku na (*not able to feel*); heiki na (*callous*).

inseparable hanásu kotó ga dekínai.

inside náka.

insight kenshiki.

    person of insight kenshiki áru hito.

insignificant tsumaránai (*unimportant*); muími na (*meaningless*).

insincere séii no nái.

insinuate (to) sore to náku iu (*hint*).

insist (to) kyoochoo suru; iiháru.

    He insisted on this point. Káre wa kono ten o kyoochoo shita.

insistence kyoochoo; shuchoo.

inspect (to) shirabéru (*examine*); ken'etsu suru (*view officially*).

inspection ken'etsu (*official viewing*); chóosa (*critical examination*).

install (to) ninmei suru (*place a person in office*); sóochi suru, toritsukéru (*put in position for use*).

installment bunkatsubárai (*a portion of money paid at stated times*).

instance réi (*example*); baai (*occasion*).

instant *adj.* kyuu na. —*n.* sókuji (*precise moment*); shunkan (*moment*).

instantaneous sókuza no.

    instantaneous death sokushi.

instantly sókuza ni, súgu.

instead (of) kawari ni.

instigate (to) sosonokásu (*incite*).

instinct hónnoo.

instinctive honnooteki na.

institute kyookai, gakkai (*institution, society*).

institute (to) setsuritsu suru (*establish*).

institution setsuritsu (*establishment*); seitei

(*of law*); séido (*system*); kanrei (*custom*); gakkai (*learned society*).

instruct (to) oshieru (*teach*); kyóoju suru (*educate*).

instruction júgyoo (*a lesson*); yoohoo (*a teaching or precept*).

instructor kyóoshi.

instrument doogu (*for work or means*); gakki (*musical*).

insufficiency fujúubun (*inadequacy*); futékitoo (*incompetency*).

insufficient fujúubun na (*not sufficient*); futékitoo na (*inadequate*).

insult bujoku (*insolence*); búrei (*impoliteness*).

insult (to) bujoku suru.

insuperable uchikaténai (*insurmountable*).

insurance hoken.

    life insurance seimei hóken.

insure (to) hoken o kakéru.

integral kanzen na.

intellect chíshiki.

intellectual *adj.* chíshiki no. —*n.* chishikíjin.

intelligence chíryoku (*mental ability*); chisei (*mentality*); joohoo (*information*).

intelligent kashikói.

intend (to) –tsumori.

    I intend to marry her. Anó hito to kekkon suru tsumori désu.

intense nesshín na.

intensity kyóodo.

intention kangáe.

interest kyóomi (*pleasurable concern*); kanshin (*intellectual curiosity*); riken (*pecuniary concern*); ríshi (*rate*).

    compound interest fukuri.

    have an interest in kyóomi o mótsu.

interest (to) kyóomi o okosaséru (*attract attention*); kookíshin o hiku (*excite the curiosity of*); doojoo o hiku (*excite sympathy*).

interesting omoshirói.

interfere (to) kanshoo suru (*meddle*); chootei suru (*mediate*); jama suru (*interrupt*).

interference boogai, jama.

interior náka, náibu.

intermediate chuukan no.

international kokusaiteki, kokusai.

    international relations kokusai kánkei.

interpose (to) –no aida ni ireru.

interpret (to) káishaku suru, hándan suru (*construe*).

interpretation káishaku, setsumei (*explanation*); hándan (*judgment*); tsúuyaku (*translation*).

interpreter tsúuyaku.

interrupt (to) saegíru (*break in upon*); jama

o suru (*hinder*); chuushi saseru (*break the continuity of*).

interruption chuushi, jama.

interval kankaku.

interview menkai (*meeting*); mensetsu, íntabyuu (*job interview*), kaiken (*with reporters*).

interview (to) menkai suru.

intimacy shinmitsu.

intimate shinmitsu na (*very friendly*); kojinteki no (*personal*); shitashíi (*friendly*).

intimidate (to) obiyakásu.

into ni, no naka e.

intolerable gáman no dekinai.

intolerance kyooryoo.

intolerant kyooryoo na (*bigoted*).

intonation kóe no táka hiku, intonéeshon.

introduce (to) shookai suru (*a person*).

introduction shookai (*of a person*); jobun (*of a book*).

intuition chokkan.

invade (to) shinnyuu suru (*overrun*); shinryaku suru (*aggress*); oshiyoséru (*rush into*).

invariable kawaranai.

invasion shinryaku.

invent (to) hatsumei suru (*method, etc.*); kangaedásu (*a story*).

invention hatsumei (*something discovered after experimentation*); tsukurigoto (*a falsehood*).

inventor hatsumeika.

invert (to) hantai ni suru (*reverse*).

invest (to) tooshi suru.

investment tooshi.

invisible mé ni tsukánai.

invitation shóotai.

invite (to) shóotai suru, manéku.

invoice okurijoo, inbóisu.

invoke (to) kámi ni inóru.

involuntary muíshiki no.

involve (to) hikikómu.

iron tetsu (*metal*); airon (*for pressing*).

iron (to) airon o kakeru (*clothes*).

irony híniku.

irregular fukísoku na.

irreparable torikaeshi ga tsukánai.

irresistible tomeru koto no dekínai.

irritate (to) íraira saseru.

irritation shigeki (*medical term*); okoraseru kotó (*exasperation, annoyance*).

island shimá.

isolate (to) kákuri suru.

Israel Isuráeru.

issue hakko o (*of a newspaper or other publication*); mondái ten (*problem*).

issue (to) hakkoo suru.

it sore (*often omitted in Japanese*).

It's late. Osói desu.

It's here. Koko ni arimásu.

Italian *adj.* Itárii no. –*n.* Itaríijin (*people*).

item koomoku.

its sono.

itself hitoride ni (*by, of itself*).

ivy tsuta.

J

jacket uwagi; jáketsu (*sweater*).

jam jámu.

January Ichigatsu.

Japan Nippón, Nihón.

Japanese *adj.* –Nippón no, Nihón no, Nipponjín, Nihonjín (*person*); Nippongo, Nihongo (*language*).

jar tsubo, kamé.

jaw agó.

jealous shittobukái.

jealousy yakimóchi, shitto.

jelly jérii.

jewel hooseki.

job shigoto (*work*); shokúgyoo (*occupation*); chí (*position*).

join (to) awaséru (*put together*); kuttsukéru (*fasten*); renketsu saseru (*connect, link*); issho ni náru (*become united*).

joint *n.* kansetsu (*of the body*); awaseme (*seam*); tsugime (*junction*). –*adj.* kyoodoo no (*common*).

joke joodán.

joke (to) joodán o iu (*jest*); fuzakéru (*be humorous*).

jolly yúka na.

journal nikki (*diary*); nikkan shínbun (*daily newspaper*); zasshi (*magazine*).

journalism jaanarízumu (*practice of*); shinbúngaku (*study of*).

journalist jaanarísuto, shinbunkishá (*reporter*).

journey ryokoo.

joy yorokobi.

joyous ureshíi.

judge saibánkan (*public officer in a court of justice*); shinpan (*umpire*); kanteika (*connoisseur*).

judge (to) hándan suru (*estimate, conclude*); sáiban suru (*at court*).

judgment hándan (*adjudication*); hanketsu (*court decision*); hihan (*criticism*); handánryoku (*powers of discrimination*).

judicial saibanjoo no.

juice shíru, júusu.

July Shichigatsu.

jump tobiagari.

jump (to) tobu, jánpu suru.

June Rokugatsu.

junior adj. toshishita no. (opp. to senior).
just adj. tadashíi (upright); koosei na (impartial); seitoo na (lawful); tekitoo na (proper); jissai no (actual). –adv. choodo (exactly); hon no (only); yatto (hardly).
justice séigi (righteousness); kooketsu (integrity); koosei (fairness).
justify seitooka suru.

K

keen eibin na (acute).
keep káu (animals); mótsu (hold); tótte oku (hold on to).
   keep quiet shízuka ni suru.
   keep in mind obóete oku.
   Keep still! Oshízuka ni.
kettle yakan.
key kagí.
kick (to) kéru.
kill (to) korosu.
kin miyori.
kind adj. shínsetsu na (gentle).
kind shúrui (class, variety, sort).
kindly adv. shínsetsu ni.
kindness shínsetsu (benevolence); aijoo (love); kóoi (goodwill).
king oo.
kingdom ookoku (monarchical state); kuni (realm).
kiss seppun, kísu.
kiss (to) kísu suru, seppun suru.
kitchen daídokoro.
kite táko.
knee hizagáshira.
kneel (to) hizamazúku.
knife náifu.
knit (to) ámu.
   knitting amímono.
knock (to) tatáku.
   knock at the door to o tatáku.
   knock against –ni butsukaru.
knot musubime.
know (to) shitte iru, zonjite iru (humble).
knowledge chíshiki (information); gakúmon (learning).
known yuumei na.
   make known shiraseru.
Korean adj. Kánkoku no, Choosén no. –n. Choosenjín (people); Choosengo (language).

L

label fuda; rábera, retteru.
labor n. roodoo, shigoto.
laboratory jikkenjo.

lace réesu (fabric); himo (of shoe).
lack (to) fusoku suru.
lacquer urushi.
   lacquer ware nuri mono.
lady fujin.
   Ladies Fujin tearaijo (toilet).
lake mizúumi; –ko (in compound names).
   Lake Biwa Biwako.
lamb kohitsúji.
lame bíkko.
lamp dentoo (electric).
land riku (solid part of the earth's surface); jímen (ground).
land (to) jooriku saseru, jooriku suru (disembark); oríru (alight).
landscape késhiki.
language kotobá, géngo; –go (in compounds).
   Japanese language Nihongo.
lantern choochín (paper); tooroo (metal or stone); ishi dóoroo (stone).
large ookíi, ookína.
laser réezaa.
last n. ichiban áto (end of something); –adj. saikin no (most recent); sáigo no (final); –adv. owari ni (after all others); saikin (most lately).
   last night yuube, sakúban.
last (to) tsuzuku (continue); mochíkotáeru (endure); nagamóchi suru (wear well).
lasting eizoku suru (durable); fuhen no, eikyuu no (permanent).
latch kannuki.
late osoi (opp. to early); ko- (prefixed to the name of someone deceased).
lately saikin.
latter áto no, kóosha no.
laugh warai.
laugh (to) warau.
laughter warai.
lavish kimae no yói.
law hooritsu.
lawful hooritsu ni kanátta.
lawn shibafu.
lay (to) oku (put); umu (eggs).
layer sóo.
lazy namáketa; bushóo na.
lead namari (mineral); shidoo (guidance).
lead (to) annái suru (guide).
leader shidóosha (guide).
leadership shidóoryoku.
leaf ha.
leak (to) móru.
lean (to) katamúku (incline); yorikakáru (lean against).
leap hiyaku.
leap (to) tobikoéru (pass over); tobu (jump).
learn naráu, benkyoo suru (study); kioku suru (memorize).

learned hakugaku na, gakúmon no áru.

learning gakúmon (*knowledge*); hakushiki (*erudition*).

least ichiban chiisái (*in size*); ichiban sukunái (*in number or amount*).
    at least sukunáku tomo.

leather kawá.

leave yasumí (*holiday*).

leave (to) déru (*depart*); tátsu (*depart for a long trip*); azukéru (*on deposit*).

lecture koogi (*in classroom*); kooen (*in public*); setsuyu (*admonition*).

left *n.* hidari.

leg ashí.

legal hooritsujoo no.

legend densetsu.

legislation hooritsu seitei (*enacting of laws*); hooritsu (*laws*).

legislator rippóosha.

legislature rippóobu.

legitimate goohoo no (*lawful*), doori ni kanátta (*reasonable*).

leisure hima.

lemon remon.
    lemonade remonéedo.

lend (to) kasu.

length nágasa.

lengthen (to) nágaku suru (*make longer*); nobású (*prolong*).

less chiisái (*in size*); sukóshi no, sukunái (*in quantity*).
    less —yóri chiisái (*smaller than*).
    less —yóri sukunái (*fewer than*).

lesson júgyoo (*schoolwork*); gakka (*subject*); ka (*chapter*).

let (to) saseru (*allow*); kasu (*loan*).
    house for let kashiya.

letter tegami (*epistle*); jí (*in alphabet*).

level *n.* heimen (*flat surface*); heichi (*flat ground*). –*adj.* taira na (*even*); suihei no (*horizontal*).
    (at) the same level onaji tákasa (*said of height*); onaji teido (*said of degree*).

liability saimu.

liable seme o oubéki (*responsible*); fukusubéki (*subject to*); kakariyasui (*exposed to*).

liar usótsuki.

liberal hoofu na, takusan no (*abundant*); kéchi kechi shinai (*not sparing*); kimae ga íi (*generous*); shinpoteki na (*progressive*).

liberty jiyúu.

library toshókan (*public*); shosai, toshóshitsu (*private, home*).

license kyóka (*permission*); ninka (*authorization*); kyokásho, menjoo (*certification*).
    driver's license unten ménkyo.

lick (to) naméru.

lie uso.
    tell a lie uso o tsúku.

lie (to) yoko ni náru (*rest*).

lieutenant rikugun chúui (*army*); kaigun táii (*navy*).

life ínochi (*animate existence*); génki (*energy*).

lift (to) ageru (*raise*); mochiageru (*hold up*).

light *adj.* karui (*weight*); usui (*color*); yasashii (*work*). –*n.* hikarí (*beam*); akarí (*of lamp, flame*); kootaku (*brightness*).
    sunlight hi no hikarí.

light (to) hí o tsukéru.
    light the lamp akarí o tsukéru.
    light the fire hí o tsukéru.

light up terasu.

lighten (to) akaruku suru (*make bright*); karuku suru (*diminish in weight*).

lighthouse toodai.

lighting shoomei (*illumination*).

lightning inabíkari (*from cloud to cloud*).
    flash of lightning denkoo.

like *adj.* onajiyóo na (*similar*); nite iru (*alike*).

like (to) konómu, suku.
    Would you like to go? Ikitái desu ka?

likely tábun (*probably*); tekitoo na (*suitable*); tanomoshíi (*promising*); mottomo rashíi (*credible*).

likewise dooyóo ni (*similarly*); mata (*too, also*); náo mata (*moreover*).

liking *n.* konomi.

limb té ashi (*hand or foot*); eda (*branch*).

limit seigén (*in the abstract sense*); kyookai, sakái (*boundary*).

limit (to) seigén suru.

limp bíkko o hiku.

line kéi, sén, ito (*thread*); rétsu (*row*); kakei (*lineage*); iegara (*family*); michi (*course, route*); –sén (*suffixed to the name of railroad*), shóobai (*trade*).
    Tokaido Line Tookaidóosen (*The Tokaido Railroad*).

line (to) sén o hiku (*mark with lines*); rinkaku o tóru (*outline*); ichirétsu ni suru (*align*); urá o tsukéru (*cover with lining*); rétsu o tsukúru (*line up*).
    lining urá (*of dresses*).

linen rinneru.

linger (to) úrouro suru; nagabíku.

link tsunagime.

link (to) tsunagu.

lion raion, shíshi.

lip kuchibiru.

liquid ekitai.

liquor sake (*Japanese rice wine*); yooshu (*foreign*).

list mokuroku (*catalogue*); kakakuhyoo (*price*).

list (to) kakinaraberu.

listen kiku.

literary búngaku no.

literature búngaku.

little chíisái, chíisai na (*not big*); sukóshi (*quantity*); tsumaránai (*trivial*); kéchi na (*mean, petty*).

live *adj.* íkite iru.

live (to) súmu (*dwell*); ikíru (*exist*); íkite iru (*be living*); ikinagaráeru (*remain alive*); kurasu (*spend the days*).

lively génki no yói (*spirited*); yooki na (*cheerful*); kappatsu na (*brisk*).

liver kanzoo (*organ of body*); kimó, rébaa (*food*).

load omoni (*burden*); nímotsu (*on a cart*).

load (to) tsumu.

loan kashikin (*money that is lent*); shakkín (*borrowed money*).

loan (to) kasu (*lend*); kariru (*borrow*).

local chihooteki na, chíhoo no.

locate (to) mitsukeru.

location basho.

lock kagí.

lock (to) kagí o kakéru.

locomotive kikánsha.

log maruta.

logic rónri.

logical ronriteki na.

loneliness sabishísa.

lonely kodoku no (*isolated*); sabishíi (*lonesome*).

long nagái (*lengthy*); hosonagái (*elongated*); takái (*tall*).

    a long time nagái aida.

    before long mamónaku.

    long ago mukashi.

longing akogare.

look ichi moku (*glance*); yooboo (*aspect*); yoosu (*department*); kaotsuki (*countenance*).

look (to) míru (*oneself*); goran nasáru (*respect: used in speaking of another person*); miéru (*have the appearance, seem*).

    Look out! Abunái.

loose yurúi (*not tight*); darashi no nái (*lax*); fumímochi na (*wanton*); fuséikaku na (*inexact*).

loosen (to) tóku (*undo*); yuruméru (*slacken*).

lord shiháisha (*ruler*); shújin (*master*); shú (*Christ*).

lose (to) nakusu (*cease to have*); otósu (*by dropping*); makeru (*be beaten*).

loss són, sonshitsu.

lost nakushita (*gone out of one's possession*); yukue fúmei no (*missing*).

lot *adv.* takusan (*great deal*); oozéi (*multitude*).

    a lot of people oozéi no hito.

loud *adj.* oogóe no, óokina kóe no (*said of a voice*); óokina otó (*said of a sound*); soozooshíi (*noisy*); kebakebashíi (*gaudy*).

love ái (*parental fraternal*); ren'ai (*between man and woman*).

love (to) aisúru (*as a parent*); koi súru, ren'ai suru (*one of the opp. sex*).

    fall in love kói ni ochiíru.

lovely utsukushíi (*beautiful*); kawairashíi (*charming*); subarashíi (*wonderful*).

low hikúi (*not high*); yowái (*weak*); iyashíi (*in society*).

lower (to) sagéru, orósu (*haul down*); ichidan to sagéru (*make less elevated*).

loyal chuujitsu na; chúugi na.

loyalty chuusetsu; chúugi.

luck ún, kooun.

    good luck ún ga íi.

    bad luck ún ga warúi.

lucky ún ga íi, kooun na.

luggage nímotsu.

luminous hikáru.

lump katamari.

lunch hirugohan, ránchi.

lung hai.

luxurious zeitáku na.

luxury zeitáku.

M

machine kikái.

mad ki no kurútta, kichigái (*insane*); muchuu no (*infatuated*); okótta (*angry*).

madam ókusama.

madness kichigái.

magazine zasshi.

magistrate hánji.

magnificent rippa na (*grand, stately*); subarashíi (*splendid*).

maid musume (*girl*); otétsudai (*servant*).

mail yuubin.

main ómo na.

    mainland hóndo.

    main road hondoo.

    main street hondóori.

maintain (to) tamótsu, íji suru.

majesty igen (*dignity*).

    His Majesty héika.

major *adj.* ómo na.

majority daibúbun (*opp. to minority*); kahansúu (*plurality*); daitasúu (*most of, greater part*).

make (to) tsukúru; koshiraeru (*construct, manufacture*).

male osu (*animal*); otokó (*human*).

malice tékii.

man otokó (*male human*).

manage (to) keiei suru (*a business*).

management toriatsukai (*handling*); soojuu, tóogyo (*control*); keiei (*direction*).

manager shiháinin, manéejaa.

mankind jínrui (*human race*).

manner gyoogi (*deportment*); táido (*attitude*); yarikata (*method*).

manners sáhoo.

manufacture seizoo.

manufacture (to) seizoo suru.

manufacturer rseizóosha; seisákusha, seizoogyóosha.

manuscript genkoo.

many *adj.* takusán no, oozéi no.

map chízu.

maple mómiji.

March Sángatsu.

march kooshin (*parade*); kooshín kyoku (*music*).

march (to) kooshin suru (*in a parade*); susumu (*proceed*).

marine úmi no (*oceanic*); kookaijoo no (*nautical*).

mark shirushi, máaku; áto (*impression*); shimi (*stain*); kizuato (*scar*); kizu (*scratch*).

mark (to) máaku o tsukéru.

   to make a mark shirushi o tsukéru.

market ichiba, maakétto.

   bear market uri sooba.

   bull market kai sooba.

   buyer's market kaite shijoo.

   market forces shijoo no jissei.

   market index shijoo shisuu.

   market position shíkyoo.

   market price shika.

   market share shijoo sen-yuu ritsu.

   market trends shijoo dookoo.

   market value shijoo kakaku.

   marketing maaketingu.

marriage kekkon.

marry (to) kekkon suru.

marvel fushigi.

marvelous fushigi na.

masculine otoko no.

mask men, másuku.

mask (to) men o kabúru.

mason ishiya.

mass *n.* taishuu.

   mass communication masukomi.

   mass production tairyoo séisan.

mast masuto, hobáshira.

master shújin (*of the house*); shújin (*employer*); senséi (*teacher*).

master (to) joozú ni náru (*become skillful*); yóku oboéru (*learn well*).

masterpiece meisaku, kessaku.

mat tatami (*for floor of Japanese house*).

match mátchi (*for fire*); shiai (*contest*); kyóogi (*game*).

match (to) niau (*be suitably associated, fit together*).

material *n.* zairyóo (*cloth, etc.*).

maternal haha kata no.

mathematics suugaku.

matter mondai (*problem*); jíken (*event*); kotó (*thing*).

matter (to) kamau, mondai ni suru.

mattress máttoresu.

mature (to) otona ni náru (*reach adulthood*), jukusuru (*as a fruit*).

maximum saidáigen.

May Gógatsu.

may –ká mo shiremasén (*possibility*).

   It may rain. Áme ga fúru ka mo shiremasén.

   –te mo íi desu (*have my permission to*).

   You may go. (*You have my permission to go.*) Itté mo íi desu.

mayor shíchoo.

me watashi ni (*to me*); watashi o (*as obj. of verb*).

meadow bokujoo.

meal shokuji, góhan.

mean *adj.* iji no warúi, hiretsu na (*base*).

mean (to) ími suru.

   What does it mean? Sore no ími wa nán desu ka?

meaning ími.

meantime, meanwhile sono aida ni.

   in the meantime soo shite iru uchi ni.

measure sunpoo (*dimension*); monosáshi (*yardstick*).

measure (to) sunpoo o tóru (*length*), hakaru (*reckon*).

meat nikú.

mechanic kikáikoo (*worker in a factory*).

mechanical kikaiteki no; kikái no.

mechanically kikaiteki ni.

medal medaru, kunshoo (*military*).

meddle (to) kanshoo suru (*interfere*).

mediate (to) chootei suru (*arbitrate*); chuukai suru (*act as an intermediary*); tonnasu (*intercede*).

medical igakuteki no.

medicine kusuri (*a drug*); ígaku (*the science*).

mediocre nami no, táishita kotó no nái.

mediocrity heibon.

meditate (to) mokusoo suru.

meditation mokusoo (*contemplation*).

medium *adj.* chuu kurai no. –*n.* chuu kurai.

meet (to) áu, o me ni kakáru (*respect*).

meeting kai (*assembly*).

melt (to) *v.t.* tokásu; *v.i.* tokéru.

member kaiin (*of an association*).

memorize (to) oboéru.

memory kioku.
mend (to) naósu (*repair*); tsugu (*darn*);
 tsukuróu (*patch up*).
mental séishin no.
mention genkyuu.
 honorable mention hoojoo.
mention (to) iu, hanásu (*in speaking*); káku
 (*in writing*).
 Don't mention it. Doo itashimáshite.
merchandise shóohin.
merchant shóonin.
merciful jihibukái (*compassionate*).
merciless mújihi na.
mercury suigin.
mercy jihi (*compassion*).
merit n. káchi (*worth*); tegara (*deed*).
merry yukai na; tanoshíi (*joyous*).
message kotozuke (*verbal*).
messenger tsukai.
metal kane.
metallic kane no, kanamono no.
method hoohoo.
metropolis shúto (*capital*); chuushin-chi
 (*central place*).
microphone maikuróhon, máiku.
microscope kenbikyoo.
microwave oven denshi rénji.
midday hiru.
middle náka no, chuukan no (*intermediate*);
 chúui no (*medium*).
 in the middle of mannaka ni.
 Middle Ages Chúusei.
 middle class chuusan káikyuu.
midnight mayónaka.
might n. chikará (*strength*).
mighty chikara no tsuyói, táishita.
mild otonashíi (*gentle*); kandai na (*not
 severe*).
mildness odayákasa.
military rikúgun no.
milk gyuunyuu (*cow's*), míruku.
milkman gyuunyuu ya.
mill súisha (*water*); fúusha (*wind*); seifunjoo
 (*flour*).
million hyakúman.
 one hundred million ichíoku.
millionaire hyakuman chóoja.
mind kokóro (*intention*); kangáe (*thought*);
 atamá (*brain, head*).
 frame of mind kimochi.
mind (to) ki ni kakéru (*bear in mind*); sewá
 o suru (*take care of*).
mine pron. watashi no, watashi no monó.
mine n. kóozan (*for mineral*).
miner kóofu.
mineral n. koobutsu. –adj. koobutsu no.
minimum saishóogen no.
minister dáijin (*of state*); kóoshi
 (*diplomatic*); bokushi (*of religion*).

ministry –shóo (*suffix*); seishoku (*of
 church*).
 Ministry of Foreign Affairs Gaimúshoo.
mink tén, mínku.
minor miseinénsha (*legal: less than 20 years
 old*).
minority shoosuu (*smaller number*); shoosuu
 too (*opp. to majority*); miséinen (*legal
 infancy*).
minute fún (*time*).
 Wait a minute! Chótto mátte kudasai.
 Any minute now. Moo súgu desu.
miracle kiseki (*religious*).
mirror kagamí.
miscellaneous iroiro na.
mischief itazura.
mischievous itazurazuki na.
misdemeanor fugyóoseki.
miser kechinboo.
miserable fukóo na (*unfortunate*); hisan na
 (*wretched*); áware na (*pitiable*).
miserably míjime ni,
misery komátte iru kotó (*a state of being in
 distress*).
misfortune fukóo (*unhappiness*); sainán
 (*calamity*).
mishap omoigakénai dekígoto.
misprint insatsu chígai, misupurínto.
Miss –san (*same suffix as for Mr. and Mrs.*).
 Miss Yamada. Yamada-san.
miss (to) ma ni awánai (*fail to get on time*);
 nakusuru (*lose*); kizukánai (*fail to
 perceive*).
mission dendóo kai, mísshon (*religious*);
 shísetsu (*official*).
missionary senkyóoshi, dendóoshi.
mist kasumi.
mistake machigái.
mistake (to) machigáu.
Mister –san. See Miss.
 Mr. Yamada. Yamada-san.
mistrust fushín'yoo.
mistrust (to) shinyoo shinai, ayashímu.
mistrustful utagaibukái.
misunderstand (to) gokai suru.
misunderstanding gokai (*mistake*); íken no
 sooi (*disagreement*).
misuse machigátte tsukau kotó.
misuse (to) machigátte tsukau.
mix (to) v.t. mazéru (*put together*); v.i.
 mazáru, majiwáru (*associate*).
mixture mázeta monó.
mob gunshuu (*crowd*).
mobilization dooin.
mobilize (to) dooin suru.
mock (to) baka ni suru (*ridicule*); maneru
 (*mimic*).
mockery baka ni suru kotó.
mode ryuukoo, móodo.

model móderu (*photography, fashion*); mokei (*copy*); tehon (*example*); hinágata (*miniature*).

model (to) katadoru (*to copy*).

moderate onken na (*temperate*); tegoro no (*medium*).

moderate (to) sétsudo o mamóru (*keep within bounds*); yawaragéru (*one's temper*).

moderation tékido, sessei.

modern kíndai no; kindaiteki (*of the present time*); géndai no (*contemporary*); modan na (*new in fashion*).

modest kenson no (*unassuming*); shitóyaka na (*moderate, unaggressive*).

modesty kenson.

modification henkoo.

modify (to) arataméru (*alter*); kanwa suru (*lessen*); keigen suru (*tone down*).

moist shikkéta, shimeppói. –*n.* shikke.

moisten (to) shimesu (*dampen*); shimeru (*become moist*).

moment shunkan.
    Just a moment! Chótto mátte kudasái.
    Any moment now. Moo súgu desu.

monarchy kunshu séitai (*system*); kunshúkoku (*nation*).

monastery shuudóoin.

Monday Getsuyóobi.

money kane, okane.
    money order yuubin gawase.
    paper money satsu.

monk shuudóosoo.

monkey sáru.

monologue hitorigóto.
    to talk to oneself hitorigóto o iu.

monopoly dokusen; senbai.

monorail monoréeru.

monotonous tanchoo na.

monotony tanchoo.

monster kaibutsu (*dragon, etc.*).

monstrosity kikái na kotó.

monstrous kikái na.

month tsukí.
    this month kongetsu.
    last month séngetsu.
    next month ráigetsu.

monthly *adj.* maigetsu no. –*adv.* maigetsu. –*n.* gekkanzásshi (*monthly magazine*).

monument kinénhi.

monumental kinen no.

mood kíbun (*feeling*); kigen (*temper*).

moody muttsúri shita.

moon tsukí.
    full moon mángetsu.

moonlight tsuki no hikarí.

mop móppu.

moral *adj.* dootokuteki na (*virtuous*). –*n.* kyookun (*maxim*).

morale shikí.

moralist dootoku shugísha.

morality dootoku.

more mótto.

morning ása.

morsel hitó kire (*a little piece*).

mortal *adj.* kanarazu shinu (*subject to death*).

mortgage teitoo.

mortgage (to) teitoo ni suru.

mosquito ka.

most *adj.* taitei no (*greatest number*); daitai (*the majority of*); ichíban (*used for the superlative*).
    most numerous ichiban óoi.

mostly taitei.

moth ga.

mother okáasan, okáasama (*respect*); háha.

motion undoo (*opp. to rest*); téburi, míburi (*gesture*).

motionless ugokánai.

motive dooki.

motor hatsudóoki, móotaa.

motor (to) unten suru (*drive a car*).

mount yamá (*mountain*).

mount (to) daishi ni haru (*pictures*); noboru (*ascend*).
    mount a horse umá ni noru.

mountain yamá.

mountainous yama no óoi.

mourn (to) nagéku, kanashímu (*lament*).

mournful kanashimi ni shizunda.

mourning mo.

mouse nezumi.

mouth kuchi.

movable ugokásu koto no dekíru.

move ungokí, idoo.

move (to) *v.t.* ugokásu; *v.i.* ugóku, hikkósu (*change one's dwelling*).
    move back hikkoméru, hikkómu.
    move forward *v.t.* máe e dásu; *v.i.* máe e déru.

movement koodoo (*action*).

movies éiga.

moving ugokásu, kandoo saseru (*touching to the emotion*); hikkoshi (*changing one's dwelling*).

much takusan, takusán no.
    much better zútto íi.

mud doró.

muddy doró no óoi; doro dárake no (*covered with mud*).

mule rába.

multiple tasúu no.

multiply kakéru; masu (*increase*).

multitude oozéi, gunshuu.

mumble (to) bútsu butsu iu.

municipal shi no, tóshi no.

municipality jichíku, shi tóokyoku.

munitions gunjúhin.
murder hitogoroshi, satsujin.
   to commit a murder hitogoroshi o suru.
murder (to) hito o korosu.
murmur zawameki, sasayaki.
murmur (to) sasayaku.
muscle kínniku.
museum hakubútsukan.
   art museum bijútsukan.
mushroom kínoko.
music óngaku.
musical adj. óngaku no; –n. myuújikaru.
musician ongakka.
must –nákereba naránai, –nákereba ikenai (have to); –ni chigai nái (in the sense of an obvious inference).
   I must go. Ikanákereba naránai.
   Ikanákereba ikenai.
   You must have said so. Soo ittá ni chigai nái.
mustard karashi.
mute oshi no (dumb).
mutter (to) bútsu butsu iu (mumble); sasayaku (murmur).
mutton hitsuji no nikú.
my watashi no (of or relating to me); uchi no (pertaining to things or persons of one's home).
myself jibun, watakushi jíshin.
mysterious fushigi na (strange); fukákai na (inexplicable).
mystery shínpi; fukákai na kotó.
myth shinwa.

N

nail tsume (of a finger or toe); kugi (instrument).
nail (to) kugi o útsu.
naïve mújaki na (innocent); adokenái (unsophisticated).
naked hadaka no.
name namae (designation); hyooban (fame).
   first name namae.
   last name myóoji.
   My name is . . . Namae wa . . . to iimasu.
   What is your name? Onamae wa?
name (to) namae o tsukéru.
nameless na no nái.
namely sunáwachi.
nap keba (of wool); hirune (short sleep).
napkin nápukin.
narrow semái.
narrow (to) v.t. sebaméru; v.i. semáku náru.
nasty iji no warúi.
nation kokumin (people); kuni (country).
national kokumin no, kuni no.
nationality kokuseki.

nationalization kokkateki ni suru kotó, kokueika.
nationalize (to) kokuei ni suru (to have the state operate).
native adj. naikoku no (opp. to foreign); dochaku no (aboriginal). –n. naikokújin (opp. to foreigner); dojin (aborigine).
natural shizen no, shizen no mama no (nonartificial); mikáikon no (uncultivated).
naturalness kazarike no nái kotó.
nature seishitsu (character); shizen (the physical universe).
naughty itazura na.
naval káigun no.
navy káigun.
near sóba no, chikái (not far); kínjo no (around the corner).
nearly hotóndo (almost); káre kore (about).
neat kichínto shita (tidy, orderly); kozappári shita (smart, dapper); shúmi no íi (trim); seizen to shita (orderly).
neatness sappári shite iru kotó.
necessarily yamú naku, hitsuyoo ni kararete.
necessary hitsuyoo na.
necessity hitsuyoo.
neck kubi.
necklace kubi kázari, nékkuresu.
necktie nékutai.
need iriyoo (want); hitsuyoo (necessity); nyuuyoo (demand); kyuuboo (destitution).
   be in need of iriyoo désu.
need (to) iru (want); hoshíi desu (wish to have).
needle hári.
needless fuhitsúyoo na.
needy konkyuu shite iru.
negative n. uchikeshi (expression); néga (photograph). –adj. insei no (opp. to positive); hantai no (contrary).
neglect kamawánai kotó (want of attention); múshi (disregard).
neglect (to) namakéru, múshi suru.
negotiate kooshoo suru, dánpan suru.
negotiation kooshoo, dánpan.
Negro Kokujin, Níguro.
neighbor tonari.
neighborhood kínjo.
neither dóchira mo (negative).
   Neither is delicious. Dóchira mo oishiku nái.
   mo-mo . . . (negative).
   Neither apples nor oranges are expensive. Ringo mo mikan mo tákaku nái.
nephew oi.
nerve shínkei (in anatomy); daitán (pluck); yúuki (courage).

nervous shinkéishitsu na (*behavior*); shínkei no (*pertaining to nerves*); kuróoshoo no (*apprehensive*).

nest su.

net amí.

neutral chuuritsu no (*not involved in hostilities*); kooheimúshi no (*impartial*).

neuter chuusei.

never kesshite (*with a negative verb*).

nevertheless –ni mo kakawárazu.

new kóndo no (*recently appointed*); atarashíi (*recently acquired*).

news táyori (*tidings*); nyúusu, hoodoo (*newspaper news*).

newspaper shinbun.

next tsugí no, ichiban chikái (*nearest*); tonari no (*neighboring*); kóndo (*after this*).

nice íi, yói (*agreeable*); shínsetsu na (*kind*).

nickname adana.

niece méi.

night yóru.

nightmare warúi yume, ákumu.

nine kokónotsu, kú, kyuu.

no iie.
> Note that when answering a question in the negative, the usage of yes and no in Japanese is opposite to their usage in English.
> **Didn't you see it?**
> No, I didn't. Hai, mimasén deshita.
> Yes, I did. Iie, mimáshita.

nobility kázoku, kízoku (*titled group*).

noble adj. kooketsu na (*high-minded*); yuudai na (*imposing*); kedakái (*dignified*); mibun no takái (*aristocratic*).

nobody dáre mo, dónata mo (*followed by a negative verb*).

noise otó (*sound*); urusái otó (*unpleasant sound*).

noisy soozooshíi.

nominate (to) shimei suru.

nomination shimei.

none dáre mo, dónata mo (*of persons*); dóre mo (*of things*) (*followed by a negative verb*).

nonsense bakágeta kotó, bakarashíi kotó.

noon hirú, shóogo.

normal adj. atarimae no (*not strange*); hyoojunteki na (*standard*); futsuu no (*regular*); heikin no (*average*).

north kitá.

northern kita no.

northwest nishi kita, seihoku.

nose hana.

nostril hana no aná.

not –nai, –masén.
> I do not go. Ikimasén (*polite*).
> I do not go. Ikanai (*plain*).
> It is not expensive. Tákaku arimasen.

It is not a station. Eki de wa arimasén (ja arimasén).

note tegami (*a letter*); kiroku (*for later reference*); satsu (*paper money*).

note (to) shirusu (*mark down*); hikki suru (*take note of*).
note down kakitomeru.

nothing náni mo (*with a negative verb*).

notice shirase, kokuchi (*public notice*); chuumoku (*observation*).

notice (to) ki o tsukéru, chúui suru (*pay attention to*).

notify (to) tsuuchi suru (*inform*); happyoo suru (*announce*).

notion ippanteki gáinen (*general conception*); kangáe (*idea*); íken (*opinion*); ikoo (*intention*).

noun meishi (*substantive*).

nourish jiyoo ga áru.

nourishment jiyoo, jiyóobutsu (*nutriment*); shokúmotsu (*food*).

novel adj. atarashíi (*new*); kawatta (*strange*). –n. shoosetsu.

novelty kawatta mono (*thing*); kawatta kotó (*event*).

November Juuichigatsu.

now íma.
now and then toki doki.

nowadays konogoro; chikágoro.

nowhere dóko ni mo (*with a negative verb*).

nuclear káka no.
nuclear energy genshír yoku.
nuclear reactor genshíro.

nude adj. hadaka no (*naked*). –n. núudo, rataiga (*in art*).

nuisance méiwaku (*action*); yákkai na hito (*person*).

nullify (to) mukoo ni suru (*make invalid*); yameru (*cancel*); damé ni suru (*make useless*).

numb (to become) kogoeru (*from cold*); shibiréru (*from pressure*).

number suuji (*numeral*); bánchi (*indicating location*); bán (*turn*); bangóo (*for telephone or room*); –góo (*issue of a periodical*).

number (to) kazoéru (*count*).

numerous takusán no.

nun áma.

nurse kangófu.

nursery kodomo beya (*for children*); uekiya (*for plants*).

nut kurumi.

oak káshi.

oar kái.

oat karasu múgi.
oath chikai.
    to take an oath chíkai o tatéru.
obedience fukujuu (*submission*); juujun (*dutifulness*).
obedient juujun na, súnao na.
obey shitagáu, iu kotó o kiku.
object monó (*article*); mokuteki (*aim*).
object (to) hantai suru.
objection hantai (*adverse reason*).
    I have no objection to it. Hantai shimasén.
objectionable iyá na (*offensive*); mónku no desóo na (*open to objection*); omoshíroku nái (*unpleasant*).
objective *n.* mokuteki (*purpose*). –*adj.* kyakkanteki na.
objectively kyakkanteki ni.
objectivity kyakkansei.
obligation gímu (*duty*); ón (*debt of gratitude*); girí (*sense of duty*).
obligatory gimuteki, hitsuyoo na.
oblige (to) múri ni saseru (*compel*).
    be much obliged arígatoo zonjimásu.
obliging shínsetsu na.
oblique katamúita, aimai na.
obscure *adj.* bonyári shita.
obscurity aimaisa.
observation kansatsu (*notice*); kanshi (*watching*).
observatory tenmondai (*astronomical*); sokkoojo (*meteorological*).
observe (to) mokugeki suru (*catch sight of*); míru (*see*); ki ga tsúku (*notice*).
observer bookánsha; obuzáabaa (*at a conference*).
obstacle shoogai (*hindrance*); jama (*impediment*).
obstinacy goojoo (*stubbornness*); gankyoo (*persistence*).
obstinate gánko na (*stubborn*); gankyoo na (*persistent*).
obvious akíraka na.
obviously akíraka ni.
occasion orí, kikái.
occasionally tama ni (*at times*).
occupation shigoto (*employment*); shokúgyoo (*calling*); gyóomu (*business*); shóobai (*trade*); senryoo (*military*).
occupy (to) senryoo suru (*by force of arms*); súmu (*live in*); té ga fusagaru (*take up space*).
    to be occupied fusagatte iru.
occur (to) okóru.
occurrence dekígoto.
ocean úmi.
    Indian Ocean Indóyoo.
October Juugatsu.
odd hén na (*strange*); hanpa no (*not paired*).

odd number kisúu.
odor kaori (*fragrance*); niói (*smell*).
of no
    roof of the house ie no yáne.
off (*usually expressed by verbs*).
    The button is off. Botan ga hazurete imasu.
    She cut it off. Kirihanáshite shimaimáshita.
    The train is off. Densha wa déte shimaimáshita.
offend (to) *v.i.* ki ni sawaru (*displease*); *v.t.* okoraséru (*make angry*).
offense hansoku (*transgression*); tsúmi (*crime*); bujoku (*insult*).
offensive *adj.* fuyúkai na (*unpleasant*); burei na (*insolent*); iyá na (*disgusting*); kooseiteki (*aggressive*). –*n.* koogeki.
offer mooshikomi, mooshiide.
offer (to) sonaéru (*as act of worship*); sashiageru (*as a present*); mooshidéru (*make an offer*); teikyoo suru (*propose to give*); susumeru (*proffer*).
offering sonaemono (*to a deity*); kenkin (*gift of money to a church*).
office jimúsho (*in general*); yakusho (*of govt.*).
    head office hónsha, honten.
    branch office shiten.
officer yakunin (*civil*); shóokoo (*military*).
official *adj.* seishiki no (*formal*); omote muki no (*public*). –*n.* yakunin.
often tabi tabi, yóku.
oil abura.
old furúi (*of things*); toshiyori (*of persons*).
old age roonen.
old man ojíisan.
old woman obáasan.
older toshiue no.
    older brother níisan, onñisan; áni.
    older sister néesan, onéesan; ane.
oldest nenchoo no.
    oldest daughter (*among daughters*) chóojo.
    oldest son (*among sons*) choonán.
olive orííbu.
    olive oil oriibu óiru.
ominous fukitsu na (*inauspicious*); yóchi suru (*prognostic*); ken'aku na (*threatening*).
on –no ué ni, –no ué de, –no ué no.
    It is on the desk. Tsukue no ué ni áru.
once ichi do (*one time*); móto (*formerly*); máe ni (*before*).
    at once súgu ni.
    all at once kyuu ni, totsuzen.
    once in a while tokidoki.
    once a year ichínen ni ichido.
    once more moo ichido.

one hitótsu, ichí (*a single person or thing*); katáhoo (*one of a pair*); kata (*in compounds, such as;* kata me = *one eye*).

one *pron.* hito, jibun.

oneself jíshin, jibun.

onion tamanégi.

only táda (*merely, but*); tatta (*emphatic*); honno (*nothing but*).

open *adj.* hiráita, hirobíro shita.

open (to) *v.t.* akeru; *v.i.* aku.

opening kuchi (*gap*); aná (*hole*); hajime (*beginning*); kuchi, kikái, chánsu (*opportunity*).

opera ópera, kágeki.

operate *v.i.* ugóku (*function*); *v.t.* soojuu suru (*work*); kánri suru (*superintend*).

operation shújutsu (*surgical*); ságyoo (*working*); unten (*of a mechanism*).

opinion kangáe, kenkai (*notion*).

opponent hantáisha (*in debate*); aite (*in sport*); kyoosóosha (*in business*).

opportune kootsúgoo no.

opportunity kikái.

oppose (to) hantai suru.

opposite *adj.* –no mukoo no, –no mukai no (*facing*). –n. mukoogawa (*the other side*).

opposition hantai.

oppress shiitagéru, osaéru.

oppression appaku (*tyranny*); kónnan (*hardship*).

optimism rakutenshúgi.

optimistic rakutenteki.

oral kootoo no, kuchi de iu, kuchi no.
    oral examination kootoo shikén.

orange *n.* míkan (*tangerine*); orénji.

orator enzétsusha.

oratory yuuben, enzetsu.

orchard kudamono bátake, kajúen.

orchestra kangéngaku, ookésutora.

ordeal shíren (*severe trial*).

order iitsuke, meirei (*injunction*); kunrei (*instruction*); jun (*regular arrangement*); chuumon (*commission to supply*).
    in order to –táme ni.
    put in order séiri suru.

order (to) iitsukéru (*command*); chuumon suru (*give an order for*).

ordinary futsuu no (*common*); atarimae no (*not special*).

organ orugan (*musical instrument*).

organization koosei (*formation*); sóshiki (*system*); dantai (*body*).

organize (to) sóshiki suru (*to form*); sooritsu suru (*to institute*).

Orient Tóoyoo.

oriental *adj.* tóoyoo no. –n. Tooyoójin.

origin moto, kígen.

originality dokusoosei.

originate (to) hajimeru, soosaku suru (*invent*).

ornament kazari.

orphan kóji.

other hoka no (*not the same*); moo hitótsu no (*additional*).

ought –béki (*obligation*).
    You ought to go to a doctor. Isha e iku béki desu.

ounce ónsu.

our, ours watashítachi no, watashidómo no.

out sóto e (*outside*).

outcome kekka.

outdo (to) dashinúku.

outer sóto no, sotogawa no.

outlast (to) –yóri mochi ga íi.
    This outlasts that one. Kore wa sore yóri mochi ga íi desu.

outlay kéihi (*expenses*); shuppi (*expenditure*).

outlet déguchi.

outline rinkaku (*contour*); aramashi (*essential points*).

outline (to) aramashi o nobéru (*state the gist*); autorain o káku (*write*).

outlook mikomi.

output sangaku (*product, yield*).

outrage ranboo.

outrageous ranboo na, hidói.

outside sóto, omoté.

oval daen no, daenkei no.

oven óbun.

overcoat óobaa, oobaakóoto.

overcome (to) –ni uchikátsu; –ni makeru (*be overcome*).

overflow (to) hanran suru (*said of a river*); koboréru (*water in a vessel*).

overlook (to) miotósu (*omit seeing*); miwatásu (*view from a high place*); minogású (*refrain from seeing*).

overpower (to) makasu, attoo suru.

overrule (to) iatsu suru, kyakka suru (*reject, decide against*).

overrun (to) habikóru, afuréru.

overseas káigai no.

oversight miotoshi (*failure to notice*); shissaku (*mistake*).

overtake (to) oitsúku.

overthrow (to) hikkurikáesu (*upset*); uchitaósu (*knock down*); seifuku suru (*vanquish*); kutsugáesu (*subvert*).

overwhelm (to) attoo suru (*crush*); seifuku suru (*defeat*).

owe (to) –ni kari ga áru (*be financially indebted to a person*).

own *adj.* jibun no.

own (to) mótsu, shoyuu suru.

owner mochínushi (*proprietor*); ninushi (*of goods*).

ox ushi.

oxygen sánso.

oyster káki.

pace –ho, –po (*suffix: step*).
    She took two paces. Ního arukimashita.

pace (to) arúite hakáru.

pacific odáyaka na (*quiet, calm*); shízuka na (*still, as water; placid, as the sea; serene, as the mind; peaceful, as sleep*); heiwateki na (*not warlike*).

Pacific Ocean Taihéiyoo.

pack (to) tsutsúmu, nizúkuri suru.

page *n.* peeji.

pagoda tóo.

pain kurushimi (*distress*); nayami (*suffering*); itami (*ache*); fuan (*uneasiness*).

pain (to) *v.t.* kurushiméru (*cause pain to*); *v.i.* itámu (*ache, smart*).

painful itái.

paint penki.

paint (to) penki o nuru (*a house, etc.*); é o káku (*a picture*).

painter penkiya (*for houses*); ekaki (*artist*).

painting é o káku kotó (*art, hobby, vocation*); é (*that which is painted*).

pair ittsui (*of objects*); fúufu (*married couple*); hitókumi (*a set*).

pair (to) kumiawáseru.

pale usui (*of color*); aói (*of the face*).

palm tenóhira (*of the hand*).

pamphlet panfurétto.

pan nábe.

pancake pankéeki.

pane garasu íta.
    windowpane mádo no garasu íta.

pang sashikomi (*sudden sharp pain*); uzuki (*twinge*).

panic kyookoo.

panorama panorama.

pants zubón.

paper kamí.

parachute parashúuto, rakkásan.

parade kanpéishiki (*military*); paréedo, gyooretsu, kooshin (*for popular celebrations*).

parade (to) kooshin suru.

paragraph páragurafu.

parallel *adj.* heikoo no.

parallel (to) heikoo suru.

paralysis mahi.

paralyze mahi suru.

parcel tsutsumi (*package*); kozútsumi (*for mail*).
    parcel post kozutsumi yúubin.

pardon yurushí.

pardon (to) yóosha suru (*forgive*); yurúsu (*excuse*).
    Pardon me! Shitsúrei.

parents ryóoshin.

parenthesis kákko.

park kooen.

park (to) chuusha suru.

parliament gíkai.

part bún, búbun (*portion, piece*); bu (*of a book*); hen (*district*).
    the greater part daibúbun.

part (to) wareru (*separate, divide, split*); kiréru (*as a cable*); wakaréru (*take leave*).
    to part with tebanásu.
    to part from hanaréru.

partial hiiki na (*biased, not fair*); ichi búbun no (*not total*).

partially ichibúbun.

particular *adj.* soré zore no, meiméi no (*individual*); betsudan no, tokubetsu no (*special*); kichoomen na (*precise*). –*n.* kuwashíi kotó (*a detail*).

particularly tóku ni, tokubetsu ni.

party seitoo (*political*); enkai, páatii (*entertainment*).

pass tooge (*over a mountain*); pasu, kippu (*ticket*); nyuujóoken (*of admission*).

pass (to) tóoru (*go beyond*); tátsu (*time*).

passage fúne no ryokoo (*on a ship*); watashi (*across a river*); rooka (*corridor*).

passenger jookyaku (*train, etc.*); senkyaku (*ship*).

passing *adj.* ichijiteki no (*temporary*). –*n.* tsuuka (*passage*).

passion joonetsu (*emotion*), netsujoo (*intense emotion*); nekkyoo (*fervid devotion*); kanshaku (*fury*).

passive *adj.* ukemi no. –*n.* ukemi (*grammatical verb form*).

past *n.* káko (*time gone by*); rireki (*past life or career*).
    half-past seven shichiji hán.

past *adj.* káko no (*gone by*); súgita bákari no (*just passed*); ízen no (*ago*).
    the past year sakunen.

paste *n.* norí.

patch tsugi.

patch (to) tsugu.

patent tokkyo.

paternal chichi no, chichikata no.

path kómichi.

pathetic kanashíi.

patience gáman (*forbearance*); shínboo (*perseverance*).

patient *adj.* gaman zuyói, shinboo zuyói.

patient kanja (*sick person*).

patriot aikókusha.

patriotism aikókushin (*nationalism*).
patron hogósha (*protector*); kooensha,
  patoron (*backer*); hiikí kyaku (*regular
  customer*).
patronize (to) híiki ni suru.
pattern gara, moyoo (*of fabric*); tehón
  (*model*); mihon (*sample*).
pause kyuushi (*short stop*).
pause (to) *v.i.* tomaru.
pave (to) hosoo suru.
pavement hodoo.
pay kyúuryoo (*salary*); chíngin (*wages*).
pay (to) haráu.
payment shiharai (*paying*); shiharaikin (*sum
  paid*).
pea endóomame.
  green peas guriin píisu.
peace heiwa (*opp. to war*).
peaceful heiwa na.
peach momo.
peak itadaki.
pear nashí.
pearl shinju.
peasant hyakushóo (*farmer*); inakamono
  (*rustic*).
pebble jari.
peculiar tokushu no (*characteristic*); hén na
  (*strange*).
pecuniary kinsenjoo no.
pedal pedaru.
pedal (to) pedaru o fumu.
pedestrian hokóosha.
peel kawá.
peel (to) kawá o muku.
pen pén (*for writing*); orí (*sty*).
  fountain pen mannénhitsu.
penalty bakkin (*fine*); kéi (*punishment*).
pencil enpitsu.
penetrate (to) *v.t.* hairikómu *v.i.* tsukiíru.
peninsula hantoo.
penitence kóokai (*repentance*).
pension onkyuu (*government*); nenkin
  (*annuity*).
people hitóbito, hito, hitótachi (*individuals
  collectively*); kokumin (*a nation*).
pepper koshóo.
perceive (to) ryookai suru (*apprehend*);
  shikibetsu suru (*discern*); wakáru
  (*grasp*).
percentage hyakubún ritsu, paasentéeji.
perfect kanzen na.
perfect (to) kansei suru.
perfection kansei (*completion*); kanzen
  (*being unblemished*); jukutatsu
  (*proficiency*).
perfectly kanzen ni.
perform (to) suru (*do*); nashitogéru
  (*accomplish*); enjíru (*act, as in a play*).
performance suru kotó (*doing*); jikkoo

(*execution*); engeki (*of a drama*); yokyoo
  (*entertainment*).
perfume koosui.
perfume (to) koosui o tsukéru.
perhaps tábun (*probably*); hyotto suru to
  (*maybe*).
peril kiken.
period jidai (*era*); shuushífu (*in
  punctuation*).
periodical zasshi (*magazine*).
perish (to) horobiru (*suffer destruction*);
  kusáru (*spoil, decay*); sinu (*die*).
permanent eikyuu no (*lasting*); eikyuuteki
  na (*perpetual*); fuhen no (*unchanging*).
permission kyóka (*permitting*); ménkyo
  (*license*); dooi (*consent*).
permit ménkyo (*license*); menkyójoo
  (*written permission*).
permit (to) kyóka suru (*allow*).
perplex (to) *v.t.* komaraséru (*throw into
  confusion*); *v.i.* komáru (*be perplexed*).
persecute (to) hakugai suru.
persecution hakugai.
perseverance níntai.
persist (to) ganbáru (*insist on*); jizoku suru
  (*last*).
person hito; –nin (*suffix*).
  three persons sannín.
personal kójin no (*individual*); jibun no
  (*one's own*); shiyoo no (*private*).
personality jinkaku (*character*); kósei
  (*distinctive personal quality*).
perspective mikomi (*prospect*).
persuade (to) tokifuséru, settoku suru.
pertaining to –ni kán shite.
petty chiisái (*small in size*); sásai na
  (*trifling*); kéchi na (*mean*).
pharmacist kusuriya.
pharmacy kusuriya.
phenomenon genshoo.
phenomenal hijoo na.
philosopher tetsugákusha.
philosophical tetsugakuteki.
philosophy tetsugaku.
photograph shashin.
  take a photograph shashin o tóru.
photograph (to) utsúsu.
phrase kú.
physical shizen no (*natural*); nikutai no
  (*bodily*).
physician isha.
physics butsurígaku.
piano piano.
pick (to) tsumu (*flowers, grass*); erábu
  (*select*).
  to pick up hirou.
picnic pikuníkku, ensoku.
picture shashin (*photo*); é (*painting*).
picture (to) egáku.

picturesque é no yoo na.

pie pái.

piece kiré (*obtained by cutting*); kakera (*broken piece*).

pig buta.

pigeon háto.

pile yamá (*heap*).

pile (to) tsumu.

    to pile up tsumiagéru.

pill gan'yaku.

pillar hashira.

pillow mákura.

pilot mizusaki ánnai (*of a ship*); soojúushi (*of a plane*).

pin pín.

pin (to) pin o sásu.

pinch (to) tsunéru.

pine mátsu.

pink pínku.

pious keiken na (*devout*); shinjinbukái (*religious*).

pipe kiseru, páipu (*for smoking*); tekkan (*of iron*).

pitiful kawaisóo na (*touching*); míjime na (*miserable*).

pity doojoo.

pity (to) doojoo suru.

place tokoro.

place (to) oku.

    to take place okoru.

plain adj. akíraka na (*evident*); karui (*said of food*); jimí na (*unadorned*); futsuu no (*ordinary*).

plain heichi (*level ground*).

plan zumen (*drawing*); keikaku (*project*).

plan (to) keikaku suru (*devise a method or course*).

plane hikóoki (*airplane*); heimen (*level surface*).

plant shokúbutsu.

plant (to) ueru.

plaster kooyaku (*medical*); kabe (*mud*); shikkui (*sand and lime*).

plate sara (*for eating*); íta (*of metal*).

platform purattohóomu, hóomu (*for trains*); endan (*stage*).

platter oozara.

play asobi (*children's play*); shibai, engeki (*dramatic performance*).

play (to) asobu (*for amusement*); hiku (*a string or keyboard instrument*); fukú (*a wind instrument*).

plea negai.

plead (to) uttaeru.

pleasant kokoromochi no yói (*giving pleasure*); yúkai na (*cheerful*).

please (to) yorokobásu (*delight*); tanoshimaséru (*give pleasure to*).

    Please. Dóozo.

pleasure tanoshími (*delight*); yorokobi (*enjoyment*).

pledge yakusoku (*promise*); shirushi (*guarantee*).

pledge (to) teitoo ni ireru (*give as a pledge*); yakusoku suru (*promise*).

plenty takusan (*much*); juubún (*enough*).

plot jísho (*land*); inboo (*conspiracy*).

plot (to) takurámu (*scheme secretly*); inboo o megurásu (*conspire*).

plow suki.

plow (to) tagayásu.

plum ume.

plunder (to) ryakudatsu suru.

plural fukusúu.

plus púrasu, tasu.

pocket pokétto.

    pocket money kózukai.

poem shi; utá.

poet shijin.

poetic shiteki no.

poetry shi, utá.

point saki (*tapering end*); kangáe (*opinion*); ten (*dot*); pointo (*prominent feature*).

point (to) togarásu.

    to point out yubi sásu (*with the hand*); chúui o hiku (*draw attention*).

pointed togátta.

poison dokú.

poison (to) dokú o ireru (*infect with posion*); dokusatsu suru (*kill with poison*).

poisoning chúudoku.

polar kyokuchi no.

pole sao.

policeman júnsa, keikan.

policy shúdan (*method*); hooshin (*guiding principle*); seisaku (*course of action in govt.*).

    insurance policy hoken shoosho.

polish tsuya.

    shoe polish kutsúzumi.

Polish Poorandojín (*people*); Poorándo no (*country*).

polish (to) migaku.

polite téinei na.

politeness téinei.

political seijijoo no, seijiteki na.

    political party seitoo.

politics seiji.

pollution osen.

    air pollution kuuki ósen.

pond iké.

poor bínboo na (*opp. to rich*); waríi (*in quality*); kawaisóo na (*worthy of pity*).

popular ninki no áru (*liked*); hyooban no íi (*famous, talked of*); taishuuteki na (*in general favor*).

population jinkoo.

pork butaniku.

port minato.
porter mónban (*gatekeeper*); akaboo (*at railway stations*); booi (*at hotels*).
portrait shoozooga.
position tsutoméguchi (*employment*); tachiba (*circumstances*); oki dokoro (*place*).
positive *adj.* táshika na (*sure*); meikaku na (*definite*); utagai no nái (*unquestionable*); jishin no áru (*convinced*). *–n.* póji (*in photography*).
possess (to) mótsu.
possession mochímono (*thing held*).
possibility kanoosei.
possible dekíru.
post hashira (*pillar*); kúi (*a stake*); yuubínbutsu (*mail*); pósuto (*mailbox*).
postage yuubínryoo.
    postage stamp kitte.
postcard hagaki (*plain*); ehágaki (*picture*).
poster pósutaa.
posterity shíson.
post office yuubínkyoku.
pot nábe (*pan*); tsubo (*jar*); hachi (*bowl*).
potato jagaimo.
pound póndo.
pour (to) tsugu (*into glass*); hídoku fúru (*of rain*).
poverty bínboo.
powder koná.
power chikará.
powerful tsuyói (*strong*); yuuryoku na (*influential*).
practical jissaiteki na (*opp. to theoretical*); jitsuyooteki na (*useful*).
practice jitsuyoo (*opp. to theory*); kéiko (*exercise*).
practice (to) jikkoo suru (*carry out*); kéiko suru (*exercise*).
praise shoosan (*commendation*).
praise (to) homéru.
prank itazura.
pray (to) inóru.
prayer inori.
preach (to) sekkyoo suru.
precaution yóojin.
precede (to) sakidátsu.
preceding máe no.
precept kyookun.
precious kóoka na (*costly*); taisetsu na (*highly esteemed*).
precise seikaku na (*exact*); kuwashíi (*detailed*); kichoomen na (*regular*).
precision seikaku (*accuracy*); seimitsu (*exactitude*).
predecessor zennínsha.
preface jobun.
prefer –hóo ga sukí desu (*one thing to another*).
    I prefer this. Kono hóo ga sukí desu.

pregnant ninshin shite iru.
prejudice henken (*bias*).
prejudice (to) henken o motaséru.
preliminary kari no, yobiteki no.
prepare (to) shitaku o suru, júnbi o suru.
prescribe (to) sáshizu suru (*dictate*); shohoo o káku (*medicine*).
presence shusseki (*at a meeting, etc.*).
present *adj.* shusseki shite iru (*opp. to absent*); íma no, génzai no (*now existing*). *–n.* génzai (*the present time*); íma (*now*); okuimono, purézento (*gift*).
    to make a present okurimono o suru.
    for the present toobun.
present (to) ageru, sashiageru (*a gift*); shookai suru (*introduce a person*); miséru (*exhibit*); teishutsu suru (*offer*); nobéru (*state*).
preserve (to) hozon suru (*maintain*); satoozuke ni suru (*in sugar*); suzuke ni suru (*in vinegar*).
preside (to) shikai suru.
president shachoo (*of a company*); toodori (*of a bank*); daitóoryoo (*of a country*); gakuchoo (*of a university*).
press shinbun (*newspaper*); assákuki (*machine*).
press (to) susumeru (*urge*); shiméru (*squeeze*); purésu suru (*iron*); osu (*push*).
pressing purésu.
pressure atsúryoku (*compulsion*).
prestige meisei (*fame*); ishin (*dignity*).
presume (to) suitei suru (*assume*); katei suru (*suppose*); omóu (*guess*).
pretend (to) misekakéru (*lay claim*); –furí o suru (*make believe*).
pretext koojitsu (*pretense*); benkai (*excuse*).
pretty *adj.* kírei na (*beautiful*). *–adv.* kánari (*fairly*).
prevail (to) kátsu (*be victorious*); yuusei de áru (*be predominant*); ryuukoo suru (*be prevalent*).
prevent (to) samatagéru (*hinder*); mamóru (*guard against*); jama o suru (*stand in one's way*).
prevention booshi, yoboo.
previous saki no (*former*); máe no (*prior to*).
    the previous year máe no toshi.
prey gisei (*victim*).
price nedan (*charge*); daika (*cost*); bukka (*of commodities*).
    price index bukka shisuu.
pride hokori (*in something or someone*); unubore (*self-conceit*); kooman (*haughtiness*).
priest sóoryo (*Buddhist*); kánnushi (*Shinto*); bokushi (*Protestant*); shínpu (*Catholic*).
principal *adj.* dái ichí no (*first*); ómo na

(*main, most important*). –*n.* gánkin (*money*); koochoo (*of a school*).

principle gensoku (*fundamental rule*); shúgi (*doctrine, an -ism*).

print (to) shuppan suru (*publish*); insatsu suru (*to put into print*).

prison keimúsho.

prisoner shuujin (*criminal*); hóryo (*of war*).

private *adj.* watakushi no, shiyoo no (*opp. to public*); shiei no (*privately operated*); kójin no (*personal*).

privilege tokken (*prerogative*); tokuten (*peculiar right*).

prize shoohin.

prize (to) omonjíru (*esteem*); daijí ni suru (*value highly*).

probable arisóo na (*likely to be*); yuuboo na (*promising*).

probably tábun (*perhaps*); taitei (*most likely*).

problem mondai.

procedure tetsúzuki (*steps*); júnjo (*way of proceeding*).

proceed (to) susumu (*move on*); hajimeru (*begin*); tsuzukeru (*continue*).

process hoohoo (*method*); katei (*course*).

procession gyooretsu.

proclaim (to) koohyoo suru (*publish*); fukoku suru (*promulgate*); sengén suru (*declare officially*).

produce (to) seisan suru (*yield*); enshutsu suru (*as plays*).

product sanbutsu (*agricultural produce*); seisakúhin (*of industrial manufacture*).

production seisaku (*through manufacture*).

productive hoofu na (*producing abundantly*); yóku tsukuridásu (*bring forth*).

profess to hákujoo suru.

profession shokúgyoo (*a calling*); koogen (*avowal*); sengén (*declaration*).

professional shokugyoo joo no (*pertaining to work*); senmonteki (*technical*).

professor kyooju (*of a úniversity*).

profile yokogao.

profit ríeki (*pecuniary gain*); éki (*advantage*).

profit (to) éki o éru, toku o suru.

program purogúramu (*theatrical, computer, etc.*); keikaku (*plan*).

    programming purogúramingu.

progress zenshin (*movement forward*).

progress (to) shinpo suru (*improve*); zenshin suru (*advance*); tsugoo yóku iku (*get on well*); hattatsu suru (*develop*).

prohibit kinjíru (*forbid*).

prohibition kinshi (*a forbidding*).

project keikaku (*plan*); kígyoo (*industrial*).

project (to) keikaku suru (*devise*); tsukidásu (*protrude*).

promise yakusoku (*engagement*); keiyaku (*contract*); mikomi (*hope*).

promise (to) yakusoku o suru.

    to keep a promise yakusoku o mamóru.

prompt hayái, subayái (*quick*); sumíyaka na (*speedy*); sassoku no (*done quickly*).

prompt (to) unagasu.

promptness binsoku.

pronounce (to) hatsuon suru (*articulate*); senkoku suru (*announce formally*); sengén suru (*declare*).

proof shoomei (*demonstration*); shooko (*evidence*); kooseizuri (*printing*).

proper tekitoo na (*appropriate*); joohín na (*respectable*); dokutoku no (*particular*); tadashíi (*correct*).

property zaisan (*assets*); jísho (*land*).

proportion wari, wariai (*ratio*); warimae (*share*); tsuriai (*balance*).

proposal mooshikomi, teian.

propose (to) teian suru (*propound*); mooshikómu (*offer*).

prosaic sanbun no (*of prose*); omoshíroku nái (*dull, commonplace*).

prose sanbun.

prospect mikomi (*outlook*); nagame (*view*); mitooshi (*mental view*); yosoo (*expectation*).

prosper (to) sakaéru, han'ei suru.

prosperity hánjoo (*of a business*); ryuusei (*a thriving*); seikoo (*success*).

prosperous sakan na (*thriving*); ríeki no áru (*profitable*).

protect (to) hógo suru (*keep safe*); fuségu (*defend*).

protection hógo (*a protecting*); kooen (*patronage*).

protector hogósha.

protest kóogi (*dissent*); fufuku (*disapproval*).

protest (to) kóogi suru (*make a protest*); hantai suru (*oppose*); genmei suru (*declare formally*).

Protestant Purotésutantó, Shinkyoo.

proud tokui na.

prove (to) shoomei suru (*demonstrate*); tashikaméru (*make certain*); jikken suru (*experiment*).

proverb kotowaza.

provide yóoi suru (*supply*).

    provide with kyookyuu suru.

province chihóo (*place at a distance from the capital*); hán'i (*sphere or scope*).

provision chozóohin (*of food, etc.*); shokuryóohin (*supplies*); kitei (*stipulation*); júnbi (*preparation*); yóbi (*reserve*).

provoke (to) kanjoo o okosaséru (*call forth*);

okoraséru (*rouse to anger*); fungai saseru
(*exasperate*); okósu (*stimulate*).
proximity chikái kotó.
prudence yóojin, shinchoo na koto.
prune sumomo.
psychological shinrigaku joo no.
psychology shinrígaku.
public *adj.* ooyake no (*opp. to personal*);
kookai no (*open to all*). –*n.* kokumin (*the
people*).
　　to make public koohyoo suru.
publication happyoo (*public notification*);
shuppan (*publishing*); shuppánbutsu
(*published materials*).
publish (to) shuppan suru (*books, etc.*);
happyoo suru (*make known*).
publisher shuppánsha.
pull (to) hiku.
pulpit koodan.
pulse myakú.
pump pónpu.
punish (to) bassúru.
punishment bátsu (*act of punishing*);
kéibatsu (*penalty imposed by court*).
pupil séito (*school*); deshí (*disciple*); hitomi
(*of the eye*).
purchase kaimono (*that which is bought*);
toríhiki (*act of buying*).
purchase (to) kau, koonyuu suru.
pure junsui no (*unmixed*); seijun na
(*uncontaminated*); kírei na (*unsullied*),
junketsu na (*chaste*); keppaku na
(*guiltless*).
purity junketsu (*chastity*).
purpose mokuteki (*object*); –tsumori
(*intention*).
　　I intend to go. Iku tsumori désu.
purse saifu.
pursue (to) oikakéru (*chase*); tsukimatóu
(*follow closely*); jikkoo suru (*carry on*).
pursuit tsuiseki (*chase*).
push (to) osu (*opp. to pull*); oshiugokásu
(*move by pushing*); tsukidásu (*thrust*);
shiíru (*force*).
put *v.t.* oku.
　　put away shimau.
　　put off nobású, enki suru.
　　put on kabúru (*a hat*); kiru (*a dress*);
haku (*shoes*); tsukéru (*a light*).
puzzle nazo (*enigma*); pázuru (*quiz*); nandai
(*difficult problem*).
puzzle (to) toowaku saseru (*perplex*).
　　be puzzled toowaku suru.

quaint fuugáwari na.
qualify (to) tekioo saseru (*fit*); shikaku o éru

(*have the qualifications for*).
　　be qualified for shikaku ga áru.
quality hinshitsu (*degree of excellence*);
seishitsu (*property*).
quantity ryóo, bunryóo (*amount*); suuryóo
(*numbers*).
quarrel (to) kenka suru.
quarter yon bun no ichi (*one-fourth part*);
hen (*district*).
queen joóo.
queer hén na, myóo na (*strange*); okáshíi
(*funny*); okáshi na (*unusual*).
quench (to) iyású (*one's thirst*); kesu
(*extinguish*).
question shitsumon (*interrogation*); kotó
(*matter*); mondai (*problem*).
question (to) shitsumon suru, tazuneru
(*inquire*); tóu (*ask*); gimon o okósu
(*raise a doubt*); utagáu (*doubt*).
quick hayái.
quickly háyaku.
　　Come quickly! Háyaku kité kudasái.
quiet *adj.* shízuka na (*calm*); otonashíi (*of
character*); ochitsuita (*not showy*). –*n.*
shizukésa (*stillness*); kyuusoku (*repose*);
ochitsuki (*peace of mind*).
　　Keep quiet! Shízuka ni shite kudasái!
quiet (to) *v.t.* shízuka ni saseru; *v.i.* shízuka
ni náru.
quit (to) hanású (*let go*); hooki suru
(*abandon*); yameru (*cease*).
quite sukkári (*completely*); jijitsujoo
(*actually*); kánari (*somewhat*); tashoo wa
(*to a certain extent*); taihen (*very*).
　　quite good totemo yoroshii.
quote (to) in'yoo suru (*cite*); hikiai ni dású
(*refer to*); mitsumóru (*estimate*).

R

rabbit usagi.
race kyoosoo (*contest*); jínshu (*of human
beings*).
race (to) kyoosoo suru.
radio rájio.
rag bóro.
rage ikari.
ragged boro boro no.
rail réeru (*of railway*); tesuri (*of a fence*).
railroad tetsudoo.
　　railroad station éki, sutéeshon.
　　railroad train kishá, densha.
rain ame.
rain (to) áme ga fúru.
rainbow niji.
rainy ame fúri no.
　　rainy season báiu, tsuyu.
　　rainy weather úten.

raise (to) ageru (*move upward*); mochiageru (*lift up*); kakageru (*hoist*); saibai suru (*grow*).

raisin hoshibúdoo.

rake kumade.

range hán'i (*scope*); narabi (*row*); dennétsuki (*electric cookstove*); gasu kónro (*gas stove*).

range (to) *v.t.* naraberu.

rank rétsu (*row*); kaikyuu (*military*).

ransom minoshirókin (*money demanded*); kaihoo (*release from captivity*).

rapid *adj.* hayaí. –*n.* kyuuryuu (*swift current*).

rapidity sókudo.

rapidly kyuu ni, háyaku.

rapture uchooten.

rash sékkachi na.

rat nezumi.

rate wariai (*proportion*); sooba (*of exchange*); sókudo (*speed*).

rate (to) nedan o tsukéru, mitsumóru (*estimate*).

rather kánari (*tolerably, fairly*); múshiro (*instead of*); sukóshi (*somewhat*).
    rather than –yóri mo.
    rather good kánari yói.
    I'd rather go. Watakushi wa dóchira ka to iéba ikitái desu.

ration haikyuu shokuryóohin.

rational rikutsu no áru.

rave (to) tawagoto o iu (*talk wildly*); donáru (*talk furiously*).

raw náma no (*uncooked*).

ray koosen, hikarí.

razor kamisori.

reach (to) todóku (*come to*); oitsúku (*overtake*); –ni tassúru (*attain to*).

react (to) *v.i.* hannoo suru (*act in response*).

reaction handoo (*against*); hanpatsu (*repulsion*).

read (to) yómu.

reading dókusho.

ready yóoi no totonótta (*completely prepared*); yorokónde . . . suru (*willing*); kákugo no tsúita (*mentally prepared for*); tejika na (*handy*).

real hontoo no (*true*); jitsuzai suru (*actually existing*); jissai no (*opp. to imaginary*); honmono no (*genuine*).

reality shinjitsu (*opp. to fancy*); genjitsu (*actuality*).

realization jitsugen.

realize (to) jitsugen suru (*effectuate*); ki ga tsúku (*come to understand*).

really hontoo ni.
    Really! Sóo nan desu ka!

rear ushiro.

rear (to) *v.t.* sodatéru (*bring up*).

reason riséi ryoku (*intellectual faculty*); doori (*explanation*); riyuu (*cause*); dooki (*motive*); wáke (*ground*); iiwake (*excuse*).

reason (to) súiri suru (*draw a conclusion*); hándan o kudasu (*form a judgment*); kentoo suru (*examine critically*).
    by reason of –no tamé ni.

reasonable risei no áru (*endowed with reason*); múri ga nái (*justifiable*); koohei na (*fair-minded*); gooriteki na (*rational*).

reasoning riron, ronkyuu.

reassure (to) anshin saseru.

rebel muhonnin (*person*).

rebel (to) boodo o okósu (*take up arms against*); shitagawanai (*disobey*); somáku (*act against*).

rebellion hanran (*revolt*); boodoo (*riot*); hankoo (*resistance*); muhon (*treason*).

recall torikeshi (*act of revoking*); kaisoo (*recollection*).

recall (to) omoidásu (*recollect*); torikésu (*revoke*); yobikáesu (*call back*).

receipt uketori.

receive (to) uketoru.

receiver reshíibaa (*radio*); uketorinin (*person*).

recent chikágoro no (*modern*); atarashíi (*new*); saikin no (*the latest*).

reception kangei (*welcoming*); kangéikai, resépushon (*social entertainment*).

recess kyuuka (*vacation*); yasumi jíkan (*school*); kyuukei (*conference*).

reciprocal soogo no (*mutual*); okaeshi no (*done in return*).

recite (to) anshoo suru (*repeat from memory*); roogin suru (*as a poem, etc.*); monogatáru (*recount*).

recognize (to) wakáru, mitomeru.

recoil (to) handoo (*as a gun*); hanekaeri (*spring back*).

recollect (to) omoidásu.

recollection oboe (*reminiscence*); kaisoo (*remembrance*); tsuioku (*retrospection*); omoide (*that which is recollected*).

recommend (to) suisen suru.

recommendation suisen.

reconcile (to) wakai saseru.

record kiroku (*written note*); rireki (*career*); rekóodo (*phonograph*).

record (to) kiroku suru (*in writing*); rokuon suru (*in sound*).

recover (to) torimodósu (*get back*); zenkai suru (*from sickness*).

recruit shinpei.

rectangle kukei.

red *adj.* akai. –*n.* áka.

redeem (to) shookan suru.

redouble (to) issoo tsuyoméru.

reduce (to) *v.t.* –ni suru (*convert*); herasu (*make small*).

reduction waribiki (*discount*).

reed áshi.

refer (to) sankoo ni suru (*consult*); makaséru (*a matter to a person*).

reference mimoto shoomeisho (*a statement of qualifications for someone*); kikiawase (*inquiry*); kankei (*relation*).

refine (to) seisei suru (*oil, etc.*).

refinement seisei (*of oil, etc.*); joohinsa (*elegance*).

reflect (to) hansha suru (*throw back light, etc.*); arawásu (*show*); kangáeru (*ponder*).

reflection hansha.

reform kaikaku (*political*); kánka (*of persons*).

reform (to) kaizen suru (*amend*); arataméru (*make better*); kaikaku suru (*renovate*).

refrain orikaeshi.

refrain (to) sashihikáeru (*abstain from*); gáman suru (*forbear*).

refresh (to) árata ni suru (*make new*).

refreshment tabémono (*food*); karui nomímono (*drink*); sáka (*tea and cake*).

refuge hínan (*shelter*); hinanjo (*place of retreat*); hógo (*protection*).
    to take refuge hínan suru.

refund harai modoshi.

refund (to) harai modósu.

refusal kotowari.

refuse kotowáru (*decline*); jítai suru (*decline to receive*); shoodaku shinai (*reject*).

refute (to) hanbaku suru.

regard kóoryo (*consideration*); sonkei (*respect*).
    in regard to –ni tsúite.

regime tóochi (*administration*); kánri (*control*); seiken (*political power*).

regiment rentai.

register choomén (*record book*); meibo (*of names*).

register (to) káku (*a name*); kakitome ni suru (*a letter*).
    registered letter kakitome.

regret kóokai (*repentance*); shitsuboo (*disappointment*); zannén (*remorse*).

regret (to) zannén ni omóu (*be sorry for*); ki no dóku ni omóu (*deplore*); ikan ni omóu (*lament*); kóokai suru (*repent*); óshiku omóu (*be sorry for the loss of*).

regular kimatta (*according to rule*); futsuu no (*usual*); téiki no (*at intervals*).

regulate (to) choosetsu suru.

regulation kisóku.

rehearsal shitagéiko, renshuu. riháasaru.

rehearse (to) shitagéiko suru, renshuu súru.

reign jidai (*period*).

reign (to) osaméru.

reinforce (to) hokyoo suru.

reject (to) kotowáru.

rejoice (to) yorokóbu.

relapse burikaeshi (*recurrence of illness*).

relate (to) hanásu (*narrate*); kankei o tsukéru (*connect*).

relation kankei (*connection*); shinrui (*kinsman*).

relationship kankei.

relative *adj.* hikakuteki, kankei áru. –*n.* shinrui, shinseki (*kinsman*).

relax (to) kitsurógu (*take one's ease*), yurúmu (*become last*); yawaragu (*become less strict*).

relaxation kibarashi (*recreation*); kyuuyoo (*rest*); yurumi (*of muscles*); tegókoro (*of regulations*).

release (to) hanásu (*let go free*); tooka suru (*let fall from*); happyoo suru (*make public*).

relent (to) yawarágu, kandai ni naru.

relentless mújihi na.

relevant kankei no áru.

reliable táshika na.

reliance shinrai (*trust*); shin'yoo (*confidence*).

relic ibutsu.

relief kyúujo (*help*); keigen (*alleviation*); ánraku (*comfort*).

relieve (to) tasukéru (*raid*); raku ni suru (*give comfort*).

religion shúukyoo.
    Buddhist religion Búkkyoo.
    Shintoism Shintoo.

religious shuukyooteki na (*of religion*); shinkoo no (*devout*); shinjin bukái, keikan na (*pious*).

relinquish (to) suteru, hóoki suru.

relish aji (*taste*); kaori (*flavor*); fuumí (*good taste*).

relish (to) ajiwátte míru (*savor*); oishiku tabéru (*eat with pleasure*); tanoshímu (*enjoy*).

reluctance chúucho.

reluctant iyagáru, fushoo bushoo no.

rely upon tayóru (*depend upon*).

remain todomáru, taizai suru (*stay*).

remainder nokorí (*remaining part*); zanryúusha (*remaining person*).

remark itta kotobá (*anything said*); íken (*comment*).

remark (to) –ni chuumoku suru (*take notice of*); hihyoo suru (*comment*).

remarkable chuumoku subéki (*noteworthy*); sugúreta (*exceptional*); subarashíi (*striking*).

remedy kusuri (*medicine*); chiryoo (*treatment*).

remember (to) oboéru; omoidásu (*recollect*).

remembrance omoide (*recollection*); kiokúryoku (*memory*); kinen (*commemoration*).

remind (to) omoidasaséru (*bring something to mind*).

remorse kóokai (*regret*); ryóoshin no togamé (*pangs of conscience*).

remote tooi, hanáreta.
   remote control rimokon.

removal iten (*of or from house*); kaishoku (*position*).

remove (to) dokeru, torinozoku.

renew ataráshiku suru (*make new again*); irekáeru (*replace*); kurikáesu (*repeat*).

rent yáchin (*for a house*).

rent (to) kasu (*to somebody*); kariru (*from somebody*).

repair shuuzen (*act of repairing*); kaifuku (*restoration to a sound state*).

repair (to) naósu (*mend*); kaifuku suru (*restore*); teisei suru (*remedy*).

repeat (to) kurikáesu (*do once more*); sono mama tsutaeru (*tell to another*); kurikáeshite okonáu (*do over again*).

repent (to) kuíru, kóokai suru.

repetition kurikaeshi, hanpuku.

reply henjí.

reply (to) henji suru.

report hookoku, shirase (*account*).

report (to) hookoku suru.

represent (to) dairi suru (*persons, etc.*); arawásu (*as a symbol*); egakidásu (*portray*).

representation daihyoo (*delegate*); mooshitate (*petition*).

representative dairinin; daihyoo (*delegate*).

repress (to) yokuatsu suru (*suppress*); yokusei suru (*keep under control*).

reprimand shisseki.

reprimand (to) shikaru, hínan suru.

reprisal shikaeshi, fukushuu.

reproach shisseki (*upbraiding*); togame (*censure*).

reproach (to) shikaru.

reproduce (to) fukusha suru (*make a copy*); saisei suru (*remake*).

reputation hyooban, meisei.

request negái, seikyuu.

request (to) negáu (*beg*); tanómu (*ask*).

require (to) iru (*need*).

rescue sukuidashi, kyúujo.

rescue (to) sukuidásu (*deliver from*); kaihoo suru (*set free*).

research (to) kenkyuu suru, shirabéru.

resent (to) okóru, hankan o mótsu.

resentment uramí (*animosity*); fungai (*indignation*).

reservation yoyaku (*at a hotel*).

reserve júnbi (*readiness*); yobíhin (*stock*).

   without reserve fukuzoonáku (*freely*).

reserve (to) tótte oku (*set apart, keep in store*).

reside (to) súmu.

residence súmai; júusho.

resign (to) yameru (*relinquish*); dannén suru (*abandon*); jishoku suru (*give up office*); taishoku suru (*retire*).

   to resign oneself shitagáu, akiraméru (*accept one's fate*).

resignation jishoku.

resist (to) teikoo suru (*withstand*); gekitai suru (*repel*); hantai suru (*oppose*).

resistance teikoo, hantai.

resolute shikkári shita.

resolution ketsudan (*firmness*); késshin (*formed purpose*).

resolve (to) késshin suru (*determine*); kaiketsu suru (*settle*).

resort hoyóochi (*for health*).
   summer resort hishóchi.

resort (to) –ni uttaéru.

resources shígen.

respect sonkei (*esteem*); kankei (*relation*).
   in respect to –ni kanshite.

respect (to) kooryo suru (*heed*); sonchoo suru (*treat with deference*); uyamáu (*revere*).

respectful téinei na, reigi tadashíi (*well mannered*).

respective kákuji no, sorézore no.

respite yúuyo (*delay*); shikéi no shikkoo yúuyo (*reprieve*); ichijiteki chuushi (*temporary cessation*).

responsibility sekinin.

responsible sekinin ga áru.

rest nokorí (*remainder*); yasumí (*repose*); suimin (*sleep*); teishi (*cessation of motion*).

rest (to) yasúmu; suimin o tóru (*have some sleep*).

restaurant ryooríya (*Japanese*); résutoran (*Occidental-style*).

restless ochitsukanai.

restoration fukkoo (*revival*); kaifuku (*recovery*).

restore (to) móto ni modósu (*bring back*); káesu (*give back*); fukushoku saseru (*reinstate*); fukkoo suru (*reestablish*); naósu (*reconstruct*).

restrain (to) yokusei suru.

restraint yokusei.
   without restraint enryo náku.

restrict seigén suru, kagíru.

restriction seigén (*limitation*).

result kekka.

result (to) –ni owaru (*end up in*).

resume (to) futatabi hajimeru.

retail kouri.

retail (to) kouri suru.
retain (to) hóji suru (*keep*); kioku suru (*memorize*).
retaliate (to) shikaeshi suru.
retaliation shikaeshi, fukushuu.
retire (to) intai suru (*from work*); yasúmu (*rest*).
retirement intai.
retract torikesu.
retreat taikyaku (*military*).
retreat (to) taikyaku suru.
retrieve (to) torimodósu (*recover*); sukuidásu (*rescue*).
return (to) káeru (*come back*); káesu (*give back*).
reveal (to) shimésu (*disclose*); shiraseru (*make known*); bákuro suru (*divulge*).
revelation happyoo (*disclosure*); Mokushíroku (*Book of the Bible*).
revenge fukushuu.
revenue shotoku (*income of an individual*); sainyuu (*of the state*).
reverence suuhai (*veneration*); sonkei (*esteem*).
reverend bokushi (*Protestant clergyman*); shínpu (*Catholic clergyman*).
reverse abekobe, hantai.
reverse (to) abekobe ni suru.
revert (to) móto ni modóru.
review hihyoo (*critical*); fukushuu (*study*).
review (to) saichóosa suru (*view again*); kansatsu suru (*survey*); kaisoo suru (*reconsider*); hihyoo o káku (*books*).
revise (to) teisei suru (*correct*).
revision kaisei, kaitei.
revive (to) fukkatsu suru.
revoke (to) torikesu (*annul*); haishi suru (*abolish*).
revolt hanran.
revolt (to) hanran o okósu (*rebel*).
revolve (to) mawaru, kaiten suru.
revolution kakumei.
reward hoobi, hooshuu.
reward (to) –ni mukuíru (*repay*); hoobí o ataeru (*give a reward to*).
   be rewarded mukuiraréru.
rhyme in.
rib abara bone.
ribbon ríbon.
rice íne (*plant*); komé (*raw grain*); góhan (*cooked*).
rich kanemóchi no (*wealthy*); yútaka na (*abundant*).
richness yuufuku.
rid (get) torinozoku.
riddle nazo.
ride noru kotó.
ride (to) –ni noru.
ridiculous bakarashíi.

rifle shoojuu.
right *adj.* tadashíi (*correct*); mottómo na (*reasonable*); machigai no nái (*not wrong*); migi no (*direction*). –*n.* kénri (*privilege*); migi (*direction*).
   have a right to kénri ga áru.
   to the right migigawa ni.
righteous koohei na, tadashíi.
righteousness séigi, koohei.
rightful tadashíi.
rigid kyúukutsu na (*not flexible*); genkaku na (*strict*).
rigor genkaku.
rigorous genkaku na.
ring wá (*circle, link, wheel*); yubiwa (*for finger*).
ring (to) *v.t.* narasu; *v.i.* naru.
rinse (to) yusugu.
riot sóodoo, boodoo.
riot (to) sóodoo o okósu.
ripe jukúshita.
ripen (to) jukúsu (*become ripe*); jukusaséru (*make ripe*).
rise agari, shusse (*getting ahead*).
rise (to) agaru (*go up*); okíru (*from bed, etc.*), déru (*said of the sun*).
risk booken (*hazard*), kiken (*peril*).
   run a risk booken o suru.
risk (to) kiken ni sarasu (*expose to peril*); kakéru (*venture*); ichí ka bachí ka yatte míru (*take the chance of*).
rite gíshiki.
ritual gíshiki (*rite*); shikiten (*ceremony*).
rival kyoosóosha (*competitor*); teki (*enemy*), aite (*in sport*).
rivalry kyoosoo.
river kawá.
road michi, dóoro.
   main road oodóori.
   middle of the road michi no mannaka.
roar unari (*of an animal*); todoroki (*of waves, etc.*).
roar (to) unárú (*of animals*); todoróku (*of waves, etc.*); donáru (*vociferate*).
roast róosuto.
roast (to) róosuto ni suru.
   roast beef roosuto bíifu.
rob (to) nusúmu.
robber doroboo, gootoo.
robbery nusumí.
robe gáun (*gown*).
robot robotto.
robust ganjoo na.
rock iwá.
rock (to) *v.t.* yusuru; *v.i.* yureru.
rocky iwa no óoi.
rod boo, sáo.
roll maki gami (*of paper*); roorú pan (*bread*).

roll (to) korobasu (*roll over*); maku (*wind*); tsutsúmu (*enwrap*); sayuu ni yusuru (*shake from side to side*); korobu (*tumble down*).
romantic romanchíkku na.
romanticism roomanshúgi.
roof yáne.
room heyá (*of a house*); basho (*space*).
    There's no room. Basho ga arimasén.
    make room for basho o tsukúru.
root né.
rope nawá, tsuná.
rose bara.
rot (to) kusáru (*decay*).
rough zára zara shita (*opp. to smooth*); deko boko no (*opp. to level*); arai (*of the sea*); ranboo na (*riotous*); gekiretsu na (*violent*); arappói (*rude*).
round *adj.* marui. –*adv.* maruku. –*n.* maru, én (*circle*).
round off (to) shiagéru.
rouse mé o samásu.
rout (to) haisoo suru.
route tsúuro, rúuto.
routine kimatta júnjo (*fixed procedure*).
rove (to) urotsuku.
row narabi (*line*); sáwagi (*disturbance*).
    be in a row narande iru.
    place in a row ichirétsu ni oku.
row (to) kógu (*a boat*).
royal kooshitsu no.
rubber gómu.
rub (to) kosúru (*any object*); sasuru (*the body*).
rubbish garakuta, gomí.
rude busáhoo na (*unmannerly*); sóya na (*uncivil*); shitsúrei na, buréi na (*impolite*); ranboo na (*rough*).
ruin háikyo (*remains*); koseki (*historical site*); hakai (*destruction*); metsuboo (*decay*).
ruin (to) wáruku suru (*damage*); damé ni suru (*make useless*).
rule monosáshi (*measure*); jóogi (*ruler for lines*); kisóku (*principle*).
    as a rule ippan ni.
rule (to) súji o hiku (*mark with lines*); osaméru (*govern*).
ruler shiháisha (*sovereign*); jóogi (*for drawing lines*).
rumor uwasa.
run (to) hashíru, kakéru.
    run away nigéru.
rural inaka no.
rush ooísogi (*great haste*); kyuugeki na zooka (*sudden increase*).
rush (to) isógu.
    rush hour rasshu áwaa.
    rush into tobikómu.

    rush out tobidásu.
    rush toward hashítte iku.
Russia Róshiya.
Russian Róshiya no (*pertaining to Russia*); Roshiyájin (*person*); Roshiyago (*language*).
rust sabí.
rust (to) *v.t.* sabisaséru; *v.i.* sabíru.
rustic inaka no; inaka mono no (*person*).
rusty sábita.
rye raimúgi.

S

sacred shinsei na (*hallowed*).
sacrifice gisei (*surrender of a desirable thing*).
sacrifice (to) gisei ni suru (*renounce something*).
sacrilege bootoku.
sad kanashii.
sadden (to) kanashimaséru.
saddle kurá.
sadness kanashimi.
safe *adj.* buji na, anzen na (*free from danger*); táshika na (*reliable*). –*n.* kínko (*strongbox*).
safely buji ni.
safety buji, anzen.
sail ho.
sail (to) shuppan suru (*depart*); fúne de iku (*go by boat*); kóokai suru (*navigate*).
saint séija, seijin.
sake tamé; mokuteki (*purpose*).
    for the sake of –no tamé ni.
salad sárada.
salary gekkyuu (*monthly*); nenkyuu (*annual*); sarari.
sale uridashi (*bargain*); hanbai (*selling*).
    sales analysis hanbai bunseki.
    sales estimate yosoo uriage daka.
    sales force hanbai in.
    sales promotion hanbai sokushin.
    sales quota hanbai wariate.
    sales territory hanbai chiiki.
    sales volume hanbai ryoo.
salt shió, shokúen (*for the table*).
salt (to) shió de aji o tsukéru.
salute éshaku (*nod*); áisatsu (*greeting*); keirei (*military*).
salute (to) áisatsu suru.
salvation sukui.
same onaji.
    all the same mattaku onaji.
sample mihon, sánpuru.
sanctuary reihaidoo (*in a church*); shinden (*Shinto shrine*).
sand suna.

sandal sándaru (*Occidental-style*); zoori (*Japanese-style*).

sandwich sandoítchi.

sandy suna no (*pertaining to sand*); sunachi no (*land*); usuchairo no (*in color*).

sane shooki no.

sanitary eiseteki na.

sap jueki (*of trees*); génki (*vitality*).

sap (to) yowaraséru.

sarcasm hiniku, fuushi.

sarcastic hiniku na.

sardine iwashi.

sash óbi.

satellite eisei.

satiate (to) akisaséru.

satin shúsu.

satisfaction mánzoku.

satisfactory mánzoku na (*contented*); juubún na (*sufficient*); yói (*adequate, good*).

satisfy (to) mánzoku saseru (*gratify*); zénbu hensai suru (*discharge*); baishoo suru (*recompense*).

saturate (to) hitasu.

Saturday Doyóobi.

sauce sóosu (*Worcestershire*); shooyu (*soy sauce*).

saucer koohíi zara (*for coffee cup*); chataku (*for Japanese teacups*).

sausage sooséeji.

save (to) sukuu (*rescue*); takuwaéru (*hoard*); setsuyaku suru (*economize*); tasukéru (*from injury*); tameru (*put by*).
    be saved tasukáru.
    to save time jikan o setsuyaku suru.

savings chokin, ginkoo yókin (*bank*).

savior sukuínushi.

say (to) iu, ossháru (*honorific: respect*).
    Say! Chótto!

scales hakarí (*weighing instrument*); uroko (*of fish*).

scan (to) kuwashíku shirabéru.

scandal shuubun, gigoku, oshoku.

scanty sukunái, toboshíi.

scar kizu ato.

scarce sukunái, fusoku na; mare na.

scarcely karóojite (*with difficulty*); yatto (*barely*); hotóndo (*with a negative verb; almost, not*).
    scarcely know hotóndo zonjimasén (*honorific: humble*).

scare (to) *v.t.* odokasu.
    get scared odoróku.

scarf sukáafu, erímaki.

scatter *v.t.* makichirásu (*strew*); oichirásu (*disperse*).

scene késhiki (*landscape*); bamen (*movie, etc.*).

scenery késhiki; kookei (*sight, spectacle*).

schedule jikanhyoo (*timetable*); ichiranhyoo (*catalogue*).

scheme keikaku (*in a good sense*); takurami (*in a bad sense*).

scholar séito (*student*); gakusha (*learned person*).

school gakkoo.
    primary school shoogákkoo.
    junior high school chuugákkoo.
    senior high school kootoogákkoo.
    go to school tsuugaku suru.
    leave school taigaku suru.

science kágaku.

scientific kagakuteki.

scientist kagakúsha.

scissors hasamí.

scold (to) shikaru.

scope hán'i.

scorn keibetsu.

scorn (to) keibetsu suru.

scornful keibetsuteki na.

scrape (to) kezuru, káku.

scratch kakíkizu (*made by nail or claw*); kasuríkizu (*wound*).

scratch (to) káku (*an itchy place*); hikkáku (*cause a wound*).

scream sakebigóe.

scream (to) sakébu (*cry out*).

screen shikiri (*partition*); makú (*curtain*).
    folding screen byoobu.
    paper screen shooji (*in a Japanese house*).

scribble (to) nagurigaki suru.

screw néji.
    screwdriver nejimáwashi.

scroll makimono.

scruple chúucho, tamerai.

scrupulous ryooshin teki na.

scrutinize (to) sensaku suru.

sculpture chookoku.

sea úmi.

seal hán, ín, fuuin (*impression*); azárashi (*animal*).

seal (to) hán o osu; fuujíru (*close up*).

seam nuime.

search soosaku (*quest*); sensaku (*inquiry*); tsuikyuu (*close inquiry*); ginmi (*scrutiny*).

search (to) sagasu (*explore*); jítto mitsuméru (*scrutinize carefully*); saguru (*probe*); shirabéru (*examine*).

seashore kaigan.

seasickness funayoi.

season kisétsu.
    rainy season báiu, tsuyu.

season (to) aji o tsukéru.

seat koshikáke (*anything to sit on*); isu (*chair*); bénchi (*bench*); séki (*place where one sits*).

seat (to) koshikakéru.

second *n.* dái ni (*in succession*); byóo (*in time*); futsuka (*of the month*). *–adj.* ni banmé no.

second (to) sansei suru (*support*).

secondary dái ní no.

secret *adj.* himitsu no. *–n.* himitsu.

secretary hishó (*in a business office*); shoki (*recording officer; as a title*).

sect shuuha, há.

section bún (*part*); kúiki (*area, zone*).

secure anshin na (*free from care*); buji na (*safe*); daijóobu na (*sure*).

secure (to) shikkári to suru (*make fast*); éru (*obtain*); hoshoo suru (*guarantee*).

security tánpo (*for debts*); teitoo (*deposited as a pledge*); anzen (*safety*).

see míru (*look at*); miséru (*show*). *–ni au* (*meet face to face*); wakáru (*comprehend*); tamésu (*try out*).

    I see. Wakarimáshita.

seed táne.

seek (to) sagasu (*look for*); sagashimotoméru (*try to obtain*).

seem (to) miéru.

    She seems not to know it. Shiranai rashíi.

seize (to) tsukamaeru.

seldom métta ni (*with negative*).

    I seldom go. Métta ni ikimasén.

select (to) erábu.

selection sentei.

self jibun, jíshin.

    myself watashi jishin.

    by itself shizen ni.

    by oneself hitóri de.

selfish migátte na (*concerned unduly with oneself*); rikoteki na (*egoistic*).

selfishness wagamáma.

self service serufu sáabisu

sell (to) uru.

semicolon semikóron.

senate jooin (*U.S.*); sangíin (*Japan*).

senator jooingíin (*U.S.*); sangiingiin (*Japanese*).

send (to) okuru (*to a distant place*); todokéru (*nearby*); dásu (*by mail*).

senior toshiue (*in age*); senpai (*old-timer*).

sensation kankaku (*perception by the senses*), kimochi (*feeling*); kandoo (*excited feeling*); koofun (*excitement*); hyooban (*of gossip, etc.*).

sense chikaku (*perception*); íshiki (*consciousness*); kanji (*sensation*); kánnen (*mental discernment*); funbetsu (*practical judgment*); ími (*meaning*).

senseless mukánkaku na (*thoughtless*); bakágeta (*foolish*).

sensibility kankaku.

sensible kenmei na (*wise*); kashikói (*sagacious*); shiryo no áru (*thoughtful*).

sensitive kanjiyasúi (*delicate*); shinkei kabin na (*overly sensitive*); súgu ki ni suru (*touchy*).

sensitiveness shinkei kábin.

sentence búnshoo (*in writing*); bún (*gram.*); senkoku (*judgment*).

sentiment kanji, joosoo.

sentimental senchiméntaru na; kanshooteki na.

separate wakáreta (*disconnected*); betsu no (*distinct*); kóko no (*individual*); hitori hitóri no (*single*); kakuri shita (*isolated*).

separate (to) hanásu; wakéru; setsudan suru (*sever*); hikihanásu (*disconnect*); hanaréru (*disunite*); bekkyo suru (*live apart, part company*).

separately betsu betsu ni, tandoku ni.

separation bunri, dátsuri.

September Kúgatsu.

serene ochitsuita (*tranquil*); háreta (*unclouded*); uráraka na (*bright and clear*); odáyaka na (*placid*).

sergeant gúnsoo (*army*); keíbu (*in a police force*).

series shiríizu, renzoku.

serious majime na (*solemn*); juudai na (*important*); kitoku no (*dying, critically ill*).

seriously majime ni.

sermon sékkyoo.

servant meshitsúkai.

    maidservant otétsudai.

serve (to) hóokoo suru (*act as a servant*); kyúuji o suru (*wait on table*); yakú ni tátsu (*be of use*); tsugoo ga yói (*be suitable*); *–no* tamé ni hataraku (*give service to*).

service sewá (*assistance rendered*); hóokoo (*servant's occupation*); sáabisu (*treatment in hotels, etc.*); reihai (*religious*).

session káiki (*period*); kaitei (*sitting of law court*); gakki (*school term*).

set *adj.* kimatta, kitei no. *–n.* kumí (*things of the same kind*).

    complete set hitó kumi.

set (to) *v.t.* oku (*place*); tatéru (*erect*); hajimeru (*begin*); totonoéru kimeru (*fix*); *v.i.* shizúmu (as the sun).

settle (to) kimeru (*fix*); kaiketsu suru (*solve*); ochitsuku (*settle down*); imin suru (*colonize*).

settlement kaiketsu (*of an affair*); jídan (*agreement*); seisan (*liquidation*); sétsurumento (*social service*).

seven nanátsu, shichí.

seventeen juunána, juushichí.

seventeenth dái juunána; juushichi nichí (*of the month*).

seventh dái shichí; nanoka (*of the month*).

seventieth dái nanájuu.

seventy nanájuu, shichijuu.

several iro iro no (*diverse*); íkutsuka no (*various*).

   several times suukai.

severe hidói (*harsh*); kibishíi (*strict*); genkaku na (*stern*); gensei na (*rigidly accurate*); mooretsu na (*intense*).

severity gekiretsu (*harshness*); genkaku (*strictness*).

sew (to) núu.

sewer gesui.

sex séi.

   female sex mesú (*animals*); josei (*humans*).

   male sex osú (*animals*); dansei (*humans*).

sexual seiteki na.

shabby misuborashíi.

shade hikage (*of sun*); káge (*of trees, etc.*).

shade (to) káge ni suru (*cast shade upon*); hikarí ga ataranai yóo ni suru (*protect from light*); kakúsu (*screen from view*).

shadow káge.

shady káge no óoi.

shake (to) *v.t.* yusuru (*rock, swing*); furu (*by holding*); *v.i.* furueru (*tremble*).

shallow asai.

sham *adj.* nise no. —*n.* nise.

sham (to) –no furí o suru.

shame hají (*disgrace*); hazukáshisa (*consciousness of shortcoming*); fuménboku (*ignominy*); fuméiyo (*dishonor*).

shame (to) haji saséru.

shameful hazukashíi.

shameless haji shírazu no.

shape katachi (*form*); keijoo (*configuration*); súgata (*guise*).

shape (to) katachi o tsukéru.

shapeless katachi no nái.

share bún (*part*); wakemáe (*portion*); kabu (*finance*).

share (to) wakéru (*divide*); buntan suru (*partake*).

shareholder kabúnushi.

sharp *adj.* surudói (*as blades, needles*); yóku kiréru (*as edge for cutting*); saki no togátta (*pointed*); nukeme no nái (*shrewd*).

sharpen (to) tógu (*an edge*); togarásu (*a point*); kezuru (*a pencil*).

shatter (to) konagona ni kowásu (*break in pieces*); kujíku (*hope*).

shave (to) sóru (*blade*); kezuru (*plane*).

she ano onna no hito, kánojo.

shed koya

shed (to) námida o nagásu (*tears*).

sheep hitsuji.

sheer kewashíi (*steep*); mattaku no (*utter*).

sheet shikifu (*for a bed*); ichí mai no kamí (*of paper*).

shelf tana.

shell kará (*of mollusks*); kóo (*of lobster, crab, etc.*).

shelter hinanjo (*refuge*); hinangoya (*shed*); hógo (*protection*).

shelter (to) *v.t.* hógo suru (*protect*); yadorásu (*lodge*); kakumáu (*give refuge*); *v.i.* hínan suru (*take refuge*).

shepherd hitsuijíkai.

shield táte.

shield (to) hógo suru.

shift kootai (*act of taking a turn*).

shift (to) *v.t.* utsúsu, kaeru.

shine (to) hikáru (*glitter*); téru (*as sun or moon*); kagayáku (*sun*).

ship fúne.

   steamship kisen.

ship (to) fúne de okuru (*send by ship*); okuru (*send by any means*).

shipment funazumi (*ship's load*); ní (*cargo*); tsumini (*the goods shipped*).

shirt shátsu, waishatsu (*Occidental-style*); juban (*Japanese*).

shiver mibúrui.

shiver (to) furueru, mibúrui suru.

shock shókku, shoogeki (*impact*); shoototsu (*collision*); shindoo (*by earthquake*); kandoo (*of the mind*).

   have a shock bikkúri suru.

shock (to) odorokásu (*with fear*); odoróku (*be shocked*).

shoe kutsú.

shoemaker kutsúya.

shoot útsu (*as a gun*).

shooting shageki.

shop mise; –ya (*in compounds*).

   butcher shop nikúya.

shopping kaimono.

shore kaigan.

short mijikái (*not long*); hikúi (*not tall*).

   short distance shookyóri.

shorten (to) *v.t.* mijikáku suru (*make shorter*); tsuméru (*curtail*); *v.i.* mijikáku náru (*become shorter*); tsumáru (*be curtailed*).

shorthand sokki.

shot happoo (*of a gun*); chuusha (*injection*).

shoulder káta.

shout oogóe (*loud voice*).

shout (to) oogóe de yobu (*call out*); oogóe o dásu (*utter a loud cry*); sakébu, donáru (*utter with a shout*).

   to shout at donari tsukéru.

shove (to) oshiwakéru.

shovel sháberu.

show shibai, misemóno (*public show*).

show (to) miséru (*let see*); oshieru (*point out*).

shower niwaka áme (*of rain*); yuudachi (*in summer*).

shrill kandakái.

shrimp ebi.

shrine jínja (*Shinto*).

shrink (to) chijimu.

shrub kanboku.

shun (to) sakéru.

shut *adj.* shimátta, tójita.

shut (to) *v.t.* shiméru (*a door, etc.*); tojíru (*things with lids*); *v.i.* shimáru (*be shut*).

shy hazukashíi (*bashful*); uchiki na (*timid*); kimari ga warúi (*embarrassed*).

sick (be) kagen ga warúi (*unwell*).
    She got sick. Byooki ni narimáshita.

sickness byooki.

side kawa (gawa).

sidewalk hodoo, jindoo.

siege kakomi.

sigh tameíki.

sigh (to) tameíki o tsúku.

sight shiryoku (*power of seeing*); nagame (*view, scene*); késhiki (*scenery*).
    out of sight miénai.

sign sáin (*signature*); shirushi (*indication*); chookoo (*symptom*); zenchoo (*omen*); fugoo (*mark*); kanban (*signboard*); míburi (*gesture*).

sign (to) shomei suru (*one's name*).

signal shingoo, keihoo.

signal (to) shingoo o okuru.

signature shomei, sain.

significance ími (*meaning*); juuyoosei (*importance*).

significant juuyoo na.

signify (to) –o ími suru.

silence seishuku, chinmoku.

silence (to) damaraséru.

silent shízuka na.

silicon shirikon.

silk kínu.
    silk cloth kénpu.

silken kínu no.

silkworm káiko.

silly baka na.

silver gín.

silvery gin'iro no.

similar nite iru (*resembling*); onaji yóo na (*same kind*); ruiji shita (*alike*).

similarity ruiji.

simple kantan na (*not complicated*); tanjun na (*not combined*); wake no nái, yasashíi (*easy*).

simplicity tanjun, kantan.

simply tán ni.

simulate (to) –no mane o suru.

simultaneous dooji no.

sin tsúmi.

sin (to) tsúmi o okasu.

since –kara (*because*); –te kara (*after*).

sincere seijitsu na.

sincerely hontoo ni (*truly*), seijitsu ni.

sincerity seijitsu.

sinew súji.

sing utau; naku (*birds*).
    sing a song utá o utau.

singer káshu; utaite.

single táda hitótsu no (*one only*); kókono (*individual*); dokushin no (*unmarried*).

singular mezurashíi (*uncommon, rare*); hén na (*strange*); fushigi na (*wondrous*).

sinister nínsoo no warúi (*person*).

sink nagashí (*in a kitchen*).

sink (to) *v.i.* shizumu (*be submerged*); *v.t.* shizumeru (*submerge, go down*).

sinner tsumibito.

sip (to) susuru.

sir senséi (*teacher, lawyer, title of respect*).
    Thank you, sir. Arígatoo gozaimásu.

sister néesan, onéesan, ane (*older*); imootó (*younger*).

sister-in-law gí-shí, giri no ane (*older*); gimai, giru no imootó (*younger*).

sit (to) koshikakéru (*on a chair*); suwaru.

site basho (*place*); shikichi (*for a building*).

situation tsutomé guchi (*employment*); jijoo (*circumstance*).

six muttsú, rokú.

sixteen juurokú.

sixteenth dái juurokú, juurokunichí (*of the month*).

sixth dái rokú; muika (*the sixth of the month*).

sixtieth dái rokujúu.

sixty rokujúu.

size ookisa, sáizu (*dimension*); sunpoo (*measure*).

skate (to) sukéeto o suru.

skates sukéeto.

skeleton gáikotsu.

sketch sukétchi (*rough drawing*); shitagaki (*rough draft*); gaiyoo (*outline*); shasei (*from nature*).

skeptic *n.* utagai bukái hito.

ski (skiing) sukíi.
    a pair of skis sukíi hitókumi.

skill gijutsu.

skillful joozú na.

skin hifu (*human, animal*); kawá (*of animals or fruit*).

skirt sukáato (*Occidental dress*); suso, hakama (*Japanese kimono*).

skull zugáikotsu.

sky sóra.

    blue sky aozóra.

slander (to) wáruku iu; chuushoo suru.

slap hirate uchi.

    to slap (someone's) face kao o hirate de útsu.

slate n. sekiban.

slaughter tosatsu (*butchering*); gyakusatsu (*massacre*).

slave dorei.

slavery dorei séido.

sled sóri.

sleep nemuri.

sleep (to) nemuru (*slumber*); yasúmu (*rest, doze*); neru.

sleeve sode.

slender hossóri shita (*slim, opp. to stout*); kabosói (*slight*); yowái (*weak, feeble*); hinjaku na (*meager*).

slice kiré.

slice (to) usuku kíru.

slide (to) subéru.

slight kyasha na (*slender*); karui (*not severe*); sukóshi no (*small, not great*).

slight (to) keibetsu suru.

slip suríppu (*article of woman's clothing*).

slip (to) subétte korobu (*trip*); tsumazúku (*stumble*); fumihazúsu (*miss one's footing*).

slipper suríppa.

slippery subekkói, tsúru tsuru shita.

slope keisha (*slant*); koobai (*incline*); saká (*hill*); shamen (*inclined plane*); keisháchi (*sloping ground*).

slot hosonagái aná.

slovenly bushóo na.

slow osoi.

slow (to be) okureru (*get behind time*).

slowly yukkúri.

slowness osoi kotó.

slumber karui nemuri, madoromi.

slumber (to) v.i. útouto suru (*sleep lightly*); nemuru (*sleep*); utatane suru (*doze*); inemúri suru (*drowse*).

sly zurúi.

small chiisái (*not big*); hosói (*slender*).

smart kashikói (*clever*); haikara na, sumáato na (*elegant in dress*).

smash (to) kowásu.

    to be smashed kowaréru.

smear (to) nasuritsukéru.

smell niói (*odor*); kaori (*scent*); akushuu (*stink*).

smell (to) kagu (*get the odor of, exercise the sense of smell*); niói ga suru (*emit an odor*); warúi niói ga áru (*be rank*); hijoo ni kusái (*stink*).

smile bishoo, hohoemi.

smile (to) níko niko suru, hohoému.

smoke kemuri.

smoke (to) kemuri o háku (*emit smoke*); tabako o nómu (*use tobacco*).

smooth súbe sube shita (*not rough*); taira na (*level, even*); odáyaka na (*not ruffled*); dekoboko no nái (*not jagged*).

smooth (to) nobasu, nadáraka ni suru.

smother chissoku saseru (*choke*); akubi o kamikorosu (*a yawn*); kanjoo o osaéru (*an emotion*); kakúsu (*conceal*); momikésu (*stifle*).

smuggle (to) mitsuyúnyuu suru.

snake hébi.

snapshot sunappu sháshin.

snatch (to) hittakúru (*grab*); nusumu (*steal*).

sneer (to) reishoo suru.

sneeze (to) kushámi o suru.

snore (to) ibikí o káku.

snow yukí.

    snowfall yukifurí.

snow (to) yukí ga fúru.

snowstorm fúbuki.

so (thus) désu kara.

    and so on –nádo, –tóo.

    It is so. Sóo desu.

    I think so. Soo omoimásu.

soak (to) shimitóoru (*permeate*); nurasu (*drench*).

soap sekken.

sob susuri naki.

sob (to) susuri náku.

sober yótte inai (*not intoxicated*); majime na (*serious*).

sociable shakooteki na (*fond of company*); koosai jóozu na (*companionable*).

social shákai no, shakaiteki na.

society shákai (*community*); jooryuu shákai (*upper class*); tsukiai (*companionship*); dooseki (*company*); kái (*association*).

sock(s) kutsushita (*Occidental*); tábi (*Japanese*).

socket sokétto (*electric*).

soft yawarakái (*not hard*); yasashii (*not harsh*).

soften (to) yawarakáku suru (*as an object*); yawaragéru (*in feeling*).

soil tsuchí (*earth*); tochi (*ground*).

soil (to) yogosu.

soldier heitai.

sole adj. tatta hitóri no (*one and only; pertaining to persons*); tatta hitótsu no (*pertaining to inanimate things*); tandoku no (*exclusive to one*); dokutoku no (*unique*). –n. soko (*of a shoe*); ashi no ura (*of the foot*).

solemn genshuku na.

solemnity genshuku, soogon.

solicit segámu (*ask earnestly of*); kongan suru (*importune*); konsei suru (*entreat*).

solid joobu na (*strong*); katai (*hard*).

solitary hitóri de kurasu (*living alone*); tsure nashi no (*without companions*); sabishíi (*lonely*); hitodoori no mare na (*unfrequented*).

solitude kodoku (*being alone*); sabishísa (*loneliness*).

soluble tokéru.

solution káishaku (*a solving*); setsumei (*explanation*); kaiketsu (*settlement*).

solve (to) kaiketsu suru (*clear up*); setsumei suru (*explain*); kaitoo suru (*find an answer*); tóku (*a problem*).

some (*often omitted in Japanese*) ikuraka no (*an indefinite quantity*); sukóshi (*a little, a few*); ní-san (*two or three*).
   Give me some water, please. Mizu o kudasái.

somebody dónata ka (*honorific: respect*); dáre ka.

somehow dóo ni ka (*in some way or other*); nán to ka shite (*in one way or another*); dóomo (*for some reason or other*).

someone dónata ka (*honorific: respect*); dare ka.

something náni ka.

sometime ítsuka (*at an indefinite time*); sono uchi ni (*at a time hereafter*); shibáraku (*for a certain period*).

sometimes tokí ni wa (*at times*); toki doki (*occasionally*); tama ni (*now and then*).

somewhat íkuraka (*in some measure*); sukóshi (*a little*); ikubun (*to some extent*).

somewhere dóko ka ni, dóko ka de (*in or at someplace*); dóko ka e (*to someplace*); áru tokoro (*a certain place*).

son musuko.

song utá.
   popular song ryuukóoka.

soon súgu.

soot súsu.

soothe (to) nadaméru (*calm down*); nagusaméru (*comfort*); shizumeru (*assuage*).

sore adj. tadareta (*inflamed*); itámu (*painful to the touch*). —n. odéki (*boil*); tadare (*a festering*).

sorrow kanashimi, nageki.

sorry (be) kinodóku ni omóu.
   I am sorry Sumimasén. Gomen nasái.
   Excuse me. Okinodóku desu (*I am sorry for you*).

sort shúrui (*kind, class*); hinshitsu (*character, nature*).

sort out (to) yoriwakéru.

soul támashii.

sound adj. kenkoo na, kenzen na (*of healthy mind*); itande inai (*undamaged*); táshika na (*reliable*); ronriteki na (*logical*). —n. otó (*that which is heard*); hibikí (*reverberation*).

sound (to) fukú (*a wind instrument*); narasu (*another musical instrument*); áizu suru (*give a signal*); otó o saseru (*make a sound*).

soup súupu (*Occidental style*); suimono (*Japanese*).

sour suppái.

source moto (*origin*); minamoto (*of a river*).

south minami.

southeast toonan.
   Southeast Asia Toonan Ájia.

southern minami no.

southwest nansei.

sovereign kúnshu.

sow (to) máku (*scatter*); makichirásu (*disseminate*); hiroméru (*propagate*).

space aita basho (*room*); supéesu; tokoró (*place*); kankaku (*interval*); kyóri (*distance*).

space (to) kankaku o oku.

spacecraft uchuusen.

spacious hirobíro to shita (*vast, broad*); ookíi (*large*).

spade suki.

spare (to) tebanásu.

spare adj. yóbi no (*held in reserve*); yobun no (*superfluous*); fuyoo no (*not required*); hinjaku na (*scanty*); kiritsúmeta (*stinted*). —n. yóbi (*reserve*).

spare (to) oshímu (*use grudgingly*); ken'yaku suru (*economize*); yurúsu (*forbear*); sashi hikaeru (*refrain from*).

spark hí no ko, híbana (*of fire*); kirameki (*gleam*); kakki (*animating principle*).

sparkle (to) kagayáku.

sparrow suzume.

speak (to) hanásu (*narrate*); iu (*mention*).

speaker hanashité, enzétsusha (*one who delivers a speech*); kooénsha, kóoshi (*lecturer*); supíikaa (*radio loudspeaker*).

special tokubetsu no (*of a particular kind*), sen'yoo no (*private*); tokutei no (*definite*); namihazure no (*extraordinary*); tokushu no (*particular*).

specialty tokusánhin (*special product*); meisan (*famous product*); tokushoku (*special feature*).

specific tokushu na, tokutei na.

specify (to) shitei suru.

spectacle kookei (*sight*); sookan (*noteworthy scene*); misemóno (*public show*).

spectator kenbutsunin (*onlooker*); bookánsha (*bystander*).

speculate (to) kangáeru (*consider*); shisaku

suru (*meditate*); suisoku suru
(*conjecture*); tooshi suru (*invest*).
speech hanashí (*talk*); hanásu nóoryoku
(*faculty of speaking*); kotobá (*language*);
enzetsu (*public address*).
speed sokúryoku (*velocity*); háyasa
(*swiftness*).
speedy sokúryoku no hayái.
spell majinai (*charm*).
spell (to) tsuzuru.
spelling tsuzuri.
spend (to) tsukau (*pay out*); kurasu (*time*).
sphere tamá (*globe*); kyuumen (*spherical
surface*); tentai (*heavenly body*).
spice yakumi (*condiment*); kaori
(*fragrance*); kóoryoo (*aromatic vegetable
flavoring*).
spider kúmo.
spill (to) kobósu.
    to get spilled koboréru.
spin (to) tsumúgu (*yarn*); kakéru (*a web*);
mawasu (*a top*); máyu o tsukúru (*silk; by
a silkworm*).
spirit támashii (*as distinct from matter*);
séishin (*disposition of mind*); kakki
(*vigor*); nétsui (*ardor*).
spiritual seishinteki na (*concerned with
things of the mind or soul*); kámi no
(*divine*); shinsei na (*sacred*);
shuukyoojoo no (*religious*).
spit (to) tsúba o háku.
spite ijiwáru (*malice*); urami (*grudge*).
    in spite of –ní mo kakawárazu.
spite (to) ijiwáru o suru.
spiteful ijiwarúi.
splash (to) hanekakéru, haneagéru.
splendid rippa na (*imposing*); subarashíi
(*magnificent*); mígoto na (*admirable*).
splendor kagayaki, mígoto.
split (to) *v.t.* sáku (*crack*); waru (*divide*);
sógu (*cleave*); *v.i.* wareru.
spoil (to) itaméru (*damage*); damé ni suru
(*render useless by injury*); wáruku suru
(*make bad*).
sponge *n.* kaimen, suponji.
spontaneous shizen no (*natural*); jihatsuteki
no (*voluntary*); jidooteki na (*self-acting*).
spoon sají.
spoonful sají ippai no.
sport undoo, supóotsu (*recreation*);
tanoshími (*pastime*); joodán (*jest*).
spot tokoro (*place*); ten (*speck*); shimi
(*stain*).
spread (to) *v.t.* hirogeru (*in length and
breadth*); nuru (*butter*); hiromáru (*news*);
v.i. hirogaru (*to be disseminated*).
spring háru (*season*); báne (*of machinery*);
onsen (*of hot water*); izumi (*of cold
water*).

spring (to) tobu (*leap*); shoojíru (*proceed,
originate*).
sprinkle (to) máku (*with water*); furikakéru
(*with powder, etc.*).
sprout (to) mé o fukú (*put forth shoots*);
háete kuru (*spring up*).
spry subashikói.
spur (to) hakusha o kakéru (*a horse*).
spurn (to) hanetsukéru.
spy supái, kanchoo.
spy (to) sagúru.
squadron kantai.
squander (to) mudazúkai suru.
square seihóokei (*geom.*); hiroba (*in a
town*).
squeeze (to) hasámu (*between two things*);
nigiri shiméru (*in one's hand*); shibóru
(*press out liquids*).
squirrel rísu.
stable *n.* umagoya. –*adj.* shikkári shita
(*firm*); antei shita (*steady*); kyóoko na
(*steadfast*).
stack shóka (*library*).
stack (to) tsumi kasanéru.
stadium kyoogijoo, sutájiamu.
staff saó (*pole*); boo (*rod*); shokúin (*of a
business*).
staff (to) shokuin o soróeru.
stage bútai, sutéeji (*theatrical*); endan
(*elevated platform*).
stain shimi, yogore.
stain (to) *v.t.* yogosu; *v.i.* yogoreru (*get
stained*).
stair(s) dán, kaidan.
stammer (to) domóru.
stamp kitte (*for postage stamps*); hán
(*rubber stamp, etc.*); keshiin (*postmark*).
stamp (to) sutanpu o osu.
stand dái (*to set things on*); hankoo
(*resistance*); bóogyo (*defense*); uriba
(*booth*).
stand (to) tátsu (*get up*); tachitsuzukeru
(*remain standing*); tátte iru (*be in a
standing position*); oite áru (*be placed:
speaking of an inanimate thing*); áru (*be
located*); tachiagaru (*stand up*); tatéru
(*erect*).
star hoshi (*celestial*); sutáa, hanágata
(*theatrical*).
stare (to) –o mitsuméru.
start hajime (*beginning*); shuppátsuten
(*starting point*); odoroki (*shock*).
start (to) *v.t.* hajimeru (*begin*); *v.i.* hajimaru
(*begin*); shuppatsu suru (*depart*); déru (*of
trains, etc.*).
starve (to) uéru.
state kókka (*political body*); jootai
(*condition*).
state (to) iu (*say*); hanásu (*tell*); nobéru

(*express in speech*); chinjutsu suru
(*express in writing*).
stately doodóo to shita.
statement seimei.
station éki, sutéeshon (*railway*).
statistic tookei.
statue zóo.
   bronze statue doozoo.
statute kisóku (*rule, regulation*).
stay taizai.
stay (to) *v.t.* tomaru (*stop*); *v.i.* okuraseru
(*delay*).
steady shikkári shita.
steak bifuteki.
steal nusúmu.
steam jóoki, suchíimu.
steam (to) músu.
steamer kisen (*steamship*).
steel hagane, kootetsu.
steep *adj.* kyuu na, kewashíi (*precipitous*);
kyuukóobai no (*high-pitched*).
steer (to) káji o tóru.
stem kukí.
stenographer sokkísha.
stenography sokki.
step dán (*of a staircase*); ashi oto (*sound of
a footstep*); ashi áto (*footprint*); dankai
(*successive stage*).
step (to) arúku (*walk*); fumu (*tread on*).
sterile ko o umanai (*barren*); fumoo no (*not
fertile*); minori no nái (*unproductive*).
stern *adj.* genkaku na (*severe*); kakoku na
(*harsh*).
stew shichuu.
stew (to) torobi de niru.
stick boo.
stick (to) sásu (*pierce*); tsuku (*adhere*).
stiff kowabútta (*rigid*); katai (*hard*);
ugokánai (*not moving freely*).
stiffen (to) kowabáru.
still *adj.* shízuka na (*quiet*). –*adv.* máda
(*more*); yahári (*after all*); sore démo
(*nevertheless*); ima máde (*yet*).
   Keep still! Jittó shite! Ugokánaide!
stimulate (to) shigeki suru.
stimulus shigeki.
sting hári (*of an animal*); togé (*of a plant*).
sting (to) sásu, píri píri suru.
stinginess kéchi.
stingy kéchi na.
stir (to) ugokásu (*move, shake*); kakimawasu
(*liquids*).
stitch (to) núu (*sew*); kagaru (*darn*).
stock zaikohin (*goods*); shihon (*capital*);
kabuken (*shares*).
stock (to) takuwáeru.
stock exchange kabushiki torihikisho.
stocking kutsushita.
stomach i, onaka.

stone ishí.
stool koshikaké.
stop teiryuujo (*stopping place for buses,
etc.*); shuushi (*end*).
stop (to) yameru (*discontinue*); tomeru
(*cause to cease*); teishi suru (*suspend*);
jama suru (*interrupt*); yokusei suru
(*restrain*); sóshi suru (*prevent*);
owaraseru (*put an end to*); fusagu
(*block*); tomaru (*come to rest*).
store misé.
   department store depáato.
stork koonótori.
storm árashi.
story hanashí (*speech*); uwasa (*gossip*);
monogátari (*tale*); itsuwa (*anecdote*);
densetsu (*legend*).
stove sutóobu.
straight massúgu na (*opp. to crooked*);
itchókusen no (*in a straight line*).
straighten (to) massúgu ni suru.
strain kinchoo (*tension*); hijoo na dóryoku
(*excessive effort*); karoo (*overexertion*).
strain (to) múri o suru.
strange mezurashíi (*rare*); fushigi na
(*wondrous*); kímyoo na (*odd*).
stranger shiranai hito (*unknown person*);
yosó no hito (*outsider*).
strap himo.
straw wára.
strawberry ichigo.
stream nagaré (*current*); ogawa (*small
river*).
stream (to) nagaréru.
street machí (*with houses, etc.*); michi (*road,
way*).
strength tsúyosa (*vigor*); táiryoku (*bodily*).
strengthen (to) tsúyoku suru (*make
stronger*); zookyoo suru (*reinforce*);
tsúyoku náru (*become stronger*).
strenuous hone no oréru.
stress kyoochoo (*emphasis*); appaku
(*pressure*); kinpaku (*strain*).
stress (to) kyoochoo suru.
stretch (to) nobásu (*extend in length*);
hirogeru (*extend in breadth*); dásu (*reach
out*); nobiru (*lengthen*).
strict kibishíi.
stride káppo.
stride (to) káppo suru.
strife arasoi (*conflict*).
strike sutoráiki, higyoo, sutó (*work*); storáiku
(*baseball*).
strike (to) bútsu (*beat*); tatáku (*rap, knock*);
shoototsu suru (*collide*); sutoráiki o suru,
higyoo suru (*quit work*); kokóro o útsu
(*impress*).
string himo.
strip (to) hadaka ni suru (*lay bare*);

toriharáu (*divest*); kimono o núgu (*undress*).

stripe shimá.

strive (to) honeóru (*try hard*); dóryoku suru (*endeavor*); funtoo suru (*struggle vigorously*).

stroke dageki (*blow*); súji (*line*); káku (*of a Japanese character*).

stroll sanpo.

stroll (to) sanpo suru.

strong tsuyói (*having strength*); joobu na (*not easily broken*); kenkoo na (*healthy*); daijóobu na (*reliable*).

structure koosei (*construction*); kumitate (*framework*); kenchiku (*building*); soshiki (*organization*).

struggle kumiuchi (*body to body*); arasoi (*strife*); honeorí (*violent effort*).

struggle (to) dóryoku suru (*make great efforts*); mogáku (*writhe*); tatakau (*fight*); arasóu (*contend*).

stubborn gánko na (*hardheaded*); goojoo na (*obstinate*); shibutói (*perverse*); té ni oenai (*intractable*); fukutsu no (*unyielding*).

student séito, gakusei.

studious yóku benkyoo suru (*assiduous in study*); gakumonzúki no (*given to study*); nesshín na (*zealous*).

study benkyoo (*application of the mind*); kenkyuu (*research, investigation, etc.*).

study (to) benkyoo suru, naráu (*learn*).

stuff shina (*material, goods*); monó (*substance, matter*); garakuta (*rubbish*); tawagoto (*nonsense*).

stuff (to) tsumekomu (*fill with something*); tsumemóno o suru (*cooking*).

stumble (to) tsumazúku (*trip up*); yoroméku (*miss one's footing*); yóro yoro arúku (*walk unsteadily*).

stump kirikabu.

stun (to) mé o mawasaseru.

stunt kyokugei (*tricks*).

stupendous tohoo mo nái.

stupid óroka na, báka na.

stupidity baka sa, oroka sa.

stupor mahi.

sturdy shikkári shita.

stutter (to) domóru.

style ryuukoo, sutáiru (*mode of fashion*); hanashiburi (*mode of speaking*).

subdue seifuku suru (*conquer*); uchikátsu (*overcome*); iatsu suru (*render submissive*); yokusei suru (*repress*).

subject shinmin (*of a country*); mondai (*theme of discussion*); gakka (*of study*).

subject (to) shitagáeru (*subdue*).

subjective shukanteki.

subjugate (to) seifuku suru (*subdue*).

sublime suukoo na.

submission fukujuu (*subjection*); koofuku (*surrender*).

submissive juujun na.

submit (to) teishutsu suru (*turn in*); shitagawaséru (*yield*).

subordinate búka, háika.

subordinate (to) shita ni oku.

subscribe (to) yoyaku suru (*to newspapers, etc.*); sansei suru (*give assent*).

subscription yoyaku.

subside (to) shizumaru (*become tranquil*); hekomu (*dent*).

subsidy hojókin (*grant of money*).

subsist (to) kurashite iku.

substance honshitsu, hóntai.

substantial jitsuzai suru (*actual*); hontoo no (*real*); oohaba no (*major*).

substantiate (to) shoomei suru.

substitute kawari (*a person*); daiyóohin (*a thing representing another*).

substitute (to) dairi suru (*person*); daiyoo suru (*thing*).

substitution daiyoo.

subtle bimyoo na.

subtract (to) hiku (*take out or away*).

subtraction hikízan.

suburb kóogai.

succeed (to) áto o tsugu (*be a successor to*); seikoo suru (*effect one's purpose*).

success seikoo (*favorable termination*); kooun (*good fortune*).

successful seikoo shita.

succession renzoku (*sequence*); keishoo (*to a position, throne, etc.*).

successor soozókusha.

such konna (*like this, of this sort*); sonna (*like that, of that sort*).

sudden kyuu na.

suddenly kyuu ni (*abruptly*); fui ni (*unexpectedly*).

sue (to) soshoo o okósu (*take legal action*); uttáeru (*bring suit*).

suffer (to) kurushímu (*be in pain*); gáman suru (*endure patiently*); songai o koomúru (*a loss*).

suffering kurushimi (*pain*); songai (*loss*).

sufficient takusán no (*plenty*); juubún na (*enough*).

sugar satóo, osatoo.

suggest (to) omoidasaséru (*hint*); iidásu (*propose*).

suggestion kangáe; anji, hínto (*hint*); teigi (*proposal*).

suicide jisatsu.

    to commit suicide jisatsu suru.

suit yoofuku, súutsu (*of clothes*); kokuso (*legal proceedings*).

suit (to) niáu (*fit*); tsugoo ga íi (*be convenient*).

suitable choodo fi (*fitting, proper*); niáu (*becoming*).

sulk (to) mutto suru (*be offended*); sunéru (*pout*).

sullen fukígen na (*in a bad mood*); inki na (*gloomy*).

sum gáku (*quantity*); gookei (*total amount*); kingaku (*amount of money*).

summary tekiyoo sho (*brief account*); gaiyoo (*synopsis*).

summer natsú.

summit choojóo (*top*).

summon (to) shookan suru.

summons shookanjoo.

sumptuous zeitakú na.

sum up (to) gaikatsu suru.

sun hi, táiyoo.

    rising sun ásahi.

    setting sun yuuhi.

sunbeam níkkoo.

sunburn hiyake.

Sunday Nichiyóobi.

sundry iroiro no.

    sundry expenses zappi.

    sundry goods zakka.

sunny urárakana.

sunrise hi no de.

sunset hi no iri.

sunshine hinata.

superb subarashíi.

superconductor choo dendoo tai.

superficial uwabe daké no (*outward*); senpaku na (*shallow; said of persons*).

superfluous yokei na.

superintendent kantoku (*supervisor*); kanrísha (*manager*); koochoo (*of school*).

superior sugúreta (*better*); jootoo no (*of great excellence*); yuusei na (*larger*); kookyuu no (*of higher rank*).

    to be superior sugurete iru.

superiority yuushuu.

superstition meishin.

supervise (to) kantoku suru.

supper yuuhan.

supplement bessatsu (*of a book*); furoku (*of a magazine*).

supplement (to) oginau.

supplementary furoku no.

supply kyookyuu (*a supplying*); kyookyuuhin (*thing supplied*).

supply (to) kyookyuu suru.

support sasaemono (*prop*); shíji (*moral support*); fuyoo (*maintenance*).

support (to) shíji suru (*hold up*); motaseru (*maintain*); genkizukéru (*encourage*); tasukéru (*assist*).

suppose (to) soozoo suru (*imagine*); omóu

(*think*); katei suru (*assume tentatively*); suitei suru (*presume*).

suppress shizumeru (*subdue*); kinshi suru (*stop*); osaéru (*restrain*); kamikorosu (*smother*).

supreme saikoo no.

sure táshika na (*certain*); ate ni náru (*reliable*); hontoo no (*true*); joobu na (*stable*).

surely táshika ni.

surety tánpo (*pledge*); hoshonin (*sponsor*).

surf yose nami (*on the shore*); uchinami (*on rocks*).

surface hyoomén.

surgeon gekái.

surgery geka (*treatment*); shújutsu (*operation*).

surmount (to) noboru (*climb*); uchikátsu (*overcome*).

surname myóoji.

surpass (to) suguréru (*be better than*); shinógu (*outdo*); sugíru (*exceed*); amáru (*be beyond*).

surplus yojoo (*the remainder*); amari (*the rest*).

surprise odorokí (*amazement*); omoigakenai kotó (*something unexpected*).

surprise (to) bikkúri saseru (*strike with wonder*); odorokásu (*cause surprise*); fui uchi suru (*take unawares*).

surrender hikiwatashi (*of a thing*); koosan (*of a person*); koofuku (*of an army*).

surrender (to) tewatásu (*hand over*); hooki suru (*give up something*); koofuku suru (*submit*).

surround (to) torimáku.

surroundings kankyoo.

survey sokuryoo (*land measurement*); kenchi (*land surveying*); tsuuran (*comprehensive view*).

survey (to) miwatásu (*look over*); ippanteki ni míru (*take a general view*); kenbun suru (*inspect*); chóosa suru (*examine*).

survive (to) ikinokóru (*pertaining to people*); nokóru (*pertaining to other cases*).

susceptibility kanjusei.

susceptible takan na, kanjooteki na.

suspect utagawashíi hito (*suspected person*).

suspect (to) kanzúku (*have an inkling*); –de wa nái ka to omóu (*half-believe*); soozoo suru (*surmise*); utagáu (*doubt*).

suspense fuan (*feeling of*); mitei.

suspension chuuburarin.

suspicion kéngi (*distrust*); utagai (*doubt*).

suspicious utagai bukái (*distrustful*); ayashíi (*doubtful*).

sustain (to) sasaeru.

swallow tsubame (*bird*).

swallow (to) nomikomu.

swamp numá.

swan hakuchoo, súwan.

sway (to) yureru.

swear (to) chikau (*take an oath*); akutai o tsúku (*curse*).

sweat áse.

sweat (to) áse ga déru.

sweep (to) háku (*with a broom*); sooji suru (*clean up*).

sweet amai (*of taste*); kawairashíi (*of face*); yasashii (*of disposition*).

sweetness airáshisa (*of person*); amasa (*of food*).

swell (to) fukureru (*bulge out*); hareru (*become swollen*); óokiku náru (*expand*).

swift hayái.

swim (to) oyógu.

swindler sagíshi.

swing (to) yureru, bura, bura ugóku (*as a pendulum*); fureru (*use as a swing*).

switch *n.* suítchi (*elec.*)
   to switch on suítchi o ireru.
   to switch off suítchi o kiru.

sword katáná.

syllable onsetsu.

symbol shoochoo (*emblem*); fugoo (*mark, sign*).

symbolic shoochooteki.

symbolize (to) shoochoo suru (*be a symbol of*); fugoo de arawásu (*represent by symbols*).

symmetrical tsuriai no tóreta.

symmetry tsuriai, kinsei.

sympathetic omoiyari no áru (*compassionate*); ki no átta (*congenial*).

sympathize (to) ki no dóku ni omóu (*feel sympathy*); sansei suru (*agree with*); nagusameru (*condole*).

sympathy doojoo.

symptom chookoo.

syrup shiróppu.

system shóshiki (*organization*); hoohoo (*method*); chitsújo (*order*).

T

table teeburu (*European*); chabudai, (*Japanese low table*).

tablecloth teeburukúroosu, teeburúkake.

tablespoon teeburu supúun.

tacit anmoku no.

tacitly soreto náku, anmoku ni.

taciturn múkuchi na.

tack (to) byóo de tomeru.

tact josai nása, kiten.

tactfully josai náku, úmaku.

tag fuda.

tail o, shippó.

tailor yoofukuya (*for Occidental clothes*); shitateya (*for Japanese clothes*).

take (to) tóru (*get, lay hold of*); mótte iku (*carry or take to*); tsukámu (*grasp*); uketoru (*receive*); tsurete iku (*take to, lead to*).

tale hanashí; monogátari (*old story*).

talent sainoo (*special faculty*); shuwan (*natural ability*).

talk hanashí; osháberi (*a chattering*); danwa (*conversation*).

talk (to) hanásu.

talkative osháberi na.

tall takái.
   She is tall. Sé ga takái desu.

tame náreta (*domesticated*); súnao na (*docile*); juujun na (*submissive*); mukíryoku na (*dull*).

tangerine míkan.

tangle (to) motsuresaséru (*entangle*); karamaséru (*confuse*).

tank suisoo, tánku (*for water, etc.*); tánku, sénsha (*vehicle of war*).

tape téepu.
   tape recorder teepu rekóodaa.
   videotape bideo téepu.

tar koorutáaru.

tardy gúzuguzu shita, jikan ni okureru.

target mato.

tarnish henshoku.
   to be tarnished kumótte iru.

tarry (to) nagaí suru.

task shigoto (*piece of work*); hone no oréru shigoto (*toil*); tsutomé (*duty*).

taste aji (*of food*); shúmi (*for art*).

taste (to) aji o míru.

tax zéi, zeikin.
   taxation kazei.
   tax allowance zei koojo.
   tax base kazei hyoojun.
   tax deduction zei koojo.
   tax evasion datsu zei.
   tax-free income hibazei shotoku.
   tax shelter zeikin hinan shudan.
   export tax yushutsu him zei.
   import tax yunyuu hin zei.
   sales tax uriage zei.

taxi tákushii.

tea ocha (*Japanese*); koocha (*black tea*).

teach oshieru (*give instruction*); shitsukéru (*train*).

teacher senséi.

team chíimu.

tear námida (*teardrop*); kagizaki (*a rent in clothing*).

tear (to) yabúru (*rend*); mushiri tóru (*pull violently away*); yaburéru (*become torn*); hagásu (*tear off*).

tease (to) nayamásu (*annoy*); ijimeru (*torment*).

teaspoon chasaji.

technical gijutsuteki no.

technique gíjutsu, tékunikku.

tedious kudói, nagatarashíi.

telecommunications denki tsúushin.

telegram denpoo.

telegraph denshin.

telegraph (to) denpoo o útsu.

telephone denwa.
    car phone jidoosha denwa.
    cordless phone koodoresu hon.

telephone (to) denwa o kakéru.

telex terékkusu.

tell (to) hanásu (*relate*); iu (*say*); oshieru (*instruct*).

temper umare tsuki (*disposition*); seishitsu (*temperament*); kidate (*personality*); kigen (*mood*).

temperance sessei, kinshu (*moderation*).

temperate odáyaka na (*mild*); tékido no (*moderate*).

temperature óndo (*of the air*); taion (*of the body*).

tempest ooárashi.

temple miya, omiya (*Shinto*); terá, otera (*Buddhist*); komekami (*of the forehead*).

temporary hakanái (*transient*); kari no.

tempt (to) yuuwaku suru (*seduce*); sosoru (*incite*); izanáu (*induce*); unagásu (*persuade*).

temptation yuuwaku (*seduction*); tameshí (*trial*).

ten tóo, júu.
    ten days tooka.
    ten o'clock júuji.

tenacious shinboozuyói (*unyielding*); nebarizuyói (*tough*).

tenacity kyoojin-sei, gankyoo.

tenant shakuyanin (*of a house*); shakuchinin (*of land*).

tend (to) mukau (*be directed toward*); keikoo ga áru (*have a tendency*); kooken suru (*serve*); ki o tsukéru (*attend to*); káihoo suru (*watch over*).

tendency keikoo (*trend*); seiheki (*inclination*); fuuchoo (*drift*).

tender adj. yawarakái.

tennis ténisu, teikyuu.

tense jisei (*gram*).
    present tense génzai.
    past tense káko.
    future tense mírai.

tense katakurushíi (*stiff*).

tension kinchoo.

tent ténto, ténmaku.

tenth dái júu, juu banmé, júu ban.
    tenth of the month tooka.

tepid nurúi.

term kígen (*limited period*); jooken (*condition*); gakki (*of school*).

terrace takadai (*raised ground*); térasu (*of a house*).

terrible osoroshíi (*dreadful*); hidói (*awful*); hisan na (*wretched*).

terrify (to) odorokásu.
    be terrified at –ni odoróku.

territory ryóodo (*as a colony*); ryóochi (*possession of a state or individual*).

terror kyoofu.

test tameshí (*experiment*); shikén (*probe*); shikínseki (*touchstone*).

test (to) kénsa suru.

testify (to) shoogen suru (*give evidence*); shookodatéru (*attest*).

testimony shoomei (*law*); shooko (*evidence*).

text shudai; tékisuto (*of a document*).

textbook kyookásho.

than yóri, yórimo.
    less than íka.
    more than íjoo.

thank (to) rei o iu.
    Thank you. Arígatoo.
    Thank you very much. Doomo arígatoo gozaimásu.

thanks kánsha (*gratitude*).

that adj. sono, ano. –pron. sore, are.
    that person anó hito.
    That's it! Sóo da!

thaw yukidoke.

theater gekijoo.

their (theirs) ano katágata no, ano kátatachi no, anó hitotachi no.

theme daimoku, shudai (*subject*); wadai (*topic*).

themselves ano katágata jíshin.

then sono tóki, sono tóki ni (*at that time*); sore kara (*after that*); sore de (*at that point*); sono baai (*in that case*).

theoretical rironteki.

theoretically sríronjoo.

theory gákuri (*scientific principle*); riron (*opp. to practice*); gakusetsu (*doctrine*).

there asoko, achira (*places outside of immediate reach*); soko, sochira (*places nearby*).

there is (are) iru (*for animate beings*); áru (*for inanimate beings*).

thereafter sore írai.

therefore sore désu kara.

thereupon sokode.

thermometer kandánkei (*weather*); taiónkei (*clinical*).

these kono, kore.

thesis ronbun.

they ano katágata, ano katátachi, anó

hitotachi (*pertaining to people*); are (*pertaining to things*).

thick atsui (*flat things*); futói (*round things*); koí (*liquids, hair, etc.*).

thicken (to) atsuku suru, kóku suru.

thickness atsusa; kósa.

thief doroboo.

thigh mómo.

thimble yubinúki.

thin usui (*flat things, liquids*); hosói (*round things*); yaseta (*persons*).

thing monó (*in concrete sense*); kotó (*abstract*).

think kangáeru (*conceive*); omóu (*suppose*); jukkoo suru (*ponder*); soozoo suru (*imagine*); shían suru (*meditate*).

third *n.* dái san, sanbanmé. —*adj.* dái san no, sanbanmé no.

    third of the month mikka.

thirst nódo no kawakí.

    to quench one's thirst nódo no kawakí o iyásu.

thirsty (be) nódo ga kawáite iru.

thirteen júusan.

thirty sánjuu.

this *adj.* konó. —*pron.* kore.

    this one kore.

thorn togé.

thorough kanzen na (*complete*); tetteiteki na (*utter*); mattaku no (*out and out*).

though ga (*but, however*).

    Though it was raining . . . Áme ga futté itá ga . . .

thought kangáe, shisoo (*that which is thought*); shisaku (*cogitation*); shían (*meditation*); án (*idea*).

thoughtful shínsetsu na (*kind*).

thoughtless karuhazumi na (*careless*); fushínsetsu na (*inconsiderate*).

thousand sén.

    three thousand sanzén.

    ten thousand mán, ichimán.

thrash (to) muchiútsu.

thread íto.

thread (to) íto o tóosu.

    thread a needle hári ni íto o tóosu.

threat kyoohaku.

threaten (to) kyoohaku suru.

three mittsú, san.

threshold iriguchi (*entrance*); shikii (*door sill*).

thrift ken'yaku.

thrifty ken'yaku na.

thrill súriru, senritsu.

thrill (to) kandoo suru; súriru o kanjiru.

thrilling wákuwaku saseru yóo na.

thrive (to) hánjoo suru.

thriving hánjoo shite iru.

throat nódo.

throb (to) dooki ga suru, dóki doki suru.

throne gyókuza.

throng gunshuu.

through *prep.* —o tóoshite (*by the medium of*); tsuranúite (*across*); —no náka ni (*in the midst of*); —juu (*during the whole period*). —*adv.* hajime kara owari máde (*from beginning to end*); zutto (*all the way*).

throughout *prep.* —juu (*periods of time*). —*adv.* sukkári, dóko mo ka mo (*everywhere*).

throw (to) nagéru (*fling*); hooru (*hurl*).

thumb oyayubi.

thunder (to) kaminari ga naru.

thunderbolt kaminari.

Thursday Mokuyóobi.

thus kono yóo ni, koo iu fúu ni (*in this manner*); désu kara (*so, therefore*); shitagátte (*accordingly*).

thwart (to) jama suru.

ticket kippu, kén.

    ticket of admission nyuujóoken.

    ticket window kippu úriba.

tickle (to) kusuguru.

ticklish kusuguttái.

tide shió, chooryuu.

tidy kichín to shita (*arranged in good order*); kogírei na (*neat*).

tie musubime (*knot*); tsunagari (*connection*).

tie (to) shibáru (*tie roughly*); yuwáeru (*tie up*).

    tie a knot musubu.

tiger tora.

tight katai (*close*); kataku musunda (*compact*); harikítta (*taut*); kitchíri átta (*close fitting*).

tile kawara, táiru.

till máde.

    till now ima máde.

    till then sono tóki made.

tilt (to) katamúku.

timber zaimoku.

time tokí; jíki (*opportunity*); jikan (*hour*); kikán (*period*); jidai (*era*).

    time sharing taimu shearingu.

    time zone jikan tai.

    from time to time tokidoki.

    in time ma ni áu yóo ni.

    What time is it? Nánji desu ka?

timid uchiki na.

timidity uchiki.

tin súzu.

    tin can kán, kanzume no kán.

tinkle (to) chirín chirin naru.

tiny chíisana.

tip saki (*end*); kokorozuke, chíppu (*gratuity*); chadai (*gratuity given in Japanese inns*).

tip over (to) hikkurikáesu.

274

tire taiya (*for wheels*).
tire (to) *v.t.* tsukaresaséru; *v.i.* tsukaréru (*get tired*).
tired tsukáreta.
tireless tsukaré o shiranai.
tiresome taikutsu na.
title dái, taitoru, daimoku; shomei (*of a book*); katagaki (*rank*); kengen (*business*).
to e (*toward*); máde (*until, up to*).
　Tell him to come. Kúru yoo ni itte kudasái.
　I went to buy. Kai ni ikimáshita.
　to him sonó hito ni.
toad hikigáeru.
toast tóosuto (*bread*); kanpai (*proposing a health*).
toast (to) (bread) pán o yaku.
tobacco tabako.
today kyóo.
toe ashi no yubi.
together issho ni, minná de (*all together*).
toil honeori.
toil (to) roodoo suru; kúroo suru.
toilet habakari, gofujoo, tóire, oteárai, benjó (*washroom*).
token shirushi (*sign*); kinenhin (*souvenir*); katami (*keepsake*).
tolerable gáman dekíru.
tolerance kandai.
tolerant kandai na.
tolerate (to) oome ni míru (*permit*); gáman suru (*endure*); kandai ni toriatsukáu (*be broad-minded*).
toll zeikin (*tax*); tsuukóoryoo (*passage money*); shishóosha no kázu (*casualties*).
tomato tómato.
tomb haká (*grave*); nookotsujo (*vault*).
tomorrow ashita, myóonichi.
ton tón.
tone otó; kuchoo (*of speech*); iroai (*color*).
tongs híbashi.
tongue shitá.
tonight kón'ya.
too mo (*also*); –sugíru (*excessively*).
　too expensive takasugíru.
tool doogu.
tooth há.
toothache haita.
toothbrush habúrashi.
toothpaste hamígaki.
toothpick tsumayóoji.
tooth powder hamigakíko.
top ue (*summit*); kóma (*toy*).
top (to) ue ni náru.
topic topíkku; shudai (*subject*); wadai (*of conversation*).
torch táimatsu.
torment kashaku (*torture*).

torment (to) kurushiméru.
torture *n.* goomon (*for forced confession*); kurushimi (*anguish*).
toss (to) nagéru.
total *adj.* sookei no (*entire*); kanzen na (*complete*). –*n.* gookei (*total amount*).
totally kanzen ni.
touch (to) sawaru.
touching áware na.
touchy shínkei kabin na.
tough tsuyói (*strong*); ganjoo na (*robust*); goojoo na (*stubborn*); hidói (*laborious*); katai (*hard*).
tour ryokoo, tabí (*travel*); kankooryókoo (*pleasure trip*).
tour (to) ryokoo suru.
tourist kankóokyaku, yuuránsha, tsúurisuto.
　Tourist Agency Ryokooannaijo.
tournament shiai.
toward –no hóo e (*direction*); góro (*about: in point of time*).
towel tenugui (*Japanese*); táoru (*Occidental*).
tower tóo.
town machí, tokai (*city*).
toy omócha.
trace áto (*remains*); keiseki (*vestige*); kekka (*evidence*).
trace (to) toosha suru (*through paper*); tsuiseki suru (*track down*).
track sénro (*railraod*).
trade shóobai (*domestic*); booeki (*with foreign countries*).
　trade union roodoo kúmiai.
tradition shikitari.
traditional dentooteki na.
traffic torihiki (*commerce*); kootsuu (*movement of people, vehicles, etc.*).
tragedy hígeki (*opp. to comedy*); kanashii dekígoto (*sad event*).
tragic higekiteki na.
trail kómichi (*mountain path*); ato (*trace*).
trail (to) áto o tsukéru (*pursue*).
train kishá (*steam- or diesel-engine powered*); densha (*electric*).
train (to) kyooiku suru (*educate*); shikómu (*animals*).
training kúnren.
traitor uragirimono (*betrayer*); kokuzoku (*rebel*).
trample (to) fumiarásu.
tranquil shízuka na.
tranquility heian.
tranquilizer chinséizai, seishin'antéizai, torankiráizaa.
transaction torhiki.
　business transaction shoogyoo tórihiki.
transfer norikae kíppu (*ticket*).
transfer (to) norikáeru (*change cars*); utsúsu

(*shift*); ugokásu (*move*); yuzuru (*hand over*).

transformer henatsu ki.

transistor toranjísutaa.

  portable transistor radio keitai yoo toranjisutaa rájio.

transition hensen, súii (*change*).

translate (to) hon'yaku suru.

translation hon'yaku, yáku.

translator hon'yákusha.

transmission dentatsu.

transmit (to) watasu (*hand over*); tsutaeru (*pass on*).

transparent sukitóotta.

transport *n.* unsoo.

transport (to) unpan suru (*carry*); unsoo suru (*by ship or railroad*).

transportation yusoo (*conveyance*); unsoo (*shipping*); kootsuu no bén (*means of travel*).

trap wána.

trap (to) wána de tóru.

trash gomí, kúzu (*rubbish*); garakuta (*odds and ends*).

travel ryokoo, tabí.

travel (to) ryokoo suru.

traveler ryokóosha.

tray bon, obon.

treacherous uragiru yoo na, fuchúutjitsu no (*disloyal*).

treachery uragiri.

treason muhon.

treasure takará.

treasure (to) daijí ni suru.

treasurer kaikeigákari.

treasury shikín.

treat gochisoo.

treat (to) motenasu (*entertain*); atsukau (*deal with*); chiryoo suru (*give medical treatment*); ogoru (*treat a person to*).

treatment toriatsukai (*conduct toward*); chiryoo (*medical*).

treaty jooyaku.

  commercial treaty tsuushoo jóoyaku.

tree kí.

  evergreen tokiwági.

tremble (to) furueru.

trembling *adj.* furuete iru. –*n.* mibúrui.

tremendous taihen na.

trench mizo (*ditch*); zangoo (*military*).

trend keikoo (*general tendency*); hookoo, múki (*general direction*).

trial sáiban (*law*); shiren (*hardship*); kokoromi (*experiment*).

triangle sánkaku.

tribe shúzoku.

tribulation kánnan.

tribunal saibansho (*a court of justice*); sáiban (*that which judges*).

trick itazura, toríkku (*mischief*); sakuryaku (*stratagem*).

trick (to) damásu.

trifle tsumaránai monó (*negligible thing*); kudaranai kotó (*insignificant matter*).

trifle (to) tsumaránai kotó ni jíkan o tsubúsu.

trifling tsumaránai (*uninteresting*); kudaranai (*trivial*).

trim (to) karikómu.

trimming kazari.

trip ryokoo.

  to take a trip ryokoo ni iku.

trip (to) tsumazúku (*take a false step*); tsumazukaséru (*trip up*).

triple sanbai no.

triumph shóori (*victory*); daiséikoo (*signal success*).

triumph (to) shóori o éru.

triumphant shóori o éta.

trivial kudaranai.

troop gúntai.

trophy káppu, tórofii.

trot (to) hayáashi de kakéru.

trouble kónnan (*difficulty*); mendóo (*bother*); shinpai (*anxiety*); nangí (*distress*).

trouble (to) mendóo o kakéru (*put to inconvenience*); komaraséru (*perplex*); jama suru (*disturb*).

  Don't trouble yourself! Shinpai shinái de kudasái.

trousers zubón.

truck torákku.

true hontoo no (*opp. to false*); makoto no (*true-hearted*); shín no (*real*); jíjitsu no (*actual*); seikaku na (*exact*).

truly hontoo ni (*correctly*); chuujitsu ni (*faithfully*); jitsú ni (*really*); mattaku (*indeed*).

trump kirifuda.

trumpet toránpetto.

trunk míki (*of tree*); toránku (*baggage*).

trust shin'yoo (*faith*); gímu (*responsibility*); shinrai (*reliance*); kakushin (*confidence*).

trust (to) shin'yoo suru (*give credit to*); shinrai suru (*rely on*).

trusting shinzúru.

trustworthy ate ni náru.

truth hontoo no kotó (*correspondence to reality*); jíjitsu (*fact*).

truthful shoojíki na (*veracious*); jitchoku na (*upright*).

truthfully shoojíki ni.

truthfulness seijitsu, seikakusa.

try (to) tamésu, kokoromíru (*prove by experiment*); yatte míru (*attempt*).

  to try to go ikoo to suru.

tube kúda, chúubu.

Tuesday Kayóobi.

tumble (to) korobu (*of persons*); taoréru (*of things*); ochíru (*roll over*).

tumult oosáwagi (*uproar*).

tune senritsu, shirabé, fushí (*melody*).

tune (to) chooshi o awaséru (*adjust*); choowa suru (*be in harmony*).

tunnel tonneru.

turf shíba, shibafu.

turkey shichimenchoo.

turmoil sóodoo.

turn junban (*order*); kaiten (*turning*); káabu (*curve*); hookoo ténkan (*in direction.*).

turn (to) mawasu (*cause to revolve*); mawaru (*revolve*); magaru (*swerve*). **Turn left.** Hidari e magatte kudasái.

turnip kabu, kabura.

twelfth dái juuni. **twelfth of the month** juuninichí.

twelve juuní.

twentieth dái níjuu. **twentieth of the month** hatsuka.

twenty níjuu.

twice nidó.

twilight yuugata, tasogare (*poetic*).

twin futago.

twist (to) nejíru (*distort*); yoriawaséru (*intertwine*); orikómu (*interweave*).

two futatsu, ní.

type katá (*specimen*); móderu (*model*); tenkei (*pattern*); táipu, katsuji (*printing*).

type (to) táipu suru.

typewriter taipuráitaa.

tyranny ooboo, gyakusei.

tyrant bóokun.

U

ugliness migurushíi kotó.

ugly mittomonái.

ulcer kaiyoo.

ulterior hyoomén no, sotogawa no.

ultimate sáigo no.

ultimately sáigo ni.

umbrella kása.

umpire shinpánkan, anpaiya.

umpire (to) shinpan suru.

unable dekínai. **I'm unable to do it.** Suru kóto ga dekimasén.

unanimity manjoo itchi.

unanimous onaji kangáe no (*agreeing in opinion*); manjoo itchi no (*consent of all*).

unanimously íku dooon ni (*with one voice*); manjoo itchi de (*with a unanimous vote*).

unaware kizukánai.

unbearable tamaranai (*unendurable*); gáman dekínai (*not able to be born*).

unbelievable shinjirarénai.

unbutton botan o hazusu.

uncertain fukákutei na (*undecided*); gúra gura shita (*unsteady*); táshika de nái (*not sure*); abunai (*risky*); hakkíri shinai (*not settled*).

uncertainty hakkíri shinai kotó.

unchangeable fuhen no.

uncle oji, ojisan.

uncomfortable kokoromochi no warúi, rakú de nái.

uncommon métta ni nái (*infrequent*); hijoo na (*extraordinary*); mezurashíi (*rare*); fushigi na (*strange*).

unconscious kizetsu shita (*having lost consciousness*); kizukánai (*unaware*).

unconsciously shirazu ni.

uncover (to) futa o tóru (*take off a lid*); ooí o tóru (*take off a covering*).

undecided kimatte inai.

undeniable hitei dekínai, mooshíbun no nái.

under –no shitá ni, –no shitá de, –no shita no.

underdeveloped country teikaihátsukoku.

undergo ukéru; shújutsu o ukéru (*undergo an operation*).

underground chiká (*subterranean*); himitsu no (*secret*).

underline (to) shita ni sén o hiku (*underscore*); kyoochoo suru (*emphasize*).

underneath –no shitá ni, –no shitá de, –no shita no.

understand (to) wakáru; ríkai suru.

understanding *adj.* wakari no yói. –*n.* ríkai.

undertake (to) hikiukéru (*take upon oneself*); kuwadatéru (*attempt*).

undertaking shigoto (*task*); jígyoo (*enterprise*).

undesirable nozomáshikun nái.

undignified omomi no nái, hin no nái, fukínshin na.

undo (to) móto ni káesu (*reverse*); torikesu (*annul*); hazusu (*unfasten*); tóku (*a knot*); akeru (*open, as a parcel*); núgu (*take off*); muda ni suru (*bring to naught*); tokéru (*come undone*).

undress (to) kimono o núgu (*oneself*); kimono o nugaséru (*make someone else undress*).

uneasiness fuan.

uneasy fuan na; ochitsukanai (*restless*).

unemployed shigoto no nái (*out of work*); shiyoo shinai (*unused*).

unequal fukóohei na, fubyóodoo na.

uneven fusóroi na (*not in line*); deko boko na (*rough*).

uneventful buji heion na.

unexpected omoigakenái (*not expected*); yóki shinai (*unforeseen*); totsuzen na (*sudden*); igai na (*surprising*).

unexpectedly igai ni, fui ni (*abruptly*).

unfailing tsukínai (*inexhaustible*); shinrai no dekíru (*sure*).

unfair fukóohei na (*biased*); tadáshiku nái (*not right*).

unfaithful fuchúujitsu na.

unfamiliar yóku shiranai (*not well known*); shirarenai (*unknown*); keiken ga nái (*inexperienced*).

unfavorable yóku nai (*not good*); fúri na (*not satisfactory*); tsugoo no waruí (*inconvenient*).

unfit tekishínai (*unsuitable*); funíai na (*unbecoming*).

unfold (to) hirogeru.

unforeseen fui no, omoigakénai.

unforgettable wasurerarenai.

unfortunate fukóo na.

unfortunately ainiku (*unluckily*); zannen nagara (*regrettably*).

ungrateful arigátaku omótte inai.

unhappily fushiáwase ni.

unhappiness fushiáwase.

unhappy fushiáwase na.

unharmed buji na.

unhealthy karada no yowái (*sickly*); dokú ni náru (*harmful to the health*).

unheard of máda kiitá koto no nái.

unhesitatingly chúucho sézu ni.

unhoped for boogai no, kitai shinákatta.

unhurt kega no nái.

uniform *adj.* onaji yóo na (*about the same*); soroi no (*of the same pattern*). –*n.* yunifóomu, seifuku.

uniformity kin'itsu, kakuitsu.

uniformly dooyoo ni.

unify (to) tooitsu suru.

unimportant daijí de nái, tsumaránai (*worthless*).

unintentional kói de nái.

unintentionally kói de náku, muíshiki ni.

uninviting ki no susumanai.

union kumiai (*association*); gappei (*combination*); engumi (*marriage*).
    labor union roodoo kúmiai.

unique hitotsu kirí no (*single, sole*); dokutoku no (*peerless*); subarashíi (*wonderful*).

unison itchi, kyoodoo.

unit tán'i.
    unit price tánka.

unite (to) awaséru (*join into one*); ketsugoo suru (*combine*); gappei suru (*amalgamate*); gattai suru (*coalesce*).

united rengoo shita.

United Nations Kokuren.

United States Amerika Gasshúukoku.

unity tooitsu, itchi.

universal zen sékai no (*covering all the world*); ippan ni okonawaréru (*widely practiced*).

universe úchuu.

university daigaku.

unjust fukóohei na.

unjustifiable iiwake no tatánai, tóo o énai.

unkempt darashi no nái.

unkind fushínsetsu na.

unknown shirarete inai.

unlawful fuhoo no, hooritsu ni hansúru.

unless –nákereba (*if not*).
    Unless you come ... Anáta ga kónakerebe ...

unlikely arisóo de nái, hontooráshiku nái.

unlimited saigen no nái, seigén no nái.

unload (to) tsumini o ageru (*a ship's cargo*); ní o orósu (*take down from a truck or train*).

unlucky ún no waruí.

unmask (to) bákuro suru.

unmistakably machigai náku.

unnecessary yokei na (*superfluous*); múeki na (*useless*); muda na (*of no use*); fuhitsúyoo na (*not necessary*).

unoccupied aite iru (*untenanted*); yooji ga nái (*disengaged*).

unofficial hikóoshiki no (*informal*).

unpack (to) ní o tóku, nímotsu o hiráku.

unpleasant fuyúkai na (*disagreeable*); iyá na (*offensive*).

unpublished shuppan sarete inai.

unquestionably táshika ni.

unravel (to) tóku, hodóku (*disentangle*); kaiketsu suru (*solve*).

unreal hi-genjitsuteki na.

unreasonable wáke no wakaránai (*not governed by reason*); hoogai na (*exorbitant*).

unrecognizable wakari kanéru, mitomegatái.

unreliable ate ni naránai.

unrest fuon, fuanjóotai.

unrestrained kimama na, yokusei no nái.

unrestricted muséigen no.

unroll (to) toku, hirogeru.

unsafe abunai (*dangerous*); anzen de nái (*not safe*).

unsatisfactory fumánzoku na (*not satisfactory*); fujúubun na (*inadequate*).

unsatisfied fumánzoku na, manzoku shite inai.

unscrupulous buénryo na, mukóo mizu no.

unseemly mittomonái.

unseen kakúrete iru, miénai.

unselfish rikoteki de nái, jibun o wasureta.

unspeakable iiyoo no nái.

unstable fuántei na.

unsteady shikkári shinai.

unsuccessful seikoo shinai, fuséikoo no.

unsuitable futekítoo na (*inappropriate*); niawánai (*not becoming*).

unthinkable kangaerarénai.

untidy darashi ga nái.

untie (to) hodóku.

until máde.
    until now ima máde.

untiring tsukarénai.

untrue úso no, hontoo de nái.

untrustworthy ate ni naránai.

untruth úso.

unusual ijoo na (*uncommon*); mare na (*rare*); métta ni nái (*not frequent*); nárete inái (*unfamiliar*); mezurashíi (*strange*); reigai no (*exceptional*).

unwarranted hoshoo no nái, fukakújitsu na.

unwell guai ga warúi.

unwholesome kenkoo ni yóku nai, kenzen de nái.

unwilling fuhón'i no (*disinclined*); ki ga susumanai (*reluctant*).

unwise óroka na, kashikóku nai.

unworthy kudaranai (*wanting merit*); fusawáshiku nái (*unsuitable*).

unyielding gánko na.

up ue, ue ni.
    eat up tábete shimau.
    give up akiraméru.

upheaval dooran

uphold (to) saseru, shíji suru (*support*); kakunin suru (*court decision*).

upkeep ijíhi (*expense*); íji (*maintenance*).

upon –no ué ni, –no ué de, –no ue no.

upper ue no.

upright tátte iru (*erect*); shoojíki na (*honest*).

uprising boodoo (*revolt*); íkki (*riot*).

uproar oosáwagi (*disturbance*); soozooshíi kóe (*clamor*).

upset (to) kutsugáesu (*overturn*); taósu (*overthrow*); shippai saseru (*frustrate*); awatesaseru (*make nervous*).
    to be upset roobai suru.

upside down sakasama (*topsy turvy*); abekobe (*reverse*).

upstairs nikai.

upward uwamuki no.

uranium uranyúumu.

urge (to) susumeru (*incite*); isogaséru (*hasten*); karitatéru (*press*); hagemásu (*exhort*).

urgency seppaku, kinkyuu.

urgent isogi no, kinkyuu no.

urinate (to) shooyoo o suru, shoobén suru.

us watashítachi.

U.S.A. Amerika Gasshúukoku.

use tsukaikata (*manner of using*).
    to be of use yakú ni tátsu.

use (to) tsukau.

used to –monó da (*habitual in the past*).
    She used to go there everyday. Mainichi itta monó da. –ni nárete iru (*accustomed*).
    I am used to dangerous places. Abunai basho ni nárete iru.

useful yakú ni tátsu (*serviceable*); chóohoo na (*handy*); yuuyoo na (*good for something*).

useless muyoo na (*of no service*); damé na (*fruitless*); muda na (*futile*).

usher annái, annainin.

usher (to) annái suru.

usual futsuu no (*commonplace*); ítsu mo no (*habitual*).

usually ítsu mo, taitei.

usurp (to) ooryoo suru, shingai suru.

utensil doogu.

utility jitsuyoo, yuuyoo (*usefulness*); kooeki jígyoo (*public utility*).
    The rent includes utilities. Yáchin ni wa suidoo-gásu-dénki ga haitte imasu.

utilize riyoo suru.

utmost adj. sei íppai no (*maximum effort*); kyókudo no (*extreme*).

utter tetteiteki na (*total*); kanzen na (*complete*); mattaku no (*entire*); mujóoken no (*unconditional*).

utter (to) iu (*say*); hanásu (*speak*); iiarawásu (*express*).

utterly zenzen (*absolutely*); mattaku (*totally*); sukkári (*completely*).

V

vacant kara no (*empty*); aite iru (*unoccupied*); karite no nái (*untenanted*).

vacation yasumí.

vague hakkíri shini (*indefinite*); aimai na (*ambiguous*).

vain yakú ni tatánai (*useless*); muda na (*fruitless*); unbore no tsuyói, kyóéishin no tsuyói (*conceited*).
    in vain muda ni.

valiant isamashíi (*brave*); yúuki no áru (*courageous*).

valid táshika na (*well founded*); yuukoo na (*effective*).

validity seitoo sa, kakujitsu sa.

valley tani.

valuable kóoka na (*precious*); neuchi no áru (*in terms of money, materially*).
    valuables kichoohin.

value neuchi (*worth*); atai (*cost*).

value (to) nebumi suru (*appraise*); sonchoo suru (*rate highly*); daijí ni suru (*think important*).

valued kichoo na.

valve bén, bárubu.

vanilla bánira.

vanish (to) kieuséru (*disappear*); usuréru (*fade away*); nakunaru (*cease to exist*).

vanquish seifuku suru (*conquer*); makasu (*defeat*).

vapor yúge (*of water*); kitai (*gaseous state of liquid or solid*).

variable kawariyasúi.

variance fúwa (*antagonism*); hendoo (*deviation, discord*); fuítchi, chigai (*divergence*).

vanity kyoéishin, unubore (*conceit*).

variation hénka, chigai (*modification, change*).

varied samazáma no.

variety hénka ni tómu kotó (*diversity*); kuichigai (*difference*); shúrui (*kinds*).

various iroiro no.

varnish (to) urushi o nuru.

vary (to) kaeru, chigaeru (*alter*); hénka o soéru (*diversity*).

vase tsubo.

  flower vase kabin.

vast hirói.

vault kínko (*safe*).

veal koushí no nikú.

vegetable yasai.

vehemence hageshísa.

vehement hageshíi, nesshín na.

vehicle norimono.

veil makú (*curtain*); béeru (*for face*).

veil (to) béeru o kakéru.

vein joomyaku (*blood vessel*).

velocity sokúryoku, háyasa (*speed*).

velvet biroodo, berubétto.

venerable sonkei subéki, rippa na (*respected*).

venerate (to) uyamáu.

veneration sonkei.

vengeance fukushuu.

venom dokú (*poison*); uramí (*ill will*).

venomous doku no aru.

ventilation kazetooshi, tsuufuu.

ventilator tsuufúuki.

venture kiken na kuwadate.

venture (to) kiken ni sarasu (*risk*); omoikítte yaru (*brave danger*).

verb dooshi.

verdict hyooketsu (*of law*); hándan (*judgment*); kettei (*decision*).

verge hashi (*edge*); herí (*brink*); kyookai (*borderline*).

  on the verge of –ni hínsuru.

verge (to) chikazúku.

verification kakunin.

verify (to) shoomei suru (*prove*); tashikaméru (*ascertain*).

versatile tagei no, bannoo no.

verse shi (*poem*); ku (*line of a poem*).

version hanashí (*of a story*); hon'yaku (*translation*); íken (*opinion*).

vertical suichoku no, táte no (*perpendicular*).

very taihen, táisoo, hijoo ni, hanahadáshiku, totemo.

vessel fúne (*ship*); iremono (*receptacle*).

vest chokki.

vex (to) urusagaraséru (*annoy*); okoraséru (*provoke*); nayamásu (*distress*).

via –keiyu.

vibrate (to) yureru (*oscillate*); furueru (*quiver*).

vice fudóotoku (*depravity*); akuheki (*evil habit*).

vice-president fuku daitóoryoo (*of a country*); fuku káichoo (*of a society*); fuku sháchoo (*of a firm*).

vice versa abekobe, hantai.

vicinity kínjo (*neighborhood*); chikái kotó (*nearness*).

victim higáisha (*injured one*); soonánsha (*sufferer*); giséisha (*one who is a sacrifice*).

victor shoorísha.

victorious shoori no éta, kátta.

victory shóori.

video bídeo.

  video camera bídeo kámera.

  VCR bii-sii-áaru.

  video disc bídeo disuku.

  video game bídeo geemu.

view késhiki (*prospect*); íken (*opinion*).

view (to) míru; yuuran suru (*sightseeing*).

vie (with) (to) kisóu.

vigor séiryoku (*vitality*); génki (*energy*).

vigorous génki na (*energetic*); tsuyói (*strong*); kappatsu na (*active*).

vile katoo na.

village murá.

villain warumono.

vindicate (to) béngo suru.

vindictive shuunen bukái.

vine tsúru.

vinegar sú.

violence bookoo (*outrage*); bóoryoku (*exertion of physical force*).

violent hageshíi, hidói (*wild*).

violet n. sumire (*flower*); murasaki iro (*color*).

violin baiorin.

virtue toku (*moral excellence*); zenkoo (*opp. to vice*); misao (*chastity*); kooketsu (*uprightness*).

virtuous dootoku no takái (*morally good*); kooketsu na (*honorable*); dootokuteki na (*moral*).

visibility shikái.

visible mé ni míeru.

visibly me ni míete.

vision shíryoku (*actual sight*).

visit hoomon (*call on someone*); omimai (*to sick people*).

visit (to) tazunéru, hoomon suru (*a person*); kenbutsu suru (*museums, etc.*).

visitor okyakusáma (*guest*).

visual shikaku no.
   visual education shikaku kyóoiku.

visualize (to) kokoró ni egáku.

vital séimei no (*of life*); hijoo ni juudai na (*very ímportant*); kan'yoo na (*indispensable*).

vitality táiryoku.

vivacious kaikatsu na (*jovial*); yooki na (*lively*); génki na (*spirited*).

vivid hakkíri shita.

vocabulary tango (*individual words*); gói (*list of words*).

vocal kóe no.

vocation shokúgyoo (*profession*); shóobai (*business*); teishoku (*regular employment*).

vogue hayarí, ryuukoo.

voice kóe.

voice (to) kóe o dású (*utter*); íken o háku (*give expression to*).

void kóoryoku no nái (*not binding*); mukoo no (*nullified*).

void (to) dású (*throw, send out, empty*).

volume yóoseki (*of a solid*); ryóo (*quantity*); -kán, -satsu (*counter for books and magazines*).
   one volume issatsú.

voluminous kasabáru.

voluntary jihatsuteki.

volunteer shibóosha.

vomit (to) háku.

vote hyoo.

vote (to) toohyoo suru.

vouch for (to) hoshoo suru (*guarantee*); hoshóonin ni náru (*stand sponsor for*).

voucher uketori (*receipt*).

vow seiyaku (*promíse*); chikai (*oath*).

vow (to) seiyaku suru (*promise*); dangén suru (*assert*); chikau (*pledge*).

vowel boin.

voyage kóokai.

vulgar gehín na.

vulnerable yowami no áru.

W

wade (to) wataru.

waffle wáffuru.

wag (to) furu.

wage chíngin.

wager kakégoto o (*act of betting*); kaké (*bet*).

wager (to) kakégoto o suru.

wages chíngin (*pay*); kyúuryoo (*salary, payroll*).

wagon kuruma.

waist koshi.

wait mátsu kotó (*act of waiting*).

wait (to) mátsu.

waiter wéetaa.

wake (to) okósu.
   be awakened okosaréru.

walk sanpo.
   Go for a walk (take a walk). Sanpo suru.

walk (to) arúku.

wall kabe.

wallet saifu (*purse*); satsu-ire (*for paper money*).

walnut kurumi.

waltz wárutsu.

wander (to) aruki mawáru.

want ketsuboo.

want (to) iru (*need*); hoshíi desu (*want to have a thing*).
   want to go ikitai.

war sensoo.

war (to) sensoo o suru.

warble (to) saezúru.

ward bóogo (*guard*); mihari (*watch*); kyoodoo byóoshitsu (*in a hospital*); ku (*division of a city, borough*).

wardrobe tansu.

ware, wares saikumono (*handicraft*); toojíki (*chinaware*).

warehouse sóoko.

warfare sensoo (*war*).

warm atatakái.

warm (to) atatákaku suru (*keep warm*).

warmth atatákasa.

warn (to) chúui suru (*caution*); imashiméru (*admonish*).

warning chúui, kunkai (*admonition*); yokoku (*notice*).

warrant hoshoo (*guarantee*); shooméisho (*certificate*).

warrant (to) hoshoo suru.

warrior héishi (*soldier*); yúushi (*distinguished soldier*).

wary yoojinbukái.

wash sentaku (*washing*).

wash (to) arau.

washroom benjó, oteárai, habakari, tóire.

waste amarimono (*waste material*); kúzu (*refuse*).
   wastepaper kamikúzu.

waste (to) muda ni suru.

watch tokei (*timepiece*).
   wristwatch udedókei.

watch (to) bán o suru (*guard*); ki o tsukéru (*pay attention*).

watchful yoojinbukái (*cautious*).

water mizu.

water (to) mizu o yaru (*plants*).

waterfall taki.

waterproof *adj.* mizu no tooránai. –*n.* boosui, taisui.

watt wátto.

wave namí.

wave (to) yureru (*sway*); hirugáeru (*flutter*); furimawásu (*brandish*).

waver (to) tameráu (*hesitate*).

wax róo, wákkusu.

way michi (*road*); toorí (*street*); hoohoo (*method*).

we watashítachi, watakushidómo.

weak yowái.

weaken (to) yówaku suru (*make weak*); yówaku náru (*get weak*).

weakly yowayowashíi, byóoshin na (*sickly*).

weakness kettén (*weak points*).

wealth zaisan (*riches*); tómi (*fortune*).

wealthy kanemóchi no (*rich*); yútaka na (*well off*).

weapon búki.

wear (to) kiru (*coat, dress*); haku (*pants, shoes*); shiméru (*girdle*); kabúru (*hat*); hameru (*ring, gloves*); kakéru (*spectacles*).

weariness híroo (*fatigue*); taikutsu (*tedium*).

weary tsukáreta (*tired*); ákita (*bored*); taikutsu na (*tedious*).

weather ténki.

  rainy weather áme, úten.

  cloudy weather kumorí.

weave (to) óru.

wedding kekkónshiki (*ceremony*).

wedge kusabi.

Wednesday Suiyóobi.

weed zassoo.

weed (to) zassoo o nuku.

week shúu (*counter for weeks*).

  this week konshuu.

  next week raishuu.

  two weeks nishúukan.

weekend *n.* shuumatsu, wiikuéndo.

weekly shuukan zásshi (*periodical*).

weep (to) naku.

weigh (to) mekata o hakáru.

weight mekata.

welcome kangei.

  You're welcome. Yóku irassahimáshita. (*Glad that you've come.*) Dóo itashimáshite. (*Nothing at all. Don't mention it.*)

welfare fukúshi (*well-being*); han'ei (*prosperity*).

well ído (*for water*).

west nishi.

western nishi no.

wet nureta, nurete iru.

wet (to) nurasu.

whale kujira.

what *pron.* nán, náni. –*adj.* dóno (*which*).

  What is it? Nán desu ka?

  what he said itta kóto (*that which he said*).

whatever nán de mo.

  whatever he saw nán de mo míta monó.

  whatever he heard nán de mo kiita kotó.

wheat komúgi.

wheel kuruma, wá.

when ítsu (*interrogative*); –tokí, tokí ni (*at the particular time that*); –tára (*if, when*); –to (*whenever*).

  When I went to Kyoto . . . Kyóoto e itta tóki . . .

  When I asked Mr. Yamada . . . Yamada-san ni kiitára . . .

  When I have a headache . . . Atamá ga itái to . . .

whenever –to, tabí ni (*every time*); ítsu mo (*always*); ítsu de mo (*at all times*).

where dóko ni, dóko de, dóko e (*in what place*); dóchira (*pol, used like dóko*); dóko e (*whither*).

wherever dóko—demo; dóko—temo.

  Wherever we go, there are many people. Dóko e itté mo hito ga óoi.

whether ka, ka dóo ka, –mo –mo.

  I don't know whether the library is open today. Toshókan wa kyóo aite iru ka dóo ka shiranai.

  I intend to go whether it rains or snows. Áme ga futtémo, yukí ga futtémo iku tsumori désu.

which *pron.* dóre (*of several*); dóchira (*of two*). –*adj.* dóno.

while –uchi ni; –aida ni.

  Wait a while. Chótto mátte kudasái.

whim kimagure.

whimper (to) shikúshiku naku.

whine (to) nakigoe o dásu.

whip múchi.

whip (to) múchi de útsu (*lash*); sékkan suru (*flog*).

whisper sasayaki.

whisper (to) sasayáku (*speak softly or under the breath*); naisho bánashi o suru (*speak in secret*).

whistle fue (*instrument*); kuchibue (*made with the mouth*).

whistle (to) kuchibue o fukú.

white *adj.* shirói. –*n.* shíro.

who *n.* dónata, dáre (*interrogative*).

whoever dáre de mo.

whole *adj.* zen- (*prefix*); -juu (*suffix*); zénbu no. –*n.* zénbu.

wholesale oroshí, oroshiúri.

wholesome kenkoo ni yói (*salubrious*); kenzen na (*sound*).

whom dáre ni, dónata ni (*as indirect object*); dáre o, dónata o (*as direct object*).

whose dónata no, dáre no.

why náze, dóo shite.

wicked warúi (*bad*); yokoshima na (*sinful*); ijiwáru na (*ill-tempered*).

wide hirói.

widen *v.t.* hirogeru; *v.i.* hirogaru.

widow mibóojin.

widower otoko yámome.

width haba.

wife tsúma; ókusama (*your wife*); kánai (*my wife*).

wig katsura.

wild yasei no (*opp. to domestic*); areháteta (*uncultivated*); arai (*untamed*); ranboo na (*lawless*); kyóoki no (*frantic*).

wilderness arano.

wildness ranboo sa.

will íshi (*the faculty*); íshi no chikará (*willpower*); kétsui (*determination*); negai (*wish*); kiboo (*desire*); yuigónjoo (*testament*).

will (to) yuigon o nokósu (*bequeath*).

willful kói no.

willing yorokónde . . . suru.
 I'm willing to go. Yorokónde ikimásu.

willingly yorokónde.

win shóori, kachí.

win (to) tóru (*prizes*); kátsu (*races*); hakusúru (*fame, etc.*).

wind kaze.

wind (to) makú.

window mádo.

windy kaze ga fukú.

wine budóoshu, wain (*grape*); sake (*Japanese; made from rice*).

wing hane (*of birds*); yóku (*airplane*).

wink mekúbase, mabátaki (*blink*); isshúnkan (*instant*).

winner shoorísha (*victory*); jushóosha (*recipient of an award*).

winter fuyú.

wipe (to) fuku.

wire harigane (*metal*); denpoo (*telegram*).

wire (to) denpoo o útsu (*send a telegram*).

wisdom fúnbetsu (*prudence*); chié (*intelligence*).

wise kashikói (*sagacious*); shíryo no áru (*sensible*); hakushiki na (*learned*).

wish negai (*longing*); nozomi (*hope*).

wish (to) –ga hoshíi (*wish for something*); nozómu (*hope*).

wit kichí (*smart utterance*); ríchi (*intelligence*); fúnbetsu (*sense*).

witch miko, májo.

with –to, –to issho ni (*together with*); de (*by means of*).

withdraw (to) hikisagéru (*take back*); sáru (*remove*); hikiagéru (*evacuate*).

withdrawal hikisage, tekkai; hikidashi (*bank*).

wither (to) kareru.

within –no uchi ni, náka ni (*internally*); ie no náka ni (*in the house*); okúnai ni (*indoors*).

without –nashi (*not with*);
 I went out without any money. Okane náshi de giashutsu shita.
 –nai de (*without –ing*).
 I went to school without having breakfast. Asagóhan o tabénai de gakkoo e itta.

witness shooko (*testimony*); shoogen (*verbal evidence*); mokugékisha (*eyewitness*); shoonin (*legal*).

witness (to) mokugeki suru (*be a spectator*); shimésu (*show*); shoonin to shite shomei suru (*sign as a witness*).

witty ki no kiita, kashikói (*clever*).

woe kunoo (*affliction*).

wolf óokami.

woman onna, onna no hito, fujin (*lady*).

wonder odoroki (*feeling*); fushigi (*cause of*); kiseki (*miracle*).

wonder (to) odoróku (*be surprised*); fushigi ni omóu (*take as strange*).

wonderful fushigi na (*strange*); subarashíi (*splendid*).

wood kí; zaimoku (*lumber*).

woods hayashi.

woodwork kizáiku.

wool yoomoo (*coat of sheep*); keito (*yarn*); ke (*material*).

woolen keori no.

word kotobá (*speech*); yakusoku (*promise*); táyori (*news*).
 word for word ichiji ichíji.

word processor waapuro.

work roodoo (*manual labor*); shigoto (*mission, job*); shoku (*employment, occupation*); chosaku (*literary work*).

work (to) shigoto o suru, hataraku.

worker roodóosha (*wage earner*); shokunin (*craftsman*).

work of art geijutsu sákuhin.

workshop shigotoba, seisakujo.

world sékai (*earth*); chikyuu (*the globe*); séken (*society*).

worldliness zokushuu.

worldly kono yo teki na.

worm mushi.

worry shinpai (*care*); kúroo (*trouble*); mendóo (*difficulty*).

worry (to) *v.i.* shinpai suru; *v.t.* shinpai saseru (*make one worry*).

Don't worry! Shinpai shináide kudasái.

worse –yóri mo warúi, sára ni warúi.

worship reihai (*religion*); suuhai (*admiration*).

worship (to) reihai suru, ogámu.

worst ichiban warúi.

worth *adj.* neuchi ga áru, kai ga áru (*worthwhile*). –*n.* káchi, neuchi.

worthless neuchi no nái.

worthy kachi no aru (*good enough for*); –ni fusawashíi (*deserving*).

wound kegá (*injury*); kizu (*scratch*).

wound (to) kizutsukéru (*injure*); kegá o saseru (*hurt*).

    get wounded kegá o suru.

wounded kegá o shita.

wrap (to) tsutsúmu.

wrathful ikidóotte iru.

wreath hanawa.

wreck nanpa (*of a ship*).

    a wrecked ship nanpasen.

wreck (to) hakai suru (*demolish*); kowásu (*bring disaster on*).

    to be shipwrecked nanpa suru.

wrestle (to) sumoo o tóru (*Japanese-style*); résuringu o suru (*Occidental-style*); kutoo suru (*struggle with*).

wrestler sumóotori (*Japanese-style*); résuraa (*Occidental-style*).

wrestling sumoo (*Japanese-style*) résuringu (*Occidental-style*).

wretched míjime na.

wring shibóru.

wrinkle shiwa.

wrinkle (to) hitai ni shiwa o yoseru (*one's forehead*).

    to wrinkle with age toshi o tótte shiwa ga yoru.

wrist tékubi.

    wristband udewa.

write (to) káku.

writer chósha (*author*); sakka (*novelist*); shoki (*clerk*); káita hito (*one who wrote*).

writing hisseki (*handwriting*); káita monó (*that which is written*).

    to state it in writing káita monó de nobéru.

    to put in writing shomen ni suru.

written kaite áru, kakáreta.

wrong *adj.* warúi, yóku nái (*bad*); ayamátta, machigátta (*mistaken*); fusei na (*not moral*). –*n.* fusei, fúgi.

wrong (to) fusei o okonáu.

Y

yacht yotto.

Yankee yánkii.

yard niwa (*garden*); yáado, yáaru (*measure*).

yarn íto.

    wool yarn keito.

yawn akubi.

yawn (to) akubi o suru.

year toshí, –nen.

    this year kónne, kotoshi.

    ten years júnnen.

    per year nén ni.

yearly mainen no (*every year*); nén ni ichidó no (*once a year*).

yearn for (to) –ni kogaréru.

yearning akogare.

yeast íisuto, kooji.

yell sakebigóe.

yell (to) sakébu.

yellow *n.* kiiro. –*adj.* kiiroi.

yen én (*Japanese currency*).

yes hai, ee, sóo de gozaimásu (*extra pol.*).

yesterday kinóo, sakújitsu.

yet máda (*still*); soredémo (*nevertheless*).

    and yet sore ná noni.

yield (to) sansúru (*produce*); yurúsu (*grant*); ataéru (*give over*); shitagáu (*follow*).

yielding juujun na (*compliant*).

yoke kubiki.

yolk tamágo no kimi.

you anáta (*sing.*) anatagata (*pl.*); kimi (*used by men to close men friends*).

young wakái.

your anáta no (*sing.*); anatagáta no (*pl.*).

yours anáta no, anáta no monó (*sing.*), anatátachi no, anatátachi no monó (*pl.*).

yourself jíshin, jibun.

youth wakái tokí (*the period*); wakái otokó (*young man*).

youthful wakawakashíi.

youthfulness wakawakáshisa.

Z

zeal nésshin.

zealous nésshin na.

zero zéro, réi.

zipper zíppaa, jíppaa.

zone chitái, chíiki (*area*); –tai (*in compounds*).

    temperate zone ontai.

    safety zone anzen chitái.

zone (to) chíiki o kugíru.

zoo doobútsuen.

zoology doobutsúgaku.

Glossary of Geographical Names

Africa Afuríka.
Algeria Arujeria.
Alaska Arasuka.
Alps Árupusu.
America Amerika, Beikoku.
  North America Kita Amérika, Hokubei.
  Central America Chuuoo Amérika,
  Chuubei.
  South America Minami Amérika,
  Nanbei.
Argentina Aruzénchin.
Asia Ájiya.
Atlantic Ocean Taiséiyoo.
Australia Oosutoráriya.
Austria Ōsutoria.
Bombay Bónbei.
Brazil Buraziru.
Burma Bíruma.
Canada Kánada.
Chile Chíri.
China Chúugoku, Shína.
Commonwealth of Independent States
  Dokuritsu Kókka Kyoodootai.
Cuba Kyúuba.
Czechoslovakia Chékosurobakiya.
Denmark Denmáaku.
Egypt Ejiputo.
England Igirisu, Eikoku.
Europe Yooróppa, Óoshuu.
France Furansu.
Geneva Junéebu.
Germany Dóitsu.
Great Britain Igirisu.
Greece Gírisha.
Hawaii Háwai.
Hokkaido Hokkáidoo.
Hong Kong Hónkon.
Hungary Hungárii.
Iceland Aisurándo.
India Índo.

Indochina Indo shína.
Indonesia Indonéshia.
Iran Íran.
Iraq Íraku.
Ireland Airurándo.
Israel Isuráeru.
Italy Itárii.
Japan Nippón, Nihón.
  Japan Sea Nihónkai.
Kobe Kóobe.
Korea Kánkoku (South); Choosén (North).
Kyoto Kyóoto.
Kyushu Kyúushuu.
London Róndon.
Malaya Maree.
Manila Mánira.
Mexico Mekíshiko.
Moscow Mósukoo.
Netherlands Oranda.
New York Nyuu Yóoku.
New Zealand Nyuu Jiirándo.
Norway Nóruuee.
Osaka Oosaka.
Pacific Taihéiyoo.
Pakistan Pakísutan.
Peiping Pékin.
Persian Gulf Perushiáwan.
Philippines Fíripin.
Poland Poorando.
Portugal Porutogaru.
Russia Róshiya.
San Francisco San Furanshísuko.
Siberia Shiberiya.
Singapore Shingapóoru.
South Africa Mihami Afuríka.
Southeast Asia Toonan-Ájiya.
Spain Supéin.
Sri Lanka Suriránka.
Sweden Suéeden.
Switzerland Súisu.
Taipei Taihoku.
Taiwan Taiwán.
Thailand Tái.
Tokyo Tookyoo.
Turkey Tóruko.
United States Gasshúukoku.
  U.S.A. Amerika Gasshúukoku, Beikoku.
Washington, D.C. Washínton.